The
EZRA POUND
Encyclopedia

The
EZRA POUND
Encyclopedia

Edited by
Demetres P. Tryphonopoulos
and Stephen J. Adams

Greenwood Press
Westport, Connecticut • London

Library of Congress Cataloging-in-Publication Data

The Ezra Pound encyclopedia / edited by Demetres P. Tryphonopoulos and Stephen J. Adams.
    p.   cm.
    Includes bibliographical references and index.
    ISBN 0–313–30448–3 (alk. paper)
    1. Pound, Ezra, 1885–1972—Encyclopedias. 2. Poets, American—20th century—Biography—
Encyclopedias. 3. Critics—United States—Biography—Encyclopedias. I. Tryphonopoulos,
Demetres P., 1956– II. Adams, Stephen, 1945– .
    PS3531.O82Z459   2005
    811'.52—dc22   2004028176

British Library Cataloguing in Publication Data is available.

Library of Congress Catalog Card Number: 2004028176
ISBN: 0–313–30448–3

First published in 2005

Greenwood Press, 88 Post Road West, Westport, CT 06881
An imprint of Greenwood Publishing Group, Inc.
www.greenwood.com

Printed in the United States of America

The paper used in this book complies with the
Permanent Paper Standard issued by the National
Information Standards Organization (Z39.48–1984).

10 9 8 7 6 5 4 3 2 1

Copyright Acknowledgments

The editors and publisher gratefully acknowledge permission to use excerpts from the following material:

Published poetry and prose by Ezra Pound used by permission of New Directions Publishing Corporation.
Unpublished material by Ezra Pound © 2005 by Mary de Rachewiltz and Omar S. Pound.

*Ma Virgilio n'avea lasciati scemi
di sé, Virgilio dolcissimo patre . . .*

For Hugh Kenner (1923–2003)
and Carroll F. Terrell (1917–2003)

Contents

List of Entries

Preface

Pound is an inescapable fact. His oeuvre is enormous, unmanageable. As "the editor of the twentieth century" (T. S. Eliot's phrase), his influence touches hundreds of other writers, great and small. As one of the prime mediators between West and East, he is a herald of global Postcolonialism. Any serious student of Modernism, of twentieth-century poetry and literature in general, must come to terms with him. But as an author, Pound is notoriously difficult to enter. One must contend with the sheer volume of work, the range of reference, not to mention his habit of apparently willful obscurity and use of an array of foreign languages. Add to this the notoriety, in his later career, of his fascist politics, his funny-money obsessions, his anti-Semitism, and his questionable sanity, and many would-be readers find him simply repellant.

Accessible bits there are, and many content themselves with a handful of imagist pieces, a poem or two from *Cathay*, selected portions of *The Cantos*, perhaps "Mauberley" (or parts of it), a few of the politer essays. The serious reader who ventures beyond these safe havens, especially into *The Cantos*, is apt to encounter in the beginning as much frustration as reward in quest of a Poundian *paideuma*, or education. Even the specialist who has devoted considerable time to Pound is unlikely to feel equally at home in every corner of this terrain: The student of Pound's economics, say, or his Chinese translations may feel forgivably shaky discussing his prosody or his engagement with medieval philosophy. To the beginner the task is, well, encyclopedic.

This *Encyclopedia of Ezra Pound* benefits from more than half a century of assiduous scholarship. The word *encyclopedia* itself derives from the Greek *enkyklios paideia*, "a well-rounded education"—an education that encompasses a wide range of geographic and historical knowledge and a variety of languages and disciplines. It was during the 1950s that the first major study of Pound's work, Hugh Kenner's *Poetry of Ezra Pound* (1951), appeared, and the painstaking process began that led first to the *Annotated Index to the Cantos* (1957) of John Edwards and William Vasse and ultimately to Carroll F. Terrell's comprehensive two-volume *Companion to the Cantos of Ezra Pound* (1980, 1984). During and since that time a whole library of monographs, biographies, introductions, controversies, and highly specialized studies has arisen. The crude early maps have been displaced by more sophisticated ones, and large areas of *terra incognita*—though some remain—are dwindling. While the specialized study continues, now seems the time for taking stock.

This may be the opportune moment for such an encyclopedia. It not only appears during a period of consolidation, but it follows soon after the deaths of the two pioneers in Pound studies, Hugh Kenner and Carroll F. Terrell. Kenner, in fact, had promised a contribution to this work but died before he managed to complete the task. The two men died just a few days apart, late in November 2003. Kenner, the dean of Anglo-American Modernist studies, brought his career to a peak with *The Pound Era* (1971), and Terrell, tireless organizer and enthusiast that he was, founded *Paideuma: A Journal Devoted to Ezra Pound Scholarship* in 1972. Now, the reorganization of *Paideuma*, newly subtitled *Studies in American and British Modernist Poetry*, signals that much of the preliminary scholarship on Pound has been completed—the major sites excavated, the peaks scaled—and it is now just possible to see his work whole.

When the editors first confronted the task of putting this work together, we wanted to provide materials to help orient new readers of Pound and Modernism but also to refresh even experienced readers. The challenge was to sift through innumerable potential topic headings and come up with a more or less systematic plan and a manageable number of entries. This process of inclusion and exclusion involved difficult decisions: It was guided by a desire to address what was essential for comprehensiveness while realizing that, given spatial limitations, it was impossible to encapsulate every single work or theme in a writer who is himself encyclopedic, interdisciplinary (even before the term was invented), and polyglot, a writer important for both his poetry and his criticism. Early on, we decided that we could not, after the model of other editors in this series, offer individual entries on every single poem—an impossibility that would be self-evident to anyone who has examined the ninety-plus-page index to Donald Gallup's authoritative *Ezra Pound: A Bibliography*. Instead, Pound's works are presented volume by volume, with individual poems and cantos discussed in the appropriate places. There are entries on Pound's contemporaries—writers, personal associates, and a few literary scholars—who figure significantly in his personal world. And there are topical entries that offer brief overviews of particular corners of Pound's multifarious interests. Most entries include a bibliography for citations that may also point toward further reading.

For references to Pound's poetry and prose, we have used the most readily available New Directions editions. As for references to *The Cantos*, we decided finally (following Massimo Bacigalupo's prudent advice) to eliminate page numbers and cite merely the number of the canto. Given the many editions of the poem already, and the possibility of more in the future, keying page numbers to a specific edition would be of limited use, and most of the cantos are brief enough not

to cause problems. We use abbreviations for Pound's primary texts as they have become established in *Paideuma*. The selected bibliography lists these texts and abbreviations, plus the most commonly cited secondary works: This list makes no pretense of being comprehensive.

Working with more than a hundred contributors has proved to be as wonderful as it has been protracted, occasionally frustrating, and exhausting. We have allowed contributors to claim their own voices and points of view, resisting as much as possible any effort to achieve uniformity. We have made every effort to detect errors of fact, but contradictory opinions have been allowed to stand. Limited space does not allow us to convey a full sense of the achievements of our many contributors; but the listing should suggest, nonetheless, what a diverse and international lot the Poundian scholarly community is—our contributors come from the world over, the United States, Canada, Great Britain, Europe, South America, Japan, Australia. We are pleased that this group includes many of the most distinguished Modernists writing today, as well as many new voices. We are delighted to include among them Pound's son Omar, contributing the entry on himself. Our debts are owed to many people for this work: for various kinds of assistance and encouragement, to our colleagues (especially librarian Stephen Sloan) and our institutions (the University of New Brunswick and the University of Western Ontario); for their forbearance and continued support, to our publishers at Greenwood (especially our editor, George Butler, Senior Project Manager Nicole Azze, and Permissions Coordinator Marcia Goldstein); and for their professionalism and expert advice, to John Donohue of Westchester Book Services and copyeditor Susan E. Badger—but our greatest debt of gratitude is to the contributors themselves.

POLICY ON THE BIBLIOGRAPHY

If one were to imagine that a current bibliography of major translations of Pound's work into Greek (which would not include the publication of translations of single poems in journals and periodicals) and of essays in Greek about his work would include more than 400 items, and that a similiar bibliography of work appearing in Italian would be much more extensive than one in Greek, one may begin to understand the nature of the impossible task of constructing a comprehensive Ezra Pound bibliography. Here, works written in languages other than English have been included on a highly selective basis where appropriate.

In other words, our bibliography makes no attempt to be complete. Rather, we have limited our selected bibliography to (1) full citations of those primary sources useful to readers for the purpose of reading this encyclopedia (with abbreviations for primary texts indicated where appropriate) and (2) a list of secondary sources that includes books but excludes scholarly articles such as those that for over thirty years (1972–2004) have appeared in the pages of *Paideuma*. References to various editions of Pound's work may be found in specific entries of this volume. For full bibliographical details on primary sources, the reader is referred to Donald Gallup's *Ezra Pound: A Bibliography*. Where appropriate, individual entries are followed by a brief bibliography containing specific items keyed to that entry. However, we have not deemed it necessary to repeat in these bibliographical listings such information as the citation of the standard biographies, like that by Humphrey Carpenter, used by many of the contributors.

The

EZRA POUND

Encyclopedia

A

ABC of Economics

The longest of Pound's money pamphlets began as a series of lectures given at the Università Commerciale Luigi Bocconi in Milan in March 1933. The book's stated aim is to "express the fundamentals of economics so simply and clearly that even people of different economic schools and factions will be able to understand one another" (*SP* 233). Most readers, however, will find the book anything but clear; in fact, it is a confused and confusing document, far from being the "brief, formal treatise" it claims to be. One wonders what Pound's Italian audiences could have made even of a fuller version. The poet seems to be thinking out loud, following his thoughts where they lead, periodically reining them in and reducing them to lists of elements. It is unconventional, off-the-cuff, as though written under deadline pressure. However disorganized the final result, the patient reader can find in *ABC of Economics* Pound's core economic assumptions and characteristic remedies for social ills.

The method of the book is to insist on the proper "dissociation" of ideas; an Aristotelian at heart, Pound is for making distinctions. Here he dissociates property from capital, inflation from steady increase—the one being "disproportionate," the other "natural." This has important implications for Pound's sense of usury. Usury is always "unnatural" and disproportionate, but "interest" may be correlated to natural increase. The basis of Pound's economy is always "nature."

Published by Faber and Faber in 1933, *ABC of Economics* is manifestly a response to the Great Depression. It is unique among Pound's money propaganda in that it appears to have been written before he had been influenced by German economist Silvio Gesell—at any rate, Gesell is not mentioned. It is the most "Douglasite" of Pound's pamphlets; yet, even here, Pound is thinking for himself; when he does refer to Major C. H. Douglas he seems to be recalling conversations of years earlier, not referring to the major's printed matter (221). The most evident contemporary influence in *ABC of Economics* is Dexter Kimball's *Industrial Economics* (1929). The technocratic strain is noticeable when Pound suggests that "the brains of the nation . . . to be used in discerning WHAT work is most needful, what work is necessary and what is desirable" (231). Pound does not get more specific than that. He says he does not care what sort of government a state has, so long as it is honest (231). The secret government of bankers is manifestly not honest, Pound thought, and the depression proved it; but the paranoia that affects Pound's later economic work is little in evidence here.

Pound's principal concern is with "distribution"—a more just distribution of work, money, and goods. "Probably the only economic problem needing emergency solution in our time is distribution," Pound writes (204). Convinced (correctly) that the problems of production have been solved, he wonders aloud: "Why should anyone starve?" (204). "The 'science' or study of economics," Pound argues, "is to make sure no one does" (205).

The pamphlet is a mixture of concrete proposals and technical remedies. Following Kimball, Pound repeatedly suggests that the working day be limited to four (or five) hours in order to distribute work more generally. Since Pound believes that "time is not money, but it is almost everything else" (213) and because he sees that job security for the many, even at reduced hours and wages, has more social value than full-time jobs for the few, he argues that the potential benefits of free time outweigh the potential loss of income. Pound is for "controlled inflation," yet he also assumes that because the amount of money in circulation reflects actual production, halving the working day in order to employ twice the number of workers ought to keep production stable. Pound's remedy would seem to double the amount of money in circulation but keep its buying power the same—there is a contradiction here. Nonetheless, Pound's idea of putting more money into circulation to cure industrial depression was a good one. It is now agreed that lack of purchasing power, not "overproduction," was what kept the world in depression. Later in *ABC of Economics* Pound will return to the problem of inflation by pointing out that a steady increase of money to account for increased production cannot be inflationary; it is a question of "proper augmentation" (230).

Bibliography

Marsh, Alec. *Money and Modernity: Pound, Williams, and the Spirit of Jefferson*. Tuscaloosa: U of Alabama P, 1998.

Surette, Leon. *Pound in Purgatory: From Economic Radicalism to Anti-Semitism*. Urbana: U of Illinois P, 1999.

Alec Marsh

ABC of Reading

Pound's *ABC of Reading* (1934) is a "school book" on "how to study poetry." In three sections, it begins with a discursive introduction in which Pound explains the rationale behind the book's middle section—a sparsely commented array of roughly a dozen exemplary small poems and excerpts, arranged chronologically. The work ends with a rather sketchy "Treatise on Metre" in which Pound eschews technical detail and instead stresses the need to listen, emphasizing the relationship of poetry to music as well as the development of the students' own critical

faculties. "The question of the relative duration of syllables has never been neglected by men with susceptible ears. . . . The way to learn the music of verse is to listen to it" (56).

Pound hangs the discussion of his literary "exhibits" on three technical terms he had introduced in "How to Read": *phanopoeia* (the casting of images, moving or static, upon the imagination); *melopoeia* (plying the musicality of word-sounds); and *logopoeia* (the use of the word in relation to accustomed contexts to achieve complex, often ironic effect). "The maximum *phanopoeia* is probably reached by the Chinese," Pound writes, "due in part to their particular kind of written language" (42). The Chinese written sign or ideogram is "the picture of a thing; of a thing in a given position or relation, or of a combination of things. It *means* the thing or the action or situation, or quality germane to the several things that it pictures" (21). The highest achievements in *melopoeia* Pound finds in the poetry of ancient Greece, in the troubadour poetry of the south of France during the Middle Ages, and in the *canzone* of Renaissance Italy. Shakespeare, the "supreme lyric technician" (101), had benefited from study of Italian songbooks. For the sophisticated use of *logopoeia*, Pound mentions Propertius and Jules Laforgue but cites no specific examples.

Though considered by Pound to be "impersonal enough to serve as a text-book" (11), *ABC of Reading* is, however, a continuation of the iconoclastic educational reform agenda of "How to Read"; it embodies Pound's personal tastes and opinions as practicing poet and critic: "Villon, the first voice of man broken by bad economics" (104); Chaucer was "the greatest poet of his day" (101); Mark Alexander Boyd's "Fra bank to bank, fra wood to wood I rin" is "the most beautiful sonnet in the language" (134); Golding's Ovid "the most beautiful book in the language" (58); in Browning's *Sordello* there is "a certain lucidity of sound. . . . [Y]ou very well may have to retire as far as the *Divina Commedia* for continued narrative having such clarity of outline" (191); and "The dirtiest book in our language is a quite astute manual telling people how to earn money by writing" (89).

In the preface to *ABC of Reading*, Pound acknowledges that its predecessor, "How to Read," had been considered "a controversial pamphlet summarizing the more active or spiky parts of the author's earlier critical skirmishing" (11). *ABC of Reading* has its "spiky parts," too. Pound opens with this warning:

> The harsh treatment here accorded a number of meritorious writers is not aimless, but proceeds from a firm conviction that the only way to keep the best writing in circulation, or to "make the best poetry popular," is by drastic separation of the best from a great mass of writing that has been long considered of value, that has overweighted all curricula. (13)

His overarching goal is to keep the best writing in circulation, that is, to keep the tradition alive. "The honest critic," Pound writes, "must be content to find a VERY LITTLE contemporary work worth serious attention; but he must be ready to RECOGNIZE that little, and to demote work of the past when a new work surpasses it" (91). Pound sees himself an unsparing critic following in the tradition of Alexander Pope:

> A great deal has been written about Pope's bitterness in attack, by people who neglect to note, or at any rate neglect to mention, that these attacks coincided with expressions of respect to the better authors (as Dryden and Swift for example) whom he attempts to weed out from writers who were nuisances in his day and who are now so forgotten that his work needs footnotes longer than the text itself. (168)

He also sees himself in the tradition of the Japanese emperor who, finding that there were too many Noh plays, "picked out 450 and the Noh stage LASTED from 1400 or whenever right down till the day the American navy intruded, and that didn't stop it" (92). Pound's critical goals and reformist educational agenda coincide in *ABC of Reading*:

> In the main I don't see that teaching can do much more than expose counterfeit work, thus gradually leading the student to the valid. The hoax, the sham, the falsification become so habitual that they pass unnoticed; all this is fit matter for education. (192)

Many canonical poets (Spenser, the Romantics, among others) are excluded from Pound's list of "exhibits" because their works do not display to his satisfaction the virtues of efficiency (every word must contribute to the meaning), clarity (natural word order, words used precisely and accurately), and singability (the words, their rhythms, the weight and duration of syllables, sustaining the musical phrase).

The academic establishment fares only a tad better in *ABC of Reading* than it did in "How to Read." Pound lambastes the established poetry anthologies for their lack of critical plan and copycat quality—their unexamined repetition of choices of earlier anthologists. He rails against the *Oxford Book of Verse* in which a poem he holds in the highest regard, John Donne's "The Ecstasy"—which, he says, is "worthy to set beside Cavalcanti's 'Donna mi Prega' for its precision"—is truncated, without notice to the reader. "It would take a bile specialist," Pound says, "to discover why" (140). The *Oxford Book of XVIth Century Verse* omits Gavin Douglas, a fact that "sheds no credit on either the press or their anthologist" (120). Pound derides "misguided ink-page scholars" who are obsessed with the personal lives of authors and do serious damage to the cause of good literature in drawing attention away from the works themselves: "One of the great maladies of modern criticism is this first rush to look for the person, and the corresponding failure EVER to look *at* the thing" (147).

Tim Romano

Active Anthology

Published by Faber and Faber on 12 October 1933, *Active Anthology* presented poems by W. C. Williams, Bunting, Zukofsky, Aragon (in a translation by Cummings), Cummings, Hemingway, Moore, Oppen, Bridson, Eliot, and Pound. Pound noted in his drafts for the preface that his own work was included "at the publisher's request." Pound at one point considered titling his anthology "The Active Element: A collection of poems unfamiliar to British readers." He stated in the preface to *Active Anthology* that he had selected this particular group of poets because "[t]hey have mostly, if not accepted, at any rate faced the demands, and considered the works, made and noted in my 'How to Read' " (23). In his drafts for the preface he also distinguished *Active Anthology* from *Profile*: "[M]y purpose in *Profile* was largely narrative. I was telling the story of what had happened to the texture of poetic expression during a given period. . . . The present collection displays the field of experiment as occupied by a small number of writers who have 'kept at it,' and to whom the title of the volume is still applicable." Among the poets whom Pound considered "active" but did not include was Gordon McLeod, on the grounds that McLeod's long poem *The Ecliptic* had been published already in Britain. Pound seemed chiefly intent on putting the work of Zukofsky and Bunting before the British public. In his drafts for the preface he commented, "Bunting is possibly the white hope of Britain, or possibly isn't," and Zukofsky "is making serious experiments in form which are of interest to a old stager like myself tho I have already made several other experiments." At least one of the contributors had no advance notice of Pound's intentions: D. G. Bridson wrote Pound on 20 September 1933 that he had recently visited the offices of Faber and Faber: "While chez Faber, I found myself in *Active Anthology*. As I knew nothing at all about it, I was very bucked up by the discovery." *Active Anthology* was not widely reviewed; when it was, the judgments were not favorable. Even the reviewer for the *New English Weekly*, who might have been expected to welcome the volume, found it "as pretty a collection of junk as I've yet coped with." Eliot, who had been in the United States when *Active Anthology* was being assembled, wrote to Pound shortly before its publication that, with the exception of the preface (reprinted in *SP* as "Prefatio Aut Cimicium Tumulus," 389–400), the volume was "Tripe."

Bibliography

Aiken, Conrad. "Personae." *Poetry* 44.5 (1934): 276–279.

Beevers, John L. "Active and Preliminary." *New English Weekly* 4.9 (1933): 210–211.

Leavis, F. R. "The Case of Mr. Pound." *Scrutiny* 2 (December 1933): 299–301.

Barry Ahearn

Agamemnon [posthumous]

According to his own date at the bottom of a typescript copy, Pound made an attempt at translating Aeschylus's *Agamemnon* around 1919 but never finished it. This may be the reason why Donald Gallup gave his edited version published in *Paideuma* in 1986 the title "Ezra Pound's 'An Opening for *Agamemnon*.' " It must be noted, however, that the Beinecke typescript has "OPENING FOR AN AGAMEMNON," which seems to underline more clearly how Pound regarded his attempt as a "criticism by translation." Although he regarded this play as probably the best of the surviving examples of Greek drama, all of his references to Aeschylus throughout his writings generally denounce the playwright as "agglutinative" and "verbose" (*LE* 273), most obviously because his magniloquence and habit of making compound words clashed with Pound's own Imagist preferences. His accounts of his treatment of the *Agamemnon* in the *Dial* of March 1923 (277–278) and in *Guide to Kulchur* (92–93) therefore describe how he changed Aeschylus's highly rhetorical language into "nigger and cockney," that is, living speech, and how he used "every [possible] el[l]ipsis and elimination" (93). Pound's fragment thus has only 56 lines of speech for the original 366 lines, its most important deletion being the entire Parodos (ll. 40–257) in which the Chorus describes the Trojan expedition and gives the famous address to Zeus. Pound, however, probably never finished his translation because he never found a solution to overcome the dilemma expressed in *Guide to Kulchur*: "No one with a theatric imagination can conceive [the *Agamemnon*] holding now as a stage play IF you leave in all the verbiage. But as an entity it stands rock-like" (93).

Bibliography

Aeschylus. *Agamemnon*. Studio City: Players, 1995.

Gallup, Donald. "Ezra Pound's 'An Opening for *Agamemnon*.' " *Paideuma* 15.2–3 (1986): 117–120.

Pound, Ezra. "Paris Letter. February, 1923." *Dial* 74.3 (1923): [273]–280.

Peter Liebregts

Agresti, Olivia Rossetti (1875–1961)

The daughter of W. M. Rossetti and thus niece of D. G. and Christina Rossetti and a cousin of Ford Madox Ford, Agresti (b. London, 1875; d. Rome, 1961) was one of the last survivors of the second English-born generation of the Rossettis. A socialist, anarchist, and agnostic in her early life, she has recorded her experiences in *A Girl among the Anarchists*, a novel coauthored with her sister Helen and published under the pen name of Isabel Meredith. In 1897 she married Antonio Agresti, a Florentine writer, and settled in Rome. From 1921 to 1943 she worked for the Italian Association of Joint Stock Companies, whose monthly journal she edited, writing often on twentieth-century economic issues. Her friends in Italy numbered among them many important literary and political personalities of the time; she was well versed in the great writers of England and Italy, and she had a special fondness for Dante.

In 1904 she met David Lubin (1849–1919), a Polish Jew from California, who was a pioneer in the movement for world economic organization; with Agresti assisting him, Lubin went on to establish in 1906 the International Institute of Agriculture, a forerunner of the UN Food and Agricultural Organization. Her reflections on Lubin's life and ideology are recorded in *David Lubin: A Study in Practical Idealism* (1922), a book that, at her insistence, Pound read in 1949 and commented on.

Agresti and Pound corresponded for over twenty years (1937–1959), met many times in Rome, and became steadfast friends. A devout Catholic, loyal Italian citizen, fascist sympathizer, and astute commentator on social and economic issues, especially those of contemporary Italy, Agresti served as an ideal sounding board for Pound—especially during his St. Elizabeths years. Their exchanges—in which Agresti holds her own and often challenges Pound—shed light on his political, economic, and religious views of the period. When upon his return to Italy in 1958 Pound discovered that Agresti was in need of money, he made a gift of their correspondence to her; sold to Yale

for $600, theirs were the first original Pound letters to be acquired for the Ezra Pound Papers in the Beinecke Rare Book and Manuscripts collection.

Bibliography

Agresti, Olivia Rossetti. *David Lubin: A Study in Practical Idealism*. Boston: Little, Brown, 1922.
Agresti, Olivia Rossetti, and Helen Rossetti Angeli [Isabel Meredith]. *A Girl among the Anarchists*. London: Duckworth & Co., 1903.
Gallup, Donald. *Pigeons and the Granite: Memories of a Yale Librarian*. New Haven: Yale UP, 1988.
Pound, Ezra. *"I Cease Not to Yowl": Ezra Pound's Letters to Olivia Rossetti Agresti*. Ed. Demetres P. Tryphonopoulos and Leon Surette. Urbana: U of Illinois P, 1998.

Demetres P. Tryphonopoulos

Aldington, Richard (1892–1962)

Richard Aldington was a British poet, novelist, translator, and critic. In April 1912, Aldington (a lawyer's son and University of London student) schemed with Pound and H. D. at a Kensington tea shop to create the Imagist movement (or *mouvemong*, as he later called it, mocking Pound's French accent). Through Pound, he published three poems in the second *Poetry* issue. He lived on Church Walk across from Pound and above H. D. and married H. D. in October 1913. The marriage is portrayed in H. D.'s novel *Bid Me to Live* (1960). Aldington contributed ten poems to *Des Imagistes* (1914), edited by Pound. In 1916 he enlisted as a private in the British army, rising to captain by 1918 but serving mostly in the trenches. He was demobilized in February 1920. He was not the father of H. D.'s daughter Perdita (b. 1918); they separated in 1919 and were divorced in 1938. In the 1930s he lived with the Irish novelist Brigit Patmore. Often "butting" against Pound—whose work, he notes in his memoirs, "can be abrupt and barbarous" but whom he considers "a pleasant companion and the most generous of men"—he remained devoted. Twice he satirizes Pound in fiction—as painter Frank Upjohn in *Death of a Hero* (1929) and as musician Charlemagne Cox in "Nobody's Baby" (*Soft Answers*, 1932). Aldington also edited *Imagist Anthology*

1930: New Poetry of the Imagists (1930), but Pound would not contribute.

Bibliography

Aldington, Richard. *Life for Life's Sake*. New York: Viking P, 1941; London: Cassell, 1968.

Doyle, Charles. *Richard Aldington: A Biography*. Carbondale: Southern Illinois UP, 1989.

John Gery

Alfred Venison's Poems

Published like a number of other works under a pseudonym, Pound's collection carries the subtitle "Social credit themes by the poet of Titchfield street." Printed by Stanley Nott in 1935 as "Pamphlets on the New Economics, No. 9," the collection brings together poems that first appeared serially between February and November 1934 in A. R. Orage's Social Credit journal the *New English Weekly*. With the exception of two poems printed in Orage's journal in 1935 and 1936, these poems were included as part of Appendix II in *Personae* (1949; see Gallup A27b) and the Faber edition (1949; see Gallup A27c).

Demetres P. Tryphonopoulos

America, Roosevelt and the Causes of the Present War

Originally a pamphlet published in Italian as *L'America, Roosevelt e le cause della guerra presente* (1944) as part of Pound's propaganda effort on behalf of the Salò Republic, it was translated by John Drummond into English in 1951 and published by Peter Russell. It is most accessible, albeit in a censored form, in *Impact* (1960)—edited and introduced by Noel Stock— where it is called "America and the Second World War." The tract has little to do with Roosevelt or the world situation in 1944. It is very much in the American populist tradition with a simple thesis: "This war is part of the secular war between usurers and peasants, between the usurocracy and whomever does an honest day's work with his own brain or hands" (*America, Roosevelt* 5). Pound does not rest with the implication that all wars are such; the pamphlet rehearses the populistic history of the United States, with its creditor versus debtor version of

class struggle, which Pound had absorbed through numberless sources. Pound shows how the American Revolution was caused by the evil policies of the Bank of England, which suppressed paper money in the Pennsylvania Colony; how the revolution was betrayed by Alexander Hamilton and the financial interests; how the Civil War was fought over Southern debt to New York banks; and how Lincoln was shot at the behest of the bankers for financing the war via greenback (therefore debt-free) currency. All this "true" history of the United States has been covered up by the money power. The German-Italian Axis, of course, has picked up the struggle against the usurers. Properly appreciated, the Fascist Revolution is the continuation of the American Revolution. In this way, Pound's booklet extends the argument of *Jefferson and/or Mussolini* (1935).

Tim Redman, who devotes several pages to this pamphlet, notes, "Despite constant talk of usurers and usocracy, there is very little overt anti-Semitism in this work" (246). *America, Roosevelt and the Causes of the Present War* should be compared to Pound's "An Introduction to the Economic Nature of the United States," another tract written during the same year and available in *Selected Prose* (167–185).

Bibliography

Pound, Ezra. *America, Roosevelt and the Causes of the Present War*. Trans. John Drummond. London: Peter Russell, 1951.

———. *L'America, Roosevelt e le cause della guerra presente*. Venezia: Casa editrice della edizioni popolari, 1944.

———. *Impact*. Ed. Noel Stock. Chicago: Henry Regnery, 1960.

Redman, Tim. *Ezra Pound and Italian Fascism*. New York: Cambridge UP, 1991.

Alec Marsh

American History: Colonial to Nineteenth Century

Pound's sense of history is linked to his theory of culture, which dispenses with the cataloguing of fact and broad generalizations of conventional scholarship in favor of a focus on what he calls the "luminous detail." Thus one cannot find either in his prose or in his poetry any chronologically organized vision of American history. Under the influence of Brooks Adams, Pound placed his view under the sign of tragic decay. The roots of American democracy are to be found in the ethics and politics of the first settlers and later in the Declaration of Independence, but he sees American industrialization in the nineteenth century as nothing but a perversion of the original ideals. The fundamental purpose of the American state has been lost in the process, and according to Pound, it has been lost to "usura," the key concept in his historicism.

For Pound, this is particularly obvious in nineteenth-century America and is contrary to the ideals of the eighteenth century. The political philosophy that informs the works of John Adams and Thomas Jefferson, his only sources on the American Revolution and the subsequent birth of the nation, is colored with the Enlightenment's valorization of the individual, democracy, and equality. From these works he derives his faith in the power of the individual to generate massive political change and his protest against what he sees as the degenerate world of industrial America.

Several texts document this vision, but three stand out as the repositories of Pound's vision of American history. In *The Cantos*, he often quotes from Adams or Jefferson, as he does at length in Canto 21, when he transcribes a letter by Jefferson; but the major sequence devoted to the heroes of the construction of the United States of America is Cantos 62–71, the so-called Adams Cantos. By calling their letters "a shrine and a monument," he pays homage to their skills not only as politicians but also as prose writers. He uses the figure of John Adams to revile not only the corruption that jeopardized political construction but above all the corruption he sees around him in his own time. Some other passages of *The Cantos* are devoted to the followers of those two heroes: Canto 37, for instance, deals with Martin Van Buren. The decline of the values of such Jeffersonians after the Civil War is seen as the cause of the decline of America. This sequence is at the center of the whole work

of *The Cantos*, and the theme is later at the end of *The Pisan Cantos* linked to the emblematic ideogram "chung," the unwobbling pivot (of early American law) as well as "l'asse che non vacilla" (of the fascist regime in Italy).

And indeed the most articulate formulation of Pound's view of American history in the nineteenth century is to be found in two prose works published in Italy. In *Jefferson and/or Mussolini* (1935) he draws a parallel, which he admits is far-fetched, between the American Revolution and the fascist revolution carried out by Mussolini. Basing his comparison on what he presumed to be both men's attachment to good order, he explains that what is happening in Italy in the 1920s and 1930s is the resurgence of the spirit that animated the Founding Fathers and the presidents in the first half of the nineteenth century. However, his most explicit account of his vision of American history occurs in the controversial *L'America, Roosevelt e le cause della guerra presente* (1944), published at the time of the demise of Italian fascism. In this booklet, he focuses on the nineteenth century, emphasizing the links he sees between the succession of events and an enduring war between usurocracy and the proletariat. He cites economic details such as Jackson's and Van Buren's struggles with the banking system and affirms the need for the state to hold a monopoly over credit (a Jeffersonian but also Douglasite notion). If America is seen as free from the oppression of usurocrats (embodied in the Bank of England's preventing the colonies from having control over credit through a currency of their own) between the Revolution and Lincoln's assassination, the latter event marks for Pound the success of a conspiracy to submit America to high finance. Pound read the rest of the nineteenth century as proof of this decay of democracy and freedom, leading to the disasters of the twentieth.

As he considered the American nineteenth century, Pound modified its accepted interpretation of history to suit his personal certainties and illustrate his economic and historical theories. The link he proposes between Jeffersonian America and Mussolinian Italy bears little credibility but is to be inscribed in his totalizing vision of mankind's evolution as "a VORTEX, from which, and through which, and into which, ideas are constantly rushing" (*GB* 92).

Bibliography

Flory, Wendy Stallard. *Ezra Pound and The Cantos: A Record of Struggle.* New Haven: Yale UP, 1980.

Nicholls, Peter. *Ezra Pound: Politics, Economics, and Writing: A Study of The Cantos.* Atlantic Highlands: Humanities P, 1984.

North, Michael. *The Political Aesthetic of Yeats, Eliot, and Pound.* Cambridge: Cambridge UP, 1991.

Redman, Tim. *Ezra Pound and Italian Fascism.* New York: Cambridge UP, 1991.

Vettori, Vittorio. *Ezra Pound e il Senso dell'America.* Rome: ERSI, 1975.

Hélène Aji

American History: Twentieth Century

During Ezra Pound's lifetime, the United States slowly developed into the dominant world power of the twentieth century. In "Patria Mia" (1913), Pound spoke proudly of a muscular America full of opportunity. By 1937, however, his evaluation had changed. According to his new reckoning, Pound was born during "the period of despair . . . 1870–1930" (*SP* 147). What led to such a turnaround?

Pound's original assessment was the product of the Progressive Era of American history, a period of vigorous political change. Ezra's grandfather Thaddeus Pound, a former Wisconsin lieutenant governor and congressman, advocated government intervention in the national economy. Thaddeus's politics as well as his experimentation with "extra-statal money" and his example as "a positive figure of creative energy" (Marsh 175–176) had a lasting influence on Ezra, though the younger Pound's first published poem (1896) was a limerick sympathetic to another Progressive, William Jennings Bryan, whose free silver campaign Thaddeus opposed (Redman 250–251). Pound retained an ambivalence toward Bryan, seeing him as "continuing an honest tradition" (*SP* 179) but lumping him with "other plagues of our capitol" who practiced "degrading concepts of government" (*SP* 218–219). Pressure by Bryan and the Democrats eventually led to Republican Theodore Roosevelt's Progressive reforms, which championed the public good over that of corporations; Woodrow Wilson's New Freedom policies, including the Federal Reserve Act, capped the Progressive Era. While Pound had little to say about Roosevelt, he denounced Wilson throughout his life, claiming that "[a]ll American and republican principles were lost during the damnable reign of the infamous Woodrow" (*SP* 243).

American isolationist voices delayed the entry of the United States into World War I. America's reluctance to enter the war "on the side of civilization . . . against barbarism," Pound believed, led to Henry James's "deathbed" renunciation of his U.S. citizenship (*LE* 295–296). After the war, Wilson solidified America's international position through his leadership in the Versailles negotiations. Domestically, the 1920s saw unprecedented economic and industrial expansion, leading to an overvaluation of stocks that eventually resulted in the 1929 stock market crash.

The crash intensified Pound's postwar turn toward economics. During the 1920s, Pound was advocating general solutions to social problems: "The job of America for the next twenty years will be to drive back the government into its proper place" (*SP* 221). By 1932, the darkest year of the Great Depression, industrial production had declined by 51 percent from its 1929 peak, and unemployment had risen to nearly 25 percent. To help, Pound proposed more specific measures, including the "shortening of the working day to four hours," claiming that "no other single and simple move will solve so much of the present 'trouble' with so little bureaucratic infamy, meddling, piddling," since the shorter workday would increase hourly wages and leisure time, decrease unemployment, and increase consumption ("The Depression Has Just Begun" 4). Newly elected Franklin D. Roosevelt's response was similar. He shortened the workday, resulting in decreased unemployment and increased weekly wages. He also suspended the gold standard and inflated the currency to relieve debtors and stimulate production, creating the so-called commodity dollar. Pound supported the commodity dollar, but when Roosevelt, pursuing his New Deal policies, showed no interest in experimenting with Social Credit, Pound became disillusioned with Roosevelt's ability to see the root cause of economic crises.

At the same time, Pound discovered Brooks Adams's *The Law of Civilization and Decay*. Adams's belief that the usurer class, through legislation, had become by the mid-1800s the unrivaled power in Europe and America gave voice to Pound's own views. He began to see American culture in a state of decline beginning with the Civil War, becoming "less *nationally* American as the usurocracy came into steadily more filthy and damnable control of the Union" (*SP* 161). Adams's cultural history also corresponded to the history of Pound's family, which "claimed an impeccable American pedigree" but "were now perceptibly descending in the world" (Carpenter 5).

Pound's disappointment in what he saw as a declining American culture intensified with America's entrance into World War II. He had searched for the cause of World War I and found his culprits in banks, financiers, and usurers, as had many others, and he attributed the same cause to World War II: "The war was started for gold, to maintain the fetish value of gold" (*"Ezra Pound Speaking"* 285). Believing that only economic reform would work, Pound broadcast: "This is my war all right, I have been in it for 20 years. My Grandad was in it before me" (120). His war was also against Roosevelt whom he now saw as perpetrating "a scheme . . . to grab world monopolies" (299). Pound's bitterness toward Roosevelt lasted long after the president's death in 1945. As late as 17 October 1957, writing to John Theobald, Pound still spoke of Roosevelt with vitriol: "[Y]ou are FAIRLY wet. Refusing to see Roosevelt a cad, and a liar who perjured himself every time he took oath of office" (*Ezra Pound/John Theobald Letters* 104).

The dropping of the atomic bombs on Hiroshima and Nagasaki closed one war but inaugurated several others for the United States, both foreign and domestic. The uneasy cooperation between the United States and the Soviet Union during the war broke down completely after the Soviets established satellite governments in Eastern Europe. An edgy peace exposed an unsettled domestic question: African American rights. In 1948, the Democratic Party split over the issue of civil rights, foreshadowing the controversies of the following decade, highlighted by the Warren Supreme Court's decision to strike down segregation in 1954. In response, advocates of segregation organized White Citizen's Councils (WCCs) that sought to stir up unrest among southern whites. Among Pound's more intimate associates during his St. Elizabeths years was bookseller John Kasper, who, along with David Horton, published the *Square Dollar Series* of books, which Pound used as a means of disseminating political and economic ideas. Believing mandated integration to be part of a Jewish conspiracy, Kasper organized the Seaboard WCC in Washington, D.C., and instigated mob demonstrations against integration in Clinton, Tennessee. Pound supported Kasper's activities insomuch as Kasper shared Pound's belief that "the NAACP [was] being run by kikes not by coons" (*"I Cease Not to Yowl"* 235), the real source of racial unrest being the desire of the usurocracy to maintain its money monopoly.

After leaving St. Elizabeths, Pound returned to Italy. In 1960, on the cusp of silence, he lamented that decades of expatriate life had blinded him to the changes the United States underwent during that time: "One is transplanted and grows, and one is pulled up and taken back to what one has been transplanted from and it is no longer there" (Hall 243).

Bibliography

Carpenter, Humphrey. *A Serious Character: The Life of Ezra Pound*. Boston: Houghton Mifflin, 1988.

Hall, Donald. "*Paris Review* Interview: Ezra Pound." *Remembering Poets: Reminiscences and Opinions: Dylan Thomas, Robert Frost, T. S. Eliot, Ezra Pound*. New York: Harper and Row, 1978. 222–244.

Marsh, Alec. "Thaddeus Coleman Pound's 'Newspaper Scrapbook' as a Source for *The Cantos*." *Paideuma* 24.2–3 (1995): 163–193.

Pound, Ezra. "The Depression Has Just Begun." *Contempo* 1.16 (15 January 1932): [1], 4.

———. *Ezra Pound/John Theobald Letters.* Ed. Donald Pearce and Herbert Schneidau. Redding Ridge: Black Swan, 1984.

———. *"Ezra Pound Speaking": Radio Speeches of World War II.* Ed. Leonard W. Doob. Westport: Greenwood, 1978.

———. *"I Cease Not to Yowl": Ezra Pound's Letters to Olivia Rossetti Agresti.* Ed. Demetres P. Tryphonopoulos and Leon Surette. Urbana: U of Illinois P, 1998.

Redman, Tim. "Pound's Politics and Economics." *The Cambridge Companion to Ezra Pound.* Ed. Ira B. Nadel. Cambridge: Cambridge UP, 1999. 249–263.

Michael J. Alleman

American Literature: Colonial to Nineteenth Century

In many ways, Pound's assessment of the state and development of American literature in the late eighteenth and early nineteenth centuries runs counter to his assessment of the state and development of American society of the same period. Whereas Pound defines the period of "American civilization" as 1760 to 1830, and characterizes the period 1830 to 1860 as one of "thinning, of mental impoverishment" (*SP* 147), he seems to assert the reverse when considering American literature. With the exception of Jefferson and Adams themselves, whose letters display "an excellent prose which has not . . . been surpassed in our fatherland" (*SP* 148), Pound has almost nothing to say about the merit of American writers in the period 1760 to 1850. They are perhaps the least represented group in *The Cantos*—Hawthorne receives just a single mention, and that by way of the fact that his funeral attracted such literati as Emerson and Longfellow (103). This is no doubt partly attributable to Pound's privileging of poetry over prose and to the relative scarcity of noteworthy poets before the mid-nineteenth century. It is also likely related to Pound's aversion to eighteenth-century verbalism, an affront that apparently continued well into nineteenth-century American literature; but it is probably most deeply embedded in Pound's sympathy for those who struggle to produce art while "wholly surrounded by roughnecks" (*LE* 391).

Pound's "luminous detail" approach to history may be loosely equated with his color sense approach to literary theory, and there is little doubt that the first American making a significant contribution to the palette is Walt Whitman, "the only one of the conventionally recognized 'American poets' who is worth reading" (*SP* 145). Despite his claim that "no American poet is of any use for the palette" (*LE* 218), Pound discovered in Whitman a kinship of purpose in their respective attempts to tell the tale of the whole tribe: "We have one sap and one root" ("A Pact," *P* 89). Pound repeatedly refers to Whitman as his spiritual father, like Dante a man who wrote "in the language of his people" (*SP* 146), eventually coming to refer to himself as "a Walt Whitman who has learned to wear a collar and a dress shirt" (*SP* 145). This last comment hints at the curious duality that exists in Pound's response to Whitman. Although enthralled by the scope and ambition of Whitman's project, Pound seems to have been much less impressed by the quality of Whitman's verse. Curiously, given the obvious impact of Whitman's verse on the development of vers libre, Pound says little to recommend Whitman's poetic practice. More taken with the concept than the execution, Pound ultimately notes that Whitman's "crudity is an exceeding great stench" (*SP* 145).

In most respects Whitman stands apart from his contemporaries in Pound's esteem. William Carlos Williams draws praise largely because of his failure to "resemble any member of the Concord school" (*LE* 391), while Emerson is damned with the faintest of praise: "Even Emerson had sufficient elasticity of mind to find something in the 'yawp'" (*LE* 384). The "cult of Poe" is dismissed as "absurd" (*LE* 218). The only other nineteenth-century American to fall within the range of writers with color sense is Henry James, though, again, Pound seems much more impressed with James's yearlong letter-writing campaign "to bring America on the side of civilization," and subsequent death of apoplexy, than with *"gli occhi onesti e tardi"*

(*LE* 295). Ultimately, despite the best efforts of Whitman, James, and the artists of the Carman-Hovey period, at the dawn of the twentieth century, America remained for Pound, "from the White House to the gutter," a land "still dominated by 'puritanical' hatred to what is beyond its understanding" (*LE* 219), the writers of the period manacled by the roughneck mentality.

Lance Callahan

American Literature: Twentieth Century

Given the fact that Pound and his coterie in exile represent a key voice in twentieth-century literature, it is difficult to separate Pound's pronouncements regarding the work of his American contemporaries from his socioartistic mandate and well-honed strictures on the art of literary composition. This is particularly true of his response to American literature in the early part of the century when his brief stint at Wabash College in Crawfordsville, Indiana, tended to color his response to all things American, seeing in them little save parochialism and narrow-mindedness. Seeing himself as one of those "[w]ho bear the brunt of our America" ("To Whistler, American," *P* 235), Pound set out for Italy and England in 1908 armed with a steadfast belief that "the young gents of literature in America" (Canto 67) were for the most part derivative insouciants whose banality allowed them to be suffered by a usurist publishing industry. This, coupled with his belief that "when a creative act occurs in America 'no one' seems aware of what is occurring" (*LE* 393), meant it was easier for him "to emigrate than for America to change her civilization" (*LE* 385).

But it is unfair to suggest that Pound summarily dismisses the American literature of the period out of hand. Key to Pound's response is the clear demarcation he draws between the talents of American writers and the lack thereof of American publishers, the "hair oil boys" driven by "contempt for and oblivion of whatever national culture exists" (*SP* 163). Pound's reproach of the industry may be based partly on his Social Credit economic and political beliefs, that the publishers are little more than propogandists for, and champions of, the usuroc-racy. But Pound's is primarily an attack on the industry's provincialism, which manifests itself in four ways: "The absurd aping of foreign modes"; "fear of accepting foreign work in an unknown mode"; "neglect of high-grade work done at home"; and "back-scratching and boosting of tosh *because* it is produced at home" (*SP* 163). This critique holds true to Pound's belief that without constant experiment literature dies. Because of the attempt to fix, then cater to the popular taste, and thus maximize profits, little is published save that which has proven formulaically successful: "The seventh issue of any of the hair oil organs is identical with the first" (*SP* 163). This stagnancy means that "the typical American editor of the last twenty years has resolutely shut his mind against serious American writing" (*LE* 384).

Thus it is not simply a matter of empathy that leads Pound to reserve his highest praise for expatriate Americans and for those whose work was first published in Europe. "Jefferson could not imagine an American going voluntarily to inhabit Europe" (*SP* 161), but Pound certainly could. And notwithstanding his claim that "in an age of pestilence like our own there is little but the great art of the past to convince one that the human species deserves to continue" (*SP* 430), Pound clearly saw a great deal of American literature that he considered great art, principally the work of William Carlos Williams, the "sole known American-dwelling author who could be counted on to oppose some sort of barrier" (*LE* 390) to the dilatory effects of the hair oil boys. Williams's genius may be partly rooted in his English/Danish/French/Spanish pedigree, that "he has not in his ancestral endocrines the arid curse of our nation" (*LE* 391); but it is his method, his attempt to "understand something in its natural colors and shapes," so akin to the Poundian attempt to grasp the thing in itself, that cements Williams's position as the great American writer. He and Joseph Gould serve as the sterling examples of the "non-Mabie, non-Howells type of author" (*LE* 393) America needs. Robert Frost receives similar praise, Pound going so far as to call it "a sinister thing" that such "a talent as that of Robert Frost should have to be exported before it can find due encouragement and recognition" (*LE* 384). Pound considers it an equal travesty that H. D. and Fletcher have been subjected to a similar fate. Pound's appreciation of Frost, to the extent that he helped Frost publish, is particularly telling since the two poets' work is so different. And indeed, "Mr. Frost's work is not accomplished, but it is the work of a man who will make neither concessions nor pretenses" (*LE* 386). Pound clearly admired those American writers he considered principled, even when those principles conflicted with his own. In the end, however, it is Frost's ability "to paint the thing, the thing as he sees it" (*LE* 382) that draws Pound's esteem, more so than his refusal to do "monkey tricks" (*LE* 386). A similar principle no doubt underlies Pound's assessment of "Steve" Crane as the finest American writer of prose fiction.

Delineating just what Pound considers "American" in literature is rather more speculative. As he points out, many "take Browning for an American" (Canto 48), while Williams starts his investigation of America "where an European would start if an European were to write about America" (*LE* 392). Still, Pound is clear that there are distinctly American authors, chief among them Frost and Gould—Frost because of his use of "a definite type and set of ideas and sensibilities, known and established in his ancestral demesne," while "Gould is no less New England" (*LE* 390). Sounding rather like Williams's in his own pronouncements on the topic, Pound notes that it is not a matter of subject but of approach, of "the difference between regionalism, or regionalist art and art that has its root in a given locality" (*LE* 390). Ultimately, the most American of writers seem to be those possessing the traits Pound so admired in eighteenth-century settlers, "driven by the desire for Freedom of Conscience, hardened by privations, favoured and betrayed" (*SP* 167).

Lance Callahan

Anglo-Saxon Translation

"He fished by obstinate isles," British no less than Aegean. Anglo-Saxon is a stubborn language, its poetry not only remote in subject matter and speech but preserved in corrupt codices. At a time when much of the leading scholarship was conducted not in Britain or the United States but in Germany and Scandinavia, Pound's exposure to Anglo-Saxon was exceptional. He studied it in 1904 under his mentor Joseph Ibbotson. Pound published his version of the best-known poem preserved in the Exeter Codex, "The Seafarer," in the November 1911 issue of A. R. Orage's *New Age* as the first installment of "I Gather the Limbs of Osiris." The next installment outlined Pound's proto-ideogrammic method of scholarship, "the method of Luminous Detail": "[C]ertain facts give one a sudden insight into circumjacent conditions, into the causes, their effects, into sequence, and law" (*SP* 22). Specific texts, including "The Seafarer," constitute just such "details."

In the same article Pound explained that he "sought in Anglo-Saxon a certain element which has transmuted the various qualities of poetry which have drifted up from the south" (*SP* 24). That element would work its way into the accents and idioms of Canto 1 and lend a refrain to Pound's eulogy to Ford, Yeats, and Joyce in the first of *The Pisan Cantos*: "Lordly men are to earth o'ergiven" (Canto 74). He would interpolate "The Seafarer" into *Cathay*, noting that Li Po and the anonymous Anglo-Saxon poet were approximate contemporaries.

Anglo-Saxon poetry rhymes not on the homophony of line-ending syllables but on the alliteration of initial accented consonants or, exceptionally, vowels. In Anglo-Saxon verse Pound could recuperate an aboriginal English precedent for verse freed from closed forms, from the "sequence of a metronome" (*LE* 4), and from Victorian fustian. Hence the argument, in "How to Read," that since Chaucer "English literature lives on translation. . . . [E]very allegedly great age is an age of translations" (*LE* 34–35).

Pound discovered in Anglo-Saxon poetry what Doughty and Hopkins had discovered: A native word-hoard plastic, compact and forceful. Hopkins of course would not be published until 1918, but by 1914 Pound was reciting Doughty's epic *The Dawn in Britain*, written in a "pure" (un-Latinate) English, to Yeats at Stone

Cottage. The precursor peeks out of "The Seafarer": "Delight 'mid the doughty" (l. 80). Pound meanwhile found in the Old English seafarer a North Sea Odysseus who "went down to the ship, / Set keel to breakers, forth on the godly sea" (Canto 1). And when the seafarer extols a vanished age of heroes (ll. 82–87), he is very much a modernist hailing the primary energies of the archaic.

Translating, probably without a crib, "from the Anglo-Saxon" (*SP* 35), Pound may commit blunders—at the very least storms falling "in icy feathers" (l. 24) seem no improvement on the original ("There answered them the tern, icy-feathered"). However, in the light of Louis Zukofsky's homophonic translations of Catullus and of Plautus's *Rudens* ("A"-21), readers can appreciate Pound's pioneering attempt to translate less for sense than for sound. Usually this involves no great offense to the literal meaning: The cry of the solitary bird "whets for the whale-path the heart irresistibly" (l. 63), much as it does in Anglo-Saxon: "hweteþ on hwael-weg hreðer unwearnum." Sometimes, especially when Pound wishes to omit Christian references, the translation is hapless: "And his laud beyond them remain 'mid the English" (l. 78)—"amid the angels," rather—("ond his lof siþþan libbe mid englum"). Pound's omission of the poem's concluding twenty-two-line homily is, however, hardly renegade. This was consistent with the widespread scholarly view that the poem's Christian motifs were corruptions introduced during scribal recension. Sweet's *Anglo-Saxon Reader* (1876), likely Pound's source, omits the poem's last sixteen lines.

Pound's aim is renovation. Translation here is *nekuia*: By giving blood to the dead, the dead may disclose futurity and possibility. "The Seafarer" offers Pound the possibilities of compound nouns (e.g., "breastlock": hreðerlocan), a freer verse, parataxis (the structural principle of *The Cantos*), a non-Christian vitality, and shortly before proposing "A Pact" with Whitman, a song of the open (whale-)road.

Finding in a thousand-year-old codex a modern poem, and creating a homophonic translation from it, Pound, as boldly as Hölderlin in his versions of Sophocles, achieves fidelity by preserving rather than eliding the alien character of the translated text. The result exemplifies Schleiermacher's call for translation as estrangement. Key verbal figures are reproduced intact. Pound thus translates most appearances of *mod* ("spirit," "heart," German *Mut*) as "mood." In preserving etymology in defiance of contemporary usage, Pound recovers the archaic sense. By its final appearance—"My mood 'mid the mere-flood" (l. 59)—this act of lexical syncresis is complete: "Min mod-sefa mid mere-flode." A transitory English mood has become the spirited Anglo-Saxon *mod* again. Here is one way to purify the language of the tribe. Walter Benjamin asserts that translation should reshape the host language in conformity with the original. In "The Seafarer" Pound reshapes English to conform to English.

Bibliography

Adams, Stephen J. "A Case for Pound's 'Seafarer.' " *Mosaic* 9 (Winter 1976): 127–146.

Krapp, George Philip, and Elliot Van Kirke Dobbie, eds. *The Exeter Book*. New York: Columbia UP, 1936.

Robinson, Fred C. " 'The Might of the North': Pound's Anglo-Saxon Studies and 'The Seafarer.' " *Yale Review* 71 (1982): 199–224.

Andre Furlani

Antheil, George (1900–1959) and *Antheil and the Treatise on Harmony*

Pound's fascination with George Antheil is often dismissed as a mistake because the young American composer never fully realized his aspirations; but the Antheil of the 1920s was an exceptionally promising talent. When Pound met him in 1923, Antheil was already gaining a reputation as composer, pianist, and provocateur. He had published an article in *Querschnitt* describing himself as a "neofist," or "neo-futurist," criticizing the noise music of the futurists for its lack of rhythmic organization; on this basis, Pound recognized Antheil as the composer missing from the Vorticist movement. Antheil was also impressed with Pound's violinist friend Olga Rudge and composed a series of three violin sonatas for her, which they performed together. These works feature complex additive rhythms, clusters, and percussionistic effects, the second even incorporating a drum (which Pound performed on, on at least one occasion). In 1924, Antheil wrote out the score for Pound's opera *Le Testament*, in extraordinarily complex rhythmic notation.

The major work of Antheil's career, *Ballet Mécanique*, was composed as score for the celebrated film by Fernand Léger and Dudley Murphy—itself a landmark in cinematic history. Conceived for pianolas and percussion ensemble (including, notoriously, an airplane propeller), it too features complex, driving rhythms. For technical reasons, it was never performed with Léger's film; but its Paris premiere in 1926 was a *succés de scandale*, with rioting in the audience that recalled the premiere of Stravinsky's *Le Sacre*. This piece is a major achievement, and it has been successfully revived. In 1927, however, the American premiere at Carnegie Hall was an embarrassing fiasco. Antheil, driven primarily it seems by a need to succeed and a desire to please, abandoned his avant-garde manner and turned to a popular jazz-flavored neoclassicism. His opera *Transatlantic*—the first American opera ever mounted by a European company—was attended by Pound and Leo Frobenius in Frankfurt in 1928, but neither was impressed. Pound and Antheil never again met after 1929.

In the 1930s, Antheil ended up in Hollywood composing movie scores, beginning with *The Scoundrel* (1935) and the Gary Cooper western *The Plainsman* (1936). If his earlier music is often too close to Stravinsky, his later concert music, including six symphonies, is too obviously marked by Prokofiev and Shostakovich. Antheil also pursued a writing career, publishing a murder mystery called *Death in the Dark* (1930), which includes a character based on Pound. In 1945, when Pound's reputation was at its nadir, Antheil published *Bad Boy of Music* (1945), an entertaining but self-serving and unreliable autobiography. Antheil is mentioned in *The Cantos* only once, as the "ebullient" (Canto 74).

Antheil and the Treatise on Harmony (Paris 1924; Chicago 1927) was intended to boost Antheil's reputation but is often said to have done more harm than good, and Antheil distances himself from it in his autobiography. At the time, however, he was clearly involved in its production. The book is cast in four sections: "The Treatise on Harmony" is the most interesting part; "Antheil" is an effort to explain the composer's procedures; "William Atheling" is a selection from Pound's reviews, with Antheil's rather uninformative marginalia interspersed; and "Varia" gathers assorted anecdotes. The American edition of 1927 adds (without headings) two brief articles, "George Antheil 1924–1926" and "Workshop Orchestration."

The salient ideas of Pound's theory—and it is impossible to separate his original ideas from Antheil's—rise from his Vorticist critique of Debussy's Impressionism. Debussy's music violates the Vorticist principle of "primary pigment" in trying to make music too pictorial; and his music, which rises "like steam from a morass," lacks rhythmic definition. Both Antheil and Pound perceived that the noise music of the futurist Luigi Russolo, with its imitations of natural and mechanical sounds, was likewise too pictorial and likewise lacked rhythmic definition. Pound dismisses it with the deft phrase "accelerated impressionism" (38).

The originality of this theory lies in its turning away from traditional notions of harmony and tonality, and searching for the organizing principles of music elsewhere, in rhythm. For this reason, Pound's editor Murray Schafer values Pound's little manifesto equally with the monumental theories of Heinrich Schenker, who abstracted musical tonality, and Arnold Schoenberg, who sought to escape tonality. (Unknown to Pound and Antheil, the composer Edgard Varèse was also experimenting with rhythmic procedures for organizing sound.)

Thus, Pound is uninterested in "chords" or "dissonance": A sound "of any pitch or any combination of such sounds" may be followed by any other, "providing the time interval between them is properly gauged" (10). Music is made up not of pitches but of sounds. The piano is treated as a percussion instrument. Chords should not be considered as static aggregates of pitch but as the consequences of "lateral motion," as in early contrapuntal music.

This rhythmic concept of music Antheil framed within a concept of "time-space" (41), borrowing from Albert Einstein's recently acquired prestige. On a macroscopic level, the entire duration of a musical work is imagined as a space filled with rhythmic dynamisms—combinations and recombinations of additive rhythms as in Stravinsky, a bell or a siren sounded for specified periods, percussive counterrhythms, measured silences. Antheil, seeing no real limits to musical time-space, was projecting new pieces four hours and ten hours long. On a microscopic level, Pound plays with the acoustic fact that pitch itself is rhythmic, reducible to the frequency of vibration; likewise timbre, so that the harmony for one instrument may not be appropriate for another, and percussion can enter the harmony like any other note. (These notions remain somewhat obscure, and Antheil himself dismissed them.)

Antheil's music, like Stravinsky's, thus consists of "hard bits of rhythm," "mechanisms," varied and repeated (*GK* 94). Pound justly saw in this a parallel with the geometric "form motifs," the defined planes and masses, in the sculpture and paintings of Lewis and Gaudier-Brzeska. These hard bits of rhythm constitute the composer's invention, so they are notated with precision, leaving nothing to the performer. They are propelled with a rhythmic unity that Pound dubbed "great base" (thus spelled in "Workshop Orchestration"), a somewhat obscure concept that recalls the figured bass of the Baroque and the unitary tempos of much early music. If Antheil's music is an art of machines, it is no accident that musicologists apply the term "motor rhythm" to Pound's beloved Vivaldi.

Bibliography

Adams, Stephen J. "Musical Neofism: Pound's Theory of Harmony in Context." *Mosaic* 13 (1980): 49–69.
Antheil, George. *Bad Boy of Music*. Garden City: Doubleday Doran, 1945.
———. "The Musical Ethic of the Future, Musical Neofism." *Querschnitt* 3 (1923): 51–53.
———. "My Ballet Mecanique: What It Means." *Querschnitt* 5 (1925): 789–791.
Fisher, Margaret. "Great Bass: Undertones of Continuous Influence." *Performance Research* 8 (2003): 23–40.
Henderson, Archie. "Ezra Pound: Composer." *Paideuma* 12.2–3 (1983): 499–509.
Whitesitt, Linda. *The Life and Music of George Antheil, 1900–1950*. Ann Arbor: UMI, 1983.

Stephen J. Adams

Anti-Semitism (See Racism and Anti-Semitism)

Arabic History

Both the geopolitical and philosophical history of the Arab world are significant to Pound. The incursion of the Arab world into Europe is explored in *Thrones*. This series of cantos narrates the peace negotiated between Abd-l-Malik and Justinian II late in the seventh century (see Migne), when Arab pressure on Byzantium and the Eastern Roman Empire was mounting. Conversely, Pound also mentions the Arab invasion of Europe, repelled at the Battle of Tours in 732 (Canto 96; Terrell 595).

The transmission of Neoplatonism to medieval Europe owes a debt to Arabic philosophy. The tradition of *amor* bears Sufic sources (*LE* 95) and informs European lyric, particularly in strophic form and rhyme scheme, via the medieval courts of Andalusia (*SR* 100). This tradition is inherited by Cavalcanti (but not, significantly, by Dante) from Averroes and Avicenna, where it reflects the divine principle in human life (*LE* 149, 158–159). Pound's notions of "precise definition" and "the light of the intelligence" are informed by Arab Neoplatonism and optics, transmitted through the work of Grosseteste.

Pound's travels in Morocco (1898) and Spain (1898, 1906, and 1908) gave him direct, if limited, exposure to Arabic culture and architecture (*GK* 52–53).

Bibliography

Migne, J. P. *Patrologiae cursus completus*. Vol. 95, Paul the Deacon. *Historia Miscella*, lib. XIX, XX. Paris, 1851.
Renan, Ernest. *Averroès et l'averroïsme: Essai historique*. Paris: A. Durand, 1852.

Mark S. Byron

Architecture

When Charles Tomlinson attempted to explain to E. M. Forster what he meant by referring to the imputed mausoleum of Galla Placidia in Ravenna as "a Poundian building," describing "haltingly the effect of that lucid darkness," he recognized an important aspect of Pound's sensibility (107): the satisfaction he found in coherently—often idiosyncratically—realized buildings with significant ornamentation. Of that building Pound had cited an opinion that he translated as follows: "Of religion it will be enough for me to say . . . 'every self-respecting Ravennese is procreated, or at least receives spirit or breath of life, in the Mausoleum of Galla Placidia'" (*SP* 322). The domed design of the compact structure—"Galla's Rest" (Canto 110)—had marvels of mosaic within: "gold fades in the gloom, / Under the blue-black roof, Placidia's" (Canto 21). When Pound commemorates significant buildings in the Byzantine style, these are hard three-dimensional examples often in Italy in contrast to W. B. Yeats's idealized and introspective vision of Byzantium. The "Byzance"-inspired buildings recur, and one reappears in a late canto "to affirm the gold thread in the pattern / (Torcello)" (Canto 116), which relates back to the sixteenth-century Santa Fosca church in the Venetian Lagoon. The exterior mosaic Madonna moves Pound to address the building as "thy quiet house at Torcello" (Canto 110); it is described in *Venice: Knopf Guides* as "the perfect expression of the Byzantine idea of space emerging from structural coherence and unity. To crown it all, the church is bathed in a light of unearthly clarity."

But Pound could also praise the Tempio Malatestiano, an eccentrically layered building that echoed the congeries of his cantos. As Carroll F. Terrell points out, "Pound's defense of Sigismundo from the charge of stealing is therefore not devoid of a self-serving element" (45). Hence, Pound took pleasure in the recycling of "marble, porphyry, serpentine" (Canto 9) stolen from Sant Apollinaire in Classe (534 C.E.), the port a short distance from Ravenna, by order of Sigismundo Malatesta for the construction of his Tempio in Rimini—"*templum aedificavit*" (Canto 8) Pound asserts in Latin, lengthening the longevity of its importance. Within the temple stood Santa Maria in Trivio by the decision of the architect Alberti, who " 'built a temple so full of pagan works' / i.e. Sigismund / and in the style 'Past ruin'd Latium' / The filigree hiding the gothic, / with a touch of rhetoric in the whole / And the old sarcophagi, / such as lie smothered in grass, by San Vitale" (Canto 9). Nonetheless, Pound wrote that the Tempio is both "an apex and in verbal sense a monumental failure" (*GK* 159).

Among the towns having medieval buildings in southern France that the young Pound explored is Poitiers (Pound's Poictiers) with two churches cited in Canto 45 in a Litanized proclamation as coming to be "Not by usura St Trophime / Not by usura Saint Hilaire." Of the latter Pound had observed more softly in Canto 4: "The sunlight glitters, glitters a-top, / Like a fish-scale roof, / Like the church roof in Poictiers / If it were gold." The Romanesque properties of the latter particularly delighted him. Of the Hall of Justice of Poitiers as well as St. Hilaire, Pound wrote, "Here the architect has invented. The cunning contrivance of lighting and the building of chimneys is, at least for the layman, something there invented, something that has no known fatherhood" (*GK* 109).

When Pound was in Italy in 1911 with Edgar Williams, younger brother of William Carlos, who was on a travelling scholarship to study architecture, they were "Veronizing," as Pound named it. He had already (1910) praised San Zeno in Verona as "pure magic . . . its toned brown-pink outside & the inside is proportion lifted to a kind of divinity" (Carpenter 144). Now he took notice of "columns [*sic*] with the artisan's signature at the base. Thus: 'Me Mateus fecit.' That is what we [in America] have not and can not have where columns are ordered by the gross" (*PM* 32). Once more, a matter of an artistic object "made to sell and sell quickly with usura" (Canto 45).

Cogently, not only "the painted paradise on his church wall" was prevented by usura but "a house of good stone / each block cut smooth and well fitting / that design might cover their face" (Canto 45). Not only expressions of supreme architecture through churches occupied Pound's imagination but also a sound contrivance for a human dwelling. As he declared in 1918, "I am more interested in the 'normal' house or shop than in the occasional building" (*New Age*, 24 October 1918, 414; signed B. H. Dias). This assertion is perplexing, but it appears to be backed up by Pound's activities four decades later by his "interest in, and acquaintanceship with, modern architecture and city-planning . . . his . . . advising the three co-editors on the founding of the journal Diapason, later Agora [*sic*], which was to have been devoted to literature inspired by the city and urban life" (Brogunier 421).

Whence came Pound's love of architecture? As a first-year student at Penn his work was outstanding only in solid geometry. "I passed my last *exam* . . . on sheer intuition. I saw where the line *had* to go, as clearly as ever I saw an image," he wrote in his appreciation of Gaudier-Brzeska (*GB* 91). In the same book Pound quoted from Gaudier-Brzeska's "Vortex," which had been published in the June 1914 issue of *BLAST* where he discussed ancient man: "Religion pushed him to the use of the VERTICAL which inspires awe. . . . He preferred the pyramid to the mastaba" (*GB* 21). Pound himself had written earlier of Manhattan: "Has it not buildings that are Egyptian in their contempt of the unit? For that is the spirit of the down-town architecture as surely as it was the spirit of the Pyramids. The Egyptian monarch despised the individual slave as effectively as the American despises the individual dollar" (*PM* 27).

What is one to understand of Pound's frequent recourse to Latin when he speaks of architecture? In a broadcast in later life he said, "Comin' from a duckboard country I was interested in LATIN order. Order in stone work" (*RSWWII* 137). Given such strong aesthetic preferences, Pound had no patience for imitations in the sense of reruns. He wrote in 1912: "There are, within a mile or two of my home [Wyncote, Pennsylvania], a castle something like Hawarden [the Wanamaker Mansion, Lyndenhurst], and one something like

Blenheim, and a great manor house (Elizabethan) and none of this is architecture" (*New Age*, 12 September 1912). Pound's eye had been trained by early exposure to Europe to tell the faux from the authentic.

Meanwhile, what was happening in New York? For Pound for whom architecture was "[t]he first of the arts" (*PM* 27), its arrival signaled to him "our first sign of the 'alba'; of America, the nation, in the embryo of New York. The city has put forth its own expression." As if brought by a muse "[a]rchitecture that has never wholly perished from the earth, that has scarcely ever slept for so long a period as the other arts, has appeared among us. It is natural that she should first appear." Ever aware of the driving force of economics, Pound adds, "For is she not more closely allied to use and to the sense of property than are the other arts?" (*PM* 28).

Beyond the practicalities, Pound recognized in New York—especially at night—the aspirations of Modernism made possible by massive application of electricity: "Squares after squares of flame, set up and cut into the aether. Here is our poetry, for we have pulled down the stars to our will" (*PM* 33).

Pound cited a few New York buildings that were not reruns in contrast to the neoclassical Public Library, which was "botch . . . of false construction" (*PM* 31). Perhaps the incorporation of the campanile as seen in Venice at San Marco—now made possible "with the advance of steel construction"—to serve a different purpose contributed to his praise for the Metropolitan Life tower as "[t]he real architectural achievement" in the company of the "great" Pennsylvania R.R. Station patterned after the Baths of Caracalla (Pound suggests "the baths of Diocletian, or some such person") (*PM* 32). They seemed to him comparable to "the palaces of the Renaissance." He trusted his ideas had been vindicated as he wrote in the late Canto 113: "No more the pseudo-gothic sprawled house / out over the bridge there / (Washington Bridge, N.Y.C.)."

Although Pound had rejected the pseudo-Gothic, his daughter Mary had labored to make the Tyrolean castle she and her husband had taken over after World War II into a fitting home and stage for a great poet. Sadly, the setting and lifestyle did not fit Pound's complicated situation: The reality of Brunnenburg collided with Pound's. Many of his final years were spent in Venice with his companion Olga Rudge in her small house, which had been built for a fisherman.

Pound is buried in the cemetery of San Michele dell'Isola within the Venetian Lagoon not far from his beloved churches at Torcello.

Bibliography

Bacigalupo, Massimo. *The Forméd Trace: The Later Poetry of Ezra Pound*. New York: Columbia UP, 1980.

Brogunier, Joseph. "Note on Ezra Pound's *Letters to William Watt*." *Paideuma* 32.1–3 (2003): 421.

Carpenter, Humphrey. *A Serious Character: The Life of Ezra Pound*. Boston: Houghton Mifflin, 1988.

Morris, James. *The World of Venice*. New York: Pantheon Books, 1960.

Pound, Ezra. *Ezra Pound and the Visual Arts*. Ed. Harriet Zinnes. New York: New Directions, 1980.

Robinson, Peter. "Ezra Pound and Italian Art." *Pound's Artists: Ezra Pound and the Visual Arts in London, Paris and Italy*. London: The Tate Gallery, 1985. 121–176.

Tomlinson, Charles. *Some Americans: A Personal Record*. Berkeley: U of California P, 1981.

Venice: Knopf Guides. A Borzoi Book. New York: Alfred A. Knopf, 1993.

Evelyn Haller

Arnaut Daniel [unpublished]

Pound planned a volume of *The Canzoni of Arnaut Daniel* as a companion to his *Sonnets and Ballate of Guido Cavalcanti* (1912). Next to translations, the book was to hold studies of the "lost art of polyphonic rhyme," maps of France and facsimiles of medieval music associated with Daniel's songs, retrieved from the *Bibliothèque nationale* in Paris and the *Biblioteca ambrosiana* in Milan. Upon the imprisonment in 1912 of the first intended publisher (Granville of Swift & Co.), the project was entrusted to Seymour of Chicago, who eventually decided against publication and returned only part of the material to Pound. A third attempt at publication failed as the manuscript sent to C. C. Bubb's Clerk's Press in Cleveland in 1918 never reached its destination.

Instead, Pound's translations and prose studies of Daniel were published in the *New Age* (December 1911–February 1912), *Little Review* (1918), and *Instigations* (1920). A number of previously unpublished translations are printed in Charlotte Ward's edition *Forked Branches: Translations of Medieval Poems*; Ward has also provided us with published and unpublished translations and variants in her variorum edition of Pound's translations of Daniel.

Bibliography

Pound, Ezra. *Forked Branches: Translations of Medieval Poems*. Ed. Charlotte Ward. Iowa City: U of Iowa P, 1985.

———. *Pound's Translations of Arnaut Daniel: A Variorum Edition with Commentary from Unpublished Letters*. Ed. Charlotte Ward. New York: Garland, 1991.

Line Henriksen

B

Barnard, Mary (1909–2001)

Mary Barnard is best known for her elegant poetic translation of Sappho. Her work encompasses poetry, translations, short stories, a collection of essays on the origins of myths, and a literary memoir.

Pound and Barnard corresponded for several years and met on a few occasions. With his usual generosity, Pound offered encouragement and practical help to the budding poet. He got Barnard into print and introduced her to other poets such as William Carlos Williams and Marianne Moore and to editors such as Harriet Monroe. Their correspondence began in 1933 when the young Barnard sent some of her poems to Pound, asking for his advice. In addition to the study of music and Greek metrics, Pound urged Barnard to hone her poetic skills on translation. Years later, Barnard took the latter suggestion to heart and began translating the lyric remains of Sappho.

In Sappho, Barnard found the poetic style she herself had been seeking for years, one combining a high degree of musicality and an intensity of emotion with simple diction in the cadence of natural speech. It was five years before Barnard's *Sappho* found its way into print: It was first published in 1958, and remarkably, it remains in print and in demand—surely a testament to its enduring elegance.

The 1994 special issue of *Paideuma* is devoted to Mary Barnard and includes a complete bibliography of her works.

Bibliography

Barnard, Mary. *Assault on Mount Helicon: A Literary Memoir*. Berkeley: U of California P, 1984.

———. *Collected Poems*. Portland: Breitenbush Books, 1979.

———. *Sappho: A New Translation*. Berkeley: U of California P, 1958.

———. *Three Fables*. Portland: Breitenbush Books, 1975.

Gordon, David, ed. *Mary Barnard*. Special Issue of *Paideuma* 23.1 (1994): 7–198.

Anita George

Barry, Iris [Iris Sylvia Symes Crump] (1895–1969)

Iris Barry was an English poet, novelist, and film historian. In 1916, impressed by Barry's poems in Harold Monro's magazine *Poetry and Drama*, Pound wrote to her, asking to see more of her work. Between 1916 and 1917, he and Barry corresponded extensively (see *L*). Pound offered much writerly advice. Especially interesting in his letters is the syllabus he devised in response to Barry's questions about what an aspiring writer should read: He called the program "KOMPLEAT KULTURE." During this time, Pound also helped Barry to place her work in such magazines as *Poetry* and *Others*. When she moved to London at his urging, he introduced her to compatriots such as Yeats, Eliot, Ford, May Sinclair, and Wyndham Lewis (for her recollections of this era, see Barry, "The Ezra Pound Period"). From 1918 to 1921, living with Lewis, Barry bore him two children. In the 1920s Barry wrote film criticism, poetry, and novels; cofounded the London Film Society; and served as film editor for *The Daily Mail* (1925–1930). After taking a position as a librarian at New York's Museum of Modem Art in

1932, she established and became curator of MOMA's Film Library (1935–1950). Barry's work on film includes *Let's Go to the Pictures* (1926).

Bibliography

Barry, Iris. "The Ezra Pound Period." *The Bookman* (October 1931): 159–171.

Meyers, Jeffrey. *The Enemy: A Biography of Wyndham Lewis.* London: Routledge and Kegan Paul, 1980.

———. "New Light on Iris Barry." *Paideuma* 13.2 (1984): 285–289.

Miranda B. Hickman

Bel Esprit

Bel Esprit was a scheme proposed by Pound in association with Natalie Barney and other writers in Paris in 1922, the first aim of which was to enable T. S. Eliot to devote his energies wholly to literature. It was motivated by the following ideas: That Eliot's talent, evident in his recent masterwork *The Waste Land*, was being wasted in banking; that the regeneration of Europe and restart of civilization depended on such masterworks; that the few capable of recognizing and benefitting from them should be willing to support their production by subscribing $50 or £10 a year; and that this was the appropriate form of patronage for the modern era. Bel Esprit would fulfill the Confucian idea that "when the Prince shall have called about him all the artists and savants his resources will be put to full use" and would be a practical application of Social Credit's call "to release more energy for invention and design." The scheme foundered when Eliot withdrew.

Bibliography

Eliot, T. S. *Letters of T. S. Eliot.* Vol. 1, *1898–1922.* Ed. Valerie Eliot. San Diego: Harcourt Brace Jovanovich, 1988. 513–613.

Pound, Ezra. "Credit and the Fine Arts . . . A Practical Application." *New Age* 30.22 (1922): 284–285.

———. "Paris Letter." *Dial* 73.5 (1922): 549–552.

A. David Moody

Bird, William (1888–1963)

Biographers and scholars commonly characterize Pound's relationship with Buffalo-born American expatriate writer, journalist and publisher William Bird as that of author to editor. This is not wrong, as Bird's Parisian Three Mountains Press famously crafted the first limited (to ninety copies), deluxe volume of cantos, *A Draft of XVI Cantos for the Beginning of a Poem of Some Length* (1925). Although this was brought off to mutual satisfaction—Pound called it "a bhloody ghood job, after awl your night sweats"—Bird proved reluctant to publish the second installation of the chryselephantine epic. No longer personally operating Three Mountains, he explained that K. Friend, its current operator, was "disinclined to do any heavy work," and while he "might, MIGHT, be persuaded [to] bite off Vol. 2 . . . probably wouldn't masticate it. Myself have BOTH teeth working overtime holding onto livelihood, absolutely unable [to] tackle ART."

Despite Bird's professed inability to tackle further art, their personal relationship continued for years after their professional one had ended. In fact, the unnamed correspondent commenting on *Mercanti di Cannoni* in chapter XXIII of *Jefferson and/or Mussolini* is Bird. Still reporting for the Consolidated Press Association and New York *Sun*, he was more knowledgeable about the state of contemporary politics than the increasingly isolated poet and arguably no less radical in his economic views—as he himself argued in January 1933 when he admonished Pound, "Don't go high-hatting me about Economics. I was a Technocrat 'way back in 1919 (before they had found that stylish name for it)." In this he was one of a very few well-informed correspondents who endeavored early on to dissuade the poet from his uncritical adherence to Benito Mussolini. The tone of their debate degenerated, however, as Pound's commitment to Italian fascism hardened, breaking down with Bird's flat censure of Mussolini in December 1935, ending not only that conversation but their friendship as well.

Bibliography

Surette, Leon. "Ezra Pound's Fascism: Aberration or Essence? The Correspondence with William Bird." *Queen's Quarterly* 96.3 (1989): 601–624.

Matthew R. Hofer

BLAST

First appearing in the summer of 1914, *BLAST* proclaimed itself the "Review of the Great English Vortex," and the two numbers of the magazine are perhaps best known both as vehicles for the writings and visual art of Wyndham Lewis and as manifestations of the most coherent statements of Vorticist principles. In an attempt to distance his specific techniques of abstraction from the broader aesthetics of the Italian futurists, Lewis found a willing collaborator in Ezra Pound. By the end of 1913, Pound had soured on the various applications of Imagism, and he sought to rearticulate his own aesthetic principles in a more vigorous form. While there is no doubt that Lewis made the loosely connected movement his own, Pound coined the term "Vorticism" and spoke about the fledgling impulse at Lewis's Rebel Art Centre in February 1914. Moving beyond what they saw as the motionlessness of Cubism, Vorticists privileged a focal point in the creative artifact while stressing the need for a dynamic engagement with its audience. As he was doing for other literary magazines at the time, Pound helped promote *BLAST*, and he sought out material for inclusion in its pages. But because he played more than a coincidental role in establishing the principles behind its inception, Pound occupied a more central position in its execution. This arrangement was, in itself, a welcome relief from the frustration he felt in his dealings with most magazine editors. Lewis and Pound wrote manifestos and statements of principle for Vorticism, and this creative activity culminated in the publication of the first number of *BLAST*, dated 20 June 1914. In fact, the magazine, already put back from its announced launch in April, was delayed further by a furor over Pound's verse. After the magazine was printed, publisher John Lane objected to lines in the poem "Fratres Minores." Distribution had to be postponed while lines like "With minds still hovering above their testicles" were manually blacked out at the Bodley Head. The format of the first number was hardly less controversial: its 157 pages were 12 1/2 by 9 1/2 inches in dimension, much of its type was thick and stark, and its cover was a color Pound described as "steam-calliope pink." Other contributors like Henri Gaudier-Brzeska, Ford Madox Hueffer, and Rebecca West joined in the blast against European civilization and established artistic practice. The outbreak of World War I conspired against the ambitions of the Vorticists: Instead of appearing as a quarterly, only one additional number of *BLAST* was printed in July 1915. This "War Number" was a little over 100 pages in length, and it was again dominated by Lewis's art and Pound's verse. But in publishing "Preludes" and "Rhapsody on a Windy Night," *BLAST* furthered Pound's support of T. S. Eliot's early efforts, and the magazine also printed one final statement on the "Vortex" from Gaudier-Brzeska, who had been killed at the front the previous month.

Craig Monk

Bollingen Prize for Poetry

With Pound's committal to St. Elizabeths Hospital in 1946, many awkward literary and political issues seemed indefinitely and conveniently shelved. But in 1949 the Fellows in American Letters of the Library of Congress gave the Bollingen Prize in Poetry to *The Pisan Cantos*. The award stirred many responses, for and against. Two groups stand out.

In an editorial in the April *Partisan Review* William Barrett asked, given "the ugly human attitudes" (fascism, anti-Semitism) found in the poem, "how far is it possible, in a lyric poem, for technical embellishments to transform vicious and ugly matter into beautiful poetry?" The May *Review* published a range of thoughtful comment by Auden, Orwell, and others on the bearing of Pound's politics and anti-Semitism on the poem and the prize.

In June Robert Hillyer published in the *Saturday Review of Literature* two diatribes whose titles are self-explanatory: "Treason's Strange Fruit" and "Poetry's New Priesthood." After tracing the alleged conspiratorial influence of T. S. Eliot, Hillyer ended, "[I]n the Bollingen award to Pound the clouds of an intellectual neo-Fascism and the new estheticism have perceptibly met."

Along with supporting editorials, the next issues of the *Saturday Review* had columns of letters for and against Hillyer's attack and modern poetry and criticism generally. But the journal would not accept a letter of protest by eighty-four writers and critics, from E. E. Cummings to Lionel Trilling. Also not accepted was a letter from Archibald MacLeish, who went on to write *Poetry and Opinion*, a dialogue between Mr. Saturday and Mr. Bollingen. Other material criticizing and correcting Hillyer's two essays was gathered later in 1949 in *The Case against the Saturday Review of Literature*.

Bibliography

Barrett, William. "A Prize for Ezra Pound." *Partisan Review* (April 1949). *Casebook.* 49–53.

Committee of Fellows of the Library of Congress in American Letters, ed. *The Case against the Saturday Review of Literature.* Chicago: Modern Poetry Association, 1949.

Hillyer, Robert. "Poetry's New Priesthood." *Saturday Review of Literature* 25 (18 June 1949): 7–9.

———. "Treason's Strange Fruit." *Saturday Review of Literature* 24 (11 June 1949): 9–11.

MacLeish, Archibald. *Poetry and Opinion: The Pisan Cantos of Ezra Pound.* Urbana: U of Illinois P, 1950.

O'Connor, William Van, and Edward Stone, eds. *A Casebook on Ezra Pound.* New York: T. Y. Crowell, 1959.

Weintraub, Stanley. *The London Yankees.* New York: Harcourt Brace Jovanovich, 1979.

Lauriat Lane Jr.

Bunting, Basil (1900–1985)

One of the two "strugglers in the desert," to whom Pound dedicated his *Guide to Kulchur*, Basil Bunting always gratefully acknowledged the influence and sponsorship of Pound. When the latter died in 1972, Bunting helped to organize a memorial concert in Newcastle-upon-Tyne at which he read from a number of Pound's works, including *Homage to Sextus Propertius*. That was a significant work for Bunting, the first by Pound to catch Bunting's attention when he arrived in London, a still impenitent rebel against conscription, from Winchester Prison in early 1919. *Homage* he called "the first poem which is consciously using the rhythmic mate-

rial of music in the manner in which it was used, in a small number of his best poems, by Walt Whitman" (Reagan 73). Whitman Bunting had discovered for himself by chance in his early teens at Ackworth School (though Bunting critics disagree on the school) in Yorkshire; his deep and abiding appreciation of music came, he believed, from his family initially and later from being "in contact" with Dr. W. G. Whittaker, director of the Newcastle Bach Choir in the early 1920s (Mottram 7). Bunting thus seems independently to have evolved an interest in verse composed, as Pound famously put it, "in the sequence of the musical phrase, not in sequence of a metronome" (*LE* 3), and to favor melopoeia: "If you're interested in sound—and unless you're interested in sound, you're not likely to write good poetry—if you're interested in sound, you're almost certainly going to be interested in music too" (Mottram 6). In *Homage* he found not so much a model to follow as evidence that a new kind of poetry—one more allied to music than to rhetoric—was indeed possible. Reflecting in later life on his debt to Pound, Bunting denied that it was the older poet's "highly individual voice and set of structures" that affected him; rather, "Pound has provided a box of tools, as abundant for this generation as those that Spenser provided for the Elizabethans, and a man who is not influenced by Pound, in the sense of trying to use at least some of those tools, is simply not living in his own century" (Mottram 8).

In a poem written "On the Fly-Leaf of Pound's Cantos" (1949), Bunting suggests something of the commanding presence of Pound and the difficulties faced by writers and readers who must confront his work. "There are the Alps," it begins: "What is there to say about them? / They don't make sense." The point is not Pound's superficial obscurity but the dumbfounding magnitude of his example, from which *"le refrain joyeux et leger"* emanates and which represents a full and almost incomprehensible creativity: "Who knows what the ice will have scraped on the rock it is smoothing?" The poem disparages those who would seek to avoid the Alps—and, by suggestion in the title, the lessons of

Pound—and recommends acceptance, though the ending is ambivalent. "There are the Alps, / fools! Sit down and wait for them to crumble" implies that the attempt to write in the shadow of Pound is simply futile in the life span of ordinary people; but there is some hope in the sentence that precedes these: "It takes some getting used to."

Assuming that such a reading is viable, and that at some level the Alps in this poem are *The Cantos* and not the Alps, Bunting's praise of Pound is certainly hyperbolic. But if Pound's example can be gotten "used to," it is clear he has not brought poetry to an end; mountains will crumble, disclosing and sustaining a changed landscape of artistic possibility. Bunting's sense of alternative possibilities was strong, notwithstanding his admiration for Pound and the clear affinities that existed between the two men. If Bunting's poetry nevertheless still lends itself to critical definition as a distinctly British variant of Poundian Modernism, his political views—oriented as far to the Left as Pound's inclined to the Right—stand as a caution against the homogenizing drift of literary historiography. He resembled Pound in no manner more closely than in being militantly and intractably individual.

Bibliography

Alldritt, Keith. *The Poet as Spy: The Life and Wild Times of Basil Bunting*. London: Aurum P, 1998.

Bunting, Basil. *Collected Poems*. Oxford: Oxford UP, 1978.

Corcoran, Neil. *English Poetry since 1940*. London: Longman, 1993.

Forde, Victoria. *The Poetry of Basil Bunting*. Newcastle: Bloodaxe Books, 1991.

Mottram, Eric. "Conversation with Basil Bunting on the Occasion of His 75th Birthday, 1975." *Poetry Information* 19 (Autumn 1978): 3–10.

Reagan, Dale. "An Interview with Basil Bunting." *Montemora* 3 (Spring 1977): 67–80.

Patrick Deane

C

The Cantos: Introduction

The Cantos is one of the major and most controversial poems of the twentieth century. Its early installments emerged from the Imagist and Vorticist poetics of the pre–World War I years, with the discovery of new forms and subjects. "Three Cantos," published in 1917, anticipated if not Joyce's *Ulysses*, which was already in progress, at least Eliot's *The Waste Land*, which, like "Three Cantos," is a poetic sequence with various characters, episodes, quotations, and connections of the mythical and the contemporary. When the early cantos were collected in book form in the two expensive in-folios of 1925 and 1928 and in the limited edition of 1930, they mirrored the insouciance of the Jazz Age, when everything seemed possible to the survivors of the war and one could live from day to day without thought of the future. This changed dramatically in 1929 with the Great Depression, and the cantos of the 1930s are much more political and eventually "totalitarian." Like many other socially conscious writers, Pound found that one had to take sides and think about politics, economics, and history. He decided to underwrite Benito Mussolini's New Deal, imagining that the brusque Italian leader had genius and a sincere concern for making a better society. Always happy to get into a fight, Pound became only more ardent in his support as Mussolini became progressively more isolated and finally decided to follow Hitler in challenging the rest of the world. Even when the Italians themselves demoted Mussolini in July 1943 and signed the Armistice in September 1943, Pound confirmed his allegiance in the two impassioned Italian cantos of 1944–1945; and when finally the Duce was executed and lynched, Pound opened the *Pisan Cantos* with an elegy for "Ben and La Clara," that is, the woman who was killed with him. Now he could elegize the fascist "dream" and its "enormous tragedy in the peasant's bent shoulders" (74). Mussolini was the son of peasant Romagna, and World War II, Pound imagined, had been fought by the capitalists against the agriculturalists—like the Civil War in the nineteenth century. This is the historical myth of *The Cantos*, where everything is made to fit in because this was Pound's vision of history. His concern for the poetry of Provence and Tuscany was germane to the scheme because Pound saw this poetry as an expression of Mediterranean myths and societies living at peace with nature and persecuted for their "heresies" (the Albigenses). The China of Confucius and the early emperors was another example of a benevolent hierarchical society founded on agriculture and on a respect for the good things of this world as against "the life after death." Judaism and Christianity were largely to be condemned except when they had expressed a local religion of the family and community—hence the "fertility cantos" of the 1930s and the beautiful "lynx chorus" of Canto 79, evocations of collective celebrations of life, beauty, stillness, and love, their common model being the anonymous Latin poem *Pervigilium Veneris*. In the post–World War II cantos, Pound only added further examples to his gallery of benevolent rulers and "magic moments" (as he called them in a 1927 letter to his father): Apollonius of Tyana, the wise magus, in 94; Edward

Coke, the cantankerous but creative Elizabethan lawmaker, in 107–109; and so on. In a late burst of creativity he again returned to the Provençal-Tuscan world of love and "fair women" in Cantos 90–95, perfecting a dense language made of sudden revelations and, as always, musically organized as litany, chant, and prayer. In the very last fragments he was still mentally traveling over "the roads of France" and the China of the Na-Khi peasants and putting down words and fleeting impressions as he had done from his first volume, *A Lume Spento* (1908).

Thus *The Cantos* is seen to be unified by a single historical myth, which was developed through the years but is self-consistent. While many readers have criticized the poem for its alleged lack of unity, one could argue instead that it is precisely its insistent unity that is a problem, so determined is Pound to make everything fit into his picture and interpretation of the world. Inevitably, if we look more closely at the materials he deploys, we often find that they do not support Pound's theses or interpretation of them. (For example, one of his heroes is Salmasius, author of *De Modo Usurarum* [1639]—Pound never having found out that Salmasius wrote in *defense* of usury.) More worrying is Pound's naive assumption that he is fit to pass judgment on all periods, persons, religions, and systems, thus issuing blanket condemnations of Taoism or Judaism. Lacking in historical sense, he does not realize that systems and religions are the product of complex processes that should be understood rather than judged on the basis of a few notions. Hence Pound may be said to have had a medieval set of mind, and in this *The Cantos* is truly close to its model *The Divine Comedy*, where in fact judgments are pronounced ahistorically, and all time is present, though indeed Dante shows tolerance for the great dead of classical times. In *The Pisan Cantos* Pound returned to the Bible of his Episcopalian upbringing, telling himself (and his readers) to "pull down thy vanity" and noting with justice and repentance: "How mean thy hates / Fostered in falsity" (Canto 81).

It is true that Pound was at times blinded by hate, and he revealed his intellectual inadequacies (for example, in the anti-Jewish passage that opens Canto 52), but there is an element of childish fighting and irresponsibility in his indignations that allows the reader to take them with some indulgence, as so much sound and fury incident to his genius for the effective line and image and for the moving canticle. Thus *The Cantos* reflects the paradoxes and contradictions of modern history and of the modern mind and remains the self-portrait of an exceptional individual as he struggles along to make sense of history and of his life. He never gives up, even when he looks with despair upon his "many errors," and he holds out a glimmer of hope: "a little light, like a rushlight" (Canto 116).

In fact, Pound was always a romantic optimist and did not share the "crepuscular spirit." Like Whitman, he wanted to believe in the glory of the world. In this he was much unlike T. S. Eliot, who thought that the only hope for humans was in the promise of Christianity, without which the world would only be darkness. Pound believed that Confucius, Cavalcanti, and others like himself belonged to a tradition of light and that sexual acts, or the processes of generation, were the mystery at the center of it all. In this he was in accord with D. H. Lawrence. So, after all, in his struggling with *The Cantos* Pound wrote a long poem of many delights and with a happy end: the bed of Venus, "thou with dark eyelids" (Canto 1).

Bibliography

Bacigalupo, Massimo. *The Forméd Trace: The Later Poetry of Ezra Pound*. New York: Columbia UP, 1980.

———. "Pound's Pisan Cantos in Process." *Paideuma* 27.2–3 (1998): 93–106.

———. "The Strange Textual Case of Ezra Pound's Cantos." *English Studies in Africa* 42.1 (1999): 63–68.

Eastman, Barbara. *Ezra Pound's Cantos: The Story of the Text*. Orono: NPF, 1979.

Gibson, Andrew, ed. *Pound in Multiple Perspective*. London: Macmillan, 1993.

Pearlman, Daniel D. *The Barb of Time: On the Unity of Ezra Pound's Cantos*. New York: Oxford UP, 1969.

Pound, Ezra. *I Cantos*. Ed. Mary de Rachewiltz. Milan: Mondadori, 1985.

Massimo Bacigalupo

The Cantos: The Ur-Cantos

By the time Ezra Pound published his first collected volume of cantos (*A Draft of XVI. Cantos of Ezra Pound*), he had been redrafting the poem's opening for ten years. Manuscripts and typescripts of fragments of a set of Cantos 1–5 dating from 1915 can be found at the Beinecke Library and contain some material never finally incorporated into later cantos (for example, sections on *The Mahabharata*'s "Vyasa's Wood" and the Cynewulf episode from the *Anglo-Saxon Chronicle*).

Pound worked up the bulk of these drafts into the *Three Cantos* (sometimes called the *Ur*-Cantos) he published in *Poetry* for June, July, and August 1917, then tinkered with the texts in versions that appeared in the American edition of *Lustra* (1917) and in the magazine *Future* for February, March, and April 1918. Between October 1919 and January 1924 Pound went on to publish small press or magazine versions of individual cantos that closely correspond to the canonical Cantos 4–13. It was not until shortly before the publication of *A Draft of XVI. Cantos*, however, that he recast the first three poems into their final (or near-final) form.

Three Cantos I begins with a theoretical proem addressed to Robert Browning:

> Hang it all, there can be but one *Sordello*!
> But say I want to, say I take your whole bag of
>   tricks,
> Let in your quirks and tweeks, and say the
>   thing's an art-form,
> Your *Sordello*, and that the modern world
> Needs such a rag-bag to stuff all its thought in[.]

How, in other words, can one write a long, narrative poem in the twentieth century? How would it combine Romantic subjectivity, philosophical amplitude, Symbolist compression, and the vividness and solidity of history? The answer, the proem suggests, involves a self-consciously dialectical method ("I stand before the booth, the speech; but the truth / Is inside this discourse—this booth is full of the marrow of wisdom"). *Three Cantos* II, then, goes on to project and interrogate voices from various times and places (Renaissance Mantua, elev-

enth-century Provence, the China of Li Po, classical Rome, the Spain of El Cid, the Portugal of Camoens, Pound's own youth in Indiana). Ultimately, *Three Cantos* III implies, these add up to a sophisticated form of visionary poetry of the kind once written by Layamon, Chaucer, John Heydon, and Lorenzo the Magnificent. *Three Cantos*'s last and most extended example is also the earliest in the Western tradition—the *nekuia* (or descent into Hades) from the eleventh book of the *Odyssey*, when with the aid of Tiresias Odysseus raises the "impetuous, impotent dead." So situated, Homer's story of pouring blood for the ghosts becomes a parable of a complicated interchange between imagination and world, self and other, past and present, culture and culture, language and language. In January 1925, Pound removed his discursive preliminary, relocated Odysseus to the opening lines of a new Canto 1, and allowed the Homeric tale to communicate its implications without commentary.

Bibliography

Bush, Ronald. *The Genesis of Ezra Pound's Cantos*. Princeton: Princeton UP, 1976.

Froula, Christine. *To Write Paradise: Style and Error in Pound's Cantos*. New Haven: Yale UP, 1984.

Gibson, Mary Ellis. *Epic Reinvented: Ezra Pound and the Victorians*. Ithaca: Cornell UP, 1995.

Longenbach, James. *Modernist Poetics of History: Pound, Eliot, and the Sense of the Past*. Princeton: Princeton UP, 1987.

Pound, Ezra, and Harry Strater. *A Draft of XVI. Cantos of Ezra Pound*. Paris: Three Mountains P, 1925.

———. "Three Cantos." *Future* (February 1918; March 1918; April 1918).

———. "Three Cantos. I, II, III." *Poetry* 10.3 (1917): 113–121; 10.4 (1917): 180–188; 10.5 (1917): 248–254.

———. *A Variorum Edition of "Three Cantos" by Ezra Pound: A Prototype*. Ed. Richard Taylor. Bayreuth: Boomerang P, 1991.

Ronald Bush

The Cantos: A Draft of XXX Cantos

Ezra Pound's epic poem *The Cantos* asserts a universal moral vision wherein the muddied forces of greed and materialism struggle against those of natural process, intellectual clarity, and spiritual light. In its portrayal of this struggle, the long poem defies the boundaries of time and space by assuming that everything occurring in time and space is interchangeable, recurrent, and best seen in its relationship to the same essential truth that governs both the seen and unseen worlds. This essential truth equates to an understanding of universal beauty, and Pound's long poem serves as a historical and poetic commentary on the difficulty of creating, maintaining, or even recognizing such beauty. But how would he begin such a poem? How would he make clear his understanding of the struggle?

Pound had been looking for a way to start his long poem since 1915, when he first began writing versions of what have come to be known as the three *Ur*-Cantos. These took their final form in 1925, having been recast as a result of Pound's independent publication of Canto 4 in 1919. This canto confirmed that Pound's poetic intent was to convey meaning through the conceptual interplay of juxtaposed images rather than through the more typical means of using a mediating narrator or voice. The canto thus offers stark and contrasting images concerning smoldering Troy, athletic triumph, mythic marriage, the founding of Thebes, and much more. It includes the kinds of paradisal imagery found recurring throughout the later cantos, as well as details from violent tragedies recorded in myth, literature, and life. Mythic Acteaon, for example, turns into a stag and is devoured by his own hunting dogs. Seremonda's husband kills her lover, the medieval troubadour Cabestan, and serves his cooked heart to her in a dish. Philomela and her sister Procne kill the son of Tereus, Procne's husband, and serve him to Tereus for dinner to avenge a rape, escaping afterward through the air following their transformation into birds by the empathetic gods.

Collectively, the details in Canto 4 illustrate the changing and seemingly unpredictable nature of human and divine circumstance. They suggest that humankind cannot defeat fate, the gods, or the forces of human passion and self-interest. Yet at the same time, amid fated circumstance, humanity nevertheless continues to live, to build, to try: Cabestan loves Seremonda;

Cadmus builds Thebes; marriages take place; and crowds lead athletes in triumph through the streets to the resounding rhythms of poetry and song. These human triumphs amid horror and excess somehow occasionally evoke the human movement toward beauty. They do so despite the assertion at canto's end that "No wind is the king's wind" (Canto 4). Control of circumstance presumably lies somewhere beyond human ken.

Thus Canto 4 traces the course of human sensibility toward and away from the light. In doing so, it also suggests one of the key means by which Pound would attempt to make his poem cohere. Ensuing cantos would depend on recurring patterns of what Pound thought to be essential aspects of human character, transmuted by circumstance and time. His sometime protagonist Odysseus, for example, recurs in aspects of other sailors and personalities; his goddess Aphrodite likewise surfaces in the transmuted forms of the ancient Greek Helen of Troy, in the medieval Eleanor of Aquitaine, in the "well tressed" goddess Kalypso, and much later, in a young unnamed Italian girl, described as "benecomata dea"—a well-tressed goddess— driving her pigs home at sunset (Canto 76). All things change, it seems, but everything essential remains.

Once under way, Pound published Cantos 5, 6, and 7 in 1921 and 8 in 1922. In 1923, he published Cantos 8–11, the "Malatesta Cantos." In these, Pound addresses another problem related both to his method of delivering meaning and his attempt at envisioning beauty existing within the human condition. He uses a wealth of archival historical materials to tell the story of Sigismundo Malatesta, fifteenth-century Lord of Rimini. Yet before Canto 8 delves into the historical record, a fight takes place between Truth and Calliope, muse of epic poetry. The jagged edge of Truth wins out over the artificially seamless reality proposed by the traditional epic form defended by Calliope.

Truth's victory is key for Pound. Traditionally, epic poets alert their readers to the end of the story in the beginning, thereby safeguarding their tales and their readers from unexpected intrusions and endings. By having Truth triumph,

Pound in effect asserts in Canto 8 that he intends to create a bolder kind of epic tale. His tale will unveil a new reality rather than reiterate an old one. It will assert a truth of the kind that Pound suggested elsewhere could be "beaten down" by the imposition onto truth of such a predictable structural form as that of the traditional epic. Thus by 1923 not only had Pound decided against using a single mediating sensibility to bring coherence to his long poem, but he had also formally announced his intent to stray from the traditional epic plan for the sake of greater human truth.

Cantos 12 and 13 were published together in 1924. The first offers a twentieth-century American merchant named Baldy Bacon as yet another protagonist cut partly in the recurring figure of Odysseus, who appears throughout *The Cantos* in such guises as Malatesta, the Chinese philosopher Confucius, the American presidents Adams and Jefferson, the Italian fascist Mussolini, and others. Collectively, Pound sees all of these figures as manifestations of the "factive" personality. They are the doers of the world, men and women of vision who are often stopped short of fulfilling their visions as a result of the dark and imbecilic forces of their day. Yet even as failures these men and women move human culture toward beauty. Malatesta builds a temple, the outside of which is covered in well-wrought art; Adams, Jefferson, and Mussolini create nations; and Confucius promotes a universal harmony based on order, civility, and intelligence.

Canto 13 introduces Kung, or Confucius. From his first appearance Confucius serves as a uniquely stable manifestation of the factive personality. He is envisioned in the canto with his students amid peaceful cedar groves, considering how men and governments can stand firm against all of the difficulties that blow into the world. As such, Confucius is one of the few characters whose vision is sufficiently important to Pound that he refers to him here and there throughout the cantos, long after references to other factive personalities have ceased. In Canto 13 Pound adds his own closing lines indicating that he, too, like Confucius, will oppose chaos

and stupidity with order, intelligence, and beauty. " 'The blossoms of the apricot / blow from the east to the west,' " Pound writes, " 'And I have tried to keep them from falling' " (Canto 13). The very next cantos, however, suggests that doing so will be a daunting task.

The Dantean "Hell" Cantos 14 and 15 and the "Purgatory" Canto 16 were first published when Pound in 1925 brought all of his revised cantos together under the working title *A Draft of XVI. Cantos*. Cantos 14 and 15 are replete with unpleasant images of self-serving, corrupting, unproductive people surrounded by fecal matter and water slugs, their "faces smeared on their rumps" (Canto 14), their penises limp, their condoms "full of black-beetles" (Canto 15). Canto 15 ends with another human protagonist being led through the oozing fetid mud of Hell to safety, then being washed in acid to remove all traces of his experience. Canto 16 begins with the same protagonist at "hell's mouth," where he meets Romantic poet and painter William Blake, who is running about and howling against evil (Canto 16). The Purgatory of Canto 16 is a place for flawed heroes such as Malatesta and for past thinkers and builders. It also contains men who died or who fought in World War I—a real-life hell described by Pound as having been created by the forces of self-interest, ugliness, and corruption.

These same forces appear to struggle with clarity, truth, and beauty in Cantos 17 and 18. Canto 17 envisions a divine energy capable of overcoming the dark forces. According to Eugene Paul Nassar, the presence of this divine energy is often invoked by Pound through his switch from a normal to an elevated lyrical mode of poetic expression. It is also embodied in the character of certain gods, goddesses, and symbols and is associated with fertility, creation, and all kinds of growth. Thus in this canto Dionysius, Venus, Athena, Persephone, and others traverse a land and seascape abundant in bounding white hounds and loping porpoise, where gulls cry above cresting waves and bees fly amid vines bursting under a still paradisal light, "not of the sun" (Canto 17). In this manner, the canto moves spatially toward an idealized Venice—one of the first historical cities wherein Pound tries to locate permanently his sense of earthly beauty. Even here, however, historical Venice proves incapable of sustaining elevated beauty and instead succumbs to the forces of darkness. Borso and Carmagnola, for example, two fifteenth-century Italians to whom Pound refers as "men of craft" (Canto 17), are separately attacked in Venice: Borso has arrows shot at him, and Carmagnola is betrayed and executed.

Canto 18 opens with the thirteenth-century Mongol Kublai Khan bringing cultural and economic order to his kingdom. Khan employed paper currency rather than heavy gold coin to promote economic exchange. In this way, the figure of Khan introduces what would become for Pound an obsession with the belief that the human struggle against self-interest, ugliness, and corruption needed to include the re-creation of economic principles as part of its task. Yet in the same canto in which sound economics is heralded as part of the solution to human problems, Pound suggests that just the opposite also is true. Weapons makers and munitions dealers of World War I vintage feed the human penchant for war and, for their efforts, are rewarded economically and socially by a society that on one level appears unable to tell the difference between philanthropists and criminals. As the poet notes in disgust at the end of the canto, "War, one war after another / Men start 'em who couldn't put up a hen-roost" (Canto 18).

Despite the perceived difficulty of solving societal problems in his cantos, by the mid-1920s Pound had solved several problems concerning the intention and design of his long poem. He had been bold in his attempt at writing a new kind of epic, one proceeding without a mediating sensibility, without a traditional structure, and without a fixed protagonist. He had been even bolder in his attempt to write such an epic while using as both resource and subject all of human and divine endeavor, manifest through time and space. The result was an unexpected and exciting new kind of poetry; but at the same time, this new poetry drew charges of incoherence and artlessness from critics. They were

kind to Pound at first but soon began to wonder. In 1918, the three early *Ur*-Cantos were explained by one critic as part of Pound's meditative autobiography, and the poet T. S. Eliot called them a "rag-bag" of Pound's readings, somehow containing a "positive coherence." By 1925 the critical mood had changed, and perhaps anticipating further charges of incoherence, Pound announced that he did not want anyone yet commenting on his work.

In 1928, and doubtless under even more pressure to explain his poetic plan, Pound suggested to his friend and fellow poet W. B. Yeats that his long poem's structure was much like a "Bach fugue." In 1929, Pound wrote his father that the poem was to operate musically, somewhat like "subject and response and counter response" (*L* 210). After several such attempts at explanations, it began to seem clear to many that Pound really did not have an answer to questions concerning coherence—yet all the while his poem became more ambitious and daring. Between 1925 and 1928, eleven new cantos were written and published as *A Draft of Cantos 17–27* in 1928.

Cantos 18–28 continue to chronicle the contention between clear and muddied human action and illustrate Pound's belief that even in those who possess clarity, right action is often beclouded by personal flaws or by the dark actions of others. In Canto 19 a man with an invention that will benefit people is convinced by a big company to sell out, move into a mansion, and forget that his invention is kept off the market. In Canto 20 Niccolo d'Este, ruler of fifteenth-century Ferrara and a great peacemaker, beheads his son Ugo and wife Parasina in a jealous rage and falls prey to remorse. Joe, an American craftsman in Canto 22, cannot compete in a work environment driven by capitalism and characterized by mass production. His work is too well and carefully done. And in the sixteenth-century Venice of Canto 25, civic leaders watch while two caged lions copulate, unaware of how separate they have become from the kinds of action that produce new life and growth.

Yet Cantos 18–27 also suggest that humanity can control its own destiny through recognizing the connection between mind, nature, and action. Canto 23, for example, begins with the Latin phrase *Et omniformis omnis intellectus est*. Taken from the third-century C.E. Neoplatonist Porphyry's *De Occasionibus*, the phrase translates "and every intellect is capable of assuming every shape." In related fashion, Canto 25 recalls that the Neoplatonic understanding of the Greek term νοῦς suggests that intelligence is the active divine agent of the universe. Together, these and like assertions link human and divine intellect, natural process, production, clarity, and an insistent, vibrant pulsing of the blood. Such alliances throughout *The Cantos* are also continually linked to natural proliferation and ritualized traditions such as the ancient Greek Eleusinian mysteries, a "blood rite" (Cantos 21 and 25) that delivers to those who undergo it an *epoptea*, or emotional and intellectual "awakening" to their immortal place within the universe. Awakenings of this sort create a paradise in the mind and heart, and once there, Pound variously suggests, an earthly paradise cannot be far behind.

Pound added three more cantos and in 1930 published *A Draft of XXX Cantos*. Three years later, he formally declared the "ideogrammic method" as the one he was using in his lengthening poem. The roots of Pound's ideogrammic method can be traced to his study of Ernest Fenollosa's theory concerning Chinese poetry, beginning in 1912. While it is uncertain whether Fenollosa's theory served as a mediating or organizing force in the first thirty cantos, there can be little doubt that after 1933 Pound began creating cantos in accordance with his understanding of it. This resulted in the composition of increasingly large blocks of textual images intended to deliver a multivalent understanding or "ideogram" of a subject or topic. Yet sometimes Pound's text-blocks spanned several pages and cantos. For many of his devoted readers, the ensuing results often stretched the limits of their imagination and their sense of poetics.

Pound's last canto in *A Draft of XXX Cantos* envisions a fight wherein the precise and pitiless goddess Artemis triumphs over a materialistic and chaotic Madam X. For many of Pound's readers, however, the true outcome of that fight would remain forever unclear. Even after another thirty or so years had passed, and another eighty-six or so cantos had been written, Pound's long unfinished poem may be said to serve more as a testament to his enduring system of beliefs than it does to any clear and finite outcome he may have had in mind. For him, the struggle of those who believe in a beautiful world created and maintained through artistry, intellect, and natural process must continue, and while that struggle will be a difficult one, any success makes the world a better place, if even for a fragment of time.

Bibliography

Akehurst, F.R.P., and Judith Davis. *A Handbook of the Troubadours*. Berkeley: U of California P, 1995.

Albright, Daniel. "Early Cantos I–XLI." *The Cambridge Companion to Ezra Pound*. Ed. Ira B. Nadel. Cambridge: Cambridge UP, 1999.

Barthes, Roland. *S/Z*. Trans. Richard Miller. New York: Hill and Wang, 1974.

Géfin, Laszlo. *Ideogram: History of a Poetic Method*. Austin: U of Texas P, 1982.

Kerenyi, Carl. *Eleusis: Archetypal Image of Mother and Daughter*. Princeton: Princeton UP, 1967.

Nassar, Eugene Paul. *The Cantos of Ezra Pound: The Lyric Mode*. Baltimore: Johns Hopkins UP, 1975.

Nolde, John J. *Blossoms from the East: The China Cantos of Ezra Pound*. Orono: NPF, 1983.

Surette, Leon. *A Light from Eleusis: A Study of Ezra Pound's Cantos*. Oxford: Clarendon P, 1979.

Robert E. Kibler

The Cantos: Eleven New Cantos XXXI–XLI

Pound's first venture after *A Draft of XXX Cantos*, individual cantos in this new collection appeared separately between the years of 1931 and 1934. They were collected as a volume in 1934 by Farrar & Rinehart in New York and one year later by Faber. Pound was writing as economic reformer carrying the banner of Social Credit, as American patriot, and as ardent supporter of Mussolini. But the dates are vital, because they place the collection prior to Pound's virulent anti-Semitic turn, which Surette has dated convincingly to early 1934, and prior to Mussolini's invasion of Abyssinia in October

1935, which raised the outrage of the world against him. These events may be read into these cantos only by hindsight.

Often overshadowed by the relatively self-contained achievement of the first thirty cantos, plus the flowering of the *Fifth Decad* and the *Pisans*, these cantos nevertheless contain some of Pound's most fascinating achievements. The documentary method developed in the Malatesta cantos is retained, but the focus shifts noticeably from the Renaissance to the Enlightenment, from the Old World to the New.

These cantos weave three strands: (1) an American group, foreshadowed in Canto 21 with a citation from Jefferson's correspondence: "Could you . . . / Find me a gardener / Who can play the french horn?" (Canto 21) (the abrupt emphasis on America beginning in Canto 31 is nonetheless startling); (2) an economic/journalistic group, dealing with present-day issues and Pound's economic crusades; and (3) a lyrical/mythic group, juxtaposing the cult of *amor* as represented by Cavalcanti in Canto 36, Circe in Canto 39, and concluding with the Odyssean "periplum" of Hanno in Canto 40. The whole is framed by Jefferson in Canto 31 and Mussolini in Canto 41, thus reflecting Pound's fanciful parallel between these to leaders in *Jefferson and/or Mussolini* (1935).

At the beginning of the volume, Pound links the Renaissance with the American Enlightenment by quoting Malatesta's motto, "Tempus loquendi / Tempus tacendi" (Canto 31). As early as 1912, he held out hope that an "American Risorgimento . . . will make the Italian Renaissance look like a tempest in a teapot!" (*L* 10). Like his *Patria Mia* (serialized in 1912), these cantos display continued hope for the possibility of America creating a new world order. Pound's interest is clearly in the early American *paideuma* as a whole, overriding partisan lines, holding up for admiration the Democrats Jefferson and Van Buren as well as the Federalists John Adams and his son John Quincy. His methodology is largely a collage of quotations from the Founding Fathers, but at this point in *The Cantos*, the gist of each quotation, while

sometimes obscure, is often relatively comprehensible—though, as always, access to the larger context is apt to throw light on Pound's intentions. Tim Redman has argued that this method of referring to external texts constitutes a kind of "protohypertext" (117); but he also observes (119) that passages selected often involve Pound's own preoccupations as well as those of the authors—Jefferson's reference to "English papers . . . their lies" (Canto 31), for example, or John Adams's frustrated "Litterae nihil sanantes" (literature curing nothing) (Canto 33).

In Cantos 31 and 32, the emphasis in the Jefferson/Adams pairing falls, conventionally, on Jefferson, a proverbial "Renaissance man." Pound's interest in the Founding Fathers had a long history, but it was undoubtedly kindled by an inspired birthday gift from Eliot, a complete edition of Jefferson's *Writings*. Here, he is exhibited as a proponent of modernity in sculpture, a visionary foreseeing the Erie Canal, friend of the radical Paine (whom John Adams deplored), architect, critic of French mistranslation, despiser of Napoleon's ignorance of commerce, and so on. In a snippet from an 1813 letter to "Mr. Eppes," he is shown to be an opponent of the National Bank. Jefferson is, in Pound's term, *polumetis*. Adams, already shown to be contemptuous of the historical ignorance of great French reputations—Lafayette, Turgot, La Rochefoucauld, Condorcet—continues to appear in Canto 32, though the focus remains on Jefferson. Within a few years, Pound's interest would shift to the relatively neglected Adams, resulting in the John Adams Cantos, 62–71 (1940). In the process, Pound discovered the Jefferson/Adams correspondence, which he declared, justly, "a shrine and a monument" to true American civilization, which he dated from 1760 to 1830 (*SP* 147). The first half of this collection concerns practical matters of European diplomacy; but then, after a hiatus of bitter political animosity, a new correspondence begins in which the two, unexpectedly bound by a warmth of friendship, exchange observations and speculations at the highest intellectual level.

The second pair displays an odder coupling, John Quincy Adams in Canto 34 and Martin Van

Buren in Canto 37. The two were divided not only by partisanship but also by a personal animadversion that Pound mostly elides. Both have been vastly underrated by historians. Van Buren has been represented as a political opportunist and fence-sitter (see the comments on his tariff speech [Canto 37]); but Pound represents his truly principled struggle against the renewal of Nicholas Biddle's private National Bank. Biddle retaliated by calling in debts and creating a politically motivated depression and numerous bankruptcies ("obtaining by panic / control over public mind" [Canto 37]), but Van Buren won—for the moment. Pound's source is Van Buren's *Autobiography*, but the story is confirmed in Arthur Schlesinger's classic history *The Age of Jackson*. Quincy Adams is more problematic—a man of genuine principle, an extension of his father's *paideuma* (he condemned Jackson's disgraceful treatment of the Cherokee [Canto 34]), Pound seems to represent him as an opponent of the appalling Biddle, though he was in fact a defender of the National Bank.

Canto 33 plays a special role in the sequence, a synoptic view of history traced in William Chace's still definitive "The Canto as Cento." Canto 33 begins with a collage of letters, many but not all derived from the Jefferson/Adams correspondence. A second block moves to Karl Marx's denunciation of the avarice and cruelty of British industrialism, circa 1842 to 1871. A third derives from Bessedovsky's *Revelations of a Soviet Diplomat* (trans. 1931) detailing the Stalinist regime's politically corrupt and financially inept efforts to export its revolution. Finally, a fourth block returns to America, citing a 1931 speech by Senator Brookhart of Iowa denouncing, in the depths of the Great Depression, the actions of the Federal Reserve Bank. The canto thus charts the failure of two great idealistic revolutions, the American and the Russian, confounded by corruption and big money.

Canto 33 anticipates the first of the journalistic pieces, Canto 35, "Mitteleuropa," the weakest canto in the volume. It is filled with Jewish anecdotes—related in a quasi-jocular tone, not the venomous rant that Pound adopted later but still offensive. Even more, Pound appears to dismiss a culture, or rather a diversity of cultures, of which he has little experience or understanding. Matters fare better in Canto 38, in which journalistic ephemera—some obscure, some very funny—are interspersed among ominous anecdotes about the lives of the idle rich and the manufacture and trade of armaments. At the heart of this canto, however, is Pound's economic crusade—a snippet from Dexter Kimball on the first page but, more important, an extended passage from Major Douglas (Canto 38). This is the gravitational core of the canto.

Three extended lyrical and mythical passages punctuate this collage of historical documents and contemporary journalism. Most important is Canto 36, presenting Pound's second translation of Cavalcanti's "Donna mi prega"—the poem that Rossetti had excluded from his *Early Italian Poets* because it was full of "metaphysics." Pound himself did not attempt it until 1928, when he was preparing his scholarly edition of Cavalcanti. Meanwhile, he set the poem to music as centerpiece of his opera *Cavalcanti*. This, the most familiar canto in the volume, a rare passage of formal versification, has attracted a wealth of commentary, much of which focuses on translation. Interpretation of the thematics of the canto usually follows Pound's lead to medieval commentaries and suspicions of Cavalcanti's heresy (hence the references to Aquinas and Aristotle in the notes following the translation): Cavalcanti, Pound remarks, "does not definitely proclaim any heresy, but he shows leaning toward not only the proof by reason but toward the proof by experiment" (*LE* 149). Love itself is a kind of knowledge. Furthermore, Pound's allusion to Grosseteste relates Cavalcanti to Pound's imagery of paradisal light. Other critics emphasize the complementary relationship between the intellectual love in Canto 36 with the highly sexual Canto 39. There, the central figure Circe, surrounded by Dionysian big cats, has turned Odysseus's companions into swine but meets her match in *polumetis* Odysseus himself, who couples with her not for immediate porcine gratification but as an equal to the goddess. By implication, true sexuality should be a fusion of both the rational and the sensual. This canto, the most overtly sexual in *The Cantos*, extends a complex web of allusions to the *Pervigilium Veneris*, Catullus, Egyptian fertility goddess Hathor, the medieval English "Alisoun," and elsewhere. The passage "By Circeo, by Terracina, with the stone eyes / white toward the sea" (Canto 39) recalls Pound's desire to replace the statue of Venus there in the belief that "a light from Eleusis persisted throughout the middle ages and set beauty in the song of Provence and of Italy" (*SP* 53). This comment further ties the canto to Cavalcanti's canzone.

Canto 40 focuses on *The Periplus of Hanno* (c. 570–470 B.C.E.), a parallel to Odysseus's sailing into unknown knowledge. Hanno sails not by abstract navigation but by the ancient empirical method of hugging the coast, thus leaving a brief but valuable record of cities founded and natives observed. Canto 41 spends half of its extent holding up Mussolini for praise—for understanding money, draining marshes, complimenting Pound's poetry, and other signs of intelligence. The canto features a number of journalistic anecdotes, including disparaging references to Churchill and Feldmarschall von Hindenburg. One passage introduces the Monte dei Paschi, foreshadowing the *Fifth Decad*, while a passing reference to Woergl, in Austria, is the first sign in *The Cantos* of Pound's awareness of Gesell's stamp scrip (Surette 176 ff). The canto closes full circle with further exempla from the good Jefferson.

Bibliography

Anderson, David. *Pound's Cavalcanti: An Edition of the Translations, Notes and Essays*. Princeton: Princeton UP, 1983.

Chace, William. "The Canto as Cento: XXXIII." *Paideuma* 1.1 (1972): 89–100.

Lash, John. "Making Sense of Donna Mi Priegha." *Paideuma* 15.1 (1986): 83–93.

Pound, Ezra. "The Jefferson-Adams Letters as a Shrine and a Monument." *SP* 147–158.

Redman, Tim. "An Epic Is a Hypertext Containing Poetry: *Eleven New Cantos* (31–41) by Ezra Pound." *A Poem Containing History: Textual Studies in The Cantos*. Ed. Lawrence Rainey. Ann Arbor: U of Michigan P, 1997.

Schlesinger, Arthur, Jr. *The Age of Jackson*. Boston: Little, Brown, 1945.

Surette, Leon. *Pound in Purgatory: From Economic Radicalism to Anti-Semitism*. Urbana: U of Illinois P, 1999.

Terrell, Carroll F. "The Periplus of Hanno." *Paideuma* 1.1 (Spring 1972): 223–228.

Stephen J. Adams

The Cantos: The Fifth Decad of Cantos XLII–LI

Pound writes these cantos between 1935 and 1937, relatively stable years in his own life even as Europe is moving closer to war, and Italy is becoming increasingly isolated from England and America; and so it is not surprising that *The Fifth Decad of Cantos* exhibits both a supreme confidence and an urgency. Most likely operating under the assumption that his "long poem containing history" would be complete when it reached 100 cantos—the perfect number of Dante's epic—Pound was conscious of bringing the first half of his life's work to a close, and in this sequence, he does manage to achieve a vision that unites the various themes he had been working on from the inception of *The Cantos*. The wandering hero who begins the poem in Canto 1 becomes identified with his own person who is desperately trying to present "his case" against usury and for a proper understanding of contemporary politics.

Having established in the previous sequence of cantos a relationship between early American history and contemporary Italian politics, with Mussolini presented in Canto 41 as a current manifestation of a possible epic hero, Pound begins this sequence with a series of cantos devoted to the founding of a "legitimate and just" (Canto 42) bank in Siena in the seventeenth century, a bank founded on the wealth produced and made possible by the grazing lands south of Siena. This grounding of value in the land itself is a principle Pound discovered in both Jefferson and Mussolini. In fact, the main reason Mussolini is a potential hero for *The Cantos* is that he reclaimed the land as the source of value, literally, by draining the marshes and, from that once useless land, providing grain, water, and room for the people. The *Monte dei Paschi di Siena* is an earlier example of Italian political sense and responsible leadership. The founding of this bank was to be guaranteed by the income generated by the Sienese grasslands, and so this bank is in direct contrast to the Bank of England whose moneys are made *"ex nihil"* (Canto 46). And unlike usurious banks, the Bank of Siena was able to keep interest rates low and paid dividends to the community every five years from its profits.

The General Council of Siena created this bank "having chief place and desire that the / citizens get satisfaction (siano soddisfatti) contentment / and [were] fully persuaded of / what for the common good is here being dealt with" (Canto 43). Canto 43 includes a celebration in response to the erection of this bank, and the next canto continues with the people's enthusiastic and spontaneous response:

Flags trumpets horns drums
and a placard
    VIVA FERDINANDO
and were sounded all carillons
with bombs and with bonfires and was sung TE
    DEUM
in thanks to the Highest for this so
provident law. (Canto 44)

The purpose of good law and responsible leadership, then, is to create a happy people living in a state founded on economic justice. Snippets from the documents that went into the founding of this "natural" bank are presented to indicate the careful and apparently unheroic attention to practical affairs required for such a state and for such a people to be constructed. If such a bank managed to function for centuries despite the machinations of the Medicis and the violence of the French Revolution and the Napoleonic wars, then such an institution is possible again.

These three cantos end with a phrase that leads Pound into his perhaps most famous canto: " 'The foundation, Siena, has been to keep a bridle on usury' "(Canto 44). The Bank of Siena was erected to fight the civil influence of a corrupt economic system, one in which money is founded on nothing at all and so is

fundamentally fraudulent; and Canto 45 is a powerful presentation of what "Usura" has done to the world—or more properly, what it has prevented in the world:

With *Usura*
With usura hath no man a house of good stone
each block cut smooth and well fitting
That design might cover their face, . . .
with usura
seeth no man Gonzaga his heirs and his concu-
    bines
no picture is made to endure nor to live with
but it is made to sell and sell quickly.

For Pound usury is neither a symbol nor an allegory for evil but something defined literally as "a charge for the use of purchasing power, levied without regard to production" (Canto 45). It is not a mysterious force but a corrupt system of economic exchange that has led to evil by preventing the construction of beauty in the world: in the homes we live in, the bread we eat, the pictures we admire, the language we use. This canto retrieves Pound's earlier emphasis on esthetics, now to be fully integrated into his political position: The creation of a state designed to foster the ability to appreciate and enjoy the beauty of the world is the great goal of Pound's politics, and usury is a system designed to prevent the construction of the beautiful and the circulation of sensual pleasure. Here his early life as an esthete and his developing political interests come together.

In Canto 46 Pound continues this integration of the esthetic and the political by presenting himself as a possible embodiment of the figure of hero in the poem. This canto begins with a challenge to the reader to decide whether Pound or Eliot has devised a "more natural language" and which one of the two will bring the reader successfully through the "hell" of the modern world. As if to pick up this challenge, Pound then writes lines that are "poetic" as opposed to "political":

That day there was cloud over Zoagli
And for three days snow cloud over the sea
Banked like a line of mountains.
Snow fell. Or rain fell stolid, a wall of lines

So that you could see where the air stopped
   open
and where the rain fell beside it
Or the snow fell beside it. Seventeen
Years on this case, nineteen years, ninety years
   on this case.

Most of us have been desensitized by usury, but the poet can still see and record the beauty of nature in these simple, direct, and lucid lines. The poet's special skill of perception and expression of beauty is what qualifies him for conducting his investigation into the causes of economic corruption, the "case" he has been working on for what seems the past ninety years. That the snow cloud is "banked" is a wonderful pun that brings his political concerns into his poetic sensibility. He presents his own body in this canto, fuzzy and long-legged, to emphasize not only the role of *the* poet in the cause of economic justice but also the role of *this* poet presenting *this* case. And he has discovered in his investigation of Major Douglas's theory of Social Credit the basis for a just economic system capable of doing for the present what the Bank of Siena did for its time: " 'pay[ing] dividends . . .' / 'Instead of collectin' taxes' " (Canto 46).

That he is on a case suggests that he is either a private detective searching for clues in a mystery or a lawyer in a courtroom presenting that evidence to a jury; and in this canto, and in *The Cantos*, he is both. He has discovered, and now presents as evidence, quotations from the very men who have founded and controlled the financial institutions of usury: "Said Paterson: / *Hath benefit of interest on all / the moneys which it, the bank, creates out of nothing* (46). This is perhaps the key piece of evidence, a quotation from the chief founder of the Bank of England in 1694 in which he simply states the fact that the banking system he is inaugurating is based on nothing. Pound quotes one of the Rothschilds as having said in the middle of the Civil War:

    "Very few people
"will understand this. Those who do will be
   occupied
"getting profits. The general public will probably not
"see it's against their interest." (Canto 46)

Pound has found the evidence of a conspiracy against the public good by a handful of usurious financiers and presents it to the jury of his readers. This poet is taking us through hell slowly, teaching us the facts about the economic system under which we live that has made the world the unhappy place it has become for the majority of its inhabitants. It is a poet's sensibility that has discovered the truth about economics and politics.

In Canto 47 Pound returns to his opening theme and opening figure, the heroic wanderer Odysseus seeking his way back home. As he repeats this theme now in the middle of these economic cantos: The heroic journey has become a journey back to an original relation to the earth itself as the source of all wealth and the ground of all values. To accomplish this return, Odysseus journeys to participate in what appears to be Pound's own version of the Eleusinian mysteries. Odysseus is drawn, beyond his own will, to the woman who awaits for him, as captivated by her power as moth or bull is drawn to its destruction by its urges:

To the cave art thou called, Odysseus,
By Molü hast thou respite for a little
By Molü art thou freed from the one bed
   that thou may'st return to another.

Odysseus is freed by the magic charm called Molü to leave one bed and return to a first and lost bed, freed from the bed of the woman who has lured him to the cave back to the bed of the mother. One needs the grace provided by Molü for this return, for a return to the mother is a violation of the primal taboo that threatens castration for the offender. This sexual journey back to the mother is to be understood as an effort to return us to an original relation to the world, as the lines quoted above move into lines from Hesiod's *Works and Days* that deliver instruction about farming, instruction that is for Hesiod and for Pound worthy of poetic treatment (Canto 47).

One must dare to violate the codes of one's culture that prohibit a relation with the mother and seek to regain that original union that usury has rendered completely broken. Though threatened with castration, "Scylia's white teeth" appear "less sharp" (Canto 47) as the wanderer continues to violate this prohibition. The woman who is one's sexual partner becomes Tellus, the Roman goddess of the earth's fruitfulness, as the personal act of sexual daring becomes a cultural symbol for a return to an agrarian world that values the earth as the source of all goodness and worth. The heroic wanderer who began *The Cantos* has violated usura's law that prohibits union with the earth, as we return to a relation to the earth as mother on whose body we lovingly labor and enjoy the fruits of that act of union. It is this act of epic daring that grounds the poem's economics, as we must see the earth as the mother upon whose body all wealth is grounded.

The climax of this canto presents the wanderer in ecstatic union with the earth:

> By prong have I entered these hills:
> That the grass grow from my body,
> That I hear the roots speaking together,
> The air is new on my leaf
> The forked boughs shake with the wind.
>   (Canto 47)

Canto 49 brings this theme to a further climax, as the wanderer emerges from this union and achieves a vision of a "people of leisure" (Canto 49) who live in harmony with nature and enjoy their life on the earth. "And by no man these verses" is Pound's way of indicating that the wanderer of Canto 47 has become the poet, now beyond personality as "no man," who can present to the politician the proper goal of his activity, a state of stillness in which people are unaware of any imperial power and who live without any fear that the state will intrude on their unhurried lives. The poetry of this canto is unmatched in its simple and lucid depiction of the world:

> Comes then snow scur on the river
> And a world is covered with jade
> Small boat floats like a lanthorn,
> The flowing water clots as with cold. And at
>   San Yin
> they are a people of leisure.

The implication is that only a people of leisure can see the world this way: clearly and directly and simply. The poet's special capacity to perceive the beauty of the world recorded in Canto 46 has become actual for the whole people by the creation of a state that does not steal a people's labor from them and that allows them to work in harmony with nature:

> Sun up; work
> sundown; to rest
> dig well and drink of the water
> dig field; eat of the grain
> Imperial power is? and to us what is it?
>   (Canto 49)

The proper use of power is for the people to be almost totally unaware of its exercise; the proper goal for power is a people who enjoy the fruits of their own labor on the body of the earth with whom they have an intimate relation.

This vision of "a people of leisure" living in "the dimension of stillness" (Canto 49) does not end the sequence, though its poetic beauty might have led another poet to end with this climax. Pound chooses to end with Pietro Leopoldo's efforts against usury rather than the poetic vision of Canto 49, perhaps to underscore the necessity of what seems prosaic activity as the only way for the poetic vision ever to be realized. After the poet's vision, the politician must still take action. What *The Fifth Decad of Cantos* establishes is that the poet is at the center of the process of realizing the vision of a just economic state and a happy people living within it. Pound's esthetics, his politics, and the theme of the epic wanderer come together in this sequence that ends the first half of *The Cantos*.

Bibliography

Brooke-Rose, Christine. *A Structural Analysis of Pound's Usura Canto*. The Hague: Mouton, 1976.

Sicari, Stephen. *Pound's Epic Ambition: Dante and the Modern World*. Albany: State U of New York P, 1991.

Tryphonopoulos, Demetres P. "'The Fourth; the Dimension of Stillness': D. P. Ouspensky and Fourth Dimensionalism in Canto 49." *Paideuma* 19.3 (1990): 117–122.

Stephen Sicari

The Cantos: Cantos LII–LXI

Cantos LII–LXI (known as the Chinese History Cantos) were composed between November 1937 and March 1939 and first published in January 1940 in one volume with Cantos 62–71 ("the John Adams Cantos"). The following are the main source materials for these cantos: (1) Canto 52 (from l. 50): *Li Ki*, the Confucian book of rites and folk customs, in Couvreur's edition (Ho Kien Fou, 1899—Chinese text with translations into Latin and French). *Li* signifies behaviors that make for order in nature and society. Rites and customs rather than legislation were the guiding principles of Confucian China. (2) Cantos 53–61 (apart from ll. 1–27 of 59 and a few lines elsewhere) are Pound's condensation (6,376 pages into about 2,500 lines) of the thirteen-volume *Histoire Générale de la Chine* by J.-A.-M. de Moyriac de Mailla (Paris, 1777–1785). De Mailla (b. 1669), a French Jesuit scholar, went to Peking in 1700, was attached to the court of Manchu emperor Kang-Hi and his successors (see Cantos 59–61), and died there in 1748. His history of China as recorded by Confucian scholars was completed in 1735. Confucian historians, while chronicling events accurately, aimed so to mirror the conduct of emperors and their officers as to make of them examples of wise rule or of misrule for the instruction of a new dynasty. Their measure of good government was the ethic embodied in *Li Ki*: to respect nature and distribute its abundance equitably among the whole people. Bad government lets individual interests come before the common good—hence the Confucian hostility to palace eunuchs and to Taoism and Buddhism. Under good rulers, the empire flourished; under weak rulers, it fell apart. Publication of de Mailla's *Histoire* (with some editorial additions) coincided with the American and French Revolutions with their similar assertions of natural reason against arbitrary law and dogma and their convictions that the good life should be enjoyed on earth by all and not just by the privileged few. Pound's version continues the infusion of the Confucian into the European Enlightenment. It is meant to shape the conduct of rulers—Pound sent a copy to Mussolini with that intention.

The main theme of the decad is stated at the start: "the abundance of nature / with the whole folk behind it"—an idea in accord with Confucian *Li*. Its negative is usury, or what is for private gain and against nature's increase. The other nine cantos trace the core drama of five millennia of China's history: the origins and foundations of its order, down to Confucius or Kung (53); the struggle to maintain that order against its internal enemies (54); decadence and disorder (55); partial restoration of order by Tartar invaders (56); worse breakdown into wars and disasters (57–58); full return to Confucian order by new Tartar invaders, the Manchu (58–59); Kang Hi's reception of useful knowledge from Europe while safeguarding the integrity of China's own culture (60); and his succession by exemplary upholders of the founding ethic (61). That ethic has been shown to be a viable force for good order in China through all its vicissitudes down to 1776.

Read as narrative history, these cantos will seem bafflingly fragmented. They require to be read as *histoire morale*: That is, the reader must make out the *ethical* relations of the fragments. Details seemingly taken at random will then be found to have been sorted and arranged to prompt a more discriminating understanding. For example, the opening section of 53 traces the gradual steps by which China advanced from primitive ignorance to "abundance." The next section (48 lines) has as its center and pivot "Day by day make it new" and shows what that axiom involves and why it is necessary. The center and pivot of the entire canto is the Chou dynasty ideogram, surrounded by praise of its exemplary achievements. The previous 100 or so lines have been building up to this, and the next 100 or so show the falling off. Of the final 100 lines, the middle 48 are devoted to Confucius, with 26 lines of disorders preceding and 26 lines on efforts to renew order following. There is a composer's sense for structure and organization throughout these cantos: Pound's aim was to transform history into a kind of music. (Compare his version of the Odes, *The Classic Anthology Defined by Confucius*, especially parts III and IV.)

Bibliography

Bell, Ian F. A. "Middle Cantos XLII–LXXI." *The Cambridge Companion to Ezra Pound*. Ed. Ira B. Nadel. Cambridge: Cambridge UP, 1999. 92–108.

Cantrell, Carol H., and Ward Swinson. "Cantos LII–LXXI: Pound's Textbook for Princes." *Paideuma* 17.2–3 (1988): 111–144.

Driscoll, John. *The China Cantos of Ezra Pound*. Uppsala: Ubsaliensis S. Academiae, 1983.

Gordon, David. " 'Confucius, Philosophe': An Introduction to the Chinese Cantos 52–61." *Paideuma* 5.3 (1976): 387–403.

———. "The Sources of Canto LIII." *Paideuma* 5.1 (1976): 122–152.

Nolde, John J. *Blossoms from the East: The China Cantos of Ezra Pound*. Orono: NPF, 1983.

Terrell, Carroll F. "History, de Mailla and the Dynastic Cantos." *Paideuma* 5.1 (1976): 95–121.

A. David Moody

The Cantos: Cantos LXII–LXXI

Cantos LXII–LXXI (the John Adams Cantos) were composed between June 1938 and March 1939 and first published in January 1940 in one volume with Cantos 52 through 61 (the Chinese History Cantos). Canto 61 carried the history of China down to about 1776 and looked forward to "our [American] revolution" and "the rise of the Adamses." Pound's portrait of John Adams, in almost exactly the same number of lines as his entire history of China in 52–61, presents him as an American version of the Confucian good governor, in effect living and legislating by the principles of the *Ta Hsio* (Great Digest).

The ten cantos are made up of material from a single source, the ten-volume *Works of John Adams*, edited by Charles Francis Adams (Boston, 1850–1856). John Adams (1735–1826) was a leading light of the American Revolution of 1776, first vice president of the United States under Washington (1789–1796), and second president (1797–1801). His *Works* consist of a biography by his son John Quincy Adams and grandson Charles Francis Adams (vol. 1); his own diaries and autobiographical writings (vols. 2–3); his political essays (vols. 3–6); and his official letters, messages, and public papers (vols. 7–10). By following this arrangement Pound

reads Adams in five distinct perspectives and gives a five-part structure to the decad:

1. 62–63.37: the biographers' Adams as first overview (spanning 1628–1826);
2. 63.38–66.64: Adams's public service "as the protagonist saw it" (1756–1796);
3. 66.65–68.47: Adams's pivotal ideas of government (1765–1791);
4. 68.48–70.49: the official record of Adams's public service (1771–1801);
5. 70.50–71: Adams's retrospective views "in the mirror of memory" (1773–1818).

Pound's John Adams is the man who above all others brought about the birth of the United States as an independent nation. He is characterized by the Greek word *THUMON* (that which animates: breath, spirit, force of mind and will), implying that he was a vital force in the shaping of America by virtue of his passionate commitment to the rule of law as the basis of liberty, together with his clarity of mind and firmness of purpose. He made the revolution "in the minds of the people" by convincing arguments and exemplary actions. His weapons were his lawbooks, his care for the precise definition and exact observance of words, and his personal integrity— "fairness, honesty and straight moving." Pound's governing concern is almost exclusively with discerning his guiding principles and ideas (his *paideuma*) as manifest in his conduct. The familiar incidents and narratives of the war for American independence—the Boston Tea Party, the Battle of Lexington, and the rest of that history—are scarcely noticed. The struggle for liberty appears as a struggle for enlightenment against the despotism of minds darkened by narrow interests. Adams's principal antagonist is Alexander Hamilton, who represents the putting of private profit before equity. "THEMIS CONDITOR" (Canto 71) sums up what John Adams stands for: the tradition of common law as the founding principle of the American and (as Pound hoped) permanent revolution. That is what places him in the line of succession to the exemplary emperors of the Confucian history of China.

Such an abstract gives no idea of how these cantos actually work. In composing them Pound skim-read the *Works*, picked out phrases and fragments, a half-line here and a line or two there, and wrote them down one after the other just as they occurred. The drafts show little or no revision or rearranging and little or no respect for the original contexts. The result can appear an overlong cascade of random bits with no logic or coherence. But it is not random, Pound maintained in an interview with Pier Paolo Pasolini: It is a form of music in which "themes find each other out" (*si ritrovano*) (Anderson 332). Yeats thought of it as "impressions that are in part visual, in part metrical . . . related like the notes of a symphony" (Yeats xxiv). One might call it a music of verbal effects. There are patterns, orderings, structures (see Kay Davis on this). One basic principle in the arrangement of the material is contrast, or similarity and difference. Another is progression in "rings" or vortices—as a rule the writing is organized about centers and does not make for closure and conclusions. An example of the arrangement by which themes find each other out might be represented by the formula $a : b : c : b : a$. (This would apply also to the overall structure of this decad.) This is evidently a new way of writing requiring a new way of reading. The reader who would follow Pound's representation of Adams must become an intensely active participant in the process of dissociating the note-fragments one from another, grasping the nature of each one, and perceiving how they relate to each other (or what they add up to). Thus the reader is not being given a predigested meaning (as in the abstract above) but is necessarily involved in the process of "moral analysis" that John Adams considered the only purpose of historical writing.

Bibliography

Anderson, David. "Breaking the Silence: The Interview of Vanni Ronsisvalle and Pier Paolo Pasolini with Ezra Pound in 1968." *Paideuma* 10.2 (1981): 331–345.

Bell, Ian F. A. "Middle Cantos XLII–LXXI." *The Cambridge Companion to Ezra Pound*. Ed. Ira B. Nadel. Cambridge: Cambridge UP, 1999.

Davis, Kay. *Fugue and Fresco: Structures in Pound's Cantos*. Orono: NPF, 1984.

Makin, Peter. *Pound's Cantos*. London: Allen & Unwin, 1985.

Moody, A. D. "Composition in the Adams Cantos." *Ezra Pound and America*. Ed. Jacqueline Kaye. New York: St. Martin's P, 1992.

Pound, Ezra. "The Jefferson-Adams Letters as a Shrine and a Monument." *SP* 147–158.

Rabaté, Jean-Michel. *Language, Sexuality, and Ideology in Ezra Pound's Cantos*. Albany: State U of New York P, 1986.

Yeats, W. B. *The Oxford Book of Modern Verse 1892–1935*. Oxford: Oxford UP, 1936.

A. David Moody

The Cantos: Cantos LXXII–LXXIII

After publishing *Cantos LII–LXXI* in 1940, Pound planned a final volume of paradisal cantos and began researching it, reading Erigena, corresponding with George Santayana, writing prose on "European" (versus Semitic) religions, and translating in Italian the Confucian classics. He also made many verse notes, including lines on Erigena's "lights" and Kung's "whiteness," and evocations of fertility rites. Two of these wartime fragments, "The Evil is Usury" and the beautiful "Now sun rises in Ram sign," were reprinted in *Drafts and Fragments of Cantos CX–CXVII*.

Pound's plans for his paradisal cantos were delayed by the war, which Italy entered in June 1940. He continued to address England and America in his radio broadcasts from Rome but also discovered a new Italian audience by writing articles for *Il Meridiano di Roma*, a prominent literary weekly. When Italy signed the armistice in September 1943, the Germans set up Mussolini as token head of an "Italian Social Republic" (RSI) in the North, and Pound maintained contacts with officials in Saló and Gardone and wrote frequently for an RSI paper, *Il Popolo di Alessandria*. In this period of suspension before the final defeat of Hitler and his European allies (April 1945), living in Sant' Ambrogio near Rapallo and thinking of Confucius, Pound turned again to poetry and composed with great vigor and speed two cantos, 72 and 73, written in Italian because by then his only audience was Italy and because they were an homage to his favorite Italian poets, Dante and Cavalcanti.

Canto 72 is written in a somewhat archaic Italian and uses a free rhyme scheme reminiscent of Dante's tercets. It was occasioned by the death of the founder of Futurism, Filippo Tommaso Marinetti (2 December 1944), a strong supporter of Mussolini who died after returning from the Russian front. Pound imagines that the spirit of his friend appears to him and asks to continue the fight against Italy's enemies. (This is also reminiscent of Japanese Noh plays.) Then Pound hears another voice, which seems to belong to Manlio Torquato Dazzi, a friend who translated a Latin tragedy (by Albertino Mussato) about Ezzelino da Romano, a tyrant mentioned by Dante. Ezzelino, a kind of Herculean or Promethean figure, appears in person and denounces the traitors and enemies of the fascist cause (including Pope Pius XII), while naming Italian officers who have died gallantly; he also speaks obscurely of the long-standing conflict between church and state. His invective is interrupted by a few evocative lines spoken by Galla Placidia, the Roman princess buried in Ravenna, but Canto 72 closes with Ezzelino (a projection of "Ez" the angry prophet) reaffirming his willpower and his certainty of final victory. Though Pound's Italian is occasionally clumsy, Canto 72 is a cogent performance, full of his combative spirit and his message. A short passage was published by Pound's friend Ubaldo degli Uberti in *La Marina Repubblicana*, an obscure periodical, on 15 January 1945, with an amicable notice and the title "Presenza di F. T. Marinetti."

Canto 73 appeared in its entirety in the following issue of *La Marina Repubblicana* (1 February 1945), with the title "Cavalcanti—Corrispondenza Repubblicana" (the latter was the name of the official RSI news agency). It is written in the style of Cavalcanti's famous doctrinal canzone of love "Donna me prega," with short rhyming lines, and is in fact spoken by the ghost of Cavalcanti. He tells Pound that he has recently encountered in Rimini the spirit of a local girl who, having been raped by Canadian soldiers, led them through a mined field and was killed with them. This story, probably an invention, had appeared in *Corriere della Sera*, Italy's chief newspaper, on 1 October 1944 and was the subject of a cover illustration of the popular weekly *Domenica del Corriere* for 15 October. Pound was struck by the tale of the heroic girl, an heiress of the Romagna spirit of Malatesta and Mussolini. He stresses her buxom beauty, which is also typical of the region. Cavalcanti concludes with fervid praise for the courageous boys and girls that wear the black fascist uniform. Very simple in its emotions, Canto 73 is nevertheless effective and connected by many themes to the rest of the poem. (Malatesta's Tempio, badly damaged by bombs according to reports of June 1944, is also mentioned wistfully.)

After 72–73, Pound went on to make extensive drafts for further Italian cantos in early 1945 but abandoned them and reworked their essential episodes in *The Pisan Cantos*. Cantos 72 and 73 he withheld for reasons of expediency, though his friends knew them, and Scheiwiller offered to publish them. They were eventually included in the New Directions *Cantos* in 1986, and in 1995 an English translation, by Pound, of Canto 72 was appended to the Italian text. Unfortunately, this translation is a crib drafted by Pound in the 1960s and does not convey the spirit of the original. It also contains several inaccuracies. Cantos 72 and 73 should be read in Italian. They will seem strange to English-speaking readers, but they are equally puzzling for Italians. In this they are no different from all of Pound's poetry, though having been written with so distinct and immediate a purpose they show Pound in the somewhat rare mood of speaking to be understood.

Bibliography

Accame, Giano. *Ezra Pound economista*. Rome: Europa Libreria, 1995.

Bacigalupo, Massimo. "Ezra Pound's Cantos 72 and 73: An Annotated Translation." *Paideuma* 20.1–2 (1991): 9–41.

Hesse, Eva, ed. *Die ausgefallenen Cantos LXXI und LXXIII*. Zurich: Arche, 1991.

Pound, Ezra. "Canto LXXIII: Cavalcanti—Corrispondenza Repubblicana." *La Marina Repubblicana* 2.3 (1 February 1945): 7.

———. "Presenza di F. T. Marinetti." *La Marina Re-pubblicana* 2.2 (15 January 1945): 2.

Turris, Gianfranco de. "L'insegnamento morale di Pound durante la R.S.I." *Ezra Pound educatore.* Ed. Luca Gallesi. Milan: Terziaria, 1997. 251–274.

Massimo Bacigalupo

The Cantos: The Pisan Cantos LXXIV–LXXXIV

The Pisan Cantos, a parenthesis of personal crisis in *The Cantos'* examination of Western culture, grew out of Pound's dire circumstances toward the end of World War II. Under indictment for treason since July 1943, Pound could not help but see that the inevitable fall of Mussolini's Salò Republic would mean the end of his dream of a better society, the destruction of much that he held dear, and the possibility of his own execution. By the end of May 1944, the war had turned definitively against the Axis, and Pound and his wife Dorothy, forced to flee their flat in Rapallo, moved into an excruciating menage à trois above the city on the cliffs of Sant' Ambrogio in the home of Pound's lifelong companion Olga Rudge. It was here, in the midst of running friction between the two women he loved, that Pound read the news that many of his sacred places had been blasted. The worst came on Sunday, 4 June, when he read that bombs had severely damaged his touchstone of Renaissance civilization, the Tempio Malatestiano in Rimini. From then on, Pound's state of mind, strained by his domestic relations, turned to lamentation over a world in ruins and the potential consolation of a landscape suffused with Greek and Confucian presences and swung between phases of defiant denial and passivity bordering on the sense of an afterlife.

The defiance appears in the Italian Cantos 72 and 73. As Pound had since 1943 been translating a selection of his earlier work into Italian in the company of his daughter Mary, he attempted his new cantos in an Italian flexible enough to incorporate colloquial rage and the philosophical inflections of Dante and Cavalcanti. In fact, Canto 73 represents Cavalcanti's own voice as he returns from the sphere of Venus to witness the heroism of a young girl who sacrifices her life for her country by leading Canadians who had raped her into a minefield. Canto 72 is longer and required more work. It depicts the appearance of the recently deceased Tommaso Marinetti's spirit, who asks to appropriate Pound's body so that Marinetti can continue to fight in the war. Marinetti, though, is first displaced by Pound's friend Manlio Torquato Dazzi, then by the ferocious figure of Ezzelino da Romano, the early-thirteenth-century Ghibilline whom Dante sees boiling among the tyrants of *Inferno* XII. It is in Ezzelino's suitably angry voice that Pound calls for the damnation of treacherous Italian peacemakers and for the revenge of the monuments at Rimini.

Pound went on with Italian sequels even before Cantos 72 and 73 saw print. These were the further drafts Pound referred to when he wrote to his daughter at Easter 1945 that he had made numerous notes for more cantos but had decided not to use them. Yet, as Mary de Rachewiltz adds in her account of his letter, the drafts contain visionary moments her father was to draw upon that summer and fall (*I Cantos* 1569). Pound's abandoned Italian cantos included manuscripts and multiple typescripts for two partially achieved cantos, 74 and 75, both of which grew out of Canto 72 and absorbed the extended preparations for a Paradiso that Pound had already made. (One of their recurrent characters is Ezzelino da Romano's sister, Cunizza, whom the troubadour Sordello courted and who— Pound believed—spent her old age in the house of Guido Cavalcanti when Dante was a boy.)

Pound's winter 1945 drafts are set among the natural beauties of Sant' Ambrogio, from whose cliffs they register the disintegration of Italy. In one of his holograph manuscripts, Pound speaks of hearing "the ancient voices" (*"le vetuste voc[i]"*) louder than ever before (*"più che mai prima"*). He claims that, "clear and more frequent" (*"chiare e più sovente"*), these voices came to him, "even as if it were divine / a fountain" (*"pur se'l divin era, / fonte"*). As the world falls apart around him, he reassures himself that these ancient voices represent a paradisal bedrock in human experience that cannot be destroyed. And in the Italian Canto 75, he portrays this ancient wisdom emanating from the figure of Cunizza, who appears at the *triedro*, the crossing of three paths near an olive grove.

Before Pound could polish these Italian verses, though, he found himself a prisoner of the American army. The Americans vacillated about what to do with him but finally ordered him incarcerated, aged nearly sixty, at the U.S. Army Disciplinary Training Center, a prison camp located near the Viareggio road just north of Pisa. From 24 May to a day or two before 13 June, he stayed in a concrete-floored, wire isolation cage in the open air of a fierce summer and slept under constant illumination until he suffered acute symptoms of confusion, anxiety, and fatigue. He was then transferred to an officer's tent in the medical compound, where he remained until 16 November, when he was put without warning on a plane to Washington.

Pound intended, while in custody, to continue the translations into English of Confucius's *The Great Digest*, *The Unwobbling Pivot*, *The Analects*, and *The Classic Anthology* he had begun in Rapallo, and he had managed to bring with him materials including Legge's bilingual edition of the Confucian texts and a small Chinese dictionary. Now terrified, however, that his breakdown might be causing him to lose his memory, he set aside the translations for a period (though they remained always in his mind) and began composing new cantos.

The English cantos Pound wrote at Pisa incorporated much of the Italian drafts in an unfolding visionary quest for internal peace. They begin with the salutation now occupying lines eleven and twelve of Canto 74—"The suave eyes, quiet, not scornful, / rain also is of the process"—and go on to telescope a vision of the *stil-novisti* beloved with a mystical reading of Confucius very like the one that concludes his contemporary translation of *The Unwobbling Pivot*: "The *unmixed* functions (in time and space) without bourne. This unmixed is the tensile light, the Immaculata. There is no end to its action" (*Confucius* 187). Pound's "suave eyes" initiate a poem that is intent upon the redeeming energies of light and reason and that proceeds

through intuitions of "la luna" to the healing power of "pale eyes as if without fire" in Canto 80 and to unexpected forgiveness of masked eyes in Canto 81. Like Cunizza's eyes in the Canto 75 typescript, the latter are "in costume" and "senz' ira"—without anger. In *The Pisan Cantos* they herald a final crisis when, reappearing in Canto 83 after a dark night of the soul in Canto 82, the eyes "pass and look *from* mine," effecting a miraculous return of compassion and peace.

It is noteworthy here that Pound did not discover in the Pisan landscape the apparitions that he now celebrated: They are (in several senses) translations. Nevertheless, as he recast and elaborated his Italian verses into English, he suffused his wartime visions with an apprehension of natural process so intensely felt that critics of the poem were convinced the one had grown out of the other. Quite deliberately, Pound orchestrates his symbolic sequence with a series of finely drawn observations of the quotidian world, so that the atmospherics of the light and the goddesses seem to be one with the solidity of ordinary creatures: "if calm be after tempest / that the ants seem to wobble / as the morning sun catches their shadows" (Canto 80).

The result is a kind of twentieth-century *Walden* in which, as Forrest Read put it in an early but still remarkable essay, "purification of [the poet's] will" follows first upon powers released by natural observation and then upon a discovery of the "paradisal energies which move nature." The whole effect is grounded in the everyday, as Pound signals when, near the end of Canto 78, he remarks, "[A]s for the solidity of the white oxen in all this / perhaps only Dr Williams (Bill Carlos) / will understand its importance, / its benediction. He wd/ have put in the cart."

A second and perhaps more enduring part of *The Pisan Cantos'* appeal appears continuous with its symbolic texture but in fact draws on quite different sources of style and value. Driven by a terror of losing his identity, Pound extemporized a poetic idiom nervous and flexible enough to articulate the moment-by-moment shiftings of a diary or a reminiscence. (In part his practice was based on the lyric and episodic *Testament* of Villon. Pound took his cue especially from lines from stanza XXIX: "Where are those laughing comrades / that I was with in former days, / who sang so well, talked so well / and so excelled in word and deed? / Some are dead and stiff— / nothing now remains of them: / may they find peace in Paradise, / and may God save the rest.")

Yet, as Pound explained in a "Note to [the] Base Censor," he wrote to assure the camp authorities that his typescripts were not encoded sedition but that there was something more involved as well. Interspersed with his memories, Pound recorded interruptions from the life of the camp around him. In Pound's words, "The form of the poem and main progress is conditioned by its own inner shape, but the life of the D.T.C. passing OUTSIDE the scheme cannot but impinge, or break into the main flow. The proper names given are mostly those of men on sick call seen passing my tent."

Pound thought he had finished his work when on 2 October he wrote his wife Dorothy that "I have done a Decad 74 / 83 . . . which don't seem any worse than the first 70." He then, though, received a letter from her mentioning that J. P. Angold, a correspondent and promising poet, had died and that several fascist collaborators were facing death. Pound was sufficiently moved to compose a new canto—a coda to the sequence he had completed. He began with a cry of grief, and before he knew it, the new canto (84) had turned into a bitter farewell to "il Capo [Mussolini], / Pierre [Laval], [and] Vidkun [Quisling]." In effect, this unforeseen conclusion reframed the sequence, and Pound completed the job by moving ten angry and as yet unplaced lines beginning "The enormous tragedy of the dream in the peasant's bent shoulders" to the beginning of Canto 74. Thus Pound's elegy to Mussolini, the dramatic opening of *The Pisan Cantos* as published, announces a much more political and programmatic poem than the one he thought he had completed. The Mussolini lines send *The Pisan Cantos* on their way, bristling with self-protective hostility and hurtling toward Canto 84. Tuning our ear to them, we

hear not openness or generosity but only what Peter Nicholls has called a "proud and intransigent . . . stoicism" that helps Pound "to control and order" his chaos and his despair (166).

Nevertheless, without *The Pisan Cantos* and his last sequence, *Drafts and Fragments*, Pound would probably now be known as a fellow traveler of the Eliot of *The Waste Land* who had self-destructed, like so many others, on the ideological reefs of the 1930s. It was his ability to portray moments when "the mind swings by a grass-blade" (Canto 83) that made a new generation regard him not as a patriarch but as an outcast who lived long enough to doubt his strongest convictions and make haunting poetry of the remaining disarray.

Bibliography

Bush, Ronald. " 'Quiet, Not Scornful': The Composition of the *Pisan Cantos*." *A Poem Containing History: Textual Studies in The Cantos*. Ed. Lawrence Rainey. Ann Arbor: U of Michigan P, 1997. 169–211.

Carne-Ross, D. S. "The Music of a Lost Dynasty: Pound in the Classroom." *Boston University Journal* 21 (1973): 25–41. Reprinted in *Instaurations: Pindar to Pound*. Berkeley: U of California P, 1979. 193–218.

Kenner, Hugh. *The Pound Era*. Berkeley: U of California P, 1971.

Nicholls, Peter. *Ezra Pound: Politics, Economics, and Writing: A Study of The Cantos*. Atlantic Highlands: Humanities P, 1984.

Read, Forrest. "The Pattern of the *Pisan Cantos*." *Sewanee Review* (1957): 400–419.

Ronald Bush

The Cantos: Section: Rock-Drill de los Cantares LXXXV–XCV

In form and structure the *Rock-Drill* Cantos (1955) is most closely related to *The Fifth Decad of Cantos XLII–LI* (1937) in that the first five cantos contrast with the following six. Both volumes develop slowly and in a self-consciously concentrated mood, then shift abruptly in subject matter and speed, as well as intensity, before pausing and then rising at the end to a sense of climax and closure. *The Fifth Decad* turns on the "Usura" Canto 45 and contrasts the ebullient pageantry and economic order of Renaissance

Tuscany with Confucian/Taoist harmonies and West Asian mythologies. In *Rock-Drill* the turning point is the poet's personal reinvigoration through his relationship with Sheri Martinelli. The style and metric of the 1954 volume is, however, different from anything that had gone before: It is far more terse in expression and extremely elliptical in all its references. Pound had already shifted from his earlier poetic mode in the Pisan sequence and now develops that new style even further. In "Ezra Pound's Later *Cantos* and His Early Work: Modes of Time and the Example," Kai-Ulrich Deissner has documented the development of the volume from a preliminary outline of references and quotations that repeat and recall basic themes already incorporated in earlier publications. In the actual writing, however, Pound rearranged the order of thematic rhymes as he fleshed them out and incorporated them into the subject matter at hand. After he came under the influence of Sheri Martinelli, everything changed.

In Canto 85 we find a selective distillation of Chinese history that goes far beyond the chronological recital in the Chinese History Cantos (52–61) or the more personal past and preoccupations that recur in *The Pisan Cantos* (74–84). Here the principles of good governance are reduced to outline form, the key concepts that account for hierarchical order and ethical probity in a Confucian view of the universe. A vast array of references to people and incidents from the whole panoply of European history are also interwoven in an effort to demonstrate the multilayered nature of human achievement. The references, however, are opaque and always require explanation in order to uncover the associative links that bind them together. For example, the lines at the end of the canto do make sense: "Dead in the Piazzale Loreto, / In Holohan's case, murder protected. / Jury trial was in Athens. / Tyrants resisted." After Mussolini had been captured and executed by partisans, his corpse was hung by the heels in a public square at Milan; despite John Holohan's testimony at the court-martial that followed Abraham Lincoln's assassination as to her innocence, Mary Surratt, too, was hanged and without benefit of

trial by jury—which had originated in ancient Athens. "Even tyrants resisted such injustice" seems to be the point here, and a number of other examples follow.

Canto 86 extends the argument but concentrates on negative aspects and incidents. The next canto returns us to early-nineteenth-century America and the conflicts over the establishment of the Bank of America. As in Chinese history, heroes and villains contend with one another in a welter of detailed references, and this story is pursued through Canto 88. The last canto in the series, 89, acts as a reprise, juxtaposing historical Chinese protagonists with those of Federal America, and Classical Athens with early-nineteenth-century Washington, while the sense of closure becomes insistent.

The first four of the following set (Cantos 90–93) are obviously love poems, celebrations of nature and the metaphor of light as manifestations of a newly perceived joy and spirituality. Sheri Martinelli (1918–1996) had been a *Vogue* model, painter, and well-known Greenwich Village eccentric, not to mention a New Age enthusiast before that term was even invented. In these cantos she is represented as Sibylla-Beatrice, Kuthera (Aphrodite), Kwanon, Ra-Set, Leucothoe, Leucothea, and Undine (among others) and is frequently associated with Castalia, the sacred pool or spring of cosmic understanding and poetic inspiration at Delphi. As idealized woman, she embodies both love and redemption, mediating between the poet and a spiritual universe that now becomes his *paradiso*. Richard St. Victor (an early Church Father whom Dante had admired) is invoked at the outset: The soul is not itself love, but love flows from it; it does not delight in itself but rather in the love that flows from it. A further reference, although not a literal quotation, occurs in Canto 90: " 'Birds for the mind' said Richardus, / 'Beasts for the body, for know-how.' " Elsewhere he translates the original Latin, "Watch birds to see how the mind works, *studia spiritualia*—animals for outside things, *exercita animalia corporalia*" (*La Destra* November–December 1972). A more exact translation would read: "Therefore in birds one sees spiritual exertion, in animals bodily exercise [work]."

Obscure philosophers such as Ocellus, Erigena, and John Heydon are also invoked as there is a perceived pattern in their understanding of the relationship between the spiritual and material worlds; but all this elaboration really has to do with the rituals Pound and Sheri Martinelli enacted on the lawns of St. Elizabeths, an asylum for the criminally insane where the poet had been incarcerated since 1945. That federal institution had been established on the grounds of an earlier arboretum that Pound and Martinelli came to think of as their sacred grove. On a small flat stone that served them as an altar they burned incense (olibanum) to various gods and later imagined a vision of a classical altar, of which Pound made a sketch (11 May 1954) that was meant to be reproduced between "Faunus, sirenes" and "the stone taking form in the air" (Canto 90). Unfortunately his publishers disappointed him, but that was hardly the first instance. The introduction of Leucothoe, daughter of Orchamus (Cantos 98 and 102), whose disastrous love affair with Helios was glossed over by her transformation into an incense bush, makes great sense in this context, as do references to Leucothea (formerly Ino, Cadmus's daughter and sister to Semele who was transformed into a sea goddess and figures in Homer's epic). In Pound's version, she brandishes a bikini rather than a veil when rescuing Odysseus (Cantos 91, 98, and 105). H. D. records the fact that Martinelli had taken a photograph of herself in a mirror, wearing a bikini, and had given it to Pound (*End to Torment* 52): " 'A spirit in cloth of gold' / So Merlin's moder said" (Canto 91). La Martinelli, who preferred her identification with Undine to all others, resurfaces in *Drafts and Fragments* as a "[g]old [not cold] mermaid" (Canto 111). There are also a number of obscure references to her in *Thrones* (Cantos 104 and 106)—the latter of which refers to a Martinelli painting. There are, however, far too many specific references to Martinelli in *Rock-Drill* to be identified and elaborated upon in so brief a space.

During this period, Pound wrote three prayers.

The first was "Prayer for a Dead Brother" on the occasion of Buddy's (Walter Brennan's) sudden death in rather questionable circumstances. A reference to Castalia is carried over into *The Cantos*. It was published posthumously in the *Antigonish Review* (1972). The others were unpublished prayers for both Pound and Martinelli, traditional and sentimental in both cases and both quite out of character. Pound had already had recourse to his early experience of Presbyterian Bible knowledge, particularly the syntax of "Psalms" in the Usura Canto 45 and the "pull down thy vanity" sequence (Canto 82) in *The Pisan Cantos* that derives from *Ecclesiastes*; but in *Rock-Drill* he reverts to the High Church Anglican–Roman Catholic liturgy—as he had in the earlier "Kyrie eleison" quotation (Canto 79). The repetition of *"m'elevasti"* (you lifted me up) with reference to Sybilla in Canto 90 is noteworthy and later repeated in both the *"oro [pro nobis]"* and "have compassion" responses of Canto 93. There is only one negative/obsessive outburst in the sequence, and that occurs in Canto 91: *"Democracies electing their sewage."*

The last two cantos of the decad (94 and 95) combine the themes of spiritual love and its manifestation in nature with public/political heroes and social order. The first of these ends in a celebration of both love and light, not personal, sexual love but rather the more universal concept of *agape*, which alone illuminates the human condition. Canto 95 continues the theme of an abstract, spiritual love but very explicitly returns to Martinelli as inspiration of art, intellect, and morality. It ends in personal pathos, rehearsing the destruction of the poet/Odysseus's known world that had already been made explicit in *The Pisan Cantos* but now with thanksgiving that he had been rescued (Canto 95).

Bibliography

Deissner, Kai-Ulrich. "Ezra Pound's Later *Cantos* and His Early Work: Modes of Time and the Example." Diss. Cambridge U, 1998.

Grieve, Thomas. "The Seraphin Couvreur Sources of *Rock Drill*." *Paideuma* 4.3 (1975): 361–509.

H. D. *End to Torment: A Memoir of Ezra Pound.* Ed. Norman Holmes Pearson and Michael King. New York: New Directions, 1979.

Pound, Ezra. "Appunti inediti per i 'Cantos.' " *La De-stra* 2.11–12 (1972): [146]–149.

———. "Prayer for a Dead Brother." *Antigonish Review* 8 ([1971–]1972): 27.

Richard Taylor

The Cantos: Thrones de los Cantares LXVI–CIX

The sequence Pound titled *Thrones de los Cantares* (1959) was written from St. Elizabeths Hospital in the last years of the poet's detention there and published in 1959, the year after his release. Bearing grim marks of his long years of confinement, these cantos exploit to the breaking point that paradoxical dimension of the Poundian method that stresses the need for pedagogical directness ("get it across e poi basta" [Canto 79]) at the same time as its materials become ever more recondite and privatized. In one notorious prose aside, Pound tells us, *"One demands the right, now and again, to write for a few people with special interests and whose curiosity reaches into greater detail"* (Canto 96), an assertion indicative of the often imperious tone of *Thrones* and of the poet's sense of a small but trusty band of readers who have the tenacity to follow him into the difficult paradisal regions of his poem.

In some respects, Pound had become comfortable in the "bug house," as he called it, sustained by a stream of often sycophantic visitors and left relatively free to pursue his increasingly rarefied interests. But the sense of being in this way marooned, cut off from the life of the capital to which he was, geographically, so close, also made these late cantos turn in on themselves and seem remote from the contemporary world. This remoteness was something Pound himself attributed to a conspiracy of silence as the money powers worked to "black out" the vital facts and ideas that his long poem sought to make available. He had always felt that it was his mission to unearth knowledge that had been driven underground by interested parties, and in *Thrones* his dedication to this task was coupled with a more emphatic sense of the poem as a kind of secret history, one often requiring protocols of reading that only the dedicated elite

could master. If *Thrones* is actually "unreadable," as many critics and readers have felt it to be, that is not only because Pound's conflicted inner world has become his sole source of intellectual and emotional sustenance but also because the very assumption of "readability" is undermined by forms of haruspication (foretelling) that focus attention on words and image clusters rather than on syntactical structure.

In the opening lines of Canto 96, Leucothea, having saved Odysseus by giving him her veil, disappears beneath "the dark waters" (the allusion is to the *Odyssey*, V, 351). This descent into darkness sets the tone for Pound's own plunge into the murky eighth-century histories of Paul the Deacon, though the act of textual exhumation is quickly linked with a more clearly visionary image: "Aether pluit numismata / Tellus vomit cadavera" (Canto 96)—as the earth gives up its dead, so the coins raining from the heavens signify wealth and the possibility of some transcendent justice. For *Thrones* will be primarily concerned with the conjunction of visionary insight and civic wisdom; Pound is thus attempting to follow Dante's example, as he explained in a 1960 interview with Donald Hall:

> The thrones in Dante's *Paradiso* are for the spirits of the people who have been responsible for good government. The thrones in the *Cantos* are an attempt to move out from egoism and to establish some definition of an order possible or at any rate conceivable on earth. (58)

The first example of such an order will be Byzantium, not the "symbolist" city of Yeats but a city representing, in Pound's view, a model of economic justice. *Thrones* begins with Paul's history of the Lombards in Italy and moves to Byzantium through the medium of the so-called *Eparch's Book* of Leo the Wise. Canto 96 sets out from the collapse of the Roman Empire, attempting to gauge whether the Roman wisdom of law and government could survive the turn to a new religion and the invasions of Italy by barbarian armies. The Eastern Empire, with its auratic capital Byzantium, now occupies center stage since it exemplifies for Pound the codification of Roman law and the maintenance for close to a thousand years of the old currency ratio of silver to gold.

This brief summary might indicate several significant features of *Thrones*. First, there is an almost allegorical tendency in Pound's writing at this point, with a widening gap between the mass of local detail, on the one hand, and the abstract principle for which it stands, on the other. In this case, the ratio of silver to gold operates almost as a Platonic form within the turbulent history it seems to transcend. Second, for all Pound's emphasis on the need to "get it across," much of the language of *Thrones* exhibits a countervailing tendency toward indirectness and self-censorship. Reminiscent of some parts of the Adams sequence, these cantos often produce twisted locutions as if in response to a need for secrecy and veiled speaking. Pound quotes Lenin to illustrate his own predicament: "Aesopian language (under censorship) / where I wrote 'Japan' you may read 'Russia' " (Canto 100), but in contrast to a simple encoding, Pound's idiom makes a habit of deferral, cautiously holding back grammatical elements that would make a statement immediately intelligible: "Not that never should, but if exceeding and / no one protest, / will lose all your liberties" (Canto 100). Such extreme contortions usually result from Pound's traffic with American historical records where, prisoner in the capital that he is, the pressure of secrecy seems greatest.

At the same time, though, certain details retain their luminosity and shine forth from the demotically presented "history" that provides their context. As we move into Canto 97, where Pound launches into an elliptical "reading through" of Alexander Del Mar's *History of Monetary Systems* (1895), these details are increasingly ones of monetary value and measure: "8 stycas: one scat," "20 scads to the dinar, / 100 scads to the mark" (Canto 97), and so on. Such formulations seem to offer points of absolute identity and stability, much as the ideogrammic inscriptions of *Section: Rock-Drill* had sought to do. *Thrones* is in this sense moved by a desire to abolish social complexity in the name of some sovereign act of performative utterance,

as in "that 6 4/5ths pund of bread *be* a farden" (Canto 97; my emphasis). Those instances of speech as a sort of willing-into-being determine many of the historical examples deployed in *Thrones*, at once allowing continued covert celebration of Mussolini and also, of course, expressing the last great hope of *The Cantos*. For the possibility of any large-scale systematic coherence had long since receded, even though the first thirty cantos still announced that possibility in their title. By the mid-1950s, in fact, Pound was finding it difficult to remember the location of particular passages in the earlier parts of the poem, and as he turned his sights toward home, his longing was now for an absolute transparency of utterance that would bring about the truth it proclaimed through the precision of its own articulation. His discovery of *The Sacred Edict of K'ang-hsi* (emperor from 1662 to 1723) offered one route toward the stability Pound needed, and Cantos 98 and 99 presented an idealized world of moral fixities and down-home values (critic Peter Makin has observed that we may also find in these cantos "the mutual moral surveillance of the early New England communities" [283]). Pound's Confucianism now exhibits an extreme commitment to the local (we may recall his wartime condemnations of Jewish "nomadism"): "Earth and water dye the wind in your valley" (Canto 98); "Establish the homestead" (Canto 99); "One village in order" (Canto 99); and so on. "The plan," we are told, "is in nature / rooted" (Canto 99), and the social order is likewise organic and external: "The State is corporate / as with pulse in its body" (Canto 99).

This excursion into what Bakhtin calls "folk-loric" time rather than history establishes the poet's deep desire for quietness and order, and while there is irascibility and "Ole Ez" humor enough here, the real emphasis falls once more on those moments of stasis and identity that show "powers converging" (Canto 99): "The state: order, inside a boundary; / Law: reciprocity" (Canto 99). Yet the poem has not ended; nor, apparently, can it now end without a shift from Byzantium as economic model to the more purely lyric evocation in the final *Drafts and Fragments* of "Byzance, a tomb, an end, / Galla's rest, and thy quiet house at Torcello" (Canto 110). Instead, Cantos 100–109, with a remarkable renewal of energy, plunge us back into American and European history, *Thrones* finally coming to a close in an almost philological exposition of Thomas Coke's Institutes ("Coke: the clearest mind ever in England" [Canto 107]). Yet there are other movements at work, too, as Pound conjures up the remote landscapes of the Na Khi kingdom of Southwest China and the "wind sway" rites used to expiate the spirits of lovers who have committed ritual suicide. These moments of natural beauty carry with them a desire for ending ("[T]his is a dying," we are warned in the *Drafts and Fragments* that follow [Canto 113]), but the poem cannot easily bring itself to face silence.

And justifiably so, perhaps, for among the passages of self-involved, slipshod writing in *Thrones*, there are still ample traces of the "old cunning" where a sudden complexity of vision opens up to illuminate the dark reaches of the poet's anger and insistence. In Canto 107 (to take just one example) we read of "the sky's glass leaded with elm boughs." It is more than just a felicitous image. Into this one line Pound compresses complex feelings about the relation of nature to artifice (the "sky's glass"), though the sky is also seen, literally, through glass, the glass of a window in St. Elizabeths. In this context, the word *leaded* may connote something oppressive, at the same time as it may also recall the leaded windows of more aristocratic dwellings, perhaps in the England of Pound's early days, as remembered in *The Pisan Cantos*. In addition to its figurative significance, the line also conveys a powerfully precise visual image of the branches framing the windows like lead. And coupled with all this, there is a subtle connection here between the idea of confinement, of being imprisoned behind glass, and an implied and compensatory freedom gained by the precise beauty of the image. Lines such as this keep the reader's attention keenly attuned, and in doing so, they offer a sort of leverage against the more blatant rhetorical attempts to persuade us of some dogmatic truth. Even in *Thrones*,

then, where the pressure of frustration and distrust is so great, a fineness and delicacy of perception persist, opening momentarily for the reader a space of reflection and discrimination that the larger, more clearly ideological movements of the sequence seek to withhold.

Bibliography

Hall, Donald. "Ezra Pound." *Writers at Work: The Paris Review Interviews*. 2nd Series. Ed. Malcolm Cowley. New York: Viking, 1963. 35–59.

Makin, Peter. *Pound's Cantos*. London: Allen & Unwin, 1985.

Peter A. Nicholls

The Cantos: Drafts and Fragments of Cantos CX–CXVII

Drafts and Fragments (1969) represents the last poems Pound wrote for *The Cantos*. The volume's contents have been surrounded by debate since its publication as an individual text in 1968–1969, two years before its first inclusion in the entire *The Cantos* in 1970. That debate, in fact, makes it difficult to describe any single *Drafts and Fragments* text, for none exists. Essentially it contains poems after *Thrones de los Cantares* (100–109) and therefore begins with Canto 110. Its termination is more difficult to identify, with various editions shifting uneasily among Canto 116, "CXVII et seq.," and "CXX" between 1968–1969 and 1986. Recent editions of *The Cantos* add "Fragments (1966)," dedicated to Pound's companion Olga Rudge, in which the poet states that these "lines are for the / ultimate CANTO."

Thrones de los Cantares appeared in 1959. By that time, Pound had written portions of what would become the first two cantos of *Drafts and Fragments*: Canto "CX" and "Notes for CXI." Between 1958 and 1960 he wrote other material with numbers above 111, none of which reached a form sufficient, in Pound's view, to be published. Pound was famous by this point in his life. The Bollingen award in 1949, the treason charge, the years of incarceration in St. Elizabeths, the exile to Italy—all these had raised his profile by the early 1960s, sometimes in an unwanted manner, not only within the literary world but also in the larger political arena.

One result of this high profile was a 1962 *Paris Review* interview with Pound conducted by poet Donald Hall. Pound sent Hall versions of the post–*Thrones* cantos he had written by that time, from which Hall was to extract passages to be carried with the *Paris Review* interview.

This material, composed of versions of Cantos 110–116, eventually found its way to New York, where it was pirated by "Fuck You/Press" in a 1967 mimeographed volume titled *Cantos 110–116*. Between 1962 and 1967 Pound published other versions of these poems in several journals. James Laughlin, Pound's New Directions publisher and editor, immediately responded to the 1967 pirated edition by initiating a New Directions volume whose title, *Drafts and Fragments*, was intended to reflect the unfinished character of its poems. The situation by this point was complex: Various versions of the poems existed; the piracy demanded an "authorized" text as quickly as possible; Pound was ill and increasingly withdrawn from the editorial process of the New Directions volume; and the act of creating a close to *The Cantos*, whose principles of Imagism and Vorticism were contrary to closure, was proving difficult for him. The New Directions volume appeared in 1968–1969 and was then incorporated into the 1970 *The Cantos*, though in each case the extent of Pound's participation is difficult to determine.

Perhaps the most contentious textual issue involved a Canto "CXX," which appeared in a journal in 1970 authored by "The Fox" and was included in the New Directions 1972 *The Cantos* after Pound's death that year. The poem asks for forgiveness—"Let the gods forgive what I / have made / Let those I love forgive / what I have made"—lines that proved significant in the debate swirling around the issue of the *The Cantos'* fascist and anti-Semitic dimensions. After a fitful journey through many editions and printings, the poem was permanently removed from that important terminal position in 1981 and placed among the "CXVII et seq." fragments, its authorship and intended inclusion by Pound in *The Cantos* questionable for many readers.

It is not surprising that the volume has been interpreted in many often conflicting ways as a contrite end to a politically charged poem, a failed attempt at a paradisal close, or an appropriately fragmentary resolution to a complex poem that never sought coherence. Despite these many problems of textual instability and the interpretive difficulties stemming from them, some characteristics of this last stage of *The Cantos* can still be articulated. Pound attempts to render a paradise of natural, private, and poetic harmony there, and some of the passages are among the most limpid and lyrical of *The Cantos*. Reducing, for the most part, the complex intertextuality that pervades so much of *The Cantos*, *Drafts and Fragments* often revisits scenes of particular personal and poetic significance in its author's life and is also frequently troubled by present personal disharmony and self-doubt. Perhaps most profoundly, the poems are deepened and dignified by Pound's sense of their failure to "cohere" (Canto 116) or be understood, a failure he felt went beyond the fluid boundaries of Cantos 110–117 to encompass much of the poem and its author.

Bibliography

Hall, Donald. "Ezra Pound." *Writers at Work: The Paris Review Interviews*. 2nd Series. Ed. Malcolm Cowley. New York: Viking, 1963. 35–59.

Pound, Ezra. *Cantos 110–116*. New York: Fuck You/Press, 1967.

Stoicheff, Peter. *The Hall of Mirrors: Drafts & Fragments and the End of Ezra Pound's Cantos*. Ann Arbor: U of Michigan P, 1995.

Peter Stoicheff

The Cantos: Posthumous Cantos

In 2002 the Italian publisher Mondadori brought out a volume titled Ezra Pound, *Canti postumi*. This is a bilingual selection from the drafts for *The Cantos*, covering the whole period in which Pound's major work was in progress. The selection, as the editor explained in the introduction, was based on considerations of poetic interest, the aim being to offer a manageable volume of Pound's uncollected drafts that would be rewarding to read in its own right, besides throwing light on *The Cantos* as published.

Canti postumi opens with the "Three Cantos" of 1917 in which Pound discussed his project

and offered a series of fine vignettes and evocations, most of which found their way into the
final version. However, the description of
Sirmione in "Three Cantos I" remains one of his
finest and should be read in its early and fuller
version. Part II, "Paris: 1920–1922," includes
three variant beginnings for what was to become
Canto 2. Of special interest is a passage in
which Pound compares himself to the cliff
dwellers at Les Eyzies in Périgord: "nameless
drawer of panther / so I in narrow cave." In another canceled passage from the Malatesta cantos, first discussed by Peter D'Epiro, Pound
remembers his meeting in Verona in 1922 with
T. S. Eliot and meditates on the "empires" that
"slide to nothing here / in the marsh drift."
These and other excerpts are arranged by the editor in chronological sequence, identified by the
first line and commented on extensively in the
endnotes. Thus the Eliot/Pound exchange in
Ravenna is titled (in the index) "By the arena,
you, Thomas amics, Galla Placidia, and the
Roman."

Part III, "Rapallo and Venice: 1928–1937,"
includes eleven selections from drafts related to
The Fifth Decad. Two drafts of Canto 47 speak
of the Ligurian landscapes that Pound used to
evoke a natural peasant community and its religion and reflect on the wonders and perils of
womanhood (Circe): "by her dost thou mount
the stars." Two fascinating canceled openings
for Canto 49 speak of the Chinese tradition of
painting set scenes and of Pound's visit to Por-
tovenere in the steps of Byron and Henry James
("From this grotto, winch"). Other passages related to Canto 51 take us to Venice and the
theme of usury epitomized by John Law ("is
burried the great financier"), who was to recur
ambiguously in Canto 100. This passage helps
us to understand the later mention, besides offering an entertaining vignette of Antonio Vivaldi, with whom Pound identifies to some
extent ("an impresario composer with ballerine,
or with a ballerina, / with troubles about re-
hearsals"). Vivaldi is briefly mentioned in Canto
92, though we know that Pound was much taken
with him, so this discarded draft fills out the
record. Indeed, some of these passages are by

no means inferior to the writing in the published
cantos: They were set aside or forgotten for
many reasons in Pound's complex journeying
through many lands and many drafts.

Part IV, "Voices of War: 1940–1945," includes seventeen passages written as Pound was
planning a final volume of cantos on "belief"
but was distracted by the war and began making
notes of dramatic events and things seen and
heard. Among these is the report of an Italian
war veteran, of pacifist import: "So that he put
up a saw mill, and they took him / to fight over
in Africa." A long draft, "So that in august, of
the year ex-XXI," compares Mussolini's fall and
rescue by the Germans to Napoleon's return
from Elba in 1815, lifting quotations from the
Gazzetta di Genova of that year. The theme is
the repeat in history. Other drafts are simply
evocations of the stillness among the Rapallo
hillside "as against the sound of the olive mill."
A short note celebrates with little foreknowl-
edge Italy's declaration of war against France
and England, which was to spell the beginning
of the end of Pound's political dream: "Never
was the olive blossom so thick."

Part V, "Italian Drafts: 1944–1945," reprints
most of the verse Pound wrote in Italian together with, or after, Cantos 72–73. These drafts
were left in a very unfinished state, so the editor
had to choose between variants and various versions of the same scenes to create a readable
text. For example, the passage beginning "Il
Sole grande ammiraglio conduce la sua flotta"
was rewritten many times and was eventually to
appear in English at the beginning of *The Pisan
Cantos*: "The great periplum brings in the stars
to our shore." Another recurring episode is the
encounter among the olive groves with a bare-
footed girl ("la scalza" of Canto 76), who is
revealed to be a goddess, both the Japanese
Kwannon and the Virgin Mary. In the most
beautiful of these drafts, "Mai con codardi (co-
dini) sarà l'arte monda," she says that she had to
escape her ruined churches (like the Rapallo
basilica near the Pounds' apartment, which was
damaged by bombs in July 1944): "thus I am
lunar / protectress of cocoons; humble / lasting
/ The little boy loves me, whom I feed / I am

the Moon." Pound was to pick up this plaintive and broken vision in Canto 80 ("At Ephesus she had compassion on silversmiths"), but this evocation in Italian is one of his more lyrical flights. Other passages evoke an earthly paradise in which Pound places Dirce and friends like "Vail de Lencour" and even Eliot's Jean Verdenal ("e i fiocchi giacciono e fondono").

Part VI, "Pisa: 1945," includes the only two major excisions from *The Pisan Cantos* typescript: the plangent opening of Canto 84—"Yet from my tomb such flame of love arise"—and the long passage that originally ended Canto 84—"Night rain and a Biddle sky," which presents Pound at his polemic and poetic best but was cut perhaps to make Canto 84 shorter and pithier. The first and more elaborate draft of the vision of Canto 81 ("there came new subtlety of eyes") is also included.

Part VII, "Prosaic Verses: 1949–1960," gives twelve somewhat disjointed passages from Pound's postwar notebooks, related to the themes of *Rock-Drill* and *Thrones*, which show Pound chiefly worried by economics, with some brief glimpses of paradise. One selection, "And might be lost if I do not record them," concluded a draft of Canto 112 after the final line as printed in *The Cantos* and has a series of quotations from the Italian Renaissance moralist Francesco Guicciardini. The final section of *Canti postumi*, "Lines for Olga: 1962–1972," prints four addresses to Pound's companion, which evoke some precious moments of their life together ("For the contrejour of her with her violin"), bringing together, as always in Pound's best moments, the epic and the lyric.

Bibliography

Bacigalupo, Massimo. "America in Ezra Pound's Posthumous Cantos." *Journal of Modern Literature* 27.1–2 (2003–2004): 90–98.

———. "Ezra Pound's Cantos 72 and 73: An Annotated Translation." *Paideuma* 20.1–2 (1991): 9–41.

D'Epiro, Peter. *A Touch of Rhetoric: Ezra Pound's Malatesta Cantos.* Ann Arbor: UMI, 1983.

Pound, Ezra. *Canti postumi.* Ed. Massimo Bacigalupo. Milan: Mondadori, 2002.

Massimo Bacigalupo

Canzoni

Canzoni, Pound's fifth book of poems, was published in London in 1911 with a print run of 1,000; it was dedicated to Olivia and Dorothy Shakespear. Thirteen of these poems had been published the year before, in *Provença*, the American edition that included selections from the two previous collections, *Personae* and *Exultations*. A second, smaller run was issued in 1913 by Pound's British publisher, Elkin Mathews, as part of a joint edition with *Ripostes*. As suggested by this print history, *Canzoni* is a transitional work that, while technically part of Pound's pre-Imagist writings in that it relies on "studies in form," begins to move toward the modern, characteristic voice of *The Cantos*, one that Pound would claim more fully in *Ripostes*. As Longenbach has shown, its arrangement moves chronologically from the Middle Ages toward the modern period.

Canzoni is often understood as a collection about translation. It notably follows his 1911–1912 series of articles "I Gather the Limbs of Osiris" (see *SP* 19–43), which contain his initial, literal translations of troubadour poets Guido Cavalcanti and Arnaut Daniel. After *Canzoni*, Pound was to diminish his reliance on imitation and traditional form, but these "studies" allowed Pound to experiment with free translations of, among others, the canzone, sonnet, and ballad forms. Several of these poems—for example, "Sonnet: Chi e questa?" a rendering of Cavalcanti's "Sonnet VII"—revisit previously translated pieces through the lens of emotion rather than content, giving Pound an opportunity to escape the crafted, impersonal voices of *Exultations* and *Personae* and discover a more personal expression of his poetics and translation methods.

The length of the canzone itself allows sustained emotional development, encouraging the reflection of the individual poet while providing security of structure. Pound bases his renditions on Daniel's canzoni, offering variations on a form that commonly consists of six seven-line stanzas and finishes with a three-line envoi. Pound's increased attention to feeling and musical rhythm rather than linguistic accuracy suggests his emerging sense of a modern lyric sequence determined by the primary emotion in a poem or passage. Although Pound cut fifteen pages of poems from *Canzoni* before publication, many of which—like "Redondillas"—illuminated the modernizing direction of the work, the collection still succeeds in offering a sense of cohesion that prefigures the long sequence. Love and the Lady, often evoked through images of light, become important tropes for this emotional cohesion, love serving as a means of channeling the divine and the past into the modern world.

The final two poems, "Translations from Heine" and "Und Drang," are pivotal pieces. The first poem continues Pound's experiments with translation while avoiding some of the more stringent constraints of the "studies in form." Although this poem appears to imitate the seven-part division of the canzone, Pound frees himself from the form by permitting each section to contain a varying number of stanzas. He continues to work with the emotional impetus of his poetic model and succeeds not only in reflecting Heine's craft and persona but also in introducing a taste of the present through more conversational, contemporary diction that includes wordplay and humor. The short "Translator to Translated" gives the narrator/poet an opportunity to address Heine directly, allowing him to enter the poem as a persona in his own right.

"Und Drang" takes a further leap away from imitation and moves toward long, polyvocal poems such as *Hugh Selwyn Mauberley*. It innovatively addresses the difficulties of contemporary culture, a subject that would form the basis for *The Cantos*. Pound uses sequencing in order to express the dichotomy between the modern world and the idealized values of medieval society. The twelve parts, equally divided between present and past, explore the poet's concerns through a series of different voices that build on and interrogate each other. The central current, however, like that of the "studies in form," can be understood to be private and emotional, contrasting the values of old and new through the eyes of love and the lover and contributing to the creation of the voice of a modern poet who is aware of his present constraints and historical influences.

Bibliography

Fogelman, Bruce. *Shapes of Power: The Development of Ezra Pound's Poetic Sequences*. Ann Arbor: UMI, 1988.

Grieve, Thomas F. *Ezra Pound's Early Poetry and Poetics*. Columbia: U of Missouri P, 1997.

Longenbach, James. "Ezra Pound's *Canzoni*: Toward a Poem Including History." *Paideuma* 13.3 (1984): 389–405.

Witemeyer, Hugh. *The Poetry of Ezra Pound: Forms and Renewal, 1908–1920*. Berkeley: U of California P, 1969.

Madeline Bassnett

Carta da Visita

Written in Italian, *Carta da Visita* was published in Rome in 1942 by Giambattista Vicari. A new edition was published in Milan in 1974 by Vanni Scheiwiller, and an English version, in a translation by John Drummond and titled *A Visiting Card*, was published in London in 1952. This translation was reprinted, with some revisions, in *Impact* (1960), pages 44–74, and without the revisions in *Selected Prose 1909–1965* (1973), pages 306–335.

Carta da Visita consists of some thirty headwords, apparently disjointed but with a certain internal coherence, dealing with economics, politics, history, and culture. The concept of the nation, its control of the economy, its monetary system and policies (the right to coin and to lend money, the introduction of stamp script), and its falling under hostile forces such as international monopolism and usurocracy govern Pound's choice for headwords. Characteristically Pound traces the history of his favorite conflict through positive and negative models: Monte dei Paschi di Siena and the monetary experiment of Wörgl versus Bank of England. He also points to the affinities between the American and the Fascist Revolutions. As regards culture, he advances his "canon" (Homer, Sappho, the Latin elegists, Troubadours, Cavalcanti, Dante, etc.) in a dense but imprecise language for whose renewal and reinvigoration he is hoping.

Stefano Maria Casella

Cathay

As a headnote indicates, *Cathay*—first published in London in April 1915—is "[f]or the most part from the Chinese of Rihaku [Li Po], from the notes of the late Ernest Fenollosa, and the decipherings of professors Mori and Ariga"(*P* 130). Pound met Mary McNeil Fenollosa, the widow of the American Orientalist Ernest Fenollosa (1853–1908), in the fall of 1913. The two decided that Pound was to acquire Fenollosa's notes and manuscripts and edit a book on Japanese Noh drama and an anthology of Chinese poets. From the Fenollosa papers that arrived in late 1913 and 1914 Pound brought out, besides *Cathay*, *Certain Noble Plays of Japan* (1916), *"Noh," or Accomplishment* (1917), and *The Chinese Written Character as a Medium for Poetry* (1920).

Pound had no knowledge of the Chinese language in 1914–1915 when he first worked on Fenollosa's notes that record a series of Chinese poetry sessions with Mori and other tutors in Japan. Yet, reflecting on *Cathay* in 1935, he insisted that "Fenollosa's work was given to me in manuscript when I was ready for it" (*MIN* 8). Pound's claim is justified in view of several facts. Shortly before *Cathay*, in 1909–1912 Pound had been initiated into the aesthetic standards of China via the British Museum collection of Chinese and Japanese art and its dedicated keeper Laurence Binyon (1869–1943). The Chinese art objects that had impressed his eye could serve as a guide clarifying settings, situations, and states of mind essential to a comprehension of classical Chinese poetry. After he was introduced to Mary Fenollosa and before he received the Fenollosa papers, Pound had studied Giles's *A History of Chinese Literature* (1901) and adapted four of Giles's Chinese poems—"After "Ch'u Yuan,'" "Liu Ch'e," "Fan-piece, for Her Imperial Lord," and "Ts'ai Chi'h." He had by 1914 managed to find a language suitable for Chinese poetry. In a letter of 4 January 1917 to Kate Buss, he pointed out that "all the verbal constructions of *Cathay* [were] already tried in 'Provincia Deserta' " (*L* 101).

Pound's *Cathay* enterprise coincided with his move toward Vorticism. His initial choices from nearly 150 poems were accordingly made under the impact of his Vorticist notion of the Image. In Li Po and other Chinese poets he found a model that at once mirrored and challenged his developing poetics. In his 1918 essay on "Chinese Poetry," he makes it clear that he translates Chinese poetry precisely "because Chinese poetry has certain qualities of vivid presentation; and because certain Chinese poets have been content to set forth their matter without moralizing and without comment" (*EPPP* 3.84). Put together in the beginning of World War I, *Cathay* also registers Pound's antiwar sentiment. Originally, the sequence consisted of twelve poems of which only one, "Song of the Bowmen of Shu," was about war. Shortly before the manuscript was sent to press, probably because the war was getting worse, Pound added "Lament of the Frontier Guard" and "South-Folk in Cold Country" to the sequence to augment its antiwar theme. In 1916, when incorporating *Cathay* into *Lustra*, Pound had an opportunity to append four more poems—"Sennin Poem," "Ballad of the Mulberry Road," "Old Idea of Choan," and "The Unmoving Cloud."

It is true that the poems of *Cathay*, considered as translations, include numerous deviations. One example of this is the conflation of two separate poems by Li Po into "The River Song." Pound could have mistaken a new poem in one of Fenollosa's "Rihaku" notebooks as more of "The River Song," but he might also have done this on purpose to create a piece in the form of "superposition." Soon he was to rehearse the technique in his "*Ur*-Cantos." When one compares carefully the poems of *Cathay* with the corresponding Chinese texts and Fenollosa's notes (at the Beinecke Libary, Yale University), one becomes aware, however, that many of the misrepresentations are attributable to Mori's flawed cribs and Fenollosa's rough translations. In his reworkings, Pound has, in fact, corrected a considerable number of mistakes. Wai-lim Yip has used "Lament of the Frontier Guard" as illustration to show that "Pound has occasionally (by what he calls 'divine accident') penetrated below a faulty crib to the original and come out right" (84). In preparing "Exile's Letter," "The

River-Merchant's Wife: A Letter," and other *Cathay* poems, Pound has similarly gone beneath Fenollosa's fragmented notes and recaptured for us much of the original poetic charm and energy. Pound is able to do so partly because he and the Chinese poets share a poetics of reticence and partly because in rendering the pieces he rightly focuses on reproducing the whole image instead of local details.

T. S. Eliot is substantially correct in calling Pound "the inventor of Chinese poetry for our time" ("Introduction," *Selected Poems* xvi). It was *Cathay* that first introduced the twentieth-century English reading public to Chinese poetry. In it Pound created a proper vehicle for getting Chinese poets across to his contemporaries, disregarding their "rhymes" and "tones" while following their verbal constructions and methods of presentation. Succeeding translators of Chinese poetry from Arthur Waley to Gary Snyder all owe a debt to Pound for providing a sound model. Nonetheless, *Cathay* should not be seen merely as a translation. After all, it played a positive role in the evolution of Pound's Modernist poetics, and it was in *Cathay* that he completed his adaptation of a poetic idiom for *The Cantos*. Indeed, the vers libre in *Cathay* (with its beauty, simplicity, and supreme power) resurfaces not only in sections of the Chinese cantos—Cantos 13, 49, 53–61, 98–99, and so on—but in countless other parts throughout the modern epic.

Bibliography

Kenner, Hugh. *The Pound Era.* Berkeley: U of California P, 1971. 192–222.

Qian, Zhaoming. *Orientalism and Modernism: The Legacy of China in Pound and Williams.* Durham: Duke UP, 1995.

Xie, Ming. *Ezra Pound and the Appropriation of Chinese Poetry: Cathay. Translation, and Imagism.* New York: Garland, 1999.

Yip, Wai-lim. *Ezra Pound's Cathay.* Princeton: Princeton UP, 1969.

Zhaoming Qian

Catholic Anthology

Catholic Anthology 1914–1915 (London: Elkin Mathews, 1915; 500 copies printed; cop-

ies remained unsold in 1936). One of five such poetry anthologies Pound edited—the others were *Des Imagistes* (1914), *Profile* (1932), and *Active Anthology* (1933), and *From Confucius to Cummings: An Anthology of Poetry* (1964; with Marcella Spann)—it was intended chiefly to promote T. S. Eliot's new work and, according to S. Foster Damon, perhaps to compete with Amy Lowell's *Some Imagist Poets* (1915). Aside from four early poems by Eliot, including "The Love Song of J. Alfred Prufrock," the collection featured work by Williams, Sandburg, Yeats, Pound, and others. The title, meant to connote inclusivity, antagonized Catholic writers such as Francis Meynell. Although Conrad Aiken reviewed it favorably in *Poetry Journal* (April 1916), Arthur Waugh derided it in the *Quarterly Review* as the anarchistic performance of "literary 'Cubists'" (October 1916); Pound responded to Waugh's charges in the *Egoist* (June 1917).

Miranda B. Hickman

Cavalcanti

An opera in three acts (about one hour) by Ezra Pound, *Cavalcanti* was composed in 1931–1933 at the request of E.A.F Harding, Pound's *Le Testament* producer at the BBC. Asked to exploit the new radio technique, Pound chose for his subject the poet Guido Cavalcanti (c. 1250–1300). Texts from Cavalcanti's ballate and canzone are augmented by two love poems of the Italian troubadour Sordello (d. 1269?). Pound wrote additional dialogue and radio announcer's script. With Olga Rudge in attendance, Robert Hughes produced and conducted the *Cavalcanti* world concert premiere on 28 March 1983 in San Francisco with the Arch Ensemble for Experimental Music, featuring Thomas Buckner in the title role and John Argue as the radio announcer.

Set against the internecine strife of the Guelph party at the end of the thirteenth century, the opera's first two acts are based on the few recorded facts of Cavalcanti's life. Act I replays an anecdote recorded by Boccaccio as "The Ninth Tale of the Sixth Day" in *Il Decameron*. The agile, witty Guido Cavalcanti, leader of a fiery group of young nobles from some of the best families in Florence, finds himself cornered in a cemetery by his enemies, led by the equally powerful Corso Donati. Donati's man Betto sings "Sol per pietà," an early song of Cavalcanti's, capping it off with the bravura of a high C#. Cavalcanti replies, "Derivative!" throwing his enemies off balance with harsh judgments of his own youthful artistic follies. He insults Donati's men, suggesting they are at home surrounded by monuments to the dead, and leaps over a tomb to escape. Act II depicts a scene recalled by Franco Sacchetti in his "Novella LXVIII" from *Trecentonovella*. The mature Cavalcanti, at the height of his powers, is pinned down, this time by friends, who insist he recite his best, most serious work, "Donna mi prega," though they confess they do not understand it. The friends joke about "cantus firmus," promising to set him free at the envoi. At the end of the act a proclamation signed by Dante Alighieri orders Cavalcanti exiled from Florence for the sake of restoring peace to the city. For Act III Pound revised the historic fact of Cavalcanti's death in Florence to a deathbed scene in the castle prison at Sarzana. A personal anecdote from Canto 20 provides the scaffold for the interchange between the dying Guido and his page Ricco. Cavalcanti attempts to send a last message to his party in Florence. The message is concealed within the music of the poetry, but the page fails to learn the tune before Cavalcanti expires. Borrowing the voice of the seneschal, the prison guard, to make her presence known, the goddess Fortuna sings of her power over man's fate ("Io son la donna"). Because one has to see and hear the goddess's voice emanate from the burly seneschal to fully appreciate the scene, Pound apologized in his notes to the work that until the availability of television, still in its experimental stage in 1932, the significance of the scene would be lost to the BBC radio audience. Closing the opera, Fortuna animates a statue of herself, singing of the loan that is life, which all must repay when the loan is called in.

The opera is composed of solo and group numbers—trios in Acts I and II, duets in Act III.

The numbers are: "Overture" (drawn from Pound's *Ghuidonis Sonate* for solo violin, composed in the fall of 1931); Act I: "Poi che di doglia" (Cavalcanti); "Sol per pietà" (Betto); "Gianni quel Guido" (trio); "Guarda ben dico" (Cobbler); "Era in pensier" (Cavalcanti); Act II: "Se m'hai del tutto" (Cavalcanti); "In un boschetto" (trio); "Donna mi prega" (Cavalcanti); "Tos temps serai" (Vanna); Act III: "Ailas" (French soldier); "Quando di morte" (Cavalcanti); "Perch'io non spero" (Ricco, a boy soprano, and Cavalcanti); "Io son la donna" (Seneschal and Fortuna). "Sol," "Guarda," and "Io son" have since been attributed to poets other than Cavalcanti. "Ailas" and "Tos temps," two poems by Sordello, supply musical contrast and further the plot. Pound considered his setting of "Tos temps serai" true to the character of thirteenth-century music.

Much of the music conveys the beauty of the poetry through a bel canto presentation of the texts. The opening numbers of Act I employ an extended vocal range to provide the principals with a dramatic platform for virtuosic singing, a technique Pound had earlier rejected in *Testament*. Cavalcanti, a baritone, has a range from G, bottom line of the bass staff, to A in the middle of the treble staff; and Betto, a tenor, from D below middle C to a minor ninth above middle C. The three soprano voices in Acts II and III are distinctive: Vanna's clipped, rhythmic Provençal, Ricco's breathy adolescent voice, and Fortuna's ethereal delivery.

Cavalcanti was scored with radio in mind, availing itself of fewer instruments and staying within a frequency range less likely to be distorted or lost by radio transmitters and receivers. Defending the slight orchestration but insisting it would suffice for radio, Pound planned larger performing forces for eventual stage and television production. His instrumentation for radio is flute, English horn, bassoon, trombone, violin, violoncello, contrabass, and percussion (three timpani, drums, and cymbals).

Pound had recently resumed his studies on Cavalcanti begun two decades earlier; since 1928 he had been preparing a comprehensive edition of the poetry, issued ultimately in January 1932 as *Guido Cavalcanti Rime*. The book presents the first of several attempts to translate Cavalcanti's philosophic canzone "Donna mi prega," a poem at the center of Pound's canon of literary texts. Pound's second translation of the canzone comprises almost the entirety of Canto 36, published in 1934 in *Eleven New Cantos*. Between the two translations he set the poem to music, making it the keystone of an opera about a poet who "glows with reason's fire." Pound's first translation of the poet's envoi reads, "Safe may'st thou go my canzon whither thee pleaseth / Thou art so fair attired that every man and each / Shall praise thy speech / So he have sense or glow with reason's fire, / To stand with other hast thou no desire." Writing for a mass radio audience, Pound had reason to be more conciliatory toward the "other" than did Cavalcanti. The unorthodox plot of Cavalcanti depends on its secondary characters: Friends, enemies, and mendicant soldiers who do not fully understand the poetry inadvertently perpetuate Cavalcanti's legacy and a lyric tradition that might otherwise be lost. In Act III, a poem of Sordello's sung by a foot soldier outside the castle walls reminds Cavalcanti that poetry may live through its music even when the meaning is not understood. Cavalcanti's cryptic utterance, "That I must drag life out of death," is typical of Pound's brief "joins" between arias; it is a line memorable for its own sake, more akin to film intertitles than to traditional dialogue that propels the action or furthers the plot. While snippets of dialogue between and during arias contain puns on musical terms, and humor accents the narrator's script, literary themes dominate the opera, often eclipsing the dramatic impulse. Upon receipt of the libretto, Harding responded that he found less action than in *Testament* and approved the use of a narrator, a device he rejected in the case of the former opera in order to make the action seem more immediate.

Pound composed the music autonomously, sending his finished arias to Agnes Bedford in London for comment, though he did not always heed her advice. For example, she found his setting of "Donna mi prega" monotonous. The song conforms to his category of a "music of representative outline"; it relies on repetitious scalar ascents and descents to conflate the mesmerizing flame of "reason's fire" with the troubadours' "fuoco d'amore." The "fire" created by intense contemplation was described in Canto 20 as "the bright flames, V-shaped."

The fact that Pound composed for literary reasons explains the pronounced dissimilarities in the musical construction of his two operas. *Le Testament* was written to capture the vital speech rhythms of Villon's poetry; *Cavalcanti* was written to revive an appreciation of a lyric poet whose reputation remained in the shadow of Dante. More confident of both his composing skills and the viability of music composition as a form of literary criticism, Pound injected into this second opera numerous musical gestures to revisit critical debate regarding, for example, the use of secret communications among the "dolce stil novo" poets, the physical reality of the poet's "donna," and the philosophical sources of Cavalcanti's poetry. Though the rhythm, melody, harmony, instrumentation, and theatrical shape of *Le Testament* were recast for *Cavalcanti*, Pound's unity of vision was unequivocal: "As with his Villon the poet here continues to follow his intention: that is, to take the world's greatest poetry out of books, to put it on the air, to bring it to the ear of the people, even when they cannot understand it or cannot understand it all at once. The meaning can be explained but the emotion and the beauty cannot be explained" (preface to the *Cavalcanti* score). Additionally, radio became for Pound a second medium onto which he could map the intersection of voices, ideas, and historical periods, as in *The Cantos*.

Indefinitely postponed by the BBC, the opera was never performed in Pound's lifetime. "Tos temps serai" and "Ailas" were sung at Hampstead on 28 June 1933 by Raymonde Collignon (who sang "Mère au Saveur" for the 1931 BBC *Testament*) and at Pound's Rapallo concert series on 8 May 1934 by Lonny Meyer.

Holographs of Pound's music are archived in the Ezra Pound and Olga Rudge Collections at the Beinecke Library at Yale University. No conductor's score has been located. A performance edition was published in 2003.

Bibliography

Anderson, David. *Pound's Cavalcanti*. Princeton: Princeton UP, 1983.

Fisher, Margaret. *Ezra Pound's Radio Operas: The BBC Experiments 1931–1933*. Cambridge: MIT P, 2002.

Hughes, Robert, and Margaret Fisher, eds. *Cavalcanti: A Perspective on the Music of Ezra Pound*. Emeryville: Second Evening Art, 2003. Essay and full score.

Pound, Ezra. *Ego Scriptor Cantilenae: The Music of Ezra Pound*. San Francisco: Other Minds (#1005–2), 2003. Audio CD and Booklet (essay, opera texts, and translations).

Margaret Fisher and Robert Hughes

Chinese History

Pound's knowledge of Chinese history is fragmented, due to the inadequacy of his Chinese and access to sources on Chinese history; as a result, Pound has been castigated by scholars as a bad historian, which of course seems like blaming a peach for not tasting like an apricot. Pound's interest in Chinese history is evident in some short poems as well as translation of Chinese political and philosophical writings, though *The Cantos* is the place where such historical curiosity finds extensive expression. In "Date Line" Pound proclaims, "An epic is a poem including history" (*LE* 86). True to his words, Pound's appropriation of Chinese historical material—which is inseparable from his engagements with Chinese literature—finds fragmented representation in many cantos, notably the so-called Chinese History Cantos, 52–61. According to Achilles Fang, the "China Cantos" owe their genesis to Couvreur's *Li Ki* (Book of Rites) and to the late-eighteenth-century French work *Histoire générale de la Chine, ou Annales de cet empire* (237).

But as Christine Brooke-Rose argues, "*The Cantos* are not history as we are taught at school" (174): "For *The Cantos* are . . . achronological as regards history" (178). Brooke-Rose points out that from history Pound took "what he needed and no more; . . . he tells us what he thinks is the best . . . [and] what is wrong with modern civilization. . . . He is picking out the best from the flux, the whirling spiral, he is picking out the activating forces which he considers as true and permanent and workable at any time, in any conditions, in any society and in any one man" (179). In Canto 89, Pound himself explains why history is important: "To know the histories / . . . to know good from evil / And know whom to trust." Indeed, Pound's interest in Chinese history is itself historical: Very little evidence exists of his interest in modern China. His knowledge of Chinese history is manifest in some salient historical facts as well as individual figures of China: Confucius, Mencius, Chuang Tzu, Chu Hsi (thinkers, philosophers, and educators); Ch'u Yuan, Tao Yuanming (Tao Ch'ien), Mei Sheng, Wang Wei, Li Po (poets); Yao and Shun (legendary emperors), the First Emperor of Chin, Liu Ch'e (Emperor Wu of Han), and Emperor Kung Hsi of Tsing, to name only the most familiar. Some of his historical knowledge Pound gleaned from literary works—Li Po's poetry, for example.

Pound's views of Confucius, indisputably the most influential figure in Chinese history, are derived from comparisons with Western philosophers such as Aristotle and Plato. In his "Procedure" for *The Confucian Analects* Pound writes, "The study of the Confucian philosophy is of greater profit than that of the Greek because no time is wasted in idle discussion of errors"; and "One must take them [the *Analects*] in the perspective of Voltaire: 'I admire Confucius. He was the first man who did *not* receive a divine inspiration.' . . . Confucius was a Chinaman, not born of a dragon, not in any way supernatural, but remarkably possessed of good sense" (191). Liu Ch'e, Emperor Wu of the Han Dynasty, appears in the title of a poem of that name, as well as in the *Cathay* poem "Old Idea of Choan by Rosoriu" (Japanese transliteration for Lu Chao-lin). Emperor Kung Hsi appears in Canto 49, the "Seven Lakes Canto." The presentation of Chinese history in this canto is short but closely resembles the "huaigu" tradition (nostalgic of the old and the ancient) in Chinese literature. As this author pointed out in a 1993 essay in *Paideuma*, Pound uses this part of Chinese history to celebrate prosperity: The Chinese Empire scaled another height of prosperity when Emperor Kung Hsi reigned around 1700 (Huang 108).

As quoted earlier, Pound's "To know the histories" is a means "to know good from evil"; in the case of Canto 49, that is to know good from bad. While the achievement of prosperity is reason for celebration, economic and political decline is cause for concern. Beginning with stanza five, Pound presents the "bad" things in Chinese history; words such as *debt*, *Geryon*, *pleasure*, and *canal* (the building of the Chinese Grand Canal, like that of the Great Wall, is a historical project whose cost included the loss of many lives as well as enormous sums of money) suggest a prosperity on the decline. "China enjoyed one of its golden days under the rule of the Tsing but also suffered the most disgrace under the late Tsing. Pound's 'get into debt' and 'This is infamy' adeptly summarize this period of Chinese history" (Huang 111). Does the poet use history to illustrate the antithesis of good and bad through such presentation? The answer could not be clearer.

Bibliography

Brooke-Rose, Christine. *A ZBC of Ezra Pound.* Berkeley: U of California P, 1971.
Fang, Achilles. "Fenollosa and Pound." *Harvard Journal of Asiatic Studies* 20 (1957): 213–238.
Huang, Guiyou. "Ezra Pound: (Mis)Translation and (Re-)Creation." *Paideuma* 22.1–2 (1993): 99–114.

Guiyou Huang

Chinese Literature

"Chinese literature" in Poundian scholarship is a fascinating, vast topic, as well as an intriguing and difficult one. Pound, who had degrees in Romance languages from the University of Pennsylvania and Hamilton College, was much more fluent in some European tongues than Chinese and Japanese, two Asian languages that he struggled to master but never truly did.

Pound derived his knowledge of Chinese literature from three major sources: (1) the famous essay on Chinese poetry prepared by Ernest Fenollosa, *The Chinese Written Character as a Medium for Poetry* that Pound edited and published in 1920 and again in 1936; (2) some notes on Chinese poems that Fenollosa took from his Japanese instructors that Pound later made into *Cathay*; and (3) an early-twentieth-century Sinological work by Herbert A. Giles, *A History of Chinese Literature* (1901). The importance of these sources to Pound's approach to Chinese language and literature cannot be overemphasized, for it is largely from these works that Pound learned to "explicate" Chinese characters and to appreciate classical Chinese poetry, especially that of the Tang Dynasty represented by Li Po (701–762 C.E.) and from which he ultimately recreated a poetics from a literature that was handed down from antiquity. While Pound studied and translated Chinese works from over 2,000 years ago, notably Confucius's *Analects*, *The Classic Anthology Defined by Confucius* (*The Book of Songs*, or *Shijing* in Chinese), and *Ta Hio* (also known as *The Great Learning*, one of the Four Books), it is from poets of the Tang Dynasty, especially Li Po and Wang Wei, that Pound formulated his articulation of a new poetics.

Pound acquired the Fenollosa manuscripts in 1913; edited and published *Cathay* in 1915; published his two-part essay "Chinese Poetry" in *Today* in 1918; and published Fenollosa's *The Chinese Written Character as a Medium for Poetry* in 1920. At the outset of his essay "Chinese Poetry," Pound explains why he translates Chinese poetry: because it possesses "certain qualities of vivid presentation" and also because he believes that certain Chinese poets write "without moralizing and without comment" (54). Pound discusses what he believes to be commendable qualities in Chinese poetry, qualities that he finds in one particular poet, Li Po. Li Po is not only the pivotal example Pound uses to illustrate qualities of Chinese poetry; this eighth-century Chinese poet also makes up two-thirds (eleven of fifteen) of the poems in *Cathay*. In this Chinese Romantic poet, Pound finds examples of the three qualities of Chinese poetry: First, "the Chinese *like* poetry that they have to think about, and even poetry that they have to puzzle over" (55); second, Chinese poetry is "full of fairies and fairy lore" (93); and third, there is a sort of "completeness in Chinese" (95). From this presentation one can clearly see that Pound admires qualities of simplicity and directness that are in strict keeping with his Imagist principles as set forth in his "A Few Don'ts by an Imagiste." Undoubtedly Pound's handling of Chinese poetry contributes directly to his formation as an Imagist and Modernist poetics.

According to Achilles Fang, Pound turned to Giles's *History of Chinese Literature* because he had exhausted Fenollosa's notes (236). Giles devoted a large portion of his book to translation, to enable the Chinese author, "so far as translation will allow, to speak for himself" (v). From reading Giles's history (and James Legge's "The Four Books" and Guillaume Pauthier's *Confucius et Mencius: Les Quatre Livres*, to a lesser extent), Pound garnered a usable knowledge of Chinese literature.

Fenollosa's *The Chinese Written Character*, which was called "a small mass of confusion" by George Kennedy (25), nonetheless taught Pound about Chinese literature as well. From it he learned one important skill—the ability to explicate Chinese characters, correctly or erroneously—and one quality of Chinese poetic language—the directness of expression, a quality that Pound practiced in his own writing throughout his poetic career. It is thus safe to say that Chinese literature, poetry in particular, helped define Pound's "less-traveled road," by way of China, to success as a poet.

Bibliography

Fang, Achilles. "Fenollosa and Pound." *Harvard Journal of Asiatic Studies* 20 (1957): 213–238.

Giles, Herbert A. *A History of Chinese Literature.* New York: Frederick Ungar, 1901.

Huang, Guiyou. "The *Shanshui* Tradition in Pound: From China to America." *Whitmanism, Imagism, and Modernism in China and America.* Selinsgrove: Susquehanna UP, 1997. 110–128.

Kennedy, George. "Fenollosa, Pound and the Chinese Character." *Yale Literary Magazine* 126 (1958): 24–36.

Pound, Ezra. "Chinese Poetry." Part I, *To-Day* 3.14 (1918): 45–57; Part II, *To-Day* 3.15 (1918): 93–95.

Guiyou Huang

Chinese Translation

A great many things—positive and negative—can be said of Pound's Chinese translation, and indeed, much has been written on this inexhaustible topic. To say the least, Pound's achievement in Chinese translation is a mixed blessing. Whether it is awkward, inaccurate, unfaithful, distorted, half-understood, or misunderstood, almost all critics and scholars agree that Pound is above all *inventive*, a view represented by Hugh Kenner in his "The Invention of China," which in turn echoes T. S. Eliot's famous statement that Pound "invented" China. This entry considers some of Pound's major Chinese translations, mainly *Cathay*, and offers a contextualized assessment of them, so that the less specialized reader may gain a sense of the scope, depth, and nature of Pound's unconventional practice as a poet-translator.

Despite Pound's inadequacy in Sinological matters, he demonstrates audacity and originality in all of his translation enterprises in Chinese. Starting around 1913, ever since he acquired the Fenollosa manuscripts given to him by the late professor's wife, Pound's engagement with Chinese never ceased. As Achilles Fang points out in his introduction to Pound's translation of *The Classic Anthology Defined by Confucius*, "The poet Pound's career as a translator of Chinese poetry was launched with the publication of *Cathay* (1915), with which volume he became, says T. S. Eliot, 'the inventor of Chinese poetry for our time' " (xiii). Then came *Ta Hio: The Great Learning* in 1928, the first of the Chinese Four Books, which Pound proclaims in "Date Line" to believe in: "As to what I believe: I believe the *Ta Hio*" (86). *The Unwobbling Pivot* and *The Great Digest* followed in 1947. In 1950 his rendition of Confucius's *Analects* was printed in *Hudson Review*. *The Classic Anthology Defined by Confucius* (*Shijing*; also known as the *Book of Songs*) appeared in 1954. Of all these translations done over a span of some forty years, that which has received the most critical and scholarly attention is *Cathay*, though an understanding of Pound's career as a poet and Chinese translator, and of his contribution to the formation of high Modernism, would not be complete without a knowledge of his important role in the publication of Fenollosa's *The Chinese Written Character as a Medium for Poetry*. Indeed, many consider this controversial essay as a collaborative product rather than a single-author work. From Fenollosa's treatise on Chinese language and poetics, Pound learned to explicate Chinese characters based on Fenollosa's notes taken from two Japanese professors of Chinese; undoubtedly, during his engagement with Fenollosa's manuscripts, Pound also learned much of the basics of Chinese syntax and poetic composition.

The 1915 version of *Cathay* is "[f]or the most part from the Chinese of Rihaku [Li Po], from the notes of the late Ernest Fenollosa, and the deciphering of the professors Mori and Ariga" (title page). This little volume consists of fifteen poems, of which fourteen are Chinese in origin and one Anglo-Saxon, "The Seafarer," intentionally translated and placed there for comparative purposes: Pound believes that classic, ancient Chinese poetry shares many qualities with Anglo-Saxon poetic writing. And of the fourteen Chinese pieces, eleven are by Li Po, whom Pound, like most contemporary Chinese readers, considers China's greatest poet (Arthur Waley, Pound's friend and competitor in Chinese translation, ranks Li Po much lower on the poetic ladder of Chinese literature, though he authored a book on him, *The Poetry and Career of Li Po*). There is no question here that Li Po (a Romantic poet in the Wordsworthian sense), arguably the greatest Chinese poet (often paralleled with Tu Fu, Li Po's friend and usually considered a Realist poet), occupies the center of Pound's translation efforts in *Cathay*; in addition, in his essay "Chinese Poetry" (in two parts) Pound uses Li Po as a prime example to illustrate the good qualities of Chinese poetry, using them to justify his partiality to Li Po.

Other poets Pound translated for *Cathay* include Ch'u Yuan, Mei Sheng, and Wang Wei. Later versions of *Cathay* also include Tao Yuanming (Tao Ch'ien), Kuo P'u, and Lu Chao-lin. Michael Alexander divides Pound's translations into two kinds: Copies, "which stick close to their original," and Remakes, "which edit and reshape their original, and cast into the English style Pound forges for it" (1108); by this definition, *Cathay* represents the best of Pound's Remakes. This author has also argued elsewhere ("Ezra Pound") that Pound's creativeness in translation leads to successful re-creations that can be easily called original composition. Hsieh Wen Tung, on the other hand, discusses "the dangers of over-literalness and misdirected attention to characters" as well as "the dangers of unwarranted freedom" (409); as anyone who is familiar with Chinese and Pound's *Cathay* will attest to, both dangers are clear and present in Pound's Chinese translations. George Kennedy, while harshly critical of Fenollosa's handling of the Chinese language, especially in poetry, and indirectly, Pound's translation based on Fenollosa's notes, joins some others in calling the translations "translucences" (24). Discussing Pound's miscellaneous Chinese translations and comparing them with other Sinologists' work, especially James Legge's, Kennedy remarks that

> Pound has in large measure taken over philologist Legge and dressed up the English that was sadly unpoetic. In *The Classic Anthology* (1954) Pound's English has loosened itself completely from any Chinese mooring. And in the *Rock-Drill* Cantos (1956), particularly Canto 85, the Chinese has become a decoration with no intelligible meaning. (36)

Taking as example Pound's rendering of the famous first sentence from *The Analects*, "xue er shi xi zhi, bu yi yue hu"—"Study and then constantly review [or practice] what is studied, is that not a pleasure?" (my translation), for which Pound has, "Study with the seasons winging past, is this not a joy?"—Kennedy concludes, "Undoubtedly this is fine poetry. Undoubtedly it is bad translation. Pound has the practice, but not the learning. He is to be saluted as a poet, but not as a translator" (36).

One can reasonably disagree with such a facile conclusion: Pound did translate Chinese texts, and many of his translations are very readable; more important, Pound, among all translators and poet-translators into English, demonstrates a remarkable ability in his translation to bring to life both the original and his own reworking of it, which is the greatest accomplishment that any translator can achieve. If out of errors, "creative" mistakes, and mistranslations wonderful re-creation and invention issue forth, then from at least an aesthetic perspective this might be a blessing. If one wishes translation of poetry to read, sound, feel, and look like poetry, then Pound has offered the best specimens of such translation. As Hsieh Wen Tung observes, "For what he lacked in lingual access . . . Mr. Pound almost made up in an astonishing interpretative acumen, by which he often penetrated through the veil of an alien text to the significant features of the original: tone, poetic intention and verbal felicity" (423).

Hugh Kenner opens his short essay "Ezra Pound and Chinese" with a laconic statement: " 'Translate' is a blurry word" (38). In "The Invention of China" Kenner further asserts that *Cathay* not only influenced subsequent translators but also "inaugurated the long tradition of Pound the inspired but unreliable translator" (27). Ultimately, many critics would agree that regardless of errors, mistakes, deviations, infidelity, misunderstanding, or distortion in Pound's Chinese translations, he undoubtedly invented a new poetics for English; ironically, without those questionable or problematic elements prevalent in Pound's translations, Modernist poetics would have taken a longer time to form, if they formed at all. And as a final word for thought, Pound's harshest critics of his Chinese translations seem to be those with limited knowledge of Chinese; interestingly and perhaps ironically, too, the more affirmative, if not defensive, critics of Pound appear to be Chinese critics with a solid bilingual knowledge (Chinese and English), such as Achilles Fang, Hsieh Wen Tung, and Wai-lim Yip, among others.

Bibliography

Alexander, Michael. "Ezra Pound." *Encyclopedia of Literary Translation into English*. Ed. Olive Classe. London: Fitzroy Dearborn Publishers, 2000. 2:1107–1110.

Fang, Achilles. Introduction. *The Classic Anthology Defined by Confucius*. Trans. Ezra Pound. Cambridge: Harvard UP, 1954. ix–xvi.

Huang, Guiyou. "Confucius." *Encyclopedia of Literary Translation into English*. Ed. Olive Classe. London: Fitzroy Dearborn Publishers, 2000. 2: 303–305.

———. "Ezra Pound: (Mis)Translation and (Re-) Creation." *Paideuma* 22.1–2 (1993): 99–114.

———. *Whitmanism, Imagism, and Modernism in China and America*. Selinsgrove: Susquehanna UP, 1997.

Kennedy, George. "Fenollosa, Pound and the Chinese Written Character." *Yale Literary Magazine* 126 (December 1952): 24–36.

Kenner, Hugh. "Ezra Pound and Chinese." *Agenda* 4 (October–November 1965): 38–41.

———. "The Invention of China." *Spectrum* 9.1 (Spring 1967): 21–52.

Tung, Hsieh Wen. "English Translations of Chinese Poetry." *Criterion* 17.68 (April 1938): 404–424.

Guiyou Huang

The Chinese Written Character as a Medium for Poetry (See Fenollosa, Ernest)

Collected Early Poems of Ezra Pound

This resource (New Directions, 1976; Faber, 1977) is indispensable for anyone seeking to trace Pound's development during the earliest portion of his career. The text and notes for the *Collected Early Poems* (*CEP*) were prepared primarily by Michael John King, under the direction of Louis L. Martz, who wrote the introduction, and Donald Gallup, bibliographer of Ezra Pound and former curator of American Literature at Yale University's Beinecke library, who edited one portion of the collection. The project was completed under the auspices of The Center for the Study of Ezra Pound and His Contemporaries at the Beinecke library.

Although the collection includes early work from 1902 to 1917, it focuses chiefly on work from between 1908 and 1912. It presents a wealth of hitherto uncollected poetry, much of it material from six of Pound's earliest books that he omitted when preparing the *Personae* of 1926. Altogether, the collection offers ninety-nine such poems Pound rejected from *Personae*, twenty-five poems that, before their publication here, appeared only in periodicals or miscellanies, and thirty-eight previously unpublished poems.

The collection concentrates, in other words, on poetry Pound later dismissed in 1965 as the "stale creampuffs" of his youth—work that many readers are not likely to find today because the widely available current New Directions *Personae* is based on Pound's 1926 selections. We might also think of this collection as representing the period that Pound inscribed and exorcised in his autobiographical *Hugh Selwyn Mauberley* sequence, when he was "out of key with his time," bent on "wringing the lilies from the acorn." Accordingly, much of the poetry features highly mannered, archaic language and inverted syntax; but as the volume proceeds, there is a clear trend toward simplification of diction and technique. When his daughter Mary de Rachewiltz was preparing the volume *A Lume Spento and Other Early Poems* (1965), Pound himself said of many of these early poems, "As to why reprint? No lessons to be learned except the depth of ignorance." De Rachewiltz, however, was able to persuade him otherwise. In her preface to that 1965 edition, reprinted in the appendixes to the *Collected Early Poems*, she noted, "When recently I suggested that while this early work may not help 'the young' technically, the feelings expressed in it might teach a lesson in this age of rage and cynicism, and that therefore it can be offered not merely as a 'literary curiosity' but as further evidence of what stuff a young poet's dreams should be made of, he seemed satisfied" (*CEP* 315–316).

As Martz notes in the introduction, this collection shows Pound in the process of striving to break free of the poetic idioms of predecessors like Swinburne, the Pre-Raphaelites, and the successors of the Pre-Raphaelites in the 1890s. Pound suggests this effort in the title of his "Revolt: Against the Crepuscular Spirit in Modern Poetry." However, most of the poetry in *Collected Early Poems* still reflects that Swinburnian language and thus remains markedly distinct from the poetry of "hard light" and "clear edges" Pound advocated as he worked with Imagism and Vorticism from 1913 to 1915. The early poetry here is also not as dominated by the influence of Browning as readers might assume it would be. As Martz remarks, Pound's final selection for *Personae* of 1926 tended to favor those early poems that displayed Browning's imprint, when this collection shows that in fact these Browningesque poems were nested among equally many that exhibited no accent of Browning at all.

The collection thus includes five major kinds of poems by Pound:

1. All poems that Pound published—in books, periodicals, or miscellanies—through 1912, the year that witnessed the significant event of the publication of *Ripostes*. The editors note that in *Ripostes* "Pound first demonstrates his firm departure from the Victorian idiom, and his achievement of a new mode, original, colloquial, imagist" (289). Poems from six early volumes have been reprinted: *A Lume Spento* (1908), *A Quinzaine for This Yule* (1908), *Personae* (1909), *Exultations* (1909), *Canzoni* (1911), and *Ripostes* (1912). The collection does not feature Pound's volume of 1910, *Provença*, but this is because, as the editors explain in the Notes, it in fact contains a subset of material from *Canzoni*. (This is somewhat confusing, since the Notes imply that the *CEP* contains poetry from "Pound's first six books" up to 1912, when in fact, by 1912, including *Provença*, Pound had published *seven* books of poetry.) Thus *CEP* includes ninety-nine poems from these collections that Pound omitted when selecting material for the 1926 *Personae*.

2. Twenty-three hitherto unpublished poems from *San Trovaso Notebook*—the resource from which Pound drew when preparing *A Quinzaine for This Yule*—thus completing publication of all fifty poems from that notebook. With assistance from de Rachewiltz, Gallup oversaw the editing of this San Trovaso section of the collection. The Notes supply the table of contents of the *San Trovaso Notebook*, a facsimile of a page from the notebook, prose commentary from the editors, and de Rachewiltz's introduction to *A Lume Spento and Other Early Poems*, which discusses the San Trovaso notebook.

3. Eleven poems hitherto available only in manuscript form—ten of them from the

Pound Archive at Yale and one from the Harriet Monroe Collection at the University of Chicago. The editors comment that these eleven were selected from more than a hundred such poems by Pound known to exist only in manuscript form—because, the editors note, they "seem to have a special interest . . . with relation to Pound's career."

4. Six poems, five hitherto unpublished, from the proof sheets of *Canzoni*, from the Harry Ransom Center at the University of Texas at Austin. These poems, as Gallup's bibliography notes, were omitted from the published edition of *Canzoni*.

5. In an appendix, a small group of fifteen miscellaneous published poems dating from the years 1913–1917, not previously collected, which, the editors maintain, seems "worthy of preservation." These appeared in such magazines as *BLAST*, *Others*, *Poetry*, and *Smart Set*.

The title pages of the six books of Pound's mentioned are reproduced in facsimile; the dedications to them are reproduced as well, as are Pound's notes to the poems. This collection, however, does not allow readers to understand the complete contents, in order, of each of these six early books. This is because, as the editors explain, whereas Pound reprinted many poems from collection to collection, each poem appears in this collection only once. The notes for *CEP* do provide a listing of the contents, in order, of *Personae* and *Exultations*, but readers seeking the full content of each of the early books, along with what George Bornstein has called the "contextual code" of each book—the order in which its selections originally appeared—should instead consult Donald Gallup's bibliography.

Worth bearing in mind as well is that although the Notes promise that a "[h]istory of the publication of each poem is provided through 1926," some of the poems are not listed in the notes. Poems seem to be omitted because they display no significant variants in either manuscript or published versions. Thus while readers seeking to reconstruct different versions of some of the poems will find the

Notes rewarding, readers looking for further information about each poem may be disappointed.

Previously unpublished poems especially of interest here include the following:

1. Two versions of "The Alchemist," one published in *Umbra* (1920) and the other a manuscript version hitherto unpublished;

2. Poems attesting to Pound's ambivalent relationship to his predecessors, such as "The Decadence," about poets of the 1890s; poems responding to Swinburne, such as "Salve O Pontifex!" Pound's tribute to Swinburne, as well as "Swinburne: A Critique"; and a poem engaging with the Celtic Twilight and titled " 'It Is a Shame'—With Apologies to the Modern Celtic School";

3. Three poems titled "Xenia"; and

4. "To E[lizabeth] B[arrett] B[rowning]."

Bibliography

Fogelman, Bruce. *Shapes of Power: The Development of Ezra Pound's Poetic Sequences*. Ann Arbor: UMI, 1988.

Grieve, Thomas F. *Ezra Pound's Early Poetry and Poetics*. Columbia: U of Missouri P, 1997.

Miranda B. Hickman

Confucius: *The Analects (Lun Yu)*

A collection of fragments rather than a philosophical treatise, *The Analects* (first published in the *Hudson Review* in 1950) is composed of 482 chapters grouped into twenty books. As in the case of *The Great Digest* (1947) and *The Unwobbling Pivot* (1947), Pound based his translation on nineteenth-century translations by Guillaume Pauthier and especially James Legge, diverging from these cribs at crucial junctures to investigate the etymology of particular words; in these cases, Pound relied heavily on the pictographic definitions offered in Morrison's Chinese-English dictionary, which he and Dorothy Pound had acquired around 1915. For *The Analects*, Pound also consulted Mathews's *Chinese English Dictionary*, which he acquired in late 1946 or early 1947.

Also like *The Great Digest* and *The Unwobbling Pivot*, *The Analects'* topics include government, taxes, circulation and distribution of goods and money, the "process" or *dao (tao)*, and verbal fidelity. But *The Analects* introduces many new topics as well: the importance of rites, of love and friendship, of learning, conscience, and beauty; the proper attitude toward illness, death, the death penalty, war—very resonant themes for Pound in the aftermath of World War II—and more than in Pound's earlier translations, the ideal of humaneness and "the humane man." In many respects, *The Analects* is antitranscendental, and it deemphasizes the Confucian "totalitarianism" of *The Great Digest* and *The Unwobbling Pivot*. Instead, it is concerned with the integrity of the individual—that is, with the importance of self-knowledge and of aligning one's actions appropriately with the human, social, and political realms. "Rites" in *The Analects* pertain to social custom based on social class and rank as well as to ceremonies performed to the spirits of the earth, air, and ancestors. "Reverence" is "respect for the kind of intelligence that enables grass seed to grow grass, the cherry stone to grow cherries," a definition that relies on the intelligence and on natural processes rather than on a more romantic or antiintellectual sense of the mystical. A number of the book's themes are especially poignant for Pound in this period after World War II: About war, for instance, Confucius says that "to send an untrained people to war is to throw them away" (XIII, end); and careful, conscientious study and planning are prized above premature action: "Love of boldness without love of study, leads to chaos" (XVII.8.3).

The Analects is the third of Pound's four Confucian translations. If he had translated all of what are grouped as the four "Confucian classics," he would have also translated *Mencius* in full. After *The Analects*, however, he turned instead to another Confucian text, the *Shi Jing* or *Book of Poetry*, which he titled *The Classic Anthology Defined by Confucius* (1954). Like *The Analects*, this work was done at St. Elizabeths Hospital.

Mary Paterson Cheadle

Confucius: *The Classic Anthology Defined by Confucius*

The Chinese book of *Odes*, the *Shih-ching*, was thought by ancient Chinese scholars to embody the essential rules governing the stars, the planets, and thus the minds of humans. For this reason, Confucius (551–479 B.C.E.) thought them a necessary object of study. The "Classic Anthology," as Ezra Pound called it, contains 305 ancient poems that promote good government and virtuous behavior. They come mostly from the ancient Shang (1766–1122 B.C.E.) and Chou (1122–255 B.C.E.) dynastic periods of Chinese history, and collectively they suggest a simpler time—a golden age of recognizable human truths. So prized were the *Odes* that they survived the famous T'sin Dynasty (255–206 B.C.E.) burning of the books that took place in 213 B.C.E.

The *Odes* survived the flames because they were deeply inscribed in the memories of so many Chinese scholars that the work was impossible to eliminate. All of the other great classics of Chinese antiquity underwent radical alterations after the famous book burning of 213 B.C.E., but when the T'sin fell, and the restoring Han rose, the Shih-ching immediately reappeared, complete, in three versions, resurrected from three different parts of the realm. Soon a fourth version appeared, the text of *Mao*. It divided the *Odes* into four sections: folk songs, lesser odes, greater odes, and odes for the temple and altar. This version was presented to the Han court in 129 B.C.E. and, by virtue of superb organization and clarity, became the canonical text.

Like most translators, Ezra Pound followed the four-division pattern set by the *Mao* version when he undertook his own translation of the *Shih-ching*, first published in 1954. Since Pound did not know Chinese, however, he needed more than a good pattern to help him deliver the *Odes* to a twentieth-century audience. He thus consulted the works of the great nineteenth-century translators Pauthier, Legge, and Lacharme, among others. But Pound's version of the *Odes* is no monkey to the work of others. He took poetic control of the material and freely altered it when he saw fit to do so. In this way he is in good company. Even the most learned translators of ancient Chinese script are sometimes charged with largely shifting for themselves. Indeed, doing so is often necessary.

Few languages allow as broad a range of interpretations as does ancient Chinese, and few translators assumed so wide an interpretive range as did Pound. Many Chinese characters, for example, have widely varying meanings, depending on their syntactical and sense relationships to other characters. As a result, Pound's free-ranging interpretations of widely interpretable material often results in remarkable eccentricities of sense and phrase and thus presents the same mix of weaknesses and strengths attributed to so much of his other poetry. At times, Pound is capable of delivering his subject with elegance and understanding. Yet often an informed reader begins to wonder if Pound should ever have undertaken the task of recreating this greatest of anthologies at all. In his attempts to bring the ancient material to a twentieth-century audience, he often quite simply misses the mark.

Even if Pound's intention was to resituate the *Odes* for a Western, popular audience, his light and comical usage of the ballad form sometimes misses the tone appropriate to an ode's subject. In Ode 167, for example, sung by soldiers tired of war and desperate for food and home, Pound begins with "pick a fern, pick a fern, ferns are high." This is not the way to introduce a sense of human desperation; Pound's tone is too light and carefree for his received subject. He had translated this same poem as the "Song of the Bowmen of Shu," years earlier, as the opening poem in *Cathay*, his 1915 volume of translations from the Chinese. A comparison of the two versions readily suggests what may at times be lost as a result of Pound's interpretative methods. Yet in other ways he is powerfully successful. For example, he is able to present the inner life of the ancient Chinese in a way that few others have proved capable of doing.

Whether we can attribute what Westerners consider to be an inner life to Shang and Chou Dynasty China is still very much the subject of scholarly debate. Nevertheless, Pound's handling of the *Odes* often produces stunning and believable results. In Ode 1, for example, his repetition of the phrase "dark and clear" is richly applied to the natural images of fish-hawks, tree boughs, water reeds, and moving streams; yet at the same time, the phrase nimbly underwrites the conclusion that all of those observances are "darkened" by the unfulfilled sexual passion of a prince who dreams of and seeks the woman who will be his bride. By drawing this connection out of the ode Pound suggests the link between nature and humanity, perception and desire, individual and cosmic truth. The *Odes* have suggested such linked truths as these for thousands of years and continue to presume that the very movement of the stars confirms them.

Bibliography

Cheadle, Mary Paterson. *Ezra Pound's Confucian Translations*. Ann Arbor: U of Michigan P, 1997.

Dembo, L. S. *The Confucian Odes of Ezra Pound: A Critical Appraisal*. Berkeley: U of California P, 1963.

Nolde, John J. *Blossoms from the East: The China Cantos of Ezra Pound*. Orono: NPF, 1983.

Sarra, Edith. "Whistling in the Bughouse: Notes on the Process of Pound's Confucian Odes." *Paideuma* 16.1–2 (1987): 7–31.

Schwartz, Benjamin. *The World of Thought in Ancient China*. Cambridge: Harvard UP, 1985.

Robert E. Kibler

Confucius: *Ta Hio (Da Xue), The Great Digest*

Pound produced three versions of this ancient Confucian text, believed to have been composed by Confucius's grandson, perhaps in the late fifth century B.C.E. Pound's translations are the *Ta Hio, The Great Learning* (1928), *Confucio, Ta S'eu, Dai Gaku, Studio Integrale* (1942), and *The Great Digest* (1947). The 1928 translation was based not on the Chinese source, which Pound had not yet begun to study, but on a nineteenth-century French version by Guilluame Pauthier. The 1942 translation was a new effort, in Italian, based on the Chinese text, which was published alongside it bilingually;

in 1944 this Italian translation was republished without the Chinese text. *The Great Digest* (1947) is Pound's second English translation, completed in the fall of 1945 (with *The Unwobbling Pivot*) at the Disciplinary Training Center near Pisa, in the same notebook in which he composed the Pisan Cantos. In the mid-1930s, Pound had begun working with Morrison's Chinese-English dictionary. Since 1937, Pound had been working with the Confucian texts in Chinese, using Morrison's dictionary and the nineteenth-century English translations of James Legge as his guides. The essay "Mang Tsze (The Ethics of Mencius)" of 1938 is the first fruit of that study (*SP* 81–97).

The Great Digest is a philosophical tract in prose, composed of seven paragraphs of text followed by a much longer section of commentary. It contains the basis of the Confucian order, an order that begins both on the individual level extending outward and on the imperial level extending in. Self-discipline is the basis of familial order, familial order the basis of social order, and social order the basis of order within the state and empire. Simultaneously, imperial order is the model of order within the state, order within the state is the model for familial order, and familial order is the model for self-discipline. Crucial to the concept of self-discipline in Pound's translation is his definition of the Chinese word for sincerity: *Cheng* is "precise verbal definitions" or "the sun's lance coming to rest on the precise spot verbally," according to Pound's pictographic interpretation of the Chinese word, and verbal precision is arrived at through knowledge. The importance of finding the precise word for one's intention and acting according to one's word is that this is the basis of order at any level, from the personal to the social and imperial. This doctrine is restated throughout Pound's Confucian translations and recurs in *The Cantos*, as in Canto 51.

Other important themes in *The Great Digest* are the importance of agriculture as the basis of an economy, the circulation of goods and money, revolution and the concept "make it new" (which comes from a proclamation quoted in Chapter II of *The Great Digest*), and the Con-

fucian *dao* (*tao*) or "process." *The Great Digest*'s philosophy is "totalitarian" in the sense that it values the wholeness or integrity of the object, individual, society, or system. Though Pound's advocation of "totalitarianism" is not identical to fascist totalitarianism, it is also true that the chief impetus for his Italian translation of the *Da Xue* in 1942 was to guide, correct, and bolster Mussolini's fascist project. After the fall of the Axis Powers in 1945, the significance of *The Great Digest* (1947) is its statement of a Confucian order based on precise verbal definitions, a "totalitarian" vision Pound believed was important to the post–World War II West.

Mary Paterson Cheadle

Confucius: *The Unwobbling Pivot (Zhong Yong)*

The Unwobbling Pivot, Pound's translation of the Confucian prose text *Zhong Yong*, develops the totalitarian vision first outlined in *The Great Digest*. Like *The Great Digest*, it, too, was first translated by Pound in Italian, appearing first in the journal *Il Popolo di Alessandria* in 1944 and early 1945 and later as *L'Asse Che Non Vacilla* (1945). The English translation was completed at the Disciplinary Training Center near Pisa, where Pound was initially held on charges of treason against the United States. This English translation was first published in 1947; in 1951 it was republished with *The Great Digest*, this time with the Chinese text on facing pages.

The *Zhong Yong* is considered by Sinologists to be the most metaphysical of the Confucian texts, composed sometime after Confucius's death in 479 B.C.E. Though Pound insists that Confucianism in general is practical and that *The Unwobbling Pivot* in particular presents ideas that can be "precisely understood," its approach is nonetheless metaphysical, even transcendental. Among the "nine rules" for governing families and kingdoms, for instance, are self-control, respect for ministers and "men of honest talent," affection for relatives and "the people," and courtesy toward artisans and foreigners. In order to govern well, the ruler must begin with integrity based on self-knowledge. Action based on this self-knowledge is the Confucian *dao* (*tao*) or way and leads, in its fullest expression, to a conjunction of man with earth and heaven. "Equity" or fairness is important in *The Unwobbling Pivot*—and so is the concept of the "heavenly mandate" or, according to Pound, "fate" or "destiny." The pivot or axis, the *zhong*, is a center around which everything else moves, and it is very difficult to grasp: Only the *jun-zi* or man "in whom the ancestors speak" can stand "firm in the middle of what whirls."

In *The Unwobbling Pivot* Pound develops a Confucian light philosophy that is influenced by his long-standing Neoplatonism. In fact, he ends his translation seven chapters before the end of the Chinese text, with a strikingly Neoplatonic vision of light that compares the ancient king Wen's virtue with the "unmixed," "unending," "tensile" light coming down from heaven. Metaphysical and "totalitarian" in respect to its vision of the entirety or integrity of the individual, the empire, and man's ideal "partnership" with earth and heaven, *The Unwobbling Pivot* marks the end of Pound's hopes that a fascist Italy could herald a Confucianism renaissance in the twentieth-century West.

Mary Paterson Cheadle

Cravens, Margaret (1881–1912)

Born into a wealthy family in Madison, Indiana, Margaret Lanier Cravens studied piano in Boston and Florence before going to Paris in 1907 to study with Ravel, Harold Bauer, and possibly Pound's friend and music collaborator Walter Rummel. In Paris, Cravens knew artists and writers and pursued mystical thought, modern languages, and Italian poetry. She met Pound through Rummel in March 1910 and shortly afterward arranged to provide the young poet with a sum of around $1,000 a year. Pound wrote to her often of his travels, friends, and hopes for an American Risorgimento of the arts and discussed his work on *The Spirit of Romance* and his Cavalcanti translations.

Cravens funded Pound for two years. Ill health, depression, and a family history of suicide contributed to Cravens's suicide in June 1912. Pound learned the news while on a walking tour of southern France. One of her final notes suggested that she had loved Rummel. It was also rumored that she had just received a telegram message from Pound, "I sleep with my love tonight," which some of her friends believed had upset her. But these words, if sent at all, likely alluded to some aspect of Pound's initial encounter with troubadour country. In *Patria Mia*, Pound paid indirect tribute to Cravens's patronage by urging "the American individual" to assist American artists: "I suggest that a sane form of bequest would be an endowment of 1,000 dollars per year, settled on any artist whose work was recognized as being of value to the community." Pound recalls Cravens in "His Vision of a Certain Lady Post Mortem," "Dans un Omnibus de Londres," and Cantos 7 and 77.

Bibliography

H. D. *Asphodel*. Ed. Robert Spoo. Durham: Duke UP, 1992.

Pound, Ezra. *Ezra Pound and Margaret Cravens: A Tragic Friendship 1910–1912*. Ed. Omar Pound and Robert Spoo. Durham: Duke UP, 1988.

Spoo, Robert. "'Authentic Sisters': H. D. and Margaret Cravens." *H. D. Newsletter* 3.1 (1990): 35–43. Also available at http://www.well.com/user/heddy/hdrs31.html.

———. "Pound's Cavalcanti and Cravens's Carducci." *Paideuma* 20.1 (1991): 77–88.

Robert Spoo

Criterion

Published between October 1922 and January 1939, the *Criterion* fulfilled T. S. Eliot's ambition of editing a critical review. Financed initially by Lady Rothermere, Eliot hoped the venture would facilitate further his acceptance into English intellectual circles. The eventual involvement of the Faber and Gwyer firm, later Faber and Faber, brought with it Eliot's job in publishing. Through the middle of the 1920s, Ezra Pound found the magazine a suitable venue for articles explicating the music of George Antheil for readers in London. But generally, Pound viewed the *Criterion* as too staid for his tastes, an opinion punctuated with a series of cranky letters about fellow contributors. Pound did agree to review some books for Eliot throughout the period of his involvement, and although Pound criticized on the pages of the magazine Eliot's unwillingness to embrace Social Credit, the *Criterion* did print some of Pound's thoughts on economics in essays like "Murder by Capital." The magazine turned out to be an apt venue in which Pound could publish a number of cantos, and in the years before World War II, he printed some of his most lucid essays from this period: "Memoriam: A. R. Orage" appeared in April 1935 and "For a New Paideuma" appeared in January 1938.

Bibliography

Harding, Jason. *The Criterion: Cultural Politics and Periodical Networks in Inter-War Britain*. Oxford: Oxford UP, 2002.

Craig Monk

Critical Reception: 1908–1920

Pound's reception has always been complicated. He has always had vigorous, and often influential, supporters, especially among fellow writers; but just as often, he has provoked puzzlement, resistance, even outright hostility, especially from mainstream readers and the literary establishment. The early part of his career presents a microcosm of this mixed reception. Initially, Pound was hailed as a young poet with great promise, but by the time of his departure from London in 1920, he was already, to a large extent, an outsider.

Reactions to his first volume, *A Lume Spento*, privately published in 1908, were few and largely lukewarm. *A Quinzaine for This Yule* (1908) drew the attention of Elkin Mathews, who became Pound's publisher. His next volume, *Personae* (1909), drew serious and positive attention, including praise from Edward Thomas in the prestigious *English Review*. Through Mathews, Pound was also making the rounds of London's literary circles, meeting Laurence Binyon, Maurice Hewlett, and later, Ford Madox Hueffer (Ford). *Exultations* (1909) did not win uniform approval, but the "Ballad of the Goodly Fere" received praise from many quarters, including a public endorsement by W. B. Yeats.

The Spirit of Romance (1910), Pound's first prose book and the first to be published in America, did not significantly advance Pound's reputation, but his next collection of poems, *Provença* (1910), earned an enthusiastic review from H. L. Mencken in *Smart Set*, who praised Pound's energy and technical skill. Two poems from *Provença* ("Portrait" and "Ballad for Gloom") were also selected for inclusion in *The Oxford Book of Victorian Verse* in 1912.

Pound, however, was turning away from the antiquarianism that had supported his success thus far. In 1911, he began frequenting gatherings led by T. E. Hulme, and through him, he became affiliated with A. R. Orage's *New Age*. The next year, he launched the short-lived Imagist movement, which eschewed poetic diction for "direct treatment of the thing." *Ripostes* (1912), which collected these more modern works, left some readers confused and others hostile. Pound's appointment as foreign correspondent for *Poetry* in 1912 drew further criticism. His promotion of modern poetry, including his own, drew attacks in the *Nation* and the *Dial* that accused him of making *Poetry* "a thing for laughter." *Poetry*'s editor, Harriet Monroe, came to Pound's defense, but Pound by then had become a target for those who resisted modern trends in poetry. His contributions to the two numbers of Wyndham Lewis's aggressively avant-garde journal *BLAST* (1914–1915) confirmed Pound's opposition to mainstream tastes and vice versa.

The Chinese-inspired poetry of *Cathay* (1915) earned praise for its restraint, but *Lustra* (1916) again pitted Pound against prevailing values. In the repressive atmosphere of World War I, Mathews insisted on omitting several "nasty" poems and on changes in others to make them less offensive. The volume was published, but the incident opened a rift that eventually led to Pound's seeking other publishers. When it did appear, *Lustra* was poorly received, being attacked by Louis Untermeyer in the *Dial* as "poetry in pantomime."

Despite these setbacks, Pound remained energetic, supporting himself as a literary journalist by maintaining a furious pace of contributions to periodicals, including the *Egoist*, the *Little Review* (as foreign editor), the *New Age* (where he reviewed art and music pseudonymously), and the *Future* (as a book reviewer). He was also vigorously promoting the work of other writers, including T. S. Eliot, whom he first met in 1914, and James Joyce, who was recommended to Pound by Yeats. Pound was instrumental in getting early works by these and other authors published.

These efforts were reciprocated in 1917 when Eliot produced the first extended study of Pound's work. *Ezra Pound: His Metric and Poetry*, published anonymously in January 1918, attempted to draw attention to Pound's technique and urged readers to view his work as a whole. Eliot also praised Pound's use of translation and of the tradition generally to revitalize the poetry of the present. Eliot and Pound worked together closely in the following years, and Eliot continued to defend Pound's work in reviews in *To-day* (1918) and the *Athenaeum* (1919).

Even with the support of fellow writers, however, the general reception of Pound remained poor. The prose collection *Pavannes and Divisions* (1918) was sharply criticized by Untermeyer again and by Conrad Aiken in the *Dial*. *Homage to Sextus Propertius*, published in part in *Poetry* and then as part of *Quia Pauper Amavi* (1919), was attacked by University of Chicago classics professor W. G. Hale, who assailed Pound as "incredibly ignorant of Latin" in his rendering of Propertius. Despite Pound's protests that he had never intended literal translation, as well as supportive efforts by Eliot, Orage, and Lewis, critics seized on Pound's supposed faults in translation as grounds for a wholesale dismissal of his work. Robert Nichols of the *Observer* went so far as to declare that Pound "is not, never has been and almost, I might hazard, never will be a poet" (Homberger 167).

In his final years in London Pound grew more isolated and more disillusioned, an attitude reflected in his last major work of this period, *Hugh Selwyn Mauberley* (1920), in which he characterizes himself as "out of key with his time." The response to this indictment of contemporary culture was predictable. Even critics inclined to agree with Pound's judgments criticized the poem for its obscurity and Pound for his all-too-obvious disdain for the common reader. Appearing the same year, *Umbra*, intended as the definitive collection of all of Pound's earlier poetry, was virtually ignored by critics.

Late in 1920, Pound was offered a position as foreign correspondent for the *Dial*. Traveling to the continent in this official capacity prompted Pound's permanent departure from London in December, which effectively closes this phase of his career.

Bibliography

Eliot, T. S. *Ezra Pound: His Metric and Poetry*. New York: Knopf, 1917 [1918].

Homberger, Eric, ed. *Ezra Pound: The Critical Heritage*. London: Routledge, 1972.

William Cole

Critical Reception: 1920–1945

The period 1920 through 1945 saw Pound publish several major poetical works (*Hugh Selwyn Mauberley*, *Homage to Sextus Propertius*, Cantos 4 through 71), important prose works (*Make It New*, *Jefferson and/or Mussolini*, *ABC of Reading*, *Confucius*, *Guide to Kulchur*), the edition of *Cavalcanti*, anthologies of others' poetry, and many reviews. Critical response to these works was as diverse as the works themselves, ranging from fiery censure to cool dismissiveness to high encomium.

In the early part of the period, which was an isolationist era of American history, critiques focused largely on Pound's expatriation (from America and from England) and on his works' constantly changing tenor—even from writers traditionally viewed as Pound's allies. William Carlos Williams found it necessary in a 1927 review to place Pound's expatriation at the center of a positive review (*New York Post Evening Literary Review* [19 February 1927]). Harriet Monroe in *Poetry* 26 (1925) spoke of Pound as a poet whose best work had already been penned and who had begun to drift from the style she so admired. Fewer critics in the 1920s and early 1930s, Ford Madox Ford among them, perceived in Pound's work praiseworthy qualities, including the vitality of his constantly changing style and the strength of his devotion to history.

Throughout, some critics chided Pound for his bookish obscurity. Even in positive reviews, critics often noted the difficulty of keeping pace with Pound's demands on the reader (Fitts in *Hound & Horn* 4 [Winter 1931], Walton in *New York Times Book Review* 2 [April 1933]). Perhaps for these difficulties, criticism of the period was frequently expository, offering plot or theme summaries for readers of the works (Wescott in *Dial* 79 [December 1925]).

Critiques of *The Cantos* throughout the period almost universally recognized the importance of Pound's work even if the critics did not praise the poem itself. Marianne Moore recognized in *A Draft of XXX Cantos* the "tautness" of Pound's spare style (*Criterion* [April 1934]). As subsequent collections of *The Cantos* appeared, critical response diverged along two distinct paths: On the one, praise for Pound's continuing experiment grew louder (Schwartz in *Poetry* 51 [March 1938]; MacLeish in *Atlantic Monthly* 163 [June 1939]); on the other, critics grew bored and frustrated with the work (Ransom in *Saturday Review of Literature* 11 [19 January 1935]; Jarrell in *New Republic* 103 [9 December 1940]).

Reviewers of the prose works were generally much more positive both about their intellectual quality and about Pound's vital presence as author. Very early in the period, H. L. Mencken, reviewing *Instigations*, called Pound "the most extraordinary man that American literature has seen in our time" (*Smart Set* 62 [August 1920]). G. K. Chesterton praised both Pound's learnedness and his "furious likes and dislikes," reviewing *Make It New* for *Listener* (28 November 1934). Widespread admiration of the prose appears even in the lukewarm and qualified praise for *Guide to Kulchur*: Williams and the often acerbic Dudley Fitts, despite their indications that the *Guide* is less than successful, nevertheless called it respectively "one of those essential books" (*New Republic* 99 [28 June 1939]) and "breathless and stimulating" (*Saturday Review* 20 [13 May 1939]). Other critics of this work shared a similar opinion, pointing out its crude scholarship and chatty tone even as they admired its engaging and interesting nature.

Of the translations, critics almost universally expressed admiration both for Pound's outstanding (if sometimes liberal) translations and for his ability as both poet and editor to translate poetically. This is especially true of *Propertius*, in which Stephen Spender, for instance, recognized "creative critic[al]" ability to reproduce the *"quality"* of the original (Spender's emphasis; *Spectator* 103 [14 December 1934]).

Bibliography

Homberger, Eric, ed. *Ezra Pound: The Critical Heritage*. London: Routledge, 1972.

Stock, Noel. *The Life of Ezra Pound*. 1970. San Francisco: North Point P, 1982.

Sutton, Walter, ed. *Ezra Pound: A Collection of Critical Essays*. Twentieth-Century Views STC-9. Englewood Cliffs: Prentice-Hall, 1963.

Jonathan Ausubel

Critical Reception: 1945–1980

At the close of World War II, Pound's reputation was at its nadir. It had been slipping prior to the war as installments of *The Cantos* found fewer and fewer readers. T. S. Eliot was viewed as the preeminent living poet, and the New Critics who had so crowned him were not sympathetic to Pound's project. Even among other writers, Pound's position was at a low. The prominent younger poets of the day—W. H. Auden, Dylan Thomas, Stephen Spender, Robert Penn Warren—owed little to Pound's influence, while those who did, like the Objectivists, were as little read as Pound himself.

To this aesthetic isolation, Pound added political outrage. His support of the Mussolini regime in Italy and in particular his broadcasts for Rome Radio during the war had earned him an indictment for treason, for which he was arrested by U.S. troops in May 1945 and returned to Washington for trial in November. Some in America were seriously calling for Pound to be executed as a traitor ("Should Ezra Pound Be Shot?" appeared in the *New Masses* in December 1945). Supporters, including Eliot, Robert Frost, E. E. Cummings, and William Carlos Williams, rallied behind Pound, but the insanity defense that was offered and that may have saved Pound's life was nearly fatal for his reputation as a serious poet. Found unfit to stand trial, Pound was confined to St. Elizabeths Hospital for the Criminally Insane in Washington, D.C., from 1945 to 1958.

Yet it was from these improbable circumstances that the resuscitation of Pound's reputation began. At the very least, he was more accessible than he had been in Italy. Visiting Pound became a kind of pilgrimage first for his friends and later for young writers and critics of all sorts. His visitors at St. Elizabeths included Eliot, Marianne Moore, Allen Tate, Randall Jarrell, Thornton Wilder, Stephen Spender, Elizabeth Bishop, Katherine Anne Porter, Langston Hughes, Robert Lowell, Allen Ginsberg, Marshall McLuhan, and Hugh Kenner.

Pound also remained prolific in his writing. *The Pisan Cantos*, which had been drafted during Pound's confinement immediately following his arrest in Italy, was published in 1948. The new cantos immediately drew attention for the more personal, almost repentant quality of the poems, which renewed many readers' hope for the overall project. Early in 1949, *The Pisan Cantos* was awarded the Library of Congress Bollingen Prize "for the highest achievement in American Poetry." The award reopened the treason controversy, with many objecting to an accused traitor receiving such an honor. Robert Hillyer attacked the award jury, which included Eliot, Porter, Lowell, and others, in a pair of articles in the *Saturday Review of Literature*, accusing them of a conspiracy to control literary culture. The award jury defended their choice by insisting on a strict separation of "poetic achievement" from all other considerations. This solution, of insisting on Pound's worth as a poet independently of his activities as a man, would form one of the major strains of Pound criticism for many decades. While in many ways a contradiction of Pound's own insistence on the political and moral dimensions of his poetry, this approach nevertheless cleared a space for a less emotional assessment of Pound's poetic achievements.

During the 1950s, critical appreciation for those achievements began to appear. Kenner's *The Poetry of Ezra Pound* (1951) broke new ground in making Pound the subject of serious academic scholarship. This lead was picked up by others willing to do the scholarly spade-work to elucidate Pound's poetry. John Hamilton Edwards, who wrote a critical biography of Pound as a doctoral dissertation in 1952, edited the *Pound Newsletter* from 1954 to 1956 and collaborated with William W. Vasse on *An Annotated Index to the Cantos of Ezra Pound* (1957). John Espey's *Ezra Pound's Mauberley* (1955) remains an indispensable study of the complex bases of that poem. In 1963, Donald Gallup produced a comprehensive bibliography of Pound's writing up to that point.

Such scholarly detective work was supplemented by Pound's publishers, who issued a steady stream of unpublished and out-of-print materials: *The Selected Letters of Ezra Pound, 1907–1941* (1950, edited by D. D. Paige); *The Translations* (1953, introduced by Kenner); *Literary Essays* (1954, edited and introduced by Eliot); *Pavannes and Divagations* (1958). Besides making available hard-to-find materials by Pound, these volumes helped to rebuild Pound's reputation as an important and influential literary critic. Eliot argued in his introduction to *Literary Essays* that Pound was the most important contemporary critic of his kind.

Although academic interest in Pound's work was growing, opinions remained divided on the nature of his achievement. At least one school of thought saw Pound as having reached his peak in the *Propertius/Mauberley* period. *The Cantos* was still viewed by many with skepticism, and neither *Section: Rock-Drill* (1955) nor *Thrones* (1959) received especially favorable reviews, even from sympathetic critics. Both volumes were criticized for being too disorganized and fragmentary, and critics regretted the turn away from the lyricism of *The Pisan Cantos*. Pound's lack of production, due to a series of mental and physical health problems following his release from St. Elizabeths, further contributed to the sense that *The Cantos* was falling apart. Donald Davie, in *Ezra Pound: The Poet as Sculptor* (1964), attacked *The Cantos* as misguided, sterile, and ultimately doomed by its own ambitions. Pound's own admissions of regret and failure privately and in the final *Drafts and Fragments* (1969) did little to upset that popular opinion.

Only after Pound's death in 1972 was his place as one of the most important poets of the century finally secured. While a number of scholars—including Christine Brooke-Rose, Ronald Bush, Davie, Timothy Materer, Stuart McDougal, Noel Stock, Leon Surette, Carroll F. Terrell, and James J. Wilhelm—made important contributions in the 1970s, Kenner's *The Pound Era* (1971) remains the single most important critical work on Pound. Kenner presented not only a sympathetic reading of Pound's full poetic and critical oeuvre but also a powerful argument for him as the central figure of an international Modernist movement. While subsequent critics have challenged both Kenner's assessment and methods, his work is a reference point for virtually all subsequent scholarship and remains essential reading for Pound scholars new and old.

Bibliography

Homberger, Eric, ed. *Ezra Pound: The Critical Heritage*. London: Routledge, 1972.

Kenner, Hugh. *The Pound Era*. Berkeley: U of California P, 1971.

Norman, Charles. *The Case of Ezra Pound*. New York: Funk and Wagnalls, 1968.

Sullivan, J. P., ed. *Ezra Pound: A Critical Anthology*. Harmondsworth: Penguin, 1970.

William Cole

Critical Reception: 1980–2000

The early 1980s saw an explosion in Pound scholarship, with *The Cantos* receiving most of the attention. Perhaps this flurry of study reflects the efforts of scholars to assure the poem's value, which in previous decades had been contested. Volume I of Carroll F. Terrell's *A Companion to the Cantos of Ezra Pound* (1980) covers the first seventy-one cantos. With the assistance of other leading Poundians, Terrell provides a tripartite list of sources, background, and exegesis. Volume II of what one critic calls Terrell's "Herculean effort" appeared in 1984. Also exemplary of the kind of scholarship that appears at an almost unassimilable rate in the

early 1980s is Guy Davenport's 1961 Harvard dissertation, *Cities on Hills: A Study of I–XXX of Ezra Pound's Cantos* (1983). Davenport provides readings of individual passages and emphasizes Pound's affinities with Blake and Ruskin.

Once the poet's reputation is unquestionably secure, Pound scholarship, which tended toward glossing and expounding on his difficult works, begins to look outward: Critics become less interested in source study than in comparative research that positions Pound within reigning contemporary critical theory. Thus, poststructuralist readings of Pound prevail into the mid-1980s. Early poststructuralist analyses of Pound's politics and poetics follow one of two predictable lines: that Pound understands the arbitrariness of signs and practices a liberating poetics of indeterminacy or, more typically, that Pound does not understand the arbitrariness of signs and practices a totalitarian poetics of logocentricity. Indeed, one or the other of these positions is detectable in Paul Smith's *Pound Revised* (1983), Joseph G. Kronick's *American Poetics of History* (1984), and *Ezra Pound and History*, a collection of essays edited by Marianne Korn (1985). However, attempts to connect Pound to poststructuralist theory are only worthwhile if there is critical payoff, something Donald Davie addresses in "Poundians Now" (1985). Davie's article, which chastises critics who subordinate poetry to ideology, calls for a more cautious application of contemporary theory to Pound's works. Jean-Michel Rabaté's *Language, Sexuality and Ideology in Ezra Pound's Cantos* (1986) is arguably such a careful study of Pound's poetics.

Pound's centenary year 1985 was cause for many celebrations. The vortex of activities surrounding these events is chronicled in special issues of journals such as the *Iowa Review*, *Field* (Oberlin, Ohio), *Los Cuadernos del Norte* (Oviedo, Spain), and of course, *Paideuma*. The centenary year inspired pause for reflection on how Pound fits within the context of his contemporaries; consequently, many of his correspondences were brought forth, including the *Pound/Lewis* (1985) letters, edited by Timothy

Materer, and the *Pound/Zukofsky* (1987) letters, edited by Barry Ahearn. (This interest in Pound's correspondence saw the publication of over twenty collections of letters before the end of the century.) Similarly, Margaret Dickie's *On the Modernist Long Poem* (1986) and Marjorie Perloff's *The Futurist Moment* (1986) demand that the reader consider Pound within a broader literary and cultural context.

By the late 1980s critics seemed to be getting a better handle on how in *The Cantos* Pound's poetry and politics interrelate on all levels. Perhaps this accounts for the increased interest in general studies regarding Pound's political involvement and the simultaneous slowdown of criticism dealing primarily with *The Cantos*. Pound's ideology, especially his fascism and anti-Semitism, becomes an overriding concern, and into the early 1990s there are as many attempts by critics to mitigate Pound's anti-Semitism and fascism as there are to condemn him. Robert Casillo's *The Genealogy of Demons: Anti-Semitism, Fascism, and the Myths of Ezra Pound* (1988) charges the "Pound industry" with ignoring the centrality of anti-Semitism and fascism in Pound's life and work, while Reed Way Dasenbrock's *Imitating the Italians: Wyatt, Spenser, Synge, Pound, Joyce* (1991) emphasizes that Pound's interest in Italian art gives us a better understanding of "Pound's Italy" and explains his turn toward fascism. Tim Redman's *Ezra Pound and Italian Fascism* (1991) is a thorough chronicle of the economic proposals that accompany Pound's involvement with Mussolini, while Michael North's *The Political Aesthetic of Yeats, Eliot, and Pound* (1991) is a more theoretical investigation of Pound's fascism.

The relative decline in Pound criticism during the early 1990s, perhaps a result of what one critic calls "the passing of the heroic age of discovery, annotating and basic decoding of the Cantos," results in an increased interest in how Pound figures into an ongoing revaluation of Modernism. While critics try to account for the heterogeneity of the Modernist movement, it seems that there is no single methodology or topic predominant in Poundian studies. Of the many general studies that discuss Pound within a revaluation of "Modernism" are K. K. Ruthven's *Ezra Pound as Literary Critic* (1990), Vincent Sherry's *Ezra Pound, Wyndham Lewis, and Radical Modernism* (1993), Leonard Diepeveen's *Changing Voices: The Modern Quoting Poem* (1993), and Stan Smith's *The Origins of Modernism* (1994).

The heightened self-reflexivity of Modernist scholars perhaps initiates the trend in critical investigations that enter previously uncharted terrain, including studies of Pound's metaphysics, his involvement with the occult tradition, and his relation to Neoplatonism. For instance, Demetres P. Tryphonopoulos's *The Celestial Tradition: A Study of Pound's The Cantos* (1992) and Leon Surette's *The Birth of Modernism: Ezra Pound, T. S. Eliot, W. B. Yeats, and the Occult* (1993) guide us through Pound's employment of various hermeticisms, including Gnosticism, the Cabala, Swedenborg, and Theosophy. Pound figures into Michael Bell's *Literature, Modernism and Myth* (1997), which claims that "mythopoeia" is "the underlying metaphysics of much modernist literature."

Materialist criticism at this time is informed by the predominance of occult studies insofar that it insistently problematizes Pound's political ideology by posing new complications once thought answered. Increased emphasis on Pound and the occult, which implies that there can be no encompassing critical discursive, allows for more complex cultural and ideological investigations into Pound's works. A major collection of essays, *A Poem Containing History: Textual Studies in The Cantos* (1997), edited by Lawrence S. Rainey, is most valuable for revealing that any critical edition of *The Cantos* must inevitably be an interpretation of the whole poem and for reminding us how provisional the text is. Peter Wilson's *A Preface to Ezra Pound* (1997) addresses some issues previously not often ventured into such as the poet's sexual politics as well as "making new" some issues such as Pound's economics and interest in fascism. The important topic of Pound's eccentric economic theories is explored in detail in two groundbreaking books, Alec Marsh's *Money* and *Modernity: Pound, Williams, and the Spirit of Jefferson* (1998) and Leon Surette's *Pound in Purgatory: From Economic Radicalism to Anti-Semitism* (1999). Rainey's *Institutions of Modernism* (1998) is an exemplary work of materialist criticism in which the author downplays his own ideological commitments. The end of the century also inspires retrospective criticism that is keen to take stock of poets and the troubled century in which they wrote. Ira Nadel's *The Cambridge Companion to Ezra Pound*, which contains fifteen essays by leading Pound scholars, is such a work.

So Michael Coyle, in *Ezra Pound, Popular Genres, and the Discourse of Culture*, writes that the best criticism in the later phase of Poundian study resists either the merely contentious dismissal of his ideological allegiances or the uncritical adoration of his poetic accomplishments. Thus, the kind of criticism that emerges at the end of the century confirms that Pound studies are more than ever a heterogenous field of activity.

Bibliography

Bell, Michael. *Literature, Modernism and Myth: Belief and Responsibility in the Twentieth Century.* Cambridge: Cambridge UP, 1997.

Coyle, Michael. *Ezra Pound, Popular Genres, and the Discourse of Culture.* University Park: Pennsylvania State UP, 1995.

Davie, Donald. "Poundians Now." *Paideuma* 14.2–3 (1985): 167–177.

Dickie, Margaret. *On the Modernist Long Poem.* Iowa City: U of Iowa P, 1986.

Diepeveen, Leonard. *Changing Voices: The Modern Quoting Poem.* Ann Arbor: U of Michigan P, 1993.

Kronick, Joseph G. *American Poetics of History: From Emerson to the Moderns.* Baton Rouge: Louisiana State UP, 1984.

Nadel, Ira B., ed. *The Cambridge Companion to Ezra Pound.* Cambridge: Cambridge UP, 1999.

Perloff, Marjorie. *The Futurist Moment: Avant-garde, Avant Guerre, and the Language of Rupture.* Chicago: U of Chicago P, 1986.

Sheri Benning

Cummings, E. E. (1894–1962)

Cummings was already a great admirer of the older poet when they first met in Paris in 1921.

Their relations, though cordial, did not become close until 1933, with the publication of Cummings's account of his tour through Russia, *Eimi*. The dim view of life under Soviet rule in *Eimi* accorded with Pound's growing distaste for communism. As Pound commented in "E. E. Cummings Alive," "Does any man wish to know about Russia? 'EIMI!' Does any man wish to read an American author who the present harassed critic has read and can re-read with pleasure?" Pound came to value Cummings's talent as a social commentator and hoped to persuade him to join the fight for a renewed Western culture. For many years he pressed Cummings to write an account of the United States to match *Eimi*. Cummings grew used to Pound's advice and admonitions but mostly resisted his friend's attempts to enlist him in campaigns.

Where Cummings parted company with Pound was over the question of the role of the artist. Pound believed the artist was obliged to take sides with those who wanted to make the world safer for individual liberty, even if some of the allies were political leaders—such as Mussolini. Cummings, for his part, had no use for direct political action beyond entering a voting booth. His persistent reluctance to join Pound's campaign was accompanied by a notable lack of enthusiasm for *The Cantos*. At times it appeared that Cummings did not enjoy any of Pound's poetry composed after 1920. Nevertheless, Cummings throughout his life insisted that Pound was a true poet. Pound was similarly selective about Cummings's work: He singled out for praise only those poems that appeared to agree with his own views about world affairs. For example, Pound repeatedly praised "plato told"—and even included it in *Confucius to Cummings*—because it seemed to deplore the greed of armaments manufacturers and other war profiteers.

Despite the occasional friction caused by their differing opinions about the duties of the artist, Cummings and Pound remained on good terms personally. One indication of Cummings's friendship for Pound occurred in 1945, when Pound was brought to the United States. His lawyer, Julien Cornell, went to New York to see if Pound's friends could be of assistance. Cummings promptly turned over to Cornell a check for $1,000, money that Cummings himself badly needed at the time. About this time, too, Cummings contributed a note on Pound to Charles Norman's newspaper article on Pound. In his note Cummings somewhat cryptically suggested that Pound's wartime radio broadcasts could be defended under the principle of freedom of speech. The fundamental respect Pound and Cummings had for each other pervades their letters. On Pound's side one finds little of the condescending tone that could appear when he wrote to younger authors. Clearly he regarded Cummings as someone with whom he could speak on almost equal terms.

Bibliography

Cummings, E. E. *Eimi*. New York: Covici-Friede, 1933.

Pound, Ezra. "E. E. Cummings Alive." *New English Weekly* 6.10 (1934): 210–211.

———. *Pound/Cummings: The Correspondence of Ezra Pound and E. E. Cummings*. Ed. Barry Ahearn. Ann Arbor: U of Michigan P, 1996.

Regier, Willis Goth. "Ezra Pound and E. E. Cummings: Confrontation between Tradition and the Avant-garde." Diss. U of Nebraska, 1978.

Barry Ahearn

Cutting, Bronson (1888–1935)

Cutting (1927–1935), a U.S. senator from New Mexico, corresponded with Pound from November 1930 until April 1935, approximately one month before Cutting died in a plane crash. Their correspondence indicates that the majority of Pound's political and economic concerns during the first half of the 1930s were clearly within the bounds of national debate. The letters, most of them from Pound, focus on a variety of issues, including postal censorship, passport regulations, copyright, child labor, working conditions, and the economic remedies proposed by C. H. Douglas and Silvio Gesell. There are indications the politically powerful Progressive Republican took a number of Pound's concerns seriously, and in 1935 the latter contributed seventeen items to a column titled *Ez Sez* that appeared only in Cutting's newspaper the Santa Fe *New Mexican*. Pound saw in Cutting a possible Social Credit candidate for president, and he refers to the senator in *Guide to Kulchur* and quotes him in Cantos 86, 98, and 102.

Bibliography

Lowitt, Richard. *Bronson M. Cutting: Progressive Politician*. Albuquerque: U of New Mexico P, 1992.

Surette, Leon. *Pound in Purgatory: From Economic Radicalism to Anti-Semitism*. Urbana: U of Illinois P, 1999.

Walkiewicz, E. P., and Hugh Witemeyer, eds. *Ezra Pound and Senator Bronson Cutting: A Political Correspondence 1930–1935*. Albuquerque: U of New Mexico P, 1995.

E. P. Walkiewicz

D

Dance

After seeing a Fred Astaire movie in Venice, Pound was inspired to dance all the way home, and since he continued to dance after arriving home, he had to be reminded of the neighbors before he would desist. Although observers as well as opponents attest to Pound's lack of coordination in tennis and fencing, Pound enjoyed spontaneity in movement unlike the military drilling that he could not stand at Cheltenham Military Academy in his early youth.

However, his interest in dance extended to the form making of the art. Pound's acquaintance with Michio Ito, who performed in Yeats's "At the Hawk's Well," inspired him to design a dance sequence named *The Birth of the Dragon, a choreograph* (Carpenter 224). Ito's biographer insists, however, that Ito never made a public spectacle of himself in front of the cage where hawks were confined at the London Zoo. "Ito's decorum never forsook him. . . . Further . . . he did not create dances by dancing them but rather by thinking, imagining, visualizing, meditating" (Caldwell 164).

Indeed, Terpsichore should be counted among Pound's muses whom he acknowledged when he wrote, "Poetry is a centaur. The thinking word-arranging, clarifying faculty must move and leap with the energizing, sentient, musical faculties" (*LE* 52); and, more emphatically, "Music begins to atrophy when it departs too far from the dance . . . poetry begins to atrophy when it gets too far from music."

Not only his personal enjoyment of dance but dance itself remained in his memory in old age. Olga Rudge wrote of dancing with Pound to Vivaldi on the gramophone—"His idea!" (Conover 240). Rudge also recorded a dream Pound had of her "dancing in a window." When she asked, "What kind of dancing," he replied, "Oh, that Ceylonese bending" (Conover 240). Pound would have been aware of the popular appeal of dances from India and Southeast Asia in both amateur and professional performance in America and Europe. But Pound was also alert to the interest in dances from exotic cultures brought about in large part by the popularity of Diaghilev's Russian ballet and its designer, Leon Bakst, to whose "stage scene" he refers in "Our Respectful Homages to M. Laurent Tailhade." Moreover, Pound recognized that the Russian dancers provided a litmus test for bourgeois sensibility as demonstrated in his poem "Les Millwin" (1913), whose title sardonically refers to the ballet tradition of French nomenclature: "The little Millwins attend the Russian Ballet. / The mauve and greenish souls of the little Millwins / Were seen lying along the upper seats / Like so many unused boas." In contrast, "art students— / Exulted they beheld the splendours of *Cleopatra* (one of *The Three Erotic Ballets*)," while "the little Millwins . . . / With their large and anaemic eyes . . . looked out upon this configuration."

While Pound was scarcely a balletomane, he praised Pavlova not only in his poem "The Garret" in 1913 ("Dawn enters with little feet / like a gilded Pavlova") but also in a review in *Athenaeum* in 1920 when he wrote of "her own delicate and very personal comment of emotion upon the choreographic lines of Fokine which won her the myriad hearts." Reflecting on sexual mores, Pound commented, "The Russian dancers present their splendid, luxurious paganism, and everyone with a pre-Raphaelite or Swinburnian education is in raptures. What 'morality' will be like in two hundred years hence is beyond all prediction" (*SP* 103). For Pound dance was the primal art.

Bibliography

Caldwell, Helen. *Michio Ito: The Dancer and His Dances*. Berkeley: U of California P, 1977.
Conover, Anne. *Olga Rudge and Ezra Pound: "What Thou Lovest Well . . ."* New Haven: Yale UP, 2001.

Evelyn Haller

Davenport, Guy (b. 1927)

Guy Mattison Davenport, Jr., to whom Hugh Kenner refers in *The Pound Era* as "polumetis," published some of the first essays arguing for Pound's preeminent place in the Modernist canon. Davenport visited Pound at St. Elizabeths Hospital from 1952 until 1957 and, as Archibald MacLeish's graduate assistant at Harvard, helped to gather the signatures of Frost, Hemingway, and Eliot in 1957 for the influential letter sent to the attorney general asking for Pound's release.

Essayist, short-story writer, translator of ancient Greek poetry, graphic artist, and teacher, Davenport was born in Anderson, South Carolina. He received his B.A. from Duke University in 1948, attended Oxford as a Rhodes Scholar from 1948 to 1950, and earned a Ph.D. at Harvard in 1961. His dissertation "Cities on Hills: A Study of I–XXX of Ezra Pound's Cantos" was published in 1983. He taught at Washington University, at Haverford College, and from 1963 until his retirement in 1991, at the University of Kentucky.

Davenport's first publication on Pound was "Pound and Frobenius" in *Motive and Method in the Cantos of Ezra Pound* (1954). He has published essays on Pound in various journals. *The Geography of the Imagination* (1981), containing many fine essays on one of Davenport's favorite subjects, High Modernism, includes four essays specifically about Pound. Referring to Pound, Joyce, Picasso, Stravinsky, and others, Davenport argues, "What is most modern in our

time frequently turns out to be the most archaic." In the collection of stories *Da Vinci's Bicycle* (1979), "Ithaka" includes an account of Davenport's visit with Pound in Rapallo in 1963.

Davenport gave the inaugural lecture at the Beinecke Library on the founding of its center for Pound Studies in 1975. His drawings appear in, for example, his books of fiction, books by Hugh Kenner, and on the covers of *Paideuma* and the *Kenyon Review*. He was awarded a MacArthur Fellowship in 1991.

Bibliography

Crane, Joan. *Guy Davenport: A Descriptive Bibliography, 1947–1995*. Haverford: Green Shade, 1996.
Davenport, Guy. *Cities on Hills: A Study of I–XXX of Ezra Pound's Cantos*. Ann Arbor: UMI, 1983.
———. *Da Vinci's Bicycle*. Baltimore: Johns Hopkins UP, 1979.
———. *Every Force Evolves a Form*. San Francisco: North Point P, 1987.
———. *The Geography of the Imagination*. San Francisco: North Point P, 1981.

Robert Merritt

Davie, Donald (1922–1995)

British poet, critic, and a leading member of the 1950s "Movement," Davie lived and taught in the United Kingdom, Ireland, and the United States. Asked by Reuben Brower to interpret Pound "for the common man," he wrote *Ezra Pound: Poet as Sculptor* (1964), a lucid reading of Pound's poetry, prose and translations considered chronologically through *Thrones*. Among the most influential early Pound studies, the book examines formal technique—the juxtaposed diction/imagery as verbal/visual discoveries, the reconstituted verse-line whose "surge" slows down reading yet allows different "perceptions" to follow quickly—to critique Pound's aesthetic and social vision. In his memoirs, Davie calls *The Cantos* a "contraption" that "fascinated and exasperated" him for years. Other works include *Ezra Pound* (1975), a series of essays that wrestle with questions ranging from *The Cantos'* rhythms to the ethics behind Pound's drive to create a literary civilization; *Studies in Ezra Pound* (1991), which collects

Poet as Sculptor with eleven later essays; and some half dozen poems, with one imagining Pound at Pisa, another invoking "Ole Uncle Ez, the crustiest sort / Of Yankee at King Arthur's Court." Though he often explores Pound's relation to continental and American writers, Davie's major contributions are his "pedestrian" investigations of individual works, where he scrutinizes both "*res*" and "*verba*," what the poetry presents and how it is said, in order to illuminate Pound's achievement.

Bibliography

Davie, Donald. *Collected Poems*. Chicago: U of Chicago P, 1990. Expanded ed. Ed. Nel Powell. Manchester: Carcanet, 2002.

———. *Ezra Pound*. Chicago: U of Chicago P, 1975.

———. *Ezra Pound: Poet as Sculptor*. New York: Oxford UP, 1964.

———. *Studies in Ezra Pound*. Manchester: Carcanet, 1991.

———. *These the Companions: Recollections*. Cambridge: Cambridge UP, 1982.

John Gery

Des Imagistes

Des Imagistes was the name Pound gave to the first Imagist anthology, edited by him and published in New York in 1914. It included much of Pound's poetry of the Imagist type, along with the poetry of ten other poets and writers he admired. The title implied a connection with the earlier French poetic school known as Les Symbolistes, a group of highly diverse but gifted poets who started what would come to be called Modern poetry. Pound understood that Imagism was rooted in Symbolism as a poetic theory and wanted to stress the connectedness of French and English poetic movements, since he was always trying to promote a new Renaissance that would equal the earlier European Renaissance as an international and interlingual rebirth of artistic greatness. However, in choosing the works to be included in *Des Imagistes*, he was not only publicizing a new poetic school but also promoting the best writers he knew. *Des Imagistes* brought together such diverse literary artists as James Joyce and Ford Madox Ford along with William Carlos Williams and H. D.

All were gifted writers, but all were not necessarily Imagist poets.

Pound deftly arranged the eleven poets in *Des Imagistes* to place the Imagists first, so that the anthology served its primary purpose of presenting the new poetic school of Imagism in its most favorable light. Richard Aldington was awarded first place and also the largest selection of poems in the book: ten in all, beginning with "Lesbia," one of Pound's favorites and a style-setting Imagist poem, which ends with the arresting line, "You morsel left half cold on Caesar's plate"—actually a line he distilled from Anthony's words to Cleopatra in Shakespeare's play, "I found you as a morsel cold upon / Dead Caesar's trencher." H. D. was awarded seven poems, including those Pound had used for her debut as an *Imagiste*: "Hermes of the Ways," "Priapus," and "Epigram," lyrics echoing the *Greek Anthology*. Then came F. S. Flint with five poems, among them his definitive Imagist portrait of "The Swan"; Skipwith Cannell with six "Nocturnes"; Amy Lowell with "In a Garden"; William Carlos Williams with "Postlude"; and James Joyce with "I Hear an Army Charging," already published in his *Chamber Music*. Pound chose six of his own poems, most of them with a definite Imagist stamp: "Δώρια" (from the Classical Greek), "The Return" (from Henri de Régnier, a minor French Symbolist), and four classic Chinese poems, "After Ch'u Yuan," "Liu Ch'e," "Fan-Piece for her Imperial Lord," and "Ts'ai Chi." Thus Pound demonstrated that Imagism derived from a wide variety of earlier poetic styles, foreign as well as English. He rounded out the anthology with Ford Madox Ford's "In the Little Old Market-Place," Allen Upward's "Scented Leaves from a Chinese Jar," and John Cournos's "The Rose."

It seems clear that Pound's intention was for *Des Imagistes* to be the vanguard of a new poetic movement, and he achieved his aim, since it remains the best of the four anthologies produced during the Imagist decade, the other three being Amy Lowell's editions of *Some Imagist Poets*, limited to six poets of her choosing who were allowed to publish whatever they liked, Imagist or not. By incorporating Joyce and Ford,

Pound deliberately extended the range of Imagism beyond a narrow coterie of poets, while keeping the literary quality high. As it turned out, *Des Imagistes* proved to be both a beginning and an end of Imagism for Pound.

William Pratt

Dial

Soon after Scofield Thayer and James Watson took over the operation of the *Dial* at the end of 1919, they were urged by T. S. Eliot and John Quinn to engage Ezra Pound as a correspondent for the magazine in Europe. In addition to his annual salary of $750, Pound was for a time able to print his own poetry and prose, and the *Dial* helped promote both Eliot's *The Waste Land* and James Joyce's *Ulysses*. But Pound's influence waned after the first year, and he was soon represented only by a regular column, a "Paris Letter" that began appearing after the poet settled in France. Thayer tired of Pound's proselytizing style, and the poet was replaced in 1923. After Marianne Moore joined the editorial staff in the mid-1920s, Pound's relationship with the magazine was reestablished, and subsequently he was awarded the $2,000 Dial Award for 1927.

Bibliography

Joost, Nicholas. *Scofield Thayer and the Dial*. Carbondale: Southern Illinois UP, 1964.

Pound, Ezra. *Pound, Thayer, Watson, and the Dial: A Story in Letters*. Ed. Walter Sutton. Gainesville: UP of Florida, 1994.

Craig Monk

Diptych Rome-London

Published in 1958 in a luxury limited edition, *Diptych Rome-London* consists of two long poems that had appeared separately about thirty years earlier: *Homage to Sextus Propertius* and *Hugh Selwyn Mauberley*. These are Ezra Pound's longest poetic series outside *The Cantos*. Both poems address the problem of the artist in a civilization in decline, and *Diptych* may have represented Pound's disappointment in the two cities that framed his career. *Propertius* and *Mauberley* are natural companion pieces, and Pound's publication of them soon after his release from St. Elizabeths may have been intended to prove his enduring worth as a poet following the controversy over his having been awarded in 1949 the Bollingen Prize for *The Pisan Cantos*.

Bibliography

Litz, A. Walton. "Introduction." *Diptych Rome-London*. New York: New Directions, 1994. 1–6.

Patricia A. Cockram

Discretions: Ezra Pound, Father and Teacher

Pound's devoted daughter Mary de Rachewiltz published this autobiographical memoir in 1971. One of the few truly indispensable background books, it presents "several realities playing in counterpoint": the story of the author's own unusual and highly independent life; the story of Pound's life as it impinged on and profoundly influenced her; together with a vivid personal record of peasant life in the Tyrol and of an experience of the 1939–1945 war in the Tyrol and northern Italy. Mary, born 9 July 1925 in Bressanone to Olga Rudge and Pound, and named Maria Rudge, was brought up by foster parents on their farm in the Pustertal. Apart from 1941–1943 when she lived with her parents above Rapallo, that was her home until she married Boris de Rachewiltz, and they made their home in Schloss Brunnenburg, Tirolo di Merano. Her education, however, was overseen by her parents and most influentially by Pound. He formed her outlook (see "Laws for Maria" 69–70); directed her studies; and trained her as a writer and translator. Well pleased with her, he wanted her to be his literary heir and executor. Her memoir is as he taught her a work of art should be, "nothing superfluous, nothing wasted, nothing sloppy." It deals in the significant detail of what she knows at firsthand with a contemplative objectivity. *Discretions* contains a good deal of illuminating information about *The Cantos* as well as about Pound as father, educator, poet, propagandist, and prisoner. The flavor throughout is of the author's own original and intensely passionate intelligence. The work amounts to a double portrait of father and daughter, which brings to mind Pound's definition of the Chinese character *Ming*[2]: "The sun and moon, the total light process, the radiation, reception and reflection of light; hence the intelligence" (*Confucius* 20).

A. David Moody

Dolmetsch, Arnold (1858–1940)

Arnold Dolmetsch, a musicologist, through meticulous editing of musical texts and reconstruction of authentic instruments, demonstrated to the modern era the profound significance of preclassical composers such as John Jenkins, William Lawes, and François Couperin. Dolmetsch was one of the first musical influences on Ezra Pound, who was involved with music in one way or another for most of his life.

Pound, formulating his personal critical agenda in London between 1910 and 1920, assimilated many of the qualities of the music of the sixteenth and seventeenth centuries into an aesthetic that he applied to literature, music, and the visual arts. Pound valued especially (1) the effect of medium on overall meaning; (2) "impersonality"; (3) concentration; (4) a fundamental tension between chaos and regularity; (5) the value of sharp, distinct form; and (6) a moral connection between art and society. When Pound said "poetry begins to atrophy when it gets too far from music" (*ABCR* 14), much of what he meant by "music" he learned from Dolmetsch.

Born in Le Mans, France, Dolmetsch was at fourteen repairing keyboard instruments in his father's workshop. From 1885 to 1889, he taught violin at Dulwich College and published arrangements of music by Corelli, Handel, and Purcell. In 1889, Dolmetsch restored a viola d'amore and discovered that the abundant viol music of the Elizabethans had been stored undisturbed for nearly 300 years, much of it in the British Museum. Dolmetsch's concert on 21 November 1890 was the first instance in modern times of sixteenth-century music being played on the instruments for which it was written.

Dolmetsch built his first lute in 1893, his first clavichord in 1894, and at the suggestion of William Morris, his first harpsichord in 1896. He made harpsichords, clavichords, lutes, and viols for Chickering and Sons in Boston from 1905 to 1911, and he worked for the Gaveau piano company in Paris from 1911 to 1914. He returned to England and published *The Interpretation of the Music of the XVIIth and XVIIIth Centuries* in 1915, which, according to *Grove's Dictionary*, is "still a landmark." Dolmetsch moved to Haslemere in 1917 and established a school and workshop, where he, his wife, and their four children gave chamber concerts, often in Elizabethan costume. In 1914, Pound heard Florence Farr recite poems accompanying herself on a psaltery Dolmetsch had built for Yeats, visited Dolmetsch at Haslemere, and commissioned a clavichord upon which he later composed much of the music for his opera *Le Testament de Villon*.

Pound published four essays specifically about Dolmetsch (see Schafer). The first, published on 7 January 1915, discusses a Dolmetsch concert. Three others, published in July and August of 1917, comment on *The Interpretation of the Music of the XVIIth and XVIIIth Centuries.* Pound, discovering that in old music rhythm could be measured by quantity and duration, concluded "simply that vers libre existed in old music." Also in the summer of 1917, Pound published in *Poetry* the preliminary versions of the first three cantos, in which he wrote: "Dolmetsch will build our age in witching music."

Dolmetsch continued to be important to Pound throughout his life. Pound recalled the world of early music while he was incarcerated for treason at Pisa in 1945, careful to identify explicitly the old instruments in the "libretto" of Canto 81:

> Has he tempered the viols wood
> To enforce both the grave and the acute?
> Has he curved us the bowl of the lute?
> *Lawes and Jenkyns guard thy rest*
> *Dolmetsch ever be thy guest.*

Back in Italy in 1959, Pound still was somehow in possession of the clavichord Dolmetsch had built for him in 1915. He wrote to Dolmetsch's son for some new strings, got them, and planned to have a clavichord built for Omar.

The two men shared characteristics that affected the way they were accepted by the public. Both men were committed to making knowledge from the past available to the present, but they could not muster sufficient respect for or from the professional scholars who could have helped to give their projects respectability and larger audiences. They both wanted to teach but were unable consistently to get their messages to a culture uncommitted to the belief that poetry and music, precisely and honestly rendered, were essential to its well-being.

Bibliography

Campbell, Margaret. *Dolmetsch: The Man and His Work.* Seattle: U of Washington P, 1975.

Haskell, Harry. *The Early Music Revival: A History.* London: Thames and Hudson, 1988.

Luckett, Richard. "Meaning and Motion: Old Music and Some Modern Writers." *Essays and Studies* 30 (1970): 88–91.

Merritt, Robert. *Early Music and the Aesthetics of Ezra Pound: Hush of Older Song.* Lewiston: Edwin Mellen P, 1993.

Schafer, R. Murray, ed. *Ezra Pound and Music: The Complete Criticism.* New York: New Directions, 1977.

Robert Merritt

Doolittle, Hilda (1886–1961)

Born in 1886 in Bethlehem, Pennsylvania, the daughter of an astronomer father and a musical, mystical mother, Hilda Doolittle grew up "in the penumbra of the light of my father's science and my mother's art." As an undergraduate at Bryn Mawr College near Philadelphia, she formed close friendships with Marianne Moore, William Carlos Williams, and most notably, Ezra Pound, to whom she was briefly engaged. When she traveled to Europe in 1911 for a planned four-month visit that would end up lasting a lifetime, it was Pound who introduced her to the London literary circles in which she would play a prominent role. And it was Pound who, in the British Museum tea shop in 1912, famously scrawled "H. D. Imagiste" on a sheaf of her poems before shipping them off with an enthusiastic cover letter to Harriet Monroe at *Poetry*, thus simultaneously creating her new literary moniker and sponsoring her first publication. H. D.'s fraught relationship with Pound during those early years is recorded in several autobiographical novels, including *Her, Bid Me to Live*, and *Asphodel*.

Pound's "Imagiste" label has stuck to H. D. ever since, despite the fact that even her earliest poetry frequently resists such a narrow categorization. Pound praised her work as "direct—no excessive use of adjectives, no metaphors that won't permit examination. It's straight talk, straight as the Greek!" (*L* 11). But H. D.'s poems from the 1910s and 1920s are seldom as spare, crystalline, and "direct" as Pound's propaganda might indicate, and their classical Greek setting masks only very thinly their references to contemporary situations. Poems such as "Sea Garden" and "Oread" depict harsh, combative landscapes that seethe with emotional intensity: "Whirl up, seas— / whirl your pointed pines, / splash your great pines / on our rocks, / hurl your green over us, / cover us with your pools of fir" (Pearson, x). And "Eurydice," far from merely echoing classical accounts of the Orpheus myth, offers a feminist rebuttal to a seemingly romantic but, in H. D.'s view, deeply misogynist tale. Biographically, "Eurydice" can be read as H. D.'s anguished response both to the marital infidelities of Richard Aldington, the British poet whom she had married in 1913, and to the poetic arrogance of her close friend D. H. Lawrence, who admired her poetry but advised her to "stick to the woman speaking." Explicated in more universal terms, the poem expresses the rage and bitterness of an articulate female poet relegated by patriarchal society to the role of a silent muse.

By the early 1930s, although she would remain best known for her finely crafted lyric poetry, H. D. was actively working to redefine herself as a writer, producing novels, short stories, essays, book reviews, and translations of Greek drama. With her lifelong companion Bryher (Winifred Ellerman), the wealthy British novelist who had "rescued" her in 1919 from her failed marriage to Aldington, she became involved in avant-garde filmmaking, contributing regularly to Bryher's film journal *Close-Up*, and acting in experimental films such as Kenneth MacPherson's *Borderline*, in which she shared star billing with fellow expatriate American Paul Robeson. In 1933 and again in 1934, thanks largely to Bryher's influence and affluence,

H. D. traveled to Vienna to undergo several months of intensive daily psychoanalysis with Sigmund Freud. Freud's sympathetic encouragement, together with her own revisionist reading of his masculinist analytic theories, equipped her with the self-confidence to regard several unexplained visionary experiences from her past not as dangerous "symptoms" of psychic derangement but as evidence of special poetic powers. Decades later, Pound would criticize her idealization of Freud: "You got into the wrong pig stye, ma chère." But H. D. took a very different view, granting "the Master" direct credit for helping her develop a new poetic voice: "And it was he himself, he who set me free / to prophesy."

With the advent of World War II, H. D. moved back to London (she and Bryher had been living primarily in Switzerland) and began to "prophesy" in earnest. Throughout the 1930s, she had been reading extensively in Moravian mysticism, astrology, alchemy, and other occultist lore, some of which she was already familiar with through her youthful friendship with Pound. In the early 1940s, she joined the London Society for Psychical Research, attended lectures on Spiritualism, and took part in a weekly séance circle. Her spiritualist and occult interests served as the crucible, and the war itself as the catalyst (to borrow her own alchemistic vocabulary), for some of H. D.'s finest and most complex work, including *The Gift* (1944), a mystical novel/memoir about her childhood; *Tribute to Freud* (1956), a lyrical, multilayered meditation on her psychoanalytic sessions in Vienna; and *Trilogy* (1942–1944), a long, visionary poem in which she perceives mystical symbols of regeneration amidst the ruins of Blitz-torn London.

Following the war, H. D. returned to Switzerland, where she composed such major works as *Helen in Egypt*, a revisionist, feminist epic that many critics consider her greatest masterpiece, and *Hermetic Definition*, an impressionistic long poem about spiritual desire and fulfillment. She also undertook a series of retrospective projects, revising long-abandoned earlier works and penning several intricate memoirs, including

End to Torment: A Memoir of Ezra Pound. Written in 1958 but first published in 1979, with the poems of Pound's 1907 *Hilda's Book* as an appendix, *End to Torment* weaves together H. D.'s youthful memories of Pound; her recollections of their occasional correspondence and encounters through the years; a daily record of her own limited existence as an elderly sanatorium patient recuperating from a bad fall; and her ruminations on poetry, politics, and the symbolic significance of Pound's just-announced release from St. Elizabeths: "The prison actually of the Self," she writes, "was dramatized or materialized for our generation by Ezra's incarceration."

H. D. died in 1961, one year after receiving the Gold Medal from the American Academy of Arts and Letters for her contributions to American poetry. Since then, and especially since the publication of her *Collected Poems* in 1983, her work and reputation have enjoyed an extraordinary renaissance, resulting in the publication or reissuance of many previously unavailable poems, novels, stories, and memoirs. To remember her solely as "H. D. Imagiste," noted Hugh Kenner in 1972, is "as though five of the shortest pieces in *Harmonium* were to stand for the life's work of Wallace Stevens." Today, few readers would be likely to make such an error.

Bibliography

Guest, Barbara. *Herself Defined: The Poet H. D. and Her World*. New York: Doubleday, 1984.

H. D. *Collected Poems, 1912–1944*. Ed. Louis L. Martz. New York: New Directions, 1983.

———. *End to Torment: A Memoir of Ezra Pound*. Ed. Norman Holmes Pearson and Michael King. New York: New Directions, 1979.

———. *The Gift*. [1944]; published as *The Gift by H. D.* Ed. June Augustine. Gainesville: UP of Florida, 1998.

———. *Tribute to Freud*. New York: New Directions, 1984.

———. *Trilogy*. New York: New Directions, 1973.

Korg, Jacob. *Winter Love: Ezra Pound and H. D.* Madison: U of Wisconsin P, 2003.

Pearson. Norman H. "Foreword." H. D., *Tribute to Freud*. New York: New Directions, 1984.

Helen Sword

Douglas, Major Clifford Hugh (1879–1952)

Born in Scotland, Douglas worked "as Chief Reconstruction Engineer for the British Westinghouse Company in India, as Deputy Chief Engineer for the Buenos Aires and Pacific Railway Company in South America, as Railway Engineer for the London Post Office (tube) Railway," and during World War I, as Assistant Director of the Royal Aircraft Works at Farnborough (Kenner 301). But Douglas is best known for his work as an economist and as the inventor of Social Credit, a scheme of economic reform that promised to democratize credit and to create economic justice through a fairer distribution of goods. This was to be accomplished by revising the meaning of money itself, by basing its value not on gold but on the social credit manifest in the heritage of industrial and cultural techniques.

Douglas is an economist poised between the great expanding industrial world of steam and steel of the nineteenth century and the dawning age of consumer capitalism. He was one of the first thinkers to see that consumer goods must become the engine of economic growth and that the older canons of value, which stressed saving and endless toil as the basis of virtue, were not only bound to fail but must be overcome to avoid the collapse of capitalism itself.

During World War I, Douglas oversaw production of airplanes for the Royal Flying Corps. He noticed that "war is a consumer whose necessities are so imperative they become superior to all questions of legal and financial restriction" (*Social Credit* 134). Under wartime conditions, "finance has to follow production instead of, as is the normal case, production having to follow finance" (135). Douglas realized that "immediately [as] production is expanded at anything like its possible rate, the idea that the financial costs of the expansion can be recovered in prices is seen in its full absurdity" (135–136). In fact, it appeared that prices could never recoup the putative costs of production.

Douglas described this structural contradiction in his "A + B theorem" (read by Pound virtually verbatim into Canto 38). Douglas divided the payments made by factories—what economists now call the "income stream"—into two groups:

Group A—All payments made to individuals (wages, salaries and dividends).
Group B—All payments made to other organizations (raw materials, bank charges, and other external costs).

The substance of this critique of "the present system" is based on the following formulation of the interrelationship and meaning of these two groups:

Now *the rate of flow of purchasing power to individuals is represented by A, but since all payments go into prices, the rate of flow of prices cannot be less than A + B. The product of any factory may be considered as something which the public ought to be able to buy, although in many cases it is an intermediate product of no use to individuals but only to a subsequent manufacture; but since A will not purchase A + B, a proportion of the product as at least equivalent to B must be distributed by a form of purchasing power which is not comprised in the descriptions grouped under A. . . .* [T]his additional purchasing power is provided by loan-credit (bank overdrafts) or export credit. (*Economic Democracy* 21–22; Douglas's emphasis)

It is clear that "the external factor," credit (23), stands between the product and the purchaser. Credit finances both the production of the means of production and those consumer goods and wages created by production (A + B). Because they are all produced by borrowed money, the money we buy them with goes to extinguish the debt; but it itself is derived from credits that have been borrowed by banks, and consequently its value must reappear in selling prices somewhere. "They must be recovered again from the consumer [in the form of taxes] if the banks are to be repaid their advances. *It is clear therefore, that one credit is only cancelled by the creation of another larger credit* (*Economic Democracy* 22; my emphasis). Credit, in Douglas's account, wields a despotic power over the distribution of purchasing power by continuously sucking value out of the system in the form of profits and taxes. Under such a system, bank credit—that is, the price paid for access to money—determines prices. Thus aggregate prices will always be higher on average than aggregate purchasing power: The consequence is poverty. Douglas concluded that private bank credit produced poverty as surely as it underwrote more "efficient" productive capacity.

Douglas's remedy was to alter the basis of credit and thus to alter the nature and meaning of money. Money, he argued, should function only as a means of exchange, *not* as a measure of value. The "money problem," he wrote, "*is not a problem of value measurement. The proper function of a money system is to control and direct the production of goods and services.* As 'effective demand,' a money system is, or should be, an 'order' system, not a 'reward' system" (*Social Credit* 61–62; Douglas's emphasis). Money should act as an effect, not a cause. Money ought to function much like a railway ticket, which "distributes transportation" (62). A bank should be like a railroad's ticket department; its "proper business" should be "to facilitate the distribution of the product in accordance with the desires of the public and to transmit the indications of those desires to those operating the industrial organization, to whom is committed the task of meeting them" (*Social Credit* 63).

Putting himself beyond the pale of economic orthodoxy of the time by contradicting Say's Law, Douglas showed that "purchasing power is not, as might be gathered from the current discussion of the subject, an emanation from the production of real commodities or services much like the scent from a rose, but, on the contrary, is produced by an entirely distinct process . . . the banking system" (*Social Credit* 23).

A reform of the banking system resulting in its democratization was, therefore, the remedy. Money was to be limited to the means of exchange; it was not to represent a store of value. In short, money should be the sign of production, not of credit. A unit of money ought to be a share of the gross national product—its aggregate book price. This sort of money simply measures a "fraction" of "material assets," the "price" of which is a function of its potential quantity. Such money is a ration ticket, demystified of its claims

to be wealth (*Social Credit* 132). So conceived, money cannot be a measure of value in things; rather, the *potential* production of things ("useful productive capacity") would determine the value of money. Douglas equates financial wealth with material assets and *prospective production*—not actual production. Douglas seems to mean that money signifies real capital + credit, assuming credit is based on the social credit embodied in productive potential, *not* on bank debts.

Social Credit, then, insofar as it measures prospective production, must be the sum of past knowledge and technique. Social credit is cultural and technical capital. As such, it belongs to no one and everyone; it is the shared heritage of all. This cultural wealth should be distributed to all. Rather than collecting taxes—in effect, forcing people to pay for access to social benefits, including money—governments should distribute money as a social dividend based on the social credit of the society.

Douglas met A. R. Orage, then a guild socialist, in 1918 and converted him to his social credit scheme to democratize capitalism. With Orage's able editorial help, Douglas's books began to appear in serial installments in *New Age* from 1919 onward. Pound met Douglas in the *New Age* offices at this time. Eventually Social Credit became an international movement. It was adopted by the Scottish National Party and achieved electoral (if not practical) successes in Canada and New Zealand. A Social Credit Party governed in Alberta, Canada, from 1935 to 1971, and the party had success in British Columbia as well. In New Zealand a Social Credit Party was elected in 1935. The American Social Credit Movement (ASCM), founded by the literary critic Gorham Munson, was active in the later 1930s, when Orage himself was in New York. William Carlos Williams and Jean Toomer were two U.S. writers involved.

Unfortunately, Douglas lacked any political skills. He was an inarticulate man, touchy and doctrinaire in his ideas. Much to Pound's consternation, he failed to form alliances with other non–Social Credit constituencies of economic reformers. A meeting with U.S. congressional figures in 1935, organized by Senator Bronson

Cutting, was anticlimactic because of Douglas's reticence. When the Rev. William Aberhart was elected on a Social Credit platform in Alberta in 1935, he invited Douglas to work as his economic adviser; but Douglas refused. (Pound offered to go in his place.)

Though Social Credit as such is not anti-Semitic, Douglas was himself a Christian anti-Semite, as were some of his fellow travelers, notably Arthur Kitson and, much later, Pound himself. Now a right-wing fringe movement, Social Credit has become associated with anti-Semitism and fascism; but in its essence, the movement is as antifascist as it is anticommunist.

Social Credit is still a fringe party in Canada, so Major Douglas's books are still in print. The most important of these are *Economic Democracy* (1919) and *Social Credit* (1924).

Bibliography

Bush, Ronald. *The Genesis of Ezra Pound's Cantos.* Princeton: Princeton UP, 1976.

Douglas, C. H. *Economic Democracy.* London: Institute of Economic Democracy, 1919.

———. *The Monopoly of Credit.* London: Chapman and Hall, 1931.

———. *Social Credit.* 1924. Vancouver: Institute of Economic Democracy, 1979.

Kenner, Hugh. *The Pound Era.* Berkeley: U of California P, 1971.

Marsh, Alec. *Money and Modernity: Pound, Williams, and the Spirit of Jefferson.* Tuscaloosa: U of Alabama P, 1998.

Redman, Tim. *Ezra Pound and Italian Fascism.* New York: Cambridge UP, 1991.

Sieburth, Richard. *Instigations: Ezra Pound and Remy de Gourmont.* Cambridge: Harvard UP, 1978.

Surette, Leon. *A Light from Eleusis: A Study of Ezra Pound's Cantos.* Oxford: Clarendon P, 1979.

———. *Pound in Purgatory: From Economic Radicalism to Anti-Semitism.* Urbana: U of Illinois P, 1999.

Alec Marsh

Dudek, Louis (1918–2001)

Canada's preeminent Modernist poet, critic, and cultural worker, Louis Dudek was born on 6 February 1918 in east-end Montreal of immigrant parents. After graduating from McGill University in 1939, Dudek began a lifelong commitment to small magazines, teaming up with Irving Layton, John Sutherland, and Raymond Souster to modernize Canadian poetry. From those beginnings in the early 1940s, Dudek went on to become the dean of Canadian small-press publishing, launching many of the well-known poets in Canada in the 1950s and 1960s and establishing himself as one of the country's finest poets.

Dudek began a close study of Ezra Pound's aestheticism while at Columbia University in 1943, and after a year of correspondence, the two met at St. Elizabeths in 1950. A steady flow of letters continued until 1953 and then slowly declined. Dudek's importance is in his close application of Poundian dicta to remaking Canadian poetry. Among Canadians, only Dudek possessed Pound's energy for cultural reorganization and his zeal to evoke the beautiful in history and civilization.

Bibliography

Davey, Frank. *Louis Dudek & Raymond Souster.* SCL #14. Vancouver: Douglas & McIntyre, 1980.

Goldie, Terry. *Louis Dudek and His Works.* Toronto: ECW P, n.d.

Pound, Ezra. *Dk/Some Letters of Ezra Pound.* Ed. Louis Dudek. Montreal: DC Books, 1974.

Tremblay, Tony. "Git yur / eye off Canada / and into internat criteria /': Exploring the Influence of Ezra Pound on the Cultural Production of Louis Dudek." *Essays on Canadian Writing* 74 (Fall 2001): 26–52.

Tony Tremblay

Duncan, Robert (1919–1988)

The poet was born Edward Howard Duncan, in 1919, in Oakland, California, and first published under his adopted name, Robert Edward Symmes. But Robert Duncan claimed his poetic birthright from Ezra Pound and H. D. Like Pound's, his poems are revelations of a Catholic learning; like H. D.'s, they are hermetic inquiries into the condition of love. Among his contemporaries, including Charles Olson, Robert Creeley, and Denise Levertov, Duncan is unique for his practice of the gnostic traditions stemming from Pound and H. D. *The H. D. Book*, his meditation on the literary inheritance from the lives and texts of H. D. and Pound, was lovingly published chapter by chapter in small magazines over the years.

Duncan first read Pound's *A Draft of XXX Cantos* while briefly a student at the University of California at Berkeley. Quitting school to pursue a lover, a male instructor he met at Berkeley, Duncan was drawn to a commune, in Woodstock, New York, where the *Phoenix*, a magazine dedicated to the work of D. H. Lawrence, was being produced. His work as a contributing editor brought him into the circle of Anaïs Nin. He was drafted into military service in 1941 but sent home from boot camp because of his homosexuality. His subsequent position statement, "The Homosexual in Society" (1944), is his most important early publication. He returned to Berkeley following the printing of his first book of poems, *Heavenly City, Earthly City* (1947). His first success with the serial poem came in 1947, when he wrote *Medieval Scenes*, ten poems written over ten consecutive evenings. In 1948, Duncan wrote his breakthrough poem "The Venice Poem" in which he can be seen to practice what he and Charles Olson would later call an "open field" poetry.

That same year, Duncan hitchhiked once again across the country—this time to visit Pound at St. Elizabeths. Two years later, he wrote the first of his many letters to H. D., mostly describing his audience with Pound. (The letters of H. D. and Duncan have been edited by Robert Bertholf.) Back in California, Duncan gradually supplanted Kenneth Rexroth as the central figure in what would be known as the San Francisco Renaissance. Robert Cree-ley's Divers Press printed Duncan's *Caesar's Gate* (1956) for its last book. In London, in January 1956, Duncan wrote the first version of his signature poem "Often I Am Permitted to Return to a Meadow." That spring, Olson invited Duncan to come to Black Mountain College to teach, replacing Creeley. It was at Black Mountain that Duncan wrote most of the poems that would be collected in *The Opening of the Field* (1960). The trilogy of books upon which his reputation rests was realized with the publication of *Roots and Branches* (1964) and *Bending the Bow* (1968).

A self-proclaimed "derivative poet," Duncan learned the collagist's art from his reading of Pound and through the painting of his longtime companion Jess Collins. In a major piece, "A Poem Beginning with a Line from Pindar," he creates one of his grandest collages from the story of Pound's internment at Pisa and the tale of Psyche sorting her seeds. Duncan's method, in the "Structure of Rime" and "Passages" series, was to arrange passages by collage and whole poems by series. This is a Postmodern master's response to the dilemmas of how to sustain the long poem and how to write a lyric of reference, first proposed by Duncan's reading of Pound's *The Cantos*, H. D.'s *The Walls Do Not Fall*, and William Carlos Williams's *Paterson*.

Bibliography

Bertholf, Robert J., ed. *A Great Admiration: H. D./ Robert Duncan Correspondence 1950–1961*. Venice: Lapis P, 1992.

Richard L. Blevins

E

Economics

Pound understood his intellectual mission as a delineation and critique of a "histoire morale contemporaine" through the medium of his long poem *The Cantos*. He not only aimed to "include history" in his poetry but also wanted to understand and represent the often secret or neglected underpinnings of historical developments. The political education he received from A. R. Orage in the offices of the magazine the *New Age* during and after World War I persuaded him that economics was a hidden current determining the flow of history. This is why, starting with *Eleven New Cantos* (1934), his poetry, together with his journalism and correspondence, took an economic and political turn. Pound started his involvement in economics as a disciple of C. H. Douglas and his theory of Social Credit. In the 1930s, however, he extended his field of interest to other programs of reform and tried through his poetry and journalism to make them known both to the literary community and to political and public opinion.

Pound met Major Douglas in the offices of the *New Age* in 1918. He was present at the conversations between Douglas and Orage and witness to the first expositions of Social Credit theory. Douglas's first series of articles in the *New Age* started in June 1919 and was republished in book form under the title *Economic Democracy* in 1920. Douglas had worked as an engineer in a Royal Air Force factory and observed that what purchasing power a factory distributed through wages, dividends, and profits was smaller than the price of the factory's product, since the latter also included other costs, not reflected in the wages: interest on bank credits, costs of materials and tools, junk and scrapped material. In Pound's words, "*that* company was creating prices FASTER than it gave out power to buy" (*Social Credit* 18). This observation was in stark contradiction to an axiom of classical economics called "Say's Law," which maintained that in a given economy aggregate demand would be able to buy the aggregate production (Surette 35). The system created a gap between prices and purchasing power, only temporarily bridged over by more loans, which in their turn raised prices and widened the gap, instead of closing it.

Douglas believed that it was a mistake to define wealth by current production, since the economic system relied on a mass of inventions that the community had been able to devise and use along its history. This accumulation, which Douglas called the "cultural heritage," was the basis of production. On the financial side, Douglas considered credit to be the money equivalent not simply of current economic activity but of this heritage plus new production. Credit therefore rightfully belonged to all the citizens of the community and not to a limited number of banks. Every individual had the right to benefit from the wealth of this accumulated heritage and would receive a "national dividend" by virtue of being a citizen. In the Social Credit system, the community itself would manage its finances through an agency called the National Credit Office, which would assess the wealth of the nation, watch the flow of assets and liabilities, and issue or cancel credit accordingly. Production would be tailored to meet the real needs of individuals, instead of creating goods that are not wanted and too expensive to the consumer. Douglas called these real needs "effective demand" and believed that both production and credit should be tailored to meet it. According to him, money should be issued in the same way as railway tickets and have the same neutral, distributive function.

Douglas's second important proposal, apart from the national dividend, was the "just price," a formula through which companies received a compensation from the National Credit Office to lower their prices to the consumer. Both measures, the national dividend as well as the just price, implied a change in the nature of money. Douglas's analysis entailed the abandonment of the gold standard, which in the 1920s was still operating in the liberal economies and international trade. In the Social Credit system, money was not to be backed by another commodity regarded as possessing intrinsic value but was to be fiat money; that is, it was to rely on the cultural heritage. Additionally, money was not to be conceived as interest bearing loans benefiting banks but as a political and administrative instrument whereby the community would distribute credit fairly. Pound took over these ideas from Douglas and centered his economics on the problem of just distribution. There was, however, a significant difference between them: Douglas was against the concentration of power, whether economic or political, and insisted on such terms as "community" and "decentralisation," while Pound, under the influence of fascist ideology, considered that "the state" is responsible for the issue and fair distribution of purchasing power.

Starting with 1933, Pound's pursuits took an economic turn: His basis was still Social Credit, but he added other theories to it in order to arrive at a more personal vision on the political function of money and the reforms necessary to correct the financial and hence the economic system.

A new element that Pound added to Douglasite economics in 1933 was Silvio Gesell's concept of "free money," a kind of currency that steadily lost a percentage of its value. The possessor of Gesell's kind of notes had to stick a stamp on them every week or month in order to restore them to their original denomination. Since the stamp was a kind of tax, this kind of money changed hands more quickly, thus offering a powerful incentive for consumption. The free money scheme had worked very well in a small town in Austria called Wörgl, from 1932 to 1933, when the central bank stopped it and put the mayor in prison. Pound referred to the Wörgl experiment in *The Cantos* (41, 74, and 78) and reviewed Gesell's *The Natural Economic Order* in the Social Credit organ, the *New English Weekly*, in January 1935. The Wörgl experiment had an international resonance, and versions of Gesell's money, called "stamp scrip" in America, were used in a number of towns in the Midwest in 1932 and 1933.

Gesell was particularly important to the way in which Pound came to regard the issue and distribution of money. By 1934 Pound had reached a formula in which Social Credit and Gesellite theory could be reconciled: He advocated the payment of the national dividend, taxes, civil works projects, and Social Security in stamp scrip. This money could be created by the state at minimal cost and was not an interest-bearing loan from banks; it circulated more quickly than normal money and could not be hoarded or rented at interest; and finally, it had an inbuilt mechanism through which it automatically canceled itself—hence, it could not lead to inflation.

For Pound, stamp scrip was antiusurious: While augmenting the money supply in the times of the depression, it radically disadvantaged the banks. Through this lens Pound observed and criticized President Franklin D. Roosevelt's New Deal policies. Roosevelt seemed to realize that the economic crisis of 1929–1933 was caused by a shortage of purchasing power that had to be alleviated by an expansion of the money supply. However, he decided to increase it in the liberal way, by borrowing the country's means of circulation from the banks. In this respect, he disappointed the hopes that Pound had vested in him.

Pound observed that the New Deal programs were "conservative" solutions (*EPPP* 6.311) designed to adjust the system to a crisis: Begin by creating artificial scarcity in order to push up prices; use heavy government borrowing to generate jobs in large-scale national projects; create new taxes to pay back the loans and finance the new Social Security entitlements. Pound discovered in these measures the familiar mechanism of usury: Faced with a national emergency, the state gets indebted to the banks in order to create or redistribute wealth; these new debts are paid from additional taxation. This is why for Pound the "Nude Eel" was "hooey": He pointed out that instead of burdening the nation with a huge debt, Roosevelt could have used stamp scrip. The measure would have distributed the purchasing power that was so sorely needed, and in addition, the money would have consumed itself in eight years, leaving the nation free of debt ("The Individual in His Milieu," *SP* 280). In his opinion, Roosevelt's solution to "make more work" was also a fallacy: As Douglas had advocated, the working day had to be shortened to keep pace with mechanical invention; the available labor could then be redistributed. The gap between wages and prices had to be bridged by a national dividend. But instead of the subvention of prices, Roosevelt introduced a sales tax. It becomes clearer now why and in what way Pound objected to the whole liberal solution to the problem of distributive justice: It was based on national debt to private banks and increased taxation.

The various reformers with whom Pound corresponded on economics were partisans of solutions in which there was no need for the state to borrow. Social Crediters in America favored the solution of state money, as the Constitution allowed: Like the greenback, this money would not have been an interest-bearing loan from a central bank but would have been guaranteed by the government on pledges of taxes. But the motions to nationalize the Federal Reserve, coming from Senator Bronson Cutting in 1934, from Congressman Alan Goldsborough in 1935, and from Congressman Jerry Voorhis in 1939, were rejected by Congress (Surette 133–135).

In *The Pisan Cantos* Pound put forth his own synthetic formula of economic and political jus-

tice. It contained what he had learned from Douglas about effective demand, as well as the principle of Gesell's free money:

"No longer necessary," taxes are no longer
    necessary
in the old way if it (money) be based on work
    done
    inside a system and measured and gauged to
        human
requirements
inside the nation or system
and cancelled in proportion
        to what is used and worn out
à la Wörgl. (Canto 78)

Pound's final statement on economics is his 1953 affirmation that money is the key attribute of national sovereignty. Since money is the main lever of national economic development, it should be controlled by the state, not by the monopoly of a private corporation ("Sovereignty," *SP* 352).

Bibliography

Douglas, C. H. *Economic Democracy*. New York: Harcourt Brace and Howe, 1920.
———. *Social Credit*. 1924. Vancouver: Institute of Economic Democracy, 1979.
Gesell, Silvio. *The Natural Economic Order*. 1914. Trans. Philip Pye. San Antonio: Free-Economy Publishing, 1934.
Redman, Tim. *Ezra Pound and Italian Fascism*. New York: Cambridge UP, 1991.
Surette, Leon. *Pound in Purgatory: From Economic Radicalism to Anti-Semitism*. Urbana: U of Illinois P, 1999.

Roxana Preda

Economics: Usury

Pound provided one definition of *usury* as a footnote to Canto 45: "A charge for the use of purchasing power, levied without regard to production; often without regard to the possibilities of production." It is a definition that Pound arrived at as a consequence of his education in Social Credit. Douglas observed that new production cannot function without bank loans, whose interest is reflected in higher prices. The manufacture based on credit caused an ever-increasing gap between prices and what the consumer was able to buy with wages. In principle, nothing could be simply produced and offered on the market without a tax (call it interest charge) levied by the banks on the purchasing power of every citizen. Since credits are needed before production, they must be repaid irrespective of whether something has been produced adequately or in sufficient quantity so that producers can continue their activity.

This definition points to an economic system, commonly called *finance capitalism*, which Pound named "usury." In this system nothing can be produced and sold without interest charges, which function as a hidden tax levied on the community. But this is only the mere surface of usury. The core of the system, as Pound saw it, resided in the possibility of a private central bank to have the monopoly on the issue of money ex nihilo. Pound quoted Paterson, the founder of the Bank of England, in Canto 46: The bank would have *"benefit of interest on all / the moneys, which it, the bank, creates out of nothing."* The principle of usury is that a private corporation has the monopoly over the creation of money. The sovereign state is a mere borrower of the country's means of circulation. The consequence of this principle is that money, under all its forms except metal coins, circulates as interest-bearing loans.

For Pound the world was divided into producers and usurers. The producers create something new, using natural or industrial resources. The usurer uses money to acquire more money through speculation, pyramiding, and monopoly. Pound protested against the current understanding in which money is said to "generate," "multiply," or "grow" through investment or interest. He pointed out that this is a misuse of words, since no two banknotes put together would generate a third. He dissociated between the natural increase (Amor) and usura, which is an economy of the same. (See the classical associations of usury with homosexuality and sodomy, which Pound takes up in his usura cantos, 45 and 51.) For Pound usury had disastrous effects on culture, since it promoted mass production and quick, slipshod manufacture to the detriment of art and craftsmanship. Under the

pressure of time and worry about selling, the producers' concerns for quality and the creation of new designs were forgotten. Invention, especially literary invention, had to be promoted and sustained in a constant battle with the system and its commercial outlets geared to the cheap and the cliché.

Since the national banks, like the Federal Reserve or the Bank of England, have the privilege of creating notes by a dash of the pen, they also have the power to control the value of money and change it at will, thereby influencing economic development and politics down to everyday life. Pound lived through two such changes, the revaluation of the pound sterling in Britain in 1925 and the devaluation of the dollar against gold in 1933. He repeatedly referred to this aspect in *The Pisan Cantos* by quoting Aristotle's "METATHEMENON TE TON KRUMENON," "if those who use a currency give it up for another" (Cantos 74, 77, and 78).

Pound's final lesson in matters of usury is that the creation and circulation of money should be controlled by the state, as stipulated in the American Constitution, where the power of coining and the regulation of the value of currency is a prerogative of Congress. The essence of sovereign power resides in the possibility of the nation to control its financial resources without paying rent for the use of its money to financial corporations.

Bibliography

Marsh, Alec. *Money and Modernity: Pound, Williams, and the Spirit of Jefferson*. Tuscaloosa: U of Alabama P, 1998.

McNaughton, William. "New Light on the *Pisan Cantos* and *Rock Drill*: Milton Friedman and Herman Kahn." *Paideuma* 16.3 (1987): 23–51.

Surette, Leon. *A Light from Eleusis: A Study of Ezra Pound's Cantos*. Oxford: Clarendon P, 1979.

———. *Pound in Purgatory: From Economic Radicalism to Anti-Semitism*. Urbana: U of Illinois P, 1999.

Roxana Preda

Education: Personal

Ezra Pound's schooling began in institutions then known as "dame schools," small private schools run by a woman, often on her own but sometimes with a small staff. Pound attended Miss Elliott's school and Chelten Hills, run by the Heacock family. In 1895, aged ten, he enrolled at provisional and then official versions of the Wyncote Public School, where he formed a strong attachment to a teacher named Jean Ridpath. His secondary education was completed at Cheltenham Military Academy, though some evidence suggests a year (1900–1901) spent at the Cheltenham Township High School. Pound's alumnus folder at the University of Pennsylvania, however, records enrollment at the military academy from 1897 to 1901. For further detail, readers are referred to the standard biographies (Carpenter, Stock, and Wilhelm); for local source material from Wyncote and surrounding neighborhoods, the Carl Gatter Collection of clippings and other memorabilia at the University of Pennsylvania is valuable. Pound appears to have been an excellent, even precocious student. At age six, his nickname was "Professor."

On more than one occasion Pound declared that, by age fifteen, he had decided to learn as many languages as possible in his preparation to become a poet. American higher education at this period was well suited to his aims: Language study and philology were strong components of the liberal arts. He began his postsecondary education at the University of Pennsylvania, an institution with which he would always have a troubled relationship. After a mediocre performance in a range of introductory, general studies courses, he transferred in 1903 to Hamilton College, receiving his baccalaureate degree in 1905. At Hamilton he studied with the Reverend Joseph Darling Ibbotson, professor of English literature, Anglo-Saxon, and Hebrew, and took forty units of language study (in French, Italian, Spanish, and Provençal) with William Pierce Shepard. He returned to Hamilton in 1939 to receive an honorary doctoral degree.

In 1905 Pound enrolled at the University of Pennsylvania for graduate study in Romanics and continued there through the academic year 1906–1907, including a period of travel and study in Spain on a Harrison Fellowship. University records and Pound's correspondence indicate that the most important teachers for him in this period were Felix Schelling, his graduate adviser, Cornelius Weygandt, professor of poetry, and Hugo Rennert, the professor of Romanics who makes an appearance in Cantos 20, 28, and 94. He also formed lasting bonds with two contemporaries: William Carlos Williams, then a medical student, and Hilda Doolittle, whose father was a university astronomy professor.

Having returned from Spain and travels in Italy and France, Pound learned his fellowship for doctoral study would not be renewed. In 1920, Pound's father Homer submitted *The Spirit of Romance* (1910) in fulfillment of requirements for his son's Ph.D., but Pennsylvania declined to award the degree. Throughout his life, Pound viewed Pennsylvania as a "beanery," that is, an educational factory that failed to recognize unusual gifts, adhered uncritically to rules, and obstructed original thought. He had, in general, little positive to say about American educational institutions.

Pound held a teaching position in Romance languages at Wabash College in Crawfordsville, Indiana, from September 1907 until his dismissal in January 1908. His formal teaching henceforth would be limited to occasional lectures (at the Regent St. Polytechnic, London, 1909–1910, and the Università Bocconi, Milan, 1931). His propensity for informal teaching, however, is one of the most notable aspects of his character, remarked by nearly everyone with whom he came into contact, from the young artists of prewar London to the students at his "Ezuversity" in Rapallo to his visitors at St. Elizabeths Hospital in Washington, D.C.

A survey of Pound's education cannot therefore end with formalities of degrees conferred, for teaching and learning were central occupations of his life. Like Whitman before him, Pound was an avid student not only of poetry but also of a wide array of subjects: American and Italian history, music, art, mythology, economics, Chinese philosophy. *The Cantos* form a record of his energetic and occasionally wayward autodidacticism. His intellectual relationship to figures of history (Dante, John Adams,

Confucius, Thomas Jefferson) and to contemporaries or near-contemporaries (W. B. Yeats, T. S. Eliot, Ford Madox Ford, Katherine Ruth Heyman, Henri Gaudier-Brzeska, Arnold Dolmetsch, George Antheil, Ernest Fenollosa, C. H. Douglas) was shaped by his lifelong pursuit of the "luminous detail." (See **Education: Philosophy**)

Bibliography

Hoffman, Daniel, ed. *Ezra Pound and William Carlos Williams: The University of Pennsylvania Conference Papers.* Philadelphia: U of Pennsylvania P, 1983.

Kenner, Hugh. "Classroom Accuracies." *A Homemade World: The American Modernist Writers.* New York: Morrow, 1975.

McDonald, Gail. *Learning to Be Modern: Pound, Eliot, and the American University.* New York: Oxford UP, 1993.

Gail McDonald

Education: Philosophy

Donald Gallup's bibliography documents Ezra Pound's sustained and passionate commitment to education. The poet's conviction that education is critical to living well and to doing good, and his numerous schemes for alternative modes of education from "literary kindergartens" conducted at Hamilton to the Ezuversity at Rapallo, place him squarely in the company of optimistic American reformers of the Progressive period. Like John Dewey and other theorists of pedagogy, he believed that the beginnings of education lay in the natural curiosity observable in children and that the aim of education should be both to prepare students to live in the world and, where possible, to improve it. Works like *Guide to Kulchur* and *ABC of Reading*, the anthologies he assembled, the journals, presses, and writers he promoted—all these energetic efforts may be viewed as Pound's attempts to correct flaws or fill voids in institutions of higher learning. Beyond the better-known texts are scores of other discussions, critiques, and screeds about the subject—in private and "open" letters, long and short prose pieces, essays collected and uncollected, in magazines central to Modernism (e.g.,

Egoist), and in those known to very few (individual college newsletters). Two sources in particular are useful for understanding Pound's educational philosophy: "I Gather the Limbs of Osiris," a multipart essay in which he outlined his "New Method in Scholarship" (*New Age* 1911–1912), and the "Preliminary Announcement of the College of Arts" (first outlined in "America: Chances and Remedies," *Egoist* 1913). Both these works come early in Pound's career, but they outline a philosophy that remains strikingly consistent.

Pound's views on education correspond to his rules for Imagist poetry, his attraction to constructs like the ideogram, and his methods of praise and condemnation in *The Cantos.* Foundational to all these theories are two principles: First, true learning requires an active perception of relationships among particular facts; and second, such perceptions generate new knowledge. If a pattern of relationship is observed between detail A and detail B, that observation produces new knowledge that is neither A nor B but a third, separate idea. Learning is thus dynamic and creative. Pound's dicta for the acquisition of knowledge, clearly relevant to his poetic method, also bear important parallels to his views on money. An honorable use of money creates goods and progress; a dishonorable one (with usury most frequently cited as example) will create only more money, not a truly generative enterprise by Pound's lights. Readers familiar with the Hell Cantos (14–15) will see evidence of the poet's condemnation of those who exhaust resources without replenishing them. Thus teachers and scholars who remain satisfied with rote memorization or acquisition of facts without critical inquiry into their value fall short of the proper goals of study. Pound's quarrel with philology, as he perceived it to be practiced during his graduate study at the University of Pennsylvania, was its failure to produce "live" thought from its findings about the nature and development of language. Absent from this larger enterprise, the scholar was comparable, he believed, to a piece-worker in a factory.

Though Pound claimed no particular admiration for Ralph Waldo Emerson, his views are comparable to those expressed in "The American Scholar." In particular, Emerson's discussion of "creative reading" seems pertinent. Like Emerson, Pound asserted repeatedly that the mind is not a passive recipient of knowledge but rather a dynamic participant in its making. What one brings to the reading of a book, therefore, will be integral to what one takes away; the mind not only receives patterns but makes them. There is room within Pound's philosophy for an intuitive, even mystical, kind of learning. The "swift perception of particulars" is as likely to arrive by flashes of insight as by labored logic. Pound asserted that the aim of study is "revelation," which, he explained to his former professor Felix Schelling, "is always didactic" (L 180).

For Pound, obstacles, whether personal or institutional, that hinder the inherently creative process of learning are by definition corrupt and antiintellectual. In particular, he repeatedly condemned those aspects of academic professionalization that led to narrow specialization and protectionist territoriality within the disciplines. While approving the elevation of professional standards and a strong work ethic, he decried those aspects of a businesslike mode of conduct causing the professoriate to attend to issues of status, money, and self-advancement to the detriment of a free exchange of ideas. Barriers of self-interest made the professors no better than the "[h]oggers of harvest" Pound rebukes in Canto 88. For a typical example of Pound's views on the dangers of overspecialization, the reader is referred to "Reorganize Your Dead Universities" (Delphian Quarterly 21.2 [April 1938]: 20–22, 28).

Nowhere is Pound more idealistic than in his visions of a model college, expressed most succinctly in his proposal for a College of Arts, published in the Egoist in 1913. In brief, the imagined structure of the college would take shape from the pursuit of the "luminous detail," that is, not simply knowledge, but knowledge that illuminates other knowledge and thus creates new knowledge. His desiderata for an educational utopia included an urban setting that lay before students not only the offerings of a specific school but also the museums, libraries, and

people that make cities living universities; an ethos of generosity whereby students and teachers worked in concert toward knowledge; the free circulation of ideas among artists, students, and print media; an emphasis on firsthand knowledge (art taught by artists, art history through direct observation of paintings, music through the playing of instruments); authority established not by institutional hierarchy but by achievement; disregard for disciplinary boundaries and encouragement of collaboration; access to any serious learner, based on an intellectual meritocracy. The dedication of Guide to Kulchur is an index of Pound's regard for those who seek knowledge but have not found it in conventional schools. Pound's teacher-heroes included Louis Agassiz, the Harvard biologist who championed direct observation; the legendary Abelard, who challenged intellectual authority; and potentially, any teacher whose mission included care for the precise use of language.

Pound's idealism on the subject of education may seem to be at odds with aspects of his thought and life tending more toward authoritarianism, elitism, and prejudice. These contradictions cannot be easily resolved, but it should be noted that an uneasy mixture of autocracy and democracy characterized much of the educational and social reform of Pound's era.

Bibliography
McDonald, Gail. Learning to Be Modern: Pound, Eliot, and the American University. New York: Oxford UP, 1993.

Gail McDonald

"Eeldrop and Appleplex"

"Eeldrop and Appleplex" is a two-part prose sketch by T. S. Eliot begun in the issue of the Little Review that announced Pound's acceptance of the post of Foreign Editor. It was Eliot's first contribution to the journal. The protagonists of the title bear a slight resemblance to Eliot and Pound, respectively. Both characters seek "to apprehend the soul in its concrete individuality" and discuss the majority's failure to be more than "generalized men."

Bibliography

Eliot, T. S. "Eeldrop and Appleplex." Part I. *Little Review* 4.1 (May 1917): 7–11.
———. "Eeldrop and Appleplex." Part II. *Little Review* 4.5 (1917): 16–19.

William Cole

Egoist

The *Egoist* was a magazine begun in London as the *New Freewoman* in 1911 by Dora Marsden of the Women's Social and Political Union. Ezra Pound became its literary editor during the summer of 1913, working alongside Harriet Shaw Weaver and Rebecca West. In the autumn, he launched into a serious reevaluation of literary values on its pages, creating a palpable tension with the magazine's original emphasis on the philosophical concerns of the "new woman." The decision to change the publication's name to the *Egoist* in January 1914 suggests how successful Pound was in realigning the magazine's editorial direction. Financial difficulties soon forced Weaver to take greater responsibility for the running of the *Egoist*, and working with Pound she would go on to serialize pieces of James Joyce's *A Portrait of the Artist as a Young Man* and *Ulysses*. The magazine became increasingly interested in using its imprint for the publishing of books, importing American copies of *Portrait* and printing T. S. Eliot's *Prufrock and Other Observations*. Indeed, the magazine remained an important vehicle for Pound and his closest collaborators during this second decade of the twentieth century: Eliot began an important period in the development of his criticism by accepting a post as assistant editor in 1917. Amid rising costs, the *Egoist* ceased publication at the end of 1919.

Craig Monk

Egyptian Literature

In 1958 Pound discussed with his son-in-law, the Egyptologist Boris de Rachewiltz, matters Egyptian and, presumably, hieroglyphs, for they appear in *Rock-Drill*. "Conversations in Courtship," included in *Love Poems of Ancient Egypt* (1962), which reads easily as colloquial American English despite Latin and Italian bits, is grounded on translations of the hieroglyphic texts into Italian by Boris published in 1957 in Milan. Pound's illness prevented his work on the other poems in the collection, which was completed by Noel Stock. These poems are presented as complete, although they derive from fragments on papyrus and pottery (dated 1567–1085 B.C.E.) in the British and Cairo Museums.

Bibliography

Love Poems of Ancient Egypt. Trans. Ezra Pound and Noel Stock. Norfolk: New Directions, n.d. [The date is possibly 1962, the year of Stock's copyright; Pound's copyright is 1960.]
Rachewiltz, Boris de. *Liriche Amorose degli Antichi Egiziani.* Milano: Vanni Scheiwiller, 1957.

Evelyn Haller

Elektra

In 1949, Pound at St. Elizabeths Hospital made a translation of Sophocles's *Elektra* together with Rudd Fleming. This version only appeared under the latter's name, perhaps because the poet was afraid that his ability to translate Greek would make him "sane" enough to stand trial, or perhaps because the figure of Elektra was a *persona* too intimate to reveal. After all, Pound regarded line 351—rendered as "Need we add cowardice to all the rest of this filth?"—as the key phrase of the play, a fact that emphasizes the poet's desire to maintain the courage of his convictions despite their having been shown to be failing or to be going against the currents of contemporary history and society.

As in his later *Women of Trachis* (1956), Pound in his *Elektra* used a broad linguistic spectrum to convey the "feel" or energy of the original. He generally adopted slang or colloquial speech to give his version a certain emotional thrust and to emphasize that decencies of language are no longer viable for the characters who find themselves in a situation in which social and familial conventions are violently broken. On the other hand, Pound at times resorted to formal, archaic diction in certain of the speeches and choric passages. Unlike *Women of Trachis*, *Elektra* emphasizes the melopoeic quality of the original Greek by preserving a

considerable number of Greek lines in transcription. As a result, Pound's version has 1,802
lines against Sophocles's original 1,510.

Bibliography

Syros, Christine. "Beyond Language: Ezra Pound's
Translation of the Sophoclean *Elektra*." *Paideuma*
23.2–3 (1994): 107–139.

Peter Liebregts

Eliot, Thomas Stearns (1888–1965)

One of Pound's closest friends and literary
collaborators, American-born, Harvard-educated
T. S. Eliot lived in England from 1914 and became the leading English-language poet, critic,
and man-of-letters of his day. He met Pound in
London on 22 September 1914. He had already
written most of the poems later collected in
Prufrock & Other Observations (1917) but could
not get them published, and Pound at once saw
that Eliot's work was "modern" and arranged
publication in *Poetry* (Chicago), *BLAST*, and in
his own *Catholic Anthology* (1915). Pound also
determined the order of the poems in the
Prufrock volume, helped with the cost of publication, and promoted it in a powerful review.
Around 1917 they agreed that vers libre had become slack in the work of their fellow practitioners and staged a return to the rigor of rhyme:
Eliot in his quatrains in *Poems* (1920) and
Pound in *Hugh Selwyn Mauberley* (1920).
Pound continued to advise Eliot on his poetry up
to *The Waste Land* (1922), where his work on
the drafts, as Eliot said, transformed "a jumble
of good and bad passages into a poem." For that
Eliot dubbed him, as their common master
Dante had dubbed Arnaut Daniel, "*il miglior
fabbro*," the better craftsman. Thanks to Pound's
recommendation, Eliot was appointed literary
editor of the *Egoist* in 1917—his "Tradition and
the Individual Talent" (1919) appeared in its final issues. Throughout the years 1914–1922
Pound was Eliot's generous mentor and contributed immensely by his conversation, convictions, and example, as well as by practical
support, to the rapid and powerful development
of Eliot's criticism and poetry.

Pound counted Eliot among "the men of
1914," along with Wyndham Lewis, Joyce, and

himself, that is, as one of the revolutionary geniuses whose work was bringing about a modern
renaissance. He regarded *The Waste Land* as the
justification of their Modern movement and
tried through Bel Esprit to free Eliot from his
career in banking for full-time creative work.
Eliot, however, had his own ambitions.
Throughout those years he had been forming
other connections, notably with the Bloomsbury
circle and with Middleton Murry, and had been
establishing an independent position in the London literary world. While Pound was bent on
promoting the work of a group of the most creative minds of his generation, Eliot was achieving individual preeminence with *The Sacred
Wood* (1920), *The Waste Land* (1922), and the
founding of his own literary quarterly the *Criterion* (1922–1939). Pound, beaten in his war to
establish a reign of intelligence, said farewell to
England in 1920. Eliot remained to become an
increasingly dominant presence among its intel-
ligentsia, in spite of a profound opposition to
many of its values.

Eliot was developing a standpoint profoundly
at odds with Pound's—and, for different reasons, with that of most of his contemporaries—
one based on Christian faith and dogma. Pound
wanted a good society based on "the abundance
of nature / with the whole folk behind it," a
paradiso terrestre. In reply to Eliot's "but what
does Mr Pound believe?" he recommended Ovid
and Confucius as sacred texts and declared his
faith in "a light from Eleusis." For this Eliot
judged him to be "after strange gods." He himself was after the Christian ideal of the City of
God. From this religious difference there followed a political difference. Pound trusted in
Mussolini and fascism to fulfill his program for
a good society, but Eliot placed no faith in political leaders or parties. His City of God could
come about only in a life of prayerful submission to God's will. He showed a positive interest
in Pound's economic ideas but maintained a
sceptical detachment from his politics. He
showed no sympathy whatsoever for Pound's
anti-Semitic propaganda.

These profound differences did not break
their friendship but did limit their literary

collaboration. Pound contributed occasionally to the *Criterion*, while protesting that Eliot had not followed the program they had agreed for it. When Eliot left the bank for Faber and Gwyer, that firm became the principal publisher of Pound's poetry and literary essays but rejected *Jefferson and/or Mussolini*. Pound included one part of *Sweeney Agonistes* in his *Profile* anthology (1932), and the other in *Active Anthology* (1933), as evidence of a continuing development in Eliot's work but largely ignored *Ash-Wednesday* and his religious drama. Pound remarked that if he himself stood for the revolution, then Eliot was the counterrevolution. Yet in their letters to each other they were consistently high spirited and good humored, Eliot playing Possum to Pound's folksy Brer Rabbit.

They were most divided in the war of 1939–1945. Pound was in Italy, convinced that the Allies were on the side of the evil usurers and that right was with the Nazi-Fascist Axis; Eliot was in blitzed London, convinced that the war offered a rare chance of spiritual purgation. Out of their utterly contrasting views and experiences each produced his finest poetry, Eliot his *Four Quartets*, Pound his *Pisan Cantos*. Equally contrasting were their prose productions: Eliot's *Idea of a Christian Society* (1939) and *Notes towards the Definition of Culture* (1948), as against Pound's wartime pamphlets and radio speeches.

In 1945 Pound was arrested by the American authorities on the charge of treason and spent thirteen years incarcerated in St. Elizabeths, an institution for the criminally insane, in Washington, D.C. Eliot in those years was being universally honored: the British Order of Merit and the Nobel Prize for Literature in 1949, honorary degrees and prestigious awards in many countries, and ultimately (in 1964) the U.S. Medal of Freedom. He used the influence that came with his prestige and his impeccable respectability, discreetly and diplomatically, to support efforts to secure Pound's release. He was instrumental in publishing *The Pisan Cantos*, and collections of his literary essays and translations, with the intention of helping Pound's cause by presenting him in his best light. And he went to see him

in St. Elizabeths on his now-regular visits to America. When Pound was finally released in 1958, Eliot was enjoying his late happy marriage and the minor success of his last play, *The Elder Statesman*, though he was aged and emphysemic. He tried to cheer Pound up when he heard of his depression by telling him that his poetry would last and that all contemporary writers were in his debt. But it was Pound who had the last word. On Eliot's death in January 1965 he made the journey from Venice to be present at the memorial service in Westminster Abbey and later in a brief written tribute declared with his old graceful generosity, "His was the true Dantescan voice."

Bibliography

Eliot, T. S. *Selected Letters of T. S. Eliot*. Vol. 1, *1898–1922*. Ed. Valerie Eliot. San Diego: Harcourt Brace Jovanovich, 1988.

Gallup, Donald. *T. S. Eliot & Ezra Pound: Collaborators in Letters*. New Haven: H. W. Wenning/C. A. Stonehill, 1970.

Kenner, Hugh. *The Invisible Poet*. New York: Citadel P, 1959.

Moody, A. David. "Peregrine in England." *Tracing T. S. Eliot's Spirit: Essays on His Poetry and Thought*. New York: Cambridge UP, 1996.

———. *Thomas Stearns Eliot: Poet*. 1979. New York: Cambridge UP, 1994.

A. David Moody

English History: Middle Ages through the Eighteenth Century

Pound's interest in old English history was focused on the legal tradition that led to the American political institutions. He saw this line initiated by the Magna Charta and the writings of Bracton and Glanvil, continued by the key figure of Edward Coke, who worked during the reigns of Elisabeth, James I, and Charles I, and fulfilled in the political work of John Adams. Two sections in *The Cantos* illuminate this tradition: the one dealing with Adams's biography (63–67) and the so-called Coke Cantos (107–109).

Edward Coke (1552–1634), the most famous English jurist, was a member of Parliament, Speaker of the House of Commons, and Attorney General during the reign of Elisabeth I. He was also Chief Justice of England under James I. His major work, the four *Institutes* (1628–1634), is the foundation of the English common law. The prime principle laid down by Coke was that "Law is the subject's birthright," a principle upheld by Adams (Canto 64). The *Institutes* rely on the work of Bracton, Glanvil, and Littleton, that is, on all former charters in which the laws of the land were laid down and commented by Coke's predecessors. It is particularly the second *Institute* that is important to Pound, since it contains Coke's commentary on the Magna Charta in one of its later versions (1290). During the reigns of James I and Charles I, Coke fought for the charter against kingly abuses like illegal arrest, imprisonment without trial, forced loans, and confiscations of property. This political struggle culminated with the "Petition of the Right" made by the Parliament to Charles I in 1628 (Canto 108). The Petition was a document upholding the decisions of the Magna Charta for the protection of property and against the right of the king to tax without the approval of Parliament. Charles attempted to resist the implementation of the document by refusing to say the granting words: "Soit droit fait comme il est desiré." It was Coke who settled the matter by enlisting the help of the House of Lords. Under the pressure of both houses, Charles was forced to give in and grant habeat corpus. The king, therefore, lost the privilege to tax and imprison arbitrarily. His own revenue was determined by the vote of Parliament.

Coke's insistence that the common law was to be considered higher than the king's will or even the laws approved by Parliament had the greatest relevance to the American political system of checks and balances. After he had studied and compared various systems of government, ancient and modern, Adams concluded, "no distinct separation of legislative, executive and judicial / heretofore save in England" (67/394). England and the principles of right upheld by the common law were to be emulated and followed by the young republic.

There is a dark spot in English history, however. The creation of the Bank of England in 1694, a direct consequence of Parliament's refusing to vote new taxes for William of Orange's war with Louis XIV, led to the reign of usury, a shadow power that, in Pound's view, undermined and corrupted the English political system, ultimately favoring economic crises, wars, and the disintegration of the British Empire.

Bibliography

Gordon, David. "The Azalea Is Grown." *Paideuma* 4.2–3 (1975): 223–299.

Hollis, Christopher. *The Two Nations: A Financial Study of English History*. 1935. New York: Gordon P, 1975.

Roxana Preda

English History: Nineteenth Century

This was the century of usury, the time when usury got respectable and changed its name to "finance." According to Brooks Adams, whose *Law of Civilization and Decay* Pound greatly admired, the Industrial Revolution was not due to the invention of the steam engine (other important human inventions had lain dormant for centuries) but to the coupling of industry and finance, which made long-term investment possible (256–258). Within this system, deflation was especially favored by bankers, because it brought more profit to their credits, whereas an inflationary trend, which brought higher prices, was more suitable to the producers. Adams also pointed out that until 1810 the interests of the producers had prevailed. After Waterloo, however, the interests of the banks led to the establishment of the gold standard through the Peel Acts of 1819 and 1844, whereby finance could control both the state debt, which had kept increasing since 1694, and the productive activity of the nation. The main method was restricting the monetary supply through the demonetization of silver and the linking of the monetary unit to a specific quantity of gold (268–273). In this conflict, Pound was totally on the side of the producers, paraphrasing Hume: "[P]rosperity depends not on the quantity of money in a country but on its *constantly increasing*" (*SP* 260).

Pound considered that the usurious system that the English had brought upon themselves with the creation of the Bank of England had led them to forget the principles underlying their political institutions. One of these principles had been Parliament's control over taxation and finance, a principle that had been first stated in the Magna Charta and continued in the struggle between king and Parliament during the reign of the Stuarts. In the century of usury it was possible that the Bank of England, a private corporation, was allowed to tax indirectly through the instrument of the national debt. As to coins, the portcullis was nominally struck by the crown, but monarchs from Charles II to Victoria had surrendered the prerogative to private hands (Canto 97). As a luminous detail illustrating this state of affairs, Pound introduced a reference to the British acquisition of shares in the Suez Canal into *The Cantos* (89, 104, and 108). Disraeli and Rothschild had settled this business at dinner, without the knowledge or approval of the Parliament.

England in the nineteenth and early twentieth centuries can be considered as the most important illustration of everything Pound said at various times about usury. Usury causes the decline in the living standard of the producers; moral degradation; erosion of artistic and cultural standards; ignorance, not only of economics but also of history and national tradition. For Pound it was only the best Victorian artists who had been aware of this decadence. Even if they had had a limited perspective, not reaching to the financial causes of evil, they had nevertheless protested against the spiritual decadence of the age. The luminaries, as Pound saw them in *Guide to Kulchur*, were Swinburne and Pre-Raphaelites Hardy and Browning.

Bibliography

Adams, Brooks. *The Law of Civilization and Decay.* 1896. New York: Vintage, 1955.

Roxana Preda

English History: Twentieth Century

For Pound, England in the twentieth century was under the sign of economic, moral, and spiritual decadence. If we take the *Guide to Kulchur* as one of his most comprehensive affirmations of belief, here is a collage of snapshots: England is a "suffocated nation" stifled by

orthodoxy and immobility (*GK* 106). In it the artist can observe "Victorian fugg, insularity, a meagreness, a dwindling" (227). In Pound's view, those governing the country had no moral courage, no desire to face new unfamiliar ideas or to heed warnings dangerous to the status quo. "[H]abits of servility" (242) were strong. English law was so ambiguously worded that it made crime, instead of preventing or punishing it (186). The Anglican Church was "a mass of sinecures" (258) and "interfered 'neither with a man's politics or his religion' " (290).

For Pound, the most important event of recent British history was World War I. The best men had fought and died for the ideals of a civilization already decadent, for an "old bitch gone in the teeth" (*Hugh Selwyn Mauberley*). This prewar life had been the usurer's matrix, a repertoire of images that was very effective in sending 5 million men to their deaths, among them two good friends, T. E. Hulme and Henri Gaudier-Brzeska. After 1918, Pound learned from C. H. Douglas that usury is responsible for wars. Douglas thought that the production of armaments is very profitable to the banks, since in times of war there is no glut of weapons, and the market demands ever increased quantities of them. On the other hand, banks profit from the credits they give to the state, which repays the debt out of postwar taxation.

In 1918, the Coalition government of Lloyd George appointed the Cunliffe Committee to decide about the best strategy for the financial future of the nation. The committee, formed entirely of bankers, recommended the return to the gold standard, which had been suspended in 1914, and the return to the "honest" prewar pound. According to Arthur Kitson, one of Pound's favorite authors, the treasury notes that had functioned during the war were to be replaced by Bank of England notes. The state had to cease interfering with monetary issue, and the former monopoly was to be restored to the bank. It also had to resume the power to dictate the discount rate, that is, the rate of economic growth and employment (Kitson 48). The administration accepted this recommendation in 1920, and Winston Churchill reestablished the gold standard in 1925, in spite of the already ruinous deflation of about 20 percent, which had caused a homemade crisis felt throughout the empire (Canto 77). The deflation raised the value of the pound sterling to prewar levels, thus increasing the profits of creditors. Douglas argued that the banks had bought certificates of the war loan from individual subscribers and thus concentrated the state debt into their own hands (*Social Credit* 140–143). Because of its ruinous effects on the economy, Britain left the gold standard again in 1931. For Pound, changing the value of money was the ultimate form of usury. Churchill, who out of ignorance or corruption allowed this, acquired pride of place in the gallery of rogues populating *The Cantos*.

Only in *The Pisan Cantos* does Pound allow himself a whiff of nostalgia for early twentieth-century London and a certain hope for the future of England (Canto 80), seeing that Churchill was finally out of office and the Labor government had nationalized the Bank of England.

Bibliography

Douglas, C. H. *Social Credit.* 1924. Vancouver: Institute of Economic Democracy, 1979.

Kitson, Arthur. *The Bankers' Conspiracy! Which Started the World Crisis.* London: Elliot Stock, 1933.

Roxana Preda

English Literature: Medieval and Renaissance

Ezra Pound campaigned tirelessly for a study of world literature; he required of literature that it both participate in and contribute to culture. For Pound "every allegedly great age is an age of translations," and Chaucer merits the title of "Le Grand Translateur" (*LE* 35). Due at least in part to his insistence that translation be recognized as a sign of literary merit, the canon as Pound saw it would remove Shakespeare from the center of English literary history. While several "Englishmen who died before 1620" (*LE* 34) are given Pound's attention, Chaucer is the one to replace Shakespeare.

Chaucer belongs to the first of the four English literary periods as enumerated by Pound in *ABC of Reading*, "when England was part of Europe" (132)—poetry before him requires a glossary (58)—and his voluminous work already contains much of what would be considered great in later authors; in other words, he serves as a measure for future English poetry: "No one will ever gauge or measure English poetry until they know how much of it, how full a gamut of its qualities, is already THERE ON THE PAGE of Chaucer" (102). Shakespeare's canonical prominence is the result of England's questionable love for the glamour of the theater and the slothful notion that Chaucer's language is not English; when these crutches are knocked out from under him by a more scientific and practical criticism—Chaucer had both a wider and a deeper "knowledge of life than Shakespeare" (99), which can be demonstrated both by the scope of his learning and by a simple comparison of both authors' works—Chaucer takes his place of prominence. There is little medieval competition; Gower's "hesitation" (101) keeps him out of the running, while the anonymous ballads are not a part of a great work.

Once Chaucer is seen in his proper light (i.e., out of Shakespeare's shadow), he can be compared with his European contemporaries. Pound considered him to be part of the same culture as the Troubadours: He "was not a foreigner. It was HIS civilization" (*ABCR* 101). He is "better than Chrestien de Troyes" (*LE* 214); he is "more compendious than Dante" (*ABCR* 101); he "should be on every man's shelf" (*LE* 216); he "was the greatest poet of his day" (*ABCR* 101). "After Chaucer, come Gavin Douglas, Golding and Marlowe with their 'translations'" (*ABCR* 59), and these, as well as Shakespeare, must be considered great *because* they translate. After the early period of the *Seafarer* and *Beowulf*, "English literature lives on translation, it is fed by translation" (*LE* 34), and it may be best to consider Chaucer "the father of 'litterae humaniores' for Europe" (*ABCR* 103)—not merely for England.

In contradistinction to Chaucer's work, which reaches out into the larger European literary history as a contribution to culture and a great feat of translation, the Anglo-Saxon poetry was for Pound indigenous English material that must *be* translated. Thereby it feeds directly into his own work: As a participant in culture much as Chaucer was, Pound used the Anglo-Saxon both as material to be translated and incorporated into his opus and as source material for revamping meter and verse in English.

Chaucer "ended the Anglo-Saxon alliterative fashions" (*LE* 92), and Pound is largely responsible for bringing the character, if not actually the alliteration, back to poetry in English. "Even today," says Daniel Albright, "translations of Old English tend to echo (or play off) the abrupt, overstressed voice that Pound established in 1911 in 'The Seafarer'" (59). Pound engaged with the language of the original while taking liberties in order to give his translation a poetic force on its own, creating what he considered a faithful translation and at the same time adopting the poem as one of his own personae. Thus there is a direct personal relationship between Pound and Anglo-Saxon poetry that cannot be found with later English poetry until Browning.

Pound had more of a fondness for the shorter "lyrics" such as "The Seafarer" and "The Wanderer" than he did for *Beowulf*, but the meter and idiom of all Anglo-Saxon poetry informed his poetics, contributing a great deal to his attempt at avoiding Latinate construction and the iambic pentameter that reigned from Chaucer onward, in favor of an English rhythm. Pound moves past mere translation in the opening to *The Cantos*: The rhythm, diction, and even alliteration in "Sun to his slumber, shadows o'er all the ocean" and "swartest night stretched over wretched men there" clearly echo the Old English in a poem that itself speaks clearly about the way in which Pound engages with medieval texts. A passage from Homer taken from a Latin crib and turned into a poem in its own right is the most appropriate opening for a poet who admires Chaucer's multitextual retellings; but the rhythm and diction—the backbone—are from the original English that disappeared with Chaucer and were not reinstated until Ezra Pound, Le Grand Translateur.

Bibliography

Albright, Daniel. "Early Cantos I–XLI." *The Cambridge Companion to Ezra Pound*. Ed. Ira B. Nadel. Cambridge: Cambridge UP, 1999. 59–91.

Matthew Robinson

English Literature: Restoration and Eighteenth Century

In Pound's list of the "sequence of authors through whom the metamorphosis of English verse writing may be traced" (*ABCR* 173), of twenty-four, five are French, and only three English writers are from the Restoration and eighteenth century. The Earl of Rochester is the Restoration representative, with Pope and Crabbe in the eighteenth century, the latter on the cusp of the next period. As much as he admired the intelligence of the period, "the age of politics" (167) gets short shrift in Pound's canon. His interest in translation occasionally leads him to look back, especially to Pope, largely intent on doing a better job with his own. As for the original writing, "in a highly superior and accomplished way the WHOLE of 18th century literature was a cliché" (*GK* 180).

The chapter "Human Wishes" in *Guide to Kulchur* begins well enough, finding value in "the perfectly weighed and placed word. Its general statements, slickingly epigrammatic, give the reader what he himself brings to the text" (179). Pope's and Johnson's "positive implication is the value of intelligence, the right to be impatient with fools, the value of being undazzled" (179). Pound, always after the pithy epigram and ready to denounce a fool, must tacitly agree, although he complains of the Dunciad, "Even if one does remember a particularly lively crack it is almost too much trouble to find it again (confession of present author, looking for a few lines he would like to quote)" (*ABCR* 169–170). This criticism (and accompanying confession) could well be leveled against Pound as well but not without heeding the meat of his complaint: Eighteenth century writing is "intellectual gongorism" (*GK* 180); the "well-express't" thought "is NOT thought at all by the expressor during or preceding the moment of expression. It is picked up and varnished, or, at best, picked up and rubbed, polished, etc." (181). And that, for Pound, is all there is. "There are scores of lines in Pope that hundreds of people can quote, each person meaning thereby something different, or something so vague and general that it has almost no meaning whatever" (*ABCR* 167); the poems are long and boring, containing only jewels to be plucked out and inserted into quotation books. "Such reading is not even training for writers," he says of *The Dunciad*. "It is a specialized form of archaeology" (170).

Pound admires Pope's desire to weed out second-rate authors and point out the better ones, but "Pope, even Crabbe all take us to a DATED world" (*ABCR* 172), and, what's worse, "Pope isn't informative!" (170); that is, he does not even provide any substantial information, dated or otherwise, in his polished verse. And Johnson is no better; his epigrams are wonderful for what they are, but "the total statement is buncombe": "human wishes are not vain in the least" (*GK* 180). The poems do not work as wholes; all but the most patient readers may as well skip to the best lines, which turn out to be abstractions that, upon closer scrutiny, are often not informative and sometimes just plain wrong. "The age was decadent. It was going bust" (182). While Pound (often tacitly) gives credit to the intellectual spirit and intelligence of the age, he would prefer to look back or forward. Pope's England was for Pound an island, separate from Europe, itself a highly polished gem: pretty from certain angles but largely useless.

Matthew Robinson

English Literature: Nineteenth Century

In Ezra Pound's response to nineteenth-century British literature, four predecessors loom large: John Ruskin, Dante Gabriel Rossetti, Walter Pater, and Robert Browning. In them, Pound discovered an already complex response to the earlier poetics of British Romanticism as he developed his own poetics and, eventually, worked toward his own understanding of the post-Romantic epic. Pound's response to his Victorian and Romantic predecessors was

necessarily mediated by late-nineteenth-century culture and the rise of the Georgian poets, among them the early W. B. Yeats of the Rhymers Club.

Like Ruskin, Rossetti, Pater, and Browning, Pound was deeply concerned with the nature of aesthetic experience and its social implications, with the relationship of art to society. Though differing from each other, these four Victorian writers were responding to the changing—and as they saw it the ambiguous, even imperiled—role of the artist in industrial capitalism. All four turned to history to rethink the role of art, and all except Browning treated the historical past as an alternative to or measure for the deficiencies of the present.

For Pound, the relation to one's predecessors as expressed in the creation of a canon was essentially the act of right naming or correct words; this notion owed much to Ruskin in "Of King's Treasuries" as well as to Confucius. To use the language well was the poet's essential task as Pound conceived it; correct language leads to right social relationships. Pound's crucial debt to Ruskin was precisely his belief that the health of art and the health of society are inextricable; in Canto 45 and in the treatment of money and credit in *The Cantos* generally, Pound's views are very much in Ruskin's tradition. Following his own predecessor Thomas Carlyle, Ruskin had preached to his Victorian audience a stringent critique of the social and political arrangements of laissez-faire capitalism; he sought, as Pound did later, to substitute a hierarchical model of social obligation for commodified art and debased social relationships.

Pound's approach to his predecessors was grounded in these large questions, but he understood such questions as entailing questions of poetic language and poetic form. From among his predecessors he created his own canon of nineteenth-century literature, looking to the novelists Henry James and Gustave Flaubert to provide a measure in prose style for the quality of language he sought in Romantic and Victorian poetry. The many pronouncements on the nineteenth-century canon in Pound's prose and letters are not an altogether reliable guide to his poetic practice; but clearly in his letters and in such essays as "How to Read," Pound created a dichotomous view of his predecessors, pitting Browning, Crabbe, Landor, Beddoes, and Hardy against what he characterized as the "Macaulay-Tennyson" approach to history and the Keatsian approach to poetic diction. Though he admired and was influenced by D. G. Rossetti's and Algernon Charles Swinburne's poems and translations, Pound argued in his canonical polemics for another kind of language, one he associated with Flaubert and with Browning, whom he acknowledged as "son père," his poetical father. To Tennyson, Pound attributed a romanticized view of history, especially medieval history, and a Keatsian ideal of beauty that he believed had balefully influenced the Georgian poets. In rejecting Tennyson in favor of Browning and Hardy, Pound attempted to distance himself from his more immediate predecessors who were writing what he called "crepuscular" poetry at the turn of the century. Browning, by contrast, he associated with what he came to call, with Ford Madox Ford, the "prose tradition in verse." The "prose tradition" marks the dichotomy Pound saw between Realism and Romanticism and between social engagement and aesthetic detachment.

Yet in Pound's poetry these distinctions are more complex than his prose sometimes indicates. Pound's early poetry was much influenced by Swinburne and Rossetti. His first volume, *A Lume Spento*, echoed Swinburne, Rossetti, and Browning in equal measure, and he was drawn to the Provençal poets by Rossetti's translations of the early Italian poets as well as by Browning's *Sordello*. Ultimately, Browning became the most important of Pound's nineteenth-century predecessors, for Pound thought Browning's meter, diction, and treatment of history a better starting point for an experimental poetics than the Pre-Raphaelites' more conventional metrical practices and more aestheticized view of history. Moreover, Browning's monologues often confronted the very issue of aestheticism itself. Browning's history and his rough diction, nonetheless, share common ground with Pater's aestheticism, for both worked in a tradition of contextual or existential historicism. This historical view, based in an understanding of the historicity and therefore the contingency of historical knowledge itself, emphasizes not historical narrative and teleology but the historian's affective encounter with the past. Pound's defense of "luminous detail" and his Imagist manifestos owe much to this understanding of history. The historian, like Browning in *The Ring and the Book*, Pater in *The Renaissance*, or Pound in "Near Perigord" or *The Cantos*, assembles the past from fragments, establishing weblike patterns of interconnection. This rapt contemplation of the past, for Pound as for Browning and Pater before him, is at once attractive and problematic. It can easily become a kind of aesthetic detachment that eschews historical judgment or social action. Such aestheticism evokes nostalgic or elegiac impulses. Pound's approach to the Victorian and Romantic poets was framed by this crisis in the role of the aesthetic itself.

As he responded to the work of his predecessors, Pound assimilated contradictory impulses, uniting Browning's rough diction and metrics with a utopian desire for order more characteristic of Ruskin or Carlyle and more amenable than historicist detachment to epic ambition. In *The Cantos* epic meets elegy, teleology combines uneasily with historical contextualism, and Pound finds a poetic diction and a metrical complexity surpassing even Browning's inventiveness.

Bibliography

Bornstein, George. *Poetic Remaking: The Art of Browning, Yeats, and Pound*. University Park: Pennsylvania State UP, 1988.

Christ, Carol. *Victorian and Modern Poetics*. Chicago: U of Chicago P, 1984.

de Nagy, N. Christoph. *The Poetry of Ezra Pound: The Pre-Imagist Stage*. 1960. Bern: Francke Verlag, 1968.

Gibson, Mary Ellis. *Epic Reinvented: Ezra Pound and the Victorians*. Ithaca: Cornell UP, 1995.

Longenbach, James. *Stone Cottage: Pound, Yeats, and Modernism*. New York: Oxford UP, 1988.

Mary Ellis Gibson

English Literature: Twentieth Century

Pound's influence reaches to both ends of the twentieth century: His own writing aside, his dialogue with older writers, contemporaries, and emerging authors and his tireless efforts at translating, editing, anthologizing, publishing, promoting, proofreading, financing, soliciting, scouting, and educating earn him a position in literary history that contemporary attitudes about canon and politics cannot revoke. Many of the ways of thinking now considered essential to an understanding of both Modern and Postmodern thought, such as textual self-awareness, the blurring of genre distinctions, and openness to the various influences of both non-Western traditions and nonmainstream Western influences (the occult, "low" culture, cultural theory) are all present in his work and his criticism. He is consciously Modern and made every effort to help forge a consciously Modern arts community, placing such a stamp on the first half of the century that Hugh Kenner's designation "The Pound Era" is still of use, even where not in use. He cofounded Imagism, and although Pound, H. D., and Amy Lowell, its chief writers, were American expatriates, the English F. S. Flint and Richard Aldington were among the group that first produced poems with distinctly Modern poetics, structured by successions of images. Pound had gone to England in order to connect with a literary world that the United States could not offer, and by the time he met T. S. Eliot in 1914, he had already developed a Modern poetics that served not only as a tool for his own work but also as an antenna with which to seek out other self-consciously Modern poets.

Among the important authors Pound met when newly arrived in Europe were Ford Madox Hueffer (later Ford) and W. B. Yeats. Pound had sought out Yeats as a colleague and mentor, believing him to be the best living poet working in the English language, and ended up acting as his secretary at Stone Cottage for the winters of 1913–1916. Yeats introduced Pound to a wide literary circle through his Monday Evenings (it seems he met everyone he wanted to except Charles Swinburne), but Pound was even more affected by their winters, during which time they immersed themselves in discussions about the modernization of poetry, studied Japanese Noh plays and the Chinese written character, and solidified Pound's idea of an esoteric tradition of poets existing timelessly through the ages.

Yeats introduced him to his Irish compatriot James Joyce. Pound's positions in various little magazines (*Poetry*, *Egoist*, *BLAST*, *Little Review*, *New Age*) throughout the 1910s helped advance their respective careers. He campaigned to get Joyce published and fought a hard battle—especially in the case of *Ulysses*—to publicize it and get it past the censors.

But aside from a respect for Ford, Wyndham Lewis, Joyce, and D. H. Lawrence, Pound had little interest in the British novel, limiting his literary influence to poetry, translation, and the essay. Greek, Japanese, and French drama receive more attention from Pound than English; perhaps his preoccupation with the focusing of English into something like the Chinese written character (as he perceived it) kept him bent on poetry. No matter whether it was poetry or prose, Pound sought innovation when he read; in his coevals' prose he found new ways of seeing, brought about largely by the new science of psychology, and these he integrated into his own work along with his own later additions from the "science" of economics. When Pound states, "The English prose fiction of my decade is the work of [Joyce and Lewis]" (*LE* 424), he means that these authors do something new while continuing in the tradition after Flaubert and Dostoevsky, but he also means that there is nothing else. While Pound wrote a great deal of prose, it was punchy, it attempted to mimic the direct conciseness of the ideogram, and it was not fiction. He was a great reader and writer of essays, but he read few novels and wrote none.

The innovations to poetry he helped initiate began with the Imagist's paring away of nineteenth-century imprecise verbiage and ornament, of rhythm based on "the musical phrase, not in sequence of a metronome," and of "direct treatment of the 'thing'" (*LE* 3) via the image. This was intensified through Vorticism and extended through time and space in its application to the long poem *The Cantos*. In this latter work images are strung together, their resonance with one another accumulating meaning in an attempt to gel its many fragments through its own organic structure. His subversion of form and genre and his work on language to make it as simple and natural as possible, using the right words and in a rhythm based on English rather than Latinate syntax, are concerns he shares with other Modernists and that his successors have taken up to make their own innovations. It must be realized that to a large extent these common concerns are the result of efforts to create a literary community, and despite his belief in individual nations' distinct characters, his efforts at building a community always worked against the insularity of nation-bound literature and sought out a global community as unfettered by time as by space.

Because of his desire to form such a community, Pound was an avid anthologist. From the early *Des Imagistes* (1914) onward, he attempted to shape literature's history by selecting and ordering it. He dashed off copious lists, not just of contemporary literature but of as much as he could access through his learning of language and history. His ultimate goal was to achieve a working list of writing, from the ancients to the moderns and spanning the globe, that would be readable in less than a lifetime and that would be complete, in that it would include all the major innovations to literature necessary to render its reader up to date. Pound's ambition collided with British conservatism; as he tells it, he could not get published for years in Britain after criticizing Palgrave's *Golden Treasury*, and two years later another publishing house, upon reading his proposal for an anthology, sent word that it was "too ambitious" and that they were looking for something "more in the nature of gems" (*LE* 18). By that time Pound was in France, his days in England past.

Matthew Robinson

English Review

The *English Review* was a monthly magazine founded in London in 1908 by Ford Madox Heuffer (later Ford Madox Ford). Heuffer proved himself an important contact for Ezra Pound among the elite of London's literary circles, but his magazine was also noteworthy for printing "Sestina: Altaforte," Pound's first poem placed in an English periodical. Frustrated by the insipidness of Edwardian literary publications, Ford began his magazine with the financial backing of Arthur Marwood; although the magazine continued until it merged with the *National Review* in 1937, the end of Ford's tenure as editor coincided with the purchase of the periodical by Sir Alfred Mond in 1909.

Bibliography
Goldring, Douglas. *South Lodge: Reminiscences of Violet Hunt, Ford Madox Ford, and the English Review Circle*. London: Constable, 1943.

Craig Monk

Epstein, Sir Jacob (1880–1959)

In 1920, Pound called Jacob Epstein "the greatest sculptor in Europe." It bothered Pound that his contemporaries did not appreciate Epstein as he did: He condemned popular taste that preferred the "carressable" pretty art of ancient Greece over Epstein's emotional and intellectual explorations of "form, not the *form of anything*." And while the Tate Gallery's refusal to purchase Epstein's work (despite its dedication to modern British art) angered Pound, he could not abide their refusal of a gift of Epstein's work. Pound knew that the formal innovation, abstraction, and primitivism of Epstein's sculpture might mystify the "man in the street," but he relied on such institutions as the Tate to help people appreciate modern art. Like the Futurists, Epstein brought motion and mechanism into sculpture, as seen in his monumental *Rock Drill* (1913). His work shows the influence of the arts of Egypt, India, Greece, Assyria, Africa, and Mongolia, as seen in *Tomb of Oscar Wilde* (1912), the controversial *Maternity* (sculpted for the British Medical Association), and his many portrait busts, which Pound praised as "not merely portrait busts, but the concentration of race into; the expression of race by means of; the single head" (*EP&VA* 140).

Bibliography

Black, Robert. *The Art of Jacob Epstein*. Cleveland: World Publishing, 1942.

Cork, Richard. *Jacob Epstein*. Princeton: Princeton UP, 1999.

Pound, Ezra. *Ezra Pound and the Visual Arts*. Ed. Harriet Zinnes. New York: New Directions, 1980.

Catherine E. Paul

European History: Ancient

Unlike Pound's extensive use in *The Cantos* of almost the entire history of China, or of various specific historical periods such as Renaissance Italy and the early years of the United States, he never seems to have had the same amount of profound interest in the ancient history of Europe, that is, the history of the western European and Mediterranean regions up to the fall of the Roman Empire in 476 C.E. This is all the more remarkable since ancient Greek and Roman literature constitute a major element in all of Pound's prose and poetry.

The beginning of Pound's interest in ancient history coincided with his more serious study of general history in the 1930s. Pound's "classical" interest cannot be dissociated from his generally socioeconomic approach to history as a source of evidence to justify and prove his own tenets. From the various discussions scattered throughout his prose writings, of which in this case *Selected Prose* and *Guide to Kulchur* are the most relevant, we may infer the following Poundian sweeping analysis of ancient history:

Contrasting classical Greece with Rome, Pound favored the latter. In his view, Greece lacked communal responsibility and morality as it stressed individuality at the cost of social order, despite the fact that Plato and Aristotle discussed rules for conduct. Rome, on the other hand, generally displayed a sense of responsible rule by establishing an effective order and by a recurrent concern for economic justice. In Pound's view, the Roman Empire, in contrast to Greece, tried to put certain concepts into action.

With regard to classical Greece, Pound favored Sparta over Athens. He regarded the latter as the home of monetary fraud, whereas Sparta had recognized the "true nature of money" as a medium of measure, not simply as a medium of exchange, by having the state in power of giving credit.

Judging from their recurrent use in his oeuvre, only three events from ancient European history seem to have engaged Pound's interest over a longer period of time. Needless to say, all of these three show the same general socioeconomic approach:

First, as Pound claimed in his Italian prose tracts *Carta di Visita* (1942) and *Oro e Lavoro* (1944), the decisive battle between Greece and the Persian Empire at Salamis in 480 B.C.E. was made possible because of the decision by the polis of Athens to loan money to the shipwrights, thus enabling them to build the fleet. This is a recurrent refrain in *The Pisan Cantos* (74, 77, and 79), as it exemplified one of Pound's major beliefs (in line with the theory of Social Credit), which he emphasized time over and again in his work, namely, that the extension of credit should be the prerogative of the state, not of private individuals or banks.

Second, a major refrain in *Rock-Drill* is the notion that Alexander the Great "paid the debts of his soldiery" (Cantos 85, 86, 89, and 95). Pound's own allusion to Arrian in Canto 86 refers us to Lucius Flavius Arrian (second century C.E.), whose *Anabasis of Alexander* recounts in seven books the history of Alexander the Great (356–323 B.C.E.) from his accession to his death.

Arrian VII.5 informs us how Alexander announced at Susa in 324 B.C.E. that he would pay off the debts of the entire army, presumably not only the arrears of pay but also the debts outstanding to creditors following the army such as traders and women. Alexander assured his soldiers that their names and debts would not be registered and that all debts would simply be paid. This largesse apparently represented for Pound a supreme example of what a benevolent man of action could do for his followers.

It is therefore not surprising, as one may infer from *Guide to Kulchur* and several essays included in *Selected Prose*, that Pound believed that Alexander's death and subsequent fall of his empire was as great a blow to the civilization of the Western world as the fall of Rome many centuries later.

And third, throughout *The Cantos* and in *Selected Prose* and *Guide to Kulchur*, Pound championed the reign of Antoninus Pius (138–161 C.E.) as the "apex" of the Roman Empire (Canto 88) for various reasons. It was a reign of "23 years without war" (Canto 96)—indeed, as many historians agree, Antoninus's rule marked a period of stability, prosperity, and relative peace. In addition, Pound often presented Pius as being distressed by the fact that at sea the law of Rhodes, not Roman law, was followed (Cantos 42, 46, 78, 87, 89, and 94). As Rhodes was the center of the sea trade in the Mediterranean, its laws were designed by commercial interests. One of these laws prescribed an interest of 30 percent (instead of 6 percent in customary Roman law) on capital lent for marine purposes. Finally, Pius was also indignant that the state should have advantages from certain misfortunes like shipwrecks. He therefore supported stricter maritime laws and insurance policies (*GK* 40–41; 34). Pound furthermore regarded Pius as a just and wise emperor for his lowering of the interest rates (Canto 98), calling his rate of 4 percent "the summit of Empire" (Canto 88). Therefore, Antoninus Pius in *The Cantos* is put on a par with such other Poundian heroes as Confucius (Canto 106) and Alexander the Great (Canto 107).

Pound believed that historians had disregarded the achievements of Pius in fighting economic malpractice and usury: "of Antoninus very little record remains" (Cantos 89, 97. See also Canto 107). The poet in this respect wanted to set the record straight since he thought, by basing himself on Claudius Salmasius's *De modo usurarum* (1639), that the reign of Pius, despite the emperor's efforts, marked the beginnings of usury in the Western world.

Given the above, one may state that in his study of classical history Pound simply evaluated certain periods as negative or positive by looking at the way in which the state prerogative of issuing and controlling money was used or abused and by looking at the height of the interest rates.

The following works contain some interesting discussions of European ancient history: "The Individual in His Milieu" (*SP* 242–243); "A Visiting Card" (*SP* 284–285); "Gold and Work" (*SP* 312); and *Guide to Kulchur* (23–43, 268–270).

Peter Liebregts

European History: Medieval and Renaissance

Pound's view of the past was not conventional. He was much more concerned with the "Paideuma" (*GK* 57) of the past than events. Nor was his view of history necessarily a linear one. In addition to a timeline, Pound seemed to think of history as composed of equally available nodes of significance that provide the energy for a *paideuma*. For the most part, these nodes of significance are individuals rather than the political events and armed conflicts that normally populate histories.

In Pound's view, the never-ending conflicts within the Christian churches of late antiquity had covered valuable pagan knowledge under the scabs of Christian theological argument. Certain individuals throughout the Middle Ages, though, become energetic nodes of protection for the ancient knowledge and carried it through to its rebirth. The Middle Ages, then, are important as a voyage of ancient pagan knowledge to the Renaissance.

Pound placed the beginning of the medieval era with the end of the Western Roman Empire and the retirement of Cassiodorus, circa 540 C.E., to his monastery at Vivaria (*SR* 11). Cassiodorus serves Pound not only as a place marker but also as a reminder of the pearls to be found in seldom visited literature and as a subtle reminder of paganism. Pound thought Cassiodorus one of the great conservators of knowledge (*SR* 239).

When Rome left Europe the area reverted to the tribal organization that had been its political and social structure before Roman authority. Germanic tribes known collectively as the Franks spread throughout Europe from the English Channel on the North to the Alps on the South. This time of conquest, known as the Merovingian age, resulted in a society of many independent small kingdoms. In these the beginning of feudalism can be detected as very local centers of secular power. Authority over these local centers was consolidated in a petty king, who then owed allegiance to a more powerful superior. Canto 68 refers to an observation by John Adams that the Franks had never decided whether their assemblies or their kings had sovereignty. This coalescing of power culminated with Charlemagne, circa 768 C.E., and the Carolingian Empire. Canto 96 gives a rapid-fire account of Byzantium from the failure of Rome until circa 900 C.E. and ends with a discussion of the "Eparch's Book" of economic regulations that Pound thinks foretells Mussolini's economic plan.

About 610 C.E., in Arabia, a Meccan merchant named Mohammed began preaching a religion of revelation. This new religion faced severe persecution, and about 622 Mohammed fled with his followers to Medina. By 630 Mohammed was powerful enough to conquer Mecca, and Islam began to spread throughout the world. There was no tradition of political unity beyond tribal loyalty in Arabia, and as Islam grew, a system of statehood developed known as the Caliphate, which was soon replaced by the Umayyads. Islam expanded across North Africa and finally into southern Spain, which was to remain Islamic until the European Renaissance.

In Europe the end of the Carolingian Empire began the real flowering of the side-by-side systems of feudalism and monasticism. During this flush of aesthetic vigor Pound found some of his most interesting nodes of luminescent energy. Pound was to see special significance in the importation of Neoplatonism to Europe and the role Scotus Erigena (ninth century) was to play in the integration of Neoplatonism (a pagan philosophy) into European Christianity. As the Carolingian Empire disintegrated, local lords reasserted their power, and the feudal manorial system began. The manors began another period of coalescing into empire resulting in the Holy Roman Empire. The monastic system responded to the disintegration of the Carolingian Empire by solidifying independence

from secular authority and thereby providing a firm foundation for separate papal authority in Europe. Where the arts and literature were patronized by the secular lords, scholarly learning centered in the monasteries. Ancient pagan learning protected by Islamic scholars and available to the Byzantine Empire began to enter Europe both from Spain into France and from the western Middle East into Italy. In Italy the resultant bloom of aesthetic energy was to blossom eventually into the Renaissance. During the high Middle Ages the region of Provence located in southeastern France near northern Italy became a center of this aesthetic exuberance. Roaming poets/singers known as troubadours sang of love and chivalry. It was their Provençal language that was Pound's interest as a student, and he was to translate numerous troubadour poems before his Imagist/Vorticist period and later work on *The Cantos*.

Ancient pagan learning also came to Europe with the returning crusaders. Throughout the high Middle Ages the kings of Europe sent crusades in an effort to conquer Palestine from Islam. Crusades, however, were not targeted just against Islam. Pope Leo X sponsored a crusade to defeat the Cathars, a heretic group in Provence. The returning crusaders also served to spread a European *paideuma* throughout Europe. The flowering of the humanities, the Renaissance, was a climax of aesthetic energy within this *paideuma*. Pound's two operas, *Le Testament* and *Cavalcanti*, are centered in the Renaissance. Pound's essay "The Renaissance" (*LE* 214–226) is a brief prose guide to his ideas, positive and negative, concerning the Renaissance. The "Malatesta" Cantos (8–11) are some of Pound's most beautiful poetry and display much of his thinking concerning the late Middle Ages and the Renaissance.

The Renaissance ended the Middle Ages when it started in Italy, riding upon the aesthetic vanguard of Dante and Cavalcanti. Dante's use of the pagan Virgil as a guide for "pilgrim" Dante (Renaissance man) in a Christian allegory must have been very heartening to the pagan Pound. Dante had dramatically illustrated the permanent nature of pagan knowledge and its role as a guide to the Renaissance. The reference at the beginning of Canto 23 (see also *GK* 45) to "Gemisto" Plethon, who had tried to reconstruct a society based on the polytheism of ancient Greece, further illustrates Pound's allegiance to the ancient pagan wisdoms.

F. Richard Seddon

European History: The Enlightenment

The Enlightenment, for Pound, is a period of slow decline, punctuated by individuals who retain a sense of culture and a hierarchy of values (*SP* 150). It sees the rise of mercantilism and the rule of usury, the decline in arts and letters from Renaissance heights, and the diminished impact of the few clear thinkers in philosophy and literature. Ethics is reduced to the straitened morality of puritanism, with sexual conduct as the sole measure (*GK* 185). France looks to the American golden age of Jefferson and Adams and attempts to bring about its own cultural liberty. Both nations ultimately fail.

Mercantilism and usury became institutionalized in banking: The Monte dei Paschi in Siena, founded in 1624, gave credit a legitimate measure in the abundance of nature (*SP* 270, 308; Cantos 41, 45, and 51); whereas the Bank of England, founded in 1694, claimed possession of "interest on all moneys which it creates out of nothing" (*SP* 308, 338, 343). The Rothschild dynasty, founded by Mayer Amschel, is also seen by Pound as part of the conspiracy against the interests of the public (*SP* 309–310, 311, 327, 339). Instances of the "Mediterranean sanity" endure, however. Milan and Venice declined war on account of its deleterious effect upon trade (*SP* 201), and English divine Herbert of Cherbury defended the principle of the just cause, albeit on grounds of strict opportunism (*SP* 305).

The decline of culture during the "heavy era" (*GK* 230) coincides with the rise to prominence of northern Europe. The French Bourbon court is slated by Pound, and Tuscan culture is eclipsed by Napoleonic aggression (*GK* 263). The "teutonic paideuma of the Leibniz-Bach episode" shines in the darkness of Europe and includes Handel, Goethe, and Beethoven (*GK* 230). Other bright spots include the time of Burke, when MPs (Members of Parliament) would quote in Latin (*RSWWII* 149) and when Berkeley and Hume would be printed in books containing Latin (*SP* 153).

For an age modeled on and read through its philosophy, the Enlightenment produced few thinkers of interest to Pound. He detects an entrenched triviality in post-Reformation reasoning (*LE* 394). The crucial exception is Leibniz, due to his effort to integrate philosophy with the church, unlike the empty doctrines of Luther (*SP* 57). He is grouped with Webster and Voltaire as a refiner of language (Canto 104), and his correspondence with Bossuet signals the last flicker of luminous thought (*SP* 156). Pound's unwillingness to engage with analytic philosophy is given expression in his opinion of Descartes, whose sole virtue lay in the invention of a geometry (*GK* 78). Likewise, Berkeley and Hume are notable simply for their grappling with issues of currency (*SP* 157, 259–260, 323; *GK* 48).

The French Enlightenment holds some interest for Pound, both in its own intellectual production and in its attitude toward the incipient American nation. Pierre Bayle, pillar of the Enlightenment and author in 1697 of the *Dictionnaire historique et critique* (Canto 28), is grouped with Voltaire in the battle against superstition. They are live repositories of the tradition handed down from the Italian Quattrocento (*SP* 150–151). The rich culture of the Encyclopaedists measures itself against a recognized order but wanes, refining cultural and human values into dry mathematical concepts (*SP* 154). An outlet for progressive thinkers lay in the American cause. John Adams circulated in Voltaire's Paris (Canto 65), on a mission to negotiate loans from European governments to bring financial independence from the British. Pierre Augustin Caron de Beaumarchais, playwright, supported the War of Independence with arms and ammunition (Canto 31). Hume's *History of Great Britain*, a rare British influence, served Adams as the rationale for an independent judiciary (Canto 67).

The Enlightenment records the final division between the state and the realm of letters. In England, the eighteenth century's stylistic signature is cliché, and the nineteenth century's is "MESS" (*GK* 183).The negative statement of Pope and Johnson, dressed in full prosodic regalia in the latter's "Vanity of Human Wishes," is finally halted by the destructive impulses of the French Revolution and Romanticism (*GK* 179–181).

In short, the Enlightenment is a contradiction in terms for Pound: It is a dark age (*GK* 261–262) in which values are degraded and distinctions blurred. Money, language, and civic principles are loosed from their cultural moorings. Yet a few voices may be heard, keeping the tradition of precise definition intact, in the shadow of a modern vulgarity.

Bibliography

Mengozzi, Narciso. *Il Monte dei Paschi di Siena e le Aziende in Esso Riunite.* 9 vols. Siena, 1891–1925.

Mark S. Byron

European History: Nineteenth Century

According to Ezra Pound, "The 'whole of the eighteenth century' was a cliché which the Romantics broke up, in disorderly and amateur manner" (*GK* 181). By "Romantics" Pound meant the writers of the first half of the nineteenth century. Later in the same volume he wrote, "18th century *in the main*, cliché. 19th century MESS" (*GK* 183). It seems somehow fitting that Pound, who was such a major figure in the twentieth century's literary revolution known as Modernism, was born late in this turbulent century.

Beginning with political revolution and ending in scientific revolution, the nineteenth century was also the century of the Industrial Revolution. The imperialistic project of Napoleon—"only a backwoods hell like Corsica could have produced him" (*SP* 201)—turned into a monumental failure and effectively cut off England from enlivening French influences. Later, Darwin's theory of evolution was published along with Marx's far-reaching economic and social ideas. Agrarian society was being exchanged, not easily, for an urban industrial one. Entire sciences such as psychology, anthropol-

ogy, and sociology saw their formal beginnings in the nineteenth century. A turbulent century of huge dislocation and remarkable intellectual advance, it was also known for the tremendous growth of nationalism and liberalism. Education was becoming a much more democratic institution, with higher education a reasonable ambition for the general population, and women were increasingly making their mark in intellectual pursuits. Concerning educational methods, Pound was always the nineteenth century's harshest critic. Pound was always to some extent a creature of the nineteenth century and seemed determined to shape the new century's literature in a fashion that would correct the "sins" of his birth century. His poetry prior to 1912 can be thought of as an attempt to carry a modified Romanticism into the twentieth century. Thankfully for Modernism, he, with the help of friends such as Ford Madox Ford, realized that a complete break was necessary and set about developing a Modern literary form for the new century.

The nineteenth was the century when the sun never set upon Queen Victoria's British Empire. Imperial power was at its most decadent. All the major European powers had colonies that they had learned to administer in a remarkably efficient, though hardly liberal, manner. The stresses generated by an increasing liberalism at home while riches were bureaucratically plundered from colonial peoples around the world were to be resolved in the twentieth century. Pound saw the nineteenth century as sowing the seeds of economic disaster. In "A Visiting Card" he quotes from Giuseppe Mazzini who circa 1850 wrote "the history of the last half-century, and the name of this half-century is *Materialism*." Pound adds in his bombastic style, "The nineteenth century; the century of usury!" (*SP* 312).

The nineteenth century saw the reunification of Italy, which was essentially in its modern form by 1870. Almost forgotten in this reunification was the final and complete loss of worldly power by the Roman Catholic Church. The Church was no longer officially a power in secular Europe.

Europe during the first two decades of the nineteenth century saw the ambitions of Napoleon Bonaparte embroil it in war after war of French imperial ambition. French imperial aims finally began to subside with the disastrous attempt, the Maximilian Affair, to make Mexico a French colony. Not needing the machinations of European imperial power, the New World had serious problems of its own. Early in the century, the "bank wars"—the ascendancy and fall of the second National Bank of the United States (1816–1836)—provided the glimmer of heroic optimism at the heart of Canto 37. But the enormous growth of the United States created complicated social strains that culminated in a tragically violent mid-century civil war over the question of slavery and whether the individual states were sovereign to the federation of states. The Civil War was a great divide: "American civilization was destroyed by and after the Civil War" (*SP* 301). Pound's aggravation with post–Civil War America seems founded in the expansion of its government and what he felt was a turning away from Jeffersonian democracy.

Japan ended its isolation in 1853 and under Emperor Mutsuhito (1867–1912) embarked on aggressive modernization. During this remarkable period Japan shifted from feudalism to a centralized constitutional monarchy and turned from a nation of fishermen and farmers to an industrial powerhouse. Their creations of an army according to Prussian specifications and a navy modeled upon the British one were to be the instruments of expansionism in the last decade of the nineteenth century and continued with tragic results into the twentieth. As Japan became part of the nations of the world, its arts and literature began to fascinate Europe. This interest culminated for Pound in the early twentieth century with Laurence Binyon's book on Japanese art and the Ernest Fenollosa notebooks on the languages of the Far East.

The first half of the nineteenth century saw the ascendancy of Romanticism, but it was the decadent Romanticism of the century's second half that Pound sought to end with his vision of a "modern" literature for the twentieth. While most of the nineteenth century's literature was not Pound's favorite reading, several writers whom Pound saw as isolated figures struggling against the current of the time were nonetheless influential. Pound wrote of his debt to Walt Whitman in the poem "A Pact"—the Whitman who had devised the free verse that was to prove the hallmark of Modernist poetry. In France, Stendahl and Flaubert sought the mot juste in fiction, while outsiders like Corbière and Rimbaud were ignored; Jules Laforgue (1860–1887) during his tragically short life wrote a number of works that made effective use of vers libre and explored the stream-of-consciousness technique immortalized by James Joyce. Pound wrote of Laforgue's use of satire, that is, "HAMLET or the Consequences of Filial Piety," in his essay "Irony, Laforgue, and Some Satire." The Italian Leopardi worked in splendid isolation, while the cosmopolitan German Heine traded in ironies. Pound respected English writers with continental affiliations, like Landor, Browning, and the Pre-Raphaelites, and he studied at the knee of the Irish Yeats whose work beginning in the late nineteenth century spelled the end of the Romantic period in literature.

F. Richard Seddon

European History: 1900–1972

In 1900, the nations of Europe were still adjusting to the enormous social changes that arose during the nineteenth century, and when Ezra Pound arrived in London in 1908, he was thrust into the social tensions produced as the older, rural, aristocratic order slowly relinquished its prestige and power to a modern mass society characterized by industrial production, urbanization, political enfranchisement, and nationalism. The development of Pound's poetry can be read as embodying many of these tensions. His early poems, exhibiting a Pre-Raphaelite influence, seem to turn from urban, industrial society toward the medieval culture out of which the aristocratic order developed, though, eventually, as in "In a Station of the Metro," Pound's poetry begins to address the circumstances of modern life.

Pound's and Europe's confrontation with the new social order was intensified by the advent of the Great War of 1914–1918. In the first decade of the century, imperialist ambition in Africa, precipitated by industrial-economic competition, combined with nationalistic self-interest to produce an increase in standing armies and navies among the major powers of Europe. The economic resources required by such a military buildup threatened nations such as France, Germany, and England with either bankruptcy or war—a fact that was not lost on Pound. In this volatile atmosphere of competition and complex alliances, the assassination of Archduke Ferdinand of Austria by a Serb nationalist (28 June 1914) triggered a series of declarations of war that brought most of Europe into the first mechanized conflict in history, though mechanization did not prevent the war from quickly becoming a four-year stalemate of trench engagements punctuated by indecisive offensives. The eventual cost ($186 billion) and casualties (37 million soldiers and 10 million civilians) were staggering to a Europe that, before 1914, understood armed conflict in terms of the Napoleonic Wars. Innocence, then, was also a casualty of the war, as were the medieval dynasties of the Habsburgs (Austria) and the Hohenzollerns (Germany). The slightly younger Romanov dynasty fell during the Russian Revolution of 1917, replaced by the Soviet Union, the first modern totalitarian state.

The direction of Pound's poetry began to change in response to modern war and modern society. The dominant themes of *Cathay* (1915) are separation and loneliness, especially, as in "Song of the Bowmen of Shu" and "Lament of the Frontier Guard," the loneliness of the soldier. That year, Pound's friend, the artist Henri Gaudier-Brzeska, with whom he had been corresponding since the latter enlisted, was killed at the front. In 1917, the year of the Russian Revolution, the United States' entry into the war, and the first large-scale tank assault in history, Pound began writing *Homage to Sextus Propertius*, which "presents certain emotions as vital to [Pound] in 1917, faced with the infinite and ineffable imbecility of the British Empire" (*L* 231,

1931). That same year, in "Moeurs Contemporaines," Pound seems to acknowledge that an age had passed away: "They will come no more, / The old men with beautiful manners" (*P* 181), a sentiment that grows bitter in his farewell to London, *Hugh Selwyn Mauberley* (1920). Section III decries significant elements of modern urban society—mass circulation newspapers, enfranchisement, democracy, mass-produced goods, and the market-driven economy—with particular attention to how they affect the arts. He concludes his critique with a furious eulogy for the war dead: "There died a myriad, / And of the best, among them, / For an old bitch gone in the teeth, / for a botched civilization" (*P* 191).

The Treaty of Versailles in 1919 established a humiliating peace for both defeated Germany and victorious Italy. The reparations and demilitarization demanded of the former contributed to the eventual rise of a militant National Socialism, while the Allies' condescending response to the latter's demand for promised compensation created a lasting resentment against France, England, and the United States. To prevent another world war, the treaty also provided for the establishment of the League of Nations, a forum for settling international disputes. In the *New Age* (8 January 1920), Pound expressed the fear that through the League "every local dispute may produce a world conflict" ("Guns; Oh Yes?" 574). Writing for A. R. Orage at *New Age* nurtured the turn from aestheticism to economics and politics in the Poundian program that began with the battlefield death of Gaudier-Brzeska, his "best hope for a new artistic era" (Redman 28).

In October 1922, 25,000 fascists marched toward Rome, while smaller groups took over local public buildings. When Premier Luigi Facta's call for martial law went unendorsed by King Victor Emmanuel III, Facta resigned. The king negotiated with fascist leader Benito Mussolini, who demanded and was awarded the prime ministry, concluding a three-year rise to power, aided by national instability, a faltering economy, and a series of strikes and land seizures in 1919–1920.

Pound had come to Europe to learn how to start a Renaissance, one that required a cultural center as well as "indiscriminate enthusiasm" and "a propaganda" or a movement (*SP* 128). In England and France he found "mental corpses . . . in the streets," but after his move to Rapallo in 1924, he discovered the seeds of an "Italian awakening" (*SP* 54) and saw in Fascist Italy the Jeffersonian principles he hoped would be part of an American Renaissance.

Mussolini impressed Pound, especially during their brief meeting in 1933, as a man who had "the capacity to pick out the element of immediate and major importance in any tangle" (*J/M* 66), and he believed, citing Frobenius, that "Mussolini's miracle had been that of reawakening the sense of responsibility" (*J/M* 39). Pound understood Italian fascism in terms of a Confucian and Dantean ethos in which the "individual virtue" of Mussolini could bring about a just society.

Economic reform assumed prominence in Pound's agenda after the 1929 New York Stock Exchange crash. The resulting Great Depression affected all of Europe. The Weimar Republic collapsed, allowing the National Socialist Party to rise to power in 1933.

The antiwar ethic driving Pound's economic writing was challenged in 1935 when an Italian army of 250,000 invaded Abyssinia in a belated attempt at colonialism. In 1933, Pound defended Mussolini against "the scare heads" of the "British bank-owned and gun-run press," claiming "that Mussolini has prevented outbreaks of war" ("Guns; Oh Yes?" 547), but with war imminent, Pound sought a justification, blaming "the present capitalist monetary system" (Redman 165) and implying that Italy's actions were a civilizing activity ("road building, etc.") among the barbaric Abyssinians (Redman 166). The League of Nations responded with a noncompulsory boycott of Italy, which pushed Mussolini toward an eventual alliance with Hitler.

Pound's belief that wars such as the Abyssinian conflict at least partly resulted from the machinations of international finance intensified during the Spanish Civil War. Pound publicly refused to support either the leftist Republican coalition of communists and anarchists backed by the Soviet Union or the rightist Nationalists supplied by Hitler and Mussolini. He accused both sides of ignoring the economic cause of the war, referring to it as "a sham conflict" (Stock 345).

Hitler stepped up his aggressive revisions of the Treaty of Versailles in 1938 with the annexation of Austria and the Munich agreement in which France and England, preferring appeasement to war, allowed Hitler to annex part of Czechoslovakia. Neville Chamberlain returned from Munich declaring "peace in our time," but the German invasion of Poland in September 1939 forced England and France into declarations of war.

In 1941, Pound began to make speeches on Rome Radio on a variety of topics of his own choosing. These broadcasts focused mostly on economic issues, poetry, and the war, for which international finance, including its stooges Churchill and Roosevelt, was to blame. In fact, once Pearl Harbor was bombed, Pound saw America's greatest "danger" not in its declared enemies but in usurers, often depicted in his speeches as Jews: "The danger to the United States as a system of government is NOT from Japan, but from Jewry. . . . The danger is not that you WILL BE invaded, it is that you HAVE BEEN invaded" (*RSWWII* 86). While Pound was making this speech, the systematic extermination of European Jewry, the plans for which were finalized at Wahnsee in January 1942, was being carried out. After the war, Pound denied that he had had any knowledge of the Holocaust.

By November 1942, German and Italian troops were in full retreat in North Africa. In January 1943, the remnant of the German Sixth Army surrendered at Stalingrad, putting the Axis permanently on the defensive. This reversal of fortune is reflected in Pound's radio broadcasts. By February 1943, his speeches had changed their focus to the British press, Brooks Adams, and the economic history of the United States.

On 10 July 1943, the Allies invaded Sicily. Doubtful of Mussolini's ability to lead, the fascists voted to end his dictatorship on 24 July.

The following day, he was arrested. In September, German commandos freed Mussolini and used him to establish a puppet fascist republic in Salò on Lago di Garda in northern Italy. Pound went north and became involved in its cultural/propaganda effort. Ironically, in March 1944, after decades of trying to make available to the public texts he thought essential for a Renaissance, the dying fascist regime, at Pound's urging, agreed to publish "an entire series on ancient Chinese history and culture" (Redman 250). This project occupied Pound for the rest of the war. On 3 May 1945, five days after partisans executed Mussolini, Pound turned himself in to American occupational forces.

In St. Elizabeths, Pound continued to disseminate his ideas through David Horton's and John Kasper's *Square Dollar Series* and the Melbourne journals *New Times* and *Edge*; but after returning to Europe in 1958, his political expressions were infrequent. In 1961, he appeared at the neofascist Movimento Sociale Italiano's May Day celebration but did not speak. The previous year, he had intimated his fear of nuclear war, stating, "It is difficult to write a *paradiso* when all the superficial indications are that you ought to write an apocalypse." He even saw the theme of the final cantos as "the principle of order versus the split atom" (Hall 241). *The Cantos* were never finished, though, and Pound spent the final, silent decade of his life as "the last American living the tragedy of Europe" (Hall 244).

Bibliography

Carpenter, Humphrey. *A Serious Character: The Life of Ezra Pound*. Boston: Houghton Mifflin, 1988.

Hall, Donald. *Remembering Poets: Reminiscences and Opinions: Dylan Thomas, Robert Frost, T. S. Eliot, Ezra Pound*. New York: Harper and Row, 1978. 222–244.

Pound, Ezra. "Guns; Oh Yes?" *New English Weekly* 3.24 (28 September 1933): 574.

Redman, Tim. *Ezra Pound and Italian Fascism*. New York: Cambridge UP, 1991.

Stock, Noel. *The Life of Ezra Pound*. 1970. San Francisco: North Point P, 1982.

Michael J. Alleman

Exile

The *Exile* was an expatriate magazine of letters and opinion founded by Ezra Pound in Rapallo in 1927. When *This Quarter* editor Ernest Walsh died in the autumn of 1926, Pound admitted to his father that the apparent loss of that magazine eliminated an important venue for American writers in Europe. The poet approached Ernest Hemingway and Robert McAlmon with the idea of starting a review, but he also remained intrigued by the idea of using existing little magazines in the United States for the dissemination of his critical prose. As early as December 1925, Pound had begun corresponding with a New York newspaperman named John Price. He charged Price with investigating the proliferation of magazines in America, and the two men together examined the cost of printing a magazine themselves. Not surprisingly, Price found that publishing in the United States was much more expensive than publishing in Europe, so when Pound finally decided in January 1927 to launch his own periodical, free from the editorial interference that had plagued his collaborations with others, plans were put in place for Pound to have the magazine printed in Dijon and shipped to New York for distribution in America. Pound and Price decided on a 100-page journal with an initial print run of 500 copies; the poet decided that no more than 200 copies could be sold in Europe, and he was unsure of the American reception awaiting the *Exile*. By the middle of March, Pound had drawn together the first number and sent it to Price. Shipping and customs costs were much higher than expected, and as a result, Pound was forced to reconsider publishing in the United States.

In fact, Pound was most concerned about securing American copyright on his material, and when this proved impossible with a magazine that was seen as "foreign" in the eyes of the government, the poet resolved to find some way to print in his home country. Pound had concluded originally that there was no reason to align himself with commercial publishers in the United States; such a small venture would not be viable for them. But when he approached Pascal Covici about publishing short monographs for him in Chicago, Covici showed great interest in printing the *Exile*, too. As a result, Covici immediately brought forward the next two numbers of the magazine, one in the autumn of 1927 and another in the spring of 1928. But by September of that year, Covici informed Pound that he would have to discontinue the *Exile*: It had proven too unprofitable. Forming a partnership with Donald Friede from Boni and Liveright, the publisher was setting up in the more competitive New York market. In spite of Pound's protests, the fourth and final number of the magazine appeared in the autumn.

Besides distributing the first number of the magazine, John Price was charged with seeking out manuscripts in the United States, a job he took very seriously. In spite of his efforts, the *Exile* did not distinguish itself by discovering new writers, as had many earlier modern little magazines. Indeed, Pound discouraged submissions by women and submissions of critical prose. Rather, Pound used the magazine to print a range of work from friends and acquaintances like John Rodker, William Carlos Williams, W. B. Yeats, and the young Louis Zukofsky. The *Exile* also gave an extensive airing to the work of Pound protégé Ralph Cheever Dunning. While the poet used the magazine to print a fragment of the twentieth canto, his work in the *Exile* was primarily critical prose. In these articles, he continued to outline the evils of American bureaucracy, responding to his recent experiences with customs and copyright officials, but the work was devoid of the factional dogma that would define his social commentary in periodicals through the 1930s.

Bibliography

Monk, Craig. "The Price of Publishing Modernism: Ezra Pound and the *Exile* in America." *Canadian Review of American Studies* 31.1 (2001): 429–446.
Craig Monk

Exultations

Pound's fourth poetry collection was *Exultations*. Some 1,000 sets of sheets were printed, but only about 500 copies were bound. It was published by Elkin Mathews in London on 25 October 1909. Dedicated to Carlos Tracy Chester (*"amicitiae longaevitate"*), the book reprints five poems from *A Lume Spento* and six from *A Quinzaine for This Yule*, adding sixteen new poems. Of the new poems, Pound retained six in *Personae* (1926): "Guido Invites You Thus," "Sestina: Altaforte," "Piere Vidal Old," "Ballad of the Goodly Fere," "Francesca," and "Planh for the Young English King." The first four of these (among the first six in *Exultations*) augment Pound's earlier series of vibrant Browningesque monologues, adopting the voices of, respectively, Guido Cavalcanti, troubadours Bertrans de Born and Piere Vidal, and disciple Simon Zelotes, while they further demonstrate his remarkable formal dexterity with the sonnet, sestina, sixain (sestet), and ballad. Despite his disclaimer in "How I Began" in 1913 that "Sestina" and "Ballad" were each composed in a single sitting and that the former's theme of praising war "could never be very important," these two poems remain among the most cited, highly praised, and anthologized of his early poems.

The other dozen poems new to this volume, while they were also exercises in "translating" and recreating Latin, Florentine, Provençal, and biblical voices, additionally reflect the influence of Yeats's *The Wind among the Reeds* (also published by Mathews, in 1899), with its pose of the jilted lover and association of the beloved with idealized beauty. Pound's themes divide between those poems celebrating "things most fragile in their loveliness" ("Sestina for Ysolt") and those expressing an "utter and beautiful weariness" with "ultimate wisdom" and "things terrene" ("Aux Belles de Londres"). In the former group—including "Hymn III," "Portrait," and " 'Fair Helena' by Rackham"—Pound also imitates Pre-Raphaelites such as D. G. Rossetti, in sometimes overly precious lines that repeatedly invoke the beloved's eyes, her hair, the wind, color, trees, red and white flowers, and shadows. In the latter group—including earlier poems together with "Nils Lykke," "A Song of the Virgin Mother," "Planh for the Young English King," "Alba Innominata," and "Planh"—he employs similar imagery and phrasing but in a decidedly more plaintive tone. Between these groups, midway through the collection stands the ten-part "Laudantes Decem Pulchritudinis Johannae Templi," with its allusion to a Ronsard sonnet (rendered by Yeats), which Pound also invoked in "Na Audiart" and, later, in "Sonnet in Tenzone" and Canto 80; the book's longest poem, it is one of its most overwrought in combining devotion to beauty with world weariness. Yet only two pages later, the thirteen-line "Francesca," using a more straightforward idiom, breaks through the artificial "sentiment" of late Victorian love poetry. Pound's practiced mannerisms led Edward Thomas to observe of *Exultations* that, after allowing "the turbulent opacity of [Pound's] peculiarities to sink down," we are likely to "see very nearly nothing at all." The *Spectator*'s reviewer praised Pound's scholarship but considered him "at present . . . somewhat weighted by his learning." Historically, the poet of this collection stands poised between the apprentice mastering his craft and the bold Modernist about to emerge.

Using an indeterminate number of the original sets of sheets (fewer than 500), Mathews reissued *Exultations* in 1913 as one volume with the 1909 *Personae*; Haskell House (New York) published an unauthorized reprint in 1973; all poems appear in *Collected Early Poems of Ezra Pound* (1976).

Bibliography

Grieve, Thomas F. *Ezra Pound's Early Poetry and Poetics*. Columbia: U of Missouri P, 1997.

Homberger, Eric, ed. *Ezra Pound: The Critical Heritage*. London: Routledge, 1972.

Jackson, Thomas H. *The Early Poetry of Ezra Pound*. Cambridge: Harvard UP, 1968.

Witemeyer, Hugh. *The Poetry of Ezra Pound: Forms and Renewal, 1908–1920*. Berkeley: U of California P, 1969.

John Gery

"Ezra Pound Speaking": Radio Speeches of World War II

"*Ezra Pound Speaking*" was the first widely distributed edition of Pound's World War II short-wave radio speeches and remains the most reliable and complete documentation of the bizarre mix of poetry, folksy reminiscences, hectoring lessons in global economics and American history, anti-Semitic diatribe, and fascist propaganda that led to Pound's arrest and imprisonment on charges of treason. Following Pound's long-standing desire to publish his radio broadcasts, in the 1970s Mary de Rachewiltz commissioned Leonard Doob—a Yale professor who had worked on American propaganda during World War II and first visited Pound at Brunnenburg in 1960 and 1961—to select and edit 120 of the "*discorsi*" that Pound typed out, recorded on phonograph discs, and broadcast internationally over the short-wave transmitters of Mussolini's Ministry of Popular Culture.

The 120 broadcasts chosen for inclusion in "*Ezra Pound Speaking*," selected from hundreds of typescripts preserved by Olga Rudge and Mary de Rachewiltz and now held at Yale, and from hundreds of recordings preserved by the National Archives, date from 2 October 1941 through 7 December 1941, from 29 January 1942 through 26 July 1942, and from 18 February 1943 through 25 July 1943, when Pound was being monitored by the Princeton, New Jersey, listening centers set up by the U.S. government. The selection unfortunately obscures the fact that Pound's radio career began much earlier and lasted much longer, in a much larger and more incriminating variety of duties than most of Pound's critics and biographers have been willing to admit. In fact, Pound made his first broadcast in 1935 and was on the air on a more regular basis by February 1940. As well, Pound wrote for Italian radio after 25 July 1943, when Mussolini's government fell, and continued to broadcast or write under pseudonyms until April 1945. It is for this reason that the several appendices in Doob's book—including quantitative analysis of a variety of themes in the broadcasts, covering World War II, economics, culture, and characters such as Roosevelt, Churchill, Mussolini, Hitler, Stalin, and Pound himself—are less-than-ideal tools for the reader interested in Pound's wartime activities. Doob's focus on the 1941–1943 period fails to include broadcasts from late in the war, when Pound's anti-Semitism was most overt and obsessive and his animus against the Allies was most on display, even as he knew that he had been indicted for treason. It is interesting to note that de Rachewiltz has also expressed reservations about *"Ezra Pound Speaking,"* but for just the opposite reason: Even in Doob's limited selection, Pound's often incoherent anger eclipses his ideas about politics and economics.

"Ezra Pound Speaking" uses Pound's original typescripts where possible, which means the reader avoids the egregious but at times hilarious errors made by the government transcribers at the Foreign Broadcast Intelligence Service's listening station at Princeton University, who mistook "Confucius" for "confusion" and "Monet" for "money." However, Pound often strayed from his printed text in the studio, effectively creating a new version of each script at the time of its recording. Moreover, Pound's speeches were written and aired in conjunction with a variety of news and music programs, context that is lost in a volume that treats the speeches as isolated and freestanding texts as opposed to performed texts with important and improvised relations to the day-to-day progress of the war—although the volume of speeches Pound planned for late in the war and even after his arrest in April 1945 made no concessions to the performed nature of the broadcasts. Finally, *"Ezra Pound Speaking"* silently corrects Pound's idiosyncratic spelling and punctuation, a fact that effaces, for example, Pound's telling inability to settle on a single spelling for the word *anti-Semitism*. Despite its flaws, *"Ezra Pound Speaking"* nonetheless remains an essential resource, yet pitifully understudied, due in part to the fact that the volume has been out of print since the 1980s, with no plans for republication.

Bibliography

Pound, Ezra. *Certain Radio Speeches of Ezra Pound.* Ed. William Levy. Rotterdam: Cold Turkey P, 1975.

———. *"Ezra Pound Speaking": Radio Speeches of World War II.* Ed. Leonard W. Doob. Westport: Greenwood, 1978.

———. *"IF THIS BE TREASON . . ."* Siena: Tip. Nuova, [1948]; Venice: Tip Litografia Armena, 1983.

Jonathan P. Gill

F

Faber and Faber

Faber and Faber has been, and remains, the principal English publisher of the works of Ezra Pound. Founded in 1925, as Faber and Gwyer, by Geoffrey Faber and Sir Maurice and Lady Gwyer, the press was notable for its choice of T. S. Eliot as the primary literary editor. After joining the firm in 1927, one of Eliot's first selections was Pound's *Selected Poems* (1928), for which Eliot also supplied an introduction. With the departure of the Gwyers in 1929, the company's name was changed to Faber and Faber, and from the 1930s to the 1960s the firm published over twenty titles by Pound. Faber and Faber has produced the first English editions of all of *The Cantos*, as well as "true" first editions of such texts as *ABC of Economics* (1933), *Homage to Sextus Propertius* (1934), *Polite Essays* (1937), *Guide to Kulchur* (1938), and *Literary Essays* (1954, with introduction by Eliot). The Faber and Faber editions of *Guide to Kulchur* and *The Pisan Cantos* (1948) are of particular note for, due to fear of British libel laws, references to such figures as Thomas Hardy, Rudyard Kipling, Winston Churchill, and the Prince of Wales were removed or altered. Today, the work of Pound makes up a substantial portion of Faber and Faber's publication list with fourteen Pound titles still in print.

Bibliography

Ackroyd, Peter. *T. S. Eliot*. London: Hamish Hamilton, 1984.

Faber and Faber. 16 November 2004. http://www.faber.co.uk/aboutfaber/history/index.cgi.

Levy, Alan. *Ezra Pound: The Voice of Silence*. Sag Harbor: Permanent P, 1983.

Stephen Cain

Fang, Achilles (1910–1995)

While at Harvard in 1949 researching "materials" (sources) of *The Cantos* for his dissertation, sinologist Fang contacted Pound to persuade him to "correct" the romanized spelling of Chinese. Pound refused, but the two collaborated to publish *The Classic Anthology Defined by Confucius* (1954). Fang's introduction emphasizes the musicality and "ballad meter" of Pound's translation as appropriate for the odes' popular subject matter and traces the etymology of *li*, important to *The Cantos*. A much anticipated scholarly edition prepared by Fang, including a Chinese seal script and a "singing key," was never published, thereby estranging the two men. Fang also wrote "A Note on the Stork Editions," included in *Confucius. The Great Digest & Unwobbling Pivot* (1951) and may have facilitated Pound's meeting Archibald MacLeish.

Bibliography

Cheadle, Mary Paterson. *Ezra Pound's Confucian Translations*. Ann Arbor: U of Michigan P, 1997.

Fang, Achilles. "Fenollosa and Pound." *Harvard Journal of Asiatic Studies* 20.1–2 (1957): 213–238.

———. "Materials for the Study of Pound's *Cantos*." Diss. Harvard U, 1958.

———. "Some Reflections on the Difficulty of Translation." *On Translation*. Ed. R. Brower. Cambridge: Harvard UP, 1959.

John Gery

Fascist Quarterly [later *British Union Quarterly*]

The *Fascist Quarterly* was founded in London in 1935 with the intention of "formulating the intellectual background of the Fascist creed." A publication of Sir Oswald Moseley's British Union of Fascists (BUF), the magazine wished to define further "an essentially British interpretation of a new dynamism." Consisting mostly of political essays, the magazine did review books and comment upon the arts from a consistent ideological perspective. While Ezra Pound had fallen out with the BUF in 1933 because the organization chose not to help him publish his *Jefferson and/or Mussolini*, the *Fascist Quarterly* soon drew his attention, and he judged it to be well edited. His work began appearing in the magazine in October 1936, but he used his first article, "A Social Creditor Serves Notice," to establish himself at some distance from the group itself, while he expounded the virtues of Italy under Mussolini. Indeed, none of his contributions ever discussed fascism directly. When the magazine relaunched as the *British Union Quarterly* in January 1937, Pound began a period as a frequent contributor that lasted nearly two years. In this time, his material dealt in general terms with topics related to his interest in politics and economics, but "The 'Criterion' Passes" in the April–June 1939 number is noteworthy for its rebuke of T. S. Eliot.

Craig Monk

Fenollosa, Ernest (1853–1908) and *The Chinese Written Character as a Medium for Poetry*

Ezra Pound described the life of Ernest Fenollosa as "the romance *par excellence* of modern scholarship" (Chisolm vii). Born in Salem, the nineteenth-century American center of Far East trade, Fenollosa was the quintessential roving Victorian scholar whose work constituted the central influence on Pound's understanding and appreciation of Oriental literature and art and whose notes provided the basis for Pound's translations of the Noh plays and the *Cathay* collection.

A devotee of Emerson, Fenollosa received a B.A. in Philosophy from Harvard and spent several years in graduate and divinity school, before leaving, in 1877, to study painting at the Boston Museum of Fine Art. While there, Fen-

ollosa's Salem neighbor Edward Morse convinced him to take one of the newly available faculty positions for Westerners at Tokyo University. In 1878, with no prior experience in Oriental studies, the twenty-five-year old Fenollosa set off to teach political economy and philosophy in a chaotic Tokyo that just ten years earlier had witnessed the fall of the Shoguns and the restoration of the emperor. Fenollosa formed an instant and enduring connection to Japanese art and culture, becoming, among other things, a Buddhist priest, a member of a traditional family guild of painters, an avid archaeologist, and ultimately, Japanese Imperial Commissioner of Fine Art. In short order, Fenollosa was transformed from a journeyman scholar with no knowledge of the Orient into the West's most prestigious critic of Japanese art, not to mention an extremely influential voice within Japan itself, reawakening local interest in such forgotten artists as Okio.

By the time the Japanese government passed the 1884 Koko Ho, the law that restricted the export of ancient art, Fenollosa had already sold his formidable personal collection to G. C. Weld, and in 1890 he returned to Boston to curate the Fenollosa-Weld collection at the Boston Museum of Fine Art. Apparently unconcerned with his new title and respectability, he married his free-spirited assistant Mary McNeil Scott (who would publish several novels under the pseudonym Sidney McCall) and, in 1897, returned with her to Japan. After several years of intensive study, the couple moved to New York in 1900, and it was here that Fenollosa wrote *The Chinese Written Character as a Medium for Poetry* and the work for which he is primarily remembered in art history, *Epochs of Chinese and Japanese Art*. He died in 1908 and was buried by the shores of Lake Biwa in the garb of a Buddhist neophyte.

One can see why Pound would have been predisposed to admire the work of Fenollosa, a man described by Henry Adams as "a kind of St. Dominic [who] holds himself responsible for the dissemination of useless knowledge by others" (Brooks 41). The widowed Mary Fenollosa presented her husband's notebooks to Pound because, according to Eliot's account, he was "the interpreter whom her husband would have wished" (Eliot 177). Pound edited and was responsible for the publication of *The Chinese Written Character as a Medium for Poetry* (1920), a work considered central to Pound's understanding of the ideogram and poetics in general.

The crux of the argument presented in *The Chinese Written Character*, and the feature of the essay that so attracted Pound, was Fenollosa's claim that the Chinese characters in particular, and ideograms in general, are "much more than arbitrary symbols" since they are "based on a vivid shorthand picture of the operation of nature" and thus evoke a reader's thoughts "far more vividly and concretely" than words. (Fenollosa 8) This position, closely aligned with Pound's belief that "the proper and perfect symbol is the natural object" (9), has been difficult for theorists to accept since it seems to postulate a direct, nonarbitrary link between the ideograms and the objects to which they refer, apparently collapsing the distinction between language and perception. Fenollosa goes on to claim that the etymology of Chinese characters may be traced back to pictorial origins, essentially sketches, and that any reader, regardless of training or experience, would be able to read Chinese, had the characters not subsequently become so stylized. Again, the suggestion seems to be that the operation of the characters allows them to function not as linguistic signifiers but as meaning in and of itself, effortlessly leaping the gap between icon and index and conveying clear and decidable significance, all of which flies in the face of most twentieth-century criticism. But it could be argued that the nonarbitrary aspect of Chinese characters to which Fenollosa refers concerns the shape of the characters and not their ability to generate meaning.

The essay clearly states that words "are only phonetic symbols" that could easily be replaced by "equally arbitrary . . . Chinese characters" (Fenollosa 8). Fenollosa ascribes a certain causal intent to the fictitious primogenitors of the language, that these originators wanted the characters to visibly resemble natural objects, a questionable claim to be sure—but he does not postulate a causal relationship between ideograms and meaning. Though Fenollosa seems to believe that ideograms represent a more transparent conveyance of significance than alphabetic language, nothing in *The Chinese Written Character* suggests that ideograms generate meaning in an intuitive, "bottom up" manner.

Fenollosa examines the workings of ideographic metaphor in a similar manner, detailing a method of imagistic juxtaposition reminiscent of Pound's paratactic poetics. The theory is based on Fenollosa's belief that every object or action in nature is related to some other object or action; thus, "in nature there is no completeness" (Fenollosa 22). Metaphor develops in response to these "objective lines of relation in nature," and not as a result of "arbitrary subjective processes" (22). This too is problematic for Modern theorists since the claim that natural processes necessitate certain literary practices seems to obscure, or deny, the discursive origins of metaphor. However, in a certain sense Fenollosa's methodology is not as dissimilar to that of later theorists as it would at first appear. Derrida also claims that "necessity operates within language and society according to the ways and powers that belong to the state of pure nature" (Derrida 271). Though this claim is a sidebar to Derrida's investigation of the manner in which discourse generates and modifies a sign, a line of inquiry that Fenollosa, writing at the turn of the century, could scarcely have imagined, it is not, in form at least, unlike Fenollosa's claim that "the observed world furnish[es] a model" for metaphor (Fenollosa 23). Even though Fenollosa clearly believes that this preexistent, nonlinguistic world is in some sense accessible, *The Chinese Written Character* never asserts that this world provides metaphor itself, nor that metaphor can be anything but a product of the system of signification in which it is produced. The essay does not so much seek to deny the discursive origins of metaphor, or claim that metaphor follows infallibly from some a priori condition of a perceiver's relation to the phenomenal, but rather argues for the existence of similar interactions and contiguities in nature. In any case, Fenollosa's recognition that isolating the origins of metaphor is not as simple as noting its first use in spoken discourse represents a fundamental break in the history of critical practice.

Bibliography

Brooks, Van Wyck. *Fenollosa and His Circle: With Other Essays in Biography*. New York: Dutton, 1962.
Chisolm, Lawerence W. *Fenollosa: The Far East and American Culture*. New Haven: Yale UP, 1963.
Derrida, Jacques. *Of Grammatology*. Trans. Gayatri Spivak. Baltimore: Johns Hopkins UP, 1976.
Eliot, T. S. "Ezra Pound: His Metric and Poetry." *To Criticize the Critic: Eight Essays on Literature and Education*. New York and London: Faber, 1965. 162–182.
Fenollosa, Ernest. *Epochs of Chinese & Japanese Art*. 2 vols. New York: Stokes, 1900.
Pound, Ezra. "A Retrospect." *Pavannes and Divisions*. New York: Knopf, 1918.

Lance Callahan

Flint, F. S. [Frank Stuart] (1885–1960)

For a time a notable poet, critic, and translator, F. S. Flint is now largely forgotten but worth rediscovering for a few poems and some sharp, polemical critical prose. He also has the distinction of having written, before Ezra Pound, a significant critical panorama of contemporary French poetry and for being one of the best-respected English intellectuals across the Channel. His contacts with many of the notable French and European writers of the early twentieth century are evidenced in a huge and fascinating array of letters that has still not been properly studied.

Born into a poor family in Islington in 1885, Flint left school at thirteen, joining the civil service as a typist five years later. Unlike many of his contemporaries in the world of letters, Flint was self-educated, studying French at night school, before going on to master several more languages, including German and Latin. In 1909 he published his first book of poems, *In the Net of the Stars*, and wrote a letter to the *New Age* attacking T. E. Hulme and the Poets' Club. Hulme replied in typically forceful manner, but

the two became friends and moved on to found the "Secession Club" (the "forgotten school" of images mentioned by Pound in *Ripostes*) and collaborated on translations and articles. Flint became one of the first Imagists, anthologized in Pound's *Des Imagistes*, as well as in the later books edited by Amy Lowell. His "Imagisme" (the famous three cardinal rules) appeared alongside Pound's "A Few Don'ts" in the March 1913 issue of *Poetry*, and Flint became a leading exponent of Imagist technique, vers libre, and a generally international attitude to poetry, before arguing with Pound over his 1915 "History of Imagism" in the *Egoist*, in which he diminished Pound's importance to the movement's beginnings. Flint's most durable poetry is his Imagist work collected in *Cadences* (1915); after this he returned to a more traditional Romantic approach. Though he continued to write reviews and essays after his Imagist period, Flint sustained a successful career in the civil service, from which he retired with distinction in 1951. Though he will never be studied in his own right, some of his poems, translations, and essays remain integral to an understanding of the forces in the air in Modernist London in the period 1910–1918.

Bibliography

Coffman, Stanley K., Jr. *Imagism: A Chapter for the History of Modern Poetry*. New York: Octagon Books, 1972.
Flint, F. S. *New Paths: Verse, Prose, Pictures, 1917–1918*. Ed. C. W. Beaumont and M.T.H. Sadler. London: Beaumont, 1918.
Hughes, Glenn. *Imagism & the Imagists: A Study in Modern Poetry*. New York: Biblo and Tannen, 1972.
Levenson, Michael H. *A Genealogy of Modernism: A Study of English Literary Doctrine, 1908–1922*. Cambridge: Cambridge UP, 1984.
Schneidau, Herbert N. *Ezra Pound: The Image and the Real*. Baton Rouge: Louisiana State UP, 1969.

Patrick McGinness

Ford, Ford Madox (1873–1939)

Ford Madox Ford was an English writer with a long career as novelist, poet, editor, and critic.

On his arrival in London in the fall of 1908, Ezra Pound was soon drawn into the circle around Ford, who was then preparing to launch the *English Review*. Close contact had been established at least by the early months of 1909, and Ford (or Hueffer, as he was then known) published several of Pound's poems, among them "Sestina: Altaforte" (June 1909). Thus began a thirty-year-long literary friendship, which withstood the vicissitudes of life and occasional manifestations of disagreement and irritation. We learn about it through their correspondence, which began with a note from Pound in 1909 and lasted till 1939 when he sent a final message. Their writings about each other also shed light on the relationship, beginning with Pound's review of the volume of verse *High Germany* (1912) and ending with his references to "Fordie" in *The Pisan Cantos* (74, 80, and 82) and *Thrones* (100 and 104) Cantos. In his important review of Ford's *Collected Poems* (1914), reprinted as "The Prose Tradition in Verse," he praised the poet for insisting "upon clarity and precision, upon the prose tradition; in brief, upon efficient writing—even in verse" (*LE* 377). It was above all Ford's *ideas* that interested him, and he claimed that for discussions of poetry he would rather turn to him than to any other man in London. Whatever disagreements there may have been between Pound the Vorticist and Ford the Impressionist, Ford was still a model of the dedicated artist as he figures in *Hugh Selwyn Mauberley* (1920).

Ford's earliest treatment of a work by Pound was a review of *Cathay* (1915), where he found "things of a supreme beauty." Throughout the years they boosted each other in various ways. Ford's reviews of *Personae* (1926) and *How to Read* (1932) were part of *his* log rolling. Pound drafted an essay (in Italian) on Ford's *Return to Yesterday* (1931), where he paid tribute to his friend's human qualities. One of Ford's most ambitious efforts was to organize and contribute to a collection of "testimonies" by several influential writers in support of *A Draft of XXX Cantos* (1930). The year after he declined to review *ABC of Economics*; this was an interest he did *not* share.

Toward the end of the 1930s Pound was becoming more explicit about who had been the chief literary mentor in prewar London. In "We Have Had No Battles," included in *Polite Essays* (1937), he says that for him and his contemporaries the "revolution of the word" began with "the LONE whimper of Ford Madox Hueffer." And in "This Hulme Business" (1939) he "rectified" a point in literary history: "The critical LIGHT during the years immediately pre-war in London shone not from Hulme but from Ford (Madox etc.) in so far as it fell on writing at all" (Kenner 307). It became a sore point with him that Ford had not received his due for the work he had done. It seemed that Ford, now in poor health and with financial problems, was being sorely neglected. In his obituary of Ford in the *Nineteenth Century and After* (August 1939), one of his most significant appraisals of his friend, he stresses the example he had set in using a clear and simple language in verse and the fact that Ford's critical acumen had been too little appreciated.

During the St. Elizabeths years and after, Ford was often in his thoughts, the memory saddened by a twinge of bad conscience, for Fordie had seen more than his contemporaries, Pound himself included, gave him credit for. In *The Pisan Cantos* Ford's significance is again restated: His conversation was better than Yeats's, for whose sake Pound had come to London in 1908. Ford's conversation consisted in "*res* non *verba*," and he had "more *humanitas*" (Canto 82). Again and again he expressed his *personal* debt to Ford the teacher, and he often came back to that first, dramatic lesson: the scene in Giessen in 1911 when Ford rolled on the floor, groaning at the archaic language of his young friend's early product *Canzoni*. It was a roll, Pound says in the obituary, that "displayed me trapped, fly-papered, gummed and strapped down in jejune provincial effort to learn, *mehercule*, the stilted language that then passed for 'good English' in the arthritic milieu that held control of the respected British circles." That roll, he concluded, "saved me at least two years, perhaps more. It sent me back to my own proper effort, namely, toward using the living tongue" (*SP* 462). It probably also led to greater self-confidence and independence. It would be hard to find another writer whose memory Pound treasured more and for whose friendship and "preachings" he was more grateful. Among the "lordly" men whom he salutes in *The Pisan Cantos*, "Old Fordie" stands out precisely for qualities that Pound the poet valued highly.

Bibliography

Kenner, Hugh. *The Poetry of Ezra Pound.* 1951. Lincoln: U of Nebraska P, 1985.

Pound, Ezra. *Pound/Ford: The Story of a Literary Friendship.* Ed. Brita Lindberg-Seyersted. New York: New Directions, 1982.

Brita Lindberg-Seyersted

French Literature and Translation

Key contemporary French writers who drew Pound's interest during his London and Paris years (1908–1925) helped to shape his emerging poetics, especially Imagism, Vorticism, and the high Modernist style of the early cantos. Pound's studies of developments in English and French poetics from the Middle Ages to the turn of the century had convinced him the French were precursors: "For the best part of a thousand years English poets have gone to school to the French. The history of English poetic glory is a history of poetic steals from the French" (*EPPP* 1.154). He sought to reform the Anglo-American Modernist canon by coordinating these "steals": As foreign editor for little magazines such as *Poetry*, the *Dial*, and the *Little Review*, he published and translated seminal works as exemplars and alerted readers to qualities and poetic techniques he considered essential to the evolution of English-language poetry.

Pound had been emulating the forms of medieval Provençal poets like Arnault Daniel since his undergraduate studies at Hamilton College. His academic work culminated in *The Spirit of Romance* (1910), but he did not become seriously interested in contemporary French poetry until he moved to London in 1908. There he joined the second Poets' Club (1909), composed of F. S. Flint, T. E. Hulme, and Florence Farr, among others, who introduced Pound to "les jeunes": Jules Romains, Georges Duhamel, Charles Vildrac,

Laurent Tailhade, Francis Jammes, Remy de Gourmont, and Émile Verhaeren; he began to value earlier poets his contemporaries had undervalued—Rimbaud, Corbière, Laforgue, and the later Gautier. Pound increasingly focused on contemporary French poets as models for Anglophone Modernists; by 1913, acting as foreign correspondent for *Poetry*, he declared in "Status Rerum" that the "important work of the last twenty-five years has been done in Paris" (*EPPP* 1.111).

In a series of writings spanning 1913 to 1925, Pound established a canon of French poets that would move English poetry out of its stymied post-Symbolist phase toward a new Realism: a more quotidian subject matter, a more natural speech-based prosody, and a more abstract treatment of form. As Scott Hamilton argues, these French poets provided Pound with models that enabled him to bring together the antithetical poetics represented by Yeats, a Symbolist, and Ford, a Realist: how to "mediate between these opposed demands of quotidian realism and a Parnassian longing for ideal beauty" (12). Pound's transition from Yeatsian Symbolism to the prose-inspired Realism of Ford coincided with his discovery of French poets who provided him with concrete exemplars. He read French poets in the context of Ford's Realism, saying Jammes's poetry was "such that the two papers by Ford Madox Hueffer . . . might have been written for the express purpose of praising it" (*EPPP* 1.162–163).

Ford derived his Realist "prose tradition in verse" from modeling poetry on the rhetoric-free "constatation of fact" he found in French prose, in particular that of Flaubert, and to a lesser extent, of Voltaire and Stendhal. Ford saw himself as the "grandfather" of literary Impressionism, a movement Pound at first embraced and defined as "a school of prose writers, and of verse writers for that matter, whose forerunner was Stendhal and whose founder was Flaubert," including Ford, Joyce, Jammes, Vildrac, and D. H. Lawrence, among others, and characterized by "clear hard prose" and "exact presentation" (*LE* 399–401). But by 1914, Pound had become critical of how Ford applied Flaubertian tenets in his own verse, which he felt lacked condensation, lyrical intensity, and complexity of form. Wanting to preserve the salutary effects of Ford's "French Flaubertian tradition" from being distorted, Pound joined Lewis in attacking Impressionism in *BLAST* as rightly superceded by Vorticism: "As to the lean belated Impressionism at present attempting to eke out a little life on these islands: Our vortex is fed up with your dispersals, reasonable chicken-men. . . . Our vortex rushes out like an angry dog at your Impressionistic fuss" (Lewis and Pound 149). In 1922, Pound named Joyce, whom he no longer identified with Impressionism, as Flaubert's true successor:

> Joyce has taken up the art of writing where Flaubert left it. In *Dubliners* and *The Portrait* he has not exceeded the *Trois Contes* or *L'Education*; in *Ulysses* he has carried on a process begun in *Bouvard et Pécuchet*; he has brought it to a degree of greater efficiency, of greater compactness; he has swallowed the *Tentation de St Antoine* whole, it serves as comparison for a single episode in *Ulysses*. *Ulysses* has more form than any novel of Flaubert's. (*LE* 403)

Despite his disapproval of Ford's verse, Pound consistently recognized Ford's importance as the first proponent of the "simple gallic doctrine of living language and the mot juste," as the man who "almost singlehandedly" reinstated the exchange with France interrupted by Napoleon:

> Our literature is always in full bloom after contact with France. . . . And the disease of both England and America during the last century is due precisely to a stoppage of circulation. Note that at just the time when Voltaire would normally have reached the English public . . . the Napoleonic wars intervened, communication was stopped. . . . France went on to Stendhal and Flaubert. England declined. . . . Her anaemia contaminated America. (*SP* 200)

In the 1929 essay "How to Read," Pound again reiterated Ford's doctrine and prescibed specific texts: "I believe no man can now write really good verse unless he knows Stendhal and Flaubert. Or, let us say, *Le Rouge et le Noir*, the first half of *La Chartreuse* [*de Parme*], *Madame Bovary*, *L'Education*, *Trois Contes*, *Bouvard et Pécuchet*. To put it more strongly, he will learn more about the art of charging words from Flaubert than he will from the floribund sixteenth-century dramatists" (*LE* 32). Similarly, in "The Renaissance" he states, "What one learns from other French poets, one might as readily learn from Voltaire and Stendhal and Flaubert" (*LE* 216).

Pound was clearly guided by contemporary French theoretical works as well as poetry. Through the second Poets' Club, Pound had regular contact with Flint and Harold Munro, founder of the *Poetry Review* (later *Poetry and Drama*), who carried on an extensive correspondence with several French poets. Most notably, Flint and Munro received large amounts of material from Alexandre Mercereau, a member of the Abbaye de Créteil group, a *phalanstère* of writers, poets, and musicians who lived together and published their own works from 1906 to 1908. Their poetic treatises defined new poetic techniques for vers librists that would better emulate natural speech, such as irregular line length, and internal rhyme and assonance as opposed to end rhyme. The Imagist manifesto, cowritten by Flint and Pound, "A Few Don'ts by an Imagiste," twice refers to Duhamel and Vildrac's *Notes sur la Technique Poétique*, whose advice on rhythm is clearly the source of the third Imagiste rule: "As regarding rhythm: to compose in the sequence of the musical phrase, not in the sequence of a metronome" (*LE* 3).

Pound's 1913 series in the *New Age*, "The Approach to Paris," and his "Editorial Comment: Paris" in *Poetry* that same year recommended key French writers and outlined qualities to be emulated: "I think our American bards would study Remy de Gourmont for rhythm, Laurent Tailhade for delineation, Henri de Regnier for simplicity of syntactical construction, Francis Jammes for humanity and the faculty of rendering his own time; and . . . intensity from Corbière" (*EPPP* 1.162–163).

"The Hard and Soft of French Poetry" (*EPPP* 3.55–58) establishes the later work of Théophile

Gautier, *Émaux et Camées* (1852), as a major turning point in French poetics. By exhorting us "to cut in hard substance, the shell or the Parian," Gautier set a standard of "hardness" and "softness" according to which poets could be categorized: "Hard" English poets are Walter Savage Landor, Lionel Johnson, good Chaucerians, Alexander Pope; "hard" French poets include Gautier, Corbière, Heredia, Samain, and Tailhade, whereas Jammes is soft. Romains, Vildrac, and Spire are soft in reaction to Gautier, having deliberately left "the ambitions of Gautier" to pursue "a new kind of French poetry" at the "dictates" of Unanimism. Interestingly, in a somewhat anti-Imagist move, Pound places his most admired writers among the "soft": Flaubert and de Gourmont for prose, Jammes for poetry, the Unanimists, Romains, Vildrac, Arcos, and most surprisingly, Pound himself. That Pound should see himself as part of those who "have left the ambitions of Gautier" and that he should examine the question of "hardness" to "ask how poetry can get on without it" indicates he was already moving away from his Imagist and anti-Symbolist stance toward what would become his more inclusive style in *The Cantos*.

Pound's 1917 essay "Irony, Laforgue and Some Satire" designates Laforgue as the poet who "marks the next phase in poetry after Gautier." Laforgue's skill as an "ironist," "purge," and "critic" makes him a great decimator of "literary poses and cliché." Laforgue was even better at purifying irony than Flaubert, having "laughed out his errors" and achieved in poetic form what Flaubert attempted in *Bouvard et Pécuchet*, an encyclopedia of the stupidities of Western civilization. By exposing human stupidity through the dross that accumulated on the language of Western civilization, Laforgue became in Pound's view "a deliverer of the nations . . . a father of light" (*EPPP* 2.279).

Qualities Pound praises in "The Approach to Paris" series reflect his Imagist and developing Vorticist poetics. Between 1911 and 1913, Pound expanded his definition of the image from an "intellectual and emotional complex in an instant of time" to "a radiant node or cluster, . . . a VORTEX, from which, and through which and into which, ideas are constantly rushing." In "As for Imagisme" he seeks to correct misconceptions about Imagist theory, which by 1915 had come to be loosely associated with Hellenism or vers libre in general: The image is "emotion" (synonymous with "energy") that "expresses itself in form" creating "pattern units, or units of design." "The image is more than an idea. It is a vortex or cluster of fused ideas and is endowed with energy" (*EPPP* 2.8). His initial emphasis on conciseness and exact diction, largely inspired by his study of Noh plays and Japanese haiku, was steadily evolving toward a definition of the image as dynamic, interactive energy as he applied Cubist and Futurist theories from the plastic arts to poetry. Pondrom notes Pound's attention to form and structural patterns in "The Approach to Paris": He praises Remy de Gourmont's *Le Latin Mystique* for its rhythmic structures, which he defined as "a geometrical pattern made up of homogenous units." Similarly, his interest in Jules Romains's "Puissances de Paris" is due to the innovative Unanimist vision of social structures as form: Our individual bodies are not units unto themselves but ever-changing components of crowds that lack physical limits, that interpenetrate, that coincide. The leader of a social unit, like the speaker in "Ode to the Crowd Here Present," is the "vortex" of his structural unit.

Although Pound claimed he was not interested in the *pathétique* of Romains's Unanimism per se and attributed it to the current "craze for crowd psychology," he devoted five different articles to explaining the movement and translated the lengthy "Reflexions" essay of *Puissances de Paris* in full. Pound's interest in Romains continued as he and Wyndham Lewis developed Vorticist aesthetics. He saw Unanimism in terms of "the development of instinct to cope with the metropolis" and likens Lewis's theory on giants and Romains's "âme collective" to the vortex or the "hypothesis of the dominant cell." He compares the energy of the Abbaye de Créteil group, who were inspired by Romains's Unanimist theories, to the *BLAST* group in England and claimed Romains and Lewis "hold the two tenable positions: the Mountain and the Multitude." In 1918, Pound reiterated that Romains's work was "perhaps the fullest statement of the poetic consciousness of our time" (*EPPP* 3.51).

Pound's hierarchy of French poets evolved with his poetics. His 1913 series "The Approach to Paris" for the *New Age* heaps inordinate praise on minor poets like Jammes ("the greatest living French poet"), Jouve, Spire, and Vildrac and yet dismisses Apollinaire's *Alcools* as merely "clever" and Rimbaud as "bitten by the pox of rhetoric" and overrated. His 1918 issue of the *Little Review*, "A Study of French Poets," would correct many of these judgments: Poets such as Jammes and Jouve he rightly termed "sentimental" and Spire "overly-rhetorical." Rimbaud, on the other hand, rose to the level of genius: "HOW, HOW, HOW! so much could have escaped me" (*EPPP* 3.31). A 1928 letter to René Taupin (author of *L'influence du symbolisme français sur la poésie américaine de 1910 à 1920*) provides a mature retrospect in which he cites the French poets who most influenced him: Villon (whose influence has been confused with Corbière's), Laforgue, Gautier, whom he "reveres," Tailhade ("superficially"), and most importantly Rimbaud, whose work Pound's systematized poetics most resembles (*LE* 216–218).

Pound greatly admired Remy de Gourmont, founder and publisher of the journal *Mercure de France* and author of the Symbolist anthology *Le Livre des Masques* (1896), as poet, philosopher, and leader of "les jeunes." As Richard Sieburth notes, "[B]etween 1912 and 1922 he was to devote more pages of enthusiastic appreciation and translation to Gourmont than any other single contemporary" (1). Pound quotes extensively from "Litanies de la Rose," remarking on the delicate accords and rhythms and crediting Gourmont with knowing "more about verse-rhythm than any man now living" and as having made "the most valuable contribution to the development of the strophe" since Arnault Daniel by creating a new "wave-length," a rhythm made of homogenous parts as opposed to parts

that differ" (*EPPP* 2.154–155). Pound's "A Distinction," his 1915 obituary on de Gourmont, defines him as having "prepared our era"; he likens de Gourmont's "gracious" mind, unencumbered by "idées reçues," to that of a scientist, and Paris to his laboratory (*EPPP* 2.133–135). He translated a collection of 224 unpublished aphorisms Gourmont had entrusted to him shortly before his death, published in nine installments as "Dust for Sparrows" in the *Dial* (1920–1921); and he devoted a special issue of the *Little Review* to him in 1919.

It is not surprising that Pound left London for Paris in 1920, since he increasingly saw Paris as the current cultural vortex of Western civilization. He quickly became involved with the Parisian avant-garde Dadaists. Initially attracted to their irreverence toward bourgeois values and journalists, he eventually incorporated some Dadaist techniques in his poetics. He made three contributions to Dadaist journals: His poem "KONGO ROUX," which appeared in *Le Pilhaou-Thibaou* (1921), is replete with erratic typography, nonsense aphorisms, and incomprehensible slogans, much like his contributions to Tzara's *Dadaphone* (1920). Pound published William Carlos Williams's Dadaist-influenced "Kora in Hell" in the *Little Review* (1921). He took a particular interest in the work of Dadaist Francis Picabia, nominating him as co-foreign editor of the *Little Review* and publishing a special Picabia issue in 1921. Pursuant to his involvement with the Dadaists, Pound's style changed significantly: He left the "strict rules of epic gravitas," adopted a colloquial, urbane tone, and began incorporating prosaic materials such as snippets of slang, invoices, and bills of lading in the Malatesta Cantos (Bush 248).

Along with the Dadaists, Pound also sought out the young Paul Morand, whom he saw as offering "the first clear eye that has been able to wander about both ends of Europe looking at wreckage" (Morand ix). Pound so admired Morand's sexual frankness, his ability to portray "race" or nationality, his "elliptical" style, and wry portrayals of European decay in the wake of World War I that he signed a contract in May

1920 to translate two volumes of his short stories, *Ouvert la nuit* and *Tendres Stocks*. Morand, who was fluent in English, liked Pound's translations *Open All Night* and *Fancy Goods* very much, and "Turkish Night" was well received when published in the *Dial* (1921). Unfortunately, the English publisher Chapman and Dodd disapproved of Pound's translation and backed out of the contract. Pound defended his "changes of idiom" and "condensation of phrase" above "a verbatim translation into stenographer's pigeon [*sic*] English" and insisted that the dialogue in the stories must be translated into "speakable phrases" (Morand xv). Pound's concern with conveying authentic voices would play a crucial role in the often-dramatic format of *The Cantos*, with its myriad of intercrossing character monologues.

Pound's prescience as literary critic rarely fails; his occasional overpraise of certain contemporary French authors may be especially indicative of concerns strong enough to have temporarily clouded his judgment. When Pound very generously compares Jammes to Dante as "one who delineates his time clearly" and who is "the acme and epitome of the . . . civilization from which he is sprung" (*EPPP* 1.184–185) or compliments Romains's unexceptional "Un Être en Marche" as "possibly the nearest approach to the true epic that we have had since the middle ages" (*EPPP* 1.158), it is more a reflection of the germs of his epic vision that would be expressed in *The Cantos* than an accurate assessment. He admired Jouve for writing in the "new jargon" about automobiles and airplanes since he conveyed the "vitality of the time" (*EPPP* 1.117). French contemporary writers helped show Pound how to combine quotidian, urban material with High Classical models of the epic gravitas and how to move Anglophone poetry out of its stymied post-Symbolist phase toward High Modernism.

Bibliography

Bush, Ronald. *The Genesis of Ezra Pound's Cantos.* Princeton: Princeton UP, 1976.

Hamilton, Scott. *Ezra Pound and the Symbolist Inheritance.* Princeton: Princeton UP, 1992.

Kenner, Hugh. *The Pound Era.* Berkeley: U of California P, 1971.

Lewis, Wyndham, and Ezra Pound. "The Improvement of Life." *BLAST* 1 [London: 20 June 1914]: 149.

Morand, Paul. *Fancy Goods; Open All Night.* Trans. Ezra Pound. Ed. Breon Mitchell. New York: New Directions, 1984.

Pondrom, Cyrena. *The Road from Paris: French Influence in English Poetry 1900–1920.* Cambridge: Cambridge UP, 1974.

Sieburth, Richard. *Instigations: Ezra Pound and Remy de Gourmont.* Cambridge: Harvard UP, 1978.

Dannah Edwards

Frobenius, Leo (1873–1938)

Ezra Pound's unearthing of Frobenius took place in 1929, around the time of his eclectic cultural interests in Confucius, in the "forgotten" composers, and in the Swiss naturalist Louis Agassiz. A German anthropologist who had made expeditions to Africa to study primitive myth and folklore, Frobenius shared his era's fascination with the theory that recently discovered Paleolithic cave drawings in Europe suggested that European culture originated in Africa and moved northward. Frobenius called this drift *Kulturmorphologie*, which Pound translated as the transformation of cultures. Frobenius's theories inform Spengler's *The Decline of the West* (1918), and his fascism is equated by Pound with Cavalcanti's, another thinker Pound was working on in the early 1930s.

Pound met Frobenius in Frankfurt on 25 May 1930 at the premiere of Antheil's opera *Transatlantic*, and with the help of Douglas Fox, Frobenius's assistant at the Forschungsinstitut für Kulturmorphologie, the two corresponded frequently in the 1930s, sharing information about tribal structure and practice. Though limited in German, Pound read parts of Frobenius's seven-volume opus *Erlebte Erdteile* (some of it in French translation), focusing particularly on the fourth volume, titled *Paideuma*.

Frobenius's use of the term *paideuma* was derived from the Greek to mean the way in which culture, as teacher, imprints itself on man, whereas Pound used the word to imply the more mystical sense of a submerged complex of ideas of any given period, those that are, moreover, constantly in action. For Pound, *paideuma* is the template of culture that people carry inside them—including assumptions, inherited biases, habits of thinking, logical defaults, and prejudices. A vital and undying energy always in the air, *paideuma* is opposite to *ideology* in that it is the people's wisdom and cannot be learned, though it is discernible by the method of close study of the natural scientist. Pound believed that *paideuma* was the innate intelligence that remained after all book learning was forgotten and that the study of the tangle of these ideas in literature, myth, and history would reveal the active principles of an age.

Other terms in the Pound lexicon derived from Frobenius are "Sagetrieb," which Kenner defines as "saying-force" (534), and "Wagadu," the lost city, from the Sudanese folktale "Gassire's Lute." Pound followed Frobenius's story of Wagadu from *African Genesis* (1938), twinning it with Herodotus's Dioce in Canto 74. Both mythical cities were to be the earthly perfections of Pound's *paradiso terrestre*.

Though fascinated by Frobenius's African esoterica, Pound was equally attracted to the anthropologist's method, particularly his thinking process. He especially admired Frobenius's skill at collecting and ordering hitherto unrelated minutiae, working from the particular, dissociating likeness, and from that, inducing general truths. Frobenius's movement from fieldwork to precise taxonomic morphologies to the discovery of intelligible orders was, for Pound, the same method of genius shared by Remy de Gourmont and Louis Agassiz. It is no coincidence, then, that at the height of his study of Frobenius, Pound wrote in the *ABC of Reading* (1934) that the proper method of studying poetry was the method of the natural scientist: close study, comparison, dissociation. Only that cognitive movement from particulars to universals would reveal the organic *paideuma* in living culture. And it is precisely this cognitive movement that Pound discerned in his next big intellectual discovery, Alexander Del Mar.

Bibliography

Davenport, Guy. "Pound and Frobenius." *Motive and Method in the Cantos of Ezra Pound*. Ed. Lewis Leary. New York: Columbia UP, 1954.

Hesse, Eva. "Frobenius as Rainmaker." *Paideuma* 1.1 (1972): 85–88.

Jahn, Janheinz. *Leo Frobenius: The Demonic Child*. Trans. Reinhard Sander. Austin: U of Texas African and Afro-American Studies and Research Center, 1974.

Kenner, Hugh. *The Pound Era*. Berkeley: U of California P, 1971.

Rachewiltz, Mary de. "Pound and Frobenius." *Komparatistische-Hefte* 2 (1980): 92–101.

Tony Tremblay

Frost, Robert (1875–1963)

Ezra Pound's active role in the English and American reception of Frost's first two books is fully chronicled in the major biographies and published selected letters of both men and in Stanley Weintraub's *The London Yankees*. To quote Pound, "I've done as much to boom Frost as the next man. . . . I reviewed [*A Boy's Will*] in two places and drew it [to] other reviewers' attention by personal letters. I hammered his stuff into *Poetry*, where I have recently reviewed his second book" (*L* 62); and to quote Frost, "Pound was a generous person who had gone out of his way to do me several favors. . . . I suppose I am under obligations to him and I try to be grateful . . . [but] Pound is an incredible ass and he hurts more than he helps the person he praises" (*Selected Letters* 148, 84, 96).

After the Frosts left England, Frost seems never to have met Pound again. But as time passed Pound may have assumed a part in some (paranoid?) Frostean literary psychodrama. Witness Frost's notorious letter from Harvard to Louis Untermeyer: "the Pound-Eliot-Richards gang in Eliot House here. I had a really dreadful letter of abuse from Pound in which he complains of my cheap witticisms at his expense. I may have to take him across my page like this: It is good to be back in communication with you on the old terms. My contribution was the witticisms: yours the shitticisms" (*Letters to Untermeyer* 277).

Much later Frost wrote Eliot, "[W]e had Ezra in common though you had much more of him than I. If I ever was cross with you it was for leaving America behind too far and Ezra not enough" (*Selected Letters* 567). Frost's role at about that time in helping to set Pound free from St. Elizabeths (not, perhaps, as full as Frost claimed) is also chronicled in biographies and letters—as is Pound's reluctant gratitude.

Bibliography

Frost, Robert. *Letters to Louis Untermeyer*. New York: Holt, Rinehart & Winston, 1963.

———. *Selected Letters*. Ed. Lawrence Thompson. New York: Holt, Rinehart & Winston, 1964.

Sokol, B. J. "What Went Wrong between Robert Frost and Ezra Pound." *New England Quarterly* 49 (1976): 521–541.

Thompson, Lawrence. *Robert Frost*. 2 vols. New York: Holt, Rinehart & Winston, 1966, 1970.

Weintraub, Stanley. *The London Yankees: Portraits of American Writers and Artists in England 1894–1914*. New York: Harcourt Brace Jovanovich, 1979.

Lauriat Lane Jr.

G

Gallup, Donald Clifford (1913–2000)

Gallup, an eminent bibliographer, editor, and art and book collector, enjoyed a thirty-three-year career as library curator at Yale (1947–1980), retiring as the Elizabeth Wakeman Dwight Curator of the Collection of American Literature at the Beinecke Rare Book and Manuscript Library. Thanks largely to him, Yale became a leading center for the study of twentieth-century American literature, acquiring and housing major collections of books, papers, manuscripts, and letters of many important writers, including T. S. Eliot, H. D., William Carlos Williams, Gertrude Stein, Eugene O'Neill, Thornton Wilder, and Ezra Pound. Among his many works are his authoritative bibliographies of Eliot and Pound; two memoirs of his days at Yale (*Pigeons on the Granite: Memories of a Yale Librarian* and *What Mad Pursuits!: More Memories of a Yale Librarian*); and various other books and editions dealing with the works of, among others, Stein, O'Neill, and Wilder. In 1987 he edited Pound's *Plays Modelled on the Noh*.

Bibliography

Gallup, Donald C. *A Bibliographical Check-list of the Writings of T. S. Eliot*. New Haven: Yale U Library, 1947.

———. *Bibliography of Ezra Pound*. 1963. Charlottesville: UP of Virginia, 1983.

———. "The Ezra Pound Archive at Yale." *Yale University Library Gazette* 60.3–4 (1986): 161–177.

———. *Pigeons on the Granite: Memories of a Yale Librarian*. New Haven: Yale UP, 1988.

———. *What Mad Pursuits!: More Memories of a Yale librarian*. New Haven: Yale UP, 1998.

"Library Curator and Noted Collector Donald C. Gallup." *Yale Bulletin & Calendar* 29.2 (15 September 2000).

Demetres P. Tryphonopoulos

Gaudier-Brzeska, Henri (1891–1915) and *Gaudier-Brzeska: A Memoir*

A French sculptor and draftsman who had an unusual background, he was born Henri Gaudier in St. Jean-de-Braye, Orléans, in 1891 and died in combat at Neuville St.Vaast, Flanders, in 1915. He received scholarships to visit England and Germany in 1908 and 1909, though he seems to have spent as much time sketching and drawing buildings, people, and animals as he did studying. Gaudier resolved to become an artist and moved to Paris in early 1910, where he studied extensively at the Louvre, the Musée Trocadero, the Musée de l'Homme, and the Bibliothèque St. Geneviève and attended the lectures of Henri Bergson. During this period he met the Polish author Sophie Brzeska, who was to become his lifelong companion. Despairing at what he saw as a narrow-minded attitude to Sophie during a visit to his home in St. Jean de Braye in late 1910, he moved with her to London and appended her name to his own, living with her as brother and sister to avoid scandal.

With few contacts in London, the early years were poverty-stricken and lonely for the Gaudier-Brzeskas, although Henri made use of the collections of the British Musuem to enhance his already impressive knowledge of European and "primitive" sculpture and drawing. Having gradually received small commissions from a circle of dilettantes surrounding the illustrator

Claude Lovat Fraser, Gaudier-Brzeska achieved his first success with the publication of some drawings in the Bergsonian periodical *Rhythm*, through the intervention of its art editor J. D. Fergusson. It is likely that Pound saw these. However, the two men did not meet until the Allied Artists' Association exhibition in the summer of 1913. By this time Gaudier had been encouraged through working at Roger Fry's Omega workshops and by a developing friendship with the American sculptor Jacob Epstein. Pound, in the company of his mother-in-law, had been making fun of the sculptor's difficult surname, unaware that Gaudier was in the room. The outraged sculptor upbraided Pound and left him unusually embarrassed and lost for words.

Despite this inauspicious beginning, the two men quickly developed a friendship, which reached a peak of intensity in January–March 1914. Pound viewed Gaudier-Brzeska as a prodigious talent and was entertained by his "alarming intelligence" and ability to think critically across different periods of cultural history. For Gaudier, Pound was a crucial contact as a cultural facilitator, sympathetic critic, and patron. Following moderate success at the Allied Artists, Gaudier gave up a day job as a clerk in the city and devoted himself full-time to his sculpture, a financial gamble that was immeasurably bolstered by Pound's support.

Although Gaudier had been friendly with artists associated with the Bloomsbury group, notably Nina Hamnett, under the aegis of Pound he quickly became central to the loose association of artists linked to the Vorticist group. This included the painters Percy Wyndham Lewis and Edward Wadsworth and the philosopher T. E. Hulme. In the intensely politicized atmosphere of the London art world in the run up to the Great War, the sculptor was unique as he maintained friendly contacts with both the Vorticist and Bloomsbury groups.

Gaudier completed a portrait bust in marble of Pound in February–March 1914, which the poet had commissioned. Pound bought a block of pentelic marble that took Gaudier weeks to prepare before the portrait could begin. Fascinatingly, the photographer Walter Benington captured the process, and these photographs proved a unique insight into Gaudier's working methods at this time.

Gaudier made sketches of Pound, in brush and Chinese ink, in 1913–1914, of which the most representative example is now in the collection of Kettle's Yard, University of Cambridge. In a few economical, assured strokes Gaudier captured the appearance of the sitter and mocked Pound's prominent forehead and neatly sculpted goatee beard. These drawings were important in the final realization of the portrait bust. Benington's photograph shows markings similar to these sketches roughed out on the block of stone as Gaudier began to carve it. In cutting directly into the block of stone, rather than modeling in clay or wax and then casting in bronze, Gaudier identified himself, and by implication Pound, in the vanguard of Modern sculpture. He had been inspired to carve by his studies of "primitive" art in musuems and under the influence of Epstein.

The process took about six weeks to complete, and during this period Pound would read his poems as the sculptor carved, and the two men talked about art politics and the Chinese ideogram. Pound later claimed that Gaudier was able to read ideogrammic drawings accurately, even though he had no formal training in the subject. The ideogram was important to the final tense, charged depiction of the poet. Gaudier reportedly said, "It will not look like you . . . [I]t will be the expression of certain emotions which I get from your character" (qtd. in Carpenter 231).

The portrait was finished by March 1914. Pound observed that "Brzeska has immortalised me in a giant marble phallic column." The portrait, indeed, mocks the manicured coiffure of Pound in the shape of a penis, although the facial features, cut deeply into the stone, produce a startling synthesis of the various preliminary sketches Gaudier had made. The choice of image, it has been suggested, derived from a fusion of Gaudier's perception of carving as a "virile art" and the bellicose rhythms of his favorite Pound poems, "Altaforte" and "The Tomb at Akr Çaar." Both sculptor and poet were captivated by the potential of an aesthetic revolution through the notion of a "modern primitive." The finished portrait presents Pound as a modern-day "primitive" idol, making manifest in three dimensions his self-perception as a "shaman" and a "djinn" about to inherit the earth with the collapse of a decadent, bourgeois urban culture. This is no idle observation, as it has been convincingly suggested that Gaudier had the Easter Island statue *Hoa-Haka-Nana-Ia*, in the collection of the British Musuem, in mind as he carved the work.

The portrait was entitled *Hieratic Head of Ezra Pound* (now in the Nasher Sculpture Center, Dallas) and joined other works by Gaudier, *Boy with a Coney* and *Stags*, in Pound's personal collection. Pound also acted as a broker for Gaudier's work with the American lawyer and avant-garde collector John Quinn. Quinn purchased *Birds Erect*, the last carving that Gaudier completed (the original is now at Kettle's Yard, University of Cambridge).

The poet also rated Gaudier very highly as a critic and historian of sculpture. The sculptor was a signatory to *BLAST* in June 1914 and contributed his "Vortex Gaudier-Brzeska," an astonishing four-page whistle-stop tour of European sculptural history. Pound later wrote: "I confess I read it two or three times with nothing but a gaiety and exhilaration arising from the author's vigour of speech"; and later he suggested that the article should be a core text in all academies of sculpture (*GB* 106).

Gaudier-Brzeska departed for the French front a few weeks after the appearance of *BLAST*. Pound and Lewis, along with a hysterical Sophie Brzeska, were among those seeing him off at Charing Cross station in London. During 1914–1915 Gaudier wrote regularly to Pound and Wadsworth, among others, and was even able to contribute a much more somber "Vortex" to the second number of *BLAST*.

Tragically, this article appeared above a black-edged death notice for the sculptor. Gaudier-Brzeska, twice promoted for bravery, was shot dead during an assault on the German lines on 5 June 1915. Pound was completely shattered at the demise of his lively friend. Introducing a memorial exhibition of Gaudier's sculpture in London in 1918, he observed: "His death in action at Neuville St. Vaast is, to my mind, the gravest individual loss, which the arts have sustained during the war" (*GB* 136).

Pound was crucial in sustaining the posthumous reputation of Gaudier-Brzeska: In 1916, he published a memoir titled *Gaudier-Brzeska* based on personal experience, letters, manifestos, and the memories of others, including photographs and a partial catalog of the sculptor's work. It also reprints Pound's article "Vorticism" from the *Fortnightly Review* (September 1914)—his most detailed account of that movement. Despite its loose appearance as a collection of miscellaneous writings, Pound's memoir contains some of his most cogent critical thought. The book is thus pivotal in Pound's own early development. Although Pound's book is heavily biased toward what he called his "squarish, bluntish style" and late work such as *Bird Swallowing a Fish* (1914; Kettle's Yard, University of Cambridge), the book was vital in preserving Gaudier's work for a generation of younger sculptors. Without Pound's memoir, which was admired by a young Henry Moore and Barbara Hepworth, among others, it is likely now that Gaudier's work would be largely forgotten, his biography obscure, and his cultural significance at the moment of Vorticism overlooked.

After Gaudier's death, Pound helped to provide for Sophie Brzeska, whose fragile mental health had been destroyed. Although Pound later discovered a new sculptural hero in Constantin Brancusi in 1920s Paris, he never forgot his friendship with Gaudier-Brzeska, and the sculptor makes appearances in his poetry and essays well into the 1930s and beyond.

Ken Russell's 1972 film *Savage Messiah* is largely based on H. S. Ede's romanticized biography of Gaudier.

Bibliography

Blackwood, Jonathan. "Primitivising English Sculpture c. 1900–32." Diss. Courtauld Institute, U of London, 2000.

Cork, Richard. *Henri Gaudier and Ezra Pound: A Friendship*. London: Anthony d'Offay, 1982.

Dasenbrock, Reed Way. *The Literary Vorticism of Ezra Pound and Wyndham Lewis: Towards the Condition of Painting*. Baltimore: Johns Hopkins UP, 1985.

Ede, H. S. *Savage Messiah*. London: Heinemann, 1931.

Lewison, J., ed. *Henri Gaudier-Brzeska, Sculptor 1891–1915*. Kettle's Yard, Cambridge, 1981.

Silber, Evelyn. *Gaudier-Brzeska: A Life*. New York: Thames & Hudson, 1996.

Jonathan Blackwood

German Literature, Translation, and *Kultur*

It was when such heavyweights of German culture as Nobel Prize winner Gerhart Hauptmann (1862–1946) were his fellow residents in Rapallo that Ezra Pound most regretted his deficient knowledge of German. What he remembered most vividly from his course at Hamilton College was Professor Hermann "Schnitz" Brandt's declaiming the *Knittelvers* (doggerel) that, for most people in the German-speaking world, is the sum total of their knowledge about Hans Sachs, that he was a "'Schuh- / macher und poet dazu" (Canto 92), unless they know him through Wagner as one of the Mastersingers of Nuremberg.

From the passages about the German lyric in Ford Madox Ford's *The March of Literature* (1938), it appears likely that it is to Ford's Heine enthusiasm that we owe Pound's only attempt at recreating the spirit of German verse, the "Translations and Adaptations from Heine" (*P* 43–47). Although he only dealt with eight Heine poems, the liveliness of his approach makes it easy for the reader to agree with what Pound interjects in "Translator to Translated": *"O Harry Heine, curses be, / I live too late to sup with thee!"* (*P* 45). The main reason why the Heine sequence from *Canzoni* (1911) does not bear comparison with Pound's two most famous "translations," *Cathay* and *Homage to Sextus Propertius*, is what happened to be pointed out to him that year, on his one notable trip to Germany, by Ford's rolling on the floor in his Giessen hotel, in pain, because of Pound's lack of "adequate English" (Demetz 291). Ford's

opinion on Pound's prose style was even worse and appears to have been responsible for his abandoning the book about his 1912 walking tour in southern France, in which he hoped to produce a "'Harzreise' with Heine left out" (*L/ACH* 3).

In "A Few Don'ts by an Imagiste," Pound advised the "candidate" to "dissect the lyrics of Goethe coldly into their component sound values, syllables long and short, stressed and unstressed, into vowels and consonants" (*LE* 5), and in "The Palette" section of his "Renaissance" article he states categorically: "After Villon, the next poet for an absolutely clear palette, is Heine" (*LE* 216). Unlike most German speakers, Pound was reluctant to give Goethe's lyrics superior status: "His lyrics are so fine, so unapproachable—I mean they are as good as Heine's and Von der Vogelweide's" (*LE* 217). Once again, it seems that Ford opened Pound's eyes to the qualities of the German *Minnesänger*, some proof of which is in Pound's singling out Ford's version of Walther von der Vogelweide's exquisite *"Under der linden"* as one of the "few beautiful poems that still ring in my head" (*LE* 14). Hence he included it, with a summary of his judgment on German verse, in the *Confucius to Cummings* anthology (82–83). Eva Hesse, whose vigorous translations of Pound's work into German have ensured his presence on the German scene, was privileged to hear Pound's powerful recitation of Walther's equally famous *"Owê war sint verswunden alliu mîniu jâr!"*

Pound insisted that he had never been able to see any advance in "German tonkunst in poetry" (*GK* 203) after the middle High German period. He was, in this respect, clearly the product of American academics brought up on that German philology that had not yet made it past the Middle Ages. What seems to have delighted him so much more than any Hölderlin or Rilke was the crude and cute stanzas by none other than the cobbler-poet Hans Sachs himself. The book, the 1934 *Insel Verlag* facsimile edition of *Das Ständebuch* (at first erroneously referred to in Canto 75 as "Stammbuch"), was a gift from Gerhart Münch, the Dresden-born pianist and composer, on whose behalf Pound established contact with the Nazi music experts to support Münch's grant application for Vivaldi research in his home town.

Having condemned, in his 1918 assessment of Henry James's contribution to international communication (*Völkerverständigung*), the German notion of "Kultur," along with philology, as "an abomination," as "an evil," like "all repressive uniforming education" (*LE* 298), Pound nevertheless used the facetious Anglo-German hybrid spelling *Kulchur* in the title of his 1938 compendium of civilization. *Guide to Kulchur* was to a large extent conceived as a companion piece to the *"Kulturmorphologie"* as preached and practiced by Leo Frobenius (1873–1938)— hence Pound's main recommendation for further reading in German was no longer the lyrics of Goethe and Heine but the *Erlebte Erdteile*, the collected papers of Frobenius, "without which a man cannot place any book or work of art in relation to the rest" (*GK* 352). Although Frobenius failed to recognize Pound as a fellow worker, Pound, upon meeting Frobenius in Frankfurt in 1930, was convinced the two of them were identical twins, *"wie aus demselben Ei geschlüpft."* The main difference, as Pound informed Eliot, was that he, unlike Frobenius, was not interested in "savages" but in "civilizations at their *most*" (*L* 336).

For Pound, Frobenius was the German who succeeded most in overcoming the sterile specialization inherent in philology by adopting the synthesizing vision of a morphology that had its roots in Goethe's *Metamorphosis of Plants*. The inclusion of the phrase "Knecht gegen Knecht" (Canto 76) in *The Pisan Cantos*, which Carroll F. Terrell identifies as deriving from line 6963 of Goethe's *Faust* ("*Sie streiten sich, so heißt's, um Freiheitsrechte; / Genau besehen, sind's Knechte gegen Knechte*"), suggests that Pound had been struck by something in *Faust*, Part II, even before he studied it more closely at St. Elizabeths for its economic wisdom (1946–1958). The antiwar sentiment the phrase expresses takes us back to Pound's 1918 observation: "Peace comes of communication" (*LE* 298). The German poet Rainer Maria Gerhardt

(1927–1954) was in 1949 the first from the "wreckage of Europe" (Canto 76) to take up Pound's peaceful cultural mission again. He ran a Pound-inspired magazine and planned to translate all of Pound's work and communicate with poets everywhere, especially in America. His death by suicide inspired Charles Olson to write "The Death of Europe: A Funeral Poem for Rainer M. Gerhardt." Before the advent of "political correctness" as the final arbiter, quite a number of critics in the German-speaking world followed Gerhardt's example and looked on Pound, in spite of all he had done, as the twentieth century's greatest poet and a force for good.

Bibliography

Baumann, Walter. "Ezra Pound and Heinrich Heine." *Roses from the Steel Dust: Collected Essays on Ezra Pound*. Orono: NPF, 2000. 163–177.

———. "Ezra Pound's Reception in the German-Speaking World." *Roses from the Steel Dust*. 155–161.

———. "The German-Speaking World in the Cantos." *Roses from the Steel Dust*. 135–153.

Demetz, Peter. "Ezra Pound's German Studies." *Germanic Review* 31.4 (1956): 279–292.

Ford, Ford Madox. *The March of Literature*. New York: Dial P, 1938.

Schneeman, Peter, "Pound's 'Englischer Brief': A Look toward Germany." *Paideuma* 7.1–2 (1978): 309–316.

Walter Baumann

Ginsberg, Allen (1926–1997)

Allen Ginsberg, the son of a minor writer of verse, grew up in Williams's Paterson, New Jersey. (Some of his letters to Williams appear in *Paterson*.) He was the last poet, after Frost, to enjoy celebrity in the United States, as a result of the controversies over his landmark poem *Howl* and in spite of his homosexuality, his open drug use, and his leftist political views. While his name is generally linked with the Beat Generation, and especially the work of William Burroughs and Jack Kerouac and the personality Neal Cassady, his *Collected Poems, 1947–1980* (1984) link his poems to the innovations of Ezra Pound. Pound remains over the years an undiminished source for the poet's imagination in poems including "Angkor Wat" and "Wichita Vortex Sutra." Ginsberg's insistence on the relevance of non-Western art to U.S. culture, along with his noun-based prosody and its telegraphic syntax, update Pound's work after Fenollosa and even imitate the abbreviated style in which Pound typed his letters. When he avoids the didacticism of Pound's most strident moments, his voice in poems can sound as prophetic as Blake's, as winsome as Whitman's.

At Columbia College, he counted Lionel Trilling, Mark Van Doren, and Raymond Weaver among his instructors. It was here that he met Kerouac, Burroughs, and Herbert Huncke. In his senior year at Columbia, in 1948, Ginsberg dedicated himself to a life in poetry after hearing the voice of Blake in a vision. Ginsberg was arrested as an accessory to Huncke's crimes and admitted to the Columbia Presbyterian Psychiatric Institute, where he spent eight months. *Howl* is dedicated to Carl Solomon, a fellow inmate. On 13 October 1955, Ginsberg's reading from a draft of this poem, at San Francisco's Six Gallery, proved to be a historical event in U.S. poetry, especially following the highly publicized trial for obscenity that ended two years later. His participation, in 1963, at the Vancouver Poetry Conference (which brought Olson, Duncan, and Creeley together for the first time) signaled his emergent status in the literary culture. But the heights of his notoriety were reached in Prague, where he was hailed as King of May in 1965, and at the 1968 Democratic National Convention, where his anti-Vietnam protests were televised to a divided nation. He was a tireless traveler and performing bard, late in life touring with Bob Dylan.

Ginsberg had three meetings with Pound during the aging poet's silent period: in Rapallo and at the Spoleto Festival in 1965 and in Venice in 1967.

In Ginsberg's address to the Ezra Pound Centennial Symposium, at the University of Maine (published in the *American Poetry Review*), he celebrated the lasting influence of Pound on his work.

Bibliography

Ginsberg, Allen. "Pound's Influence." *American Poetry Review* 15.4 (1986): 7–8.

Richard L. Blevins

Gold and Work

Gold and Work (in Italian, *Oro e Lavoro*, 1944) differs from Ezra Pound's other money tracts because it is framed as a Utopian fantasy, unique in Pound's oeuvre. Apparently, Pound composed the Utopian section of this piece on his walk north from Rome, and the republic he dreams of is an ideal Salò Republic (Redman 253). Next, Pound dips into his familiar short "history of the crime" of usurious finance capitalism—beginning with the Bank of England and ending with the "Hazard Circular," which, in U.S. Populist lore, announced the sale of the United States to the Rothschilds. Pound invokes Brooks Adams's *Law of Civilization and Decay* and shows how ignorance of the true history of Western civilization has been systematically erased by the "usurocracy."

Pound has two key points to make about money in the pamphlet. First, he calls money "the pivot. It is the middle term. It stands midway between industry and workers" (*SP* 343). As a middle term, then, money is like the hinge of a metaphor, or "is like" in a simile; it is a nonsymbolic gesture of equivalence. Pound's second point is about "work-money." He proposes that money units be "certificates of work done," *not* a "symbol of work" (346). This distinction is most important, because Pound wants money, like language, to refer directly to concrete realities. Thinking of his father's work as an assayer at the Philadelphia Mint, Pound imagines a similar assay of work. He gives no details but states the problem: "The advantage of work-money mainly derives from one fact alone: work cannot be monopolized" (345). Here we can see why Pound objected to the translation of "Oro e Lavoro" as "Gold and Labor": *Labor* has become an abstract and general economic category, while *work* suggests to Pound something personal, particular—much in line with his conception of money itself. He follows up this point by arguing for a Gesellite money that would resist commodification because it cannot be hoarded. Gesellite "stamp scrip" decays naturally, like most things, and thus cannot be deified.

The text is available in *Selected Prose*.

Bibliography

Marsh, Alec. *Money and Modernity: Pound, Williams, and the Spirit of Jefferson.* Tuscaloosa: U of Alabama P, 1998.

Redman, Tim. *Ezra Pound and Italian Fascism.* New York: Cambridge UP, 1991.

Alec Marsh

Gourmont, Remy de (1858–1915)

Editor of the *Mercure de France*, fin-de-siècle libertine, and speculative naturalist, Remy de Gourmont was a prolific poet, novelist, and critic who first came to Ezra Pound's attention in early 1912 via F. S. Flint.

Pound's writings on de Gourmont began in the *New Age* with "The Approach to Paris" in September 1913 and continued with obituaries published in the *Fortnightly Review* (December 1915) and *Poetry* (January 1916). Later Pound presided over a special edition of the *Little Review* (February–March 1919) dedicated to de Gourmont, which included Pound's well-known essay "De Gourmont: A Distinction." In addition, Pound secured *Les Chevaux de Diomède* (Paris, 1897) for the *New Freewoman* in 1913, translated into English with the author's assistance by Madame Sartoris, Natalie Barney's associate. Subsequently, Pound translated a selection of de Gourmont's aphorisms, which appeared in the *Dial* between Autumn 1920 and Spring 1921 as "Dust for Sparrows" and, in Summer 1921, *Physique de l'amour: Essai sur l'instinct sexuel* (Paris, 1903), published with Pound's idiosyncratic "Translator's Postscript" the following year as *The Natural Philosophy of Love* (see separate entry on this text).

When Pound read the *Litanies de la rose* (Paris, 1892) in 1912, the evocative musical qualities of de Gourmont's Symbolist verse profoundly impressed him. Yet in early 1912 Pound was also reading *Le Problème du style* (Paris, 1902), which was seminal in his development of a "Realist" aesthetic of disinterested observation and precise, economical presentation. These technical strictures, and de Gourmont's "Sonnets en Prose," eventually helped Pound abandon dramatic monologues, or "personae," and develop the more sophisticated, ironic narrative voice of *Homage to Sextus Propertius* and the early cantos. It was also through de Gourmont that Pound became interested in the novels of Stendhal and Flaubert and arrived at a conception of "Realism" as the authentic record of *moeurs contemporaines* and scientifically detached critique of bourgeois morality. Elaborated in *Le Culture des Idées* (Paris, 1900), de Gourmont's concept of the "dissociation of ideas" further equipped Pound with the means to dissect widely credited clichés by exposing their component parts and historical origins, showing them to be arbitrary and provisional.

Pound perused de Gourmont's compendious study of medieval and Renaissance Latin, *Le Latin mystique* (Paris, 1892), in early 1912, citing it in his *Quest* lecture "Psychology and Troubadours." There he encountered Goddeschalk's phrase *"amas ut facias pulchram,"* which he later assimilated to his de Gourmontian sense of love as an "intellectual instigation," a perception contrasted in the early 1920s with the bloodless aestheticism of Henry James in *Hugh Selwyn Mauberley* and Canto 7. *Physique l'amour* united Pound's critique of bourgeois values and his vitalist concept of the body as an avenue of illumination by deconstructing the opposition between human beings and the natural world, mind and body, to see human sexuality as an "animal" sexual instinct.

Although they never met, Pound always wrote warmly of de Gourmont's personal charm and integrity, long venerating him as a thinker of saintlike sagacity and, above all, "a man standing for freedom and honesty of thought."

Bibliography

Burne, Glenn. *Remy de Gourmont: His Ideas and Influences in England and America.* Carbondale: Southern Illinois UP, 1963.

Lindberg, Kathryne V. *Reading Pound Reading: Modernism after Nietzsche.* New York: Oxford UP, 1987.

Sieburth, Richard. *Instigations: Ezra Pound and Remy de Gourmont*. Cambridge: Harvard UP, 1978.

Anthony Leyland

Greek Literature

Throughout his life Ezra Pound denounced the mere philological approach to ancient Greek texts. Pound studied, quoted, and translated Greek literature because he believed that it disclosed formal discoveries and perceptions about the human condition that were still valid for the modern world. In this regard, Pound generally preferred poetry to prose. He rejected, for example, the *Histories* of the Greek historian Herodotus in his introductory note to *Ta Hsio: The Great Digest* (1928) as "a mere collection of anecdotes," while he dismissed Thucydides as the "first journalist," "Fleet Street muck that he is" (*L* 93). As far as Greek prose is concerned, Pound had a higher regard for Greek philosophers, particularly Aristotle and Plotinus, from both of whom he quoted with increasing frequency in his prose and poetry from the 1930s onward.

Throughout his career, Pound never ceased to admire Greek poetry for what he called its *melopoeia*, while he also believed that its wide range of complicated metrical patterns could show modern poets how to liberate themselves from the restrictions of conventional English meter. Next to this stylistic-aesthetic quality, Pound valued Greek poetry for its presentation and treatment of the gods as images for otherwise indefinable states of mind or vital forces that constitute the complexity of existence and, concomitantly, the notion of poetry as the expression of epiphanic enlightenment, whether in epic (Homer), lyrical form (Sappho), or drama (Sophocles).

In his idiosyncratic canon of world literature, which Pound kept revising throughout his life, he always included the following poets and/or poems:

1. For Pound, Homer was the Greek poet par excellence. He supplied Pound with one of his most recurrent "touchstones" of poetry, namely, the often quoted line "παρὰ θῖνα πολυφλοίσβοιο θαλάσσης" "along the shore of the loud-resounding sea" (*Iliad* 1.34). Pound recommended this onomatopoeic phrase for what he in *Hugh Selwyn Mauberley* called "the imaginary / Audition of the phantasmal sea-surge."

   Homer is the most referred to Greek poet in all of Pound's writings, both prose and poetry, early and late. *The Cantos* pays tribute to this epic predecessor not only by opening with a passage from Book 11 of the *Odyssey* but also by the great number of quotations, translations, and references to both the *Iliad* and the *Odyssey*, although the latter is far more prominent as it supplied Pound with one of the basic models for his own poem.

2. Sappho of Lesbos (second half seventh century B.C.E.) was the supreme lyrical Greek poet for Pound. He believed that the *Ode to Aphrodite* (Ποικιλόθρον', ἀθάνατ' Ἀφρόδιτα) was one of the best poems ever written, and he referred to it time and again, not only in his prose writings (e.g., *ABCR* 47; *LE* 10) but also in *The Cantos* (76). Next to the *Ode*, Pound favored Sappho's Fragment 31 with its famous opening line *phainetai moi kènos isos theoisin*, "He seems as fortunate as the gods to me," as well as the so-called "Atthis" poem, which uses one of Pound's favorite Greek words, βροδοδάκτυλος, "rosy-fingered" (see Cantos 5, 76, and 80).

   An explanation for his admiration may be that Pound attributed to Sappho's poetry the Imagist accuracy of description enabling the poetess to objectify her highly subjective, passionate experience and for her use of rhythm. In his poem "Apparuit," Pound attempted to transpose the so-called Sapphic stanza of the *Ode* to Aphrodite and Fragment 31 into English.

3. Pound regarded Ibycus (sixth century B.C.E.) as a fellow Imagist and paid his tribute by rendering the poem beginning with the line *èri men hai te Kudooniai* as "The Spring."

4. Theocritus was Pound's favorite of the poets of the Hellenistic period (323–30 B.C.E.). Pound felt a kinship with the Alexandrian poets who were very much devoted to their art and whose experiments

produced technically and metrically perfect poetry. Moreover, their use of allusion to and quotation from the work of their archaic and classical predecessors, by which these poets established their place in a continuing literary tradition, was very similar to Pound's own methods. Theocritus's *Idyll II* was a lifelong favorite of Pound's, as he regarded it as a classical precursor of the Browningesque dramatic monologue.

5. Pound also admired the *Death of Adonis* by Bion (c. 100 B.C.E.) for its *melopoeia* and claimed that no one could become an expert in the "the art of metric, the art of making verses" (*SP* 323) without knowing the *Death of Adonis*. Pound seems to have consciously adapted Bion's use of alliteration, assonance, and anaphora, as well as of syncopation in Poem IV of *Hugh Selwyn Mauberley*.

Next to these positive evaluations of Greek poetry, two negative ones are noteworthy. First, Pound, at least at first, did not have a high regard for the Greek dramatists Aeschylus, Sophocles, and Euripides. In *How to Read* Pound still saw in them a decline from Homer, while he also denounced the style of Aeschylus as "agglutinative" and "verbose" (*LE* 273), most obviously because the playwright's magniloquence and habit of making compound words clashed with his own Imagist preferences. Pound does not seem to have changed his mind, despite the fact that throughout his career he quoted from the *Agamemnon*. Although Pound at first was also critical of Sophocles, in the 1940s he changed his mind. Especially in the later *The Cantos*, we find a frequent number of quotations, while Pound during his stay at St. Elizabeths made versions of both *Elektra* and the *Trachiniae*.

Second, Pound never seems to have liked Pindar (518–c.440 B.C.E.), generally regarded as the greatest of the Greek choral poets. He denounced Pindar's art as it represented everything Pound sought to purge through Imagism: rhetoric, superfluous adjectives, and elaborate comparisons and metaphors.

Peter Liebregts

Greek Translation

Unlike Pound's command of the Romance languages, his grasp of Greek was relatively weaker, although it was not as inconsiderable as is popularly held. However, given the greater linguistic difference between Greek and English in comparison, for example, to Latin and English, and given Pound's habit to favor the transposition of the meaning and "feel" of an original text over a correct grammatical translation, his renderings from the Greek often seem to swerve more away from the source texts than his Romance versions do.

In his attempts to present an equivalence for the virtu of a foreign text, to bring out its timeless quality in a contemporary form in terms of idiom and sensibility, Pound generally used translations not so much to emphasize the "alterity" of the source text but to make its intrinsic and universal quality more accessible. In the case of Greek poetry, Pound considered its most enduring lesson for modern poets to be its *melopoeia*, the musical quality of verse. Here Homer supplied him with one of his most recurrent "touchstones" of poetry, namely, the often quoted line παρὰ θῖνα πολυσφλοίσβοιο θαλάσσης "along the shore of the loud-resounding sea" (*Iliad* 1.34). Pound recommended this onomatopoeic phrase for what he in *Hugh Selwyn Mauberley* called "the imaginary / Audition of the phantasmal sea-surge."

Moreover, Pound believed that the wide range of complicated metrical patterns of Greek poetry could show modern poets how to liberate themselves from the restrictions of conventional English meter. This aspect of Pound's poetry is still the subject of scholarly discussion. Although Pound can be said to have sometimes succeeded in adapting Greek meter for his own poetry—such as his "Apparuit" written in Sapphic stanzas, and "The Return" using the choriamb as its basic metrical unit—it generally remains debatable whether one can apply the rules of quantitative Greek verse, using syllabic length, to the writing of poetry in English, which is determined by syllabic accent.

Pound himself seemed to have been aware of the difficulty of transposing the melopoeic quality of Greek poetry, given the fact that in his canon of world literature, although it did include translations from the Latin such as Gavin Douglas's *Aeneid* and Arthur Golding's *Metamorphoses*, he did not incorporate Greek translations for the very simple reason that there was "no satisfactory translation of any Greek author" (*LE* 35). Although Pound did appreciate certain parts of Chapman's *Odyssey* and Pope's *Iliad*, he advised Iris Barry, if she could not read Greek poetry in the original, to use Latin translations, as most English translations are "hopeless" (*L* 87), with the possible exception of J. W. Mackail's *Select Epigrams from the Greek Anthology* (1890), Andrew Lang's *Theocritus, Bion and Moschus* (1880), and Henry Thornton Wharton's *Sappho* (1885). Pound very much disliked the work of Gilbert Murray, one of the most popular translators of Greek poetry of the twentieth century, and with great approval he quoted in a 1934 letter Eliot's words on Murray that the latter had "erected between Euripides and the reader a barrier more impassable than the Greek language" (*L* 263).

In his own translations, Pound often expressed his awareness of the various layers of language and cultural traditions between the ancient Greeks and modern man, of all preceding interpretations creating the gap between what Greek culture was and what we have made of it. Thus Canto 1 is not a direct translation from the opening of Book 11 of the *Odyssey*, but it is based on the late Latin version by Andreas Divus and in the archaic style of the Anglo-Saxon poem "The Seafarer." By such cultural impositions, Pound stresses how any translation is influenced by the heritage of interpretative perspectives foisted upon the original. Sometimes this overlayering is ineluctable: Catullus's Carmen 51 (*Ille mi par esse*), for example, will always stand between us and Sappho's Fragment 31 (Φαίνεταί μοι). At other times, Pound deliberately used impositions: In his belief in the many similarities between ancient Greek drama and the Japanese Noh, he superimposed his knowledge of the latter in his rendering of Sophocles's *Women of Trachis.*

Pound's main extended Greek translations from *texts* are:

1. Homer: Canto 1 (based on the first half of *Odyssey* 11 and the Second Homeric Hymn to Aphrodite in a Latin rendering [1538] by Andreas Divus and Georgius Dartona Cretensis, respectively); Canto 39 (a mixture of quotations and transcriptions of *Odyssey* 10.135–574, of literal translations into English, of adaptations of Clark and Ernestus's 1804 Latin translation, of paraphrases, and of details invented by Pound himself).

2. Hesiod (late eighth century B.C.E.): in Canto 47 (the section beginning with "Begin thy plowing"), Pound rendered Hesiod's *Works and Days* 383–391 and 448–451.

3. Stesichorus (c. 630–555): adaptation of phrases of his (fragmented) *Geryoneis* in Canto 23, including renderings of a Latin crib by Johannes Schweighaeuser (1802) and transcriptions of Liddell & Scott's *Greek-English Lexicon.*

4. Sappho (second half of seventh century B.C.E.): Pound rendered Sapphic fragments in "Papyrus," "Ἱμέρρω," and Canto 5, using translations by Richard Aldington and J. M. Edmonds's conjectural restorations in *The New Fragments of Alcaeus, Sappho and Corinna* (1909).

5. Ibycus (sixth century B.C.E.): Pound rendered his poem beginning with the line "ἔρι μεν αιτε κυδοονιαι" as "The Spring."

6. Aeschylus (c. 525–456 B.C.E.): Pound's rendering of the opening of the *Agamemnon* was published posthumously.

7. Sophocles (c. 496–406 B.C.E.): *Women of Trachis* (first published in 1954 in the *Hudson Review*); *Elektra* (1949, in collaboration with Rudd Fleming, published posthumously in 1989).

8. *The Greek Anthology*: Pound rendered epigrams in "The Cloak" and "Homage to Quintus Septimius Florentis Christianus," a series of six epigrams translated from the Latin rendering of Greek poems by Florent Chrétien (1540–1596).

Peter Liebregts

Guide to Kulchur

Ezra Pound's *Guide to Kulchur* is arguably one of the most important prose tracts written by the author during his lengthy career. Pound certainly believed as much, referring to the volume in a 1940 letter as his "best prose" (Norman 375) and placing the *Guide* alongside *The Cantos*, *Personae*, *Ta Hio*, and *Make It New* in a list of key works. While, with some exceptions—in particular Bacigalupo, Coyle, Davie, Harmon, Lindberg, and Nicholls—there has been no sustained scholarly consideration of *Guide*, Pound's critics make repeated reference to the volume in support of exegeses of the poetry and explications of Pound's political, economic, and cultural theories. Furthermore, many of the standard landmarks of Pound's intellectual topography—the doctrine of Ch'ing Ming, the ideogrammic method, *The Cantos* as "tale of the tribe," the figure of the rose in steel dust, and the term *paideuma* —enjoy sustained articulation within the pages of what was to be Pound's last lengthy prose work. Finally, the volume is an exemplary instance of Pound's paratactic, combinatory structures of writing, his patterns of associative thought, and his strategies of inductive argument. It is on these grounds that the *Guide* should not only be regarded as an indispensable key to *The Cantos* but also deserves concerted critical attention in its own right.

Guide was published by Faber and Faber in Great Britain in July 1938 and by New Directions, under the more somber title of *Culture*, in the United States in November 1938. Copies of the book had already been bound when its British publishers elected to delete or revise certain passages on the grounds that they were libelous. For example, Pound's typically acerbic reference to the seventeenth-century French bishop Jacques-Bénign Bossuet as a "tumid rhetorical parasite, hardly better than N. M. Butler" was altered to read "hardly better than some University Presidents" (*GK* 165) in order to avoid implicating Butler, a Nobel Laureate, a close companion of Roosevelt, and the longstanding president of Columbia University. The publication of the volume was delayed by one month while some fifteen offending leaves were

replaced. Pound retained five unexpurgated copies. New Directions published a new edition of the volume in 1952 (reissued in paperback in 1968), appending nineteen pages of additional materials to a photographic reprint of the first edition. Those addenda include Pound's "Sextant" and other mnemonic devices related to the volume, as well as an important lengthy statement on Pound's opera *Villon*. It is to this new edition to which most contemporary scholars have ready access.

Over a one-month period in the spring of 1937, Pound wrote *Guide* with what biographer John Tytell has called "a sense of harried desperation" (247). Indeed, Pound's self-styled "book of yatter" (*GK* 292) is written with a certain urgency—maybe not quite, yet, desperation—from Rapallo as part of an effort to instigate the "new learning" or *paideuma* that he envisioned. This broad-ranging volume, then, stands alongside Pound's Populist and pedagogical efforts during the prolific decade of the 1930s (including *ABC of Economics*, *ABC of Reading*, *Social Credit: An Impact*, and *Jefferson and/or Mussolini*) to educate his readership on the interrelationship of economics, politics, and art. *Guide* likewise serves as a likely postscript to Cantos 31–41, having been written some two months before *The Fifth Decad of Cantos* appeared in print in June 1937. It can also be argued that the *Guide* anticipates the writing of *The Pisan Cantos* in the sense that Pound here sets out to "write this new Vade Mecum without opening other volumes" (*GK* 33); in both cases, Pound struggles to create the conditions of possibility for a *paradiso terrestre* by working explicitly from memory and immediate impression with only minimal reference to particular outside texts.

The title of the volume, *Guide*, and the curious spelling of *kulchur* make oblique and possibly derisive reference to the German *Kultur* while at the same time eschewing the standard connotations of the English *culture*. In deriving this coinage, Pound at once avoids both the racial arrogance implied by the then-current Germanic sense of the term and the prescribed superficialities of the "cultured" elite of the

Anglo-American world. This revised sense of culture is central both to the volume's methodology and to Pound's attempt to instigate "the new learning" necessary to any renaissance. Culture, Pound tells us, is "when one HAS 'forgotten-what-book'" (*GK* 134) and "what is left after man has forgotten all he set out to learn" (*GK* 195). Culture, then, is largely the correlate of what Pound calls "understanding" as opposed to "knowledge," the amnesiac by-product of a totalitarian (in the sense of holistic) grasp of history, economics, politics, and the arts. At the heart of Pound's sense of "kulchur" is the term *paideuma*, which in Greek means "the taught" and which Pound defines as "the tangle or complex of the inrooted ideas of any period" and "the gristly roots of ideas that are in action" (*GK* 57–58). Pound explicitly distinguishes *paideuma* from the term *Zeitgeist*, linking the concept to the "Kulturmorphologie" of anthropologist Leo Frobenius, from whom he borrows the term. This archeological and anthropological understanding of culture demands, on the model of Frobenius's own fieldwork, an engagement with the concrete, with the particularities of cultural artifacts and documentary evidence that respects their dynamics within a larger and more inclusive network of causalities. As such, Pound's sense of culture allows him to integrate a broad interdisciplinary range of exemplary materials into a more coherent sense of what might constitute a "new paideuma," a new vitality of ideas in action, for the modern age.

Hence, the radical juxtaposition of disparate fragments that is here clearly apparent in a volume that offers tattered formulations—or what Pound calls "a heteroclite set of impressions" (*GK* 208)—that cut across and between some six parts, thirteen sections, and fifty-eight chapters. In a dizzying swirl of reference, Pound moves rapidly from one discursive and historical moment to the next, covering such varied subjects as Confucian doctrine, classical philosophies, Western metaphysics, theology and occultism, material science, pedagogical practice, mercantile economics, historical and anthropological methodologies, European cuisine, and of course, the literary, visual, plastic,

architectural, dramatic, and musical arts. Yet what might be said to hold the volume together is Pound's methodology itself and the presuppositions that inform his associative patterns of thought. Understood largely as the prose complement to Pound's long poem, *Guide* can be see as an embodiment of the self-same ideogrammic method as *The Cantos* themselves, although critical consensus on this point is far from complete. Nonetheless, in the central chapter "Zweck or the Aim" Pound himself points to the ideogrammic method as the logic of the volume in hand and uses the *Guide* as the opportunity to impart a retrospective coherence to his earlier poetic strategies. "The ideogrammic method," Pound writes, "consists of presenting one facet and then another until at some point one gets off the dead and desensitized surface of the reader's mind, onto a part that will register" (*GK* 51).

While the methodology is key, one might also regard the text in terms of its various functions, the kind of cultural work that the author intended for his volume. Pound understood *Guide* as serving particular purposes, and it is in those terms that we might best summarize, however reductively, a sprawling publication that refuses the possibility of paraphrase and mitigates against the compartmentalization of experience. The book is, as its title suggests, a program for reading and a kind of intellectual Baedeker. Pound's epigraph to the volume tells us that the book "is written for men who have not been able to afford an university education" (*GK* 6) and, as such, introduces what is both a pedagogical device and a theory of education that refuses academic abstractions of all kinds. This is to be a kind of handbook for daily living, and Pound's excoriation of traditional philosophical discourse is based on the charge that Western philosophy and academic education are too far divorced from the practice of everyday life and the practical governance of society. Pound will measure his own teachings against similar yet, according to his estimation, failed projects—Aristotle's *Nichomachean Ethics*, for example—and follow more closely the model of the Stoics and Confucian thought in grounding his guidance in concrete particulars.

This effort necessitates what Pound calls his "new historical method," which involves putting back into circulation "whole slabs of record" without regard for generic or disciplinary boundaries. Pound's effort here is toward the recovery of suppressed or forgotten texts, the "fatal lacunae" of history (*GK* 31), an effort that he sees as serving a revised historical description that relies on inductive examples of interanimating economic and political programs and their coextensive practices of the arts. Pound's attempt at inclusiveness and his insistence on the "triumph of total meaning over detail" (*GK* 92) constitute the central principle of the methodology of his "totalitarian" treatise. While *totalitarian* is used by Pound throughout the volume in this very local sense, the term nonetheless does carry the burden of Pound's ideological sentiments and his support of the Mussolini regime. Although many of Pound's critics have contested such easy correlations between form and politics—and such correlations are, indeed, vexed—it is very difficult to disavow Donald Davie's claim that *Guide* is, ultimately, "an overtly Fascist book" (125) that might be best understood in the context of Pound's contemporaneous political and economic pronouncements.

Bibliography

Bacigalupo, Massimo. *The Forméd Trace: The Later Poetry of Ezra Pound*. New York: Columbia UP, 1980.
Coyle, Michael. *Ezra Pound, Popular Genres, and the Discourse of Culture*. University Park: Pennsylvania State UP, 1995.
Davie, Donald. *Studies in Ezra Pound*. Manchester: Carcanet, 1991.
Harmon, William. *Time in Ezra Pound's Work*. Chapel Hill: U of North Carolina P, 1977.
Lindberg, Kathryne V. *Reading Pound Reading: Modernism after Nietzsche*. New York: Oxford UP, 1987.
Nicholls, Peter. *Ezra Pound: Politics, Economics, and Writing: A Study of The Cantos*. Atlantic Highlands: Humanities P, 1984.
Norman, Charles. *Ezra Pound*. New York: Funk & Wagnalls, 1968.
Tytell, John. *Ezra Pound: The Solitary Volcano*. New York: Anchor P, 1987.

Michael J. O'Driscoll

Guido Cavalcanti Rime

In his initial period of interest in Guido Cavalcanti (c. 1250–1300), which led to his translations of 1912, *Sonnets and Ballate of Guido Cavalcanti*, Ezra Pound was blind to a certain aspect of Cavalcanti's work. In *Dante and His Circle*, D. G. Rossetti had not translated the canzone *"Donna mi prega,"* the one complete canzone assuredly by Cavalcanti that has come down to us, since he considered it "perhaps the very worst of Guido's productions" and of "little true interest" because it is "filled with metaphysical jargon" and with "stiffness and cold conceits" (311). That Pound's initial interest in Cavalcanti is deeply Rossettian is shown nowhere better than by the fact that *Sonnets and Ballate* repeated Rossetti's exclusion of *"Donna mi prega,"* and in "Troubadours—Their Sorts and Conditions" (1917) Pound echoed Rossetti's dismissal.

At some point in the 1920s, Pound began to rethink this exclusion as part of a more fundamental rethinking of whether Cavalcanti's "metaphysical jargon" was indeed worthless. What followed was a second period of intense interest in Cavalcanti in which he translated *"Donna mi prega"* for the *Dial* in 1928; retranslated the poem as part of Canto 36 in *Eleven New Cantos* (1934); wrote several essays on Cavalcanti published in the *Dial* in 1928 and 1929 that were brought together in 1934 under the title "Cavalcanti" in *Make It New*; composed an opera, *Cavalcanti*, in 1932 (which was first performed only in 1983); and finally assembled a new edition of Cavalcanti's work, *Guido Cavalcanti Rime*, published by Edizioni Marsano in Genoa in 1932, which included an edition of Cavalcanti's poems accompanied by essays in English and the beginning of a new bilingual edition of Cavalcanti's poetry.

What led Pound to this renewed interest in Cavalcanti and to this second edition and translation of his work? Several factors—but above all, Pound became interested in what Cavalcanti had to say in his poetry, not just in how he said it. This involves an exact reversal of Rossetti's judgment on *"Donna mi prega"*: From being the "worst of Guido's productions," it becomes—if not the best—at least the most interesting and the most important. Reacting against a notion of medieval culture as homogenous and conformist, Pound seeks to discriminate between a medieval orthodoxy he identifies with Dante and Aquinas and the heterodoxy he sees in *"Donna mi prega,"* whose "tone of thought"—Pound asserts—"may have appeared about as soothing to the Florentine of A.D. 1290 as conversation about Tom Paine, Marx, Lenin and Bucharin would today in a Methodist bankers' board meeting in Memphis, Tenn" (*LE* 149). Elsewhere in the same 1929 essay, "Cavalcanti," Pound says that "Guido is called a 'natural philosopher,' I think an 'atheist' and certainly an 'Epicurean' " (*LE* 158). He sees Cavalcanti not as an isolated figure in this respect but as someone influenced by Averroism and as an important forerunner of the *quattrocento*, especially in being "without hell-obsession" (*LE* 153).

Pound's presentation of Cavalcanti as a figure of heterodoxy naturally raises two questions, one of accuracy and the other of motivation: Is the distinction he draws between Guido and Dante grounded in reality? And whether or not this is the case, what motivates him to make so much of this distinction? Neither question can be answered within the confines of an entry of this length. My own sense is that Pound probably overplays the contrast in both directions, leaning on every potentially heterodox moment in Cavalcanti and accepting a vision of Dante as conforming to a monolithic medieval orthodoxy that is surely in part a retrospective construction on the part of champions of Renaissance and postmedieval notions of cultural history. However, this is not to say that Pound's work on Cavalcanti is haphazard or Impressionistic: He is surely a careful reader of Cavalcanti, studied ancillary texts such as Dino del Garbo's commentary as well as the primary texts, and grounds his reading in Dante's complex if oblique, raising of this issue in *Inferno* X. What motivated this distinction, in this author's judgment, was his attempt to understand the neglect of Cavalcanti's work. The presentation of Guido as a heretic whose thought was dangerous fit into this narrative, since it enabled Pound to see a pattern of

orthodoxy neglecting heterodox genius, which he saw in many other places and times. Indeed, in the 1920s, Pound saw Eliot become the central figure in English letters and saw himself pushed to the margins—and thus there was more than a hint of self-reflection in the work on Cavalcanti, with himself as the Guido of the *novecento* and Eliot as the more orthodox and more widely acclaimed equivalent to Dante.

What is valuable here is Pound's willingness to contest received notions and ask us to rethink our habitual allegiance to them; what is less valuable is the hint of paranoia, a paranoia that grows across the 1930s and is part of what leads him to his support for Mussolini. Indeed, Cavalcanti the heretic is reconfigured by Pound into Cavalcanti the protofascist saint: The last substantive presence of Cavalcanti in Pound's oeuvre is in Canto 72 in which Guido has descended from *"dal" "terzo cielo"* to tell the story and acclaim the heroism of a *"contadinella"* who leads a group of Canadian soldiers into a minefield at the cost of her own life. Ethically, this passage comes close to being the absolute low point in all of Pound's oeuvre; it is also remarkable that Pound is willing to betray his own earlier reading of Cavalcanti in order to arrange his poetic masters into a pro-fascist orthodoxy. Surely, Pound's presentation of Guido in the late 1920s as a questioning voice and potential heretic is far closer to the mark.

This sets the intellectual context in which Pound set out to retranslate and edit Cavalcanti's works in the late 1920s. And true to Pound's self-presentation as a man out of spirit with his times, the edition ran into numerous difficulties and was only partially completed. He began work on a new bilingual edition of Cavalcanti, revising some of his earlier translations and adding a new translation of *"Donna mi prega."* But the British publisher who had agreed to publish the volume, Aquila Press, went bankrupt in 1929 with the volume only partially printed. Pound then turned to a small Italian publisher, Edizioni Marsano, with the idea of a new edition of Cavalcanti's works in Italian. But in order to save money, the pages of the Aquila edition were bound together with newly set texts of Cavalcanti in Italian. The result can only be called a hodgepodge, and the 1932 book that resulted received no attention in Italy and little in the English-speaking world, with the conspicuous exception of a lengthy and favorable review in the *Criterion* by the eminent medievalist Étienne Gilson. The mixed reception of *Guido Cavalcanti Rime* and Pound's inability to find anyone to present the opera *Cavalcanti* he worked on at the same time may have helped dissuade Pound from pursuing his interest in Cavalcanti any further: The result, though hardly central to subsequent Cavalcanti scholarship in the way Pound must have hoped, is a fascinating testament to the importance of Cavalcanti's work in Pound's poetic and intellectual development.

Bibliography

Anderson, David, ed. *Pound's Cavalcanti: An Edition of the Translations, Notes, and Essays.* Princeton: Princeton UP, 1983.

Gilson, Étienne. Rev. of *Guido Cavalcanti Rime. Criterion* 12 (October 1932): 106–112.

Rossetti, Dante Gabriel. "The Early Italian Poets." *Poems and Translations.* Oxford Standard Authors. London: Oxford UP, 1913. 173–466.

Reed Way Dasenbrock

H

Hemingway, Ernest (1899–1961)

An American writer, journalist, and outdoorsman born in Oak Park, Illinois, Ernest Hemingway was a twenty-two-year-old reporter and aspiring writer when he turned up in Paris in December 1921. Two months after his arrival, he first encountered Ezra Pound in Shakespeare and Company, Sylvia Beach's bookshop on the rue de l'Odéon. At first Hemingway was contemptuous of what he saw as the poet's self-conscious bohemianism, reflected in his shoddy living conditions on the rue Notre Dame des Champs. But a friendship between the two men soon flourished as Hemingway taught the poet to box. "Ezra was the most generous writer I have ever known," he later confessed in *A Moveable Feast*. "He helped poets, painters, sculptors and prose writers that he believed in and he would help anyone whether he believed in them or not if they were in trouble" (110). Hemingway estimated that Pound spent only one-fifth of his time on his own work, devoting the rest of his energy to promoting the careers of others. Indeed, Pound arranged for William Bird to bring forward from Three Mountains Press in 1924 a collection of vignettes titled *in our time*. The following year, Boni and Liveright published in New York an expanded version of the work as a short-story collection, and Hemingway's growing fame would make unnecessary further patronage of this kind.

Nonetheless, Hemingway remained very close with the poet and his family during the 1920s, attending the premiere of Pound's opera *Le Testament de Villon* in June 1926 and accompanying Dorothy Shakespear to the hospital for the birth of Pound's son Omar in September of that year. He also visited Pound in Rapallo, and when *ABC of Economics* was published in 1932, Hemingway wrote his friend in an attempt to dissuade him from his support of Mussolini's politics. Pound later replied that his friend's position "don't lower me respekk for Benito" (*L* 283), and he grew openly critical of all writers who did not address economic matters in their work. The poet admonished Hemingway, in particular, for a lifestyle more concerned with adventure than opposing usurious financiers. "And the buggars back of the Bank of Paris are more worth killin than pussy cats, however titanic, that ain't got no guns to shoot back with, you god damn lionhunter," he fussed. "Why not take a crack at 'em in the only god damn part where they FEEL—god rot their testicles—in their *wallet*, in the buggarin bunk account" (*L* 283).

Hemingway and James Joyce were present at a dinner in Paris in 1934 where Pound's erratic behavior led both companions to conclude that he had lost his mind. Hemingway was certain of his friend's insanity when Pound was charged with treason in 1945, but his work with T. S. Eliot, Robert Frost, and Archibald MacLeish was instrumental in arranging for the poet's eventual release from St. Elizabeths in 1958. Living in the United States himself in July 1961, Hemingway took his own life, and when Pound heard of the suicide, he characteristically lashed out at America's lack of support for—and understanding of—its most talented writers.

Bibliography

Hemingway, Ernest. *A Moveable Feast*. New York: Scribner's, 1964.

———. *Selected Letters, 1917–1961*. Ed. Carlos Baker. New York: Scribner's, 1981.

Craig Monk

Henderson, Alice Corbin (1881–1949)

Alice Corbin Henderson was a poet, editor, anthologist, and publisher. Her two volumes of poetry, *The Spinning Woman* (1912) and *Red Earth: Poems of New Mexico* (1920), were both popular. From 1912 to 1922 she was associate editor of *Poetry* magazine, the first reader of all submissions who discovered new writers like Carl Sandburg, Sherwood Anderson, and Edgar Lee Masters. She also constantly argued for the publication of poetry that was international in scope and modern in style while contributing eighty-five reviews and a score of editorials to the magazine, including a defense of vers libre. Pound particularly admired her writing and included her poem "One City Only" in his *Catholic Anthology 1914–1915*. He respected her independent critical judgment and favored her confident views, which she summarized in "Don't's for Critics" published in the *Little Review* (3 [1916]: 12–14). Pound sent her his "Three Cantos" first: Only after she read them in Santa Fe, New Mexico, where she had moved in 1916 to battle tuberculosis, did she forward them to Harriet Monroe with the warning "of course they are erudite—but there is life—and a poet's life—in it & through it all" (*L/ACH* 194).

From Santa Fe, Henderson continued to contribute to *Poetry* and write, coediting *The New Poetry* (1917) with Harriet Monroe and then fashioning a distinguished anthology of Southwest poetry, *The Turquoise Trail* (1928). Her Santa Fe publishing company, Writers Editions, quickly became a leading outlet for southwestern writers. Both she and her husband, the architect William Penhallow Henderson, became supporters of Navajo art and culture. She became the center of a group of Santa Fe writers and a friend of D. H. Lawrence, Witter Bynner, Willa Cather, and composer Ernest Bloch.

Bibliography

Pound, Ezra. *The Letters of Ezra Pound to Alice Corbin Henderson*. Ed. Ira B. Nadel. Austin: U of Texas P, 1993.

Williams, Ellen. *Harriet Monroe and the Poetry Renaissance. The First Ten Years of Poetry 1912–1922*. Urbana: U of Illinois P, 1977.

Ira B. Nadel

Hesternae Rosae, Serta II

Roses of Yesterday, a collection of nine troubadour songs issued by Augener in 1913, was a collaboration of Ezra Pound with his friend the eminent pianist Walter Rummel. The melodies are interpreted from the unmetered medieval notation according to the so-called rhythmic modes, and Rummel supplies elaborately pianistic accompaniments more or less in the style of Debussy, much dependent on open fifths. The texts include verses by Bernart de Ventadour, Williaume li Viniers (whose "Mere au Sauveour" was inserted by Pound into his opera *Villon*), and Peirol, among others, including of course the two extant melodies by Arnaut Daniel. In Canto 20, Pound tells the story of finding these melodies in manuscript, and Rummel's preface claims that they are "here published for the first time," though they had earlier appeared in a scholarly article by Antonio Restori.

The texts appear in Provençal, in Pound's English, and in the French of musicologist M. D. Calvocoressi. The effect is compromised, however, because the settings use only two of the multiple stanzas of each *canso*. Pound's translations (three of which appear in *The Translations of Ezra Pound*) struggle to adhere to Pound's ideal of word-note relationships, but success is not complete, since in the very first phrase he is forced to set the final syllable of "exquisite" under a sustained note. Nonetheless, Pound considered these songs an important part of his campaign to popularize the troubadours, and as music critic William Atheling, he induced Raymonde Collignon to sing them before a London audience.

Neither Pound nor Rummel was involved in *Serta I*, which contains nine French songs of the seventeenth century.

A similar collaboration, *Five Troubadour Songs*, was issued by Boosey in 1920. The songs are set to music by Pound's friend Agnes Bedford; the words of four are adapted by Pound from Chaucer, while the fifth is translated from Gaucelm Faidit.

Bibliography

Bedford, Agnes. *Five Troubadour Songs*. London: Boosey, 1920.

Restori, Antonio. "Per la storia musicale dei Trovatori Provenzali." *Rivista Musicale Italiana* 3 (1896): 231–260.

Rummel, Walter Morse. *Hesternae Rosae. Serta II*. London: Augener, 1913.

Stephen J. Adams

Heyman, Katherine Ruth (1874–1944)

Ezra Pound met Katherine Heyman, a concert pianist of considerable stature, around 1904 or 1905. His poem "Scriptor Ignotus" (1906), referring to a "great forty-year epic," is dedicated to her. H. D., in her autobiographical novel *HERmione*, portrays her as "Miss Stamberg," an older woman who holds the Pound character, George Lowndes, in her spell through both her music and her devotion to the occult. She may have introduced Pound to the ideas of Spiritualism, Swedenborgianism, and yoga. Traveling to Europe in 1908, Pound was briefly described as Heyman's concert manager, as he made his way via Venice to London. Thereafter her hold on Pound faded, but they remained cordial. Heyman became particularly associated with the music of the Russian Theosophist composer Alexander Scriabin, and in her later years she founded the New York Scriabin Circle.

Heyman's book *The Relation of Archaic to Ultramodern Music* (published 1921 but begun in 1916) reveals Poundian cross-influences not only in its title, which has a Poundian ring, but also in its content. The chapter "Parallels between Ultramodern Poetry and Ultramodern Music," especially, reveals a Poundian interest in relations between words and music, and the poetry in question is Imagist—Pound's, H. D.'s, and her friend Amy Lowell's. And Heyman's interpretation of music, like Scriabin's, is pervasively Theosophical ("The tone E is mana consciousness").

Heyman appears as "the american lady, K. H." in Canto 76.

Bibliography

Bowers, Faubion. "Memoir within Memoirs." *Paideuma* 2.1 (1973): 53–66.

Doolittle, Hilda. *End to Torment: A Memoir of Ezra Pound*. Ed. Norman Holmes Pearson and Michael King. New York: New Directions, 1979.

———. *HERmione*. New York: New Directions, 1981.

Heyman, Katherine Ruth. *The Relation of Archaic to Ultramodern Music*. Boston: Small, Maynard, 1921.

Tryphonopoulos, Demetres P. *The Celestial Tradition: A Study of Ezra Pound's The Cantos*. Waterloo: Wilfrid Laurier UP, 1992.

Stephen J. Adams

Hilda's Book

Hilda's Book is a small collection of verses that Pound wrote, hand sewn, bound in vellum and presented to H. D. in the early years of their romantic friendship (1905–1907). Although *Hilda's Book* is riddled with typing errors and corrections, replete with "the rambling vagueness, the imprecise use of archaic or florid diction, the pseudo-Swinburnian syntax . . . and the abuse or absence of punctuation," these are qualities one might expect in an apprentice project (King 357). The text is, however, significant as a record that Pound's earliest obsessions—with his place in the literary tradition, with things mystical, medieval, and classical, with the idea of the lady/muse, and with literary mentors such as Chaucer ("Thu Ides Til"), Dante ("Sancta Patrona"), and D. G. Rossetti ("Donzella Beata")—were all consistent with his later concerns.

Certain poems from *Hilda's Book*—"La Donzella Beata," "Li Bel Chasteus," "Era Venuta" (a.k.a "Comraderie"), and "The Tree"—were published in altered form in Pound's early volumes, and other poems—"To draw back into the soul of things. Pax" and "The Banners"—were incorporated into "Sonnet of the August Calm" and "Fratello Mio Zephyrus" in the "San Trovaso Notebook." The full text of *Hilda's Book* did not appear in print until New Directions combined it with H. D.'s Pound memoir *End to Torment* in 1970.

Bibliography

Doolittle, Hilda. *End to Torment: A Memoir of Ezra Pound.* Ed. Norman Holmes Pearson and Michael King. New York: New Directions, 1979.

King, Michael King. "Go, Little Book: Ezra Pound, Hilda Doolittle and 'Hilda's Book.'" *Paideuma* 10.2 (1981): 347–360.

Julie Dennison

Homage to Sextus Propertius

Virtually from the moment of its initial, partial publication (Sections I, II, III, and VI) in the March 1919 edition of *Poetry* magazine, the *Homage to Sextus Propertius* aroused a controversy over its putative qualities as a translation. On the one hand, philologically minded critics decried the work as an overly free distortion of Propertius's odes. So, in the very first response to the *Homage*, classicist William Gardner Hale declared Pound incredibly ignorant of Latin and proceeded to indict all the liberties he took with the original simply as grammatical mistakes. Unlike the Chinese in *Cathay*, however, Pound could actually read the Latin from which he worked to produce the *Homage*. Thus, most of his departures from the original text were purposeful. On the other hand, readers with more poetic sensibilities such as T. S. Eliot have tended to gloss over or justify Pound's intentional deviations from his source as a creatively faithful recreation in English of certain tonal or pragmatic aspects of Propertius. In this vein, J. P. Sullivan has written the most thorough analysis of the *Homage* in its complex intertextual relation to the original Latin love elegies out of which it arose, and his *Ezra Pound and Sextus Propertius: A Study in Creative Translation* (1964) remains the essential work from that perspective.

Despite their incommensurable assessments regarding Pound's treatment of Propertius, all the participants in this long-standing debate remain bound by the basic question of accuracy, whether conceived in semantic or pragmatic terms. Moreover, they share a common view of translation as a permanently and universally fixed procedure, one untouched by historical development or alteration under the forces of changing literary conceptions. Consequently, this dispute delayed significantly the realization of the extent to which, in addition to employing Propertius as a poetic persona or mask through which to address his own concerns as a writer, Pound contributed through the *Homage* to a redefinition of the very parameters of translation itself as a mode of literary production during the Modernist period. Indeed, Pound himself added to the confusion over how to characterize the work; for in his various defenses of the *Homage*, he both explicitly abjured the term *translation* yet still claimed almost complete semantic and pragmatic fidelity to Propertius's own words. Accordingly, then, Donald Davie's assertion that the *Homage* constitutes a strictly original poem fails to account for its complexities. The best approach lies in recognizing that in the *Homage* Pound aggressively blurs any simple, categorical distinction between translation and original composition by employing the reproduction of semantic meaning from a work in another language as a constitutive technique in the creation of a text with its own particular ambitions to cultural signification, a writing strategy that he would come to use extensively throughout *The Cantos*.

In his treatment of Propertius, Pound stitches together parts of separate elegies to produce different sections of the *Homage*. Exemplifying his notion of criticism by translation (*LE* 74), the *Homage* attempts to recast the prevailing image of Propertius at the time as simply a romantic elegist who evinced the values and employed the language of sentiment. Pound seeks to achieve this revision by highlighting tonal irony and amplifying the themes of antiimperialism and artistic independence. In light of such modifications to the original, the *Homage* emerges as Pound's exploration of classical erotic verse and its attendant configuration of gender roles for poetry as a crucial step toward achieving an epic poetic stance. Over the course of the poem's twelve sections, Pound not only assumes, and thereby assesses, various traditional postures of masculine expression mapped by love poetry; in doing so, he also tests the underlying model of their relation to the feminine for the process of literary production. Moreover, although through much of the poem he amplifies Propertius's ambivalence toward the historical and mythic heroic themes typically associated with epic poetry as unsuited to his own genius, by its final section the *Homage* solidifies a conception of the erotic as a logical precursor to and driving force behind epic achievement.

Containing many of the most infamous of Pound's departures from Propertius, Section I mocks imperial verse and war poetry, while also claiming a connection between poetic vocation and ritual sexual knowledge. Section II explicitly takes up the issue of genius and its relation to subject matter. In Sections III and IV, Pound deepens his exploration into the possibilities of erotic poetry by assuming two conventional postures identifiable with amatory verse: first, the male lover who bemoans the demands of his mistress, yet still extols the sanctity of his station; and second, the paramour who seeks news of his beloved through an intermediary after a quarrel. Section V again raises the concern of choosing between heroic poetry singing the praises of war and empire, on the one hand, and expressly personal erotic verse focusing on women, on the other. Section VI offers the most pointed critique of military achievement. In Sections VII, VIII, and IX, Pound again assumes conventional amatory postures, specifically those of the triumphant and despairing lover. At the same time, these sections also establish sexual desire as the originating force behind the events leading to epic through the famous example of Paris and Helen. The final three sections turn to the more social situations of love poetry. The fantasy sequence of Section X touches upon the themes of jealousy and imagined infidelity, and Section XI depicts the devastating emotional consequences of love. Section XII revives the mockery of imperial epic and, through allusions to the Trojan War and the tale of Jason and Medea, establishes sexual desire as the ultimate genesis of heroic action.

Through the *Homage*, Pound discovered an enabling, masculine posture of poetic articulation in his drive toward epic. Moreover, despite the passionate, oftentimes negative responses it aroused as a translation, the *Homage* has exerted an enormous impact on the transmission of the classics through its influence on the efforts of such subsequent figures as Robert Lowell and Louis Zukofsky.

Bibliography

Davidson, Peter. *Ezra Pound and Roman Poetry: A Preliminary Survey.* Amsterdam: Rodopi, 1995.

Davie, Donald. *Ezra Pound: Poet as Sculptor.* New York: Oxford UP, 1964.

Hale, William Gardner. "Pegasus Impounded." *Poetry* 14 (1919): 52–55.

Hooley, Daniel M. *The Classics in Paraphrase: Ezra Pound and Modern Translators of Latin Poetry.* Selinsgrove: Susquehanna UP, 1988.

Pound, Ezra. "Homage to Sextus Propertius." *Poetry* 13.6 (1919): 291–299.

Sullivan, J. P. *Ezra Pound and Sextus Propertius: A Study in Creative Translation.* Austin: U of Texas P, 1964.

Thomas, Ron. *The Latin Masks of Ezra Pound.* Ann Arbor: UMI, 1983.

Steven G. Yao

How to Read

How to Read (Harmsworth, 1931), available in Pound's *Literary Essays* (15–40), was dedicated to "Mr Glenn Frank, and other starters of ideal universities" (*LE* 22). Frank had been much in the news for establishing the Experimental College at the University of Wisconsin. After his disappointment with graduate studies at the University of Pennsylvania and the more recent lukewarm reception academic publishers had been giving him, the Experimental College must have seemed to Pound a fresh opportunity indeed: It was staffed by a team of young instructors, emphasized classic works, and was taking an interdepartmental, interdisciplinary approach, encouraging students to break down artificial academic boundaries. Pound had perhaps reason to hope the comparative literature curriculum that had been much on his mind (see *ABC of Reading*) might find a receptive audience there. If the experimental model caught on, a new generation of undergraduates could be reading the best of the best and learning to recognize good literature under his virtual tutelage.

Pound had come to the opinion that the study of letters was in dire need of reform. He found the study of literature divided up by language and period. Far too much attention was devoted to the work of minor period authors who had not advanced the art, he thought, and the sense of literature as a vital expression of the human condition had been lost. The teaching of literature was in the hands of somnolent catalogers who "make a bog, a marasmus, a great putridity in place of a sane and active ebullience. And they do this from sheer simian and pig-like stupidity, and from their failure to understand the function of letters" (*LE* 21). In the custody of such men, the study of literature becomes marginalized and inane, and its cultural purpose subverted. In Pound's view, the best writing keeps *the machinery of social and individual thought* in working order. The proper function of literature is that of

> maintaining the very cleanliness of the tools, the health of the very matter of thought itself. . . . [T]he governor and legislator cannot act effectively or frame his laws, without words, and the solidity and validity of these words is in the care of the damned and despised *litterati*. . . . [W]hen their very medium, the very essence of their work, the application of word to thing goes rotten, i.e. becomes slushy and inexact, or excessive or bloated, the whole machinery of social and of individual thought and order goes to pot. This is a lesson of history, and a lesson not yet half learned. (*LE* 21)

Drawing on the classical Western virtues of simplicity and clarity blended with Confucian notions of definition and virtue, Pound identifies precise, exact language with the spread and upkeep of civilization, "excess" and "bloat" with decadence. He challenges writers to wrest their art from these "lovers of order" and charges them with responsibility for maintenance of the language itself; they were up against publishers who were failing to bring the best new work to light and were thereby contributing to the social and cultural decline.

The academic publishers to whom Pound had been showing his proposals for anthologies and guides to literature seemed to him more interested in protecting their vested interests than in furthering the cause of good writing. With their eyes on the bottom line they had been rejecting his proposals or simply sitting on them. *How to Read* is little more than a pamphlet; it was, in fact, a much-scaled-back version of a short guide to literature that was, in turn, a far cry from the twelve-volume poetry anthology Pound had been proposing. In that anthology, which was to contain more than 300 items—an analogue to the Japanese emperor's collection of Noh plays that preserved for posterity that country's great literary masterworks—each poem would be "an invention, a definite contribution to the art of verbal expression" (*LE* 17). *How to Read* may be most important for what it might have been.

Tim Romano

Hugh Selwyn Mauberley

First published in 1920, *Hugh Selwyn Mauberley*, according to Pound's later recollections in 1932, originated in a belief shared with Eliot that by 1917 the free verse movement had gone too far in the direction of "general floppiness." As a countercurrent, they took the tightly rhymed quatrains of Théophile Gautier as a model, Pound producing *Mauberley* and Eliot the seven dense and satirical quatrain poems in *Poems* (1920). On the technical level of versification, comparison is instructive: Eliot ventures some virtuoso rhyming, including macaronic rhymes (suggested by Gautier's example), but preserves metrical strictness; Pound's rhyming goes much farther in this direction, and metrically he invents a kind of verse sometimes regular but more often freely draped over the underlying rhyme structure in no regular pattern.

Mauberley is Pound's last major poem before he turned his full attention to *The Cantos*, and it has been highly admired and widely anthologized (though sometimes only in excerpt). F. R. Leavis's influential praise in *New Bearings in English Poetry* (1932) preserved Pound's central position in the Modernist movement, even while reading the poem autobiographically as a confession of failure and rejecting *The Cantos*. Despite Pound's claim that he is no more Mauberley than Eliot is Prufrock, most critics see the Mauberley figure, correctly, in some kind of relation to Pound himself—the invented character Mauberley embodying a critique of Pound's early aesthetic stance, as the poem turns to themes of social criticism, to economics (the first appearance of the word *usury* in Pound's poetry), and unfortunately in the "Brennbaum" section, to what would later become a rabid anti-Semitism. The sequence as a whole, despite moments of hilarity, is a sour, satirical "farewell to London" (Pound's own phrase), as he left for Paris in 1920.

The critical history of *Mauberley* took a complicated turn when Donald Davie published an influential analysis of the poem in *The Pelican Guide to English Literature* (1961), a series aimed at students. Davie, relying partly on dubious external evidence, argued that some of the poem at least is meant to be spoken by the Mauberley character. Yet neither he nor any who have followed him has been able to agree on which parts of the poem were intended to be spoken by Mauberley. His principal follower, Jo Brantley Berryman, Davie's onetime graduate student, argues this view tenaciously, finding fabulous subtleties in Pound's management of persona; Davie himself, however, later admitted the difficulties of his position and, partly blaming the poem for insufficient cues and questionable ironies, explicitly disowned his early essay (1975). But he never gave up the concept of a Mauberley "persona." Though Davie's approach is still followed by some, this author finds it not only based on poor evidence but unnecessary and misleading, making particular nonsense of the eloquent poems denouncing World War I (IV and V in the first sequence).

Mauberley is set out in two consecutive poetic sequences under the subtitle "Life and Contacts"—later altered by Pound himself to "Contacts and Life" to reflect the actual order of the subject matter. The first sequence is a satirical analysis of the London scene. The difficulties of the introductory "E. P. Ode pour l'election de son sepulchre" have contributed to confusion

about the entire sequence: It is clearly *about* Pound, but there is no reason to import an alien speaker. The poem makes sense as a mock-epitaph, Pound constructing the London perspective on his own "death," that is, his rejection by the English literary establishment. (The subgenre of self-epitaph has examples enough—perhaps the best known is Swift's.) This poem also exhibits difficulties that complicate the entire sequence: highly compressed syntax, glittering ironies, allusion (often in foreign languages), and antonomasia. The name "Capaneus," for example, is syntactically isolated, leaving the reader to decide how it is connected to the poem and whether the reference recalls Greek myth or Propertius or Dante. Likewise with the name "Flaubert"—emphasis may fall on the realist, the ironist, or the stylist. The Greek phrase from Homer's *Odyssey* introduces a sea voyage or quest motif that reechoes, sometimes faintly, through the sequence. The French phrase from Villon's *Testament* aligns Pound with one of the great outsider poets of literature. Pound's language is nowhere more densely textured than here.

Sections II and III are more general statements on the laxness of present-day society. Emphasis in II falls on aesthetics, the present preference for "a prose kinema" over the "sculpture of rhyme"; section III peers into ancient history, pitting a lofty pagan against an inferior Christian ethos, then pitting both against the present ascendancy of the "press" and "franchise"—an explicit condemnation of democratic degeneracy. Against this backdrop, sections IV and V of the poem present World War I as the product of "usury age-old and age thick / and liars in public places." Pound's rhetoric intensifies his rejection of "old men's lies" and the sentimental patriotism of Horace's *"dulce et decorum est pro patria mori"* (a phrase known to every British schoolboy) but mixed with recognition of the soldiers' courage and compassion for their needless suffering. The power of Pound's language may disguise the complexity of feeling here, as the poem concludes that the Great War was fought for nothing better than "two gross of broken statues / For a few thousand battered books." The carnage calls into question the very arts and literature to which Pound devoted his life.

At this point, the first sequence of *Mauberley* presents seven anecdotal vignettes, lighter in tone, that examine English social and literary history as Pound experienced it. "Yeux Glauques" looks back to Rossetti's Pre-Raphaelitism—its ideals, its sexual looseness, and its rejection by Victorian society. The next two sections evoke the aestheticism of what Yeats termed the "tragic generation"—Dowson, Johnson, and the 1890s Rhymers' Club—and in "Brennbaum" (modeled after Max Beerbohm) the phenomenon of the dandy. "Mr. Nixon" (often taken to be Arnold Bennett) presents a philistine litterateur who discourages verse and encourages critical logrolling. Section X depicts the anonymous "stylist" (probably Ford Madox Ford), desultory and isolated. The last two sections turn to feminine society, section XI to the sheltered and conventional suburban household, and XII to the moneyed, superficially artistic literary salon.

The "Envoi" that follows the first sequence abandons the ironic mode for pure lyric, being a finely wrought imitation of both Waller's *carpe diem* anthology piece "Go, Lovely Rose" and of the troubadour's conventional benediction to his *canso*. Characteristically, Pound leaves no indication of its purpose in the sequence. It is often described as Pound's exemplum of the best tradition of poetry that England has abandoned. But such an account leaves unresolved the lyric's bearing on Pound's apparent critique of Mauberley as failed or at least limited artist, aesthete, and hedonist in the sequence that follows. Nor does it explain the intricate relationship between "Envoi" and the concluding "Medallion."

The poem's second sequence analyzes the character of the fictitious Mauberley. First he appears as an artist of admirable models but limited means—one who reveres Flaubert or Pisanello, while "lacking the skill." Verbal echoes with the opening "Ode" suggest comparison with the Pound depicted there—contrast, or parallel, or a little of both. This analysis pro-

ceeds in section II, probably the most densely obscure writing in the poem. Mauberley's failure, surprisingly, is related not to social or political inadequacies, as one might expect from the first sequence, but to some kind of sexual deficiency combined with a temperamental passivity. Pound's concocted French epigraph, his dependence on Greek phrases and bilingual punning, and his obscure metaphors ("sieve," "seismograph") seem at this point designed as much to conceal his meaning as to reveal it. "The Age Demanded" is clearer, charting Mauberley's passive drifting into subjective hedonism, an inability to relate his perception of beauty to any other reality. Section IV is Mauberley's epitaph, standing in contrast to Pound's self-epitaph in the "Ode." His life has ended in unmeaning: "I was / And I no more exist."

"Medallion," the final poem in the sequence, is another site of major critical disagreement. Even John J. Espey, who nowhere else discerns a Mauberley persona speaking in the poem, describes "Medallion" as Mauberley's "single poem" and attributes it to his voice; conversely, Jo Brantley Berryman, who insists on the Mauberley persona elsewhere, rejects it here. The poem does seem to represent Mauberley's work of art (whether a visual or a verbal portrait is not entirely clear) and stands in relation to the "Envoi": The one who there "sang me once that song of Lawes" is apparently, but not assuredly, identical with the "clear soprano" here. But to construe "Medallion" as Mauberley's own poem requires that the reader search the text for the author's characteristic failings, an approach that has not yielded satisfactory results. Much better is to leave "Medallion" in Pound's voice, like the rest of the poem; he finishes the sequence on a flat note with an ironic description of Mauberley's work of art—attractive, perhaps, but rather inconsequential.

Bibliography

Adams, Stephen J. "Irony and Common Sense: The Genre of *Mauberley*." *Paideuma* 18.1–2 (1989): 147–160.

Berryman, Jo Brantley. *Circe's Craft: Ezra Pound's "Hugh Selwyn Mauberley."* Ann Arbor: UMI, 1983.

Davie, Donald. *Ezra Pound*. Chicago: U of Chicago P, 1975.

———. "Ezra Pound's 'Hugh Selwyn Mauberley.' " *The Pelican Guide to English Literature*. Ed. Boris Ford. Baltimore: Penguin, 1961.

Espey, John. *Ezra Pound's Mauberley: A Study in Composition*. Berkeley: U of California P, 1955.

Leavis, F. R. *New Bearings in English Poetry: A Study of the Contemporary Situation*. London: Chatto & Windus, 1932.

Stephen J. Adams

Hulme, Thomas Ernest (1883–1917)

T. E. Hulme was born in Staffordshire in 1883 and died in action in Flanders on 28 September 1917. Soldier and poet, art critic and literary theorist, political thinker and philosophical popularizer, Hulme intervened in many of the key debates of early Modernism. He studied at Cambridge but left after being forced—twice—to withdraw for disciplinary reasons. His earliest works include several poems and two haunting and poetic fragmentary essays, "Notes on Language and Style" and "Cinders," written between 1907 and 1909. From 1909 onward Hulme became one of the main conduits for the ideas of the French philosopher Henri Bergson, whose lectures in Paris he attended and whose ideas he applied across a spectrum of literary, artistic, cultural, and political fields. From Bergsonism, Hulme moved toward the cultural and literary Right, notably sympathizing with L'Action Française, the right-wing, legitimist group of thinkers that included Maurras and Lasserre, who influenced, among others, T. S. Eliot and David Jones. In his most anthologized piece, "Romanticism and Classicism," Hulme argued forcefully for a new form of dry, hard classicism and attacked the European Romantic tradition for what he called, in a phrase that became famous, "spilt religion." It was his essays on cultural politics ("Romanticism and Classicism," "Humanism and the Religious Attitude," and other pieces) that led Eliot to call Hulme "the forerunner of a new attitude of mind" (231). Hulme has often been held up as the founder of Imagism, though it would be more correct to say that he elaborated many of the

movement's principles *avant la lettre* and helped focus the energies that were to culminate in *Imagisme* (as understood by Pound rather than Amy Lowell). In "A Lecture on Modern Poetry," delivered to the Poets' Club in 1908, Hulme argued for a "modern spirit" in poetry, attacking what he saw as the outmoded pomp and slither of the poetry of the period. For Hulme, language was "a large clumsy instrument" that needed to be coerced into meaning, while poetic expression derived from a constant new minting of analogies and images. But these images and analogies needed perpetual reinvention—prose, he wrote, was the "museum" where dead expressions were kept. Hulme valued brevity and precision and argued forcefully for vers libre as representative of the Modern writer's abandonment not just of the old ways but also of the old certainties that buttressed them. "Are the things that a poet wishes to say no in any way different to the things that former poets say? I believe that they are," he asserts (72).

Hulme was briefly a member of the Poets' Club, in whose 1908 chapbook he published two of his best known poems, "Autumn" and "Above the Dock." He left to found the "Secession Club," where he was joined by F. S. Flint and others such as Edward Storer and Florence Farr. Pound joined in April of the same year. This was the "forgotten school of 1909" to which Pound alludes in the note preceding "The Complete Poetical Works of T. E. Hulme" in *Ripostes* (1912). Was the inclusion of Hulme's poems (far from complete, as it turned out) an act of good fellowship, or did it signal the subsumption of Hulme into the Poundian narrative of Imagism? On this question, the critical debates have continued. In the Imagism Special Issue of the *Egoist* (1 May 1915), Flint wrote a "History of Imagism" that gave Hulme and Storer precedence over Pound in the shaping of the Imagist aesthetic. Pound objected, Flint dug in, and literary historians have battled it out ever since.

There is no record of what Hulme thought of Imagism as a movement or of the debates in which he was quoted. Though for Eliot Hulme had written "two or three of the most beautiful short poems in the English language" (231),

Hulme himself showed no special interest in being a poet, preferring the role of free-ranging troublemaker and intellectual pugilist. He enlisted as a private in 1914 and was wounded in 1915. Pound, who included Hulme's "Trenches St Eloi: abbreviated from the conversation of Mr T.E.H" in his *Catholic Anthology*, remembers Hulme fondly and with uncanny exactness in Canto 16: "And he read Kant in the Hospital, in Wimbledon, / in the original, / And the hospital staff didn't like it."

Bibliography

Coffman, Stanley K., Jr. *Imagism: A Chapter for the History of Modern Poetry.* New York: Octagon Books, 1972.

Eliot, T. S. "A Commentary." *Criterion* 2.7 (1924): 231–239.

Hughes, Glenn. *Imagism & the Imagists: A Study in Modern Poetry.* New York: Biblo and Tannen, 1972.

Hulme, T. E. "A Lecture on Modern Poetry." *Further Speculations.* Ed. Sam Hynes. Lincoln: U of Nebraska P, 1962.

———. *Speculations: Essays on Humanism and the Philosophy of Art.* Ed. Herbert Read. Foreword by Jacob Epstein. London: Routledge, 1987.

Levenson, Michael H. *A Genealogy of Modernism: A Study of English Literary Doctrine, 1908–1922.* Cambridge: Cambridge UP, 1984.

Schneidau, Herbert N. *Ezra Pound: The Image and the Real.* Baton Rouge: Louisiana State UP, 1969.

Patrick McGinness

Hutchins, Patricia (b. 1942)

Patricia Hutchins began corresponding with Pound in 1953 when she contacted him at St. Elizabeths for permission to quote his unpublished letters to James Joyce in her book *James Joyce's World* (London: Methuen, 1957). While their personal meetings were few, their correspondence developed into a focused biography, *Ezra Pound's Kensington: An Exploration 1885–1913* (1965), as well as into a valuable archival resource (housed in the British Library). Hutchins structures the biography around Pound's years in Kensington, but she also treats Pound's background and his life during and after St. Elizabeths. Quoting extensively and reproducing Pound's letters, Hutchins grounds the biography in her correspondence and discussions with Pound, his family, and his acquaintances.

Bibliography

Hutchins, Patricia. *Ezra Pound's Kensington: An Exploration 1885–1913.* Chicago: Regnery, 1965.

Ce Rosenow

I

Ibbotson, Joseph Darling (1869–1952)

Joseph Darling Ibbotson was a Hamilton College professor of English literature, Anglo-Saxon, and Hebrew. Ibbotson, nicknamed "Bib," also was college librarian for years. Pound studied Anglo-Saxon with Ibbotson and spent late nights talking with the professor about poetry and translation. In April 1936, Pound wrote to author Harold W. Thompson that "the CANTOS started in a talk with 'BIB.' " Pound was listed in the 1905 college yearbook as "Bib's Pride." Pound and Ibbotson corresponded from the mid-1930s until Ibbotson's death. Ibbotson visited Pound in Rapallo in 1937.

Bibliography

Pound, Ezra. *Ezra Pound: Letters to Ibbotson, 1935–1952*. Ed. Vittoria I. Mondolfo and Margaret Hurley. Orono: NPF, 1979.

Cameron McWhirter

Ideogram

The ideogram is a calligraphic notation capable of expressing a multitude of ideas in a very compressed, economical manner. It is traditionally found in Chinese writing and art and also was central to Japanese Noh drama and the Hokku.

Pound's interest in the ideogram was stimulated during his period as secretary to W. B. Yeats and by his involvement in a group of connoisseurs, critics, and writers interested in the culture of the Far East, centered around the British Museum in London from circa 1909. Key in this loose coalition was Lawrence Binyon, keeper of printed books at the Museum and author of the influential *Flight of the Dragon: An Essay on the Theory and Practice of Art in China and Japan*. This book appeared in 1911 and was widely read and admired, not least by Pound.

Pound's and Binyon's approaches were similar in that both men admired what they saw as the Chinese and Japanese respect for tradition, while simultaneously testing and "making it new." This was key to the development of Pound's poetry and criticism at this time and took on an urgent development in October 1913.

The Far Eastern scholar Ernest Fenollosa had died in 1911, leaving a large body of unpublished manuscript material. Pound had been impressed with the posthumous publication of Fenollosa's *Epochs of Chinese & Japanese Art* in 1912. By chance, Pound met Fenollosa's widow at a literary evening. Mary Fenollosa, having read Pound's poems, invited him to edit the papers of her late husband. This was a task Pound accepted with alacrity. In the dead scholar's manuscripts, Pound was to encounter a summation of his early interests in Confucius and Far Eastern poetry and drama. It is not difficult to see the definition of an ideogram as "the capture of the potential energy of a thing in compressed form" in Pound's later involvement with Imagism and Vorticism. Pound's definition of "The Vortex" might also read as his own personal understanding of an ideogram: "The image is not an idea. It is a radiant node or cluster; it is what I can, and must perforce, call a VORTEX, from which, through which, and into which ideas are constantly rushing" (*GB* 92).

Here was an apparatus that allowed Pound to use ancient forms of poetry and drama in his development of a modern idiom in verse. The ideogram was also of central importance to Vorticist visual art, in particular, the work of Henri Gaudier-Brzeska and Percy Wyndham Lewis. Several of Gaudier's late sketches in brush and Chinese ink can be read as modern equivalents to the ideogram.

Pound was to produce several volumes on Fenollosa during World War I. His translation of *Cathay*, derived from the scholar's notes, appeared in 1915. In the following year Pound published *Certain Noble Plays of Japan*, from the manuscripts of Fenollosa, which was introduced by Yeats, and a study of classical Noh drama. As late as 1920, shortly after his departure for Paris, Pound's *Instigations* was published in New York accompanied by *The Chinese Written Character as a Medium for Poetry*, a Fenollosa essay on the ideogram.

Bibliography

Binyon, Lawrence. *The Flight of the Dragon: An Essay on the Theory and Practice of Art in China and Japan*. London: J. Murray, 1911.

Fenollosa, Ernest. *Epochs of Chinese & Japanese Art*. London: Heinemann, 1912.

Holaday, Woon-Ping Chin. "Pound and Binyon: China via the British Museum." *Paideuma* 6.1 (1977): 27–36.

Humphries, Richard. *Pound's Artists: Ezra Pound and the Visual Arts in London, Paris and Italy*. London: Tate Gallery Publications, 1985.

Jonathan Blackwood

"IF THIS BE TREASON . . ."

"*IF THIS BE TREASON . . .*" (1948) marked the first publication of the World War II radio speeches that resulted in Pound's treason trial and imprisonment. Edited by Olga Rudge to exonerate Pound of charges of having allied himself with wartime enemies of the United States, 300 copies of six talks—"e. e. cummings," "e. e. cummings/examind [*sic*]," "James Joyce: to his memory," "A french accent," "Canto 45," and "*BLAST*"—were distributed in early 1948, shortly before *The Pisan Cantos*. The pamphlet was gathered by Rudge from Pound's written drafts, as opposed to transcripts, and seems to have been published without Pound's knowledge, although he had long supported the publication of his radio speeches.

Bibliography

Pound, Ezra. "*IF THIS BE TREASON . . .*" Siena: Tip. Nuova, [1948]; Venice: Tip Litografia Armena, 1983.

Stock, Noel. *The Life of Ezra Pound*. 1970. San Francisco: North Point P, 1982.

Jonathan P. Gill

Imaginary Letters

This volume (published in 1930) collects Ezra Pound's eight contributions (September 1917 to November 1918) to a feature of the same title that ran in the *Little Review*. Wyndham Lewis had been responsible for the first "Imaginary Letters," written by a fictitious William Bland Burn to his wife; when World War I made Lewis discontinue the charade, Pound stepped in, choosing the pseudonym Walter Villerant but initially preserving Lydia Bland Burn as his addressee. Pound's letters dismiss art for the masses (I); deride enthusiasm for postrevolutionary Russia (II, VI); satirize British *moeurs* (IV); celebrate Confucius (VII); and exculpate James Joyce of obscenity (VIII).

Bibliography

Pound, Ezra. *Imaginary Letters*. Paris: Black Sun P, 1930.

Brian M. Reed

Impact: Essays on Ignorance and the Decline of American Civilization

Published in 1960 by the Henry Regnery Company of Chicago, *Impact* was edited with an introduction by Noel Stock, and Ezra Pound proofed the galleys. Stock divided the collection into three parts: previously published essays; segments from unpublished material; and letters to various American political leaders and artists. The bulk of the writings is from the 1930s and 1940s—and while the essays range in subject matter, they keep as a general theme the importance of economics in world history and culture. Stock wrote in his introduction: "I . . . have attempted to present [Pound's] mature view as it was, say, in 1940" (xviii).

Cameron McWhirter

Indiscretions

Ezra Pound's short sixty-two-page autobiography *Indiscretions: or, Une Revue de Deux Mondes*, written when he was thirty-five and dedicated to A. R. Orage, was begun in Venice and printed in Paris at Bill Bird's Three Mountains Press in 1923 in an edition of 300 copies. Pound reports selected fragments of family history—the book is concerned primarily with Homer Pound, the writer's father—on the premise that they convey the history of the United States in microcosm. Family names are disguised, however, and much that seems fantastic has basis in fact, allowing for imprecision in what was transmitted to him such as the circus elephant that had run loose in Hailey, Idaho, as a portent of the birth of Gargantua (Pound himself). While Pound refers to "the sty of the family" (11–12), he delights in his forebears as well as their associates. His "great aunt-in-law," for example, had danced with General Grant and took him to Europe when he was thirteen. Pound approves of his ancestors, the Westovers, "for not taking passage on the Mayflower" (19). Then in an instance of reverse snobbery, "they arrived decently upon the 'Lion,' before the rush" (34). Likely seeing himself anticipated in his father, he praises Rip Weight (Homer Pound) for descending from the train for West Point, thereby escaping "a rigid complete set of values" (53).

Indiscretions first appeared in the *New Age*, in twelve installments from 27 May to 12 August 1920; it was reprinted in *Pavannes and Divagations* (1958; 3–51). As noted in Pound's "Postscript," the book was meant as a foreword to a series of five other volumes—Ford Madox Ford's *Women & Men* (1923); B. C. Windeler's *Elimus* (1923); William Carlos Williams's *The Great American Novel* (1923); B.M.G. Adams's *England* (1923); and Ernest Hemingway's *In Our Time* (1924)—published by Bill Bird's press under the general title *The Inquest*. These authors, Pound writes, "have set out from five very different points to tell the truth about *moeurs contemporaines*, without fake, melodrama, conventional editing" (62). Bill Bird did not comply with Pound's suggestion in 1924 to bind together the remaining copies of the series as *The Inquest*.

Bibliography

Carpenter, Humphrey. *A Serious Character: The Life of Ezra Pound*. Boston: Houghton Mifflin, 1988.

Pound, Ezra. *Indiscretions; or, Une Revue de Deux Mondes*. Paris: Three Mountains P, 1923. Reprinted in *Pavannes and Divagations*. New York: New Directions, 1958.

Evelyn Haller

Instigations

Published two months before *Hugh Selwyn Mauberley*, *Instigations* (1920) is primarily a collection of literary essays, most of which had appeared in various journals during 1918–1919. Although convenience more than thematic unity seems to have determined the selection and the arrangement of its pieces, there are certain topics—translation, French literature, Pound's growing frustration with British and American culture—that appear throughout the collection. It also marks the first appearance in book form of Ernest Fenollosa's *The Chinese Written Character as a Medium for Poetry*. Ultimately, *Instigations* provides the reader with some of Pound's closing statements on his London years and sheds light on Pound's post-London work, though T. S. Eliot included much of this material in *Literary Essays of Ezra Pound*.

The collection opens with "A Study of French Poets," a loose essay that Pound developed from a series of articles published in the *Little Review*, February–October 1918. This "brief anthology of French poems" (3) with comments by Pound includes work from Laforgue, Corbière, Rimbaud, Jammes, Vildrac, Romains, and others, as well as a section on *unanimisme*. The implicit goal of this study, which covers a quarter of the book's length, is to "search foreign tongues for *maestria* and for discoveries not yet revealed in the home product" (4).

The following essay, "Henry James" (*Little Review*, August 1918), presents Pound's assessment of the novelist as writer and as citizen. He sees James primarily as "the hater of tyranny" who writes "against oppression, against all the sordid petty personal crushing oppression, the domination of modern life" (107). Pound concludes the essay with a Jamesian "treatise on novel-writing" (160) abstracted from James's notes for *The Ivory Tower*.

Much of "Henry James" reads like an annotated bibliography, as does the following essay, "Remy de Gourmont, a Distinction" (*Little Review*, February–March 1919). Pound distinguishes James's concern "for the social tone of his subjects" from Gourmont's interest in his subjects' "modality and resonance in emotion" (170). Gourmont's works "taken together" are "a portrait of the civilized mind" (176). Pound also includes several extended quotations as examples of Gourmont's style.

The next essay, "In the Vortex," gathers articles on T. S. Eliot (*Poetry*, August 1917), James Joyce (*Future*, May 1918), Wyndham Lewis (*Egoist*, 15 June 1914; *Little Review*, March 1918), Lytton Strachey (*Future*, October 1918), Marianne Moore, Mina Loy, Williams Carlos Williams, and others (*Little Review*, March 1918; *Future*, June 1918). The essay ends with "The Classics 'Escape' " and "Cantico del Sole" (*Little Review*, March 1918), attacks on U.S. obscenity laws in prose and verse, respectively.

The second part of the book begins with two satirical pieces, "Our Tetrarchal Précieuse (A Divagation from Jules Laforgue)" (*Little Review*, July 1918) and "Genesis, or The First Book in the Bible" (*Little Review*, November 1918), the latter being a translation of a piece by Voltaire. "Arnaut Daniel," a collection of translations that Pound had been working on since 1911, follows these. Individual poems and Pound's introduction had previously appeared in several different journals. The last of Pound's own essays, "Translators of Greek" (*Egoist*, August–October 1918), provides some insight into Pound's use of Latin cribs and includes comments on Andreas Divus.

Instigations concludes with *The Chinese Written Character* (*Little Review*, September–December 1919). As editor, Pound claims to "have done little more than remove a few repetitions and shape a few sentences" (357). Fenollosa's study of how "Chinese notation . . . is based upon a vivid shorthand picture of the operations of nature" (362) would inspire Pound to develop the ideogrammic method, the basis for Pound's aesthetic and philosophical explorations throughout *The Cantos*.

Bibliography

Pound, Ezra. *Instigations of Ezra Pound, Together with an Essay on the Chinese Written Character by Ernest Fenollosa.* New York: Boni & Liveright, 1920.

Michael J. Alleman

Italian Literature

Ezra Pound's interest in Italian literature was lifelong and formed an indissoluble part of his love for Italian culture and indeed the people and land of Italy, where he was to live the greater part of his adult life. He traveled extensively in Italy before 1924, beginning with a trip with his aunt in 1898. He lived in Rapallo, a small city on the Ligurian coast near Genoa, from 1924 to 1945 and again after 1958; but the city with the richest Poundian associations is Venice, where he published his first book, *A Lume Spento*, in 1908 and where he died in 1972. He is buried in the small Protestant cemetery on Isola San Michele, near Igor Stravinsky, another great Modernist whose *"cammin di nostra vita"* led him from the edge of European culture to Venice.

At the center of Pound's love for Italy was his love for Italian literature, and at the center of that love stands Dante Alighieri, undoubtedly the greatest single influence on Pound's work. It has long been understood that *The Cantos* stand in a close relationship to Dante's *Commedia*, even if the details of that relationship are contested. The common view is that *The Cantos* are designed as a formal imitation of the *Commedia*, with the Early Cantos (1–30) as an *Inferno*, the Middle Cantos (31–71) as a *Purgatorio*, and the *Pisan Cantos* (74–84) and on some accounts the Later Cantos (85–117) as a *Paradiso*. Although various remarks by Pound support this reading, it does not make very much sense of his poem as we have it, which contains 117 cantos, not 100, and has no very discernible "Dantescan rising" of the kind Pound alludes to in Canto 74. One way of interpreting this lack of formal or narrative consonance is that *The Cantos* is a botch, and various remarks of Pound support this reading as well. This author would prefer to say instead that Dante's productive influence on Pound lies elsewhere than in such a formal resemblance.

One central influence of Dante on Pound is Dante's language, particularly his direct presentation of the image. Dante's language is not without figuration, of course, but Pound always stressed that Dante's figures were functional, not ornamental, and he saw in this a close resemblance to Romanesque architecture such as San Zeno in Verona. Although the *Vita Nuova* was less important for Pound than for earlier poets such as Rossetti, Pound was very interested in Dante's lyrics, the later *rime petrose* being of particular importance. He was also a careful reader of Dante's prose: *De Vulgare Eloquentia*, *Il Convivio*, and *De Monarchia* are works that profoundly affected Pound's thinking about language, poetry, and politics. Pound's close engagement with all of Dante's oeuvre can be seen in his library, which contains two heavily annotated editions of Dante's complete works and his college Dante textbook, the bilingual Temple Classics *Commedia* in three slim volumes. Finally, Pound took Dante seriously enough to use his enthusiasms as a guide for his own reading: Though Pound excoriated Virgil and consistently underestimated his importance for Dante, Dante was a crucial influence on Pound's exploration of Provençal poetry and later of Aristotle.

However, it would be a mistake to assume that Pound's engagement with Italian literature stopped with Dante, as important as he is to all of Pound's oeuvre. Pound viewed Guido Cavalcanti as second in importance only to his friend Dante. In some ways, he felt closer to Cavalcanti in spirit than he did to Dante, since he interpreted Cavalcanti as far more theologically and intellectually heterodox than Dante. Pound's lifelong exploration of Cavalcanti led to two books, *Sonnets and Ballate of Guido Cavalcanti* (1912) and *Guido Cavalcanti Rime* (1932), as well as several essays on Cavalcanti, an opera, and perhaps most strikingly, the incorporation of a translation of all of Cavalcanti's canzone

"Donna mi prega" in Canto 36. That Cavalcanti is at all known to English-language readers today is probably due to Pound's influence.

Cavalcanti and Dante are the two major figures of Italian literature for Pound, and Pound undeniably thought that the high point of Italian literature was the work of these Tuscan poets between 1280 and 1321; but that does not mean that only these writers are of influence for Pound. Pound was from the beginning very interested in Renaissance Humanism, less in the Florentine culture of civic humanism influential for later democratic thinking than the visual as well as literary culture of the Renaissance courts. It is not irrelevant here that he did not particularly like Florence and spent remarkably little time there, in sharp contrast to most expatriate denizens of Italy. Venice, Siena, Verona, Ravenna, Rimini, and Sirmione are the sites central to Pound's apprehension of Italy— Pound preferred the cities where Dante lived in exile to the city that exiled him. Among the Humanists, Lorenzo Valla was of particular importance for Pound, both because of his epicureanism as expressed in *De Voluptate* and because his exposure of the Donation of Constantine as a forgery showed the kind of effect on the world that philological and scholarly labor could have. The influence of Renaissance Humanism on Pound has not been fully understood: For instance, it seems to this author that Pound's apprehension of Dante was strongly mediated by the Renaissance reading of Dante in terms of epideictic rhetoric and an orientation toward exemplarity in epic theory. However, as critics have already argued, it was the figure of the Renaissance Prince, not the artists and scholars who surrounded him, who was finally of greatest interest for Pound. In contrast to Yeats, whose choice of Urbino and the Montefeltro court as represented in Castiglione's *Il Libro del Cortegiano* contains more than a measure of idealization, Pound knew that the culture he admired in the *quattrocento* had not been achieved by sweetness and light as much as by force and rapacity.

The figure of Sigismundo Malatesta represents this conjunction most fully for Pound, and

Pound's fascination with Malatesta and the Malatesta Cantos (Cantos 8–11) that emerged as a result have been carefully studied by a number of critics. Pound was more interested in Malatesta than in the artists he employed because he believed the role of the patron to be at least as important in the creation of art as the role of the artist and because, though confident that the modern era had the artists to match the Renaissance, he was less sure we had comparable patrons. This interest in patronage, or more broadly in the social conditions that are conducive to the production of great art, though a little off to one side of our subject here, is part of what led to Pound's fascination with Benito Mussolini and support of his regime. In a nutshell, he saw him as the Sigismundo Malatesta of our time, and this perception of an analogy was part of what crystallized Pound's commitment to Mussolini's regime, announced in *Jefferson and/or Mussolini* (1934).

On the heels of that commitment, which led him across the 1930s down the road to the broadcasts over Rome Radio during World War II in support of the Axis, his interest in the Italian past was deflected into an increasing interest in the Italian present, not what Italy had been but what Italy was and would be. However, little in Pound's voluminous correspondence or journalism suggested a substantial engagement with contemporary Italian literature. He was personally acquainted with and fond of F. T. Marinetti, and Canto 72 presents Marinetti speaking from the dead urging Pound and Italy to keep the fascist faith. There are also some favorable remarks about Gabriele D'Annunzio, who despite his complex relation to Mussolini has been claimed as the "John the Baptist" of fascism. However, these scattered references do not disguise Pound's fundamental lack of interest in and lack of knowledge of Italian literature of the twentieth century.

There are two curious exceptions: Enrico Pea and Saturno Montanari. Pea was the author of a four-volume, rather Hardyesque novel, *Moscardino*, which Pound discovered in 1941. Pound translated the first volume, "the only time in my life that I have ever wanted to translate a novel" (*L* 318). Pea lived in Viareggio, a small town on the coast in Tuscany, and Pound would visit Pea on the way to and from Rome and sought his help with the dialect in the novel. Pound's interest in Pea may have been political in origin: The passage quoted above comes from Pound's pro-fascist pamphlet of 1942, *A Visiting Card*, and Pound presents *Moscardino* as evidence that "at last, in the Year XXI of the Fascist Era, it seems to me that the Fascist style may be beginning to take root" (*SP* 318). Pound was certainly in a position to ascertain Pea's attitudes toward Mussolini's regime, but this author is unable to discern anything stylistically, aesthetically, or even politically fascist about the part of *Moscardino* Pound translated, which was in any case not published until 1955. Saturno Montanari was a lyric poet who died in 1941 at the age of twenty-three while serving in Italian-occupied Yugoslavia. Pound's translations of five of his brief and quite unremarkable lyrics were published in *Imagi* in 1951 and then republished in *The Translations of Ezra Pound* (446–448) in 1953. Pea and Montanari are extremely marginal figures in contemporary Italian literature. This author's assumption that Pound saw them as figures in a pro-fascist canon again hardly changes the impression that Pound knew little about and had no vital connection to the Italian literature of his own time.

There is a reason for this, implicit in Pound's perception of Mussolini as the great patron of the arts of our time. If a great patron was needed for a great artist, if the political and the aesthetic were as closely linked as Pound's adult thinking suggested, then Pound in fact had a vested interest in not thinking highly of the Italian literature of his time. That portion of it that was critical of fascism would of course have been unwelcome to Pound, but significant pro-fascist writers were, in this author's reading, little more welcome to Pound. Pound felt that the great epic hero, Benito Mussolini, already had a poet worthy of his patronage and ready to sing of his accomplishments—Ezra Pound. As *The Cantos* in the 1930s moves toward an epic celebration of the figure of Benito Mussolini, Pound moved closer to seeing himself as an important figure in Italian literature itself. The grotesque culmination of this perception is the wartime cantos written in Italian, Cantos 72 and 73, which celebrate fascism in an imitation of the *Commedia*. These cantos are of interest above all because Pound's hopes sunk on the shores of reality: Benito Mussolini was not the great epic hero of our time but someone who led his country to disaster. Likewise, Pound was not the great epic poet contemporary Italian literature was waiting for (and is still waiting for): He could not even write grammatically correct Italian, and this is one sign of just how oblique Pound's relation to contemporary Italy really was.

But it would be a mistake to stop there, with a simple picture of Pound having a fruitful relation to the distant Italian past and a disastrous one with the Italian present. We need to complicate it at least in the sense of asking what led Pound to and enabled him to have such a fruitful relation to the Italian literature of the past. After all, Pound did not have an unmediated relationship with Dante and Cavalcanti. Previous Pound criticism has rightly stressed both an English, largely Pre-Raphaelite, context for Pound's interest in the *duecento* lyric and an American, largely New England, context for his interest in Dante's epic achievement. Rossetti, Browning, and Longfellow are all important figures here, and the prose of Landor and Ruskin would need to be included in a full account. There is another influence here whose importance for Pound has not been sufficiently recognized—Italy's greatest lyric poet since the *trecento*, Giacomo Leopardi (1798–1837). Pound translated a Leopardi poem early in his career, "*Sopra il ritratto di una bella donna*," which he translated as "Her monument, the Image Cut Thereon" and included in *Canzoni* in 1911. Leopardi's poem is a beautiful and haunting meditation on love, death, and time. Pound's translation, suffering from the archaic and stilted tone of the other poems in this volume, is hardly a masterpiece, though it does revise Leopardi's text in some interesting ways. More important for Pound's later development than this poem in particular is Leopardi's idea of creating a book of poems of epic stature in lyric form through intelligent and

fruitful collocation of individual poems. Above all, the title of Leopardi's collection, *I Canti*, is the closest analogue to the title of Pound's major work, *The Cantos*. *The Commedia* is obviously made up of cantos or *canti* but, equally obviously, it is called something else. Pound's title echoes Leopardi's title echoing Dante in a gesture that situates both poets as belated in Harold Bloom's terminology, imitating the Italian past that they see (always in Leopardi's case, almost always in Pound's case) as greater than the Italian present.

Pound took the phrase *patria mia* from the title of one of Leopardi's poems most intensely involved in the Italian past to title his early essays about the United States (1913), which were optimistic about the possibilities for American culture. But by the end of his life, Pound's *patria* was the Italy in which he is buried as much as the United States that kept him in a madhouse for thirteen years. His commitment to a virtual binational identity, revealed above all by the macaronic texture of his correspondence, is of great fascination today as we look for a more plural, transnational form of identity. A model of this with enduring fascination is Pound's lifelong involvement with Italy and Italian literature.

Reed Way Dasenbrock

Italian Translation

Ezra Pound was a prolific translator who translated work written in Italian, Latin, Provençal, French, Greek, and Chinese, as well as work in Japanese, Egyptian hieroglyphics, and Hindi with the help of notes or other translations. His translations can be provisionally divided into two categories: translations whose primary purpose was to make the original available in English and translations whose primary purpose was to provide Pound with a foil or persona for his own work. It is work in the second category—most notably the Old English poem "The Seafarer," *Cathay*, and *Homage to Sextus Propertius*—that occasioned the most controversy and that remain the most influential of Pound's translations. Scholars have had continuous problems with Pound's "mistranslations" (how can Sextus Propertius call something

"Wordsworthian"?), while poets have delighted in the freedom Pound's example has given them—Christopher Logue's continuing dialogue with the *Iliad* being one conspicuous example. Of work in the first category, undeniably the most extensive and important for Pound's evolution were his translations of the Confucian classics, beginning with the *Ta Hio* in 1928 and extending through his wartime translations of the *Ta Hio* again and of the *Chung Yung* into Italian during the war and into English just afterward and finally his 1951 translation of *The Analects*. His final major translation, of the *Shih Ching* or *The Confucian Odes* in 1954, can be seen as an attempt to merge these two categories. The primacy of these Chinese translations does not correspond perfectly to Pound's sense of the comparative importance of the literature as much as to Pound's sense of our need to have the material translated. The pattern of Pound's translations has to be seen as a strategy of supplementarity: He devoted his efforts to the translation of Chinese because there was work that needed to be done.

Translation from Italian literature is second only to translation from Chinese in Pound's oeuvre, and virtually all of his Italian translations are in the more faithful mode of translation. Consequently, none of his translations from Italian has either the celebrity or notoriety of "The Seafarer" or *Sextus Propertius*. Moreover, we need to understand that his strategy of supplementarity was at work here as well. Consequently, Pound never translated Dante, the greatest single influence on his work, obviously because he felt that Dante was already accessible to English-language readers. His major translations from Italian were of the poetry of Guido Cavalcanti, Dante's contemporary and close friend. This work led to the publication of *Sonnets and Ballate of Guido Cavalcanti*, a bilingual edition published in Boston and London in 1912 of fifty poems of Cavalcanti, basically all of the accepted oeuvre at the time of Pound's work except for the canzone "*Donna mi prega.*" Pound returned to Cavalcanti in the late 1920s when he had developed an interest in "*Donna mi prega,*" translating it for the *Dial* in

1928 and then incorporating a second translation into Canto 36 in 1934. He also retranslated a number of poems he had done in 1912, seeking a more precise and less Rossettian idiom for Cavalcanti. This was to be part of an enlarged bilingual edition of Cavalcanti to be published by Aquila Press in London. When Aquila went bankrupt with the book partially printed, Pound incorporated these pages into an edition of Cavalcanti, *Guido Cavalcanti Rime*, published by Edizioni Marsano in Genoa in 1932. This marked the end of Pound's work on Cavalcanti, though New Directions reprinted the poems in 1966 and Pound added a new preface.

Beyond Cavalcanti, Pound translated a few poems by his contemporaries, "*Vedut'ho la lucente stella Diana*" by Guido Guinizzelli (or Guinicelli) in *The Spirit of Romance*, a sonnet by Guido Orlandi to Cavalcanti printed in the *Dial* in 1929, and finally St. Francis's "*Cantico del sole,*" also in *The Spirit of Romance*. These are essentially poetic illustrations of points being made in the prose texts in which they are contained and are not of great importance in their own right.

Pound also translated one poem by Giacomo Leopardi, his "*Sopra il ritratto di una bella donna*" from *I Canti*, translated as "Her Monument, the Image Cut Thereon" and included in his own collection of poetry, *Canzoni*, in 1911. Leopardi is a figure whose influence on Pound has not been sufficiently recognized; however, the influence is to be found above all in the way Leopardi modeled for Pound a creative involvement with the Italian past, which is not a particular theme of this poem. If Pound's reasons for translating "*Sopra il retratto*" are somewhat inscrutable, the reason for his only translation of contemporary Italian poetry, his translation of five lyrics of Saturno Montanari for *Imagi* in 1951 is even more so. Montanari is an extremely minor figure in Italian literature, and the poems themselves give no hint of what attracted Pound to them.

Finally, Pound translated two works of Italian prose, one part of Enrico Pea's four-part novel *Moscardino* and a work of economics, Odon Por's *Italy's Policy of Social Economics,*

1939–1940. The translation from Pea is significant as the only work of fiction Pound ever translated out of admiration, but the novel itself gives little clue to Pound's interest in it, since it is a work of regional *verismo* that seems to be of little calculated interest to Pound. One suspects that Pound's attraction to Pea and Montanari was political, though the actual texts provide little evidence for this, and this is clearly the case with Odon Por, who was of Hungarian origin and supported Mussolini's regime from an explicitly left syndicalist perspective.

It can therefore scarcely be said that Pound was an innovative or an important translator of Italian literature. This is a curious and insufficiently pondered fact, given the centrality of Italian literature and culture for all of Pound's work. It may well be that the very closeness of Italy for Pound prevented him from successfully engaging in translation from Italian. Certainly, his strategy of "creative mistranslation" works better when there is more distance between him and his model than there ever was between Pound and his beloved *patria*.

Reed Way Dasenbrock

J

James, Henry (1843–1916)

Pound met the American prose master Henry James in 1912. The poet's letters to his parents indicate that although the initial meeting was not exactly friendly, Pound soon developed affection for the longtime expatriate writer. The two did not have much personal contact in the ensuing years, yet Pound reiterated his respect for his older contemporary numerous times. Most of the space in the August 1918 Henry James memorial issue of the *Little Review*, for which Pound was serving as European editor, was devoted to Pound's essay on the novelist (reprinted in *LE* 295–338). The essay, which surveys nearly the entire oeuvre, is Pound's longest devoted to a single novelist writing in English. Pound's praise is not unqualified, however, for he accuses James of inconsistency and unfavorably compares some aspects of his works to those of Flaubert and other French writers. Pound's conclusion is nonetheless flattering: The best works James produced range leagues ahead of the competition in English. Pound again praises James in *ABC of Reading*, where James is included in the exclusive list of worthwhile English novelists. Perhaps most important is the influence of James on his younger compatriot's verse. He is mentioned in an explanation Pound offered for *Hugh Selwyn Mauberley* (8 July 1922 letter to Felix E. Schelling; *L* 180), he influenced the composition of Canto 7, and he is mentioned in Cantos 74, 79, and 89 as well as in "L'Homme Moyen Sensuel."

Bibliography

Holder, Alan. "The Lesson of the Master: Ezra Pound and Henry James." *American Literature* 35.1 (1963): 71–79.

Christopher K. Coffman

Japanese Literature

The history of Japanese literature goes back to the eighth-century *Manyoshu*, a collection of 4,500 poems that also includes some prose pieces. This rich lyric tradition of tanka, with thirty-one syllables, has produced a still briefer form of poetry called haiku, with seventeen syllables. Pound's debts to this tradition are evident in such poems as "In a Station of the Metro" and many other early poems but also some longer "hokku-like" poems. Pound's theory of "superposition" and his essay "A Few Don'ts by an Imagiste" are also respectively directly and indirectly inspired by the haiku.

Japanese literature also includes a number of poems written in Chinese by Japanese poets. Eight of them, composed during the Edo Period, with eight tanka and paintings on eight scenes of Sho-sho inspired Pound to write Canto 49 (see Kodama, *American Poetry and Japanese Culture* 105–120).

The narrative tradition in Japanese literature also has a long history and includes such works as *Taketori Monogatari*, *The Tale of Genji*, *The Tale of Heike*, and many other narratives. Dramatic literature is also abundant with Noh plays, some of which Pound translated into English, and *Kabuki* and *Joruri*, which are still played in traditional theaters in modern cities in Japan.

Following the Meiji Restoration (1868), European and American literatures were introduced to Japan, and they inspired Japanese writers and poets to write modern fiction, drama, poetry, and criticism. Katue Kitasono (1902–1978), one of the Modernist, avant-garde poets, had a long correspondence with Pound, who called him Kit Kat in his letters of friendly admiration (Kodama, *Pound and Japan*).

Bibliography

Kodama, Sanehide. *American Poetry and Japanese Culture.* Hamden: Archon Books, 1984.

———. *Ezra Pound and Japan: Letters and Essays.* Redding Ridge: Black Swan Books, 1987.

Sanehide Kodama

Japanese Translation

Pound's debut in Japan dates as early as 1916 when an anonymous rough translation of his "*Awoi no Uye*," with an introduction and additions, appeared in *Yokyokukai*, a magazine for the Noh students and lovers. The earliest translation of Pound in book form was *Bungaku Seishin no Gensen* (*How to Read*) by Tsunetaro Kinoshita in 1933. In the magazine *VOU* Katsue Kitasono kept translating Pound from 1936 on.

After World War II, *How to Read*, "Francesca," "A Girl," a part of *Hugh Selwyn Mauberley*, "To-En-Mei's 'Unmoving Cloud,'" "Tensone," "In a Station of the Metro," and several other early poems were translated into Japanese and collected and published in book form as *Sekai Bungaku no Yomikata* from Hobunkan in 1953. Three years later, Ryozo Iwasaki translated "Sestina: Altaforte," "The Lake Isle," "Alba," *Hugh Selwyn Mauberley*, "Cantos I and IV," and other poems, published as *Paundo Shishu* from Arechi Shuppan in 1956. All these early works were mainly based on the translators' interest in Pound as a torch-bearer of the Imagist, Vorticist, and Modernist movements.

As listed in Donald Gallup's *Bibliography*, academic interest in Pound produced a number of new and more correct translations since then, in books, anthologies, and periodicals. Among them, two books should be mentioned here:

Ezura Paundo Shishu by Toshikazu Niikura (Kodansha, 1976), a collection of translations of early poems and some twenty cantos, and *Shigaku Nyumon* by Junnosuke Sawasaki (Fuzambo, 1979), a translation of *ABC of Reading* and *How to Read*.

Special mention should be made of two more books among all other works not listed in Gallup. Masakazu Ono and Yasuo Iwahara cotranslated *A Lume Spento* as *Kieta Biko* and published it with two postscripts from Shoritsu Yamada in 1987. The same team published their complete translation of A *Quinzaine for This Yule*, *Personae*, and *Exultations* as *Kamen* from the same publisher in 1991 with two postscripts.

As for Pound's translation into English from the Japanese, his reworking of the rough English translation of the Noh plays contained in Fenollosa's notebooks needs special attention (see also *"Noh," or Accomplishment*). For example, in "Nishikigi" Pound emphasizes the image of "maples" by using the word more often in his translation than is used in the original and associates their red color with passion and their fading leaves with death. Pound then argues that the "Unity of Image" in a Noh play like this one is an answer to the following question: "Could one do a long Imagiste poem or even a long poem in vers libre?" (*Classic Noh Theatre of Japan* 27; see also Hasegawa 40).

There are more than thirty Japanese poems written by and translated into English by VOU Club members, published, with Pound's introduction, in *Townsman* (January 1938 and April 1939) and *New Directions* (1938). Pound was surprised at "the chameleon's tongue quickness" and "untrammelled clearness" of these poems, but he confessed that he did "not understand some sentences" ("Vou Club" 4). So he may have edited and reworked these poems—but research has yet to address this matter.

Bibliography

Fenollosa, Ernest, and Ezra Pound. *"Noh," or Accomplishment: A Study of the Classical Stage of Japan.* London: Macmillan, 1916 [1917].

Hasegawa, Toshimitsu. *Yeats and Noh and Modernism.* Tokyo: UC Planning, 1995.

Pound, Ezra. "Vou Club [Introduction]." *Townsman* 1.1 (1938): 4.

Pound, Ezra, and Ernest Fenollosa. *The Classic Noh Theatre of Japan.* New York: New Directions, 1959.

Sanehide Kodama

Jefferson and/or Mussolini

Ezra Pound's *Jefferson and/or Mussolini* (1935) is an attempt to undo—or, as we now say, deconstruct—the opposition between the most seemingly opposed of historical figures: "The heritage of Jefferson . . . is HERE, NOW *in the Italian peninsula* at the beginning of the fascist second decennio, not in Massachusetts or Delaware" (*J/M* 12). Jeffrey Mehlman characterizes the entire project as "maddeningly wrong-headed" (8–9), which, in one sense, it certainly is. Pound's political investments do not simply taint a greatness that nevertheless rises, Phoenix-like, above them, and both the fascism and the anti-Semitism need to be acknowledged for what they are. Yet if *Jefferson and/or Mussolini* is "maddeningly wrong-headed," so too is the impulse to dismiss it as such. Fredric Jameson argues that a politics incapable of grasping "the immense Utopian appeal" of fascism "can scarcely hope to 'reappropriate' its collective energies" (298), and if our relation to Pound's politics is to progress beyond ritual condemnation, the poet's celebration of Mussolini as Jefferson reborn must be taken as more than an individual quirk or idiocy. Pound's act of protodeconstruction was not, after all, unique to him: Roosevelt was frequently compared to Mussolini, and fascist elements were discerned in the New Deal. Giovanni Gentile, Mussolini's education minister, viewed fascism as the most perfect expression of liberalism and democracy, and the manifest absurdity of Pound's comparison should not blind us to the uncomfortable truth that there is a strong protofascist element in the tradition of U.S. Populism to which the poet was heir. Leon Surette casts Pound in the familiar (and thoroughly individualizing) role of "tragic hero": "Well-intentioned though he was, overweening self-confidence led Pound into error and sin. (I can think of no more appropriate term for his moral failure)" (11).

But if we are to have any hope of comprehending (or, better, "reappropriating") the collective energies of fascism, the vocabulary of "error" and "sin" will hardly do. (Dante might have been merciful enough, Surette speculates, to place Pound "in purgatory rather than hell, perhaps in the first terrace of Love Perverted, which is reserved for the Wrathful" [11]. Theological parlor games are not, however, a meaningful response to fascist politics.) "Gents who make guns," Pound writes in *Jefferson and/or Mussolini*, "like to sell 'em, such is the present state of the world, in the bourgeois demo-liberal anti-Marxian anti-fascist anti-Leninist system" (72). The contempt for the "bourgeois demo-liberal" establishment is palpable, yet the obvious question, which haunts every student of Modernism, persists: Why did a generalized and potentially revolutionary dissatisfaction with the liberal settlement issue in fascism? In anti-Semitism? In a 1933 article, "Murder by Capital," Pound asks: "What drives, or what can drive a man interested almost exclusively in the arts, into social theory or into a study of 'the gross material aspects' . . . of the present?" (*SP* 228–229). Of which we might ask: What drove so many modern individuals, Pound included, into reactionary social theory and practices?

Pound seeks to substantiate the highly provocative juxtaposition of his title—U.S. Democrat and/or Italian fascist—by positing "three common denominators or possibly four":

> agriculture, sense of the "root and the branch," readiness to scrap the lesser thing for the thing of major importance, indifference to mechanism as weighed against the main purpose, fitting of the means to that purpose without regard to abstract ideas, even if the idea was proclaimed the week before last. (*J/M* 64)

To reverse Pound's order: Jefferson and Mussolini are celebrated for their freedom from ideological fixity, their commitment to the life of practical action (which involves the subordination of means to ends), and their sense of the organic totality of all things. Jefferson stood for the good of the many against the special interests of the few; Mussolini's opposition to "the infinite evil of the profiteers and the sellers of men's blood for money" (*J/M* 61)—read: an international conspiracy of Jewish financiers—allegedly revives Jefferson's heritage in the here and now.

There is a sense, however, in which *Jefferson and/or Mussolini* is structured by a second, implicit juxtaposition, no less provocative than the first: "Mussolini and/or Pound." Artist celebrates artist: "I don't believe any estimate of Mussolini will be valid unless it *starts* from his passion for construction. Treat him as an *artifex* and all details fall into place. Take him as anything save the artist and you will get muddled with contradictions" (*J/M* 33–34). In "Murder by Capital," Pound complains that "no party programme ever contains enough of his [the artist's] programme to give him the least satisfaction," but the artist's interests are clearly decisive (*SP* 215). Pound evidently cast his lot with Mussolini because he believed the dictator to be engaged in a project analogous to his own. Much has been written on the relationship between the accomplishments of the high Modernists and the formalism of New Critical aesthetics, but no poem has ever less resembled a "well-wrought urn" than *The Cantos*, and perhaps no poem, certainly no modern poem, has ever labored to intervene so directly in the affairs of the world. Pound's definition of epic, "a long poem including history," still enjoys a certain currency, but it is an inadequate characterization of his own epic ambitions. For *The Cantos* do not simply "include" history as so much archival subject matter; rather, the poem hopes to effect a historical revolution. "I tried to write Paradise": Pound's ambitions are radically transitive, constructive rather than contemplative. The goal is not "an ideal republic situated in a platonic paradise" but "an arrangement possible in Italy in the year VIII or IX of the Era Fascita" (*J/M* 57). This is Pound on Mussolini, but it might also be Pound on Pound.

If a commitment to the life of practical action unites poet and dictator, so too does an alleged freedom from ideological fixity. Granted, fascism is not generally known for its intellectual or ideological fluidity; yet as Stanley Payne observes, Italian fascism developed a "codified set of doctrines only ex post facto, some years after Mussolini came to power, and then only in part" (4). *The Cantos* themselves, moreover, evince a certain openness before the unpredictability of experience and history. (Pound's epic thus serves as an exemplary caution against the facile translation of aesthetic form into ideological content. *The Cantos* resists "totalization" in the aesthetic sense, yet its politics are no less "totalitarian" for that.) Mussolini's "sense of the root and branch," his commitment to the organic complementarity of all things, was highly selective: Italian fascism respected the sanctity of capitalist property relations, even as it sought to engender "organic" or precapitalist modes of social organization.

Pound's "sense of the root and branch," however, everywhere informs his opposition to the operations of international finance capital. The ideal currency would be "no more durable than potatoes, crops, or fabrics" (*SP* 336); the closest approximation to it, Silvio Gesell's "scrip money" or "perishable currency," bears at least an attenuated relation to the rhythms of natural increase and decline. All this assumes, however, that the politician rather than the poet enjoys pride of place in the juxtaposition, that Pound was in fact engaged in a politicization of art. Quite the opposite may be the case. In the name of art the poet forgoes the realm of artistic autonomy, but only to reconstruct the "gross material" aspects of the age in the interests and image of art. Aestheticism is rendered militant, introduced into the life of historical action itself.

Walter Benjamin argues that a militant aestheticism is characteristic of fascism in general: "The masses have a right to change property relations; Fascism seeks to give them an expression while preserving property. The logical result of fascism is the introduction of aesthetics into political life" (241). Pound's celebration of Mussolini as "artifex" is an exemplary case in point: "We know what the artist does, we are, or at any rate the author is, fairly familiar with a good deal of plastic and verbal manifestation. Transpose such sense of plasticity or transpose your criteria to ten years of fascismo in Italy. And to the artifex" (*J/M* 92). Italian fascism did little to transform the class structure; it was, after all, the old elites who summoned Mussolini to power. It did, however, allow for the direct representation of specific economic interests. In 1928, the National Council of Corporations, which in theory regulated the Italian economy, changed its system of representation from the political to the occupational, which Pound held to be more representative than the old model Parliaments. And as with fascist assemblies, so too with fascist discourse: "AN AWAKENED INTELLIGENCE" animates the nation, Pound rejoices in *Jefferson and/or Mussolini*, "and a new LANGUAGE" informs "the debates in the Chambers" (73). Even Pound's economics never progressed beyond a concern with monetary representation and distribution. The question of production having been decreed solved by Mussolini, Pound gave himself over to monetarist gadgetry, the aesthetics of money, an economics of the signifier rather than the signified. The horror of Pound's political investments is frequently taken as a negative argument for the purely contemplative stance of traditional aesthetic production and consumption. But *Jefferson and/or Mussolini* suggests otherwise: The horror issues from an aestheticized politics, not a politicized aesthetic.

Pound complains in *Jefferson and/or Mussolini* that although a scholarly, ten-volume edition of Jefferson's writings was available, there was no "cheap popular edition of selected and significant passages" (12), and all his life he inveighed again "the historical blackout," the universal conspiracy to repress or destroy vital documents. It is thus ironic that his own *Jefferson and/or Mussolini* is no longer generally available or widely read. (Pound completed the text in 1933, but it was rejected by some forty publishers before it was accepted by Stanley Nott Ltd. in 1935. The book was translated into Italian in 1944; it was not published again in English until 1977.) The repression (or at least unavailability) of the text may serve Pound's reputation, but it hardly contributes to our understanding of the politics of reaction that remain, even in these Postmodern times, a persistent threat.

Bibliography

Benjamin, Walter. "The Work of Art in the Age of Mechanical Reproduction." *Illuminations*. Trans. Hannah Arendt. New York: Schocken Books, 1969.

Jameson, Fredric. *The Political Unconscious: Narrative as a Socially Symbolic Act*. Ithaca: Cornell UP, 1981.

Mehlman, Jeffrey. "Writing and Deference: The Politics of Literary Adoration." *Representations* 15 (Summer 1986): 1–14.

Morrison, Paul. *The Poetics of Fascism: Ezra Pound, T. S. Eliot, Paul de Man*. New York: Oxford UP, 1996.

Payne, Stanley G. *Fascism: Comparison and Definition*. Madison: U of Wisconsin P, 1980.

Surette, Leon. *Pound in Purgatory: From Economic Radicalism to Anti-Semitism*. Urbana: U of Illinois P, 1999.

Paul Morrison

Joyce, James (1882–1941)

In 1913, when W. B. Yeats showed him James Joyce's poems, Pound instantly saw a major writer in potential. For a decade, he helped Joyce become that writer by supporting the unpublished *Dubliners* stories and the developing novels *A Portrait of the Artist as a Young Man* and *Ulysses*, finding journal outlets for these works, helping Joyce grapple with book publishers, trying to get his play *Exiles* staged, foisting his books on friends, urging institutions and individuals to support him financially, and reviewing his works to build an audience. He also served as Joyce's occasional censor (cutting passages from *Ulysses* in the *Little Review*), medical adviser (seeking physicians for Joyce's eye problems, even offering a diagnosis), travel agent and urban guide (encouraging Joyce to move to Paris and introducing him to people there), and clothing adviser and supplier (when Eliot first visited Joyce, Pound gave him a parcel containing old shoes to deliver). Not surprisingly, Joyce called Pound a "wonder worker" (*L/JJ* 80).

Readers can follow the extraordinary saga of the relationship in the biographies of Pound and Richard Ellmann's life of Joyce and especially in *Pound/Joyce*, Forrest Read's collection of Pound's letters to Joyce and essays and articles about him. From 1913, when Yeats told Pound that he and Joyce might "have a hate or two in common" (*L/JJ* 18) and Pound wrote to Joyce, until they finally met in 1920, the connection was entirely epistolary. Robert Spoo calculated in 1995 that 95 letters from Pound to Joyce and 103 from Joyce to Pound have come to light so far. All the known Pound letters have been published in *Pound/Joyce* and Spoo's supplementary collection, but only 26 of Joyce's are in print (533). Their first face-to-face meeting in Sirmione was a muted success: Joyce worried that Pound had found him "a hopeless bourgeois" (Gorman 272), and Pound concluded that "the real man is the author of *Chamber Music*, the sensitive. The rest is the genius" (*L/JJ* 178). Pound supported Joyce because of both his writing and his difficulties with institutions, but when Pound saw changes in the writing and Joyce progressed beyond needing help, the relationship between what Spoo has described as "a pair of profoundly mismatched temperaments held together by a common drive to get *A Portrait* and *Ulysses* published" (534) declined.

For Pound, starting with Stendhal and Flaubert, "the serious art of writing 'went over to prose' " (*LE* 31), and he wrote in 1915, just as he was reading *Dubliners* and *Portrait*, that "poetry must be *as well written as prose*" (*L* 48; Pound's italics). His words for *Dubliners* and *Portrait* define well-written prose: "clear and direct" (*L/JJ* 24), "free from sloppiness" (27), "intensity, selection, and concentration" (28), "carefully avoids telling you a lot that you don't want to know" (28), "hardness and gauntness" (32), "clear, unexaggerated, realistic" (90). He arranged to have *Portrait* serialized in Harriet Shaw Weaver and Dora Marsden's *Egoist* and convinced Weaver to set up the Egoist Press to publish it as a book. Upon seeing the early chapters of *Ulysses* as Joyce finished them, he waxed ecstatic, calling the writing "Echt Joice" (128; Pound's spelling) and declaring that Leopold Bloom "answers the query that people made after *The Portrait*. Joyce has created his second character" (139). He called Bloom "*l'homme moyen sensuel*" and also "the basis for democracy; he is the man in the street, the next man,

the public" (*L/JJ* 194; *LE* 403). He arranged to have *Ulysses* serialized in the American *Little Review*, where thirteen chapters and part of the fourteenth appeared before a court declared the book obscene.

Pound consistently placed *Ulysses* in a Realist tradition, claiming that Joyce in *Ulysses* carried out "what Flaubert set out to do in *Bouvard and Pécuchet*, done it better, more succinct. An epitome" (*L/JJ* 139; *LE* 416). (Apart, though, from listing "The Wandering Jew" among Bloom's attributes, his "realism" omitted Bloom's Jewishness.) Pound trumpeted *Ulysses* as "obscure, even obscene, as life itself is obscene in places" (139; 416) but balked at Joyce's detailed accounts of urination and defecation, especially in combination with Joyce's increasingly elaborate formal and technical experiments—the end of the "Sirens" episode provoked this: "One *can* fahrt with less pomp & circumstance" (*L/JJ* 158; Pound's italics and spellings). He dismissed the use of Homer's *Odyssey* as "part of Joyce's mediaevalism and . . . chiefly his own affair, a scaffold, a means of construction, justified by the result, and justifiable by it only" (*L/JJ* 197; *LE* 406). But, these reservations notwithstanding, he supported Joyce's case when *Ulysses* was charged with obscenity for depicting masturbation, and he sought a book publisher despite the obscenity conviction. And on the back of his letter complaining about "Sirens," he wrote to Joyce, "P.S. *And* you may be right" (*L/JJ* 159; Pound's italics and underline).

Pound's increasing lack of sympathy with the second half of *Ulysses*, where the stylistic elaborations overtake the realism, disturbed Joyce, as did his eventual rejection of the entire conception and execution of *Finnegans Wake*. (He wrote Joyce, "Nothing so far as I make out, nothing short of divine vision or a new cure for the clapp can possibly be worth all the circumambient peripherization" [*L/JJ* 228; Pound's spelling].) Joyce found new supporters, and his personal suspicions about Pound mounted in the late 1920s when, despite offering to help with an international petition Joyce launched against the American Samuel Roth's piracy of *Ulysses*, he refused to sign. Joyce worked Pound into

Finnegans Wake in large and small ways (see Hayman and *L/JJ* 262–266), ranging from puns on his name, allusions to his particular interests, and references to his poetry to including him in the makeup of the figures HCE and Shaun. In the *Wake* Shaun the Post is the opposite / antagonist / rival / complement to Shem the Penman, the Joyce figure, and, in making Pound one of the components of Shaun, Joyce asserted the competitive and conflicted aspect of the relationship along with its supportive side.

Joyce repeatedly acknowledged the help Pound gave him, as in writing that, but for him, "I should probably be the unknown drudge that he discovered" (*L/JJ* 245). However, the formality of a testimonial he wrote in 1925 suggests the reserve that accompanied his appreciation: "I owe a great deal to his friendly help, encouragement and generous interest in everything that I have written. . . . He helped me in every possible way in the face of very great difficulties for seven years before I met him, and since then he has always been ready to give me advice and appreciation" (Joyce, *Letters* 3:117). Joyce separated the "wonder worker" from the poet in Pound—he hardly ever referred to Pound's poetry or even acknowledged that he was a poet (although he did parody *The Cantos* in a 1925 letter [*L/JJ* 232]). Joyce summed up his attitude toward Pound in 1927: "I never listened to his objections to *Ulysses* as it was being sent him once I had made up my mind but dodged them as tactfully as I could. He understood certain aspects of that book very quickly and that was more than enough then. He makes brilliant discoveries and howling blunders" (*L/JJ* 229).

What Pound got from Joyce is less clear than the reverse. Critics have claimed that his reading of the early chapters of *Ulysses* during his first years of work on *The Cantos* changed the shape of the poem because he reworked it to open the first canto with Odysseus (see, for example, *L/JJ* 11). Ronald Bush, however, argues that Pound revised the poem before he knew how the structure of *Ulysses* would incorporate an Odysseus figure and that Joyce influenced him

mainly by providing a model of realism and compression (193–197).

In the 1920s and 1930s Pound called "Work in Progress" (as *Finnegans Wake* was called until it was published) a work "in regress" (*L* 292), disdained what he called its "diarrhoea of consciousness" technique (*L/JJ* 257), and dismissed its lack of interest in "the present": "I can not see in it either a comprehension of, or a very great preoccupation with, the present, which may indicate an obtuseness on my part, or may indicate that Mr Joyce's present and my present are very different one from the other, and, further, that I can not believe in a passive acceptance" (251). But his descriptions of *Ulysses* in 1933 as "a summary of pre-war Europe, the blackness and mess and muddle of a 'civilization' led by disguised forces and a bought press, the general sloppiness, the plight of the individual intelligence in that mess! Bloom very much *is* the mess" (251; Pound's italics) and in 1941 as "the END, it was the completion (literarily speakin) of an era. It cooked up and served the unmitigated god damn stink of the decaying usury era" (267; Pound's spellings), especially in light of his earlier blindness toward Bloom's Jewishness, show the dark side of Pound's "present" as they barely hide his anti-Semitic analysis. He acknowledged Bloom's Jewishness only after Joyce's death, when he described *Ulysses* as "whole, entire, gentile and jew'first great book in contemporary english, insistin on Mr Blum (jew) as existin" (267; Pound's spellings). He called Joyce a "small bourgeois, to the UTMOST" (268; Pound's capitals) who "knows very little of life as it has been in the large since he finished 'Ulysses'" (256), but Joyce appears several times in the much more elegiac mood of *The Pisan Cantos* (Cantos 74 and 76).

Joyce was happy to exploit Pound's "brilliant discoveries" when they centered on him and to move on when Pound made "howling blunders." For Pound, as he wrote in one of his last statements on *Ulysses*, the book he in many important ways made possible, "it painted a dying world, whereof some parts are eternal" (*L/JJ* 268).

Bibliography

Bush, Ronald. *The Genesis of Ezra Pound's Cantos.* Princeton: Princeton UP, 1976.

Ellmann, Richard. *James Joyce.* 1959. New York: Oxford UP, 1982.

Gorman, Herbert. *James Joyce.* New York: Rinehart, 1948.

Hayman, David. "Pound at the Wake, or the Uses of a Contemporary." *James Joyce Quarterly* 2 (1965): 204–216.

Joyce, James. *Letters.* 3 vols. Vol. 1. Ed. Stuart Gilbert. New York: Viking, 1957, 1966. Vols. 2–3. Ed. Richard Ellmann. New York: Viking, 1966.

Kenner, Hugh. *The Pound Era.* Berkeley: U of California P, 1971.

Kugel, Adelaide. " 'Wroth Wrackt Joyce': Samuel Roth and the 'Not Quite Unauthorized' Edition of *Ulysses.*" *Joyce Studies Annual* 3 (1992): 242–248.

Litz, A. Walton. "Pound and Eliot on *Ulysses*: The Critical Tradition." *James Joyce Quarterly* 10 (1972): 5–18.

Materer, Timothy. *Vortex: Pound, Eliot, and Lewis.* Ithaca: Cornell UP, 1979.

Pound, Ezra. "James Joyce and Pecuchet." 1922. Trans. Fred Bornhauser. *Shenandoah* 3 (1952): 9–20.

Schneidau, Herbert N. *Ezra Pound: The Image and the Real.* Baton Rouge: Louisiana State UP, 1969.

Sherry, Vincent. *Ezra Pound, Wyndham Lewis, and Radical Modernism.* New York: Oxford UP, 1993.

Spoo, Robert. "Unpublished Letters of Ezra Pound to James, Nora, and Stanislaus Joyce." *James Joyce Quarterly* 32 (1995): 533–581.

Vanderham, Paul. "Ezra Pound's Censorship of *Ulysses.*" *James Joyce Quarterly* 32 (1995): 583–595.

Michael Groden

K

Kenner, Hugh (1923–2003)

Author of *The Pound Era* (1971), scholar and critic, prolific writer, and the foremost interpreter of Modernist literature in English, Hugh Kenner was born 7 January 1923 in Peterborough, Ontario, Canada. Educated at the University of Toronto (M.A., 1946) and Yale University (Ph.D., 1950), he had a distinguished career as a professor of English at the University of California, Santa Barbara (1950–1973), Johns Hopkins University (1973–1989), and the University of Georgia (1989–2003).

Imbued with the poetry and criticism of T. S. Eliot, and intent on examining the works of James Joyce in the course of graduate study, Kenner made a memorable visit to Ezra Pound at St. Elizabeths—in the company of Marshall McLuhan, an early mentor—in spring 1948. That first of many visits sparked Kenner's lifelong engagement with Pound's oeuvre. In a tour de force of retrospective air-clearing, in part a response to the controversy over the award to Pound of the Bollingen Prize in Poetry, Kenner wrote the first book about Pound, a keynote in the critical literature, *The Poetry of Ezra Pound*, which was copublished by New Directions (James Laughlin) and Faber and Faber (T. S. Eliot) in 1951. As Laughlin later described it, the book "was the beginning, and the catalyst, for a change in attitude toward Pound on the American literary and educational scenes."

Over the course of fifty years Kenner published scores of essays and reviews that guided and continue to guide readers to an understanding of Pound's work and his place in the Modern movement: "New Subtlety of Eyes," "In the Caged Panther's Eyes" (1949); "Prophets of Renaissance" (1950); "Praestantibusque ingeniis" (1951); "Gold in the Gloom," "Pound on Joyce," "Ezra Pound and the Light of France" (1952); the introduction to *The Translations of Ezra Pound*, "Ezra Pound and the Provision of Measures," "The Broken Mirrors and the Mirror of Memory" (1953); "Homage to Musonius" (1957); "Leucothea's Bikini: Mimetic Homage," "Ezra Pound and Money," "Ezra Pound and Chinese" (1965); "The Invention of China," "The Persistent East" (1967); "The Rope in the Knot," "Ghosts and Benedictions," "Homer's Sticks and Stones," "The Muse in Tatters" (1968); "Blood for the Ghosts," "Motz el Son" (1969); "Horizontal Chords," "Mao or Presumption," "Douglas" (1970); "The Magic of Place" (1973); "The Possum in the Cave" (1981); "Poets at the Blackboard" (1983); "The Making of the Modernist Canon" (1984); "Ezra Pound's *Commedia*," "Pound and Homer" (1985); "Modernism and What Happened to It" (1987); "Ezra Pound and Modernism" (1988); "Pound and Eliot in Academe" (1993); "Pound and the American Dante" (1998).

Alert readers in the late 1960s became aware—through early versions of a dozen or more portions published in the little magazines and quarterlies—of the great work of literary scholarship then taking shape, a study by Kenner of the Anglo-American literature of 1910–1960 and of Pound's centrality to that literature. When *The Pound Era* was published in March 1971 it was recognized as a master work of historical synthesis and literary analysis, "an X-ray moving picture of the age of Pound, Eliot, Joyce, Lewis." The book received the Christian Gauss Award of Phi Beta Kappa, one outward sign of the high esteem in which Kenner's work is held.

As a textual/editorial adviser, primarily to James Laughlin at New Directions, Kenner exercised considerable influence on the texts of Pound's works, especially *The Cantos*. (See his "Notes on Amateur Emendations," in *A Poem Containing History* [1997].) Kenner served as senior editor to *Paideuma* from its inception in 1972. As a teacher, Kenner was responsible for the nurture and cultivation of several generations of students, many of whom are now among the most productive Pound scholars.

In 1992 Marjorie Perloff wrote of Kenner that Modernism is "to a large degree his own construction"; a similar, if more eloquent summation is that of Richard Stern: "Early on, Hugh [Kenner] learned the geography of this century and drew its first rough maps. Since, he has kept exploring, drawing ever finer, larger, more beautiful maps. It will be very difficult to travel twentieth century intelligence without them. . . .

More recently it became clear that the mapmaker himself was part of the map."

The Hugh Kenner Archive, including over 125 letters from Ezra Pound, is located at the Harry Ransom Humanities Research Center, University of Texas at Austin.

Bibliography

Davenport, Guy. "Hugh Kenner: The Kenner Era." *National Review* 37.25 (1985): 89–90.

———. "The Pound Vortex." Rev. of *The Pound Era*. *The Geography of the Imagination*. San Francisco: North Point P, 1981. 165–168.

Goodwin, Willard. *Hugh Kenner: A Bibliography*. Albany: Whitston Publishing, 2001.

"Hugh Kenner." *Contemporary Authors*, New Revision Series 28 (1990): 270–272.

Kenner, Hugh. "Notes on Amateur Emendations." *A Poem Containing History: Textual Studies in The Cantos*. Ed. Lawrence S. Rainey. Ann Arbor: U of Michigan P, 1997. 21–29.

———. *The Poetry of Ezra Pound*. 1951. Lincoln: U of Nebraska P, 1985.

———. "Portrait of a Mentor." *The Elsewhere Community*. Concord: House of Anansi P, 1998. 20–47.

———. *The Pound Era*. Berkeley: U of California P, 1971.

Willard Goodwin

L

Latin Literature

While it seems natural to point to Propertius and Ovid as Pound's greatest Latin influences due to his translation of the former and praise of the latter (especially of Golding's translation), Pound's true debt to Latin literature is less obvious and far more subtle. Indeed, it lies at the very root of Pound's poetics.

As much as Pound professed dislike of Virgil, he learned from him, as he learned from Catullus and Propertius and Ovid, a poetics that revolutionized the poetry of his time and all that came after it. Like Pound, and like the Greek poets (Callimachus, Theocritus, Aratus) they emulated, these Latin poets were almost all expatriates writing in a time when they felt alienated from the community of letters—indeed, when there was no cohesive community in place. It was a time when literature had become stale and imitative. In Rome, Catullus was the first to respond with a new poetics based on the poetic program of a reactionary literary movement of third century B.C.E. Alexandria. For this, he was known as one of the Neoterics ("New Poets") and a proponent of Alexandrian poetics. Propertius, Ovid, and Virgil were to follow his lead.

Although this author's doctoral dissertation (see George) is the first extended study of the topic, the debt in poetics of Pound and T. S. Eliot to the Roman and Greek Alexandrian poets has been noted for years. As early as 1927, E. R. Curtius took Eliot's Alexandrianism for granted; in a strange reversal, Virgil and Propertius have been called "Modernists" by some Classicists. But what precisely is the Alexandrian poetic movement?

Alexandrian poetry displays a poetics of extreme difficulty and complexity, of compression and condensation. It is clean and precise in its use of language, and yet it is highly allusive, obscure, erudite, and scholarly (even bookish). It is self-conscious and aware of its status as art and concerned with literary tradition to the point of near obsession. It is a style that deliberately blurs generic, linguistic, spatial, and temporal borders. It is laboriously worked and finely drawn—hardly the swift-flowing product of romantic inspiration. It is more private than public, very musical, and keenly interested in mythology, psychology, and the pathology of eros. It incorporates unpoetic words and phrases to expand the possibilities of poetic diction and uses foreign languages and metrical innovations. Drawing upon a wide, often idiosyncratic knowledge base, the poet incorporates into the work allusions to, quotations from, and even citations to other texts. The resulting poetry possesses an unprecedented level of intertextuality and a level of obscurity ranging from the arcane to the impenetrable.

Pound was aware of the Roman Alexandrian movement, although he would not have known it by that (relatively recent) name. He read carefully both the Greek and Latin Alexandrians in the original languages. In fact, in his own literary criticism, Pound uses two of the key rallying terms of the movement: *venustas* (charm) and *lepidus* (elegance).

Like the Greek and Latin Alexandrian poets who use a collage of dialects and languages, various levels of diction, prose words, idioms and proverbs, archaisms and neologisms, literary language and rare words, Pound dispenses with linguistic barriers to indicate the continuity, the universality of the human experience. Thus *The Cantos* freely shift from English to Greek to Latin, French, Spanish, German, Chinese, and even Egyptian hieroglyphics, drawing from all manner of literature and language, from the formal diction of the presidential office to the slang of the prisoners in the Detention Training Camp at Pisa.

One of the principal innovations that Pound borrows from Ovid and Virgil is the fusion of lyric style and grand epic form to create a new style of epic poem. The result is *The Cantos*. The generic hybrid that is the Alexandrian epic freely crosses generic boundaries. For example, Ovid's *Metamorphoses* (an important model for Pound) contains elements of epic, lyric, tragedy, oratory, hymnody, love elegy, epistle, epigram, pastoral, history, and philosophy. Similarly, Pound incorporates everything from historical documents, private letters, scientific treatises, literary allusions, and popular songs in *The Cantos*. And yet, arguably, the result is a unified epic poem.

The unity of the Alexandrian epic is not linear, nor Homeric, but essentially metaphoric, or associative. It is affected by the "associative technique." Like Pound's ideogrammic method for poetry, the associative technique is a method of setting two or more things side by side in implicit comparison, of likening one thing to another. It is similar to what Pound called "subject rhyme": If two words that sound the same rhyme, then two things that *mean* the same rhyme. For example, in *The Cantos*, Eleanor of Aquitaine "rhymes" with Helen of Troy.

Associations thus created slowly accrue over the course of the long poem. The resultant unity is an aggregate perceived principally on an emotional level. It is not logical nor linear in fashion. Using this associative technique, both Pound and Ovid repeat over and over again key themes, words, phrases, and character types in different contexts to alert the reader to search for similarities between them.

Bibliography

Benediktson, D. Thomas. *Propertius: Modernist Poet of Antiquity*. Carbondale: Southern Illinois UP, 1989.

George, Anita. "The New Alexandrians: The Modernist Revival of Hellenistic Poetics in the Poetry of T. S. Eliot and Ezra Pound." Diss. U of Toronto, 1997.

Newman, J. K. *Classical Epic Tradition*. Madison: U of Wisconsin P, 1986.

Stead, C. K. *Pound, Yeats, Eliot, and the Modernist Movement*. New Brunswick: Rutgers UP, 1986.

Anita George

Latin Translation

While Pound translated the occasional poem by Horace and Catullus, he is largely known for his translation of Sextus Propertius, the Roman elegist who flourished in first century B.C.E. *Homage to Sextus Propertius* was written in 1917. Harriet Monroe published four sections of the poem in *Poetry* in 1919. It resulted in furious attacks from Latinists (most notably William Hale) who chose to overlook its title (as Pound maintained, it is an homage, not a translation in the strict sense) and accused the poet of gross ignorance of the Latin language. Despite Pound's public statement on the subject, it was and continues to be viewed as a translation of the literary—as opposed to literal—variety.

Pound's *Homage to Sextus Propertius* is perhaps the greatest contribution of the twentieth century to translation, not so much for what it brings to Propertius as for what it brings to the theory and practice of translation. Pound's innovation caused a major shift in the fundamental question: Exactly what does one translate? A poem's lexical content or its poetic content? For as any experienced translator knows, it is rarely possible to translate both. In order to answer this question, it is necessary to decide what makes a poem a poem: Is it its lexical, or information, content, or its sound, ideas, and imagery? Or as Pound would put it, *melopoeia*, *logopoeia*, and *phanopoeia*?

A poem is not just words on a page but an action, a script that lies ready for the reader to enact and bring into being. It is a series of words and sounds, images and cadences created and arranged to have a specific effect on the reader. Words are chosen not just for their denotational but also for their connotational value. Rhythms are chosen to excite the human heartbeat and thus control the reader's emotions. Before one can translate a poem, one must determine what it *does*. The challenge, then, is to write a new poem that does the same thing in the target language and culture. Usually, this is done by means of equivalences. For example, some biblical translations in Eskimo culture refer to Christ as "the Seal of God" (Eskimos being unfamiliar with lambs).

For the *Homage*, Pound shunned the Latin elegiac meter for a highly musical vers libre. While it is technically possible to write Latin elegiacs in English, Pound realized that they simply do not do the same thing in English as they do in Latin. This is because of fundamental differences in the English and Latin languages and in their respective accentual and quantitative verse systems. English verse depends on stress, while Latin depends on time, the juxtaposition of long and short syllables. Because the quantities of English vowels are so flexible and hard to determine, English is simply not the material from which one can create meters on the Latin model. At best one might manage a rough approximation. Further, the English language proliferates with consonants and monosyllabic words. This results in a scarcity of natural dactyls and a heavily spondaic, thudding line that does not come close to the rapid lilt of the Latin.

If a translated poem is not of equal caliber in its own language and culture to the original, then it constitutes no translation at all. A Fitzgerald for a Virgil is not an even trade. Hence, poets must translate poetry. Pound's success in the *Homage* has resulted in bringing a dead poet to life—making Propertius new—for an audience who never would have heard of Propertius otherwise and certainly would be ignorant of his importance in literary tradition. Such a first-rate translation can also renew interest in the discipline of Classics, just as a bad one can kill it.

While many Classicists over the years have complained of Pound's Propertius, the fact is that Pound knew his Latin very well indeed. As J. P. Sullivan's definitive study illustrates, those supposed "howlers" are not mistakes at all but rather deliberate mistranslations. For example, in an attempt to duplicate the sound of the Latin (*melopoeia*), Pound often uses English homophones for Latin words, even if they happen to mean something different: hence "mines" for the Latin *minas* ("threats"). Further, he indulges in bilingual puns (a frequent device, incidentally, of the Latin poets themselves) and allows words to play upon his poetic sensibility, creating new associations for a more vivid image. While they may not literally be in Propertius's poem in the same place and manner in which Pound sets them, these devices are not alien to Propertius's own method and ultimately serve his poetic purpose.

Pound's enormous sensitivity to the nuances of the poet's voice results in the first translation that captures Propertius's irony and his arch wit. Pound's use of everyday speech peppered with archaisms, which give the work an appropriately foreign feel for the modern reader, replicates Propertius's own daring mix of colloquialisms and traditional poetic language. This is Propertius as he might have sounded had he lived and breathed in our time.

The concept of literary translation—the imitation, the paraphrase—has been around for a long time. Pound's work pushes that concept to its limit. One might argue that Pound's translations represent a third mode of translation: They are not literal, or literary in the usual sense, but *littoral* (from the Latin word for "shore"); they accurately neither convey the lexical content of the original nor offer a strict literary equivalent for it (e.g., English elegiacs for Latin elegiacs) but, like a wave on the beach, skim the edges of the metaphorical shore of original meaning.

Bibliography

Lefevere, André. *Translating Literature: Practice and Theory in a Comparative Literature Context*. New York: MLA, 1992.

Pound, Ezra. *Ezra Pound: Translations*. Introduction by Hugh Kenner. New York: New Directions, 1963.

———. *Homage to Sextus Propertius. Dyptich.*
Rome–London. Introduction by A. Walton Litz.
New York: New Directions, 1994.
Sullivan, J. P. *Ezra Pound and Sextus Propertius: A*
Study in Creative Translation. Austin: U of Texas P,
1964.

Anita George

Laughlin, James (1914–1997)

James Laughlin was a publisher and writer.
As head of New Directions Press, Laughlin was
Ezra Pound's primary American publisher for
more than sixty years. But "Jas," as Pound called
him, was also one of Pound's closest friends
through much of the poet's life. Pound and
Laughlin's relationship was complicated, with
each man taking the respective role of mentor
and student, author and publisher, surrogate father and adoptive son, patient and caretaker, as
well as long-term friend; in addition, each party
personally benefitted from the friendship, for
the collaboration of New Directions Press and
Pound brought the fledgling publishing firm to
prominence (and solvency) and helped Pound's
poetry become central to American literary
history.

Laughlin, who came from Pittsburgh's Jones
& Laughlin steel fortune, attended Choate,
where he studied with the poet and translator
Dudley Fitts, who provided him with introductions to Pound and Gertrude Stein, among others. Laughlin met Pound in Rapallo in 1933
while on a European summer sojourn from Harvard. Returning the following year, Laughlin attended Pound's "Ezuversity," learning about
Social Credit and literary history and seeking
Pound's blessing on his own poetry. Pound,
though, felt that Laughlin's verse was substan-
dard and encouraged the young man instead to
put his energy and family money into publishing. In 1936, Laughlin founded New Directions
Press (named after his literary column in
Gorham Munson's *New Democracy* magazine)
and began publishing the *New Directions in*
Prose and Poetry annual anthologies. Throughout the rest of the 1930s, Laughlin worked for
Pound, placing the poet's works in journals,
writing articles on Pound, and finally obtaining,

from Farrar & Rinehart, the rights to publish
The Cantos and Pound's other new books.

With the 1940 publication of *Cantos LII–*
LXXI, Laughlin's approach to publishing came
into conflict with Pound's own political desires.
Knowing that American readers had little interest in Pound's historical references and even less
patience for his controversial views, Laughlin
refused to publish anti-Semitic content and demanded the inclusion of an explanatory preface
in the volume. Pound resisted these conditions.
The poet and publisher reached a compromise
on these issues, but Pound's subsequent treason
indictment, capture, and insanity plea seemed to
spell the end of the efforts of New Directions (or
"Nude Erections," as Pound often called the
company) to establish Pound as America's leading poet.

In response, Laughlin embarked upon a concerted campaign to initiate what he called a
"counter-swing" in public opinion of Pound's
poetry. Abandoning his earlier strategy of explaining Pound's beliefs in the most favorable
and moderate terms, Laughlin decided to utterly
ignore the content of Pound's works in his pub-
licity and marketing efforts and instead emphasized the aesthetic and formal qualities of
his poetry. The 1949 Bollingen controversy, in
which numerous intellectuals on both the Left
and the Right argued that political considerations should play no role in aesthetic valuation,
bolstered Laughlin's campaign. Through the
1950s, Laughlin republished Pound's older
nonpolitical works, always seeking to construct
an apolitical Pound, and also helped to nurture
the nascent school of formalist Pound criticism
whose most important figure was Hugh Kenner.

After Pound returned to Italy in 1958, his correspondence with Laughlin diminished, but the
publisher continued to improve Pound's status
in American literary history. In the late 1950s
and 1960s, for instance, Laughlin began aggressively to bring out Pound's works in the student-
friendly trade paperback format, aiming to reach
the audience that would one day become professors and critics.

Pound was by no means Laughlin's only important author at New Directions. Laughlin's

relationship with William Carlos Williams was equally long—and equally contentious—but Laughlin also worked closely with Henry Miller, Delmore Schwartz, Thomas Merton, Mary Karr, and dozens of other literary figures. In the 1950s, Laughlin took a sabbatical from New Directions, leaving Robert MacGregor in charge, to found and direct "Intercultural Publications," a Ford Foundation–funded enterprise similar to the Congress for Cultural Freedom. Intercultural Publications required Laughlin to spend extended periods of time in Burma and India, where Laughlin could both work and indulge his lifelong passion for skiing. (He also owned the Alta ski lodge in Utah for many years.) After Pound's death, Laughlin acted as the executor for Pound's literary trust and managed the often complicated financial arrangements intended to divide Pound's royalties between Dorothy, Olga Rudge, and Mary de Rachewiltz.

Although he was very successful in crafting a nonpolitical image of Pound, Laughlin himself never saw Pound's work as merely an aesthetic artifact. Notwithstanding his own conflicted attitude toward his strategy, though, Laughlin's activities were significantly responsible for Pound's attainment of a place in the American literary canon, for his apolitical, aesthetic formalist packaging of Pound's poetry gave professors, literary critics, and even popular journalists a successful argument for Pound's greatness in the conservative 1950s. After Pound's death, Laughlin grew more willing to publish Pound's political and economic writings, and in later life Laughlin wrote extensively about his personal relationship with the poet—not skipping over the controversies. Moreover, even though Pound had discouraged him back in 1933 and 1934, Laughlin continued to write his Williams- and Rexroth-influenced poetry throughout his life and made Pound the subject of some of his verse. In the end, their relationship was deeply symbiotic on many levels, satisfying to both men and suggestive to us of the profound influence a publisher can have on every aspect of a poet's life, work, and reputation.

The New Directions archive and James Laughlin's personal archive, with extensive holdings of Pound's manuscripts and letters to Laughlin from Pound, Pound's parents, Dorothy Pound, Olga Rudge, Omar Pound, Mary de Rachewiltz, is housed at the Houghton Library, Harvard University. The Houghton's collection contains copies of many of Laughlin's letters to Pound; however, the bulk of those letters are housed in the Ezra Pound collection at the Beinecke Library, Yale University.

Bibliography

Barnhisel, Greg. *James Laughlin, New Directions Press, and the Re-Making of Ezra Pound.* Amherst: U of Massachusetts P, 2004.
Laughlin, James. *The Collected Poems of James Laughlin.* Ed. Hayden Carruth. Wakefield: Moyer Bell, 1994.
———. *The Master of Those Who Know: Ezra Pound.* San Francisco: City Lights, 1986.
———. *Pound as Wuz: Essays and Lectures on Ezra Pound.* Saint Paul: Greywolf P, 1987.
Pound, Ezra. *Ezra Pound and James Laughlin: Selected Letters.* Ed. David M. Gordon. New York: Norton, 1994.

Greg Barnhisel

Law and Social Justice

Law is a significant preoccupation in Pound's writing—as attested, for example, by his recognition of the centrality of law to social "order" (Cantos 56 and 99); by his regular incorporation of references to the making and administration of laws, whether he is considering China, the Roman Empire, or medieval England; by his admiration for codifiers or compilers such as Justinian and jurists such as Coke ("the clearest mind ever in England" [Canto 107]); and by his fondness for legal terminology ("misprision," "replevin," "tenants in capite").

While not systematically developing a *legal* theory, Pound evinces a "natural law" outlook. Indeed, he apparently discerns continuities or correspondences between divine law and human law (64, 94), and even between physical laws and social norms, so that "From ploughing of fields is justice" (Canto 100; cf. Cantos 74 and 99). For him, "justice"—a recurrent theme—must lie behind law or inhere in it: "*ubi justitia non est, nec jus potest esse*" (Canto 67). He dismisses legal positivism, represented by John Austin, which emphasizes the separation of law and morals (Canto 100), and insists that the mere forms of law, divorced from morals or conduct, are vacuous or worse (Cantos 56, 61, and 97). He regularly distinguishes good law (say, "the law of the just middle" [Canto 53]) from bad law ("the worst sort of tyranny" [Canto 62]) on the basis of substantive criteria.

While prepared to extol the positive lawgiver—be it the legislature or the individual ruler or judge—whose laws are just, Pound, consistently with his naturalist inclinations, tends to see law as already given (it is "written not outside [the] natural colour" of "[h]eaven, man, earth" [Canto 99]), or as arising organically from the interactions of people within a culture. Hence, his apparent celebration of "folcright" (Canto 67)—or customary law, "consuetudines" (Canto 105)—and his interest in the preeminence, in the English tradition, of "common law," which, following Coke, he characterizes as the subject's "birthright" (Cantos 64 and 66). This latter focus on the cultural genesis of law tends to qualify the universalism of natural law: Good customs vary, may be "local" or "diverse" (Canto 105), although they must embody the same deeper principles and are therefore not radically divergent.

As for the purpose of law, Pound asserts, in *The Cantos* (Cantos 89 and 96) and elsewhere, that it is to prevent coercion—either of persons by the state or of persons by other persons. This is consistent with his general concern with the maintenance of boundaries within which the individual personality can develop freely. Pound's frequent invocation of Magna Carta ("the root is that charter" [Canto 107]) and his admiration of Coke for his defense of traditional liberties, against the incursion of the royal prerogative under the Stuarts, manifest this concern to limit the exercise of arbitrary power.

It is reflected, too, in some of his preoccupations at the level of legal procedure. Thus, he insists on the rule of laws, not men (Cantos 66 and 67); law should not be "bent to wanton

imagination and temper of individuals" (Canto 63). An aspect of this is the need for fixed and precise terminology in law (Cantos 63, 98, and 109), as elsewhere, which Pound sees as an antidote to arbitrariness and tyranny. Vague laws (Canto 85), laws inviting "construction," are dangerous to liberty (Canto 64)—and to the certainty that is, in Coke's phrase, "the mother and nurse of repose" (Canto 107). Another procedural protective of liberty upon which Pound insists is trial by jury (Canto 66).

Pound is, however, not entirely consistent in characterizing law as having these prophylactic functions (preventing coercion, drawing boundaries around the person). He does at times attribute to law a more positive or morally prescriptive role—for example, when he writes that "Laws must be for the general good, / for the people's uprightness, / their moral uprightness" (Canto 99). Moreover, he occasionally seems prepared, particularly in the Chinese context (Gordon, "Azalea" 297–298), to entrust adjudication ("deeming justice" [Canto 53]) to a good person like Chao Kong, who has cultivated "internal order" and who thus has a reliable sense of equity (Canto 53).

Another dimension of Pound's interest in "law issues" is captured in the expression "distributive justice"—the "heart of the matter" according to Terrell (564)—which he credits both Dante and Shakespeare with "mentioning" (Canto 93) and faults their expositors for ignoring. For Pound, this apparently means, on the one hand, easing social burdens—typically in the form of taxes—on the populace (Canto 54). So he espouses a sane and decent system of taxes—or, more properly, *tithes*, proportionate or "according to harvest and soil" (Canto 55). These are to be administered by tribunals (Canto 55), but not too many (Canto 56). On the other hand, distributive justice is to be achieved by the equitable allocation of social wealth, for example, via the mechanism of the "just price" ("prezzo giusto / In this sphere is Giustizia" [Canto 113]). Thus, "social justice" might be accomplished through a combination of legal protections of the sphere of autonomy and legal mechanisms permitting more accurately measured accessing of wealth generated by the social interactions identified in the notions of "cultural heritage" and "increment of association."

So described, Pound's attitude toward law appears as a version of liberalism, not easily reconciled with his fascist sympathies. Perhaps one clue to the paradox is his allusion to Justinian's codes as "inefficient," "a haystack of laws on paper" (Canto 87). What might have appeared more *efficient* to Pound was a Mussolini, encouraging informal settlement out of court, under threat of state intervention (Canto 87)—arguably the antithesis of the rule of law for which Pound contends elsewhere.

Bibliography

Furia, Philip. *Pound's Cantos Declassified.* University Park: Pennsylvania State UP, 1984.

Gordon, David. "The Azalea Is Grown." *Paideuma* 4.2–3 (1975): 223–299.

———. "*Corpus Juris* and Canto XCIV." *Paideuma* 11.2 (1982): 313–324.

Terrell, Carroll F. *A Companion to the Cantos of Ezra Pound.* 2 vols. Berkeley: U of California P, 1980, 1984.

Dennis Klinck

Lawrence, David Herbert (1885–1930)

An English novelist, short-story writer, poet, and critic, Lawrence was introduced to Ezra Pound in autumn 1909 at South Lodge, home of Violet Hunt. Although Lawrence was treated with snobbish disdain during his early years in London literary circles, he and Pound quickly became friends. Pound introduced Lawrence to other writers and critics during the period 1909–1914 and wrote two sensitive reviews of the Englishman's verse for *Poetry* and the *New Freewoman* in July and September 1913, respectively. Although Pound wrote that "there is no English poet under forty who can get within shot of him. . . . Mr. Lawrence has attempted realism and attained it" (*LE* 387–388), he deprecated what he viewed as Lawrence's tendentious, provincial subject matter and his interest in romantic love and sex. Pound was to commission stories and poems from Lawrence for the *English Review* and the American magazine *Smart Set* during 1913–1914 and was generous to the novelist when he faced financial problems. Pound was also quick to defend Lawrence over the scandal surrounding the pulping of his novel *The Rainbow* in 1916. By the time of Lawrence's departure for Cornwall in 1916, and then Italy in 1919, the friendship had withered; by the time of Lawrence's death from tuberculosis in the south of France in 1930, the two men were no longer in touch.

Jonathan Blackwood

Lewis, Wyndham (1882–1957)

Ezra Pound met Wyndham Lewis in 1909 during what he called the "British Museum era," a golden though rather stuffy age when scholars, artists, and museum officials would meet on the red plush chairs of the Vienna Café in New Oxford Street. Lewis trained at the Slade School of Art in London (1898–1901) and had been painting in Munich and Paris (1902–1909). Like Pound, he was publishing in Ford Madox Ford's *English Review*. Some of his early stories were revised and published in his brilliantly comic volume *The Wild Body* (1927). Lewis was writing a semiautobiographical novel finally published as *Tarr* (1918). In the wake of Imagism, Pound joined Lewis's Vorticism movement and contributed to the two issues of Lewis's journal *BLAST* (1914–1915). Lewis's battlefield service as a gunnery officer was memorialized by Pound in one of the "Hell" Cantos (Canto 16). While Lewis was in France, Pound arranged for *Tarr* to be serialized in the *Egoist* and then published. He also sold many of Lewis's art works to John Quinn and arranged through Quinn for a Vorticist show in New York. Lewis described Pound in *BLAST* (1914) as a "Demon pantechnicon driver, busy with removal of old world into new quarters." Pound's description of Lewis in a 1914 *Egoist* was prophetic and applied as well to Pound himself: "[Y]ou can not be as intelligent, in that sort of way, without being prey to the furies."

When Lewis returned from war, his feelings about Vorticism and avant-garde art had changed. As he wrote in *Rude Assignment: A Narrative of My Career Up-to-Date* (1950), when he saw the shell craters of the battlefield he recoiled from a landscape "so consonant with the austerity of that 'abstract' vision. . . . And before I knew quite what I was doing I was drawing with loving care a signaller corporal to plant upon the lip of the shell-crater." Pound like Lewis felt that all "*surplus* vigor was being bled away and stamped out" in England by the war. Pound left for Paris and hoped Lewis would join him there. During the years 1921–1926, however, Lewis used a small inheritance to concentrate on writing the books that became the social and literary criticism of *The Art of Being Ruled* (1926) and *Time and Western Man* (1927), as well as his gargantuan satire on literary and artistic bohemianism, *The Apes of God* (1930). (His criticism of Pound as a "revolutionary simpleton" in *Time and Western Man* only slightly strained their friendship.) Lewis extended his polemics in his virtually one-man journals *Tyro* (1921–1922) and the *Enemy* (1927, 1929).

When Pound moved to Italy, Lewis considered him "buried alive in a Fascist state." But Lewis was also drawn into the political passions of the time in a series of books such as *Hitler* (1931), *Left Wings over Europe* (1936), and *Count Your Dead: They Are Alive!* (1937). *Men without Art* (1934), with its famous critiques of Eliot ("the pseudoist") and Hemingway ("the dumb ox"), is his wittiest and most perceptive volume of literary criticism. In 1937 Lewis published the most brilliantly written and surely the most comic of all World War I autobiographies, *Blasting and Bombardiering*, where he uses the phrase "The Men of 1914" to describe the writers of his war-torn generation. Lewis's reputation never quite recovered from *Hitler* (1931), which rashly speculated that Hitler was a "Man of Peace" who would contain Bolshevist violence. Even his major novel *The Revenge for Love* (1937), in which the sympathetic characters are the victims of political manipulation, received little recognition. Nor did his career as a portrait painter thrive, and a series of illnesses and operations between 1932 and 1937 left him deeply in debt. His portraits of T. S. Eliot and Pound in 1938 and 1939 are two of his best, but in prewar times portrait commissions were few.

He left for America to seek work as a painter and writer, but when World War II broke out, he was stranded in Canada. The privations of those years are dramatized in his autobiographical novel *Self Condemned* (1954). The tragic power of this novel comes from Lewis's insight into an intellectual (the historian René Harding) whose despair at the corruption by violence of his society finally corrupts him as well. Lewis's dramatization of the "tragic fracture" of Harding's character reflects in part Lewis's understanding of Pound's character as well as his own. In Lewis's "Doppelgänger: A Story" (1954), he draws a thinly disguised portrait of Pound.

Returning to England in 1946, Lewis became the art critic for the BBC weekly journal the *Listener*. His dystopian trilogy *The Human Age* (*Childermass*, *Malign Fiesta*, and *Monstre Gai*, 1955) was successfully produced as a BBC radio drama. In *The Red Priest* (1956) he continued his preoccupation with violently political protagonists, and his short stories in *Rotting Hill* (1951) are a satiric portrait of postwar London. A measure of official recognition came to the self-styled "Enemy" when Lewis received a Civil List pension in 1952 and in 1957 a retrospective exhibition of his art at the Tate Gallery. The ill health that troubled him all his life continued as a pituitary tumor, first diagnosed in 1945, progressively blinded him. He resigned as art critic for the *Listener* in 1951 in an essay titled "The Sea Mists of Winter," which announced his blindness in terms that were both comic and deeply moving. His lifelong obsession with the disjunction between mind and "the wild body" is epitomized in this essay. Lewis's decision not to have an operation that might save his sight but would risk his mental faculties led to Pound's final tribute in Canto 115: "Wyndham Lewis chose blindness / rather than have his mind stop." Throughout his career, Pound championed Lewis's paintings and ranked *Tarr* with James Joyce's *A Portrait of the Artist* and *The Apes of God* with *Ulysses* as Modernist masterworks. In 1956 he wrote Lewis from St. Elizabeths Hospital that Vorticism was the "dominant cell in somatic development." For Pound, Lewis was chief among "The Men of

1914" who established twentieth-century Modernism.

Bibliography

Dasenbrock, Reed Way. *The Literary Vorticism of Ezra Pound and Wyndham Lewis: Towards the Condition of Painting.* Baltimore: Johns Hopkins UP, 1985.

Edwards, Paul. *Volcanic Heaven: Essays on Wyndham Lewis's Painting & Writing.* Santa Rosa: Black Sparrow P, 1996.

Materer, Timothy. *Vortex: Pound, Eliot, and Lewis.* Ithaca: Cornell UP, 1979.

Meyers, Jeffrey. *The Enemy: A Biography of Wyndham Lewis.* London: Routledge, 1980.

Wees, William C. *Vorticism and the English Avant-Garde.* Toronto: U of Toronto P, 1972.

Timothy Materer

Literary Essays of Ezra Pound

T. S. Eliot's edition of *Literary Essays of Ezra Pound* (Faber and New Directions, 1954) remains a milestone in the institutionalization of Ezra Pound as a paradigmatically *Modernist* poet. Its publication was, in important ways, the apotheosis of the very public battle that followed Pound's 1949 receipt of the Bollingen Prize for Poetry. Amplifying the critical tendencies formalized by the young Hugh Kenner's *The Poetry of Ezra Pound* (New Directions and Faber, 1951), both in Eliot's introduction and in his overall design, *Literary Essays* distinguishes between not only man and poet but also between Pound as cultural commentator and Pound as literary critic. Pound, Eliot affirms, is a particular *kind* of critic, whose preoccupation is not with understanding but with craft. This demonstration is arguably the primary work of Eliot's edition.

More than the convenience it proposes to be, *Literary Essays* dramatically redacts Pound's work and career, either eliding or deemphasizing Pound's tireless essays at changing the world. "Pound's literary criticism is the most contemporary criticism of its kind," Eliot affirms (x), "but the limitation of [its] kind is in its concentration upon the craft of letters, and of poetry especially" (xiii). This view of Pound's work is remarkable enough, but coming from Eliot and his more than thirty years' experience

of Pound's decidedly extraaesthetic tirades, it is especially striking. No argument in Eliot's career as critic was bolder—or more immediately successful. For more than half a century, now, *Literary Essays* has been the only one of Pound's critical books to remain consistently in print; and between 1954 and 1968 it was the only serious collection still in print in either Britain or America. Eliot accomplished his redaction with unprecedented agility, with a touch so light and familiar that forty years later we still hardly notice its pressure. *Literary Essays* is very much a book of its time: a book that neither Eliot nor anyone else would have thought necessary or even valuable much before World War II and a book that today no editor, not even one of Eliot's stature and skill (were such a stature possible today), could pull off without exciting howls of critical protest. *Literary Essays* is thus more a monument to the successes of what used to be called "the New Criticism" than it is to the criticism of its nominal subject.

This is not to deny, of course, that the volume collects a number of Pound's most enduring essays. But a collocation of Eliot's sources in and of itself suggests something of his project. He drew liberally from those volumes of essays that Pound himself had edited: from *Pavannes and Divisions* (Knopf, 1918) came two essays ("A Retrospect" and "Dubliners and Mr. Joyce"); from *Instigations* (Boni & Liveright, 1920) came eight essays ("T. S. Eliot," "Joyce," "Arnaut Daniel," "Translators of Greek: Early Translators of Homer," "Remy de Gourmont," "Wyndham Lewis," "Arnold Dolmetsch," and "Vers Libre and Arnold Dolmetsch"); from *Make It New* (Faber, 1934) came "Date Line" (from the head of which Eliot quietly removed Pound's fascist date line), "Cavalcanti," and "Medievalism"; and from *Polite Essays* (Faber, 1937) came four essays ("Hell," "The Prose Tradition in Verse," "Dr. Williams' Position," and "The Teacher's Mission"). Eliot reprinted two essays from his own *Criterion*, the aforementioned "Hell" and "Mr. Housman at Little Bethel," and fully ten more from the pages of Harriet Monroe's *Poetry* ("The Constant

Preaching to the Mob," "The Tradition," "The Renaissance," "Irony, LaForgue, and Some Satire," "The Hard and the Soft in French Poetry," "Swinburne versus His Biographers," "The Prose Tradition in Verse," "The Later Yeats," the second of the two reviews of Robert Frost, and "D. H. Lawrence"). The only important essay not from these sources is "The Serious Artist," which first appeared in the *Egoist* in 1913. In other words, all but six of the twenty-nine essays included in *Literary Essays* came from sources that Eliot's audience would have been prepared to accept as important: Pound's own collections or eminently reputable journals that were already a part of Modernist legend. Even the six essays not from these sources were from the *Future*, the *Dial*, or the *Egoist*. Eliot included nothing from A. R. Orage's *New Age*, or his *New English Weekly*; neither did he see fit to represent any part of Pound's Italian journalism, his contributions to politicocultural journals like *New Masses*, or the many marginal periodicals, like Ronald Duncan's *Townsman*, to which Pound frequently contributed.

In these choices, Eliot was perfectly within his rights, and doubtless simply being true to his idea of a "literary essay." As he observed in his 1923 essay on John Donne, "[S]election and order represent a criticism, the imposition of a critical taste upon the reader." In this edition, as elsewhere, Eliot proves a powerful critic indeed. But the fact remains that Pound spent most of his career working to undermine the kind of distinction between the properly literary and the politicocultural that Eliot maintains. In this way, the publication of such "counter"—revisionist or corrective—volumes as Noel Stock's *Impact* (Henry Regnery, 1960) or William Cookson's *Selected Prose* (Faber, 1973) must inevitably fail, because such separate volumes inevitably preserve the distinction.

Toward the end of his introduction, Eliot acknowledges that he omitted several "papers which [Pound] would have liked me to include" because they are "outside the frame of a volume entitled 'Literary Essays' " (xiv). In truth, Pound seems to have worried more about Eliot's criterion for such omissions than the omissions

themselves. So it was that he complained to Huntington Cairns (a trustee of the Bollingen Foundation, influential in making possible Pound's 1949 Bollingen Prize) that "Mr ElYuTT HAS stuck the narsty title of 'LITerary essays' on his whatever yu call it/Ezpurgation of Ez. or Possumation or wotNOT" (Carpenter 816). Eliot may have provided his best possible defense when he wrote, again toward the end of his introduction to the volume: "[Y]ou can't ask everything of anybody; and it is an illusion fostered by academic authorities on literature, that there is only one kind of criticism" (xiv). It might then be an accident of its own success that *Literary Essays* fosters such an illusion, and it may be that no single collection of Pound's prose could ever represent the several *kinds* of criticism he practiced. But until such a volume appears, Pound's readers will do well to use *Literary Essays* in conjunction with other Pound titles like *Selected Prose* and *Guide to Kulchur*.

Bibliography

Carpenter, Humphrey. *A Serious Character: The Life of Ezra Pound*. Boston: Houghton Mifflin, 1988.

Coyle, Michael. *Ezra Pound, Popular Genres, and the Discourse of Culture*. University Park: Pennsylvania UP, 1995.

Eliot, T. S. "John Donne." *Nation & Athenaeum* 10 (9 June 1923): 331–332.

Michael Coyle

Little Review

Founded in Chicago in 1914, the *Little Review* was the creation of Margaret Anderson, a woman whose experience in publishing came from working on the *Dial* and the *Continent*. At a time during which Anderson was questioning openly the quality of material she was receiving for her magazine, Ezra Pound wrote to her in June 1916 to ask her to print two French pieces from the Belgian poet Jean de Bosschère. Pound had already agreed to help her, and he published letters in the *Little Review* and used the opportunity to rail against American tariffs on books and related matters. But when Anderson in frustration printed her September 1916 number with blank pages, Pound saw an opportunity to seek even greater involvement. With the financial backing of John Quinn, Pound suggested that instead of launching his own magazine, he and Anderson might somehow collaborate on the *Little Review*. Looking for a venue in which he might arrange for his regular appearance and for the regular appearance of his friends, Pound officially took up his position as foreign editor in 1917. Over the next two years, the magazine was an important outlet for the work of T. S. Eliot, James Joyce, and Wyndham Lewis. Beginning in March 1918, the magazine began serializing Joyce's *Ulysses*, and through the subsequent legal challenges to the work in the United States, Anderson and her associate editor Jane Heap proved themselves loyal supporters of the Irish novelist. For a time, Pound's involvement with *Poetry* kept his creative material out of the *Little Review*, but Harriet Monroe's timidity in printing the poet's "frank" verse occasioned more and more work to appear under Anderson's auspices. Pound resigned his post with the magazine in 1919 as its money grew tight. But in 1921, as he was squabbling with Scofield Thayer over his role with the *Dial*, he agreed to resume his work with the *Little Review* as a European collaborator. Pound had some input in the magazine's relaunch as a quarterly, but his agreement with Anderson was again unsatisfactory to both parties, and it lapsed in 1924.

Bibliography

Pound, Ezra. *Pound/The Little Review: The Letters of Ezra Pound to Margaret Anderson*. Ed. T. L. Scott and M. J. Friedman, with J. Bryher. New York: New Directions, 1988.

Craig Monk

Love Poems of Ancient Egypt (See **Egyptian Literature**)

Lowell, Amy (1874–1925)

An American poet and critic, Amy Lowell was born of a prominent Boston family and worked tirelessly to advance the cause of the early-twentieth-century renaissance in American poetry. Within Ezra Pound studies, she is best known for her famous "schism" with Pound about the poetic movement of Imagism.

When she discovered Imagism in 1913, Lowell had published just one volume of poetry, the Keatsian *A Dome of Many-Colored Glass*. Though her well-connected background had allowed her access to many Boston luminaries, at that point she still felt isolated as an aspiring poet. In the March 1913 issue of *Poetry* magazine, Lowell found verses by "H. D., *imagiste*," and, by her own account, suddenly recognized that H. D. had achieved the poetic goals for which she had been striving. Learning that the "Imagistes" were in London, Lowell sailed to meet them. A mixture of English and American poets, the group consisted of Ezra Pound, its self-appointed leader, as well as T. E. Hulme, F. S. Flint, Richard Aldington, H. D., and Ford Madox Ford. Sharing poetry and ideas with them, Lowell was inspired both by their commitment to what Pound called "clarity and intensity" (*L* 79) and their resolve to enliven English poetry with infusions from French Symbolist work as well as poetry from ancient China and Greece.

After this cordial meeting, Pound asked Lowell to contribute to his forthcoming anthology of Imagist poetry. Despite a warning from friend John Gould Fletcher that Pound might be using her merely to fill out the collection, Lowell contributed "In a Garden" in Pound's *Des Imagistes* (1914). For much of 1913–1914, she sustained friendly relations with Pound, who credited her with great intelligence and charisma.

In the spring of 1914, answering a request of hers, Pound gave Lowell permission to publish her poem "Astigmatism," which condemned his poetic principles as narrow. This exchange, ostensibly convivial, reflected growing differences between them. That summer, Lowell proposed to the Imagists that they bring out another anthology, this time under her directorship. H. D., Aldington, and Flint agreed, perhaps wanting to escape Pound's leadership, but Pound himself refused: His amicable letter to Lowell explained that as she seemed to want either to control the project or govern by committee, he preferred to dissociate himself. He requested she not use the name "Imagism," as her taking it would "deprive" him of valuable "machinery" for promoting "new talent" (*L* 78).

Tensions increased when, to advertise Lowell's anthology, Houghton Mifflin circulated notices that deemed Lowell "at the forefront" of Imagism. Angry, Pound felt that his rightful place as leader of the movement had been usurped. Although Lowell assured Pound that she had tried to prevent her publisher from such inflated claims, she reminded him that no one had a patent on a movement.

A schism resulted, during which some writers left Pound and came "with" Lowell: H. D., Aldington, Flint, Ford, Fletcher, and D. H. Lawrence. Ultimately, after much debate about the title, Lowell's anthology appeared in 1915 as *Some Imagist Poets*: The dropped "e" distinguished the new Imagism from Pound's, and "Some" conveyed that there were other Imagists not included in the project. Allegedly to avert further friction, the preface eschewed direct reference to Pound. In Lowell's view, the omitted "e" also indicated a new, distinctively American version of the movement, no longer hampered by European cobwebs—but to Pound, it suggested the degradation of principles his earlier anthology had upheld.

After the split, Pound increasingly attacked both Lowell and "Amygism"—the diluted American version of Imagism that he felt had given the movement a bad name. During this period, in addition to bringing out three annual editions of *Some Imagist Poets*, Lowell also published well-received collections such as *Sword Blades and Poppy Seed* (1914) and *Men, Women, and Ghosts* (1916), as well as critical studies such as *Six French Poets* (1916) and *New Tendencies in Modern American Poetry* (1917). Lowell also helped to launch Frost's career in the United States with her favorable review of his *North of Boston* in 1915.

Until her death in 1925, Lowell worked unstintingly for American poetry, lecturing, backing projects, hosting gatherings, writing criticism and verse. In fact, although the schism about Imagism remains central to accounts focused on Pound, it should be remembered that Lowell was in many ways deeply similar to Pound—in her energy, skill for promotion, generosity, and indomitable will to make a difference.

Bibliography

Damon, S. Foster. *Amy Lowell: A Chronicle, with Extracts from Her Correspondence.* Boston: Houghton Mifflin, 1935.
Gould, Jean. *The World of Amy Lowell and the Imagist Movement.* New York: Dodd, Mead, 1975.
Lowell, Amy, ed. *Some Imagist Poets.* Introduction by Richard Aldington. Boston: Houghton Mifflin, 1916.

Miranda B. Hickman

Loy, Mina (1882–1966)

Mina Loy was a British-born poet, painter, fashion designer, stunning beauty, and provocative conversationalist. Ezra Pound's best-known essay on Loy was a review of her work along with that of Marianne Moore (1918). He termed Loy's work "logopoeic," applauding her for the way she engages the reader through her incisive language, intelligence, and biting satire.

Loy has come to be thought of as an American poet, though her life was quite international. As a member of the expatriate community in Florence in the 1910s, she was influenced by Futurists Gertrude Stein and Carl Van Vechten, who placed her earliest poems and manifestos in American avant-garde journals. Moving to New York in 1916, she was very active in artistic circles there. She met and married the Dadaist poet and boxer Arthur Cravan in 1918, moving with him to Mexico, where he mysteriously disappeared. Afterward, she lived in Europe, mostly designing lamps, until her return to New York in 1936, where she began to live more reclusively, her life ending in obscurity in Aspen, Colorado. Her most productive poetic era was the 1910s and 1920s, including the controversial "Love Songs to Joannes" (*Others*, 1917), her collected poems in *Lunar Baedeker* (1923), and *Anglo-Mongrels and the Rose* (1923–1925).

Bibliography

Burke, Carolyn. *Becoming Modern: The Life of Mina Loy.* New York: Farrar, Straus & Giroux, 1996.
Loy, Mina. *The Lost Lunar Baedeker: Poems of Mina Loy.* Ed. Roger Conover. New York: Farrar, 1996.
Shreiber, Maeera, and Keith Tuma, eds. *Mina Loy: Woman and Poet.* Orono: NPF, 1998.

Ellen Keck Stauder

A Lume Spento

Pound's first book of poems was printed at his own expense in Venice by A. Antonini in July 1908. The edition comprised 150 copies. Pound had completed the forty-four poems in the collection before he left the United States earlier in the year. Both before and after the Venice printing, he tried—without success—to find an American publisher for the manuscript. He included selected poems from *A Lume Spento* in later volumes of his work, but the book as a whole was not reprinted until *A Lume Spento and Other Early Poems* (1965) and *Collected Early Poems* (1976).

A Lume Spento is dedicated to William Brooke Smith, a young painter and art student whom Pound met in Philadelphia in 1901–1902. An admirer of Oscar Wilde and Aubrey Beardsley, Smith introduced Pound to the work of the English Decadents before dying of consumption in 1908. Pound's title commemorates the death of his friend through an allusion to Dante's *Purgatorio*, Canto 3, line 132. There, *a lume spento* ("with tapers quenched") describes the funeral procession of Manfred, son of the Holy Roman Emperor Frederick II, whose rites were dampened because the Church suspected him of heresy. Pound implies that Smith, like Manfred, led an unorthodox life.

Such allusions are typical of the poems in *A Lume Spento*. They display Pound's learning, pay homage to his sources of inspiration, and demonstrate the relationship between his work and the poetic traditions he wishes to perpetuate. Two traditions are especially important: the medieval (the Provençal and Italian troubadours of the later Middle Ages, Dante, Villon) and the late Victorian (Browning, Swinburne, Rossetti, Morris, Dowson, Symons, Yeats). His references to earlier writers, together with the archaic diction in many of his poems, earned Pound a reputation for antiquarianism and obscurity.

To link himself still more closely with the poets of the past, Pound employed the dramatic monologue. He adopted the technique from Robert Browning, to whom Pound pays tribute in "Mesmerism." By donning a mask or *persona*, Pound appears to speak in the voices of historical or legendary figures such as Miraut de Garzelas ("La Fraisne"), Cino Polnesi ("Cino"), Bertrans de Born ("Na Audiart"), François Villon (the "Villonauds"), Tristan and Isolde ("Threnos"), and a chorus of wasted Decadents ("The Decadence"). In a letter of 21 October 1908 to William Carlos Williams, Pound explains that in such poems "I catch the character I happen to be interested in at the moment he interests me, usually a moment of song, self-analysis, or sudden understanding or revelation" (*L* 4). Thus Browning's form helped Pound to impersonate ancestral spirits at defining instants of passion, ecstasy, or contemplative lucidity. His letter to Williams contains useful comments about other poems in *A Lume Spento* as well.

Pound's early work was influenced not only by his scholarly allegiances but also by the prewar fashion for the occult and esoteric. Underlying the poetic enterprise of *A Lume Spento* and *A Quinzaine for This Yule* (both 1908) is a Neoplatonic spiritualism, according to which *personae* are not so much ventriloquial Chautauqua performances as they are mediumistic channelings of, or momentary possessions by, the spirits of the past. "Thus am I Dante for a space, and am / One François Villon, balladlord and thief," Pound says in "Histrion." "So cease we from all being for the time, / And these, the Masters of the Soul, live on" (*CEP* 71). What better muse than a master-soul, temporarily reincarnated in one's own self?

The world of *A Lume Spento* thus ranges from a mystical and ethereal realm of ghosts, refracted light, and inspiring winds to a grossly material realm of carousers, quarrelers, and lechers. Between the Oversoul and its fleshly embodiments are many gradations, from the disincarnated spirits of "Aegupton" and "Prometheus" to the boon revelers of "Ballad of the Gibbet" and "A Rouse." The poems also depict movement up and down this scale. "The Tree" and "Masks" even suggest that myths and legends of metamorphosis and disguise are parables of the soul's transitions from one state of being to another.

Pound seems fondest of *personae* who are caught uncomfortably between opposing conditions of life and death, body and soul, desire and detachment. He favors lonely, alienated souls who are more confident of their divinity and creativity than of their earthly identity. They sometimes long for the companionship of kindred spirits, but among such spirits there can be little community. When the poet looks into a mirror in "On His Own Face in a Glass," he sees not one image but a "myriad." They are by turns "ribald," "saintly," and "sorrow-swept," as Pound himself has been in the various poems that constitute *A Lume Spento*. Throughout his career, Pound remained a chameleonic poet of shifting identities and voices. In this respect, as in others, *A Lume Spento* anticipates its author's future achievement.

Bibliography

de Nagy, N. Christoph. *The Poetry of Ezra Pound: The Pre-Imagist Stage.* 1960. Bern: Francke Verlag, 1968.

Fogelman, Bruce. *Shapes of Power: The Development of Ezra Pound's Poetic Sequences.* Ann Arbor: UMI, 1988.

Grieve, Thomas F. *Ezra Pound's Early Poetry and Poetics.* Columbia: U of Missouri P, 1997.

Witemeyer, Hugh. *The Poetry of Ezra Pound: Forms and Renewal, 1908–1920.* Berkeley: U of California P, 1969.

Hugh Witemeyer

Lustra

Lustra was published in London by Elkin Mathews in 1916, though most of the poems in it were composed between 1913 and 1915. These poems show Pound as a buccaneering spirit jibing at the insular culture of the center of the British Empire, coterminous with the onset and early years of World War I. For Pound, London had lost its potency as a cultural capital and the site of a coming renaissance in the arts and letters, and *Lustra* marks the beginning of his repudiation of London and its intellectual establishment, a rejection formally analyzed in *Hugh Selwyn Mauberley*. The meaning of the title is given in the epigraph to the collection and signals the rites of expiation performed by a censor at the end of his term of office, a cleansing of the sins of the people. There is a deliberate irony in this, for some of these poems were censored

by Harriet Monroe, editor of *Poetry* (Chicago), where some of them first appeared, and Elkin Mathews, the publisher of *Lustra*, anxious not to offend the sensibilities of their readers. Indeed, of the first edition of *Lustra*, 200 copies were printed "almost unabridged," and these constitute a privately printed edition, though technically not published, and included poems that alarmed Mathews because of what he considered their indecorous content. The dedication of *Lustra* to "Vail de Lencour" conceals the name of Brigit Patmore, a close friend of Pound in his London years, and the Latin quotation from Catullus reads: "To whom should I present this little book."

The poems of *Lustra* reflect Pound's Vorticist and Imagist preoccupations and his translations from the Chinese using the notes of Ernest Fenollosa. In addition, they show Pound's continuing deployment of poetic strategies and voices or personae borrowed from the Romance literatures of Europe, especially those of the Italian courtly love poets such as Cavalcanti and the troubadours of twelfth-century Provence. A satiric engagement with the mores of contemporary life underlies much of his work here in sympathy with the Vorticist enterprise to *BLAST* away the aesthetic and moral conventions in the arts and society inherited from the nineteenth century and to usher in the spirit of the new modern age. This is evident in the opening poem, "Tenzone," whose strategies surreptitiously invoke Walt Whitman's advocation of his "psalms of the self" as the embodiment of the voice of American nineteenth-century democracy, though in "Tenzone," this voice seems insistent on its uniqueness, rather than its democracy, and is content to repose on the idea of poetry as a sacred mystery, rather than the speaking voice of the "commonwealth" of the Republic, as in Whitman. "The Condolence" responds with a sense of mock irony to the reception of his early poems as virile full-blooded expressions of masculinity and locates his creativity with the ductile quality of the female, rather than braggart male sexual assertiveness.

On the other hand, sexual joy independent of moral propriety is celebrated in "The Garret" as though to remind his audience that sexual joy and creative plenitude are at peace with each other. In general, Pound's view of the morality of art is comparable to Chekhov's, whose view is central to literary Modernism: The morality of art lies in the artist's capacity to do the best job of work possible with his materials, and any subscription to the conventional morality of the times is fatal to the work of art. At the same time, some of these poems will strike an uneasy note read in the context of the present, as in "The Garden," where class snobbery and emotional poverty are vilified as symptoms of cultural malaise; yet the threat here is implicitly one of male sexual effrontery in its challenge to the closeted female. On the other hand, any poem titled "The Garden" invokes that primary site of sexual and intellectual temptation, the Garden of Eden, sufficient to call in Pound's antagonism to the pieties of conformist Christianity in favor of the sacred and profane vigor of ancient pagan deities. By contrast, "Coitus" openly celebrates the anticipatory joy of shared sexuality in a way that is sympathetic to common human experience and needs no further defense.

Walt Whitman is a dominant point of reference in these poems about sex, writing, and the relation of the poet to the world he writes for, particularly in the poems where Pound addresses his "songs," a synonym for "poem" famously deployed in Whitman's *Song of Myself* and many other poems. Pound's uneasy acceptance of his Whitmanian inheritance is briefly addressed in "A Pact," a short poem in which the disputatious son finally acknowledges the strengths of the father, that they "have one sap and one root." Pound's feelings about Whitman and America were the subject of a series of articles originally published in 1912 under the title *Patria Mia*.

The Imagist poems of *Lustra* are fine examples of this kind, especially in their avoidance of abstractions and the adjectival and adverbial excess common to much poetry published during Pound's London years. They include "Ts'ai Chi'h," "In a Station of the Metro," "Alba," "Heather," "L'Art, 1910," "Women before a Shop," and this author's own favorite, "Fan-Piece, For Her Imperial Lord," in which a woman's abandonment by her aristocratic lover is plangently evoked in three short lines. Several of these poems are versions of Chinese poems reflecting Pound's engagement with the Fenollosa manuscripts and the brilliant *Cathay* poems of 1915.

If Whitman is one presiding spirit addressed in *Lustra*, Pound's love of Provençal poets and poetry is equally important especially in the two major poems, "Near Perigord" and "Provincia Deserta," both the fruit of a visit to Provence in 1912. "Near Perigord" is a questioning poem addressed to a warrior baron and poet, Bertran de Born, with reference to de Born's poem "Dompna pois de me no'us cal," translated by Pound and published with the notes to "Near Perigord" when it was first published in *Poetry* in December 1915. De Born's poem is read by Pound as a love poem in which he consoles himself for his rejection by Lady Maent of Montaignac by constructing a fictive ideal Lady who embodies all the best quality of the ladies of Provence, a strategy that may win back Lady Maent's love. However, "Near Perigord" acknowledges that de Born's motives in his poem may be questionable, as though the endeavor to regain the love of Lady Meant is really a covert attempt to secure a power base within the warring castles and communities of ancient Provence. "Near Perigord" is thus a periplum, a physical journey into a foreign landscape through which the traveler may achieve an emotional familiarity with a past age to enlarge his intellectual familiarity achieved through the study of its literature. Pound's poem seeks to uncover the truth of Bertran de Born's poem and to debate the relative claims of art and history as a way of recovering the past and the values inscribed in it. "Near Perigord" does not resolve these questions but articulates them in a manner that anticipates Pound's pervasive concern with these issues in *The Cantos*.

"Provincia Deserta" is another periplum, here not so much a "sailing after knowledge" but a record of the feel of the Provençal landscape, its roads and its peoples in the present as Pound walks about visiting the cities, castles, churches, and other sites familiar to him from Provençal poetry, a process of physical and geographical familiarization that gives him a differently informed feel for the world transcribed in those Provençal poems. Past and present are brought into conjunction through the itemization of place names—Perigord, Ribeyrac, Sarlat, Narbonne, Cahors, Excideuil, and so on—with the record of meetings and moments on his journey, of the old in charitable care at Chalais where there is a "pleached arbour," a momentary observation that firmly anchors the poem in particulars even as it recalls a vanished world peopled by the poets of the past. Later there is a garrulous old man at an inn and an old woman willing to lend the traveler dry clothing and to listen to his talk of Arnaut Daniel. "Provincia Deserta" is a kind of love poem, recording Pound's delighted encounter with the landscape and places inhabited in the poetry he thought to be the mainspring of Modern lyric poetry. It is also, of course, Pound's own version of Whitman's "Song of the Open Road."

Bibliography

Alexander, Michael. *The Poetic Achievement of Ezra Pound*. London: Faber, 1979.

Brooker, Peter. *A Student's Guide to the Selected Poems of Ezra Pound*. London: Faber, 1979.

Kenner, Hugh. *The Pound Era*. Berkeley: U of California P, 1971.

Ruthven, K. K. *A Guide to Ezra Pound's Personae (1926)*. Berkeley: U of California P, 1969.

Wilson, Peter. *A Preface to Ezra Pound*. New York: Longman, 1997.

Lionel Kelly

M

Machine Art [unpublished]

In the latter half of the 1920s, Pound proposed a functional conception of aesthetics: Beauty coincides with function. *Machine Art* (1927–1930) is the text that establishes a new criterion of beauty for the twentieth century. Though rejected, it is fundamental for Pound's aesthetics of *technê*, dating from 1927 to the 1940s: (1) Beauty as ideal form is transformed by Pound into the notion of form as law. The beauty of the machine does not reside in its architecture but in its motor, which represents latent concentrated energy: function. (2) Pound assigns a cognitive function to the language of poetry.

The manuscript, preserved in the Pound Archive at Beinecke Rare Book and Manuscript Library at Yale University, is dated 1927 and was first reported in *Ezra Pound e la scienza* (1987). Its draft was corrected by Pound in 1930, probably for publication in the *New Review* with its monographic issue dedicated to machines (Winter 1931–1932). The principles present in *Machine Art* are operative in the 1930s and 1940s. *Machine Art* is proposed as work of Poundian aesthetics in progress, placed as it is within the Vorticist moment and the Ideogrammic Method of the 1930s but also functioning as late as *Rock-Drill*.

Bibliography

Ardizzone, Maria Luisa. *Ezra Pound e la scienza. Scritti inediti o rari*. Milano, Scheiwiller, 1987.

Pound, Ezra. *Machine Art and Other Writings: The Lost Thought of the Italian Years*. Ed. Maria Luisa Ardizzone. Durham: Duke UP, 1996.

Francesca Cadel

MacLeish, Archibald (1892–1982)

Archibald MacLeish and Ezra Pound met only twice in their long lives. But decade by decade MacLeish fought for and against Pound: in their often exasperated correspondence, in MacLeish's oral and written recollections, in his drafts of the petition for Pound's release from St. Elizabeths, in his essays on Pound's opinions and on his stature and influence as a poet, and in his own poetry.

MacLeish's personal library had at least twenty-three books by Pound (see Howland). Of these, *Lustra*, *Umbra*, and *A Draft of XVI Cantos* were at hand for MacLeish's Paris "education as a poet" in the language and rhythms of "the new challenge to the poetic tradition" (*Reflections* 22)—as were *Instigations* and Eliot's poetry and *The Sacred Wood* (Donaldson 130–131). As for Pound's direct influence, Goodwin's reference to MacLeish as "the least intelligent of Pound's imitators" (183) is unfair to his longer poems of the 1920s and 1930s.

MacLeish never denied this original debt but soon tired of Pound's dogmatism: "Pound has too many rules. . . . Pound is crazy" (*Letters* 194–196). In the 1930s he was put off by Pound's political and economic obsessions but nonetheless helped him find American publishers. He would not have given Pound the Bollingen Prize, but in *Poetry and Opinion* he did praise "the poet's vision of a tragic disorder which lies far deeper in our lives and in our time" (48). And he did more than any other in getting the treason indictment dismissed, which made possible Pound's release from St. Elizabeths.

Five years before his death Pound wrote MacLeish, "What is of importance is an old and tried friendship" (Carpenter 896). MacLeish ended his essay-eulogy on Pound: "neither dilettante nor traitor but . . . a foolish and unhappy man . . . who was a poet also . . . a master poet" (*Riders* 122).

Bibliography

Carpenter, Humphrey. *A Serious Character: The Life of Ezra Pound.* Boston: Houghton Mifflin, 1988.

Donaldson, Scott. *Archibald MacLeish: An American Life.* Boston: Houghton Mifflin, 1992.

Goodwin, K. L. *The Influence of Ezra Pound.* London: Oxford UP, 1966.

Howland, Margaret. *Descriptive Catalogue of the Archibald MacLeish Collection at Greenfield Community College.* 2 vols. Greenfield: The College, 1991–1993.

MacLeish, Archibald. *Archibald MacLeish: Reflections.* Ed. Bernard A. Drabeck and Helen E. Ellis. Foreword by Richard Wilbur. Amherst: U of Massachusetts P, 1986.

———. *The Letters of Archibald MacLeish.* Ed. R. H. Winnick. Boston: Houghton Mifflin, 1983.

———. *Poetry and Opinion: The Pisan Cantos of Ezra Pound.* Urbana: U of Illinois P, 1950.

———. *Riders on the Earth.* Boston: Houghton Mifflin, 1978.

Lauriat Lane Jr.

Make It New

Published first by Faber in 1934, and then by Yale University Press in 1935, *Make It New* collects many of Ezra Pound's essays unavailable to then contemporary readers due to their limited appearance several decades earlier in literary journals such as *Quarterly Review*, *Egoist*, and *Little Review*. Written primarily between 1912 and 1920, and ranging in subject from the troubadours to Elizabethan classicists and French poetry, the essays contained in *Make It New*, most importantly, demonstrate Pound's understanding of what literary criticism should be, what forms it can take, and how the art of writing poetry has everything to do with it. In *Make It New* Pound considers Greek translation, sifts though the prose of the nineteenth century to come out with Henry James, and looks to antiquity for lessons in poetic craft. The result of this account is a sense that criticism must at once "weed out" the lesser work of a given age, presenting only the highest examples of that age to the public, at the same time that it teaches its readers *how* to read, the aim of which is to give them a more sophisticated historical and social awareness. Toward this end, the essays in *Make It New* focus on the central notion of what each writer, or writers, accomplished that was unique to his (all the authors considered are male) historical moment and why such a development remains useful to a Modernist sensibility. As might be expected, Pound understands each poet's ability to capture the spirit of his age as a reaction against the morality and practices of that age. Pound certainly does not except himself from such a historical position and sees his criticism as performing essentially the same revolt as the texts he considers, writing in the introduction—titled "Date Line"—"As language becomes the most powerful instrument of perfidy, so language alone can riddle and cut through the meshes. Used to conceal meaning, used to blur meaning, to produce the complete and utter inferno of the past century . . . against which, SOLELY a care for language, for accurate registration by language avails" (7).

Crucially, in this sense, the volume reveals Pound's insistence on the practical political power of poetry and criticism. The works under discussion, and the way Pound discusses them, become a virtual annotation of the poetics and politics that inform and construct his primary activity undertaken in *The Cantos*. *Make It New* thus becomes an important companion piece to any sophisticated understanding of Pound's achievement, as well as his obsession with economics, the role of history, and his fall into fascism. Put simply, Pound's essays, as a tool to "make it new," reflect his sense of a certain praxis: to remake the moment—its politics and social reality—through language. The focus after all should be on the "it." It is the "it," the now, the word, that Pound wanted "new," and to be "new" and in the "now" means simply rejecting the mistakes (Pound's sense of them at least) of both the past and the present, regardless of one's particular historical moment. History in this sense is not linear. Again, as Pound writes in the introduction, "It is quite obvious that we do not all of us inhabit the same time" (19).

Bibliography

Baumann, Walter. *Roses from the Steel Dust: Collected Essays on Ezra Pound*. Orono: NPF, 2000.

Beach, Christopher. *ABC of Influence: Ezra Pound and the Remaking of American Poetic Tradition*. Berkeley: U of California P, 1992.

Singh, G. *Ezra Pound as Critic*. New York: St. Martin's P, 1994.

Joel Bettridge

Il Mare, Supplemento Letterario

Ezra Pound's collaboration with the Rapallo weekly *Il Mare* lasted from August 1932 to November 1939. Sixteen issues of the literary supplement (*Supplemento Letterario*) were published fortnightly (20 August 1932–3 March 1933). From April to July 1933, *Il Mare* appeared as the *Pagina letteraria del Mare* (eight issues).

Pound served on the weekly's editorial board in the Affari Esteri section. He wrote forty-seven articles, signed as Ezra Pound, E. P., and P. His most important contributions deal with French poetry ("Poeti francesi," eleven installments), "Vorticism" (four installments), "Appunti" (nine installments) as well as various other topics, ranging from articles on literary criticism, poetic language and style (after the Imagist theories of twenty years earlier), the Italian literary panorama (often quite old-fashioned), and newly published books deserving greater attention to comments on the common characteristics among modern arts.

In his "Poeti francesi" contributions, he generally introduces or presents a choice of poems in the original and adds brief introductions or afterwords on the specific author; the most widely discussed poet is Jules Laforgue. In the articles on Vorticism he traces the main features of the movement and points out its differences from Italian Futurism. Many of these articles recall Pound's major essays of the 1910s and 1920s.

Beginning with an August 1932 entry (signed "William Atheling," his London music critic's

pseudonym), Pound used *Il Mare* to publicize the series of Rapallo concerts organized by himself and Olga Rudge as violinist, with other musicians, including pianist Gerhart Münch. Other friends also contributed to this cause, including Basil Bunting and Father Desmond Chute. His aims were to produce great music on a modest scale, not competing with the large centers; to feature the best of new music; and, in the spirit of Dolmetsch, to revitalize the forgotten music of pre-Romantic times. In the midst of this enterprise, Pound and Olga Rudge became aware of the treasury of Vivaldi manuscripts lying in Italian libraries, and they became crusaders for the cause. These concerts thus figure significantly in the revival of early music, and it is fitting that Pound's last article before World War II bears the title "Risveglio Vivaldiano."

Stefano Maria Casella

Marinetti, F. T. (1876–1944)

The Italian Futurist (Emilio) F(ilippo) T(ommaso) Marinetti was born in Alexandria, Egypt, completed his baccalaureate in Paris, and settled in 1894 with his parents in Milan. After graduating from the University of Genoa with a law degree in 1899, he dedicated himself to literature, publishing criticism, poetry, and plays. His "Futurist Manifesto," published in *Le Figaro* in 1909, established him as an international spokesman for the Italian avant-garde. Marinetti and the Futurists rejected both the aesthetics and the morals of the past, embracing technology, speed, and aggression. Aesthetically they resembled the Cubists and Vorticists, but they were closer philosophically to the Dadaists and Surrealists.

After World War I, Marinetti endorsed Mussolini's fascism. He continued to write manifestos, now often in the service of the party. Early in his Futurist career, he had called for burning the museums and destroying all that was sentimental in art or that evoked the past; now he advocated nationalism, war, opposition to religion, and the subjugation of the individual to the state. In 1920 Marinetti broke with the fascists, after Mussolini accepted the monarchy and clergy, but he returned in 1924 and was named to the Italian Academy two years later. He volunteered to fight in World War II, despite his advanced age, and died in December 1944, shortly after returning from the front, at sixty-eight. Marinetti and Pound became friends in Italy. Pound had disapproved of Futurism, but he admired Marinetti's patriotism and courage and memorialized him in Canto 72, the first of the two "Italian Cantos."

Bibliography

Affron, Matthew, and Mark Antliff, eds. *Fascist Visions: Art and Ideology in France and Italy.* Princeton: Princeton UP, 1997.

Crispolti, Enrico, ed. *Futurismo e Meridione.* Naples: Electa, 1996.

Hewitt, Andrew. *Fascist Modernism: Aesthetics, Politics, and the Avant-Garde.* Stanford: Stanford UP, 1993.

Patricia A. Cockram

Meridiano di Roma

Ezra Pound's collaboration with *Il Meridiano di Roma*, a daily directed by Cornelio di Marzio, resulted in one of the most substantial of his wide-ranging contributions to periodicals and papers, consisting of more than 100 articles published between 24 April 1938 and 12 September 1943, with the greatest number written during the triennium 1940–1942. Thirty-five of these articles were included in *Orientamenti* (1945). These articles are devoted mainly to economic topics, such as the necessity for the State to issue stamp script (Gesellism and Douglasism). Repeated here are Pound's attacks against the international plutocratic capitalism (almost invariably identified with the great Jewish financiers) allied with the Banks and English and American politicians and leaders, against false advertising, against anti-Italian propaganda, and of course, against usura. The gold standard is strongly censured as well. Judaism is attacked for being historically allied to Protestantism and always having menaced and corrupted Christianity and its healthy and vital Mediterranean aspects derived from classical paganism. True and reliable ethics (for both the individual and the State) are represented by Confucius and the Tao. Finally, Fascist Italy is held up as an example of political, economical, social, and cultural revolution. However, the content is often tainted with propaganda. Perhaps the most valuable contributions are those on cultural matters, including his comments on the importance of classical learning and precision in terminology (*economia ortologica* and *mot juste*).

Stefano Maria Casella

Money Pamphlets

Pound began agitating systematically for economic reform along broadly Douglasite lines in 1931. The immediate motive was undoubtedly the Great Depression, which lasted in the European industrial democracies until the outbreak of World War II in September 1939. Pound correctly believed that the depression could create a war that would complete the destruction of European civilization. As international tensions mounted in the 1930s, Pound's attempt to stop the war via articles, reviews, and his voluminous private correspondence became increasingly frenzied. Even *The Cantos* were enlisted in a last-ditch effort to prevent the "cannibals of Europe" from "eating each other again" (Canto 32).

Pound devoted several pamphlets to economic problems and their political consequences. These fall into two main groups: those written in English and published in the 1930s and those written in Italian during the war. The English-language pamphlets include *ABC of Economics* (1933), *Social Credit: An Impact* (1935) and *What Is Money For?* (1939). Pamphlets in Italian include *Carta da Visita* (1942; English translation 1952), *L'America, Roosevelt e le Cause della Guerra Presente* (1944; English translation 1951), *Introduzione alla Natura Economica degli S.U.A.* (1944; English translation 1950), and *Oro e Lavoro* (1944; English translation 1951 [1952]). The last three of these pamphlets were produced as part of Pound's effort to promote and defend the short-lived Salò Republic, the German puppet state created for Mussolini after his rescue by German commandos in September 1943. The Italian pamphlets were translated by John Drummond and published in English by Peter Russell in 1951. Pound's final words on economics appeared in *Nuova Economica Editoriale* in 1962. Most of these pieces were included by Noel Stock in *Impact: Essays on Ignorance and the Decline of Western Civilization* (1960) or more carefully edited by William Cookson in *Selected Prose 1909–1965*. All except *ABC of Economics* (which had originally been published by Faber) were reprinted by the poet Peter Russell in 1951.

Pound's economic ideas were not fixed. Though it is fair to call him a Social Creditor, Pound was by no means "orthodox" in his adherence to Major Douglas's views. Pound's economic ideas evolved—especially as he absorbed the work of Silvio Gesell in the early 1930s—resulting eventually in a syncretistic amalgam of "under-consumptionist" economic criticism and monetary remedies he was already calling "Volitionist Economics" by 1933.

Certain themes are constant in the pamphlets: First and foremost they are honestly dedicated to economic and social justice with an emphasis on "distributionist" remedies to economic problems and disparities. This meant finding ways of rethinking what money means and augmenting the supply of money (Douglas and Fisher) or of increasing its "velocity" (Gesell). Following Kimball, Pound also advocated a shorter working day. Pound's negative criticism always includes a sharp attack on the financial status quo, which by creating unpayable debts makes war an economic necessity, which in turn creates more debt. This insight Pound combined with a Populist notion of a "bankers' conspiracy" to explain social injustice, which became pronounced by the mid-1930s, when the poet, after much inner struggle, accepted the arch-cabal propounded in *The Protocols of the Elders of Zion* and emerged as an open anti-Semite. As "Volitionist" suggests, Pound was sure we could have economic justice if we had the will to do so; that we did not suggested to him *abuleia*—a weakness of will, abetted by the usurocratic control and "black out" of economic truth—one reason why his economic writing is impatient, hectoring, often enraged.

Pound was angry because he thought the causes of and solution to economic injustice were quite simple. The poet's penchant for simple solutions to what he saw as a simple problem may explain why the influences of two more systematic economic thinkers, J. M. Keynes and Karl Marx, are conspicuous by their near absence from Pound's economic thinking. For a writer of the "red decade" of the 1930s, Pound has remarkably little to say about Marxism. He did read at least part of *Capital*, for Marx's shocking chapter on "The Working Day" made an impression; but Pound was not tempted by Marxist solutions to the problems of capitalism, and though he admired Lenin and even Stalin, Pound became a fervent anticommunist. According to Leon Surette, Pound read Keynes's *General Theory of Employment, Interest and Money* (1936) when it appeared, but it had no effect on his thinking (Pound in Purgatory 9).

The influences cited or detectable in Pound's pamphlets range from Thomas Jefferson to J. A. Hobson (the inspiration for Lenin's *Imperialism: The Last Stage of Capitalism*) and from David Hume to Mussolini. Pound was especially influenced by the "stamp scrip" suggested by Sylvio Gesell, which had been put into practice in Wörgl, Austria, in the early 1930s, because he felt it made the meaning of money plain. Paper money is always a fiction agreed upon, which has no other basis, Pound argued, than the credit of the community that issued it—be it a country like Italy or a town like Wörgl. Pound was fond of sending correspondents his grandfather Thaddeus C. Pound's company scrip as proof that any creditworthy enterprise could issue tickets that behaved like money.

Pound sought and found ancient precedent for his economic views, but the principal contemporary works in English from which Pound assembled his (sometimes contradictory) economic ideas include, in alphabetical order by author, the following: Brooks Adams, *The Law of Civilization and Decay* (1895); Charles Coughlin, *Money! Questions and Answers* (1936); C. H. Douglas, *Economic Democracy* (1920) and *Credit Power and Democracy* (1920); Irving Fisher, *Stable Money: A History of the Movement* (1934); Silvio Gesell, *The Natural Economic*

Order (1916); J. A. Hobson, *Imperialism: A Study* (1902); Christopher Hollis, *The Two Nations: A Financial Study of English History* (1935); Dexter Kimball, *Industrial Economics* (1929); Jeffrey Mark, *The Modern Idolatry: Being an Analysis of Usury and the Pathology of Debt* (1934); Willis A. Overholser, *A Short Review and Analysis of the History of Money in the United States* (1936); and Anonymous (but the English translation financed and promulgated by Henry Ford), *The Protocols and World Revolution [The Protocols of the Elders of Zion]* (1920).

Bibliography

Bush, Ronald. *The Genesis of Ezra Pound's Cantos.* Princeton: Princeton UP, 1976.
Marsh, Alec. *Money and Modernity: Pound, Williams, and the Spirit of Jefferson.* Tuscaloosa: U of Alabama P, 1998.
Redman, Tim. *Ezra Pound and Italian Fascism.* New York: Cambridge UP, 1991.
Sieburth, Richard. *Instigations: Ezra Pound and Remy de Gourmont.* Cambridge: Harvard UP, 1978.
Surette, Leon. *A Light from Eleusis: A Study of Ezra Pound's Cantos.* Oxford: Clarendon P, 1979.
———. *Pound in Purgatory: From Economic Radicalism to Anti-Semitism.* Urbana: U of Illinois P, 1999.

Alec Marsh

Monroe, Harriet (1860–1936)

Harriet Monroe was born in Chicago and died in Peru. Poet, biographer, dramatist, anthologist, journalist, and editor, she played a critical role in the acceptance of modern European and American poetry and art, not only by fashioning such important anthologies as *The New Poetry* (1917), coedited with Alice Corbin Henderson, but through her work as art critic on the *Chicago Tribune.* Her poetry, notably *The Columbian Ode*, written to mark the opening of the Columbia Exposition in Chicago in 1892–1893, and *You and I* received popular attention, but her most significant contribution was as editor of *Poetry, A Magazine of Verse*, which she founded in 1912 and edited until her death.

Through the publication of writers like Ezra Pound (foreign correspondent from 1912 to 1917), Joyce, Yeats, Eliot, H. D., Amy Lowell, Sandburg, Stevens, and Hart Crane, *Poetry* heightened the visibility and acceptance of Modern poetry in America. Monroe's editorials and essays in the journal provide a history and status of new movements and fresh voices, whether it was Imagism or Objectivism. Her autobiography *A Poet's Life*, published after her unexpected death in Arequipa, Peru, where she traveled to visit ancient Inca ruins following participation in the international P.E.N. conference in Buenos Aires, is a valuable account of the Chicago Renaissance in American art and letters and the founding of *Poetry.* Pound's letters to her form an important exchange that defines his aesthetic and her goals for American writers.

Bibliography

Monroe, Harriet. *A Poet's Life.* New York: Macmillan, 1938.
Williams, Ellen. *Harriet Monroe and the Poetry Renaissance: The First Ten Years of Poetry 1912–1922.* Urbana: U of Illinois P, 1977.

Ira B. Nadel

Moore, Marianne (1887–1972)

Ezra Pound's relation to Marianne Moore forms part of his productive and cooperative if at times also prickly relation with the large number of strong women editors, publishers, and writers who did so much to disseminate Modernist works. Their interaction persisted largely through a correspondence of over 400 items from December 1918 until March 1967, punctuated by occasional personal meetings. Impressed by Moore's early verse in *Poetry* and the *Egoist*, Pound responded to her submission of poems for the *Little Review* with a long and generous letter mingling sympathetic criticism ("I am worried by 'intentioned.' It is 'not English.'"), advice ("I would warn you of the very great importance of the actual order of poems in a booklet"), and curiosity about both Moore and the literary scene in New York. Moore wrote back describing her background ("I am Irish by descent . . . purely Celtic"), explaining both her stanzaic technique and her scant publishing history and offering several poetic revisions in response to Pound's suggestions. A lifelong friendship had begun.

By the early 1920s Pound considered Moore a major Modernist poet and grouped her with William Carlos Williams and Mina Loy as the three best poets working in the United States. He helped introduce her to the *Dial* crowd, and in return she cultivated his reconciliation with that circle after she became editor of the magazine from 1925 until its demise in 1929. Having herself won the *Dial* prize in 1924 for her volume *Observations*, Moore made sure that Pound himself also won it in 1927. She had wanted to award it for "services to literature," but Pound himself asked that it be given specifically for *The Cantos* or for his verse as a whole. Their mutual support continued into the 1930s, when Pound included a prominent selection of Moore's poems first in his *Profile: An Anthology* (1932) and then in his *Active Anthology* (1933) and hoped that she would succeed Harriet Monroe as editor of *Poetry*. For her part, Moore reviewed *A Draft of XXX Cantos* perceptively for *Poetry* in 1931 and the *Criterion* for 1934. Yet Moore had always regretted Pound's "promptness with the cudgels," and by this time she had severe doubts about both his politics and his pugnacity yet defended him on grounds of both genius and generosity. "Ezra Pound does wrong in the fullest sense of the word in a thousand ways," she wrote to her old friend William Rose Benet in 1933. "But one speaks up for a person who helps one." And after sixteen years of correspondence Moore finally switched her salutation from "Dear Mr. Pound" to "Dear E. P."

Pound and Moore's first personal meeting, in 1939, preceded the interruption of their correspondence by the war years. After the war, correspondence resumed, and Moore visited Pound at St. Elizabeths. She wrote a testimonial as part of the effort for his release, and he encouraged her translation of the fables of La Fontaine. Their long and fascinating correspondence ended in 1967, but they were to meet in person one more time. At an American Academy of Arts and Letters program held in the New York Public Library in 1969, the two poets approached each other after half a century of friendship and support (if occasional acerbity), clasped hands, and exclaimed, "Oh, Ezra" and "Oh, Marianne."

Bibliography

Bar-Yaacov, Lois. "The Odd Couple: The Correspondence between Marianne Moore and Ezra Pound, 1918–1939." *Twentieth Century Literature* 34 (Winter 1988): 507–527.
Bornstein, George. *Material Modernism: The Politics of the Page*. Cambridge: Cambridge UP, 2001.

George Bornstein

Mosley, Sir Oswald (1896–1980)

During the 1920s, Mosley was recognized as exhibiting "the attributes . . . wanted from a Labour leader—bold policies, unflinching courage, eloquent language, compassion, popular appeal." In Parliament (1918–1924), he served as secretary of a Peace with Ireland Council. After his time in the Labor Party (1924–1931), Mosley formed the British Union of Fascists (BUF) in 1932, the political organization to which Ezra Pound offered the opportunity to publish *Jefferson and/or Mussolini* in 1933. The BUF's unresponsiveness caused Pound to write a letter comparing Mosley's movement unfavorably with that of "the boss" (Mussolini). In 1934 T. S. Eliot warned Pound not to get involved with "that Mosley," continuing his misgivings stated in the *Criterion* (April 1931). In August 1939 Pound praised the Third Reich in an article for Mosley's magazine *Action*: "The natural civiliser of Russia is Germany. No less gutsy and active people would bother about educating the Mujik" (Heymann 75). Pound published "Sovereignty" (March 1953), "Of Misprision of Treason . . ." and "Three Poems" (both January 1959), and Canto 101 (February 1959) in the *European*, founded by Mosley (1953–1959) and edited by his second wife, Diana Mitford Mosley. Mosley remarked: "Ezra Pound I met when I was just forty. . . . He appeared as a practical person, making the shrewd observation that Englishmen of my class never grew up until they were forty" (*My Life* 226).

Bibliography

Cassels, Alan. *Fascism*. Wheeling: Harlan Davidson, 1975.

Heymann, C. David. *Ezra Pound: The Last Rower*. New York: Viking, 1976.

Mosley, Diana. *A Life of Contrasts: The Autobiography of Diana Mosley*. London: Hamish Hamilton, 1977.

Mosley, Oswald. *My Life*. London: Nelson, 1968.

Skidelsky, Robert. *Oswald Mosley*. London: Macmillan, 1975.

Evelyn Haller

Music

Ezra Pound's involvement with music was even greater than his better-known involvement with visual arts. If music plays a less obvious role than the visual arts in Pound's poetry and poetics, the reason is largely that during his formative years visual artists like the Italian Futurists Wyndham Lewis and Henri Gaudier-Brzeska were leading the vanguard of artistic experiment, while composers within Pound's range of awareness offered nothing comparable. From a musician's standpoint, Pound was a downright amateur. Though he had some keyboard skills, and in the 1920s conducted a brief flirtation with the bassoon, he was never an accomplished player. He was curious about harmony, counterpoint, and musical form, but his actual knowledge was haphazard. Yet he valued music enormously, possessed a substantial knowledge of repertoire, wrote voluminous criticism, a *Treatise on Harmony* and, most outrageously, two idiosyncratic "operas." He cultivated musical friendships throughout his life (at least until the St. Elizabeths period, when musical contacts were few), and his musical aesthetics parallel his poetics in significant ways.

While still a student in America, Pound's medieval studies, particularly of the Provençal troubadours, pointed to his deepening involvement with early music—an enthusiasm common today but quite exceptional for its time. His study of troubadour poetry was driven in part by his quest for the elusive ideal of *motz el son*, the perfect union of words and music. At the same time, Pound's friendship with concert pianist (and avid Theosophist) Katherine Ruth Heyman stimulated his interest in recent music, which Heyman championed, first Debussy and then Scriabin. In 1908, Pound made his entrance into Europe in the guise of Heyman's concert manager.

During this same period, probably in America, Pound met Walter Morse Rummel, a pianist far more celebrated than Heyman, compared in the press with Busoni and Rubinstein, and handpicked by Debussy to premiere his final piano works. Pound and Rummel, whose friendship was for a time quite close, collaborated on settings of troubadour lyrics (*Hesternae Rosae*), and Rummel set some of Pound's poems, including "The Return."

Through Pound's first decade in London, he met a large number of musicians, including Thomas Beecham (who gave him opera tickets and commissioned a translation of the libretto to Massenet's *Cendrillon*), folklorist Marjorie Kennedy-Fraser, contralto Elizabeth Grainger Kerr, and Bengali poet-composer Rabindranath Tagore. But the most important was Arnold Dolmetsch. Already an established figure in the 1890s, Dolmetsch is probably more responsible for the revival of Baroque and pre-Baroque music than any other individual; he was not merely a scholar in this then-neglected field, but he built instruments—recorders, lutes, harpsichords, clavichords (one of which Pound purchased)—and furthermore learned to play them, frequently appearing in concert with members of his family. Dolmetsch is the subject of five articles by Pound and remained one of Pound's ideals of proactive scholarship: "There are times when . . . a resurrection is equally creative or even more creative than invention" (*EP&M* 46).

Pound's musical involvements suddenly intensified when he took a position as critic for A. R. Orage's *New Age*, writing art reviews under the name B. H. Dias and music reviews under the name William Atheling—a total of sixty-one of these between December 1917 and January 1921. These high-spirited columns are rewarding for their sheer entertainment value. But Atheling's underlying purposes are clear. Although he reviewed some of the great names of the day—Arthur Rubinstein, Maggie Teyte—he concentrated on the aspiring young, primarily singers, in London's recital halls. He set out to advance the cause of early music not only by praising it in print but by seeking out young performers and encouraging them to expand their repertoire. Ever the poet-critic, he praised clarity of diction in performance and musical settings sensitive to prosodic values. Setting a poem to music, he affirmed, is an act of literary criticism. (Unfortunately, the Great War distorted his perspective on the tradition of German *Lieder*, which were performed infrequently and in translation.) Atheling was also attentive to new music, but he did not find much to admire—youthful reputations of the day belonged mainly to the English "cowpat school," Romantic pastoralists like John Ireland or Walford Davies.

During this period, Pound undertook another more surprising musical project: He set out to compose an opera. He concocted a libretto on the life of François Villon featuring passages from the poet's *Testament* and his best-known lyrics. He then attempted to compose the music, seeking help briefly from a singer, Grace Crawford, then more persistently from pianist Agnes Bedford (whom he met in 1919), to write it down. The work would not be completed, however, until Pound received help from George Antheil in 1923. The conception of this work arose, it seems, from Pound's collaboration with Yeats on his Noh-inspired play for dancers *At the Hawk's Well* (1917). Before meeting Pound, Yeats, assisted by actress Florence Farr, had for years experimented with minimalist musical settings of verse in his "cantillations" to the psaltery (an instrument constructed for him by Dolmetsch); for his play, Yeats likewise insisted on a minimalist music that would highlight and not obscure the values of his verse. This music was provided by Edmund Dulac, a musical amateur. Pound's conception of *The Testament of François Villon* is similarly Noh inspired, using masks, stylized acting, and vaguely medieval-sounding minimalist musical settings.

Pound's arrival in Paris brought three changes that intensified his musical life even further. The musical life of 1920s Paris was advanced far beyond that of the London he had left behind. Though Debussy's ghost still lurked, Stravinsky dominated the scene, and the eccentric Erik Satie was adulated by the young French composers known as *Les Six*. Second, Pound's personal life was transformed when he met in 1923 the young American violinist Olga Rudge (once reviewed by Atheling), who became his lifelong companion and mother of his daughter Mary. Third, Pound met the "ebullient" young American composer, pianist, and provocateur George Antheil, whom Pound immediately recognized as the musical Vorticist missing from the London scene. In the mid-1920s, Pound helped both Rudge and Antheil organize concerts, occasionally together, and publicized the composer in a book, *Antheil and the Treatise on Harmony* (1926). The year 1926 saw the apex of this activity: First was the scandalously successful premiere of Antheil's *chef d'oeuvre*, *Ballet Mécanique*; a few days later saw the premiere of Pound's *Le Testament*, a concert performance of about half of the music, with Yves Tinayre as principal singer. For a while, Pound agitated to have *Le Testament* performed at the Abbey Theatre and at the Met but without success.

When Antheil's music took a conservative turn after 1927, Pound's enthusiasm waned. But Pound's musical interests rekindled when in 1931, largely at the behest of Agnes Bedford, the BBC broadcasted a second and complete performance of *Le Testament*. Working on his monumental edition of Guido Cavalcanti at this time, Pound was inspired to compose first a *Sonata Ghuidonis*, for unaccompanied violin, and then a second opera, *Cavalcanti*, which was not performed until after his death.

In the summer of 1933, Pound and Olga Rudge organized a series of chamber concerts in Rapallo with the help of German pianist Gerhart Münch. These were intensive through 1935 and, after Münch left Rapallo, continued intermittently until the war. Pound had become aware of hoards of early music lying unperformed in manuscript in nearby libraries. Münch was adept at transcribing this music for violin and piano (including Francesco da Milano's version of Janequin found in Canto 75), and these were featured prominently. Pound was fond of presenting large blocks of music by a single composer: Bach, violin sonatas of Mozart, Purcell trio sonatas, and the first modern performances of English Baroque composer William Young. Recent music was also favored: piano music of Debussy, Ravel, and Scriabin; violin sonatas by Debussy, Ravel, Honegger, plus Stravinsky's reductions of *Petruchka* and *Pulcinella*. Tibor Serly arrived from Budapest with the New Hungarian Quartet to present his *Viola Concerto* plus the quartets of Bartók and lesser Moderns. Pound's activities drew considerable attention from musicians elsewhere, and he advertised their economic sense in articles like "What a Small Town Can Do" and "Money and Music."

In 1936, Pound and Olga Rudge fixed their attention on a single little known composer: Vivaldi. Münch sent photographs of manuscripts from his native Dresden, while Olga studied the 309 concertos in nearby Turin, producing the first thematic catalog of Vivaldi's *inedite*. Having taken a position at the Accademia Chigiana in Siena, Olga first founded a Vivaldi Society in Venice in 1938, performing his music there, and then agitated, through composer Alfredo Casella, to mount a "Settimana Vivaldiana" in Siena in 1939, a series of six all-Vivaldi concerts including the first modern performances of the opera *L'Olimpiade*. For a while, Olga was known as "Miss Rudge-Vivaldi." Such activities provided essential groundwork for the postwar Vivaldi revival.

Pound's active musical life effectively ended with the war and his incarceration at St. Elizabeths. In Venice, his grave is near Stravinsky's.

Bibliography

Adams, Stephen J. "The Dramatic Background of Pound's Operas." *Literary Modernism and the Occult Tradition.* Ed. Leon Surette and Demetres P. Tryphonopoulos. Orono: NPF, 1996.

———. "Ezra Pound and Music." Diss. U of Toronto, 1974.

———. "Pound, Olga Rudge, and the 'Risveglio Vivaldiano.'" *Paideuma* 4.1 (1975): 111–118.

Bucknell, Brad. *Literary Modernism and Musical Aesthetics: Pater, Pound, Joyce, and Stein.* New York: Cambridge UP, 2001.

Fisher, Margaret. *Ezra Pound's Radio Operas: The BBC Experiments 1931–1933.* Cambridge: MIT P, 2002.

Henderson, Archibald, III. "Pound and Music: The Paris and Early Rapallo Years." Diss. UCLA, 1983.

Hughes, Robert, and Margaret Fisher. *Cavalcanti: A Perspective on the Music of Ezra Pound.* Emeryville: Second Evening Art, 2003.

Merritt, Robert. *Early Music and the Aesthetics of Ezra Pound: Hush of Older Song.* Lewiston: Edwin Mellen P, 1993.

Pound, Ezra. *Ezra Pound and Music: The Complete Criticism.* Ed. R. Murray Schafer. New York: New Directions, 1977.

Stephen J. Adams

Myth and Anthropology

Pound's treatment of gods and heroes indulges the epic ambition of all with creative spirit: to remold an imperfect world in their image of the way things should be. He mythologized those perceived to inhabit his intellectual ground, muddled history, and made truth secondary to artistic purpose as he sought to convey that every age has much to teach; that divinity is tangible; and that *paradiso terrestre* is not dream but reality. Pound was convinced that the "enlightened" sense and record in art, myth, and heroic achievement the order and vitality (charged particles) of a world Vortex akin to the poetic image, a "radiant node or cluster . . . from which, and through which, and into which, ideas are constantly rushing" (*GB* 92). The consummate mythmaker, he acted on intuition and belief, discerning that sound and sense, word and thing, connect in experience beyond formulated language: the "tin flash in the sun dazzle" (Cantos 2 and 21), the seed, or the "gristly roots" (*GK* 58) he documented as top flights of mind.

Sparkling with Ovidian humor, his radiant world seldom differentiates between myth and religion. Because he believed all gods are eternal states of being accessible to the perceptive (*SP* 47–48), "graeco-roman gods welcome corresponding divinities/metaphors from all cultures" (Kearns 74–76). Myth, Pound argued, is intelligible in a "vivid and glittering sense" to those who understand Demeter, Persephone, and the Laurel—those who have "met Artemis" (*SR* 92), who are capable of discerning the "emotional colors" divinity represents (*GK* 299). More Aristotelian than Platonist, he found myth "a supple language to think in"; even landscape and weather are mythologized (Kearns 74). It is "the supreme lie," said Pound, "that the splendor of the world is not a true splendor, that it is not the garment of the gods" (*SP* 431). It is the here and now that mattered for him; from his point of view, the pagan gods were "always, whether by patronage or metamorphosis, more concretely involved with this world than the Christian god or Neoplatonic One" (Dekker 294).

East meets West in invented deities like Isis Kuanon (Canto 90), whose key attribute is compassion (divine love) and whose power—worshipped from the dawn of history—is regeneration. Kuanon is the ancient Chinese goddess of mercy; Isis, the Egyptian Queen of the Dead (identified with earth goddesses Ceres, Demeter, Persephone, and Ishtar), gathered the limbs of Osiris to restore light and life. Pound also commands another symbol of wisdom and renewal: "the viper stirs in the dust, / the blue serpent / glides from the rock pool" before the "Grove hath its altar" (Canto 90). He establishes timeless, fluid spheres wherein virtue has room to play: He illuminates what exists instead of creating ex nihilo, juxtaposes past and present, balances abstract thought with violent action, and holds his greatest lyric moments fixed. As Canto 1 closes, punctuation freezes a "tale of the tribe" in flux: Aphrodite bears "the golden bough of Argicida. *So that:*" (emphasis added). All experience flows from her. She is most alive in the later cantos as the Japanese nymph of the Hagoromo who visits Pound in the Detention Training Center (Dekker 290) and as the prophet/shaman's guide, Princess Ra-Set (Canto 91), child of a "sacred marriage" of Father Sky and Mother Earth—the Egyptian sun god Ra, symbolic of the soul's journey through the underworld toward rebirth, and Set, symbolic of chaotic, destructive forces (Rachewiltz 179–182).

Certain of Pound's esoteric beliefs became entrenched during his long friendship with Allen Upward (1863–1926), Quest Society associate and amateur religious historian who, he revealed in a 1913 letter to Dorothy Shakespear, knew "things that ain't in Frazer," who "talked sense about sun worship & the siege of Troy" (*L/DS* 259). In *The New Word* (1910), which Pound reviewed sympathetically, Upward employs etymological clues to show how contemporary language preserves "ancestral ghosts"; furthermore, he proposes a chameleon "whirl-swirl" akin to Yeats's gyre and Pound's Vortex as *logos* for divine/human interaction. In *The Divine Mystery* (1913), Upward discusses the evolution of a Divine Man or Chrestos (anointed one) from Wizard, Magician, Genius, Seer, Priest, and Prophet—archetypical hero of the human journey from darkness to light (Tryphonopoulos 74–77).

No less crucial to the development of his values, attitudes, and beliefs was the quality of the affection Pound had for his look-alike, ethnographer Leo Frobenius (1873–1938), whose theories attracted Spengler and underpin Jung's theory of the collective unconscious. Frobenius, an Odyssean figure aligned in *The Cantos* with Confucius, Erigena, and Mani (Davenport, "Pound and Frobenius" 53), influenced the poet's understanding of Ovid and Noh drama; his racial ideas and collection of African folktales—particularly one celebrating restoration of a mythological city and godhead, Wagadu—convinced Pound of the truth of *Kulturmorphologie* (organic transformation of cultures). At Pisa (Canto 74), Pound saw in the African tale of suffering the *paideuma* (*GK* 58) of Ecbatan or Dioce/Deos, a city "in the mind indestructible" to supersede Fascist Italy, his impossible dream in worldly form.

Influenced directly or indirectly by Creuzer, Nietzsche, William Robertson Smith, Karl Müller, and Emile Durkheim, classicists of the period provided insight into "irrational" origins of religion, affirming the notion of cultural evolution and firing the public imagination. E. B. Tylor's *Primitive Culture* (1871) linked heroic legend with solar myth well before Schlieman's excavations at Troy (1873) and those of Evans at Knossos (1900) lent credence to the tales of Homer. Pound's striking use of the Adonis/Thamuz vegetation rite at Rapallo (Canto 47) illustrates his debt to the fourth of twelve heavily annotated volumes of *The Golden Bough—Adonis, Attis, and Osiris: Studies in the History of Oriental Religion* (1906). Highly charged, erotic language reminds of the harsh actualities as well as the delights of human experience: "Thy day is between a door and a door." Frazer's images of sacred marriage (sexual union of male and female as sympathetic magic), his observations concerning chastity and sacrifice, and his thesis—that humankind has progressed from magic through religious belief to scientific thought—are reflected in the poet's early works, such as "The Coming of War: Actaeon," as well as *Guide to Kulchur* and the whole epic compendium of artistic and social ideas.

Jane Ellen Harrison, whose work T. S. Eliot admired, also provided evidence of ancient belief that life continued in the grave, that the power of the dead was felt to be commensurate with that exercised by the living, and that ideas of taboo (the sacredness or profanity of certain deeds or things) had withstood change. Human sacrifice, long denied by admirers of "classical" values, was revealed to have had its place in Greek religion even in historic times. Removal of impurity was often effected or guaranteed by introducing into the "infected" place a pig, cock, or human being thought to absorb the infection before being destroyed. According to Harrison, the impetus for such rites lay in a perceived need to placate ghosts, enhance fertility, or purify oneself physically and morally. Whereas primitive cults of the dead poured libations on graves to placate or purge elusive spirits, said Harrison, the Hellenists propitiated deities replete with human faults. The Olympian form of worship (of a higher, purer nature) celebrated light, beauty, and conscious intelligence; the chthonic (more intimate and instinctive) encompassed magic, witchcraft, and death. The latter found expression in mourning for the maiden, Koré (Persephone); her grieving mother, Demeter; and Dionysos, son of Semele. Olympian ritual (of the sky) separated people from divinity; chthonic ritual (distinctly of the earth) brought

the two together. J.A.K. Thomson (*Studies in the Odyssey*, 1914) built on Harrison's work, pointing to the common heritage of epos and drama. At its source, he argued, Homeric epic is the birth-song of Apollo, Olympic god of light and reason; Attic tragedy, incorporating the ecstatic spirit of the Dionysia, is lament for Odysseus—epic poet, mythic hero, king, and god derived from one figure: the leader of the magic-making tribal dance.

The Cantos reflect Olympian ritual and its chthonic predecessor. Canto 1's translation of the *nekuia* preserves Homer's superimposition of ritual elements, fireless sacrifice and consignment by fire; even after Tiresias is summoned, chthonic rites dominate the work's sacrificial acts. The poem gains immeasurably as a result. The melancholic tone established in its early lines, "Heavy with weeping, and winds from sternward / Bore us outward with bellying canvas, / Circe's this craft," is reinforced by the blood sacrifice of Odysseus and sustained. Pound was evidently aware that in the rift between primitive ritual and its Hellenistic refinements lay the stuff of tragedy. He makes the division between Olympia and Chthonos particularly clear in Canto 17 (Bush 134), wherein an Ithacan homecoming reveals the dual nature of his Homeric alter ego: "Gods, / Hermes and Athene, / As shaft of compass, / Between them, trembled." Pound's characterization of Odysseus as worshipper, ancestor, lover, tyrant, and divine hero exploits the tension between the two forms of worship in embodying more than one ancient religious impulse: As an individual in quest of knowledge, the hero sacrifices; as Osiris, Adonis, and Dionysos incarnate, he is *sacrificed* so that a group dynamic (deified in Aphrodite Urania) may be reborn.

Bibliography

Bush, Ronald. *The Genesis of Ezra Pound's Cantos.* Princeton: Princeton UP, 1976.

Davenport, Guy. "Persephone's Ezra." *New Approaches to Ezra Pound.* Ed. Eva Hesse. Berkeley: U of California P, 1969. 145–173.

———. "Pound and Frobenius." *Motive and Method in the Cantos of Ezra Pound.* Ed. Lewis Leary. New York: Columbia UP, 1954. 33–59.

Dekker, George. "Myth and Metamorphosis: Two Aspects of Myth in *The Cantos*." *New Approaches to Ezra Pound*. Ed. Eva Hesse. Berkeley: U of California P, 1969. 280–302.

Emery, Clark. *Ideas into Action: A Study of Pound's Cantos*. 1958. Coral Gables: U of Miami P, 1969.

Harrison, Jane Ellen. *Prolegomena to the Study of Greek Religion*. 1903. London: Merlin, 1980.

Kearns, George. *Ezra Pound: The Cantos*. Cambridge, Cambridge UP, 1989.

Pratt, William, ed. *Ezra Pound, Nature and Myth*. New York: AMS P, 2002.

Rachewiltz, Boris de. "Pagan and Magic Elements in Ezra Pound's Works." *New Approaches to Ezra Pound*. Ed. Eva Hesse. London: Faber, 1969. 174–197.

Surette, Leon. *The Birth of Modernism: Ezra Pound, T. S. Eliot, W. B. Yeats and the Occult*. Montreal: McGill–Queen's UP, 1993.

Tryphonopoulos, Demetres P. *The Celestial Tradition: A Study of Ezra Pound's The Cantos*. Waterloo: Wilfrid Laurier UP, 1992.

Diane Reid

N

The Natural Philosophy of Love

Coincident with his interest in the Provençal poets and troubadours, Pound's discovery of Remy de Gourmont in early 1912 was by way of F. S. Flint, whose recommendation of de Gourmont and review of Paul Delior's *Remy de Gourmont et son oeuvre* (1909) were of special interest to Pound. Pound's 1912 lecture "Psychology and Troubadours" drew on de Gourmont's *Le Latin mystique* (Paris, 1892), and Pound's essays of the period show an awareness of the older poet's *Le Problème du style* (Paris, 1902), the work that enabled Pound to move beyond the Symbolist abstractions of Yeats and Symons to a poetics rooted in the concrete and particular.

A polymath with wide cultural and historical interests, de Gourmont was editor of *Mercure de France*, author of forty books, and of ultimate interest to Pound because of his uncompromising scholarly independence. Pound admired especially in de Gourmont's writing the virtues of honesty and concision, practiced without consideration of tact and detached from institutional or ideological loyalties. With a lucidity emulating invention, de Gourmont was the elder in France that Ford Madox Ford had been in England.

In 1913, Pound began translating de Gourmont's work for the *Egoist*, and after editing a special de Gourmont number of the *Little Review* (February–March 1919), he translated *Physique de l'amour: Essai sur l'instinct sexuel* (Paris, 1903) in 1921 as part of a contract with the small New York publisher Boni & Liveright. *The Natural Philosophy of Love* was published in 1922, along with Pound's "Translator's Postscript." Like *Les Chevaux de Diomède* (Paris, 1897), *Physique de l'amour* is tepid soft porn, so effete that Pound referred to it as pornography for pastors ("pink sensuality" was Yeats's phrase). Nevertheless, its content was controversial enough that the group thought best suited to release the first English edition (1926) was The Casanova Society.

Physique de l'amour's general argument equates human sexuality with animalism, celebrating the naturalness of sex and condemning the various bourgeois moralities, Christianity foremost among them, intent on censoring, even perverting, sexual instinct. De Gourmont argues that the cults of virginity and fidelity, the perversion of abstinence, and the taboos of adultery, homosexuality, and promiscuity are a corruption of pagan sexuality and appetite and that humankind would be well served by a sexual liberation.

Pound's "Translator's Postscript" picks up de Gourmont's suggestions of the relationship between sexual and cerebral freedom and functioning and advances the more esoteric conclusion that the brain is a repository of seminal fluid, and thus the source of generative impulse, whether sexual or creative. Evident in the "Postscript" is also an idea that Pound would develop some months later in a review of Louis Berman's *Glands Regulating Personality* (1921). Describing women as passive and conservative, and men as innovative and daring, Pound uses de Gourmont's notion of cerebral spermatozoid and Berman's glandular hypotheses to propose a cultural theory of sexual biology that later theorists would take up.

Physique de l'amour and "Postscript" reflect both the intense Freudian and Darwinian speculations of the period, as well as the libertine allowances that held vogue in Paris in the early 1920s. De Gourmont's biological theory of culture would be further developed by Pound when he encountered the *Kulturmorphologie* of Leo Frobenius.

Bibliography

Burne, Glenn. *Remy de Gourmont: His Ideas and Influences in England and America.* Carbondale: Southern Illinois UP, 1963.

Bush, Ronald. *The Genesis of Ezra Pound's Cantos.* Princeton: Princeton UP, 1976.

Sieburth, Richard. *Instigations: Ezra Pound and Remy de Gourmont.* Cambridge: Harvard UP, 1978.

Uitti, Karl. *La Passion littéraire de Remy de Gourmont.* Paris: Presses Universitaires, 1962.

Tony Tremblay

"Near Perigord"

"Near Perigord" appeared in *Poetry* 3.3 in December 1915 and was reprinted in *Lustra*. It engages with the Occitan troubadour Bertran de Born's canzon *"Dompna puois de mi no'us cal,"* Ezra Pound's translation of which had been published in *Poetry and Drama* in 1914 and was reprinted with "Near Perigord" in *Poetry*. Bertran assembles an imaginary *"dompna soiseubuda,"* a "borrowed lady," by combining characteristics of various women of Provence in the hope that this "patchwork mistress" will equal Maent, who rejects him. The speaker of "Near Perigord" conjectures that Bertran's poem may conceal military ambition: "Is it a love poem? Did he sing of war?" Pound's reading of Bertran, including the identification of Maent as the troubadour's beloved, is based on the *razo* by Uc St. Circ, to whom the opening stanza refers.

"Near Perigord" is divided into three sections. Section I examines "fact" and provides a condensed rewriting of the canzon, accompanied by quotations from other poems by Bertran. Through observations of the landscape around Bertran's castle at Hautefort (Altaforte), the speaker speculates on a possible military strategy; like "Provincia Deserta," "Near Perigord" attempts to access the past through topography. Section II turns to "fiction" in dramatic scenes of the canzon's composition, performance, and reception, including a conversation between Arnaut Daniel and King Richard Coeur de Lion, contemporaries of Bertran. The italicized lines at the end of Section II provide a concentrated translation of *Inferno* XXVII, 118–142, in which Dante defines Bertran as instigator of strife. Lines 22–27 in Section I are concerned with the same passage in Dante, here narrated with inserted citations rather than translated. A keyword in Dante's text, *contrapasso*, appears throughout "Near Perigord," as "counterpass," "counterpart," and "counterthrust." In *Poetry*, Section III opens with two lines deleted in subsequent editions: "I loved a woman. The stars fell from heaven. / And always our two natures were in strife," identifying Bertran as the speaker of the section's lyrical meditation on love.

Sections I and II are related to the dramatic monologue and address a "Messire Cino": "Solve me the riddle, for you know the tale." Question marks abound and signal the hypothetical nature of the many suppositions; throughout, "Near Perigord" depends on elements of typography, including italics and quotation marks. With its patchwork of rewritten quotations, speculations, and dramatic scenes, the poem parallels Bertran's borrowed lady, as well as Section III's definition of Maent as a "broken bundle of mirrors."

The voice that assembles dialogues and condensed quotations relies on interrogatives and imperatives rather than on narrative exposition. It foreshadows the discussion in the "Ur-Cantos" of the relation of Browning's verse to historical fact, while the juxtaposition of scenes points to the technique of *The Cantos*.

The epigraph quotes lines 36–37 of Bertran's *"Un sierventes on Metz non fail,"* translated in *The Spirit of Romance* as "At Perigord near to the wall." The title thus presents a combination of metonymic condensation, topography, and literary translation characteristic of Pound's verse.

Bibliography

de Born, Bertran. *The Poems of the Troubadour Bertran de Born.* Ed. William D. Paden, Jr., Tilde Sankovitch, and Patricia H. Stäblein. Berkeley: U of California P, 1986.

Line Henriksen

New Age

The *New Age* was a weekly socialist magazine founded in London by Frederick Atkins in 1894. When A. R. Orage began editing the publication in 1907, he intended to use it to discuss all realms of culture and thought. Ezra Pound met Orage through T. E. Hulme in 1911. Pound was acquainted with Hulme's circle of poet friends, one of whom, F. S. Flint, had written of Pound favorably in the *New Age* during the previous year. Orage proved himself something of a visionary by agreeing to print in his magazine Pound's translations of Anglo-Saxon, Provençal, and Tuscan verse, while giving the poet free reign to pursue his own interests in the prose he published. Pound began to espouse his "new method of scholarship" in "I Gather the Limbs of Osiris," beginning in November 1911, and his thoughts on the United States were expressed in *Patria Mia*, the first of eleven installments appearing in September 1912. In addition to providing him a vehicle for some of his first important prose, Pound's association with the *New Age* was significant in this early period for a number of other practical reasons: Pound forged through Orage connections with yet another significant circle of intellectuals in London; the editorial policy of the magazine and the fact that Orage paid his contributors helped the poet establish a degree of professional freedom in the period before World War I; Pound's growing familiarity with the editorial procedures of the *New Age* offered the poet a period of apprenticeship that would make him a prolific periodical writer into the mid-1920s.

By 1917, Pound had been touched by the interdisciplinary approach taken in the *New Age*. He began to think seriously about socialism and a range of features of modern society. He also began to write art and music criticism for the magazine. While he disguised much of this activity under pen names and dismissed the writing as necessary to sustain himself in London, there is little doubt that his growing range of interests influenced his understanding of Modernism. At the *New Age* offices in 1918, Pound was introduced to Major C. H. Douglas. Douglas's ideas about society and economics interested Pound a great deal. Working with Douglas and Orage, Pound helped shape stray ideas into a program that would later become Social Credit. Beyond the influence of Douglas's thought on Pound, meeting Douglas reminded the poet of the necessity of systematizing one's thought.

Pound contributed regularly to the *New Age* until he left London, placing more than 300 articles there by 1921. He was informed in Paris that the magazine could no longer afford to pay him, and his involvement waned. Orage left the magazine in 1922 to work for G. I. Gurdjieff, first in France and then in the United States. The magazine continued to publish until 1938 under the editorship of Arthur Moore and, later, Arthur Brenton.

Bibliography

Martin, Wallace. *The New Age under Orage.* Manchester: Manchester UP, 1967.

Craig Monk

New Directions

Ezra Pound's "creation" of New Directions is an oft-told tale. In the summer of 1933, at the suggestion of his Choate master, Dudley Fitts, James Laughlin, a Harvard undergraduate and an heir to the Jones-Laughlin steel fortune, made a brief visit to Rapallo to meet Pound. Laughlin returned in the fall of 1934 for a stay of several months at the "Ezuversity." When Pound determined (in a rare lapse of his fabled literary perspicacity) that the young man would never "make it" as a poet, he encouraged Laughlin to "go back to Amurrica and do something useful." Pound shrewdly and sensibly told "Jaz" to complete his studies at Harvard, approach his parents for seed money, and start a publishing firm. Pound would provide contacts and encourage his friends to submit manuscripts. And essentially that is what happened. The initial

New Directions book was the 1936 anthology *New Directions in Prose and Poetry* (containing Pound's Canto 44), the first of many ground-breaking introductions of Modernist writers. *Culture* (later *Guide to Kulchur*), brought out in 1938, was the first Pound title published by New Directions. Laughlin then began to bring out the essays in collaboration with Pound's British publisher, Faber and Faber, to gradually take over the editions of poems originally done by other American publishers such as the 1933 *A Draft of XXX Cantos* (published by New Directions in 1940) and the 1926 *Personae* (ND, 1946) and to publish new sections of *The Cantos* as they were completed. There are currently twenty-eight titles by Pound on the New Directions list.

Laughlin recounted the above story on many occasions and wrote about his relationship with Pound in *Pound as Wuz*, *Random Essays*, and elsewhere. In deference to his revered mentor (always referred to as "Boss"), Laughlin obscured his own independence as a publisher; but he never let New Directions become Pound's private sounding board and stated the vital role he played in creating the audience for Modernism in general and Pound's work in particular. (Greg Barnhisel's 1999 dissertation—recently published by the University of Massachusetts Press—on New Directions is a valuable study in this regard.) Without Pound, there would not be a New Directions; and without New Directions and James Laughlin's determination to make Pound's work (and that of Pound's friends) known and keep it available, the map of twentieth-century literature would be unrecognizable.

Bibliography

Barnhisel, Greg. *James Laughlin, New Directions Press, and the Re-Making of Ezra Pound.* Amherst: U of Massachusetts P, 2004.

Laughlin, James. *Pound as Wuz: Essays and Lectures on Ezra Pound.* Saint Paul: Greywolf P, 1987.

———. *Random Essays.* Mt. Kisco: Moyer Bell, 1989.

Pound, Ezra. *Ezra Pound and James Laughlin: Selected Letters.* Ed. David M. Gordon. New York: Norton, 1994.

Peggy L. Fox

New English Weekly

The *New English Weekly* was begun in London by A. R. Orage in 1932. Orage had returned to England from the United States the year before, and he sought to resume his abandoned editorial position with the *New Age*. When this proved impossible, he planned a new magazine, and he resolved to surround himself with contributors whom he had used in the earlier venture. This arrangement proved beneficial for Ezra Pound, whose preoccupation with social and economic matters estranged him from many literary magazines through the 1930s. Pound's first contribution appeared in the *New English Weekly* in June 1932; over the next eight years, he placed nearly 200 pieces there. Although Orage died in 1934, his widow Jesse continued to publish the magazine until 1949 with Philip Mairet as editor.

Craig Monk

New Masses

An ideological successor to the similarly named proletarian magazine published between January 1911 and November 1917, the *New Masses* first appeared in New York in May 1926. Dominated through much of the late 1920s by Mike Gold, the publication reflected many of his diverse interests, sometimes to the chagrin of American socialists. By the end of 1926, the magazine caught the attention of Ezra Pound; his initial correspondence with its editors led them to exclaim, prematurely, "Pound joins the revolution." He did use the magazine to publish appreciations of George Antheil, but Pound soon argued publicly with coeditor Hugo Gellert over politics in literature. His collaboration with the magazine was quickly truncated but not before the *New Masses* aired some of his pro-fascist views to readers in the United States. In March 1936, the publication released some of Pound's correspondence with the Silver Shirt Legion of America, accusing him of functioning as "an intellectual front" for fascism.

Craig Monk

The Novel

Ezra Pound's most important contribution to the novel is probably his role as the friend, promoter, and editor of novelists. The list of novelists that Pound befriended, corresponded with, and often aided includes many luminaries, such as Henry James, Thomas Hardy, James Joyce, Wyndham Lewis, Ford Madox Ford (Hueffer), D. H. Lawrence, and Ernest Hemingway. Older novelists such as James and Ford had an effect on the formation of Pound's own critical sense. He shares with them their respect for the accomplishments of nineteenth-century French novelists. The younger prose writers Pound knew were able to benefit from his position in the literary world. The poet's connection to a number of little magazines such as the *Little Review* and the *transatlantic review* allowed him to help his novelist colleagues get published. Pound was also able to help with the more pragmatic concern of keeping the novelists fed and clothed by putting them in touch with benefactors and collectors such as John Quinn.

Pound published criticism of novelists, though he dealt with them more summarily than he did his greater interests of economics or poetry. His earliest informal statements about the genre are sometimes uninformed and often negative. In a 1914 letter to Joyce, he remarks that English prose is something he rarely peruses, aside from James, Hudson, and Conrad (*L/JJ* 24). The affection that Pound had for Joyce's art was based on the fact that Joyce's prose was characterized by the hard clarity that Pound found in the best of the continental authors, such as Flaubert. Pound later confessed that he rarely read novels, other than those of James or Flaubert, for specific purposes. Despite his relative disinterest in the novel, Pound had become appreciative enough of the novelist's art to undertake a reading of Henry James's entire canon in preparation for an essay following James's death. As with Joyce, Pound tends to evaluate James in terms of French models. In his evaluations of Joyce and James, Pound defends the prose style that he celebrated in "How to Read."

In that essay, Pound, in the footsteps of Stendhal, held up prose as a model for poetry. In prose, Pound argues, can be found language in service of effective communication, a use that is lost to contemporary English poetry. Pound proposes that not only good prose but also good modern verse can come only after knowledge of the developments of Flaubert and Stendhal. Nevertheless, Pound was capable of observing that the tenor of the two languages and relative development of their prose demanded different qualities. In "The Hard and Soft in French Poetry," Pound evaluates French and English prose by different standards. For the French, Pound argues, the measure of success is how well a norm has been achieved. For the English novelist, good prose must be adapted to the individual voice, the personal language of the creator.

By the 1930s, Pound had apparently had enough experience with novelists and the novel to include some recommendations in *ABC of Reading*. At the top of the list of practitioners in English were Fielding and Austen, with places reserved for Sterne, Trollope, James, and Ford. Pound felt that, as in poetry, many of the best examples were not written in English. In the case of the novel, the best work has come from France, where Stendhal, Flaubert, and the Goncourts have produced many of the greatest achievements. Pound also mentions and praises the Spaniard Galdos. He shows no sign of having read the Russians.

Bibliography

Carpenter, Humphrey. *A Serious Character: The Life of Ezra Pound*. Boston: Houghton Mifflin, 1988.

Pound, Ezra. "How to Read, or Why. Part I: Introduction." *New York Herald Tribune Books* (13 January 1929): [1], 6; "Part II: Or What May Be an Introduction to Method" (20 January 1929): [1], 5–6; "Part III: Conclusions, Exceptions, Curricula" (27 January 1929): [1], 5–6.

Christopher K. Coffman

O

Olson, Charles (1910–1970)

Charles Olson was the leading Postmodernist interpreter of the Modernist practice of poetry in the line of Pound and Williams and a central figure, along with Robert Creeley and Robert Duncan, in the so-called Black Mountain School of poetry. Williams appropriated Olson's manifesto, the "Projective Verse" essay (1950), for a chapter in *The Autobiography of William Carlos Williams*. His teaching and his poetry influenced a whole generation of post-Poundian writers, including Edward Dorn, Joel Oppenheimer, and Ed Sanders. His vision, after his reading of Pound and Melville, was epic and boldly speculative, especially in his four-volume *The Maximus Poems*, which, like Pound's own "poem including history," ended only with the poet's life.

Olson was thirty-five and had published only four poems when he met Pound at St. Elizabeths. He had trained at Wesleyan to be a Melville scholar (his iconoclastic *Call Me Ishmael* was published, against the advice of Edward Dahlberg, in 1947) and had given over his position in the Democratic National Party to turn to the writing of poetry. The evolution of Olson's early dealings with Pound are a paradigm for his formative thinking about poetry. In 1946, Olson published in the *Partisan Review* "This Is Yeats Speaking," his defense of Pound against charges of treason. Olson's impressions from his visits to St. Elizabeths from 1946 to 1948 were recorded in a manuscript he called "Cantos" (published in *Charles Olson and Ezra Pound: An Encounter at St. Elizabeths*). In a note Pound scribbled during the time of Olson's visits, he wrote: "Olson saved my life." By 1948, in his memoir "GrandPa, GoodBye," Olson is distancing himself from Pound's prejudices and his views of the primacy of the mind over the body, preparing to take on his rethinking of *The Cantos* leading to his *Maximus Poems* (begun in 1950). Still, in Olson's first poem in his mature style, "The Kingfishers" (1949), he will recognize his debt to Pound, his "next of kin." His 1950 trip to the Yucatan Peninsula to study Mayan hieroglyphics can be understood as an extension of Pound's interest in Chinese written characters (his field letters to Creeley are collected in *Mayan Letters*, 1953).

Olson first came to Black Mountain College, in North Carolina, at the behest of Josef Albers, in 1948. Later on, he became teacher and rector there until its close in 1956. He resided in Gloucester, Massachusetts, starting in 1957, where he wrote his *Maximus Poems* of Poundian history and Williamsonian place, leaving only to teach briefly at State University of New York at Buffalo and the University of Connecticut.

Olson's *Collected Prose* (1997) rivals Pound's speculations on culture and literature. His voluminous correspondence with Creeley, beginning in 1950, is in part a testament to the younger poet's derivation from the model of Pound. The first ten volumes have been published as *Charles Olson & Robert Creeley: The Complete Correspondence* (1980–   ).

Bibliography

Butterick, George, and Richard Blevins, eds. *Charles Olson & Robert Creeley: The Complete Correspondence*. Santa Barbara: Black Sparrow P, 1980–   .

Olson, Charles. "Projective Verse." *Selected Writings*. Ed. Robert Creeley. New York: New Directions,

1966. (Quoted extensively in William Carlos Williams' *Autobiography*, chapter 50.)

Seelye, Catherine, ed. *Charles Olson and Ezra Pound: An Encounter at St. Elizabeths.* New York: Grossman Publishers, 1975.

Richard L. Blevins

Oppen, George (1908–1984)

Although he was to break with Pound in horror of his fascist politics and epic ambitions, George Oppen remained to the end of his career perhaps the truest practitioner of Pound's principle of *phanopoeia*. In Oppen's poetry, the writer's perception—of objects, groupings, a landscape—becomes necessary poetic form. It is the poet's ethos that the clearer his perception, the truer the expression.

Oppen emerged, in New York, in the late 1920s, as an original member of the Objectivist group of poets, including Luis Zukofsky and Charles Reznikoff, who were galvanized by the Modernist manifestos of Pound. The Objectivists came to prominence after spokesman Zukofsky's "Objectivist" issue of *Poetry* (February 1931). From Le Beausset, France, he and his wife Mary Oppen worked as publishers for To Press, with Zukofsky on salary as editor. They published Pound's *How to Read* but returned to the United States, in 1933, before realizing a projected complete prose of Pound. In 1930, Oppen traveled once to Rapallo to meet Pound, who was to include him in his *Active Anthology* (1933). In the fall of that year, even while he was becoming increasingly disaffected with Pound's politics, the cooperative Objectivist Press that Oppen and Zukofsky established (at Pound's instigation) published Oppen's first book, *Discrete Series*, from poems he had begun as early as 1928. The book featured a preface by Pound, and it was reviewed by William Carlos Williams for *Poetry* (July 1934).

In 1935, his growing social concerns, especially over the rise of fascism and the economic depression, led Oppen to join the Communist Party. Refusing to be used by the Party, he began a sabbatical from writing poetry that would last until 1958. He had stopped writing, he told Harvey Shapiro, "midpoem." Oppen's active

Party membership lasted from 1936 to 1941, when he made another of the momentous decisions that characterize his life. Although he was too old for the draft, enjoyed a machinist's work exemption, and was the father of a daughter (Linda Jean, b. 1940), he was inducted into the infantry, in November 1942, eventually seeing action in the Battle of the Bulge. On 22 April 1945, he was wounded in action.

After the war, Oppen worked as a carpenter in Redondo Beach, California, until he and Mary Oppen were driven into Mexico to flee an FBI investigation in June 1950. The Oppens were at length granted U.S. passports, in 1958, and they returned to the United States, where, in May, Oppen wrote "Blood from the Stone," his first poem in nearly twenty-five years. His second book, *The Materials*, appeared to critical acclaim in 1962, followed by *This in Which* in 1965. Oppen was hailed by a generation of younger American poets as a link with the tradition of Pound and Williams. However, by 1962, Oppen's break with Pound was complete. In a rare essay, "Three Poets" (*Poetry*, August 1962), his review of Charles Olson, Allen Ginsberg, and Michael McClure, he rejects the younger poets' work because he finds it tainted by Pound's influence. Fame arrived with the 1969 Pulitzer Prize for *Of Being Numerous* (1968). The Oppens moved to San Francisco in 1967. In 1976, *The Collected Poems of George Oppen* (1975) was nominated for a National Book Award. Mary Oppen's memoir of their marriage, *Meaning a Life*, is the only biography.

Bibliography

Hatlen, Burton, ed. *George Oppen, Man and Poet.* Orono: NPF, 1981.

Oppen, Mary. *Meaning a Life: An Autobiography.* Santa Barbara: Black Sparrow P, 1978.

Richard L. Blevins

Orage, A. R. (1873–1934)

Alfred James (later Richard) Orage was born on 22 January 1873 in Dacre, Yorkshire, to an impoverished working-class family. A schoolteacher at first, he taught at a Leeds elementary school and helped found the Leeds branch of the Independent Labor Party. In 1901, with Holbrook

Jackson, he established the Leeds Arts Club. Orage moved to London in 1906 and, with A. J. Penty, founded the Fabian Arts Group in 1907. That year George Bernard Shaw and Lewis Wallace each loaned Orage and Jackson £500 to purchase the *New Age*. The new coeditors subtitled the journal "An Independent Socialist Review of Politics, Literature, and Art." Jackson parted amicably at the end of the year. From 1908 to 1922 Orage served as sole editor of what would soon become the most remarkable English-language journal of the twentieth century.

Of his changing attitudes during those years Orage wrote: "Like every intellectual in those days . . . I began as some sort of socialist" ("An Editor's Progress" 376). His socialism blended Theosophy, Nietzsche, Plato, Morris, and Shaw, though his Fabian ties were quickly abandoned. Early on *New Age* advocated partial control of various industries by their respective trade unions, an early form of Syndicalism, and, following Penty, the restoration of the guild system. It published a series of articles under the title of "National Guilds." World War I quickly put to an end the aspirations of Syndicalism and socialism as trade unions throughout Europe offered full support to their respective national sovereigns.

Orage never lost his profound empathy with the working class, and during the Great War he continually denounced the inequality of the sacrifice they were called on to make. He called for the conscription of capital as well as men, the sacrifice of war-industry profit as well as lives. The war brought to Orage the growing and often repeated understanding that "financial power precedes political power," that England was governed by a half-hidden plutocracy advancing its own interests over those of the nation. Possessing what he described as "a professional interest in economics," which led him, among other things, "to master Marx's *Das Kapital*," Orage's deepening concern with war finance prepared him for his momentous meeting with C. H. Douglas (376).

Orage later believed that his advocacy of guild socialism "and all the rest" served only as preparation for "the ideas of Douglas" (379). "I knew, without being able exactly to diagnose it, that the whole idea of National Guilds . . . was wanting in some vital part . . . the relation of the whole scheme to the existing, or any prospective system of money" (402).

Orage met Douglas during the latter part of the war and found his knowledge of economics "extraordinary" (402). "He said many things in our first talk that blinded me with light," he recalled (403). Douglas's theory of Social Credit showed "that every member of the community is justly entitled to a social dividend, work or no work," and it seemed to offer a way out of the boom- and bust-cycle of industrial capitalism, freeing the productive capacity of the nation without the need of war (404). Orage introduced Pound to Douglas in 1918. By 1919 *New Age* had become the de facto Social Credit organ.

Convinced equally of the correctness of Douglas's solution and the impossibility of its ever being realized, Orage resigned the editorship of *New Age* late in 1922 to become a disciple of G. I. Gurdjieff in France. In December 1923 he left for New York City to take charge of disseminating Gurdjieff's teachings in the United States.

Orage returned to London in 1930 and started *New English Weekly* on 21 April 1932. The journal closely resembled *New Age* and was subtitled "A Review of Public Affairs, Literature and the Arts." Once again, Orage provided Pound with one of his few outlets in the British press. *New English Weekly* published over 200 of Pound's reviews, letters, articles (including many on political and economic subjects), poems (including Canto 61 and over twenty of the *Alfred Venison's Poems*), and a regular column, "American Notes," during the period 1932 to 1940. In the first issue, in the column "Readers and Writers," Orage wrote: "As I was saying ten years ago when my literary studies were suddenly lifted to another plane, Mr. Ezra Pound is one of our very few major men of letters" (10).

After giving a radio talk on Social Credit over the BBC on 5 November 1934, Orage, the man with the liveliest mind in England, died in his sleep early the next day. Tributes were quick in coming. In the memorial issue of *New English*

Weekly, T. S. Eliot called him "the best critic of that time [1912–1922] in London." Pound recalled: "[F]or one period we seemed almost to get out the old *New Age* between us. . . . [He was] the man whose weekly guinea fed me when no one else was ready to do so, and that for at least two years" (*SP* 437). In the April 1935 issue of the *Criterion*, Pound wrote: "He was a moralist, and thence an economist." Pound's most moving tributes to Orage appear in *The Cantos*: "But the lot of 'em, Yeats, Possum and Wyndham / had no ground beneath 'em. / [ideogram for bird in flight] / Orage had" (Canto 98). "Orage held the basic was pity / *compassione*" (Canto 111).

Orage was among the first to champion Nietzsche and Freud in London. He provided Pound with a thorough education in politics and economics. He never censored his contributors' writing. His conversational skills were legendary. His greatest accomplishment, the *New Age*, still bears close examination and deep study. It possesses continuing relevance.

(*Note*: Pound's contributions to the *New Age*, starting with a letter in 1910 and running through 1922, are too numerous for brief description. Fortunately nearly the entire run of the journal is already available online, the first product of the outstanding Modernist Journals Project, http://www.modjourn.brown.edu/.)

Bibliography

Mairet, Philip. *A. R. Orage*. London: Dent, 1936.
Martin, Wallace. *The New Age under Orage: Chapters in English Cultural History*. Manchester: Manchester UP, 1967.
Orage, A. R. "An Editor's Progress: I. The New Age." *Commonweal* (10 February 1926): 376–379; "II. The Douglas Revelation" (17 February 1926): 402–404; "III. The Impossibility of Reform" (24 February 1926): 434–435; "IV. The Quest of God" (3 March 1926): 456–457.
———. *Orage as Critic*. Ed. Wallace Martin. London: Routledge, 1974.
Redman, Tim. *Ezra Pound and Italian Fascism*. New York: Cambridge UP, 1991.
Selver, Paul. *Orage and the New Age Circle*. London: George Allen and Unwin, 1959.
Taylor, Paul Beekman. *Gurdjieff and Orage: Brothers in Elysium*. York Beach: Weiser Books, 2001.
Thatcher, David S. *Nietzsche in England 1890–1914*. Toronto: U of Toronto P, 1970.

Tim Redman

Orientamenti

Comprising thirty-eight brief articles in Italian, collected in a guide to "orient" or "direct," *Orientamenti* was printed in Venice by Edizioni Popolari in September 1944. The book's distribution was held up for weeks until a decision was made to scrap the entire run—but not before the author's copy and a number of review copies had already been distributed. The decision was taken presumably because either the Salò regime objected to it or it was felt that the timing for the book's publication was wrong since it would do Pound's case no good in the face of the imminent victory of the Allies. Indeed, the 1945 FBI investigation of Pound's activities in Italy included a translation of the book into English. The text has not been reissued.

With the exception of the first three items, the rest are reprinted from *Meridiano di Roma*, comprising articles that first appeared between 1939 and 1942. Only apparently disjointed, they all deal with economics, Pound's most urgent concern of the late 1930s. (See entry on *Meridiano di Roma* for a discussion of the common themes recurring in Pound's articles.)

Stefano Maria Casella

P

Paideuma [journal]

The first issue of *Paideuma*, subtitled "A Journal Devoted to Ezra Pound Scholarship," was published in 1972, with Hugh Kenner and Eva Hesse as senior editors; Donald Davie, Donald Gallup, and Lewis Leary as editors; and Carroll F. Terrell as managing editor. The senior editors and editors supplied advice, but in fact "Terry" Terrell exercised almost total editorial control from the start. The first issue includes major articles by John Peck, Walter B. Michaels, Donald Davie, and John Espey, along with shorter notes by Hugh Kenner, Eva Hesse, and William Chace. Guy Davenport contributed a cover drawing; he also designed the typeface of the title and divider pages that have been used throughout the history of the journal. Beginning with the second issue, most issues were divided into "The Periplum" (major articles), "The Explicator" (shorter notes explaining references in Pound's text), "The Biographer" (notes by people who had known Pound), "The Documentary" (reprints of primary documents relevant to Pound's work), "The Gallery" (pictures of Pound and his associates), "The Bibliographer," and "The Reviewer."

Throughout its history the emphasis of *Paideuma* has fallen more on scholarship than on criticism: The journal tended to assume Pound's importance as a poet and thus devoted itself not to arguing for the significance of the work but rather to elucidating references in *The Cantos* and documenting the poet's career. Nevertheless, over its history the journal has also published important critical essays on Pound by, among others, John Peck, Eva Hesse, Leon Surette, David Moody, Jacob Korg, Herbert N. Schneidau, Donald Davie, Ian Bell, M. L. Rosenthal, James Powell, Kevin Oderman, Daniel Pearlman, Akiko Miyake, Angela Elliott, Walter Baumann, Peter Stoicheff, Stephen Sicari, Daniel Bornstein, Helen Dennis, Kathryne Lindberg, Marjorie Perloff, Michael Coyle, Ellen Keck Stauder, Demetres Tryphonopoulos, Peter Dale Scott, Norman Wacker, Daniel Tiffany, and many others. *Paideuma* has also published special issues devoted to Louis Zukofsky, George Oppen, Basil Bunting, and Pound and African American Modernism. Beginning with volume 31 in 2002, *Paideuma* widened its scope to include scholarship on other British and American Modernist poets along with Pound.

Burton Hatlen

Paideuma

Pound takes this word from the work of Leo Frobenius, the German ethnologist noted for his fieldwork in Africa in the early years of this century. In *Guide to Kulchur* (1938) Pound writes, "To escape a word or a set of words loaded up with dead association Frobenius uses the term *paideuma* for the tangle or complex of the inrooted ideas of any period" (57). Pound differentiates *paideuma* from the Romantic concept of the Zeitgeist and uses it to designate what he calls "the gristly roots of ideas that are in action" (*GK* 58). The word *paideuma* derives from *paedeutics*, the science or art of education, and is central to Pound's purpose in the *Guide to Kulchur*, which is concerned with a "conscious renovation of learning," and in this is like *How* to Read, *ABC of Reading*, *ABC of Economics*, and his many other prose works that constitute an unorthodox pedagogy. In *Guide to Kulchur*, *paideuma* is a descriptive term applied to all those thinkers whose work he values, from Confucius to the present, and a prescriptive term invoked as a pedagogic principle. Like the Vortex, defined by Pound as "a radiant node or cluster . . . from which, through which, and into which, ideas are constantly rushing" (*GB* 92), *paideuma* signals the illuminating energy of intellectual perception and understanding that Pound saw as native to the inductive methods of enquiry in scientists such as Frobenius and Louis Agassiz.

Pound admired Frobenius because his ideas of cultural history were derived from anthropological fieldwork rather than conceptual abstractions and were based on empirical evidence discovered in the traces left by ancient cultures in surviving artifacts and folk history in oral and written narratives, to be found in his books *The Voice of Africa* (1918), the seven-volume *Erlebte Erdteile* (1925–1929), and with Douglas C. Fox, *African Genesis* (1938). Frobenius developed the concept of "Kulturmorphologie," the idea that the defining characteristics of a particular civilization are discoverable from a limited number of its artifacts, and this corresponds with Pound's belief in the value of what he called "luminous details," fragments of historical evidence such as cave paintings, fossils, torn papyrus, and so on, which provide access to the geological, racial, and cultural characteristics of past civilizations from which the fundamental truths of human culture could be understood and communicated. Frobenius's work gave tacit support to Pound's belief in the cyclical view of human history, a narrative of the rise and fall of civilizations, and the consequential belief that to understand the "errors" of the past was to arm ourselves in the present and for the future. It is in these contexts that Frobenius is celebrated in the *Guide to Kulchur*, and if Confucius has pride of place as the indispensable thinker in human history, Frobenius is seen as a fit companion to him, along with Homer, Dante, and others.

There are five references to Frobenius himself in *The Cantos*, honorific citations indicative of his working practices and his value in bringing "the living fact to bear on the study of dead documents," in Cantos 38, 74, 87, 89, and 102; more significantly, Pound calls on Australasian and African legends—in Cantos 74 and 77—researched and communicated by Frobenius and his pupils. The first of these, in Canto 74, relates to ground drawings of the Australian folkloric figure of Wondjina said to have created the world by saying the names of things, whose prolific naming created so much that his father closed his mouth so that he could not speak. Pound deploys this in a customarily gnomic manner to suggest the necessity for silence in the face of ignorance, as in his appeal to historians to leave blanks in their histories for the things they do not know and, implicitly, to elevate verifiable truths from specious theorizing. Cantos 74 and 77 contain references to Gassir's lute and the figure of Wagadu, narratives drawn from the Fasa tribe of North Africa in Frobenius, specifically in the Soninke legend in which Wagadu is a female deity who variously manifests herself and survives as "the strength which lives in the hearts of men." Pound exploits this legend through the concept of Wagadu as an ideal city "in the mind" and connects it with other cultural manifestations of civic perfection such as Ecbatan, the fabulous city of the Median king Dioce. It should be noted that Pound's use of Frobenius in these cantos works to establish cross-cultural affiliations between legendary and recorded versions of human history, connections in themselves indicative of his belief in paideumistic learning.

Bibliography

Davenport, Guy. "Pound and Frobenius." *Motive and Method in the Cantos of Ezra Pound.* Ed. Lewis Leary. New York: Columbia UP, 1954. 33–59.

Lionel Kelly

Patria Mia

Unpublished in book form until 1950, *Patria Mia* is a reworking of "Patria Mia" and "America: Chances and Remedies"—both first published in the *New Age* from 5 September to 14

November 1912 and from 1 May and 5 June 1913, respectively. The book comprises an essay on the prospects for an "American Renaissance," an artistic efflorescence in the United States that would rival the Italian *Cinquecento*. The essay's first part laments the current, dire state of intellectual and artistic life in the country. Pound dismisses most Americans as ardent materialists unable to distinguish masterpieces from tripe. He also sharply criticizes *Atlantic*, *Century*, and other prominent journals for preferring mediocre, traditional writing to more adventurous material. He considers architecture to be America's only progressive art form and praises such impressive, monumental works as New York's Metropolitan Life Tower (1909) and Pennsylvania Station (1910). Talented, ambitious Americans who work in other media—such as Henry James and James McNeill Whistler—have rightly felt compelled to leave their homeland. The second part of *Patria Mia* argues, however, that the present-day "Dark Ages" could prove evanescent. Pound explains that millionaire-philanthropists such as J. P. Morgan and the Carnegies resemble latter-day Medicis. Handled properly, they could be persuaded to endow "super-colleges" capable of providing financial support, community, and mentorship to young artists. The result would be the rapid formation of an authentic, indigenous arts scene.

Brian M. Reed

Patronage of the Arts

Patronage was central to Ezra Pound's conception of the just society and the health of art and literature. Early in his career, he had been the recipient, for two years, of roughly $1,000 per year provided by Margaret Cravens, an American living in Paris. Although Cravens's gift was cut short when she committed suicide in 1912, her disinterested and intelligent generosity remained for Pound a model of what the relationship between the artist and the public could be.

Pound's faith in collaborative patronage was reinforced a few years later when John Quinn, the New York lawyer and art collector, responded to Pound's urging that he increase his support for living artists and writers. Before his death in 1924, Quinn had purchased manuscripts from T. S. Eliot and James Joyce and art by Henri Gaudier-Brzeska, Wyndham Lewis, Brancusi, and many others. Quinn also made outright gifts of money to artists, writers, and little magazines, occasionally in the form of a "loan" or a "salary." His indirect assistance included defending the *Little Review* editors against charges of publishing obscenity and his efforts to get Modernist authors printed in the United States. He personally saw to it that American editions of Pound's *Lustra* were issued without the deletions that had marred the English edition. Quinn's gallant, perspicacious support for living artists made him, in Pound's mind, a modern-day equivalent of Sigismondo Malatesta, the fifteenth-century Italian ruler who employed talented architects, painters, and sculptors to reconstruct the church of San Francesco in Rimini.

Pound's own support of artists and writers was generous, if sometimes disarmingly idiosyncratic. He provided cash gifts to Joyce, Eliot, Ford Madox Ford, Basil Bunting, and many others, yet his benefactions could be more concrete and direct: secondhand clothes for Joyce; meals for Eliot; a check drawn for Louis Zukofsky in the amount of a dollar. With his wife Dorothy, Pound purchased art by Lewis, Gaudier-Brzeska, and others. His most ambitious patronage scheme, dubbed "Bel Esprit," was to free Eliot from his bank job by assembling some thirty patrons to give an average of £10 per year for as long as Eliot should need it. Pound had obtained twenty-one pledges before the plan unraveled toward the end of 1922 as a result of Eliot's embarrassment and his unwillingness to throw up his bank position without a guarantee of greater financial security. Bel Esprit manifested the more quixotic side of Pound's drive to free artists from bureaucracy and drudgery. His most valuable acts of selflessness—as in his tireless work to get *Ulysses* and *Tarr* published and his brilliant editing of *The Waste Land*—are beyond monetary calculation and represent collaborative patronage in its purest form.

Pound had envisioned Bel Esprit as a sort of equity investment in genius that he likened, in a letter to Quinn, to investing in "small pearl-fishing ships . . . where there was a great deal of risk but a chance of infinite profit." With the onset of economic depression in the 1930s, Pound came to believe that support for artists must be grounded in the totalitarian state and fortified by Douglasite economics, stamp scrip, and the elimination of usury. By 1933, Pound's hopes for patronage were bound up with his faith in Mussolini, whom he saw as promoting "quality" in national production. In this respect as in others, Pound believed that Mussolini reincarnated the factive personality of Malatesta.

Pound's belief in patronage was rooted, from beginning to end, in a distrust of capitalism. His essential conception of patronage—despite the political and economic overlay of the 1930s and 1940s—was that of a voluntary collaboration of artist and benefactor that bypassed the arbitrariness and impersonality of market forces. Integrity in this relationship could be maintained if donors gave adequate but not lavish support to young writers and artists of genuine promise, thereby enabling them to concentrate solely on creating. If enough deserving beneficiaries could be brought together in cities or "super-colleges," a new Risorgimento might ensue. The antithesis of such intelligent, personalized generosity was the art world's speculation in old masters or the government's granting a stipend to a famous, aging poet. In Pound's conception, the true patron was neither speculator nor consumer but rather an equal of the artist and, in a sense, a cocreator. As he wrote Margaret Cravens in 1910 after learning of her gift to him, "[W]e both work together for the art which is bigger & outside of us" (Pound, 11).

Bibliography

Pound, Ezra. *Ezra Pound and Margaret Cravens: A Tragic Friendship 1910–1912.* Ed. Omar Pound and Robert Spoo. Durham: Duke UP, 1988.
Rainey, Lawrence Rainey. *Institutions of Modernism: Literary Elites and Public Culture.* New Haven: Yale UP, 1998.
Reid, B. L. *The Man from New York: John Quinn and His Friends.* New York: Oxford UP, 1968.

Robert Spoo

Pavannes and Divagations

Pavannes and Divagations is a 1958 collection with the stated intention of helping to "complete the record" by reprinting Pound's lighter and satiric works from the previous four decades. Most of the selections date from the period immediately after World War I: the loosely autobiographical sketch *Indiscretions, or Une Revue de Deux Mondes* (originally serialized in the *New Age*, May–August 1920, and published by William Bird's Three Mountain Press in 1923); Pound's contributions to the series of "Imaginary Letters" begun by Wyndham Lewis in the *Little Review* (May 1917–November 1918); several short prose pieces that comprised the "Pavannes" section of *Pavannes and Divisions* (1918); Pound's translation of "Twelve Dialogues of Fontenelle" (published 1917 by the Egoist Press); three selections from the short-lived Vorticist journal *BLAST* (1914–1915); "Genesis or, The First Book in the Bible" and "Our Tertrarchal Précieuse" from *Instigations* (1920); and Pound's Postscript to his translation of Remy de Gourmont's *The Natural Philosophy of Love* (1922). In addition, there are a few later prose pieces reprinted from periodicals, some short poems, and an Appendix of "Poems by 5 Friends" (Maurice Craig, Ernest Hemingway, Barry Domville, Saturno Montanari, and Jaime de Angulo).

William Cole

Pavannes and Divisions

In 1918 Knopf published *Pavannes and Divisions*, a sampling of Ezra Pound's prose. To create the volume, Pound salvaged portions of an unpublished manuscript (*This Generation*) and added work that had appeared over the previous two years in venues such as the *Little Review* and the *Egoist*. The book's title somewhat fancifully distinguishes between the two classes of writings that it features. *Pavannes* refers to a slow, stately dance in 4/4 time popular in Renaissance courts. The verb *pavaner* in modern French means to strut or prance; one etymology traces *pavannes* back to the Spanish *pavo*, or peacock. *Divisions*, in music, are variations, florid phrases derived from an original melody. Originally, *division* implied the splitting of long notes into several short ones. The "Pavannes" section of Pound's book gathers together fantastical, satirical, and virtuosic pieces. Examples include "Jodindranath Mawhwor's Occupation," "L'Homme Moyen Sensuel," "Stark Realism," and a translation of twelve of Fontenelle's dialogues. The "Divisions" section of *Pavannes*—which begins with "A Retrospect," a look back at Imagism—is more polemical and topical. It contains manifestoes, reviews, and literary criticism. Among Pound's subjects are Remy de Gourmont, James Joyce's *Dubliners*, Provençal troubadours, Ford Madox Ford, "Elizabethan Classicists," and the English music antiquarian Arnold Dolmetsch.

Brian M. Reed

Pellizzi, Camillo (1896–1979)

The founder of Italian Sociology, Camillo Pellizzi was one of the most articulate fascist intellectuals. He taught Italian at London University College (1920–1939). In 1939 he was awarded the chair of Social and Political Sciences in Rome, a position he left soon after he became president of the National Institute of Fascist Culture.

In 1936 his friend Odon Por urged him to review *Jefferson and/or Mussolini* for the prestigious *Corriere della Sera*. A "left-wing Fascist," Pellizzi did not know Pound or his work but appreciated his book and authored a review that was published on 14 February 1936. Impressed by the review, Pound wrote to James Laughlin on 15 February 1936 to say that Pellizzi "goes straight for the DANGEROUS idea," meaning monetary reform (56). Pound wrote to Pellizzi, and a twenty-year friendship ensued. Their letters—numbering over 100 and housed at the Beinecke, Yale University, and in Rome's Fondazione Ugo Spirito—document Pound's political passion before, during, and following World War II. While Pound is concerned with economic justice, Pellizzi wishes to change the way political affairs are conducted.

Following the war Pellizzi was "purged" as a former fascist and worked as a translator and journalist until 1950 when he was awarded the first Italian Chair of Sociology at the University of Florence. He continued to write to Pound at St. Elizabeths, informing him about the political and social situation of postfascist Italy. In 1949 he published *La rivoluzione mancata* (The Failed Revolution), a sort of self-analysis of the reasons for fascism's failure to change Italy.

Bibliography

Breschi, Danilo e Gisella Longo. *Camillo Pellizzi.* Catanzaro: Rubbettino, 2003.

Gallesi, Luca. "Il carteggio Pound-Pellizzi negli anni del fascismo." *Nuova Storia contemporanea* 6.3 (May, June 2002): 69–78.

Pellizzi, Camillo. *Una rivoluzione mancata.* Milano: Longanesi, 1949.

Pound, Ezra. Letter to James Laughlin, 15 February 1936. *Ezra Pound and James Laughlin: Selected Letters.* Ed. David M. Gordon. New York: Norton, 1994.

Luca Gallesi

Periplum

One of Ezra Pound's signature words in *The Cantos*, *periplum* derives from the Greek *periplus*, which means "circumnavigation," and the written account of such voyages. In Canto 40, Pound translates from *The Periplus of Hanno*, a Carthaginian explorer circa 470 B.C.E. *Periplus* is indelibly associated with Homer's *Odyssey*, one model for Pound's enterprise in *The Cantos*. The term is common to Latin and English, though Pound's use always takes the form *periplum*, a lexical pun expressing both circumference (peri) and center (plum), thus signaling his practice in *The Cantos*, which is a "sailing after knowledge" to discover and record the center of values across the spectrum of human history. *Periplum* is used some dozen times in *The Cantos*, most frequently in *The Pisan Cantos*, because Pound's circumstances during the writing of this sequence in captivity in the Detention Training Center at Pisa curtailed his physical and textual voyaging, while its composition brilliantly affirmed his power of voyaging through the agency of memory. Both meanings of *periplus* are called on. In Canto 59 *periplum* asserts the value of physical knowledge over "reading," when Pound writes "periplum, not as land looks on a map / but as sea bord seen by men sailing." This is not to devalue maps but to privilege the primacy of firsthand experience against that which depends on recorded evidence. Other uses relate to an attempt to rejuvenate Western culture by starting "a press / and print the greek classics . . . periplum" (Canto 74) and the recall of his own European journeyings in Madrid (Canto 95); but the most striking use—along with that in Canto 59—is in Canto 76, "the sun in his great periplum / leads in his fleet here / sotto le nostre scogli / under our craggy cliffs / alevel their mast-tops," one of many overt or implied references to the myth of the sun-God Helios and his temporal journeys. In this last, and in comparable usages in Cantos 74 and 82, *periplum* relates to the epic motions of the planetary system, and the natural order of winds and waves, the physical harmonics of the universe. The sense of our ceaseless human struggle within the frame of these epic motions is brilliantly summoned at the conclusion of Canto 113 where *periplum* is implied rather than cited: "Out of dark, thou, Father Helios, leadest, / but the mind as Ixion, unstill, ever turning."

Lionel Kelly

Personae (1909)

Although commonly thought to be Ezra Pound's first published volume of poetry, *Personae* (London: Elkin Mathews, 1909) was, in fact, his third, preceded by *A Lume Spento*, 150 copies of which Pound had printed in Venice in 1908 at his own expense, and by *A Quinzaine for This Yule* (1908). Nevertheless, *Personae* (1909) can be considered Pound's first "real" book of poems: It was a significant printing (1,000 sets of sheets) by a reputable publisher, and it attracted the interest of reviewers in prominent British literary journals. These reviewers agreed that, despite a tendency to affectation, the volume announced an original poetic talent notable for its "passion" and "vigorous individuality."

What these reviewers did not know, being apparently ignorant of Pound's first "vanity press" volume, was that just over half of the poems in this slim, small, sixty-page book had been previously published. At the same time as it is Pound's first major volume of poetry, *Personae*

(1909) is the first of numerous instances of his books that collect new poems together with a selection of previously published work that he saw fit to reprint. In the case of *Personae* (1909), Pound's editorial decisions on what to keep and what to reject mark his first attempt to map out a direction for his poetry.

Personae (1909) retains seventeen of *A Lume Spento*'s forty-four poems. In general, as this author has argued in detail elsewhere (see *Ezra Pound's Early Poetry and Poetics*), Pound chose to republish all the poems from *A Lume Spento* that speak through Troubadour personae—poems, that is, heavily influenced by Pound's master Robert Browning—and to reject the great majority of poems based on various literary attitudes derived from the Pre-Raphaelites, the poets of the 1890s, and the early Yeats. These latter poems Pound was to dismiss as "A collection of stale creampuffs" when he came to write a brief forward for a 1965 reissue of his early work.

Few of the sixteen new poems in *Personae* (1909)—roughly the second half of the volume—are free from the poetizing that characterized so much of his earliest verse. One of the exceptions, "Marvoil," continues the realist, revisionary medievalism of "Cino," "Na Audiart," the two "Villonauds," and "Fifine Answers" that provides the dominant theme of poems retained from *A Lume Spento* that comprise the first half of *Personae* (1909). These Browningesque dramatic lyrics in which Pound speaks through the personae of tough-minded, witty, and spirited characters, historically situated, represent his first achievement of a distinctive voice. In these poems a new sensibility enters into English poetry, one that takes direct aim at the languid, romanticized medievalism that had provided the poetic landscape for virtually all the major Victorian poets.

Another of the new poems, "In Durance," repeats, thankfully only in part, the anxious confessions and strident assertions of aspirations and allegiances of earlier poems rejected from *Personae* (1909). "In Durance," however, displays a new frankness, self-irony, and more important, self-consciousness about the writing of verse within inherited codes and conventions and about the fitting of his own drives as a poet into preexisting literary poses. Similarly, in the new "Revolt against the Crepuscular Spirit in Modern Poetry," Pound speaks expressly of the contemporary condition of the poet and of poetry. Yet this poem is riddled with bombast and with the Celtic twilight mannerisms that, ironically enough, it purports to inveigh against.

"In Durance" and "Revolt" are representative instances of the tension in *Personae* (1909) as a whole, a tension created by Pound's conflicting allegiance to two competing stances for poetry: one that sees poetry as a dream of reality out of this world, voiced in the privileged language of literature; and another that understands poetry as an activity very much in and of this world, speaking what Pound would later prize as "natural speech, the language as spoken" (*LE* 262). In *Personae* (1909) Pound takes his first deliberate step in the direction of the latter.

As Hugh Kenner aptly remarked, "The title of the 1909 *Personae* implies . . . not merely masks but a man donning them" ("Broken Mirrors" 3)—and, one should add, a man self-conscious about donning them. It is this self-consciousness concerning the enterprise of his poetry, what is new about it and unique in it, that most distinguishes Pound's third book of poems from the first two. By the time Pound came to compile the poems to be included in *Personae* (1909), he was able to see the difference between a persona and a posture and to understand how the former provided him with a means of advancing beyond the impasse of his immediate poetic inheritance.

Bibliography

de Nagy, N. Christoph. *The Poetry of Ezra Pound: The Pre-Imagist Stage.* 1960. Bern: Francke Verlag, 1968.

Grieve, Thomas F. *Ezra Pound's Early Poetry and Poetics.* Columbia: U of Missouri P, 1997.

Jackson, Thomas H. *The Early Poetry of Ezra Pound.* Cambridge: Harvard UP, 1968.

Kenner, Hugh. "The Broken Mirrors and the Mirror of Memory." *Motive and Method in the Cantos of Ezra Pound.* Ed. Lewis Leary. New York: Columbia UP, 1954. 3–33.

———. *The Poetry of Ezra Pound.* 1951. Lincoln: U of Nebraska P, 1985.

Schneidau, Herbert N. *Ezra Pound: The Image and the Real.* Baton Rouge: Louisiana State UP, 1969.

Witemeyer, Hugh. *The Poetry of Ezra Pound: Forms and Renewal, 1908–1920.* Berkeley: U of California P, 1969.

Thomas F. Grieve

Personae (1926)

Personae (1926) is one of the key texts of Modernist poetry. Here for the first time in one volume a reader will find Ezra Pound's carefully deliberated selection of his earliest verse and a virtually complete collection of his poetry from *Ripostes* (1912) on, including poems from Pound's Imagist and Vorticist phases, poems previously expurgated from *Lustra*, and the major sequences of *Cathay*, *Homage to Sextus Propertius*, and *Hugh Selwyn Mauberley*. First published on 22 December 1926 by Boni & Liveright of New York, and subtitled *The Collected Poems of Ezra Pound*, it announced itself as the "Edition to date of all Ezra Pound's poems except the unfinished 'Cantos.'" Yet the designation "Collected" is misleading if a reader understands by it that *Personae* (1926) is a complete grouping, in chronological order, of every poem from the thirteen volumes of poems that preceded it.

Pound and his publisher could have more accurately claimed that the volume was a "selection" and repeated the qualification that had graced the title page of *Umbra* (1920), an earlier attempt at a collected edition: "All that he now wished to keep in print." In compiling the poems to be included in *Personae* (1926), Pound maintained the editorial practice that began with the first 1909 *Personae*, and continued through *Provença* (1910), the American edition of *Lustra* (1917), and *Umbra* (1920), of combining a selection of previous work with new poems to compose a new volume. Interestingly, T. S. Eliot, when he edited his *Ezra Pound: Selected Poems* for British publication two years later—a volume quite similar in content and arrangement to Pound's "collection" in *Personae* (1926)—observed the distinction.

The history of just how it was collected and what was collected in *Personae* (1926) is an interesting one. "Have long wanted a collected edtn.," Pound wrote to his father, Homer Pound, on 12 September 1925. Six months earlier he had first broached the idea to his American publisher, Horace Liveright. Negotiations then ensued to secure the American copyright to *Lustra* from Alfred A. Knopf, the volume's publisher, and as various autograph letters, a typescript table of contents, and tear sheets from *Canzoni* and *Umbra* in the Ezra Pound Collection of the Beinecke Library reveal, Pound was much occupied in the fall of 1925 in selecting and arranging pre-*Ripostes* work for inclusion in the volume. By letter, he consulted Eliot and Richard Aldington, disagreeing more than agreeing with Eliot's suggestions, and apparently rescuing at least six poems from *Canzoni* and deciding on a more generous selection from his earliest work as a result of Aldington's persuasive arguments. An explanation proffered to his father in a letter of 28 November 1925 reveals the basic principle behind his selection: "The things I'm throwing out are the 'soft' stuff, and the metrical exercises."

By February 1927, Boni & Liveright reported "a good continuing sale" of "approximately 750" and that a new edition of 500 was in the works. In 1929, Pound received the grand sum of $30.80 in royalties. Since its original publication, *Personae* (1926) has gone through numerous impressions and editions of ever-increasing quantity as Pound's status as a major poet was established. These culminated in 1990 when Lea Baechler and A. Walton Litz provided a definitive revised edition: *Personae: The Shorter Poems of Ezra Pound* (New Directions). This edition, beyond providing many needed textual revisions, does the valuable service of removing chronological confusion in the arrangement of poems in the original edition and adding in an appendix "Three Cantos" (1917)—early versions of the first cantos, previously difficult to access.

In *Personae* (1926), Pound provided a record of his pre–*The Cantos* achievement. The volume enables us to trace a twenty-year path in the development of his poetry. We read Pound at the outset of his career, chafing within the derivative

style and subject matter borrowed from his master, Robert Browning, and from the Pre-Raphaelites, the poets of the 1890s, and the early Yeats. We follow him through formal experimentation, parody, translation, and the complicated exercises in self-criticism of his *personae* to his achievement of an increasingly externalized view of the role of the poet and of the scope of poetry. We see, that is, the record of how a major poet progresses away from a lyric and toward an epic conception of poetry's responsibility to its world or, to employ the poet's own terms, how the "search for oneself" is displaced by the "search for the real" (*GB* 85).

Bibliography

de Nagy, N. Christoph. *The Poetry of Ezra Pound: The Pre-Imagist Stage*. 1960. Bern: Francke Verlag, 1968.

Grieve, Thomas F. *Ezra Pound's Early Poetry and Poetics*. Columbia: U of Missouri P, 1997.

Jackson, Thomas H. *The Early Poetry of Ezra Pound*. Cambridge: Harvard UP, 1968.

Kenner, Hugh. "The Broken Mirrors and the Mirror of Memory." *Motive and Method in the Cantos of Ezra Pound*. Ed. Lewis Leary. New York: Columbia UP, 1954. 3–33.

———. *The Poetry of Ezra Pound*. 1951. Lincoln: U of Nebraska P, 1985.

Schneidau, Herbert N. *Ezra Pound: The Image and the Real*. Baton Rouge: Louisiana State UP, 1969.

Witemeyer, Hugh. *The Poetry of Ezra Pound: Forms and Renewal, 1908–1920*. Berkeley: U of California P, 1969.

Thomas F. Grieve

Philosophy: Ancient European

According to Pound, the emergence of Western philosophy from solar myths (Greek, Egyptian, and Near Eastern) and vegetal rites (Eleusinian) endows it with a source common to poetry and hermetic knowledge. The loss of such a "Mediterranean state of mind" (*SP* 150) signals the failure of philosophy: its descent into fragments and philological fussiness (*GK* 119, 127).

Pound mentions a wide range of pre-Socratic philosophers in his prose and in *The Cantos*, particularly *Rock-Drill* and *Thrones*. The Milesian philosopher Thales is notable for demonstrating the nature of economic demand, creating an olive-press monopoly during a bumper crop (*SP* 172; Canto 88). Anaximander and Anaximenes anticipate medieval philosophers "on light and diaphana" (*GK* 117). Pythagoras portends the tradition of Neoplatonist light philosophy for Pound (Canto 91) and provides an affinity with elements of Confucian doctrine (Terrell 548). Ocellus, a Pythagorean, anticipates the light philosophy of Erigena (Cantos 87 and 94). Empedokles also attracts Pound's attention in the early poem "Anima Sola" (*CEP* 19–21) and during the composition of *Thrones*, when he reads Burnet's *Early Greek Philosophy* and its quotations from Milhaud's *Les Philosophes–Géométres de la Grec* (*L/WL* 284–285). The decline of philosophy is evident in Herakleitos's monistic principle of flux being rendered abstract by his followers (*GK* 31). Pound sees philological wrangling over the pre-Socratic fragments as having totally obscured the "fire of the gods" in them (*GK* 119).

Socrates and Plato do not figure prominently in Pound's writing. Eleusis is preferred to Delphi: The latter becomes a sign of economic obfuscation, conspiracy rather than mystery (*Impact* 185). Yet Socrates is an adept in the light of mind and the crystalline νοῦς, a cornerstone for later philosophy (*GK* 33). Pound seems finally to accept Plato's theory of forms (*L/WL* 301; *GK* 44) and praises his discernment of μέλος as the union of words, rhythm, and music (*SP* 27).

Pound's extended review of Aristotle in *Guide to Kulchur* constitutes his most concentrated writing on philosophy next to his work on light philosophy in the "Cavalcanti" essay and in *The Cantos*. The "anchor" of thought for two millennia, Aristotle proposes a philosophy of action in the theory of efficient cause, a notion Pound retains throughout his life (*Impact* 244; *L/WL* 39, 236). The *Nichomachean Ethics* and *Politics* provide, along with the Four Books of China, an intellectual foundation for civilization (*SP* 350). Pound's opinion of the *Ethics*, however, is not consistent. He considers it in one instance completely worthless, except for its residually pre-Socratic mention of ενδαιμονεῖν (*GK* 307) and elsewhere as a correct and valuable determination of currency as a measuring principle (*GK* 325). It is significant for Pound that Aristotle applies his epistemology, a knowledge of "concrete particulars," by compiling 158 state constitutions for a comparative study of political systems (*GK* 343). This is seen to have a positive influence on John Adams in the foundation of the American nation (*RSWWII* 390), linking the best of classical thought to the American Constitution.

The philosophers of late antiquity form the foundation for Neoplatonism in the Middle Ages. Several are mentioned merely in passing: Synesius the Neoplatonist (Canto 99); Epictetus the Stoic for his ethic of endurance, appropriately mentioned in *The Pisan Cantos* (Canto 77); Zeno of Citium, founder of Stoicism, for placing ethics before cosmology (*GK* 122); and most spectacularly, Peregrinus the Cynic, for throwing himself onto the flames at the Olympic Games in 165 C.E. (Canto 100). Another notable precursor to Neoplatonism is Apollonius of Tyana, who figures prominently in Canto 94. He claimed a spiritual descent from Pythagoras (Terrell 554) and brought Pythagoreanism and Eastern mysticism together after traveling widely (Cantos 91 and 94). Of very few references to Latin philosophy, Lucretius warrants mention for his attempt to propound a philosophic system in *De rerum naturæ* (*GK* 193).

Neoplatonism is given due treatment in the earlier Cantos and in *Rock-Drill* and *Thrones*. Plotinus, the founding figure of Neoplatonism, distinguishes between εἶδος (eidos, form) and εικών (eikon, likeness), a precision in language admired by Pound (*L/WL* 301). Significantly, it is Plotinus who leads Pound out of Hell in Canto 15. Porphyry, the first editor of the *Enneads* and a disciple of Plotinus, recurs in *The Cantos* as author of the phrase "Omnis Intellectus Est Omniformis" (Cantos 23 and 91). Iamblichus, another Neoplatonist, posits light as the suffusing element binding human activity with divine creativity, a nexus for Pound with male sexuality and the cult of *amor* (5/17; *GK* 128, 225; Terrell 17). Neoplatonist iconography signifies divine possession and therefore poetic creativity by fire and light (Cantos 5 and 91), tracing a line through Provence, to the few post-Renaissance figures aware of the *mysterium* (Cantos 14 and 82).

Bibliography

Burnet, John. *Early Greek Philosophy*. London: A. & C. Black, 1920.

Libera, Sharon Mayer. "Casting His Gods Back into the NOUS: Two Neo-platonists and *The Cantos* of Ezra Pound." *Paideuma* 2.3 (1973): 355–377.

Philostratus. *The Life of Apollonius of Tyana*. Trans. F. C. Conybeare. 2 vols. 1912. Cambridge: Harvard UP, 1950.

Zielinski, Thaddeus. "The Sibyl." *Edge* 2 (November 1956): 1–48.

Mark S. Byron

Philosophy: Medieval and Renaissance European

Medieval philosophy marks Ezra Pound's most intense philological and philosophical engagement with the Western philosophical tradition. The link between antiquity (the Eleusinian mysteries and Neoplatonic light philosophy) and medieval thought is developed in Pound's attempts to translate Cavalcanti's *"Donna mi prega"* (Canto 36; *T* 132–141).

Patristic philosophers receive occasional mention in Pound's writing, either as forerunners of medieval light philosophy or exponents of logic-chopping and linguistic obfuscation. Historically situated between ancient science and Modern empiricism, the scholastic emphasis upon terminology serves to sharpen thought (*GK* 26, 50), and medieval natural philosophy gives rise to a world of forms (*LE* 155). While there was a clear edge to much of its philosophy, the Middle Ages was also "the darkness of decentralization" (*LE* 220).

St. Augustine is summarily dismissed by Pound (*L/WL* 284), except in providing a formula for the Trinity parallel to Cavalcanti's "memory, intelligence and will" (*LE* 178). Like Augustine, Anselm defines an image or speculum of the Trinity in the human, *mens ipsa sola* (Canto 98; Terrell 633). His importance to Pound is his thesis, in the *Monologium* of 1063, that faith and reason are compatible (Canto 105). Continuing the pattern, Pound discerns in

Richard of St. Victor three modes of thought: cogitation, meditation, and contemplation. Pound equates these modes with Hell, Purgatory, and Paradise of Dante's *Divine Comedy* (*GK* 77, 328). He discovers Richard's *De Contemplatione* via Dante (*SP* 333) and later publishes a series of quotations from it (*SP* 71–72).

Pound's use of Johannes Scotus Erigena occurs in three separate ways. This ninth-century philosopher and classicist refuted Gottschalk of Orbais on predestination and was duly condemned at the Councils of Valence in 855 and of Langres in 859. Pound initially champions Erigena as the victim of a Trinitarian controversy (*L* 304), conflating this event with his later condemnation during the Albigensian crusade by Pope Honorius III (*GK* 333; Canto 83). Erigena's reputed statement, "Authority comes from right reason," recurs in Pound's work (*GK* 75, 164, 333; *SP* 61, 78; Canto 36). Second, Erigena embodies the virtue *hilaritas* (Canto 92), chiefly through the use of Greek in his poetry in the court of Charles the Bald (Cantos 83, 85, and 87). Third and crucially, Erigena's phrase "Omnia quae sunt, lumina sunt," from his *Periphyseon*, is a hallmark of Neoplatonic light philosophy (Cantos 74 and 87; *L* 333, 334), a demonstration of medieval *virtù* (*SP* 78; Cantos 36, 74, and 100) and thus a point of contact with Cavalcanti.

Robert Grosseteste's *De Luce* is the primary source for Pound's Neoplatonic light philosophy: It represents the kind of atmosphere in which Cavalcanti wrote the *"Donna mi prega"* (*LE* 149, 158, 160–161). It is behind the movement, later in *The Cantos*, toward "the GREAT CRYSTAL" (Canto 91) or the "great acorn of light" (Cantos 86 and 116). Grosseteste derives from Arabic treatises on perspective and Neoplatonism and, like Erigena, translated the Pseudo-Dionysius (Michaels 39). Pound values him for the coherent structure of his thought (*GK* 77). The totality of light in Erigena and Grosseteste, the "plura diafana" (Canto 83), informs Cavalcanti's *diafana* (Canto 36) and renders *amor* and the Eleusinian mysteries in Neoplatonic terms (*SP* 59).

Counter to the medieval Neoplatonic tradition stands the logic and rhetoric of Aquinas's

Summa Theologica. Aquinas neglects the *mysterium*, proof of the abstract tendency of patristic philosophy (Cantos 36 and 97), and Thomist ontology is interested in things that the modern mind finds dull (*SP* 58). In 1917 Pound admits to having not read Aquinas (*L* 109). By 1939 Pound wholly rejects the "Aquinas-map" (*L* 323), but in the following year he takes issue with Aquinas in order to discredit him (*L* 339).

The Trinitarian controversies of the medieval period opened the way for the Renaissance revival of learning in Quattrocento Italy. In particular, Pound traces the revival of Neoplatonism to the figure of Georgios Gemistos Plethon, who was sent to the Council of Ferrara and Florence in 1438 (Cantos 8, 23, and 26). The Council marked an attempt to unite the Eastern and Western Churches over the issue of the Trinity, contentious ever since the Council of Nicaea in 325 C.E. (Canto 26). Gemistos's Platonism posits Neptune as the greatest of the gods, from whom all flows (Canto 83; 116; *GK* 224). He also follows the Aristotelian *universalia in re*, where universals are known in particulars (Canto 74). Under the influence of Gemistos, Cosimo de' Medici established the Florentine Platonic Academy, at which Ficino was later to teach (Canto 21) and which led the revival of Greek studies in the West (*GK* 45). On a failed military expedition to Mistra in 1464–1466, Sigismundo Malatesta brought back the ashes of Gemistos to Rimini and interred them in the Tempio Malatestiano. Pound claims spiritual kinship with Gemistos due to his own role in the revival of learning (*L/WL* 303).

Pound's relative lack of interest in Italian Renaissance Neoplatonism, compared with its medieval predecessors, indicates his preference for the earlier thinkers' originality. However, Pound explicitly links figures of the fifteenth century with medieval thinkers in a "conspiracy of intelligence" (*GK* 263) and denotes the fifteenth century as the salvation from Christian medievalism (*L/WL* 218). Ficino's role in the Florence Academy is crucial: He interprets Porphyry's *De Occasionibus* from which Pound took the phrase "Omnis intellectus est omniformis" (Canto 5 and 23), yet Pound reserves a skeptical humor regarding Ficino's eclectic pha-

lanx of classical writers (*EP&VA* 24–25). Pico della Mirandola is dismissed altogether, except for the one passage continually quoted in Pater's *Renaissance* (*EP&VA* 25, 222; *GK* 160; *LE* 331), but Pound does credit him with a cultural vision beyond Greek and Latin (*EP&VA* 25). The humanist Lorenzo Valla is a champion of historical truth for Pound, having revealed the fraud of the Donation of Constantine and having been employed as a Latinist papal secretary when such things were taken seriously (*GK* 160).

In Pound's eyes, the Renaissance declines into cloudy rhetoric (*EP&VA* 28), and the clear definition of terms is abandoned for empirical science (*SP* 65). The legacy of Eleusis and light philosophy remains with the small number of people in which a culture resides, Machiavelli's "L'Umanità vive in pochi" (*SP* 38, 304; *GK* 266).

Bibliography

Fiorentino, Francesco. *Manuale di Storia della Filosofia*. 3rd ed. Vol. 1, 3 vols. Torino, 1921.
Gilson, Étienne. *History of Christian Philosophy in the Middle Ages*. New York: Random House, 1955.
Michaels, Walter B. "Pound and Erigena." *Paideuma* 1.1 (1972): 37–54.

Mark S. Byron

Philosophy: Eighteenth Century to the Present

The Western philosophical tradition after Leibniz (1646–1716) is not held in high regard by Ezra Pound. The preponderance of "useless verbiage" (*L* 267) led to the blunting of precise definition, and the professional philosopher became "too damned lazy to work in a laboratory" or at art or was "like 89% of the since writers on philosophical subjects, just a dud or a half wit" (*GK* 78). The post-Enlightenment subjugation of philosophy to empirical method compounded its problem of loose definition (*GK* 50) and saw it trail after material science (*LE* 76, 394; *Machine Art* 120).

The German philosophical tradition of Kant, Hegel, and Marx was incomplete: "Something was lacking" (*GK* 172). Pound simply describes Rousseau as "distressing" and the eighteenth century as "a cliché which the Romantics broke up, in disorderly and amateur manner" (*GK*

181). At this time, British philosophy and French Encyclopaedism degenerated into abstract thought for Pound. The "brilliance" of Pierre Bayle and Voltaire anticipated a diminishment of principles and "gradations of value," "a musical concept of man they dwindle downward to a mathematical concept" (*SP* 154). "ETHICAL simplicity," on the other hand, makes a medieval canonist more modern than "any eighteenth-century 'intellectual' " (*SP* 151). The continued decline in nineteenth-century British thought was due to the loss of contact with the Continent after Waterloo (*GK* 227).

In political philosophy, both Marx and the Marquis de La Tour du Pin failed to perceive the role of money, as Pound states in *The Cantos* and in numerous essays (Canto 46; *SP* 154, 155, 268, 272, 273, 274, 278, 280, and 307); John Stuart Mill and Brooks Adams made a similar error, seeing "money as an accumulator of energy" (*SP* 307). The application of political philosophy to human conduct failed for Marx and Hegel (*SP* 87); Marx was also beset with the problem of acolytes "anchoring and petrifying" his thought (*SP* 282).

American intellectual life is divided into four periods by Pound: a phase of civilization (1760–1830); one of "thinning, of mental impoverishment" (1830–1860); the Civil War and its aftermath (1860–1930); and finally, a phase of possible renewal (1930–   ) (*SP* 147). Although Pound does not identify a philosophical tradition native to America, it did experience the influence of European thought in such figures as John Adams and Thomas Jefferson: "[T]hey inherit that forma mentis in an active state where definition of terms and ideas has not been lost" (*SP* 157). This growth of civilization was stunted by a lack of printing and distribution of seminal texts (*SP* 162).

Nineteenth-century European thought is glossed over by Pound. Yet he notes that Nietzsche had done no harm in France, as the French "understood that thought can exist apart from action" (*SP* 421) and were therefore immunized against that philosopher's excesses. The primary problem of intellectual life, the "art of getting meaning into words" (*LE* 32), was temporarily challenged by Darwin, science, machinery, and Nietzsche.

Bertrand Russell "or any other flat-chested highbrow" of his ilk (*GK* 166) continued the folly of philosophy in the twentieth century. His notion of logic was insufficient when abstracted from experience and anachronistic at a time when physical science and empirical method required attention to particulars in addition to the precise definition of terms already found in medieval scholastic philosophy (*GK* 166). Pound also critiques the "terminological inexactitude" fit to scandalize "a freshman of A.D. 1250" in Russell's *Outline of Philosophy* (*Machine Art* 118).

Pound's assessment of modem philosophy is not entirely negative. Although he critiques Oswald Spengler's philosophy of history for failing to demonstrate sufficiently detailed knowledge due to a desire for synthesis (*LE* 16), Pound sees the philosophical project as such as worthwhile. The reach of philosophical thought extends to Fabre and Frazer, who write at the interface of ethics, philosophy, and religion (*LE* 343). Pound also sees Dada as a mode of philosophy and praises Francis Picabia and Marcel Duchamp as the intellectual heirs of Voltaire and Bayle (*GK* 87).

Pound's closest philosophical ally was George Santayana, with whom he enjoyed a brief correspondence in 1939–1940 while researching medieval light philosophy for the paradiso stage of *The Cantos* (*L* 331). Pound admired the intellectual honesty of "Santy Yanner" (*L* 307) and mentions his materialism at several points in *The Cantos* (80, 88, 95, and 100). Pound explained his ideogrammic method to Santayana and his idea of the monad as a combination of elements: "[T]rue science, true thinking is ideogrammic in the sense that the general is composed of *definite particulars known directly* by the thinker" (*Machine Art* 158; see also 151–152). Pound's aversion to abstract terminology (*L* 333) and his corrective pedagogy had him propose to Santayana a triptych volume (along with T. S. Eliot) to be published by Faber on "the Ideal University, or The Proper Curriculum" (*L* 339).

Pound regretted the endemic decline of philosophic thought, from luminous detail and "the GREAT theory or revelation" (*Machine Art* 138) into a post-Renaissance imprecision and generality. The comparable degeneration in economic thought and in poetics stemmed from the same ignorance: "If oikos was bastardised to mean merely agora, the love of wisdom had been degraded to mean merely the discussion of generalities" (*SP* 280–281). A knowledge of post-Enlightenment philosophy serves as a guide to the serious work of reading, preventing the trickery of "fixed and petrified ideas and modes of thought" or that of rationalization and the syllogism (*Machine Art* 113).

Pound's cursory treatment of post-Enlightenment philosophy was undertaken mainly in 1937, in preparation for the paradiso section of *The Cantos*, and before the China and Adams Cantos were composed (from summer 1938). The task was not discharged with any close primary reading of the major philosophical works in question.

Bibliography

Pound, Ezra. "How to Write." *Machine Art and Other Writings: The Lost Thought of the Italian Years.* Ed. Maria Luisa Ardizzone. Durham: Duke UP, 1996. 87–128.

Mark S. Byron

Plays Modelled on the Noh

The little volume of unpublished plays written in 1916, so excellently edited by Donald Gallup in 1987, is, unfortunately, rather mistakenly titled. Pound had very little knowledge of classical Japanese theater, and Ernest Fenollosa's unpublished notes, upon which he relied, were, at best, fragmentary and, more often than not, unreliable. The idea of using so formal and fixed a musical/literary structure as that of Noh (a form of theater that demands mythic subject matter and an imaginative retreat into intense subjectivity) for blatantly realistic modern drama doomed his attempts to dismal failure. "The Protagonist," however, one of the four "rescued" plays, is claimed to have been modeled on Kyogen (brief and moderately realistic farces, performed as interludes between Noh plays). Using Dublin street scenes is not altogether unacceptable for

such an enterprise, but Yeats's imaginative *Cat and the Moon* comes much closer to the mark. Of Pound's other drafts, only "Tristan" shows even a minimal debt to the Noh, but its prologue is a poor imitation of Yeats, and the rest reads like an unintended parody of Maeterlinck's *La mort de Tintagiles* with an undisguised Henri Gaudier-Brzeska as hapless hero. The author was quite correct not to publish those texts in his lifetime, and they now serve only to demonstrate the futility of attempting to work in a form without inherent interest in its techniques or even vaguely understanding its subtleties.

Richard Taylor

Poems 1918–21

In 1921, the New York press Boni and Liveright published a selection of Ezra Pound's latest verse: *Poems 1918–21 Including Three Portraits and Four Cantos*. The "Four Cantos" are early versions of Cantos 4, 5, 6, and 7, and they are numbered as such. The "Three Portraits" section, in contrast, disregards clear structuring principles. It contains four, not three, poem sequences: "Homage to Sextus Propertius," "Langue d'oc," "Moeurs Contemporaines," and "Hugh Selwyn Mauberley." The table of contents, too, is arranged so that "Mauberley" is difficult to discern as a single work. Its discrete parts receive typographical emphasis equivalent to the collective title. Finally, whereas "Mauberley" and "Moeurs" could be considered "portraits," the other two poem sequences, consisting largely of free translation, hardly seem "portraiture," except in a very loose sense. The volume as a whole does succeed, though, in suggesting that *The Cantos* represents an extension of Pound's earlier interests in Classical antiquity, medieval Provençal, and social satire. Moreover, the relatively chaotic organization of "Three Portraits" may prepare a reader for *The Cantos*' challenge to linear, hierarchical modes of thinking.

Bibliography

Bush, Ronald. *The Genesis of Ezra Pound's Cantos.* Princeton: Princeton UP, 1976.

Brian M. Reed

Poetics

"Mr. Pound," declared T. S. Eliot in his introduction to the *Literary Essays of Ezra Pound* (1954), "is more responsible for the XXth Century revolution in poetry than is any other individual" (xi). This is no exaggeration. From his early Imagist and Vorticist manifestos to his dissemination of Ernest Fenollosa's writings on the Chinese Written Character to his later "Confucian" poetics, Pound is the poet-critic who has most fully defined what we think of as Modernist as well as Postmodernist poetry.

Take the early manifesto "A Retrospect," in which Pound puts forward the three Imagist principles:

1. Direct treatment of the "thing" whether subjective or objective.
2. To use absolutely no word that does not contribute to the presentation.
3. As regarding rhythm: to compose in the sequence of the musical phrase, not in sequence of a metronome (*LE* 3).

In the literary context of 1912, all three were remarkable. The poetry of the 1890s and 1900s, whether in Britain or the United States, urgently needed renewal. Fuzzy vague diction, conventional phrasing, circumlocution, pseudoclassical cliché, lofty sentiment, and tum-ti-tum meters: These were the order of the day. So the prescriptions "Use no superfluous word, no adjective which does not reveal something," and "Don't use such an expression as 'dim lands of *peace*.' It dulls the image" (*LE* 4–5), coupled with the matter-of-fact assertion that the poet must avoid excessive symbolism, recognizing that "A hawk is a hawk" (*LE* 9), were like a breath of fresh air. As for that third "rule," its emphasis on the musical phrase served as an important reminder that poetry was not equivalent to verse as such (the metronome). And further, this principle, together with its corollary, "Do not retell in mediocre verse what has already been done in good prose" (*LE* 5), reminds us that literary *prose* is much more than "not verse," as M. Jourdain thought, that it is itself an art form, and that even the freest "free verse" must have a raison

d'être for its rhythms and line breaks. "A rhyme," remarked Pound very sensibly, "must have in it some slight element of surprise if it is to give pleasure; . . . it must be well used if used at all" (*LE* 7).

Such prescriptions are, of course, primarily technical; their concern is less with the ontology of poetry as a form of discourse than with the *how to* embodied in such titles as *How to Read* or *ABC of Reading*. Pound's is avowedly a pragmatic poetics; the poet, in his scheme of things, is not the purveyor of great truths (indeed Pound seems curiously indifferent to the thematic component of Dante or Flaubert) but, in the classical sense, a *maker* (*poietes*) and inventor of language. All the more startling, then, that his seemingly simple formulations—"Great literature is simply language charged with meaning to the utmost possible degree" (*ABCR* 28, 36); "poetry . . . is the most concentrated form of verbal expression" (*ABCR* 36); or "Literature is news that STAYS news" (*ABCR* 29)—are so brilliantly apt. Pound seems to have been quite unaware of the existence of Ludwig Wittgenstein, but the above aphorisms are perfectly in accord with the philosopher's famous distinction, "Do not forget that a poem, although it is composed in the language of information, is not used in the language-game of giving information." It is, at its core, the distinction Roman Jakobson made between the poetic and the referential functions of language—a distinction that has, of course, come under heavy fire from contemporary Sophists like Stanley Fish, who have "proved" that one cannot pinpoint a hard-and-fast difference between, say, the language of journalism and the language of poetry. But if there cannot and should not be a quantitative measure for such differentiation, common sense—and this is where Pound is such a central poetician—tells us that "writing" that does not "stay news" is quickly expendable and replaceable by other writing. Only poetry, as he frequently said, endures.

Pound also provided us with an excellent classification of the basic kinds of poetry: *melopoeia*, "wherein the words are charged, over and above their plain meaning, with some musical property, which directs the bearing or trend of that meaning"; *phanopoeia*, "a casting of images upon the visual imagination"; and *logopoeia*, " 'the dance of the intellect among words' " (*LE* 25; *ABCR* 37). The Greek and Provençal poets, Pound believed, had excelled at the first, the Chinese (and sometimes Rimbaud!) at the second. As for the *logopoeia*— what we would now call conceptual art—it is a more modern phenomenon found in the hitherto minor genres like satire and parody. The musical, the visual, the conceptual: In most poetry all three matter, but Pound is surely right to note that the emphasis varies: Gerard Manley Hopkins, for example, is primarily a *melopoeic* poet. The offbeat poetry of Mina Loy or Louis Zukofsky, Pound understood, was essentially a case of *logopoeia*, even as his own poetry neglected the conceptual in favor of sound and imagery.

The evolution of literary forms and genres is another topic on which Pound wrote brilliantly. True, his judgments were extremely idiosyncratic—he hated Milton, had no understanding for Goethe or Hölderlin, and overrated such French Parnassians as Théophile Gautier—but he had a very clear idea as to how poetic movements play themselves out. First, he noted (*ABCR* 39), come the "inventors," those who "found a new process"; then the "masters" who solidify it, followed by the "diluters," and then "good writers without salient qualities," who produce credible work when a particular literature is healthy: For example, "men who wrote sonnets in Dante's time." Here again, Pound's practical division sheds enormous light on what is happening in poetry right now—say, language poetry, where the "diluters" have already been active and the "good writers without salient qualities" are now minding the store. The distinction also sheds light on current pedagogy that foregrounds, for ideological reasons, novels like Kate Chopin's *Awakening* without explaining that these dilutions would not exist without such earlier paradigms as *Anna Karenina* and *Madame Bovary*.

How ideological is Pound's aesthetic? To what extent is it informed by his highly questionable, if not reprehensible, politics and economics? This is a tricky question. It is true that, as many critics have argued, politics informs *The Cantos*, not just at the level of the occasional anti-Semitic slur or encomium to Mussolini; the very structure and texture of Pound's "poem including history" are colored by fascist myth and metaphor. But the irony is that, insofar as *The Cantos* can be called a fascist epic, it violates Pound's own poetics that consistently make the case for a poetry exempt from rhetoric and didacticism, a poetry in which "Dichten = condensare" (*ABCR* 36).

Where that poetics is weak, however, is in its articulation of the Image, which Pound first defined as "an intellectual and emotional complex in an instant of time" (*LE* 4). In *Gaudier-Brezska* (1916), he tried to "advance" Imagist theory by calling it Vorticist and emphasizing movement and energy: "The image is not an idea. It is a radiant node or cluster . . . a VORTEX, from which, and through which, and into which ideas are constantly rushing" (*LE* 92). Vorticism became the cornerstone for Charles Olson's later *Projective Verse*, with its definition of the poem as an "energy discharge" and of the poet's need to "keep it moving!" But whether static, as it was for the minor Imagists, or moving, as it was for Pound, H. D., and William Carlos Williams, the Poundian Image could not bear the weight imposed on it. In his writings derived from Fenollosa, Pound took the naive position that the ideogram (for him, the ultimate Image) was equivalent to the "thing itself" to which it referred, that the three ideograms for "Farmer pounds rice" really *show* the farmer performing this act. Later theorists, some of them themselves poets like the Brazilian Concretist Haroldo de Campos, himself a great admirer of Pound's, have shown that this romantic theory holds no water, that there is no way that the written sign, whether Chinese ideogram or Greek letter of the alphabet, can *be* the thing it ostensibly represents. How, for starters, can language be "charged with meaning" if there has to be one ideogram per referent as in the argument that the ideograms "man"+"tree"+"sun" combined give us the ideogram for "sun tangled in the tree's branches, as at sunrise, meaning now the East" (*ABCR* 21). And even if in such simple cases the ideogram visualizes its meaning, what about function words like *of* or *but* or *among*? The ideogram, de Campos suggests in a book on the subject, functions not to represent things in the external world but relationally within the text itself, to move from one poetic unit to another.

Pound's "invention of China," as Hugh Kenner calls it, thus did great things for his own poetry, but the "ideogrammic method," as he defined it, was always questionable. The natural object, moreover, was by no means "always the adequate symbol," as Pound suggested in his early Imagist credo. In his own poetry, certainly, the "objects" used became increasingly unnatural and hence distinctive. Questionable as well is Pound's peculiar Confucianism—his adaptation of the *Cheng Ming* or "correct denomination of names" and the "unwobbling Pivot." In *Guide to Kulchur*, Pound conflates Confucianism with Leo Frobenius's notion of the *paideuma*, defined by Pound as a "tangle or complex of the inrooted ideas of any period" (*GK* 57) and roughly equivalent to the Foucaultian *episteme*. In its attempt to define the core of what Pound called "the grisly roots of ideas that are in action" (*GK* 58), Pound oddly undercuts his own earlier emphasis on "luminous detail," "constatation of fact," and "direct treatment of the thing." Indeed, Pound's citationality—his imbrication in a given text (whether poem or essay or play) of literally countless proper names and found objects like popular songs or extracts from others' books—is less an instance of the Confucian "rectification of names" than it points to a deeply skeptical Nominalism to which Pound himself never quite owned up.

Few poets have ever used proper names as brilliantly, have devised ways of incorporating into the poetic fabric names of persons and places, real or invented, formal titles or dialect and slang names, in English or in a dozen other languages, as has Pound. Indeed, Pound's concept of "direct treatment," "luminous detail," and the ideogram finds its realization not so much in his nature images, which are often quite conventional, as in his citations of proper names

that are characterized by their astonishing variety and their total distinctiveness, their *difference* from one another even as the "phalanx of particulars" involves artful repetition and variation. It is in this sense that Pound spoke of poetry as "language charged with meaning."

However authoritarian his politics, then, however prescriptive his economics, Pound's *poetics* is characterized by a profound understanding of *language* and verbal nuance, coupled with a refreshing common sense that makes his critical essays read as if they were written yesterday. Here is Pound in 1914 on the James Joyce of *Dubliners*:

> Mr. Joyce's merit . . . his most engaging merit, is that he carefully avoids telling you a lot that you don't want to know. He presents his people swiftly and vividly, he does not sentimentalize over them. . . . He is a realist. He does not believe "life" would be all right if we stopped vivisection or if we instituted a new sort of "economics." He gives the thing as it is. . . . Mr. Joyce's *Araby*, for instance, is much better than a "story," it is a vivid waiting. (*LE* 400)

A *vivid waiting*: The descriptor fits Pound's own writing as nicely as it does Joyce's. No other Modernist poet has provided a body of writings on the art that has remained as relevant as Pound's. As he put it, when he wanted to create an audience for one of his favorites, "Read him!"

Marjorie Perloff

Poetics: Imagism

Imagism was a poetic movement of the early twentieth century that led to the style later known as Modernism. It began in 1912 in London, when two Americans and one Englishman—Ezra Pound, Hilda Doolittle ("H. D."), and Richard Aldington—agreed on certain principles for writing poetry. In Pound's view, these principles were best exemplified by some poems H. D. showed him in the British Museum Tea Room in the fall of 1912. To her astonishment, he edited them, affixed the signature of "H. D. Imagiste" to them, and then sent them off to Harriet Monroe in Chicago, to be printed in the January 1913, issue of *Poetry: A Magazine of Verse.*

Thus Imagism proper began with Pound and H. D., although a little earlier Pound had attached to his 1912 collection of poems *Ripostes* an appendix that he called "The Complete Poetical Works of T. E. Hulme," a collection of half a dozen brief poems that were really, along with his own, the first published poems in the Imagist mode—short free verse lyrics centering on a single image—and Pound introduced them with the word, in his preferred French spelling, to indicate that the future was in their hands. It was not until March 1913, however, that Pound published "A Few Dont's by an Imagiste" in *Poetry*, laying down what would become famous as the three rules of Imagism:

1. Direct treatment of the "thing" whether subjective or objective.

2. To use absolutely no word that does not contribute to the presentation.

3. As regarding rhythm: to compose in the sequence of the musical phrase, not in sequence of a metronome (*LE* 3).

To these three guiding principles of the new poetic school, Pound added a one-sentence definition: "An 'Image' is that which presents an intellectual and emotional complex in an instant of time" (*LE* 4).

Pound was certainly not the only poet of the new movement, but he was its spokesman, and he edited the first Imagist anthology, which was published in 1914. It bore a French title, *Des Imagistes*—meaning, somewhat vaguely, "Some Imagists"—which was clearly intended to bring to mind the earlier French poetic school of Les Symbolistes; and, indeed, Pound would claim in "A Retrospect," his overview of the Imagist movement published in 1918, that "we thought we had as much right to a group name . . . as a number of French 'schools' " (*LE* 3). So Imagism took its point of departure from Symbolism, though the rules and definition that Pound articulated in 1913 were his own invention rather than translations of earlier French pronouncements about poetry. To distinguish the new Imagism from the older Symbolism, Pound was

careful to insist there was nothing allegorical or ornamental about it, that "the proper and perfect symbol is the natural object," and that "[t]he image is itself the speech." It was through his definitions, and his anthology with examples of the new style, that Imagism emerged as an Anglo-American poetic movement, largely replacing its precursor, the French Symbolist movement.

Surprisingly, Pound did not publish the poem that became the touchstone of Imagism until after his anthology appeared; it was called "In a Station of the Metro," and it was only two lines long:

> The apparition of these faces in the crowd:
> Petals, on a wet, black bough.

With its appearance, and his explanation of how he composed it in Paris using a Japanese haiku as his model, Pound ended his direct involvement in Imagism. It had lasted only from 1912 to 1914, from his agreeing in 1912 on principles for a new poetic style to his 1914 publication of *Des Imagistes* and "In a Station of the Metro."

Nonetheless, the Imagist movement as a whole includes the earlier school to which Pound had belonged, which he came to call "the forgotten School of Images." It began in London in 1909 and was led by T. E. Hulme, whose position was solidified by Pound's publication of Hulme's poems in 1912 at the end of a book of his own poems. This earlier school had been English and had included F. S. Flint among its members; Pound was an American latecomer who arrived after it had started meeting in Le Tour Eiffel restaurant near the British Museum, the unlikely first headquarters of Imagism in London. When F. S. Flint, who was associated both with the earlier and the later Imagist schools, published his "History of Imagism" in the *Egoist* magazine in 1915, he spoke rather scornfully of Pound as a follower of Hulme rather than the leader of a new movement. Flint saw Pound as an enthusiast for the medieval French troubadours—not for the contemporary French Symbolists—and said he had been converted to the new poetic movement because of its discussion of and experiments with the poetic image. Hulme, who was a philosopher as well as a poet, deserves credit for the original formulation of Imagist principles, but Pound invented the term *Imagistes* and promoted the movement, especially among American poets, and Pound would later maintain he started it to publicize poems by H. D., not by Hulme.

At any rate, by 1914 Imagism had become a full-fledged, highly successful poetic movement, and characteristically, Pound lost interest in it, turning the leadership over to the forceful personality of Amy Lowell, another American newly arrived on the London literary scene. Under her direction, Imagism became what Pound disdainfully nicknamed "Amygism," a movement limited to just six poets, three of them English—Richard Aldington, F. S. Flint, and D. H. Lawrence—and three of them American—H. D., John Gould Fletcher, and Amy Lowell herself. In 1915, 1916, and 1917, she edited the three anthologies that were published in Boston as *Some Imagist Poets*, a title echoing Pound's earlier French title but conspicuously excluding him. By that time, there were other American poets experimenting with Imagism, and they were contributors to an anthology called *Others*, among them William Carlos Williams (whom Pound had included in *Des Imagistes*), Marianne Moore, and Wallace Stevens. There were also younger American poets such as Carl Sandburg, E. E. Cummings, and Archibald MacLeish who were writing poems of the Imagist type, though they did not appear in any of the Imagist anthologies.

Imagism dominated the second decade of twentieth-century poetry in English, from 1909 to 1918, and continued to be an influence on poets in later decades, as free verse prevailed and short poems centering on imagery became fashionable. Much later on, T. S. Eliot would confirm that Modernism in English verse began with Imagism, stating, "The *point de repère* usually and conveniently taken, as the starting-point of modern poetry, is the group denominated 'imagist' in London about 1910" (*American Literature and the American Language* 23).

For a summing up of Imagism by Pound, see "A Retrospect" (1918) in the *Literary Essays of Ezra Pound*, edited by T. S. Eliot (3–14).

Bibliography

Eliot, T. S. *American Literature and the American Language: An Address Delivered at Washington University on June 9, 1953*. St. Louis: Washington U, 1953.

William Pratt

Poetics: Prosody

English poetry has developed not one system of prosody but several; beginning with the native Old English alliterative line, with its accentual metric, it later developed the accentual-syllabic system of literary poetry dominant since the mid-sixteenth century. From time to time, poets have attempted quantitative meters. A pure syllabic verse was introduced in the twentieth century by Bridges and, more successfully, by Marianne Moore. Since Whitman, poets have also had the option of "free verse," poetry conforming to no metrical system. Although most poets are content to practice within one or two of these modes, few have assumed mastery of them all: Among these is Pound, who to this author's knowledge, omitted only pure syllabics from his prosodic arsenal.

Even his first volume, *A Lume Spento* (1908), shows Pound ranging from formal regularity to free verse, and within metrical poems experimenting, deliberately roughening, stretching the accepted limits of the prosodic expectation. In this, he follows an American tradition of discomfort with inherited British meters, in such poets as Emerson ("Merlin"), or Poe, with his variable stanzas ("Israfel"). It is difficult indeed to find true formal regularity in this book: The opening "Grace before Song" appears regular metrically but not in its rhyming. True, there is the virtuosic "Villonaud for This Yule," a ballade using only two rhymes. There are variants of the Italian sonnet ("Masks," "Plotinus"), irregular iambics ("The Tree," "Scriptor Ignotus"), irregular litanylike trochaics ("Na Audiart"), bumptious dactylics ("Mesmerism"). There are varied refrains ("Ballad Rosalind"). More free are poems organized largely by syntactic parallelism ("Threnos," "The Cry of the Eyes"), a device presumably learned from Whitman and later brought to perfection in the

Cathay translations. There is even a prose poem, "Malrin." A poem like "la Fraisne" appears iambically based, though it is frustrating to scan. But most prophetic of all is "Cino," a study in contrasted voices, Cino speaking for himself, mimicking others, and singing, with meters juxtaposed as well—all of which foreshadows *The Cantos.*

During the next few years, as if to remedy a defect, Pound devoted great energy to the discipline of strict forms, typically choosing as his models the most intricate of the troubadours. He essayed this challenge in several translations, as well as six poems in *Canzoni* each labeled "canzone," each modeled after a specific troubadour lyric. These poems tend to a sentimental musicality of the kind that Pound later thought "gummy," and they tend to stanzas of a single line length. Later however, circa 1917, Pound returned to Arnaut Daniel and produced translations that reproduce the rhyme and meter of fantastically intricate stanzas and a fondness for "scarce," or unusual, rhymes. In these, he seeks sharpness of sound rather than melodious smoothness, rising to the technical challenge but at the cost of uncontrollable enjambment and implausible diction. From these exercises, he concluded that such elaborate rhyming was not "impossible" but "inadvisable." In his later poetry, rhyming is rare, but if used, he advised, it should "please the expert."

As well, Pound attempted Arnaut Daniel's invention, the sestina, three times in his early work, but preserved only "Sestina: Altaforte" in the 1926 *Personae.* Typically, it is the one that takes license with the prescribed paradigm (lines 27–28 and the envoi).

Ripostes (1912) contains two of Pound's most significant experiments, his sole published attempt at pure quantitative sapphics, "Apparuit," and his celebrated translation of the Old English "Seafarer." "The Seafarer" first appeared in the "I Gathered the Limbs of Osiris" essays (1911), where it represented the elements native to English verse, as yet unmixed with continental importations. Typically, Pound did not reproduce the rules of Old English, with its patterned alliterations and Sievers types; instead, he tried to reproduce the very sounds of the original as closely as possible. "Hrim hrusan band, hægl feoll on eorþan" thus becomes "Frost froze the land, hail fell on earth then." In the process, Pound suggests the alliterative patterns and, more important, preserves the overwhelmingly falling rhythms, most of the lines dropping away from an initial stress as in the original—a feature rarely, if ever, observed in other translations. He returned to this meter in Canto 1.

The quantitative sapphics of "Apparuit" had greater consequences for Pound's prosody. Working not by rule but aural intuition, Pound attempted true English quantities, not just letting accent stand for quantity. Though at times accent and quantity do coincide, close inspection shows many occasions where an accented syllable stands in a short position ("delicately" in line 21), or an unaccented in a long position (the "-ous" in "glamorous sun," line 6). Scansion and pronunciation require some practice, and typically, Pound leaves one problematic line—line 5—that seems to violate the paradigm. Pound never repeated his experiment. But his study of classical quantities led him to bolder experiment in a related poem "The Return": Here, inspection shows a free verse deriving internal structure from varied recombinations of two rhythmic units, the classical choriamb (– ˘˘ –) and the adonic (–˘ ˘–˘). These formal units, like repeated triangles in a Vorticist structure, allow the artist to create a free form that still has a feeling of coherence. The choriamb-adonic rhythm had long rung in Pound's ear (compare "Eyes, dreams, lips, and the night goes" from "Cino"), and Pound's free verse at its most crafted often resorts to these and other rhythmic units.

Though the poems of Pound's Imagist phase pursue *phanopoeia* more than *melopoeia*, the famous Imagist Credo includes a metrical article—to compose according to "musical phrase," not the "metronome." Essentially this is a validation of Pound's intuitive practice; yet behind it stands his avowed belief in "absolute rhythm," an exact correspondence between verbal rhythm and emotion. Free verse is a means of expressing emotions not capturable by meter, a means of technical discovery. When Amy Lowell hijacked the Imagist name, however, she advanced free verse "as for a principle of liberty"—liberation, it seemed, not only from meter but from technique. Pound protested in a letter (January 1915) that "rhythm MUST have meaning," but he was fighting on two fronts, simultaneously advancing the cause of free verse and fighting advocates of technical sloppiness.

One consequence of this dilemma, *Hugh Selwyn Mauberley* was written in the belief that by 1917 the free verse movement had gone "too far." Based on the polished rhymed quatrains of Théophile Gautier, much of *Mauberley* exhibits a similar virtuosic rhyming. But unlike Eliot—whose quatrain poems, written at the same time, are metrically strict—Pound allows his meters great freedom within the rhyme scheme, now loosening, now contracting to a point. This freedom within suggestions of formal constraint is a highly original innovation but uncharacteristic of his work as a whole. Something resembling this technique appears, however, in his translation of *The Confucian Odes* (1954).

When Pound set out writing the first cantos in 1915, the so-called *Ur*-Cantos, his metrical decision was surprising: Critics have scarcely noticed that these three poems are written largely in a highly irregular Browningesque variety of blank verse. If he meant to continue in this mode, having established his metrical contract, the finished product that we call *The Cantos* would have been far different from what we know. The much-quoted line in Canto 81, "to break the pentameter, that was the first heave," may refer to this change of direction.

The Cantos as we have them present a bewildering array of formal techniques that seem to defy generalization. Much of the poem uses a very loose, colloquial free verse, but there are also many highly worked up lyrical passages. The extremes range even from "prose" (Malatesta's letters, Canto 9) through degrees of more controlled free verse to metered passages ("Tudor indeed is gone," Canto 80), at times reaching great intricacy (Cavalcanti's canzone, Canto 36). Outer extremes range from wordless music (Janequin in Canto 75) to unpronounceable visual icons (the playing cards in Canto 88). This is more than simple diversity. Arguably, *The Cantos* operates within a metrical decorum closely tied to its theme of permanent, recurrent, and casual. Furthermore, the juxtapositions seem self-conscious, making meter itself part of the subject of the poem—as in Canto 1. Narrative or journalistic material remains rough-hewn, sometimes explicable as a loose accentual meter, like the Ovidian tale in Canto 2. In lyrical passages, however, slack syllables become fewer, and patterns emerge like the classical quantitative units foreshadowed in "The Return" (though created by English stress). These patterns, usually allied to heightened diction and fragmented syntax, also prevent more familiar English meters from forming.

Pound's metrical variations remain free and intuitive, simultaneously avowing and disavowing meter. He claims the relevance of many metrical systems in a virtually thematic way but retains the poet's freedom from the constraints of any.

Bibliography

Adams, Stephen J. "The Metrical Contract of *The Cantos*." *Journal of Modern Literature* 15 (1988): 55–72.

Childs, John Steven. *Modernist Form: Pound's Style in the Early Cantos*. Selinsgrove: Susquehanna UP, 1986.

Powell, James A. "The Light of Vers Libre." *Paideuma* 8.1 (1979): 3–34.

Stauder, Ellen Keck. "Crystal Waves Weaving Together: Visual Notation and the Phrasal Music of the *Rock-Drill Cantos*." *Paideuma* 26.2–3 (1997): 93–110.

Stephen J. Adams

Poetics: Vorticism

Energy, *force*, and *dynamism* are the terms Ezra Pound associated with Vorticism. The movement developed in the wake of the Post-Impressionist and Futurist exhibitions held in London in 1910–1913. The painter Wyndham Lewis, who was exhibiting nearly abstract works as early as 1912, hoped to distinguish advanced English art from French Cubism, Italian Futurism, and German Expressionism. He founded the Rebel Art Centre and a journal, *BLAST* (two issues, 1914 and 1915), to establish an alternative to the foreign movements that were dominating the attention of English critics such as Roger Fry. *BLAST* and Vorticism were inspired by F. T. Marinetti's success in publicizing his Futurism movement in England during his visits in 1910 and 1912. Marinetti's example inspired Lewis and Pound to become the entrepreneurs of their own art. The "Blasts" and "Blesses" of people, objects, and ideas in *BLAST* were influenced by Guillaume Apollinaire's "Rose" and "Merde" list in the Futurist journal *Lacerba* (June 1913).

The nucleus of the rebels included the painters Frederick Etchells, Edward Wadsworth, and William Roberts and the sculptor Henri Gaudier-Brzeska. When Lewis's friend Pound joined the group, he lectured on poetry at the Rebel Centre, suggested the name "Vorticism" for the movement, and obtained T. S. Eliot's "Preludes" for *BLAST*'s first issue. Pound felt for the first time that he was associated with a group of artists capable of revolutionary art and leading the way to a new cultural renaissance in England. The goal of the Rebel Art Centre was to "familiarize those who are interested with the ideas of the great modern revolution," and the goal of *BLAST* was to ridicule and blow away the dead ideas of a post-Victorian age. Like Cubist art, Vorticist art was rarely completely abstract; but it emphasized geometric forms such as the triangle, arc, and circle—often organized in strongly diagonal or spiral designs.

The dynamic forms of Vorticism distinguished it from what Lewis considered the static quality of Cubist design, which he characterized as relying too heavily on natural forms and traditional genres such as the still life. Although Lewis always insisted that abstract compositions were ultimately derived from representational forms, the Vorticists looked to the machine and the city rather than nature for inspiration. *BLAST* proclaimed that Vorticist art was filled with "the forms of machinery, factories, new and vaster buildings, bridges and works." However, the Vorticists considered the modern world a dehumanized "iron jungle" and dismissed the naive praise of machines in Futurism (Lewis called it "automobilism," and Pound an "accelerated sort of Impressionism"). Rather than Futurism's speeding and blurred forms, Vorticist forms were clearly illuminated and sharply contoured. Instead of glorifying activity and change for its own sake, it sought the still center of the Vortex. Pound wrote that "the Vorticist is at his maximum point of energy when stillest" (*EPPP* 283). The Vortex was a "radiant node or cluster" through which "ideas are constantly rushing," and it did not reject the past but focused these revolutionary ideas on the present. The manifestos were divided into juxtaposed blocks and lines of print, often using parallel grammar and syntax, that were the verbal equivalent of Vorticist painting.

To Lewis, Vorticism was essentially a visual art, but Pound believed that Vorticist principles applied to all great art. Stretching the term in a way Lewis distrusted, Pound could find Vorticist principles in Chinese art or a Vortex of activity in Renaissance Italy. Pound embraced the movement as a way of distinguishing his art from the static, pictorial images that had become associated with Imagism. The term *Vorticism* suggested the greater energy and dynamism of the Vorticist image. It indicated poetry that goes beyond the mimetic to express "a world of moving energies"; the Vorticist image is not a picture but a force. In the 1914 *BLAST*, Pound declared that the Vorticists use the "primary pigment" of their art: "EVERY CONCEPT, EVERY EMOTION PRESENTS ITSELF TO THE VIVID CONSCIOUSNESS IN SOME PRIMARY FORM. . . . IF SOUND, TO MUSIC; IF FORMED WORDS, TO LITERATURE; THE IMAGE, TO POETRY . . . COLOR IN POSITION TO PAINTING" (*EPPP* 260). The primary forms of Lewis's *Timon of Athens* drawings are their "lines, and masses, and planes" rather than the armored figures that are drawn to the center of the design. Pound's master image for the Vortex was the organization that a magnet imparts to iron filings. His conception of a dynamic image helped Pound in 1914 to conceive of a long Vorticist poem (*The Cantos*) in which a pattern of images, like the "units of design" in a Vorticist painting, could be presented without representational or narrative continuity and would gain force from their juxtaposition.

The movement ended when many of the Vorticists went to fight in World War I. During the war, Pound continued to promote the movement by arranging a Vorticist show in New York (January 1917) and working with Alvin Langdon Coburn to develop Vorticist photography ("Vortography"). His *Gaudier-Brzeska: A Memoir* (1916) continued to promote the movement. However, Gaudier-Brzeska died in the war, and Lewis's postwar painting reacted against what he came to feel was the sterility of abstraction. But the movement convinced Pound that a small nucleus of avant-garde artists could create a contemporary renaissance and inspired him to continue creating poetry out of the "primary pigment" of the image.

Bibliography

Cork, Richard. *Vorticism and Abstract Art in the First Machine Age*. 2 vols. Berkeley: U of California P, 1976.

Dasenbrock, Reed Way. *The Literary Vorticism of Ezra Pound and Wyndham Lewis: Towards the Condition of Painting*. Baltimore: Johns Hopkins UP, 1985.

Materer, Timothy. *Vortex: Pound, Eliot, and Lewis.* Ithaca: Cornell UP, 1979.

Wees, William C. *Vorticism and the English Avant-Garde*. Toronto: U of Toronto P, 1972.

Timothy Materer

Poetry: A Magazine of Verse

Founded by Harriet Monroe in Chicago in 1912, *Poetry: A Magazine of Verse* quickly became a pivotal register of the most innovative writing in Modern poetry. From Imagist poets like H. D. and Richard Aldington to new American voices like Carl Sandburg and Wallace Stevens, *Poetry* became an unprecedented venue for serious writers and readers. From its beginning in 1912 to roughly 1917, *Poetry*—which continues to publish—was the preeminent American journal for the most daring international as well as American poetry.

The most important influence on the magazine was its first foreign correspondent, Ezra Pound. Responding from London to Monroe's original circular outlining the goals of the periodical, Pound challenged her to provide a serious outlet for poetry: "Can you teach the American poet that poetry *is* an *art*, an art with a technique. . . . Can you teach him that it is not a pentametric echo of the sociological dogma printed in last year's magazines?" (*L* 9). Assured that *Poetry* stood for the new and would welcome the unconventional, Pound quickly secured contributions from the well-known and unknown among his poetic circle: "I've had luck again," he wrote to Monroe in October 1912, "and am sending you some *modern* stuff by an American, I say modern, for it is in the laconic speech of the Imagistes, even if the subject is classic" (*L* 11). The work was by H. D. and soon the Imagist debate overtook the magazine, which included two important essays on the subject in 1913, F. S. Flint's "History of Imagism" and Pound's "A Few Don'ts by an Imagiste."

Controversy often characterized the journal, adding to its liveliness and interest: whether it was awarding its first poetry prize to W. B. Yeats rather than Vachel Lindsay, the War Poem contest of 1914 that featured Stevens, the constant championing of free verse, the bold positions of its reviewers confirmed by their frequent sniping at other journals, or the appearance of unorthodox works like Ford Madox Ford's "On Heaven" and poems by D. H. Lawrence, *Poetry* was the center of debate.

In the midst of such disputes, the magazine continued to discover new voices and poems, notably Lindsay's "General William Booth Enters into Heaven" (1913) and work by Sandburg, Amy Lowell, and Marianne Moore. Monroe, however, favored American Midwest poets, while Pound insisted on a more international scope, supported by the associate editor, Alice Corbin Henderson. Henderson also urged Monroe to forget schools and maintain poetry of the highest standard that might, at times, strike others as "indecent" or improper. Yet, she argued, *Poetry* must never compromise its high standards.

Notable among new work to appear in *Poetry* was Pound's "Three Cantos," received first by

Alice Corbin Henderson, then living in Santa Fe, New Mexico. She sent them on with praise to Monroe in Chicago, whose reaction was unenthusiastic: "I read two or three pages of Ezra's Cantos and then took sick—no doubt that was the cause. Since then I haven't had brains enough to tackle it" (*L/ACH* 194). She completed them a month later, admitting that they have "his quality—though more diluted than usual" (*L/ACH* 194) and suggested that they appear in serial form, which they did over the summer of 1917. Other major works to appear in *Poetry* include Eliot's "The Love Song of J. Alfred Prufrock" (June 1915), Wallace Stevens's "Sunday Morning" (November 1915), and three poems by James Joyce, the first he published in America (May 1917).

Supplementing the verse was the prose, often important critical statements by contributors like Ford, whose essay "Impressionism" appeared in 1913, or Pound, whose three-part series "The Renaissance" appeared in 1915. Editorials or reviews by Monroe and Henderson added to the critical importance of these assessments on the state of American and European poetry, often challenging received ideas about poetry and its value. The appearance of occasional special topics, like the "Objectivists" issue of February 1931 edited by Louis Zukofsky, added further controversy and luster to the journal.

The first five years of *Poetry* were its most exciting as it conveyed a new direction for writing. From 1917 on, however, it seemed to lose some of its edge, a reflection of Pound's unofficial departure from the staff, although his name remained on the roster of editors until 1919, and he acted as adviser until 1921. His conception of poetry as a weapon in intellectual controversies contrasted with Monroe's view of poetry as being inclusive and artistic. Pound had sought only genuine masterworks to publish and declined experiments in verse unless they were successful. And when the magazine did not measure up, his response was unrestrained: "*My gawddd! This* IS *a* ROTTEN *number of Poetry*," he exclaimed to Monroe in 1915 (*L* 60). His courage made the journal daring; her conservatism made it respectable. Without Pound, the

magazine began to reflect rather than initiate new movements.

Poetry paid for the work it printed, adding professionalism to the publication. It also pioneered a series of prizes and awards. Yeats won the first for "The Grey Rock," establishing a standard of excellence and underlining the need for public recognition of poetry. Later prizewinners included Eliot, Sandburg, Hart Crane, Stevens, and Moore. The pragmatism of Monroe sustained the magazine through its post-Pound era and ensured its continuation to the present. Eclecticism and diversity defined the editorial policy of *Poetry* during and following the tenure of Monroe, whose policy, as an editorial in the second issue declared, was "to print the best English verse . . . regardless of where, by whom or under what theory of art it is written" (*Poetry* 1 [1912]: 64).

Bibliography

Monroe, Harriet. *A Poet's Life*. New York: Macmillan, 1938.

Williams, Ellen. *Harriet Monroe and the Poetry Renaissance. The First Ten Years of Poetry 1912–1922*. Urbana: U of Illinois P, 1977.

Ira B. Nadel

Politics

In the last of *The Pisan Cantos*, Ezra Pound writes of the hated Franklin Roosevelt, "an' doan you think he chop and change all the time / stubborn az a mule, sah, stubborn as a MULE, / got th' eastern idea about money" (Canto 84). Pound's political views cannot be separated from his economic views, even from his earliest years. Carpenter has discovered that Pound's first published poem, in 1896, was on William Jennings Bryan's defeat: "There was a young man from the West, / He did what he could for what he thought best" (36n). More than forty years later, he was still thinking about Bryan and the lively discussions about Populist issues that he heard while growing up—the concentration of capital in the East that beggared farmers, ranchers, and miners in the West, a situation to be solved by the free coinage of silver. When, for example, he attacks Churchill for returning to "the putrid gold standard / as was about

1925" (Canto 74), he is recalling Bryan's famous "Cross of Gold Speech," delivered at the Democratic National Convention in Chicago on 9 July 1896: "You shall not press down upon the brow of labor this crown of thorns. You shall not crucify mankind upon a cross of gold." Pound's political views can only be understood by considering their origins in American Populism.

For example, Charles Macune's 1889 Subtreasury Land and Loan proposal closely resembled the fascist system of *ammassi*, which Pound supported in the 1940s. Noting that banks and the gold standard forced hardship on farmers, who sold their crops at harvest when the market was lowest, and borrowed at planting time when rates were highest, Macune proposed that warehouses be established by the federal government: Farmers would store their crops and receive certificates of deposit on which they could borrow government-issued greenbacks. They could then sell their crops when they chose. Macune believed that this reform would take control of the nation's credit away from commercial banks and restore it to the U.S. government.

Pound grew up during the heated Main Street versus Wall Street debates of the Populist upheaval, but as he turned to a doctrine of art for art's sake, he was exposed to politics and economics during his decade of involvement with the socialist *New Age*, London's premiere cultural and political weekly, and its editor A. R. Orage. Orage's central idea was that "economic power always precedes political power." Throughout the Great War, the *New Age* blasted the disproportionate sacrifices made by the working class and the privileges accorded to the financial class. Lives were sacrificed through conscription; profiteering was preserved through collusion between government and finance. The *New Age*, like *The Cantos*, inscribes an economic view of history and politics. Pound's turn to politics was reluctant, but it is clearly announced in a 1921 review of C. H. Douglas's *Credit Power and Democracy*. It is remarkable enough that Pound was reviewing a book on economics, but he articulates his change of position clearly: "The symbolist position, ar-

tistic aloofness from world affairs, is no good *now*" (*EPPP* 2.225). Pound's change paralleled Orage's, who on 6 November 1921 wrote that Douglas's Social Credit ideas fulfilled his own economic theories.

Pound's turn to politics was motivated by World War I. But his interest actually waned during the 1920s. During this time, he received a favorable impression of Lenin from John Reed, but he was absorbed in his poetry and his new passion for music. His political comments were limited to three items affecting artists: copyright protection for authors, the banning of *Ulysses* for obscenity, and the new nuisance of passports. He had little to say about Mussolini or the fascist state of Italy; world opinion of Mussolini was generally favorable until the Abyssinian War of 1935.

But by 1932, the worldwide Great Depression was clearly to be of long duration, and Pound's concern for politics and economics reawakened. Orage returned to England and in 1932 started the *New English Weekly*, to which Pound contributed 200 articles during the 1930s. The election of Roosevelt that year gave Pound a glimmer of hope for reform, which darkened quickly as Pound became convinced FDR was a tool of the bankers.

In April 1933, the *ABC of Economics* was published by Faber, its dust jacket noting that Pound had given a series of lectures at Luigi Bocconi University, Milan, "on economics, not on the mummified muses." "In politics *the* problem of our time," he writes, "is to find the border between public and private affairs. . . . In economics: to find a means whereby the common-carrier may be in such way kept in circulation" (*SP* 240). He advocated some specific remedies: shortening the workday while keeping wages the same by having the government issue paper credit and spending debt-free paper money on public works. Although he admired Marx's passion for social reform, he followed Proudhon, Gesell, and Douglas, dismissing Marx's economics because he did not understand the nature of money. Pound kept up correspondence with Douglas and wrote to American lawmakers, but the crucial event for Pound's politics at this time was his meeting with Mussolini on 30 January 1933.

By all accounts a charismatic man, Mussolini won Pound over: "Livest hour I have spent in some time," he wrote to Dorothy Pound. "Livest animal I have seen since I last saw Picabia." Pound was invited back the next day. But the meeting was canceled. Hitler had just been named chancellor of Germany, and Mussolini's day was devoted to meetings on what Italians saw as a foreign affairs crisis.

Pound has little to say about Hitler, but his admiration for Mussolini is unbounded. After the meeting he started work on his book *Jefferson and/or Mussolini*. He began dating events using the fascist-era calendar. In Canto 41, he sees Mussolini as a successful reformer whom he might persuade to realize the economic ideas of Douglas, and later of Gesell. And Mussolini's socialist roots awakened Pound's memories of his long affiliation with Orage and led him to characterize his own politics as "left-wing fascism" (Redman 157). James Gregor correctly describes the Italian regime as a developmental dictatorship and fascism as a Marxist heresy. Pound compares *Jefferson and/or Mussolini* to Dante's *De Monarchia* and draws upon his extensive experience of Italy to demonstrate that fascism was the form of government best suited to the problems of Italy. It is not, he makes clear, a system for other countries. The principal subject of the book is Mussolini; Jefferson appears partly to attract the attention of an American audience and partly because Pound had been reading Jefferson and portraying him in Cantos 31, 32, and 33. Lenin also comes in for praise—showing that the simplistic categories of "Right" and "Left" are completely inadequate to describe Pound's politics.

The book is difficult to characterize. It demonstrates the failure of Pound's largely eighteenth-century political vision to explain twentieth-century dictatorship. Pound's *directio voluntatis* was drawn from Dante, whereas Mussolini's will to power was drawn from Nietzsche. Pound dismisses complaints about the Italian loss of liberty under fascism. And he uses aesthetic criteria to judge the artform of

statecraft practiced by Lenin and Mussolini. Although the book advances valid observations on Italian history and society, it must be seen, finally, as an act of *fede fascista* in Mussolini's accomplishments: "grain, swamp-drainage, restorations, new buildings" (*J/M* 73). But Pound's faith would be betrayed when Il Duce led his nation first into Abyssinia, then disastrously into World War II.

Pound, acting as apologist for fascist Italy abroad, was particularly unhappy about its portrayal as right-wing and reactionary. In April 1934 he wrote to Ubaldo Degli Uberti, who had written for the *New Age*, that "no one has heard of the left wing of the fascist party, for ten years fascism was supposed to be reaction in the pay of bankers" (Redman 156). As Leon Surette has ably chronicled, around this time Louis Zukofsky sent Pound an article, "The Mystery of the Civil War and Lincoln's Death," that attributes these events to a Jewish conspiracy. Pound's belief in a conspiracy-based anti-Semitism began at this time, vitiating much of his subsequent writing on economics and politics.

Italy's war in Abyssinia began in October 1935. Pound's devotion to Mussolini led him to justify the war and led to a hopeless muddle in his thought. Having begun his study of economics and politics to avoid war, Pound employed the racist, colonialist rhetoric of the time, as well as his growing anti-Semitism, to explain the correctness of this particular war. His increasing frustration and anger, the result of a little-understood bipolar disorder, made his attempts to communicate more fragmentary and difficult. Sanctions imposed on Italy by the League of Nations then led to the Axis pact between Mussolini and Hitler in October 1936, and for the next nine years, the situations of Italy, Mussolini, and Pound deteriorated rapidly.

Pound meanwhile had manifested contempt for England since his departure in 1921. In correspondence from that time he described the "leprosy" of the British Empire and excoriated Churchill's decision to return to the gold standard (a critique in Pound's Populist vein, shared by John Maynard Keynes, among others). But Pound's support in the late 1930s for Sir Oswald

Mosley's British Union of Fascists led to further strain with the English. The first issue of the *British Union Quarterly* (January–April 1937) announces contributions by Wyndham Lewis, Pound, Leon de Poncins, Roy Campbell, and Vidkun Quisling. An editorial describes public disorder as product of "Red agitators acting largely at Jewish instigation" and denounces "the frenzied Jewish campaign for war" (7–8). It critiques Neville Chamberlain's decision to increase gold reserves of the Bank of England as benefitting "the international usury system" (13). In contrast, "Italy Leads the Way to Sanity" praises Italy for freeing itself from gold while focusing on national production and managed currency (14). The issue also contains Pound's article "Demarcations," which monotonously reiterates "the STATE has credit" (35), and an enthusiastic notice of *Jefferson and/or Mussolini*. The second issue prints another article by Pound, while an editorial praises "the boldness of Japan [in the Sino-Japanese conflict] in challenging the two greatest international forces in the world," finance and communism (5). Pound shared most of the journal's political philosophy.

Pound's politics increased in stridency, if not always insight, during World War II. Exceptions include pieces for the well-regarded *Meridiano di Roma*; in one, he synthesizes Social Credit with the ideals of the fascist state: "[C]redit is a collective product, that is, statal. It depends on civic order. . . . Every individual citizen has the right to participate in the gains of the State" (Redman 199). Increasingly, Pound sought ancient wisdom to address contemporary issues, in frequent appeals for study of Greek and Latin classics and especially his own translations of Confucius.

The rant of Pound's radio speeches, for which he was indicted for treason, merits little attention, even in the sanitized edition by Leonard Doob. As the war ended, Mussolini was arrested by the Italians in July 1943, then freed in September by the Germans, who established him in a Nazi puppet state, the Republic of Salò. Pound, in Rome at the time, made an arduous trek to the north to visit his daughter and make

contact with the new regime. He was encouraged by the left-wing fascism in the manifesto of the Republican Fascist Party in mid-November. But Pound's pamphlets in Italian for the Salò regime contain little new; his articles for *Il Popolo di Alessandria* contain new material only in their more vicious anti-Semitism. Of his work during this time, only his poetry (early versions of *The Pisan Cantos*) and his translations of Confucius possess enduring merit. On 3 May 1945, Pound was taken into American custody and, after imprisonment in Pisa, was flown to Washington, D.C., to stand trial for treason. Conrad Rushing has demonstrated that although Pound's insanity plea was appropriate in the political climate of the time, Pound would probably have been exonerated had he gone to trial a few years later. Nevertheless, his wartime Rome Radio broadcasts remain his most disquieting political act.

Although he avoided public comment during his years at St. Elizabeths, Pound contributed unsigned pieces to small journals run by Noel Stock, William McNaughton, and others. These pieces and his correspondence show his political allegiances unchanged. He corresponded with right-wing groups like the Defenders of the American Constitution and the Seabord White Citizens' Council. Although Pound was not racist, he supported a states' rights agenda. His views were undoubtedly influenced by Dorothy Pound's increasing concern over damage to the environment, and his antiindustrial attitudes are often congruent with those of the Southern Agrarians, as expressed in their 1930 collection *I'll Take My Stand*. Alec Marsh has noted these similarities, but they have not been widely discussed. Pound complained that discussion of fascism took place in ignorance of *fascio di sinistra* (left-wing fascism) and of the writings of Odon Por and Carlo Pellizzi. Such remarks remind us that his politics cannot be simplified and deserve nuanced exploration, as in the work of Felice Chilanti.

After the treason indictment against Pound was dismissed in 1958, he returned to Italy where, talking to reporters, he was photographed giving the fascist salute. Pound refrained from political statements during his final years. He felt insufficiently informed and was absorbed with his poetry. He lapsed into serious depression through his final decade and seldom spoke. But he attended a reception for Sir Oswald Mosley in Rome, and his mute presence on stage was eloquent enough.

Bibliography

Chilanti, Felice. "Ezra Pound among the Seditious in the 1940s." Trans. David Anderson. *Paideuma* 6.2 (1977): 235–250.

Ferkiss, Victor. "Ezra Pound and American Fascism." *Journal of Politics* 17 (May 1955): 174–195.

Flory, Wendy Stallard. *The American Ezra Pound.* New Haven: Yale UP, 1989.

Goodwin, Lawrence. *The Populist Moment: A Short History of the Agrarian Revolt in America.* New York: Oxford UP, 1978.

Gregor, James A. *Italian Fascism and Developmental Dictatorship.* Princeton: Princeton UP, 1979.

———. *Young Mussolini and the Intellectual Origins of Fascism.* Berkeley: U of California P, 1979.

Marsh, Alec. *Money and Modernity: Pound, Williams, and the Spirit of Jefferson.* Tuscaloosa: U of Alabama P, 1998.

Nicholls, Peter J. *Politics, Economics, and Writing.* London: Macmillan, 1984.

Redman, Tim. *Ezra Pound and Italian Fascism.* New York: Cambridge UP, 1991.

Rushing, Conrad. " 'Mere Words': The Trial of Ezra Pound." *Critical Enquiry* 14 (Autumn 1987): 111–133.

Surette, Leon. *Pound in Purgatory: From Economic Radicalism to Anti-Semitism.* Urbana: U of Illinois P, 1999.

Tim Redman

Il Popolo di Alessandria

From November 1943 to April 1945, Pound contributed more than sixty entries to the fascist fortnightly *Il Popolo di Alessandria*, an instrument of the Fasci Repubblicani di Combattimento. This material had been all but inaccessible until the publication of *Ezra Pound's Poetry and Prose: Contributions to Periodicals* (1991). The majority of these articles deal with economic themes, including the struggle between the international (mainly British and American) forces of plutocracy and usurocracy and young nations such as Fascist Italy (or eighteenth-century America) striving to combat economic tyranny. Pound lists the names and merits of thinkers and writers who, in his opinion, have opposed usurocracy, including A. R. Orage, C. H. Douglas, Silvio Gesell, and Brooks Adams. In these brief articles one occasionally comes across memorable statements such as "The treasure of a nation is its honesty" or other pronouncements whose value goes beyond the *hic et nunc* of the slogans of the period. Of special interest are the two installments titled "Confucio Parla" (23 December 1944 and 2 January 1945) with Pound's translations of Confucius's ethical teachings that deal with the conduct of the individual and honest government of the state or the nation.

Bibliography

Turris, G. De. "La collaborazione al 'Popolo di Alessandria' di Ezra Pound." *La Destra* (Rome) 2.11–12 (1972): 117–137.

Stefano Maria Casella

Por, Odon (1883–?)

The Hungarian-born economist Odon Por wrote to Ezra Pound to introduce himself in early April 1934. He described himself as "an old New Age–Orage man . . . trying to propagate Social Credit here" (Redman 156). Before coming to Italy, Por had lived in England, where he contributed several articles on trade unionism to the *New Age*. The correspondence between the two was one of the richest of Pound's fascist period. Earle Davis correctly observed that Por strongly influenced Pound's ideas about "the intent and execution of Mussolini's program" (Davis 157).

Por contributed articles to important Italian periodicals such as *Osservatore Romano* and *Civilta' Fascista*. He had influential friends among fascist intellectuals and politicians. Por's letters to Pound gave the poet hope that the economic reforms he advocated were being put into effect by Mussolini's regime. But Social Credit never happened in Italy, and the two friends' correspondence functioned largely to shore up each other's *fede fascista* and help each other with journalistic contacts and assignments. Editors occasionally demonstrated skepticism about Pound's economic theories: Por wrote to Pound on 14 June 1935: "The editor of *Civilta' Fascista* asks you to write him an article on anything except economics" (Redman 163).

Shortly after the outbreak of World War II, Por wrote to Pound sounding him out about contributing to Italian propaganda efforts, perhaps by writing a pamphlet to be called "Pound, an Open Letter to Americans." On 11 September 1939, Pound sent Por a mild letter addressed to the English, with a proposal for a more scathing one for the Americans. Pound was in financial difficulties at this time, and Por helped him out, finding him work translating Por's new book *Politica Economico-Sociale in Italia Anno XVII–XVIII* into English. *Italy's Policy of Social Economics 1939/1940* appeared in September 1941.

Por was proud of his work on political economy. He wrote to Pound on 22 February 1936: "I will send you my early stuff. Much of the best buried in New Age (Orage's)—of which I have no copy." Pound's own assessment of their contribution appeared in a 6 March 1939 letter to Henry Swabey: "E. P. with Por one of first to compare and correlate the DIFFERENT contemporary programmes: Corp[orate]. State, Doug[las], Gesell" (Redman, 186). Attempting to find, combine, and put into practice the best ideas in Italian fascism, C. H. Douglas's Social Credit, and Silvio Gesell's stamp scrip absorbed most of Pound's and Por's journalistic and epistolary energies during this time.

(Note: Por's articles for the *New Age* can be found online at the Modernist Journals Project. The Pound–Por correspondence is at the Beinecke Library at Yale.)

Bibliography

Davis, Earle K. *Vision Fugitive: Ezra Pound and Economics*. Lawrence: UP of Kansas, 1968.
Redman, Tim. *Ezra Pound and Italian Fascism*. New York: Cambridge UP, 1991.

Tim Redman

Pound, Homer Loomis (1858–1942)

Ezra Pound's father Homer was born in Chippewa Falls, Wisconsin, the son of a lumber and railroad entrepreneur, Thaddeus Coleman Pound, and Susan Angevin Loomis. Homer was a freethinker not particularly interested in school or work. He was accepted to West Point, despite having run away from his military school, but got off the train and returned home.

Homer's father, who had lost a couple of fortunes by the 1880s, owned silver mines near Hailey, Idaho. Hoping to employ Homer in some useful way, Thaddeus used his influence in Washington to persuade the president to open a Government Land Office in Hailey and appoint his son "Register" in 1883. In 1884 Homer married Isabel Weston of New York, whom he had met through her aunt, Frances Amelia Weston. Hailey, Idaho, proved too rugged (both physically and socially) for Isabel, and a year and a half after Ezra's birth, she returned East with their child. Homer soon followed.

Having become an expert assayer of silver, in 1889 Homer was appointed as an assistant assayer to the U.S. Mint in Philadelphia. While living in Wyncote, Pennsylvania, and working at the Mint, Homer took an active interest in his son's career and handled some of his literary and financial affairs in the United States. Ezra himself greatly admired his father's talent at judging the quality of silver, which he described as "an aesthetic perception, like the critical sense" (Carpenter 17). Homer remained at the Mint until his retirement in 1928. In 1929 he and Isabel moved to Rapallo, Italy, both to be near Ezra and to make the most of their retirement income. He died there in 1942.

Bibliography

Carpenter, Humphrey. *A Serious Character: The Life of Ezra Pound*. Boston: Houghton Mifflin, 1998.

Patricia A. Cockram

Pound, Isabel Weston (1860–1948)

Ezra Pound's mother was born in New York City to Harding Weston, a ne'er-do-well, and Mary Parker Weston, whose ancestry included a Wadsworth. Harding had served in the military but was never again employed. One of his brothers, Ezra, took in Mary and Isabel. Ezra Weston was eccentric, but he was successful enough to support his family and his brother's wife and daughter. He and his wife Frances ran an artists' colony in Nyack, New York, an enterprise that quickly failed. Afterward, they opened a boarding house in New York City, where Isabel spent most of her childhood.

Isabel was a spoiled only child, who grew up to be a pretty if affected (Pound once referred to his mother as the "Presbyterian peacock") young woman, whom Ezra's friends described as remote. She and Homer adored their son and supported him in all his undertakings, but it was primarily Isabel who encouraged his intellectual pursuits. After her marriage to Homer, Isabel found herself in the rugged Idaho Territory, where her new husband was Register of the Government Land Office in Hailey. A year and a half after Ezra's birth, Isabel took him back to the East, and Homer soon followed.

Isabel and Homer brought Ezra up at Wyncote, Pennsylvania, a suburb of Philadelphia, where Homer was employed as an assistant assayer at the U.S. Mint. After Homer's retirement from the Mint, the Pounds moved to Rapallo, Italy, in 1929. Isabel died there in 1948.

Patricia A. Cockram

Pound, Omar Shakespear (b. 1926)

Born in the American Hospital in Paris, 10 September 1926, and registered by Ezra and Dorothy Pound the following day with the French civil authorities, Omar Pound was also registered, in due course, as a U.S. citizen.

He went to London at eighteen months under the care of Dorothy's mother, Olivia Shakespear, to the Norland Institute in London where families living oversees often sent their children. In 1931 Homer and Isabel visited him there. In 1933 he moved to Sussex, where he enrolled in the local Montessori school, then in the local preparatory school. When Olivia died in 1938, Ezra went to London to settle her estate because Dorothy was in hospital, and Omar visited him at Olivia's apartment.

In 1940 Omar entered Charterhouse School in Surrey, where a dozen of his ancestors had been. On 26 June 1942, he was confirmed into the Church of England, adding "Shakespear" as his legal middle name. In 1943 he left Charterhouse to train in hotel management in London. Bombed out of London in 1944, he was evacuated to a farm in the west of England.

In 1945 he volunteered for the U.S. Army, trained in France, and served in the Army of Occupation in Germany. While in Germany he got leave to visit Dorothy in Rapallo and en route visited the Disciplinary Training Center near Pisa where he missed by a day or two Ezra, who had been taken to Washington, D.C., via Rome. Once Omar was back in the United States, he was allowed to visit Ezra for fifteen minutes at St. Elizabeths Hospital in the "Hell-Hole," their first reunion since 1938. He also attended one of Ezra's court hearings in 1946 while still in uniform.

Following his discharge he attended Hamilton College on the G.I. Bill of Rights, majoring in anthropology and French. Taking a break from Hamilton, he attended the London School of Oriental and African Studies to study Persian and Islamic history. While there he was awarded an Iranian Government scholarship to the University of Tehran to continue his study of Persian literature and language. Following his graduation from Hamilton College in 1954, he received a Rockefeller Foundation scholarship to the Institute of Islamic Studies at McGill University in Montreal, receiving his M.A. in Islamic Studies in 1958.

From 1957 to 1962 he taught at the Roxbury Latin School, Boston, and in 1962 accepted the headmastership at the American School of Tangier, Morocco. His wife, Elizabeth Stevenson Parkin, and two young children followed him in due course. His contract finished, he returned to England and taught at the Cambridgeshire College of Arts and Technology, remaining there until his move, in 1980, to Princeton University, where he taught for several years freshman composition.

While in England he published his own translations of *Arabic & Persian Poems* (Fulcrum P, 1970; New Directions, 1970), introduction by Basil Bunting; *Corby and the Rats*, a translation of a fourteenth-century Persian children's tale (various editions); and *Wyndham Lewis: A*

Descriptive Bibliography (1978), with Philip Grover. At Princeton he published *Ezra Pound and Dorothy Shakespear, Their Letters 1908–1914*, with A. Walton Litz (1984), and *Ezra Pound and Margaret Cravens: A Tragic Friendship 1910–1912* (1988), and *Ezra and Dorothy Pound: Letters in Captivity 1945–1946* (1999), both with Robert Spoo. He also published several volumes of poetry and contributions to little magazines.

In 1989 he received an honorary degree (D.H.L.) from Lawrence University, Appleton, Wisconsin, retiring shortly after. He is a founding trustee of the Wyndham Lewis Memorial Fund in England.

Omar Pound

Pound, Thaddeus Coleman (1832–1914)

Ezra Pound's grandfather Thaddeus was born in a pioneer shack in Elk, Pennsylvania. He married Susan Angevine Loomis from upstate New York, and they settled in Chippewa Falls, Wisconsin, where he worked as a bookkeeper for a lumber company. They had three children, Homer, Florence, and a son who died. Thaddeus was energetic, ambitious, and charismatic, and he soon became a partner in the Union Lumbering Company. By 1870 he had been elected lieutenant governor of Wisconsin, and in 1876 he went to Congress as a Republican representative. An outstanding orator, Thaddeus had a lively and promising career in government. He was nominated for a seat in Garfield's cabinet, but he withdrew his candidacy after a rival denounced him for leaving his wife and living openly in Washington with another woman.

He paid the employees of the lumber company in his own money, which was redeemable only in the company store, and he borrowed against this scrip to establish a railroad company; but his Chippewa Falls line fell prey to competition from the much larger Northern Pacific, which absorbed Thaddeus's railroad after it went into receivership. He failed frequently and spectacularly in business but always managed to recover. To his grandson Ezra, Thaddeus was a model of the American pioneer spirit and a warrior in the struggle against corruption and

usury. Pound mentions him both in his prose works (e.g., see *J/M* 33) and *The Cantos* (21, 22, and 28); he is "that man [who] sweated blood to put through that railway" (Canto 21).

Patricia A. Cockram

Profile

In 1932, Pound arranged to have 250 copies of *Profile: An Anthology Collected in MCMXXXI* privately printed in Milan. In an epigraph, Pound describes the work as "a collection of poems which have stuck in my memory and which may possibly define their epoch, or at least rectify current ideas of it." The anthology presents these poems in roughly chronological order, frequently interspersing terse prose commentary. Throughout, it seeks to trace the "contour" of a tradition in Modern verse, extending from the Yellow Nineties to the Proletarian Thirties, which can provide a satisfying alternative to "the mere excrement" found in the "British and American commercially-sustained weeklies."

The collection opens with Arthur Symons's late Romantic lyric "Modern Beauty." Next, poems by Pound, William Carlos Williams, and James Joyce illustrate the best work from the first decade of the twentieth century. The volume then portrays the period 1909–1914—the crucial *avant-guerre* years that saw the rise of vers libre and Imagism—as a stretch of time whose chief masters were Ford Madox Ford and T. E. Hulme. H. D. merits only two lyrics ("Hermes of the Waves" and "Oread"), which Pound unflatteringly labels "more or less static." (Robert Frost comes in for much worse: His verse is dismissed as "Sincere, very dull, without tragedy, without emotion, without metrical interest, a faithful record of [a] life [that does not] differ greatly from that of horses and sheep.") The following decade, 1915–1925, is represented by generous selections from T. S. Eliot, Marianne Moore, E. E. Cummings, Williams, and Pound himself. The section treating the latter half of the 1920s and the early 1930s is largely given over to introducing and defending younger, less well known poets. Two of these—Cheever Dunning and Emmanuel

Carnivali—were protégés of questionable merit whom Pound had touted for several years without attracting much interest. Three others— Basil Bunting, Louis Zukofsky, and the now-obscure Scottish Modernist Joseph Gordon MacLeod—justly receive more attention. They are represented, respectively, by extracts from the longer works "Villon," "Poem Beginning 'The,'" and *The Ecliptic*. Pound rounds out *Profile* with five short, socialist-themed lyrics and a group of "Negro Songs of Protest" that had appeared in *New Masses*; he downplays the politics of these pieces and emphasizes instead their robust *völkisch* idiom.

Insofar as *Profile* as a whole can be said to offer its readers a canon of Modernist poetry, it suggests that whereas a handful of writers have produced quality writing that epitomizes a particular style and historical moment (Ford, Hulme, Moore, Cummings, Zukofsky), an even shorter list of authors (Eliot, Williams, Pound) has proved capable of changing and progressing over the decades. This eminent trio is distinguished by having poems appear on three or more occasions within *Profile*'s timeline. Another impression left by *Profile*: It displays a surprising heterogeneity of taste. Not only does Pound nod to the depression-era Zeitgeist by incorporating "class poetry," but he also finds praise for such diverse figures as Padraic Colum, Alice Corbin, Thomas Hardy, Mina Loy, Walter de la Mare, and Parker Tyler.

Brian M. Reed

Provença

Provença was the first American collection of Ezra Pound's poetry, published by the Boston house Small, Maynard & Co. in November 1910. The volume provides a selection from *Personae* and *Exultations*, both published by Elkin Mathews in London in 1909, as well as material under preparation for the volume that came out as *Canzoni* with Mathews in 1911. Fourteen poems of *Canzoni* are here published for the first time in the section *Canzoniere: Studies in Form*. Apart from these, the volume includes no first-time publications but constitutes a step in the process of selection from the

early verse that reaches the stage of a definitive "Collected Poems" with *Personae* of 1926. Ten of the fourteen poems from *A Lume Spento* included in *Personae* are found also in *Provença*. The concerns of the volume largely coincide with those presented in Pound's study of Romance poetry, *The Spirit of Romance* (1910), which was prepared during the same period and in which "Provença" appears as the title of the chapter on the troubadours.

The title places a focus on the twelfth-century poetry of Provence (in contemporary academic discourse referred to as Occitania), to which are added the following centuries of verse in the Romance languages, including the Italian *trecento* and the fifteenth-century French poet Villon to whom two "villonauds" are dedicated. Translation is one strategy of reviving the past: "Planh for the Young English King" translates a song by Bertrans de Born, and "A Song of the Virgin Mother" a component from Lope de Vega's play *Los Pastores de Belen*. Another strategy is the *persona*, with which Pound hopes to have "dug up" de Born when in "Sestina: Altaforte" he borrows the stanza form that the troubadour might have employed to describe the joys of war. The *persona* comes closer to the Browningesque dramatic monologue in "Cino," which presents a Cino Polnesi, who is not the *stilnovista* of Pistoia but nevertheless a poet, wandering the roads of Italy in 1309.

The "studies in form" of the *Canzoniere* section rehearse the stanza forms and rhyme schemes of troubadours and *trecento* poets. "Canzon: The Yearly Slain" thus follows the *cobla estrampa* rhyme scheme favored by Arnaut Daniel (rhyming abcdefg-abcdefg), whereas "Canzone: Of Angels" represents the canzone as practiced by the poets of *il dolce stil nuovo* and focuses upon vision and light, features highlighted in the discussion of Tuscan verse in *The Spirit of Romance* and later in "Medievalism." Next to Occitan and Tuscan *canzoni*, the section gives us the Tuscan *ballata*, sonnets both *stilnovist* and Petrarchan, and a Petrarchan octave. The *Canzoniere* section thus represents an occasion for the study of the rhymes and stanza forms favored by the poets invoked through *personae* and translations in the first two sections of the book.

The interest in the Italian *trecento* and (to a lesser degree) the troubadours associates Pound with the previous generations of British poets. Rosetti had translated Cavalcanti and Dante; Swinburne had worked with the troubadours' *sestina*; and both had translated Villon. The influence of the nineteenth century is striking also in the verse where Pound is not evoking "the Spirit of Provence" but assuming the aesthetic stances and poetic voices of Pre-Raphaelites and the poets of the 1890s, and especially of Yeats, echoes of whom are evident in "An Idyl for Glaucus" and "Laudantes decem pulchritudinis Johannae Templi."

The emulation of the voices of the nineteenth century and the study of forms of troubadours and *stilnovisti* present us with a poet searching for a poetic voice and function. The troubadour presence narrates a nostalgia for a time that assigned a clearly defined and significant role to the poet; in 1913 Pound writes of the troubadours' verse: "[T]hese songs played a very real part in love intrigue and in the intrigue preceding warfare" (*LE* 94). The programmatic dismissal of shadows and dreams in "Revolt against the Crepuscular Spirit in Modern Poetry" seems to yearn for a poetry capable of a similar function. The highly diverse poems of *Provença*, however, include archaisms, dreams, and shadows, and their ambition remains aesthetic.

Bibliography

de Nagy, N. Christoph. *The Poetry of Ezra Pound: The Pre-Imagist Stage*. 1960. Bern: Francke Verlag, 1968.

Grieve, Thomas F. *Ezra Pound's Early Poetry and Poetics*. Columbia: U of Missouri P, 1997.

Jackson, Thomas H. *The Early Poetry of Ezra Pound*. Cambridge: Harvard UP, 1968.

Witemeyer, Hugh. *The Poetry of Ezra Pound: Forms and Renewal, 1908–1920*. Berkeley: U of California P, 1969.

Line Henriksen

Provençal Literature

Ezra Pound discovered the poetry of medieval Provence when he transferred from the University of Pennsylvania to Hamilton College in the fall of 1903. Here he encountered two professors who would have a lasting impression on him: Rev. Joseph Ibbotson, professor of English literature, Anglo-Saxon, and Hebrew, and William Pierce Shepard, professor of Romance languages. It was Shepard who introduced him to the troubadours, and before the 1905 academic year was over, Pound had published in the *Hamilton Literary Magazine* the first of many translations from Provençal, "The Belangal Alba." The poem was written in medieval Latin with a refrain in Provençal. For Pound, it represented the point of transition from Latin to the vernacular. Like the generation of scholars who preceded him, Pound viewed Provençal poetry as the first vernacular poetry in western Europe, and Provence would thus become a cornerstone for him in his search for "origins."

Through Shepard, who had done graduate work in Romance languages in Europe after receiving his B.A. from Hamilton, Pound was exposed to the extraordinary revival of interest in Provençal that had taken place in the second half of the nineteenth century, a period that saw the publication of nearly thirty editions of individual Provençal poets, as well as several anthologies. Pound would chronicle his meeting with Emile Lévy, the editor of the *Provenzalisches Supplement-Wörterbuch* in *The Cantos*: "And so I went up to Freiburg" (Canto 20). There Pound questioned Lévy about the meaning of *noigandres*, a Provençal term from which the entire *Canto* grows. In his monumental work *The Pound Era* (1971), Hugh Kenner stated that by the 1960s Provençal studies had become "dormant." Indeed they had, but the reinterest in Pound's work in Provençal in the 1960s and 1970s would be one factor in the second revival of Provençal studies that began in the 1970s and continues to this day.

Pound arrived in London from Venice in the fall of 1908, and the following January he began a series of six lectures at the London Polytechnic titled "A Short Introductory Course of Lectures on the Development of Literature in Southern Europe." The troubadours played an important part in this series, the success of which resulted in an invitation to give a full course in Romance literature at the Polytechnic. This expanded series would later become his first extended prose work, *The Spirit of Romance* (1910). In the "Praefatio ad Lectorem Electum" (1910), Pound pays tribute to Shepard, and the first chapter, "The Phantom Dawn," includes a stanza from the Provençal alba he had translated while still Shephard's student at Hamilton College. He devotes the second chapter entirely to Arnaut Daniel ("Il Miglior Fabbro"), with extensive translations and a detailed discussion of his work, and the third—"Proença"—to analyses of a handful of other major Provençal poets. A chapter added, "Psychology and Troubadours" (delivered as a lecture to the Quest Society and first published in journal form in G.R.S. Mead's *The Quest* in 1912, the essay was added to *Selected Prose* in 1932; see Gallup A33b), outlines the mystic appeal of this world to Pound.

Pound's early poetic work included translations from Provençal ("Planh for the Young English King," "Dompna Pois de me No'us Cal"), poems that used Provençal poets as masks ("Marvoil," "Piere Vidal Old"), poems that experimented with Provençal verse forms ("Sestina: Altaforte"), and meditations on Provençal sources, like "Na Audiart," that in method prefigure "Near Perigord" and *The Cantos*. In the "radiant medieval world" beginning with the Provençal poets and culminating with Dante, Pound discovered a *Weltanschauung* that he would return to over and over again throughout his career. Of the poets he translated, it was Arnaut Daniel who compelled his attention for his extraordinary craftsmanship. He published a series of translations of Daniel's lyrics in "I Gather the Limbs of Osiris" (1911–1912) and sent a collection of Daniel's lyrics in English to a publisher in 1912. This collection was not printed, but, undaunted, Pound returned to the task of translating Daniel's poetry on two more occasions before devoting himself full-time to *The Cantos*. His long essay on "Arnaut Daniel," consisting of translations accompanied by critical analysis, was first published in *Instigations* (1920) and reprinted in his *Literary Essays*

(109–148). For nearly a decade, the work on these poems was an abiding and important interest.

In 1912 Pound traveled to Provence and made extensive notes on his walking tour. He intended to publish a revised version of his notes under the title *Gironde* but apparently never completed them. A later essay, "Troubadours—Their Sorts and Conditions" (1913), is a passionate plea for understanding this "age out of fashion," and one of the ways of doing this, Pound suggests, is to "walk the hill roads and river roads from Limoges and Charente to Dordogne and Narbonne." Pound returned briefly to Provence in the spring of 1919 with his wife Dorothy and revisited some of the same sites. Many decades later Pound took the notes of his 1912 trip from his drawer and considered publishing them, but the project remained stillborn until Richard Sieburth's masterful transcription and reconstruction of these notes in his edition of 1992, *A Walking Tour in Southern France: Ezra Pound among the Troubadours*.

The earlier walking trip shaped two of Pound's important pre-*Cantos* poems, "Provincia Deserta" (1915) ("I have walked over these roads / I have thought of them living") and "Near Perigord" (1915), his meditation on Bertran de Born, Dante, and historical processes, a work that would, in many ways, prefigure *The Cantos*. Pound's last sustained look at Provence before turning to *The Cantos* was "Homage à la langue d'Oc" (1918), a work that functions in *Quia Pauper Amavi* as a companion piece to *Homage to Sextus Propertius*. Three of the five poems in the "Homage à la langue d'Oc" are albas or dawn songs, and the language—as well as the sensibility—of these poems is extremely archaic. In this respect, the sequence contrasts markedly with the other sequences in the volume.

Pound was apprenticed in Provence, and the lessons he learned there remained with him throughout his career; he wove Provence in and out of *The Cantos*, and late in his life he was still dreaming of rewalking those roads by means of a new edition of *Gironde*. Provence had become a part of Pound's "true heritage" and ours as well.

Bibliography

Kenner, Hugh. *The Pound Era*. Berkeley: U of California P, 1971.

Makin, Peter. *Provence and Pound*. Berkeley: U of California P, 1978.

McDougal, Stuart Y. *Ezra Pound and the Troubadour Tradition*. Princeton: Princeton UP, 1972.

Pound, Ezra. *A Walking Tour in Southern France: Ezra Pound among the Troubadours*. Ed. Richard Sieburth. New York: New Directions, 1992.

Wilhelm, James J. *Il Miglior Fabbro: The Cult of the Difficult in Daniel, Dante, and Pound*. Orono: NPF, 1982.

Stuart Y. McDougal

Provençal Translation

Although discussions of Pound and the troubadours have focused mainly on historical and philosophical concerns, genuine enough, they have largely ignored the craftsmanship that first attracted him. He evaluated the troubadours so highly because of their skill in what he eventually called *melopoeia*, the combining of "motz el son," words and music. When Pound discovered the troubadours in his college days, they seemed to hold the key to the art of lyric poetry.

Pound's actual translations from Provençal are confined to his early years, dating from his first published poem, the "Belangal Alba" in 1905, to the "Langue d'Oc" sequence of 1918. These translations focus primarily on Arnaut Daniel but embrace a number of other troubadours, including Bertran de Born, second to Arnaut in order of interest. They are grouped in two clusters: The earlier includes the utilitarian cribs included in *The Spirit of Romance* (1910), two groups of Arnaut *cansos* printed in "I Gather the Limbs of Osiris" (1911–1912), translations intended to be sung to music in *Hesternae Rosae* (1913), plus individual poems like Bertran's "Planh for the Young English King" (1909) and "Dompna Pois de me No'us Cal" (1916) that survived into the 1926 *Personae*. Related are the "studies in form" that appeared in *Provença* (1910) and *Canzoni* (1911), not to mention those poems that adopt troubadour masks, like "Marvoil." The later group includes a second round of Arnaut Daniel translations intended for book publication but eventually appearing in the essay "Arnaut Daniel" (1920) and the sequence "Langue d'Oc" (1918). These translations have suffered the usual scholarly condemnations for mistranslation; but issues of accuracy apart, they are a valuable guide to Pound's apprenticeship in the craft of strict formal poetry.

Pound studied the troubadours in, among others, H. J. Chaytor's anthology *The Troubadours of Dante*, and clearly he approached them through lenses Dante provided in his critical treatise *De Vulgari Eloquio*, as well as his vivid portraits of Bertran, Sordello, and Arnaut in the *Comedia*. Dante, Pound insisted, defined a canzone as words written to be sung to music; as for diction, Dante defined words in his famous "chapter of the sieve" (II, vii) as either "combed" or "shaggy" (*pexa* or *hirsuta*). Pound, in his earlier translations, remains tied to a sentimental Victorian musicality of sonorousness, as he practices the craft of marshaling words into tight frames bound by the exigencies of English rhyme. But in the later versions, he observably learned to complicate his sense of *melopoeia*.

This learning can be diagrammed through his changes in diction, in rhyme and word order, and in the overall conception of *melopoeia* itself. The diction of the earlier translations is, like his earliest poems, archaic and poetical; but the later group maintains this mode, even as Pound elsewhere was modernizing himself. In a 1922 letter he contrasts this language with that of his *Propertius*: "We are just getting back to a Roman state of civilization," he says, "whereas the Provençal feeling is archaic, we are ages away from it" (*L* 179). He even intensified the archaism, altering the earlier version of Arnaut's "Autet e bas"—"But each bird his song unwasted / Lettetth loose, / Singeth spruce"—to the later "Auzel each in tune contrasted / Letteth loose / Wriblis spruce." Thus he persisted, even to the puzzlement of his Vorticist colleagues.

Second, there is no better poetry "wherein to study the subsidiary arts of rhyme and rhyme-blending" (*LE* 215). His perceptions in this area are many: Arnaut discovered that the music of rhymes "depends upon their arrangement, not on their multiplicity" (*SR* 38). He cultivated the art of "scarce" rhymes, that is, rhymes on unusual words or with few rhyming options. Arnaut's subtle *coblas estrampas* (scattered rhymes) satisfy not only the modern ear but also the classical ear "to which rhyme seemed and seems a vulgarity" (*SR* 22). Thus even though "verbal rhythm is monolinear," rhyme can attain a contrapuntal quality "against its own echo, or against a developed expectancy" (*Antheil and the Treatise on Harmony* 47). In translation, he can attempt "a map of the relative positions" of rhyme (*LE* 127) and even forms of half rhyme as in "clamour" and "charmer" (see *L* 179–180). But he cannot reproduce the actual sounds of the language: English has enough rhymes, he says, but the word sounds are wrong—they have extra consonants, or they "go squashy" or "fluff up"; "they are not *rime agute*" (*LE* 168). Furthermore, intensive rhyming is incompatible with clear word order in English, as it is not in an inflected language like Provençal: The troubadours had only to observe "the tune and rhyme-scheme. . . . They were not competing with Maupassant's prose" (*LE* 115). Hence his efforts at translation prove that "Provençal rhyme schemes are not *impossi*ble in English. They are probably *inadvis*able" (*L* 179).

Most important, perhaps, is Pound's determination that musicality in verse is not mere sonorousness but a varied "aesthetic of sound" (*LE* 114), not superficial onomatopoeia but "a mastery in fitting the inarticulate sound of a passage to . . . that mood or passion which the passage describes or expresses" (*SR* 160). Verse can be not only legato but staccato, not "gummy" but "clear." The Provençal language with its hard consonants, unlike its French cousin, demarcates syllables rather than blurring them. Hence Arnaut's "Doutz brais e critz, / Lais e cantars e voutas" becomes in English "Sweet cries and cracks / and lays and chants inflected."

The Provençal translations may be unsatisfactory in themselves as English poems. *Melopoeia* cannot be translated "save perhaps by divine accident" (*LE* 25)—as in the exquisite alba that prefaces the "Langue d'Oc" sequence. But

Pound's efforts to translate the troubadours points us toward a body of great lyric poetry; and they hold up a model of craftsmanship that can hardly be equaled. "It is not necessary that a poem should rely on its music," he said; but if it does, "it must be such as will delight the expert" (*LE* 5). Pound absorbed the lessons of verse in formal rhyme and stanza, then chose to do otherwise. But the lessons of troubadour musicality remained with him.

Bibliography

Adams, Stephen. "Ezra Pound and Provençal Melopoeia." *Four Decades* 2.1 (1978): 27–48.
Chaytor, H. J. *The Troubadours of Dante*. Oxford: Clarendon P, 1902.

Stephen J. Adams

"Provincia Deserta"

"Provincia Deserta" appeared in *Poetry* 5.6 in March 1915 and was included in *Lustra*. Like "The Gypsy" and "Near Perigord," the poem is the outcome of Pound's walking tour of southern France in the summer of 1912 and traces what amounts to a pilgrimage through the landscape inhabited and traveled by the troubadours in the twelfth century. The title defines the province (which is also "Provence") as deserted; the poet's walking feet reflect those of meter as the poem voices an *ubi sunt* motif and muses on the impossibility of reviving the past.

The attempt at resuscitating the past through the landscape remains futile; only the proper names of the region seem to connect past and present, and geography and language. The listing of proper names of troubadours, castles, and places creates a focus on the individual connotations attached to these that foreshadows a central practice of *The Cantos*. The troubadour Giraut Riquier and the *stilnovist* Guido Cavalcanti are thus evoked as if their very names might effectuate presence: "I have said: / 'Riquier! Guido'." The story of the de Maensac brothers of Auvergne referred to toward the end of the poem returns in Canto 5 and is given with less elision in "The Troubadours—Their Sorts and Conditions" (1913), which includes further identifications of places and troubadours.

Bibliography

Grieve, Thomas F. *Ezra Pound's Early Poetry and Poetics*. Columbia: U of Missouri P, 1997.
Line Henriksen

Psychology and Psychiatry

It is in some respects impossible to separate questions of law, ethics, and medicine when investigating the matter of Pound's responsibility for actions that most judges and juries considered treason during wartime. As such, Pound's psychology not only in the 1940s but throughout his life remains a subject of lively and intense controversy among Poundians, and psychiatry remains a classic test case in the study of the relationship between morality and literature.

It has been argued that Pound's precarious state of mind in the fall of 1945 was largely due to having spent several terrifying summer months in an outdoor cage in the U.S. Army detention camp near Pisa. However, the question of Pound's sanity was not a new one in 1945. Tim Redman has speculated that symptoms of an abnormal mental condition can be seen as early as the 1910s and 1920s. Friends like H. D., William Carlos Williams, and Louis Zukofsky were in doubt of his soundness of mind in the 1930s. Even Mussolini's subordinates in the Ministry of Popular Culture thought Pound's radio broadcasts evidence of "a nebulous mind, deprived of all sense of reality." Pound himself claimed in a 1942 broadcast: "Whom God would destroy He first sends to the bughouse."

Doctors who examined Pound over almost three decades never agreed on a diagnosis. Psychiatrists at the army camp in 1945 diagnosed Pound to be suffering from extreme anxiety and claustrophobia but termed him essentially sane. Six months later, psychiatrists testifying at Pound's trial found him "insane and mentally unfit for trial" and "in need of care in a mental hospital"; but it is not clear whether Pound's condition had deteriorated or whether there was honest professional disagreement about his condition, or as some scholars have claimed, there was a conspiratorial effort to keep him out of the courtroom. Pound had himself acceded to the possibility of an insanity plea, so he was willing to accept the less drastic label "unfit for trial" and not simply because it was legally expedient. Pound openly doubted his own state of mind during this time, as do most readers, even those accustomed to his eccentric logic and rhetoric.

Sentenced to an indefinite stay in at St. Elizabeths Hospital for the Insane in Washington, D.C., Pound was eventually observed and interviewed by dozens of psychiatrists and nurses, many of whom made copious formal notes on his activities and condition during his thirteen years as a patient. The cumulative record is difficult to summarize, since Pound's behavior was so eccentric and unpredictable; but it is clear that there was considerable dispute about his soundness of mind throughout. His official diagnosis, arrived at eight years after his entry, was "psychotic disorder, undifferentiated." Pound was released in 1958 from St. Elizabeths without having been treated or tried—it was agreed by all parties that he was still unfit for trial, that he was likely to remain that way, and that his mental condition may have predated his allegedly treasonous actions, almost eliminating the possibility of conviction, should his case ever go to trial. Pound was made the legal ward of a committee of caretakers and returned to Italy claiming, "All America is an insane asylum" (Carpenter 848).

Pound's experience at St. Elizabeths seems to have reinforced a decades-old hostility toward psychiatry and psychology in general, motivated in part by his belief that the discipline was a Jewish phenomenon, with all the attendant interest in analysis, introspection, and abstraction that Pound considered to be characteristic of Jews. In the 1940s and 1950s, such ideas were directed with special intensity toward Sigmund Freud, whom he claimed to be a "Viennese savage" and "the flower of a deliquescent society going to pot" (*J/M* 100). Freud's theories were exposed in Canto 91 as little more than "kikery." It is worth noting that Freud himself, hearing about Pound from his patient H. D. in 1933, claimed that he seemed to have "very difficult Oedipal problems" and asserted, "If I had known Ezra I would have made him all right."

If Pound thrived under the benign neglect of the medical establishment at St. Elizabeths, his final years in Italy were marked by an almost crippling melancholy, suicidal anxieties, paranoia, phobic hypochondria, and a progressive dementia that resulted in an almost total silence in his final years. Treatments with a variety of crude medications, including hormones, antidepressants, tranquilizers, and sheep cell injections, had no effect on his condition and even may have hastened his decline.

Inasmuch as a single diagnosis would apply to a lifetime's worth of activities and mental states, many contemporary psychiatrists and psychologists—and judges and juries—would no doubt label Pound a victim of chronic or manic depression or bipolar disorder and therefore suffering from a brain chemistry imbalance that would be easily cured by medication, rather than someone who suffered from developmental trauma resulting in the anal retentiveness, narcissism, and hero worship characteristic of fascist anti-Semites. That is also the consensus of most scholars.

Important exceptions include Wendy Stallard Flory, who has maintained that Pound suffered from psychological traumas as an adult that resulted in a self-destructive and psychoanalytically diagnosable inability to think coherently about his actions, and E. Fuller Torrey, who asserted that Pound feigned mental illness and that his doctors were coconspirators. Most Poundians today are able to concede that Pound had some sort of psychological disorder without suspending judgment as to his absolute moral responsibilities for his language and for his actions.

Bibliography

Carpenter, Humphrey. *A Serious Character: The Life of Ezra Pound.* Boston: Houghton Mifflin, 1988.

Flory, Wendy Stallard. *The American Ezra Pound.* New Haven: Yale UP, 1989.

Norman, Charles. *The Case of Ezra Pound.* New York: Funk & Wagnalls, 1968.

Torrey, E. Fuller. *The Roots of Treason: Ezra Pound and the Secret of St. Elizabeths.* New York: McGraw-Hill, 1984.

Jonathan P. Gill

Q

Quia Pauper Amavi

This volume, published by the Egoist Press in 1919, contains four sequences of poems: "Langue d'Oc," "Moeurs Contemporaines," "Three Cantos," and *Homage to Sextus Propertius*. It is notable as the first book publication of any cantos—though these are the so-called *Ur*-Cantos, later discarded—and the first book publication of the "Homage," Pound's most misunderstood early masterpiece. It is notable as well for its purposeful design, setting the contemporary satire of the funny "Moeurs Contemporaines" beside the *logopoeic* wit of the "Homage," and both beside the more remote *amour courtois* of "Langue d'Oc." There is an implied parallel, as well as distinction, between the erotic sensibilities of the two older cultures (*LE* 151), as well as the virtual disappearance of eros from the contemporary world.

T. S. Eliot's review praises the book as Pound's "most coherent extended work" and the best demonstration of Pound's "historical method" (1065). His enlightened comments on the *Homage*—an exception to the pedantic outcries that greeted the poem elsewhere—are particularly significant, given that Eliot omitted the sequence entirely from the 1928 *Selected Poems*: "[I]t is one of the best things Mr. Pound has done," he writes, and "probably a truer interpretation of that man of letters than Professor Mackail's" (1066).

There are a few significant textual variants. "Langue d'Oc" in this collection includes a translated Arnaut Daniel *canso*, later discarded. The "Three Cantos" appear in a form printed in the American edition of *Lustra*, somewhat revised from the first *Poetry* printings, and with minor marginalia.

Bibliography

Bush, Ronald. *The Genesis of Ezra Pound's Cantos*. Princeton: Princeton UP, 1976.

Eliot, T. S. "The Method of Mr. Pound." *Athenaeum* (24 October 1919): 1065–1066.

Stephen J. Adams

Quinn, John (1870–1924)

Immediately following the Malatesta Cantos, the American John Quinn appears as "Jim X" in Canto 12, embarrassing a group of Presbyterian businessmen with a racy story. The juxtaposition of the Italian condottiere and the financial lawyer expresses Pound's sense of Quinn as a modern Malatesta, a man of action who patronized living artists and helped to forge a new civilization. He met Quinn through W. B. Yeats's father in New York in 1910. When Pound criticized him (though not by name) in the *New Age* in 1915 for buying William Morris manuscripts while living artists were neglected, Quinn wrote to defend himself to Pound as not only a collector but a patron of living artists. He was stung by Pound's criticism since he was one of the major organizers of the International Exhibition of Modern Art, which became famous as the Armory Show of 1913. As he reminded Pound, he also successfully lobbied in Washington to remove a tax on original art works. Pound answered with equal frankness, and a friendship developed through their letters. Since Quinn wished to expand his collection of English art, Quinn virtually made Pound his art agent. Through Pound, Quinn bought the works of

Jacob Epstein, Wyndham Lewis, and Henri Gaudier-Brzeska; and he organized the only exhibition of Vorticist work in America in 1916.

Quinn also supported the *Egoist* and the *Little Review* so that it could publish Pound's work and that of T. S. Eliot, James Joyce, and Wyndham Lewis. Quinn arranged for many of Pound's works to be published in the United States and meticulously edited his poems for the Knopf publication of *Lustra* (1917). He also facilitated the publication of Joyce's *A Portrait of the Artist*, Lewis's *Tarr*, and Eliot's *Poems* (1920). Eliot was so grateful for Quinn's help with the American publication of *The Waste Land* that he gave him the manuscript with Pound's annotations. When the *Little Review* was prosecuted for publishing chapters from the novel that became *Ulysses*, he defended the editors in court.

After the *Ulysses* case of 1920 sorely tried Quinn's patience with impractical artists, he had fewer contacts with Pound; and he was now interested only in French art. But they met in Paris in 1921, and Quinn helped Pound with a generous "loan." In 1923 he met with Pound, Joyce, and Ford Madox Ford in Paris and pledged his support for Ford's *transatlantic review*. He also generously contributed to Pound's Bel Esprit plan to provide an endowment for artists such as T. S. Eliot. Pound always felt that Quinn's deep understanding of art was the mark of a true patron. For example, Quinn would recite *The Waste Land* from memory for his friends, and he encouraged Pound's work on *The Cantos* at an early stage. As Quinn wearied of his career as one of New York's premier lawyers, he planned on traveling to Europe and renewing his friendship with Pound. But this was prevented by his early death from cancer in 1924.

Bibliography

Pound, Ezra. *Selected Letters of Ezra Pound to John Quinn, 1915–1924*. Ed. Timothy Materer. Durham: Duke UP, 1991.

Reid, B. L. *The Man from New York: John Quinn and His Friends*. New York: Oxford UP, 1968.

Timothy Materer

A Quinzaine for This Yule

This slender volume was the first book of Pound's to be published in London. When he arrived there from Venice in August 1908, he brought with him a manuscript of poems called the *San Trovaso Notebook* (now at Yale, it is included in Michael John King's edition of Pound's *Collected Early Poems*). Unable to find a publisher for the manuscript, he paid Pollock and Co. to print a selection of fifteen poems from it in early December (the term *quinzaine* means a group of fifteen). Then Elkin Mathews ordered 100 additional copies to be produced under his imprint in time to catch the 1908 holiday trade.

The mystic beauty of Venice between twilight and dawn is a central theme of the book, as in the rapturous lyric "Night Litany." The closing poem, "Nel Biancheggiar," compares this beauty to the playing of Katherine Ruth Heyman, an American concert pianist whom Pound knew. The exotic name "Weston St. Llewmys," which is appended to two crepuscular epigraphs in the book, is a pseudonym for Pound himself, derived from the family names of his mother (Weston) and his paternal grandmother (Loomis).

Hugh Witemeyer

R

Rachewiltz, Boris de (1926–1997)

Boris de Rachewiltz was Ezra Pound's son-in-law through his marriage in 1946 to Mary Rudge or Mary de Rachewiltz. After a classical education from the Irish Brothers in Rome, Boris attended the Faculty of Ancient Oriental Studies of the Pontificio Instituto Biblico in Rome (1951–1955) specializing in Egyptology. He also studied Vatican Diplomacy at Accademia Vaticana (1953), and with the help of fellowships from the Italian Ministry of Foreign Affairs, he studied with and worked under renowned Egyptologist Professor Ludwig Keimer at Cairo University, Egypt (1955–1957).

Following numerous archaeological and ethnographic missions to the Middle East and among the Beja of Upper Egypt and the Sudan in the 1960s, Boris added teaching to his fieldwork in the 1970s, becoming professor of Egyptology at Vatican University in 1972. Among his many and varied books, *Il Libro dei Morti degli antichi Egiziani* (Scheiwiller, 1958) and *Egitto magicoreligioso* (Boringhieri, 1961) are considered groundbreaking.

Boris and Pound shared a deep and mutual affection for each other, one that sustained Pound during his incarceration at St. Elizabeths. Not only was Boris's Tyrolean castle, Schloss Brunnenburg, the *paradiso terrèstre*, the *palazzo* that Pound had yearned for in *Exile*, but Boris's work became an important esoteric study for Pound, who used his son-in-law's Egyptian maxims and knowledge of Sumerian rituals in *Section: Rock-Drill* of *The Cantos*. Of greater consequence to Pound in the early 1950s, Boris used his training in Vatican protocol and Italian politics to arrange pro-Pound broadcasts and speeches over Vatican Radio, to generate complimentary articles and testimonials on Pound, and to pressure the Italian press into taking up Pound's cause. The 1953–1958 correspondence between Boris and Pound, as yet unpublished, is an important source of information on Pound's motives for the Rome Radio broadcasts and for the questionable fragility of Pound's mind during the years of his confinement. Among Pound's European supporters in the 1950s, Boris was as important as Olga Rudge and Olivia Rossetti Agresti.

Bibliography

Bacigalupo, Massimo. *The Forméd Trace: The Later Poetry of Ezra Pound.* New York: Columbia UP, 1980.

Rachewiltz, Boris de. "Pagan and Magic Elements in Ezra Pound's Works." *New Approaches to Ezra Pound.* Ed. Eva Hesse. Berkeley: U of California P, 1969. 174–187.

Rachewiltz, Mary de. *Discretions: Ezra Pound, Father and Teacher.* Boston: Little, Brown, 1971.

Tremblay, Tony. "Boris Is Very Intelligent and 'Simpatico' and Interested in Worthwhile Things: The Association and Correspondence of Ezra Pound and Prince Boris de Rachewiltz." *Paideuma* 28.1 (1999): 151–160.

Tony Tremblay

Rachewiltz, Mary de (b. 1925)

The daughter of Ezra Pound and the American expatriate violinist Olga Rudge, Maria was born 9 July 1925. She was conceived during the last months of Pound's sojourn in Paris, where he had met Rudge. When Pound and his wife

Dorothy moved to Rapallo, Italy, Olga followed; a few months later, she and Pound went to Bressanone in the Italian Tyrol for Maria's birth. Shortly thereafter, Pound and Olga contracted with the Marchers, a Tyrolean couple who had recently lost their own baby, to raise their child. Pound believed country life would be healthy for Maria, but the arrangement was also convenient both for Pound, who remained married to Dorothy Shakespear, and for Olga, who continued her musical career. The Marchers lived in Gaïs, in the Austro-Italian Tyrol, and Maria was raised speaking the local Germanic dialect. She called her foster parents *Tatte* and *Mamme* and referred to her own parents, whom she saw rarely, as the *Herr* and the *Frau* and later as *Tattile* and *Mamile*. Still later, she called Pound *Babbo*, northern Italian for "Daddy."

As Maria grew older, Pound and Olga became more involved in her education. They took her with them to Venice, where she was exposed to the many writers and artists they entertained. Maria's relationship with her beautiful and strict mother was never easy, but she seems to have enjoyed great warmth and encouragement from her father, who eventually came to see his daughter as his literary heir and tutored her extensively, particularly in translating his own works into Italian. In 1937, at the age of twelve, she went to a convent school in Florence, where she began to be called Mary.

After leaving school, Mary lived at her mother's home in Sant'Ambrogio, where Pound could oversee her continuing education, but returned to the Tyrol in 1943 for the rest of World War II. When word arrived of Pound's arrest, she traveled alone to the U.S. Counter Intelligence Corps headquarters in Genoa but was unable to see him. In October 1945, after two trips between Gaïs and Sant'Ambrogio in search of news, Mary received a letter from Pound indicating that she would be permitted to visit. She went to Pisa with Olga, who was unexpectedly allowed in with her. Mary then returned to Gaïs and began organizing Pound's papers.

In 1946 Mary married Boris de Rachewiltz, a young man she had met in Rome in 1943 among a group of Pound's acquaintances. Shortly after their marriage, the couple acquired and restored Brunnenburg Castle in the Italian Tyrol, where Mary still lives. They had two children, Siegfredo Walter Igor Raimondo, born in 1946, and Patrizia Barbara Cinzia Flavia, born in 1950. Mary visited her father at St. Elizabeths in 1953; after his release in 1958, Pound returned to Italy with Dorothy and lived in Mary's Brunnenburg castle for a time, but he found the climate oppressive and eventually returned to Olga's care in Sant'Ambrogio and Venice.

Mary de Rachewiltz is the author of several books of poetry and translation. In addition to her translations into Italian of much material written by and about Pound, including *The Cantos*, she has created Italian collections of the work of E. E. Cummings, Robinson Jeffers, James Laughlin, Denise Levertov, and Marianne Moore. In 1971 she published *Discretions*, a memoir of her father. She continues to write and publish poetry in English and Italian.

Bibliography

Conover, Anne. *Olga Rudge and Ezra Pound: "What Thou Lovest Well . . ."* New Haven: Yale UP, 2001.

Pound, Ezra. *I Cantos*. Ed. Mary de Rachewiltz. Milan: Mondadori, 1985.

Rachewiltz, Mary de. *Discretions: Ezra Pound, Father and Teacher*. Boston: Little, Brown, 1971.

Patricia A. Cockram

Racism and Anti-Semitism

We may define *racism* as a belief, first, that each human race possesses immutable qualities determining how any member of that group will act, and second, that one race is inherently superior to all other races. By this definition, Pound was not, in any consistent sense, a racist. Like most of his contemporaries, he tended to accept without question the pseudoscience known as eugenics. Furthermore, from the late 1930s to the end of World War II, when Pound was subject to a barrage of Axis propaganda against Jews as an alien race, he sometimes invokes race as a category of analysis. In a Rome Radio broadcast of 23 March 1942, he tells British listeners (if any) that while his analysis of usury in Britain has hitherto focused on the economic part of the picture, he has decided that "you lose by not thinking about this problem as RACIAL" (*RSWWII* 71). However, Pound never assumed that Aryans are superior to or even fundamentally different from Asians. On the contrary, when fears of the Yellow Peril were widespread in the United States, Pound celebrated the ideogrammic Chinese consciousness and argued that English and American readers should cultivate such a consciousness as an alternative to the categorical boxes within which the Western mind had locked itself; and in his work as a translator, Pound remains an important intermediary between the cultures of Asia and Euro-America. Furthermore, although blacks are the principal object of racism in America, Pound never displayed animus against blacks, seeing them rather as simple, happy, natural folk, with a heightened mythic consciousness. We now regard such stereotyping as racist; but if racism implies race hatred, Pound's attitude toward blacks is not racist. In fact, Pound's views on blacks were relatively progressive: He denounced lynching and contributed money to a defense fund for the Scottsboro Boys, the most famous victims of American racism during the 1930s.

On the other hand, from the 1930s until the 1960s, Pound displayed an animus against Jews that powerfully affected his public actions, personal relations, and writings, including his poetry. While not racist globally, then, Pound was certainly an anti-Semite. In 1967, speaking to Allen Ginsberg, Pound reportedly said, "[B]ut the worst mistake I made was the stupid suburban prejudice of anti-Semitism. All along, that spoiled everything." (Ginsberg's account of this conversation, while confirmed by Michael Reck who was present, has been questioned.) Pound's anti-Semitism from the 1930s to the 1960s goes far beyond mere suburban prejudice, but his initial attitude toward Jews may have been shaped by his upbringing in an America where Jews were banned from country clubs and admitted into Ivy League colleges only in limited quotas. The upper-middle-class British society that Pound entered upon his marriage to Dorothy Shakespear was equally anti-Semitic, and Dorothy's letters display a strong prejudice against Jews. These early influences seem to have bred in Pound a vague dislike of Jews, just

as he inherited a vague, condescending affection for African Americans. Pound's early writings reveal scattered references to presumably objectionable qualities of Jews, but these are no more frequent or hostile than similar references in writers who shared Pound's American upbringing, like T. S. Eliot and even William Carlos Williams, who had a Jewish grandparent. (In *A Voyage to Pagany*, Williams describes a stranger as a Jew of the usual objectionable type [217].) In Pound, such attitudes may have been complicated by uneasiness about his Jewish-sounding first name and his sense that he looked Jewish—these themes crop up occasionally in his letters. But if Pound had died in 1932, we would see anti-Semitism as no more than an incidental part of his literary persona.

Pound's anti-Semitism was also complicated by a lifelong antipathy toward monotheism. Despite the moralistic Protestantism of "Ballad of the Goodly Fere," Pound reacted against his Presbyterian upbringing and by 1910 had begun to define himself as a devotee of the pagan gods. An attempt to revive these gods was in the air during these years, inspired largely by Pater—see *Marius the Epicurean* and the essay "Demeter and Persephone." "The Return" (1912), a well-known early poem, envisions the return of pagan gods to the earth. Theurgic invocations of the gods are also common in the work of certain poets who were close to Pound in the years before and during World War I. H. D.'s poems of this period repeatedly invoke the gods, sometimes with wonder (Hermes, Adonis), sometimes in terror ("The God," where Mars drives out all other gods). Williams's "March" and Yeats's "The Second Coming," both written during or immediately after World War I, offer bleaker visions of the return of the pagan gods. Of all these poets, Pound's commitment to the pagan gods remained most intense. In 1930, responding to a request by Eliot that he say what he believed, Pound declared himself a resolute pagan: "Given the material means I would replace the statue of Venus on the cliffs of Terracina. I would erect a temple to Artemis in Park Lane. I believe that a light from Eleusis persisted throughout the middle ages and set beauty in the song of Provence and of Italy" (*SP* 53).

Pound recognized that monotheism is antithetical to the paganism he espoused. His denunciations of all the Abrahamic faith—Judaism, Christianity, and Islam—are often vehement; and insofar as the religion embodied in the Hebrew Bible (the Christian Old Testament) represents the foundation of all monotheisms, then Pound's animus against the Jews is partly religious.

Pound's vague suburban prejudices and his religious views may play a role in his anti-Semitism, but only in the 1930s does an overt, ideologically grounded hatred of Jews become a significant part of his literary persona. In this period vociferous outbursts of anti-Semitic rhetoric—images of sewage, filth, slime, slither, offal, and foeter—begin to erupt into his discourse. All these quoted words come from a passage in the 1938 *Guide to Kulchur* (130–132); and although Pound does not mention Jews in this passage, he clearly intends them as the embodiment of what he has come to call usury. A similar rhetorical rupture occurs at the beginning of Canto 52, dating from about the same time: The attack on the "Stinkschulds" in this passage is so extreme that James Laughlin of New Directions insisted on blacking out certain lines before he would publish the canto, and these black lines remained an integral part of the text until 1986. Both outbursts are relatively encapsulated: The passage from *Guide to Kulchur* cited above is unique within this vigorously opinionated but otherwise not particularly irrational book, and after the tirade about *"neschek"* in Canto 52 Pound turns to cantos about Chinese and American history, sequences that have little or nothing to say about the Jews. In the Rome Radio broadcasts and in such writings of the St. Elizabeths period as the letters to Olivia Rossetti Agresti, a rhetoric of filth, slime, dung-flow, always associated with "kikery," takes over almost completely, but such language remains relatively rare in *The Cantos*: Perhaps Pound instinctively sensed that he must not surrender his poem to his new obsessions. Nevertheless, a stereotyping of Jews collectively as willful destroyers of everything valuable in human life and an attendant refusal to acknowledge the humanity of individual Jews (except for Louis Zukofsky) remain characteristic of Pound's discourse from the 1930s until the 1960s, and every reader of Pound must come to terms with this fact.

What triggered Pound's sudden obsession with Jews during the late 1930s? There is widespread agreement that the shift is connected with his economic concerns. In the wake of World War I, Pound was convinced by Major Douglas, apostle of Social Credit, that an iniquitous banking system had caused the war, and in the 1930s he came to believe that this same system would soon cause another such war. As Alec Marsh and Leon Surette have both argued, there is no necessary connection between Social Credit and anti-Semitism: For example, Gorham Munson, principal spokesperson for the American Social Credit movement, explicitly disavowed anti-Semitism. Yet Douglas himself was anti-Semitic, and both in Britain and in Canada Social Credit parties veered toward anti-Semitism, as did one wing of the American movement; thus, it should not surprise us to find Pound tracing a similar path. Second, Pound was deeply devoted to Mussolini, whom he saw as the destined hero of his epic. In 1938, under pressure from his new ally Hitler, Mussolini, who had expressed no previous animosity toward Jews, adopted a set of racial laws directed against Jews, and this shift in fascist policy encouraged Pound to adopt an anti-Semitic rhetoric. However, Leon Surette has shown that an obsession with the Jews actually appears in Pound's letters as early as 1934. The principal influence here seems to have been certain right-wing American propagandists for the theory that a conspiracy of Jews was manipulating the money system to enrich themselves and to impel the nation toward war. Pound was particularly fascinated by the radio broadcasts of neo-Populist Father Coughlin, who may have provided a model for his own wartime broadcasts. We have here, then, a third important influence (along with Social Credit and the racist rhetoric of Hitler via Mussolini) on Pound's abrupt commitment, beginning in the late 1930s, to hatred of Jews as a fundamental ideological principle.

In *The Genealogy of Demons: Anti-Semitism, Fascism, and the Myths of Ezra Pound*, Robert Casillo argues that Pound's personality and writings are early and late, root and branch infected with the virus of anti-Semitism. Casillo's argument, built on psychoanalysis and intellectual history, offers evidence that Pound's utopian vision of human life as grounded in the abundance of nature requires an enemy to explain our failure to find that utopia—the enemy being first usurers and then the Jews. However, the striking shifts in Pound's attitudes toward Jews over the course of his life—shifts that Casillo recognizes—and the relatively minor role that anti-Semitism plays in *The Cantos* support the view that anti-Semitism plays a more limited and encapsulated role in Pound's psychic and aesthetic economy. Arrested by the American forces at the end of the war and charged with treason because of the Rome Radio broadcasts, Pound was found by psychiatrists in Washington unfit to stand trial on grounds that he was suffering from a paranoid state. Obviously, anti-Semitism cannot be seen, ipso facto, as a symptom of mental illness—not unless we dismiss entire societies (Europe during the Crusades, Nazi Germany) as insane. But Pound's conviction that all the ills of the world can be ascribed to Jews and the apparently uncontrollable outbursts of scatological language that came to accompany almost any reference to Jews both suggest some sort of mental breakdown consistent with paranoia. (Such a hypothesis also offers an alternative to David Moody's truly disturbing theory that Pound was not in fact an anti-Semite but, instead, that he adopted anti-Semitism as a deliberate political ploy, a strategy for stirring up the masses.) Other aspects of Pound's behavior from the late 1930s to near the end of his life also suggest mental illness. His 1939 trip to America was precipitated by a conviction that if only he could talk to the right people and say the right things to them, he could single-handedly prevent the impending war. Similar streaks of megalomania run through the postwar letters to Agresti. The repetitiveness and the manic, hectoring tone of all his letters from the St. Elizabeths period also suggest a mind that is slipping over the edge. In these respects, finding Pound's anti-Semitism a sign of mental illness seems not unfair. On the other hand, to argue as Wendy Flory and others

have done that outside of his paranoid obsessions he remains a morally perceptive and even wise man seems a dubious thesis. Sadly, both the paranoia and the megalomania affect his poetry, where the anti-Semitic passages are relatively brief and self-contained, as well as his prose writings and private letters, where the anti-Semitic rhetoric is often pervasive and obsessive.

Bibliography

Casillo, Robert. *The Genealogy of Demons: Anti-Semitism, Fascism, and the Myths of Ezra Pound*. Evanston: Northwestern UP, 1988.

Flory, Wendy Stallard. *The American Ezra Pound*. New Haven: Yale UP, 1989.

Marsh, Alec. *Money and Modernity: Pound, Williams, and the Spirit of Jefferson*. Tuscaloosa: U of Alabama P, 1998.

Pound, Ezra. *"I Cease Not to Yowl": Ezra Pound's Letters to Olivia Rossetti Agresti*. Ed. Demetres P. Tryphonopoulos and Leon Surette. Urbana: U of Illinois P, 1998.

Surette, Leon. *Pound in Purgatory: From Economic Radicalism to Anti-Semitism*. Urbana: U of Illinois P, 1999.

Williams, William Carlos. *A Voyage to Pagany*. 1928. New York: New Directions, 1970.

Burton Hatlen

Religion: Confucianism and Taoism

In the early 1910s Ezra Pound was introduced to Taoism and Confucianism—two of the mainstays of ancient Chinese philosophy; henceforth, what may be seen as Taoist and Confucian sensibilities vied for control of his work, just as the two had vied for control of the philosophical landscape of ancient China. Although Pound condemned Taoism, the allusive aspects of his literary work have affinities with it; and although he always admired Confucianism, the dogmatic aspects of his work are partly the result of its influence.

Both Confucianism and Taoism developed between the sixth and fourth centuries B.C.E. in China. In key ways, these philosophies are strikingly different. For Taoists, the Great *Tao* or "Way" is immeasurable and uncontrollable and yet not beyond human apprehension. If people would remain still in their heart, and free from willfulness and delusions of control, then they could recognize both the Great *Tao* and their own place within it. Confucianism, however, is a practical, willful, and controlling philosophy that generally suggests that humankind is the center of its own universe. Its contrast with Taoism shows through each philosophy's unique response to the significance of words. Taoists believe that words are temporary conveyances of shifting meaning. Confucians believe that words contain and control meaning; they are meaning traps, without which meaning would drift and society would fall into disorder.

By December 1913 Pound was in possession of Asian art historian Ernest Fenollosa's notes, including scores of translations of Chinese Taoist poetry. He quickly recognized that this poetry was terse, polished, and most important, emotionally suggestive. He had admired these qualities in the verse of Western classical and medieval poets such as Sappho and Dante but had been unable to achieve the same effect in his own verse. Starting in 1913, however, the character of Pound's work changed noticeably. This was especially evident in *Cathay* (1915), his volume of translations taken from the Fenollosa notes. Pound began to achieve with words what fellow poet T. S. Eliot suggested was the ability to actually modify inarticulate emotions by presenting them in precise words and images. In short, Pound's poetry developed a conceptual allusiveness. His translation titled "The Jewel Stairs' Grievance," from *Cathay*, serves as a prime example:

The jewelled steps are already quite white with
  dew,
It is so late that the dew soaks my gauze stock-
  ings,
And I let down the crystal curtain
And watch the moon through the clear autumn.

Both Fenollosa and Pound observed that the reader is never told that a woman impatiently waits for someone—yet strained impatience is precisely the emotion produced by the poem. Such an emotional movement out of details toward emotional truth is typical of Taoist poetry.

At very nearly the same time that Pound was working through the Taoist poems in the Fenollosa notebooks, he began reading G. M. Pauthier's French translations of the four classical Confucian texts. Unlike Taoist thought, which came to Pound first as poetry, Confucian thought first came to him as social and political science. Confucius was concerned with effective governance during a time of political instability in China. He proposed the maintenance of social order. This social order began with the precise definition of terms. Precise definitions were necessary in order to explain the inarticulate thoughts of virtuous men in leadership roles. Their virtuous character would thus extend outwards until it was manifest as an entire state, living in ordered harmony. As can be imagined, the social application of Confucianism in China had a spotty history. Despite the best of intentions, its emphasis on order sometimes turned into obsession and toward intolerance of difference. More than once in the history of China, Confucian philosophy served as the warrant for human oppression.

Many Sinologists maintain that the less formal approach to life and living implied in Taoist (and later, Buddhist) philosophy served as a social corrective to Confucian rigidity in China. Further, as time passed, the popular reception of the philosophies as well as the specific content of their canonical texts became crossbred with one another. Pound, however, did not have the hundreds of years of polemical contention behind him as did Chinese Confucianism and Taoism. He thus failed to recognize or obtain the kind of symbiotic understanding that the two philosophies in China had developed over time. Consequently, his work sometimes evokes a Taoist allusiveness and, at other times, illustrates the kind of rigidity to which Confucianism sometimes tended. Furthermore, in the 1920s, Pound began to combine his understanding of Confucianism with his understanding of Italian fascism. As a result, his various calls for social and aesthetic order intensified, and he began to show a willingness to subordinate the human spirit to the principle of social order. He had come to this willingness as much through his belief in Confucianism as from his belief in fascism. But it stood in stark contrast to the Taoist sensibility that he had developed through translation and his ongoing work. Something clearly had to give. Many of Pound's readers feel that it was the allusiveness in his poetry that did so.

In the late 1930s, Pound read J.A.M. de Moryiac de Mailla's *Histoire Générale de la Chine*, an eighteenth-century French translation of a Chinese history text. De Mailla's source had been a politicized Confucian account of Chinese history. It condemned Taoists and Buddhists for all social ills in China and praised Confucians for all that had gone well. Pound likewise started a campaign of invective against Taoists in his writings. This campaign corresponded in time to the intensification of his efforts to promote the Confucian-Fascist Italian State. When that state finally collapsed in 1945, so did much of Pound's Confucian vision. Many scholars note the resurgence of a Taoist sensibility in Pound's work after this time. Pound never relinquished his affinity for Confucianism. But of the two philosophies, only Taoism could have underwritten the stillness, the allusiveness, and the humility displayed in one of the last cantos, where Pound writes as one adrift within what is great and moving and unknown:

> A blown husk that is finished
>   but the light sings eternal
> a pale flare over marshes
>   where the salt hay whispers to tide's change
> Time, Space,
> neither life nor death is the answer. (Canto 115)

Robert E. Kibler

Religion: Monotheism and the Bible

Pound was born into a Presbyterian family of earnest and evangelistic tendencies. His father was an elder, a Sunday School teacher, and president of the local Christian Endeavor. The family did mission work in Philadelphia, during which time Pound may have absorbed some antiimmigrant, anti-Semitic prejudices; the young Pound read the Bible regularly and attended church through his college years. Even in the early London period he was capable of writing "Ballad of the Goodly Fere," a derivation from "muscular" or YMCA Christianity, in irritation at the "cheap irreverence" of some companions. In *Guide to Kulchur*, Pound asserts that his Christian beliefs were eroded by the "truly filthy racket" of some Kensington church bells (300). Of far more importance were his developing interests in occult traditions and pagan mysticisms.

The influence of the Bible remained traceable in the larger designs of his work and life, however. What he called his "plymouth-rock conscience" is obviously the key to his aesthetic/economic moralism; in some sense he identified himself with the Hebrew prophets, denouncing the people he loved from the standpoint of an alienated spiritual exile, issuing gnomic writings full of dire warnings. The prophets were the first writers in our tradition to identify economic exploitation with religious sin, so Pound, like Marx, was a Son of the Prophets, in spite of contempt for the "Old Testy-munk" and its "barbarous blood sac[rifice]" (Pound absorbed the usual ideas of his time about Hebraism as a religion of primitive nomads: This confusion mistakes poetic pastoral symbolism for sociological reality). Just as his life exemplified Protestant virtues such as thrift and temperance in spite of his contempt for the bourgeois, so his writing everywhere displays an impassioned moralism derived from prophetic rhetoric. See Canto 45: not only "With usura hath no man a house of good stone" but even "they have brought whores for Eleusis," which depends far more on biblical contempt for prostitution than on tolerant Greek attitudes. Prophetic rhetoric is dominated by the metaphor of idolatry as sexual sin, "whoring after other gods."

In *Guide to Kulchur* his ambivalences about the Bible were displayed floridly. On the one hand, he was Voltairean: "There is not a trace of civilization from the first lies of Genesis up to the excised account of Holophernes" (330). On the other hand, he asserted that "the forbidden fruit of hebrew story is a usury parable" (42) and showed that he had not only studied the relevant Torah on usury (Exodus 22:25, Leviticus 25:36, Deuteronomy 23:19) but even the Hebrew words. In the same work, he indulged in fantasias about medieval Catholicism having preserved some pagan mysteries, in contrast to Semiticized Protestantism, which blurs distinctions and values. However, his poetry and poetic consistently displayed a Protestant fear of ornament ("ornament is excrement" was becoming a watchword in Modernist architecture at about this time) and of rhetoric, so that an "imperfect broken statement if uttered in sincerity often tells more to the auditor than the most meticulous caution of utterance could" (*GK* 129). Here his evangelistic values were related to those of other American poets (Whitman, Dickinson, Frost, Williams) touched by antinomian impulse. In Pound's case one can trace heavy influence from Protestant literalism and intolerance of allegory (even though biblical typology clearly helped him to find the method of "repeats in history"): See D. S. Carne-Ross's analysis of Pound's avoidance of the polysemous, in order to "give back to the literal level its full significance." In this light the depressed mutism of his last years appears as Pound's mistrust of his own rhetoric: *tempus tacendi* (ultimately from Ecclesiastes 3:7) became his most enduring motto.

When in Pisa he found himself with almost no books, the available Bible became a resurrected source for the cantos. Canto 74 is especially thick with allusions to both Testaments: the Paraclete, Barabbas, Leviticus 19:35 on justice in "meteyard and measure," Jeremiah's buying a field at divine order (chapters 31 and 32). The twelve lines beginning "and the greatest is charity" (1 Corinthians 13:13) give an antinomian's credo and lead to "with justice shall be redeemed / who putteth not out his money on interest" and to other gnomic references. Pound is even capable of citing Micah 4:5, in several forms (e.g., "each one in the name of his god" [Canto 76]), throughout *The Pisan Cantos*, apparently as warrant for polytheism. It is hard to use the Bible more creatively than that.

Bibliography

Carne-Ross, D. S. *Instaurations: Essays in and out of Literature, Pindar to Pound.* Berkeley: U of California P, 1979.

Flory, Wendy Stallard. *The American Ezra Pound.* New Haven: Yale UP, 1989.

Schneidau, Herbert N. "The Antinomian Strain: The Bible and American Poetry." *The Bible and American Arts and Letters.* Ed. Giles Gunn. Philadelphia: Fortress/Scholars, 1983. 11–32.

Herbert N. Schneidau

Religion: Polytheism, Neoplatonism, and the Occult Tradition

The Cantos of Ezra Pound continues to invite interpretation as an odyssey of "world soul" conceived in pagan mystery rites reborn from "darkness" into the light of *gnosis*. Heterodox elements of religious ritual supply "binding matter" (*L* 242) for a work meant to articulate the poet's faith in a positive, dynamic course for the future and to establish Pound's forty-year epic as modern reaffirmation of humanity's potential for contact with the divine.

Early poems, notably "The Tree," "Threnos," "Plotinus," "Praise of Isolt," "Paracelsus in Exelcis," "Speech for Psyche in the Golden Book of Apuleius," "The Return," and "The Alchemist," reflect what some argue became Pound's preoccupation: union with divinity and restoration of faith in life everlasting. Convinced that "a light from Eleusis" persisted through the Middle Ages and "set beauty in the song of Provence," Pound sought to restore "Venus on the cliffs of Terracina," to erect "a temple to Artemis in Park Lane" ("Credo," *Front* 1 [December 1930]: 11). "Only in the high air and the great clarity can there be a just estimation of values"; Gods [plural] exist," he declared (*GK* 299).

Canto 1's summoning of ghosts—no less than its linguistic descent—suggests "a writer intensely responsive to ritual, to the mystery of death, to the sacred" (Woodward 9). Given the work's sustained, often troubling juxtaposition of good with unmitigated evil, however, sight of its forward movement is sometimes lost. Aspiration toward excellence is given human form in Odysseus and deified in Aphrodite Urania; yet the celebratory note of Canto 90 is disturbed by the intrusion of Elektra's infidelity and blood revenge; Aphrodite Pandemos, goddess of the sensual, is given more lines than Aphrodite Urania, goddess of sublime love. Pound's infusion of crude sympathetic magic into deep spiritual mysticism has been connected to scholarship that linked Olympian ideals with archaic sacramental rites, a resurgence of interest in Neoplatonic thought, and the poet's personal "belief in a *'Theos'* that transcends human consciousness" (Materer 71–72).

Pound was evidently attracted to, yet suspicious of, occult speculation: "Rest me with Chinese colors, / For I think the glass is evil" (*P* 95). With the Great War, Restoration magus John Heydon, whose *Holy Guide* was discussed with practicing occultist W. B. Yeats at Stone Cottage, loses the pride of place he has in Canto 3 (1917); although Heydon is "resurrected" in 87 and 91, *ominformis omnis intellectus est* (every intellect is capable of assuming every shape) emerges as "a general theory of imagination rather than a specific belief in reincarnation" (Materer 60–62). Pound's interest in the heterodox, which predates his friendship with Yeats, was in part stimulated by early reading that H. D. described as "an avalanche of Ibsen, Maeterlinck, Shaw, Yogi books, Swedenborg, William Morris, Balzac's *Séraphita*, Rossetti and the rest of them" (Doolittle 46–47). Influenced by French Rosicrucian Joséphin Péladan, who characterized Quixote and Parsifal as tragic heroes (Surette, *Light from Eleusis* 34–39), Pound became convinced of the existence of underground mystery cults and linked Albigensianism with Eleusis (*SR* 90). His interest has also been traced to the complex interactions of the French Romantic movement with occultism (Materer 18–20) and to occult interpretation of Nietzsche's *Birth of Tragedy* by three Quest Society associates: researcher of primitive mysticism G.R.S. Mead (secretary to Theosophist Madame Blavatsky), A. R. Orage, and Allen Upward (Surette, *Light* 37, 192–195; Tryphonopoulos 74–78). Mead, who published Pound's 1912 Quest Society lecture "Psychology and Troubadours," believed spiritual insight to be a product of archaic ritual; early publication of parts of Mead's study of Gnosticism, *Doctrine of the Subtle Body*, provided the poet a composite model of initiatory ritual structures (Tryphonopoulos 82–100).

As Pound himself pointed out, there is "nothing particularly new in describing the journey of a living man through Hell"; indeed, it may be regarded as "a literary habit of the race" (*SR* 161). Symbolic descent into chaos ("dying") as a condition of new birth or resurrection distinguishes sacred ceremonies: Divine creative power is invoked to restore the energy of the infant cosmos, to inspire participants to "higher" spiritual life. Death herein becomes a *positive*—a means to a worthy end: transcendence of human limitations, complete freedom (a universal desire). In-

volving purification (fasting), nourishment, and hierogamy (sacred marriage), the harvest rites at Eleusis (a fixture of Greek culture for centuries) approximated the rape, abduction, and subsequent return of Koré (Persephone). In *The Cantos*, negative (often irreverent) forces ("Usura" or "Geryon") are often opposed to life-giving, creative forces exemplified by the Eleusianian spirit (Cantos 49, 51, 88, etc.), the loss of which, Pound felt, "reduced the collective consciousness of Europe to atheism" (Tryphonopoulos 2–3). Allusions to the myths of Dionysos, Orpheus, and Osiris, as well as hierogamic sexual encounters such as that of Zeus and Danäe (4), serve to remind of Usura's destructive power and of the possibility of *palingenesis*—restoration of, and delivery into, divine presence.

Christianity's development (which recognizes only the one, all-powerful male god of Islam and the Hebrews) forced suppression of religious activities contrary to accepted practice, but Neoplatonic and polytheistic ideas—among them, the concepts of life after death and transmigration of souls (reincarnation)—have surfaced over the years in "pagan" opposition to Christian orthodoxy. Possibly imported from Egypt by Thales, Orphic and Mithraic doctrine empowering the individual emerges in Stoic doctrine, Pythagoras, Plato ("The Allegory of the Cave"), Virgil, Ovid, Pythagorean disciples Plotinus and Porphyry, and Proclus (c. 418–485)—the enlightened of Pound's "tradition" whose achievements are celebrated in his lyric poetry, *Guide to Kulchur* (1938), and *The Cantos*. The resurrecting divinity of *Rock-Drill*, in keeping with Pound's pantheism, is the poet himself: "out of Erebus, the deep-lying / from the wind under the earth, / m'elevasti" (Canto 90).

Akiko Miyake shows how Pound turns, in *Rock-Drill* and *Thrones*, to Neoplatonist Johannes Scotus Erigena (fl. 850) to unite heaven and earth, paralleling the Confucian vision of the Chinese History Cantos. The dawn ideogram signals the elevation of soul (Isis) into *nous* (divine mind or transcendent love), a condition the poet identified with responsible government (197–223). Another soul mate, Georgios Gemistos (Plethon), was recovered during Pound's research for the Malatesta Cantos (8–11). Political reformer and Byzantine philosopher Plethon, like Pound, sought to fortify a civilization by replacing "dead" Christian values with Greek polytheism—in Plethon's case, against invasion by Ottoman Turks. In his 8 September 1953 letter to Olivia Rossetti Agresti, Pound suggests Plethon's participation in the Council of Ferrara-Florence (1438–1439) influenced Cosimo de' Medici and spurred debate that flowered as the Italian Renaissance.

Colin McDowell, who has argued against reconciling references to the afterlife to construct an "Aquinas-map," acknowledges the difficulty of the poet's roads to felicity: The soul's way is "[b]y no means an orderly Dantescan rising" ("Bridge over Worlds" 175). Scholarly phobia long obscured the impact of nineteenth-century occult speculation on Pound's metaphysics and on Modernism as a whole (Surette, *Birth of Modernism* 289–290), but insight has been provided into how Platonic and Hellenistic ideas about salvation animate *The Cantos*, as well as Joyce's *Ulysses* and Eliot's *The Waste Land*. All have been interpreted as occult texts—perhaps rightly so, given Orphism's influence on Western culture. The Homeric *Hymn to Demeter*, Pindar's second Homeric ode, Plato's concept of temporal and permanent worlds, Cicero, Hermetic writings, and Clement of Alexandria assume the possibility of human elevation to a state of being at one with, or equal to, the gods. Pound knew that belief in illumination by means of initiation (metamorphosis) is also a distinctive feature of Freemasonry and other secret societies for men—groups that his hero Leo Frobenius suggested grew in response to matriarchal economic, social, and religious supremacy (Eliade 73). He knew, too, that symbols of, and allusions to, initiatory rites (the perilous descent to Hell) are ubiquitous in the Grail quest of Celtic origin (Arthurian romance, tales of the Fisher King) and ceremonies of the Albigenses and Knights Templar, as well as thirteenth-century Provence's *fidèle d'amour*. He therefore appropriated with confidence what G.R.S. Mead called "fragments of a faith forgotten."

Pound's occult borrowings, like his range of mythical devices, serve a creative scheme meant to ignite a civilization—to transform what the Modernists understood as "the decadence and enfeeblement of Western life, the deliquescence of Christianity into a form of sentimentalism, the need for some rich and imaginative form of life in a world grown pale, mechanical and abstract" (Righter 31). The poet's choices were clear: Reject the trappings of this world in favor of a higher reality or order the fragments as he saw fit. The occult preserve simply provided a new language to interrogate the human condition, one meant to thwart the Hobbesian beast.

Bibliography

Doolittle, Hilda. *End to Torment: A Memoir of Ezra Pound.* Ed. Norman Holmes Pearson and Michael King. New York: New Directions, 1979.

Eliade, Mircea. *Rites and Symbols of Initiation: The Mysteries of Birth and Rebirth.* Trans. Willard R. Trask. New York: Harper & Row, 1958.

Materer, Timothy. *Modernist Alchemy: Poetry and the Occult.* Ithaca: Cornell UP, 1995.

McDowell, Colin. " 'As Towards a Bridge over Worlds': The Way of the Soul in *The Cantos.*" *Paideuma* 13.2 (1984): 171–200.

———. "Literalists of the Imagination: Pound, Occultism, and the Critics." *Paideuma* 28.2–3 (1999): 7–107.

Miyake, Akiko. *Ezra Pound and the Mysteries of Love: A Plan for the Cantos.* Durham: Duke UP, 1991.

Rachewiltz, Boris de. "Pagan and Magic Elements in Ezra Pound's Works." *New Approaches to Ezra Pound.* Ed. Eva Hesse. Berkeley: U of California P, 1969. 174–197.

Righter, William. *Myth and Literature.* London: Routledge, 1975.

Surette, Leon. *The Birth of Modernism: Ezra Pound, T. S. Eliot, W. B. Yeats, and the Occult.* Montreal: McGill–Queen's UP, 1993.

———. *A Light from Eleusis: A Study of Ezra Pound's Cantos.* Oxford: Clarendon P, 1979.

Tryphonopoulos, Demetres P. *The Celestial Tradition: A Study of Ezra Pound's The Cantos.* Waterloo: Wilfrid Laurier UP, 1992.

Woodward, Anthony. *Ezra Pound and the Pisan Cantos.* London: Routledge, 1980.

Diane Reid

Ripostes

Ripostes was first published by Stephen Swift and Company in 1912 and was the sixth collection of Pound's poems. Dedicated to the American poet William Carlos Williams, the title is taken from the sport of fencing, where a riposte is a counterblow against an opponent, and in common usage is a sharp or barbed verbal or written response. This collection is commonly regarded as a breakthrough volume in Pound's early career, a move away from the courtly diction and phraseology of his earlier work, steeped as it was in the Romance literature of Europe, toward a more contemporary language as the proper vehicle for poetry, a move in sympathy with the theory and practice of Imagism. In *Ripostes*, Pound's metrical and technical expertise in the use of traditional verse forms still signals his debt to what he called "the tradition," but there is now what T. S. Eliot called a new restraint and maturity in *Ripostes* displacing the "romantic" passion of the earlier work. Pound is moving here from a "subjectivist" tradition of a poetry of the self toward a harder, more concisely phrased "objective" poetry, so that *Ripostes* marks a transitional moment in Pound's poetics that leads eventually to *Homage to Sextus Propertius, Hugh Selwyn Mauberley,* and the early cantos. The first edition of *Ripostes* contained twenty-six poems by Pound and a curiosity, "The Complete Poetical Works of T. E. Hulme," five Imagist poems by the English philosopher and essayist whose writings in the years before World War I advocated classical ideals of clarity and precision against Romantic subjectivism in art. Hulme, whose essays contributed substantially to the theory of Imagism, was killed in action in France in 1917. In later printings of Pound's early poetry, some of the twenty-six poems of the original edition are omitted from collections under this title, and one much-admired poem included, "The Alchemist," though it first appeared in *Umbra,* Pound's 1920 collection of the early poems he then wished to keep in circulation.

Three poems about women in *Ripostes* show the new and the old in Pound's practice: "Portrait d'une Femme," "A Girl," and "A Virginal."

"Portrait d'une Femme" is an objective portrait of a patroness of the arts, written in rhymed and half-rhymed iambic pentameters. It is an analysis of what has become of a figure sacred to the arts throughout history, the patron, here reduced from the classical examples of the Roman and European Renaissance worlds to the lady who presides over a "salon." In this it anticipates poem twelve of *Hugh Selwyn Mauberley*. Critical, yet with a grudging acceptance of what she represents, the poem is obliquely indebted to Henry James's great novel *The Portrait of a Lady* (1881) and bears comparison with Eliot's dramatic monologue "Portrait of a Lady." While Eliot's poem proceeds by narrative self-revelation in the manner of the dramatic monologue, Pound's poem is a study in contemporary cultural mores in a vocabulary and syntax near to everyday language yet replete with verbal signifiers of the culture of the past. "A Girl" is a brief celebration of the metamorphosis of Daphne, pursued by the love-struck Apollo and metamorphosized into a laurel tree to escape his clutches. The myth of Daphne has long been cherished by poets as the ideal of chastity, and in this poem there is an implied conjunction between chastity and the high ideals of true art, both ignored by the world. "A Girl" delivers a version of this myth in everyday language, so that while it invokes the "tradition," its treatment of its subject is contemporary. By contrast "A Virginal" maintains the romantic subjectivism of Pound's earlier manner. A rhyming love sonnet, it uses archaic forms such as "hath" and syntactical inversion as in "As winter's wound with her sleight hand she staunches." To this extent it is an unexceptional poem in the tradition of courtly love poetry. For a much finer example of Pound's writing about the inspirational love for a woman, see his versions of Guido Cavalcanti's "Donna mi Prega," especially that in Canto 36.

The most notable poems of *Ripostes* are "The Seafarer," "The Return," and "The Alchemist." "The Seafarer" is a translation of an eighth-century Anglo-Saxon poem and, as with many of Pound's translations, it has upset scholars and historians who complain of Pound's blunders in the translation of particular words, or his ignorance of the cultural context of the original. Yet

Pound's practice in his translations has been inspirational for poets throughout the twentieth century in cases too numerous to name here. The defense of Pound is that he did not work for a literal translation of the original but, in this case, through what has been called a "phonic simulacrum," a homophonic translation that recreates the reading experience of the Anglo-Saxon in the way the sounds of the words and the rhythmic pattern of the poem emulate the original. Of course this defense cannot be tested by one who cannot read Anglo-Saxon, but it is indisputable that Pound's version will give a reader the felt experience of an exiled wanderer in a storm-tossed seascape whose world-weariness, contempt for worldly power, and the illusory consolation of earthly riches are powerfully and eloquently rekindled in this fine poem.

"The Return" is a free verse celebration of the survival of the pagan Gods of ancient mythology into the present and thus foreshadows Pound's polytheistic convictions in *The Cantos*. In this poem Pound gives an intuitive sense of their return, as though emerging from some underworld into the light of day in which the form of the poem imitates their hesitant movement, like wary animals sniffing the air for danger but also acknowledging their ancient power. W. B. Yeats praised "The Return" as "the most beautiful poem that has been written in the free form" and admired its "real organic rhythm," the way in which the meaning of the poem is expressed through its form (Carpenter 174).

"The Alchemist" is a poem that particularly needs chanting aloud to truly hear its vibrant rhythmic effects, despite the unfamiliarity of the names to the English ear. They are the names of women to be found in the literatures of southern Europe, except for the first named, Saïl of Claustra, a twelfth-century Provençal poetess. To chant these beautiful names is to achieve the transformatory power of the alchemist, whose desire was to turn base metals into gold. Here the transformation will lead not to material riches but to the creative riches of the poetic process of which the idealized woman is the muse or intercessor, the love of whom is inspirational. "The Alchemist" is therefore a kind of courtly love poem, remarkable for its verbal ingenuity, its pace, and its dynamic rhythmic power. Again it anticipates some of Pound's central concerns and compositional methods in *The Cantos*.

Bibliography

Alexander, Michael. *The Poetic Achievement of Ezra Pound*. London: Faber, 1979.

Brooker, Peter. *A Student's Guide to the Selected Poems of Ezra Pound*. London: Faber, 1979.

Carpenter, Humphrey. *A Serious Character: The Life of Ezra Pound*. Boston: Houghton Mifflin, 1988.

Grieve, Thomas F. *Ezra Pound's Early Poetry and Poetics*. Columbia: U of Missouri P, 1997.

Ruthven, K. K. *A Guide to Ezra Pound's Personae (1926)*. Berkeley: U of California P, 1969.

Wilson, Peter. *A Preface to Ezra Pound*. New York: Longman, 1997.

Witemeyer, Hugh. *The Poetry of Ezra Pound: Forms and Renewal, 1908–1920*. Berkeley: U of California P, 1969.

Lionel Kelly

Rudge, Olga (1895–1996)

An American concert violinist and Vivaldi scholar, Olga Rudge was born in Youngstown, Ohio, but raised and educated almost entirely in Europe. Her mother had been a famous singer, and her father was an industrialist, who apparently did not mind supporting his wife and children while they lived abroad. Olga gave concerts in London (1916–1920), one of which Pound reviewed for the *New Age* in November 1920; but they first met in Paris in 1923. Pound introduced her to the American composer George Antheil, whom he persuaded to compose two (eventually three) violin sonatas for her, which Antheil and Olga performed in Paris in December 1923. Pound and Rudge became lovers and remained romantic and intellectual companions to the end of his life. She followed Pound to Italy and lived in Venice and Sant'Ambrogio, a hillside village outside Rapallo. Working at the Accademia Musicale Chigiana in Siena, she did much to promote Vivaldi's music. In 1925 Olga gave birth to a daughter, Mary (now Mary de Rachewiltz), who was raised by a peasant couple in the Italian Tyrol. During the 1930s Olga assisted in planning the Pound-sponsored Concerti Tigulliani (after the Bay of Tigullio) and performed in them with other musicians. The repertoire of these concerts included modern composers like Debussy, Satie, and Stravinsky, as well as pioneering presentations of early music by Bach, Domenico Scarlatti, and William Young (a recently rediscovered Baroque composer). Later in the decade, Olga became aware of hundreds of unknown Vivaldi concerti in manuscript in a nearby library, prepared the first thematic catalog of Vivaldi's works, and became a major force in the revival of Vivaldi's modern reputation.

When toward the end of World War II the Germans, in anticipation of an Allied invasion, evacuated the Rapallo seafront where the Pounds lived in via Marsala, they moved into Olga's small house at Sant'Ambrogio—a not altogether happy arrangement as evidenced by Pound's line in Canto 116: "If love be not in the house there is nothing."

During Pound's confinement in Washington, Rudge remained in Italy, apparently at his insistence. From there she worked incessantly to clear his name of the treason charge. After his release, he and Dorothy returned to Italy and lived for a time with Mary at Brunnenburg Castle in the Italian Tyrol, but he soon returned to live with Olga in her small house in Venice, where he died in 1972. His many words of tribute to Olga include the following in the last one of *The Cantos* titled "FRAGMENT (1966)": "That her acts / Olga's acts / of beauty / be remembered. // Her name was Courage / & is written Olga."

Olga lived her last years with her daughter at Brunnenburg. Late in her long life, according to Mary, she looked out the window of her room in the castle and said, "I have always been surrounded by beauty."

Bibliography

Adams, Stephen J. "Pound, Olga Rudge, and the 'Risveglio Vivaldiano.'" *Paideuma* 4.1 (1975): 111–118.
Conover, Anne. *Olga Rudge and Ezra Pound: "What Thou Lovest Well . . ."* New Haven: Yale UP, 2001.
Pound, Ezra. *Ezra Pound and Music: The Complete Criticism.* Ed. R. Murray Schafer. New York: New Directions, 1977.

Patricia A. Cockram

Rummel, Walter Morse (1887–1953)

A pianist and composer, Rummel was first taught piano in Berlin by his father, after whose death he moved to Washington, D.C., continued his musical studies, and acquired U.S. citizenship. In 1904 he returned to Berlin to study piano with Leopold Godowsky and composition with Hugo Kaun. He then moved to Paris, where he became a friend and champion of Debussy, giving the first performances of at least ten of his works. From 1918 to 1921 he performed in joint recitals throughout Europe with the dancer Isadora Duncan. During the 1920s he lived in London, where he was an active recitalist, and in the 1930s he moved to Brussels, where he received the support and friendship of King Leopold III. In the early 1940s he performed regularly in Germany and the occupied countries and in 1944 took German citizenship. After the war, he returned to live in France. His recordings include striking interpretations of Bach, Liszt, and Chopin, and his published works—including forty songs and a series of Bach transcriptions—achieved some popularity.

Ezra Pound's friendship with Rummel dated from around 1908, when they first met in America. In 1910 they spent time together in New York City and on a visit to Pound's parents in Pennsylvania. During the next two years, Pound was Rummel's frequent houseguest in Paris "for months at a stretch," and they also shared a house in London for a time in 1911. Rummel became friends with Dorothy Shakespear, Pound's future wife, and he often visited and performed at her home in London. In May 1911 Pound and Rummel attended the premiere of Debussy's *Le martyre de Saint Sébastien* together in Paris. In 1910 Rummel introduced Pound to Margaret Cravens, a budding American musician studying in Paris, and the three became close friends. When she committed suicide in 1912, she left notes addressed to both men. Pound remembered her years later in Canto 80.

Rummel's professional relations with Pound include their settings of nine troubadour songs in *Hesternae Rosae. Serta II* (1913) and Rummel's settings of *Three Songs of Ezra Pound*

(1911) and "The Return" (1913). Pound dedicated "Maestro di tocar" (from *Canzoni*) to Rummel and also referred to him in Cantos 80 and 104. After their respective marriages, the two saw each other only once again, in Paris around 1927. By then, Pound felt that Rummel's early promise as a composer had not been fulfilled and that he had been "reduced to the status of a pianist" (as he expressed it in a letter of 31 March 1925 to Henry Allen Moe). Early in 1936, however, the two corresponded about Vivaldi's music, and Rummel sent Pound the edition of Vivaldi's cello sonatas that he had coedited. Pound's appreciation was evident in a subsequent address he gave in Rapallo, referring to Rummel as "my great friend." And in November 1948, Pound wrote the poet H. D. to seek confirmation that Rummel was still alive.

Although he was not involved with the first volume of *Hesternae Rosae* (1911), which consisted of Rummel's settings of French chansons of the seventeenth century, Pound's contribution to the second volume was threefold: He made English translations of the nine troubadour songs; he rediscovered two melodies by the twelfth-century composer Arnaut Daniel; and he helped Rummel to determine the proper rhythm of the songs, thus influencing to some extent the rhythms of Rummel's piano accompaniments. The accompaniments include driving ostinatos, new countermelodies, cadenzas between strophes, and even a four-octave glissando. As Stephen J. Adams has observed, "Rummel and Pound wanted more to be persuasive in the cause of this ancient music than to approximate how it once sounded."

Bibliography

Adams, Stephen J. "Ezra Pound and Music." Diss. U of Toronto, 1974.

Pound, Ezra. *Ezra Pound and Margaret Cravens: A Tragic Friendship 1910–1912*. Ed. Omar Pound and Robert Spoo. Durham: Duke UP, 1988.

Timbrell, Charles. "Claude Debussy and Walter Rummel: Chronicle of a Friendship, with New Correspondence." *Music & Letters* 73 (1992): 399–406.

———. "Walter Morse Rummel, Debussy's 'Prince of Virtuosos.'" *Cahiers Debussy* 11 (1987): 24–33.

Charles Timbrell

Russian and Slavic Literatures

Pound's knowledge of Russian literature, as his friend Robert McAlmon commented (231), was neither broad nor deep. His reading experience seems to have been limited primarily to a handful of the great nineteenth-century novels. Of twentieth-century Russian Modernism Pound was evidently unaware. He condemned most of Russian literature as containing "no problems that are of interest to any man with two grains of lucidity" ("Paris Letter" 276). Pound made exceptions for Turgenev, Chekhov, and to some extent, Dostoevsky. In "Remy de Gourmont" and "The Rev. G. Crabbe, LL.B.," Pound praises Turgenev's novel *A Nobleman's Retreat (Une nicheé de Gentilshommes, Dvoryanskoye gnezdo)*, citing a phrase uttered by the character Marfa Timofeevna Pestov, whom he mistakenly calls "Maria Timofevna," perhaps confusing her with Maria Timofeevna Lebyadkina in Dostoevsky's *The Devils (The Possessed, Besy)*. Pound considered "that Chekhov was a great writer, trying to remedy the chaos [of Russian life] by showing it its face in the mirror" ("Paris Letter" 275). As regards non-Russian Slavic literature, Pound reacted favorably to the work of the Bohemian poet Petr Bezruč, "poet of the mines," whose "*Songs of Silesia* have the strength of a voice coming *de profundis*" ("Bohemian Poetry," *EPPP* 1:105).

Bibliography

McAlmon, Robert. *Being Geniuses Together*. Ed. Kay Boyle. London: Hogarth P, 1984.

Pound, Ezra. "Bohemian Poetry." Rev. of *An Anthology of Modern Bohemian Poetry*, trans. P. Selver. *Poetry* 1.2 (1912): 57–59.

———. "Paris Letter." *Dial* 74.3 (1923): 273–280.

———. "Remy de Gourmont." Part 1. *Fortnightly Review* 98 (n.s.) (1 December 1915): 1159–1166.

———. "The Rev. G. Crabbe, LL.B." *Future* 1.4 (1917): 110–111.

Archie Henderson

S

San Trovaso Notebook (See *Collected Early Poems of Ezra Pound*)

Science

Any consideration of Pound's uses of science must be qualified: Certainly his manifold curiosity extended to the scientific developments of his day; yet of the hundreds of personal contacts he formed over the years, none was with a working scientist. He valued science for its process of empirical observation—its certitude and preciseness. But his exempla are more apt to be ancient than modern. He praised the pragmatic Enlightenment interest of, say, Jefferson in the propagation of seedlings as a sign of useful knowledge. Linnaeus and Louis Agassiz receive honorific mention in the later cantos. Typically, though, in resuscitating the name of Agassiz, an important naturalist in his time, Pound seems uninterested in Agassiz's resistance to Darwinism (the reason he is now forgotten) and emphasizes only his insistence on precise observation (*ABCR* 17–18). Pound's references to contemporary scientists are rare: The Curies make a brief appearance in Canto 23, but they are exceptional. And if Pound believed, literally, that the human brain is a "great clot of genital fluid," as he notoriously avers in his Postscript to Gourmont's *Natural History of Love* (*PD* 203), his knowledge of anatomy was ludicrously inadequate.

Still, Pound from his earliest years was fond of using the antisentimentalist rhetoric of science in his critical writings as a metaphor for accurate observation—and occasionally as a sign of occult truth. In two passages, for example, he advances aesthetic notions as types of mathematical formulas: "Poetry is a sort of inspired mathematics which gives . . . equations for the human emotions" (*SR* 14). Great works of art contain equations that "cause form to come into being" (*GB* 92). And though Pound participated in Lewis's scoffing at the Italian Futurists' interest in modern technology as mere "automobilism," he eventually by the 1930s developed a complex theory of "machine art."

Maria Luisa Ardizzone's *Ezra Pound e la scienza: Scritti inediti o rari* (1987), edited in the original English with Italian translation, is primarily a collection of documents from the Pound Archives at Yale University's Beinecke Library. They are published together with a number of articles that had never appeared before in a comprehensive volume, in a chronological frame that extends from 1908 to 1958. *Machine Art and Other Writings* (1996) contains different material, but the center of both collections is the draft of Pound's unpublished book on Machine Art, circa 1927–1930. Pound increasingly developed his interests in the relationship between science and poetry from the end of the 1920s to the beginning of the 1940s. It took the years at St. Elizabeths to organize these materials in a more coherent way and finally led Pound to identify the links between poetry, language, and science as a veritable natural paradise. Thus the language and ceremonies of the Na-Khi (a people of southwest China) are used by Pound as a final metaphor for paradise in the *Thrones* (Canto 104).

Various authors molded Pound's theories about science, nature, language, and poetry: the Aristotle of the Physics and Ethics (who informs Cavalcanti's "Donna me prega"), Bacon, Leibniz, Vico, Rousseau, Jefferson, Emerson (*The*

Natural History of Intellect [1893]), Whitman, John Heydon, Gourmont, Fenollosa—not to mention Confucius. Earliest manuscripts, from circa 1908, including a list of minerals and an embryonic reflection on Dante's *Paradiso*, attest to Pound's early interest in nature. Pound develops his premises in opposition to metaphysics: "In nature are signatures / needing no verbal tradition" (Canto 87). For Pound, poetry *is* science, something he expresses beginning with his essays of the 1910s ("Psychology and Troubadours," "The Serious Artist," "Vorticism"). Movement—that which flows—is the essence of nature and language, in agreement with science and according to Fenollosa's statement, "In diction and in grammatical form science is utterly opposed to logic. Primitive men who created language agreed with science and not with logic. Logic has abused the language which they left to her mercy" (Fenollosa 28) Pound agrees with science and not with logic.

Fenollosa implies that the Chinese language, organized on the centrality of the verb/action/movement, is closer to nature and poetry than Western languages. This was exactly what Pound was looking for with his early research on the ideogram, as he retrospectively figured out in *ABC of Reading* (1934):

> Example of ideogrammic method used by E. P. in "The Serious Artist" before having access to the Fenollosa papers.
> I was trying to indicate a difference between prose simplicity of statement, and an equal limpidity in poetry, where the perfect simple verbal order is CHARGED with a much higher potential, an emotional potential. (96)

Following Cavalcanti, poetry for Pound gives the equations of human emotions and in this sense is part of science: "Art for art's sake, no, art for propaganda, no, art is part of biology" (*EP&S* 164).

In his reflections on de Gourmont—his essays of 1915 and 1920 and his 1922 translation of *Physique de l'amour*—Pound finds his way back to Cavalcanti, with his translations of the late 1920s. His Postscript to Gourmont's *Physique* and an unpublished "Suggestions on

the Psychology of Pleasure" (*EP&S* 98–101) imply further assimilation of Cavalcanti's poetry into Pound's own world and poetics on the new basis of de Gourmont's theoretical system (abetted by Dr. Berman's popular book on the endocrine glands). Love and "sensibility"—sexuality—are for Pound part of nature's energies. "Happiness" is a physical emotion and a fully bodily potential. It is here and now, in a concrete, earthly, biological past/present/future time, within bodies of nature: "The thesis in my translation of Gourmont's *Physique de l'amour* is worth considering. The skull doesn't hold all the human intelligence" (*EP&S* 98). Cavalcanti was for Pound the "physicus" poet par excellence, since he put at the center of his poetics what in medieval culture was considered an accident: love without any metaphysical implication. The sources for Pound's reading of "Donna me prega" are Aristotle's *De Anima* and Dino del Garbo's comment on Grosseteste's *De Luce*. Virtue from "sensibility" and love as a passage of light will be at the center of Pound's *paradiso* in his late cantos. Pound did elaborate in a productive way Dante's ethical model—"Letizia, Dante, Canto 18 a religion / Virtù enters. / Buona da sè volontà. / Lume non è, se dal sereno" (Canto 100)—together with Cavalcanti's lesson: "Than Guido Cavalcanti no psychologist of the emotions is more keen in his understanding, more precise in his expression. . . . *La virtù* is the potency, the efficient property of a substance or person. Thus modern science shows us radium with a noble virtue of energy" (*T* 18).

In "Debabelization and Ogden" (*EP&S* 198–205), "A Problem of (Specifically) Style" (188–197), "Leo Frobenius" (174–179), and an unpublished "Addenda" (154–157), Pound confronts his contemporaries on the specificity of language. In agreement with neoempiricist and pragmatist postulates, language is for Pound an instrument of knowledge and clarity, which finds in poetry its highest possible scientific use, realizing through *technê* its cognitive function. What Pound calls "monetary function" (1936 Letter to Bertrand Russell, 218–221) is part of his theories on *res* and *verba* (1934 Letter to Albert Einstein, 216–217), questioning in an economic direction the link between usury and language (1937 Letter to Douglas Fox, 186).

Bibliography

Bell, Ian F. A. *Critic as Scientist: The Modernist Poetics of Ezra Pound*. London: Methuen, 1981.

Berman, Louis. *The Glands Regulating Personality*. New York: Macmillan, 1921.

Fenollosa, Ernest. *The Chinese Written Character as a Medium for Poetry*. Foreword and Notes by Ezra Pound. 1920. London: S. Nott, 1936.

Pound, Ezra. *Ezra Pound e la scienza: Scritti inediti o rari*. Ed. Maria Luisa Ardizzone. Milano: Libri Scheiwiller, 1987.

———. *Machine Art and Other Writings: The Lost Thought of the Italian Years*. Ed. Maria Luisa Ardizzone. Durham: Duke UP, 1996.

Francesca Cadel

The Selected Letters of Ezra Pound [Paige ed.]

D. D. Paige's pioneering work in the general correspondence of Ezra Pound enjoys an immense prestige in the community of scholars. Since it provides a good range of information on Pound's views on literature and the arts, it is used as reference in teaching as well as research.

Paige's edition (whose original title was *The Letters of Ezra Pound 1907–1941*) is not simply a volume of general correspondence but a work firmly rooted in the time in which it was undertaken. Paige was a graduate of the University of Pennsylvania who corresponded with Pound in the early St. Elizabeths years. He started work on the volume in 1948 with Pound's blessing, who told him what correspondents to contact. The poet also gave him free access to his own carbon copies of letters he kept in his apartment in Rapallo. Paige crossed the Atlantic and saw himself confronted with an immense mass of correspondence, a goldmine no one had touched until then. It took him two years to make a selection (about 4,000 typed pages of transcript), which the editor of his publishing house, Harcourt, Brace and Co., further cut to the dimensions of the present volume, first brought out in 1950 (Carpenter 787).

Paige's personal relationship with Pound as well as the generally hostile attitude toward the poet's output in America left their marks on the principles of selection operating in the volume. This is not an authentic cross-section of the Poundian correspondence but a synthesis slanted toward the literary and artistic point of view (Burns 35). The volume emphasized Pound's *ars poetica* as well as his roles as a teacher, translator, and editor. If we had only Paige's edition available as a source of information on Pound as an economist or politician, we would not be able to understand the views that led to his indictment for treason.

Starting with the early 1930s, Pound corresponded with American politicians like Bronson Cutting, George Tinkham, and William Borah (these three correspondences are now available in individual volumes), wrote letters to Roosevelt and Mussolini, and had an enormous correspondence on economics with Social Crediters, like C. H. Douglas, A. R. Orage, M. Butchart, H. Swabey, and Odon Por; with Gesellites like Hugo Fack and E. S. Woodward; and with liberal economists like Irving Fisher and Lionel Robbins. This political and economic side of Pound's letter writing is not reflected in Paige's edition.

The editorial policy of the later volumes of Poundian correspondence has diverged from the Paige model. Editors have concentrated on collections or selections of individual correspondence, which had the advantage of the biographical or historical interest. Paige's edition remains the only selection of general correspondence available. In it, Pound's idiosyncrasies of spelling, lineation, and punctuation were to a large extent standardized or erased in order to ease the work of the reader. This obscures the character and moods of Pound's epistolary style, as well as its development over the years. Later editors have attempted to preserve these particularities and to standardize as little as possible so as to give a more accurate picture of the individual character of Pound's correspondence.

Bibliography

Burns, Philip J. " 'Dear Uncle George': The Pound-Tinkham Letters." *Paideuma* 18.1–2 (1989): 35–65.

Carpenter, Humphrey. *A Serious Character: The Life of Ezra Pound*. Boston: Houghton Mifflin, 1988.

Roxana Preda

Selected Poems (1928)

The 1928 *Selected Poems* was the first of many books by Ezra Pound to be published by the eminent London house of Faber and Faber (known in 1928 as Faber and Gwyer). Poetry editor T. S. Eliot selected the contents of the volume and wrote the introduction. Eliot's text (with a few changes) remained the basis of subsequent British editions of the *Selected Poems* until 1975, when a new and different edition appeared.

Packaging and marketing Pound to an audience that he had systematically insulted since 1914 was no easy task. Eliot began with Pound's own selection of his work for the 1926 New York edition of *Personae* but changed that selection to make it more appealing to British readers. He added five poems published before 1912, the year of Pound's turn toward the Modern. He highlighted the popular *Cathay* translations ("Pound is the inventor of Chinese poetry for our time"). He deleted the *BLAST* satires, some of the *Lustra* epigrams, and the controversial translation *Homage to Sextus Propertius*. He regretted that he was unable to include any of *The Cantos*. Eliot's strategy of softening Pound's edges for general consumption was successful and has since been followed by other editors and critics.

Bibliography

Fletcher, John Gould. "The Neglected Assessment." *Criterion* 8 (April 1929): 513–524.

Hugh Witemeyer

Selected Poems (1949)

In 1946, James Laughlin, founder and managing editor of New Directions, commissioned the American poet and critic John Berryman (1914–1972) to make a selection of Ezra Pound's poetry for a paperback edition. It took Berryman more than two years to complete the task. Published in October 1949, *Selected Poems* has probably introduced more American readers to Pound's verse than any other book. With some changes, it is still in print today.

Pound wanted the edition to showcase the poetry he wrote before 1922, with only 20 to 25 percent of the contents drawn from *The Cantos*. But Laughlin, who recognized *The Cantos* as

Pound's masterwork, added more passages from the epic, bringing its proportion of the volume to 43 percent. Laughlin also wanted the book to have an introduction, but this proved impracticable. The one Berryman wrote was too recondite for general readers, and another penned by the American poet and translator Rolfe Humphries (1894–1969) was unacceptable to Pound because Humphries insisted on disclaiming Pound's political views. The controversy generated by the award of the Bollingen Prize to Pound in February 1949 made all parties sensitive to the political implications of every decision concerning the making of *Selected Poems*.

Bibliography

Berryman, John. "The Poetry of Ezra Pound." *Partisan Review* 16 (April 1949): 377–394.

Gilman, Richard, and Michael Paul Novak, eds. *Poets, Poetics, and Politics: America's Literary Community Viewed from the Letters of Rolfe Humphries, 1910–1969.* Lawrence: UP of Kansas, 1992.

Haffenden, John. *The Life of John Berryman.* London: Routledge, 1982.

Witemeyer, Hugh. "The Making of Pound's *Selected Poems* (1949) and Rolfe Humphries' Unpublished Introduction." *Journal of Modern Literature* 15 (Summer 1988): 73–91.

Hugh Witemeyer

Selected Prose 1909–1965

Issued in 1973 by New Directions and Faber, *Selected Prose* is an attempt, according to editor William Cookson, "to show the unity of Ezra Pound's vision and the integrity of his concerns" (7); it gathers sixty-six works by Pound, ranging from essays on economics and history to previously uncollected literary essays to short, aphoristic statements he published later in life as clarifications of earlier writings. The British edition also includes "Statues of Gods" and "The Treatise on Harmony," while the American edition omits these and includes instead *Patria Mia*. Cookson organizes the essays into five sections according to "the main themes of the *Cantos*" (7) and arranges each section chronologically. (Two other sections each contain single, longer essays.) Cookson's collection allows the reader access to many of Pound's most important individual essays, and his chronological arrangement produces a record of the development of and changes in Pound's thinking from "What I Feel about Walt Whitman" (1909) through the book's forword, which Pound wrote four months before his death in 1972. Cookson's introductory essay serves two functions: On one level, it provides a brief guide to the major themes of the collection and how they relate to *The Cantos*. On another level, it is an *apologia* for the more controversial elements of a body of work that "records the fight to preserve the individual human spirit, and 'to keep the value of a local and particular character' against all forms of oppression and blurring of distinctions, throughout history" (8–9). Cookson also furnishes the essays with annotations that identify Pound's sources, provide additional information on a subject, and direct the reader to relevant cantos. What follows is a general description of each section, highlighting important essays.

Part One: *I Gather the Limbs of Osiris*. Cookson edited this single essay from a series of articles published in the *New Age* from 7 December 1911 through 15 February 1912. *Osiris* proposes "the method of Luminous Detail" (21) for a more accurate study of literature and history. At this early date, Pound was already working out some of his most important poetic and philosophical ideas. As Cookson points out, Luminous Detail prefigures Pound's "ideogrammic method."

Part Two: *Religio*. The second section collects Pound's essays on religion, beginning with "Religio or, The Child's Guide to Knowledge," a pagan catechism originally published in *Pavannes and Divisions* (1918). In addition to several shorter pieces, the section also includes "Axiomata" (*New Age*, 13 January 1921)—a more serious and systematic expression of Pound's religious thinking—and three critiques of religion in the West: "Terra Italica" (*New Review*, Winter 1931–1932), "Ecclesiastical History" (*New English Weekly*, 5 July 1934), and "On the Degrees of Honesty in Various Occidental Religions" (*Aryan Path*, October 1939). These later essays are particularly concerned with comparisons of paganism, Christianity, and Confucianism as well as the economic and cultural role of the Catholic Church in European history.

Part Three: *Confucius and Mencius*. These two essays on Confucian philosophy—"Immediate Need of Confucius" (*Aryan Path*, August 1937) and "Mang Tsze (The Ethics of Mencius)" (*Criterion*, July 1938)—attempt to locate European, and more specifically Dantescan, affinities to a Confucian "hierarchy of values" and demonstrate the "medicinal" and "hygien[ic]" benefits of adopting Confucian ethics in "the Occident."

Part Four: *Patria Mia*. This lengthy early essay is a revision of two articles originally serialized in the *New Age*: "Patria Mia" (5 September–14 November 1912) and "America: Chances and Remedies" (1 May–5 June 1913). It presents Pound's most optimistic analysis of the United States and "its chance for a Renaissance" (102). In the essay, Pound frequently and proudly identifies himself as American.

Part Five: *America*. This is a relatively short but revealing collection of essays on America. Written in 1909, "What I Feel about Walt Whitman" is the earliest essay in the book and reads like an expanded version of "A Pact": "The vital part of my message, taken from the sap and fibre of America, is the same as his" (145). The other essays in this section were all written in or after 1937, and Pound's growing frustration with America's "deafness" to his political and economic ideas is revealed in their frequently urgent and pessimistic tone and a willingness to engage in "the 'decline and fall' method in writing history" (155). "The Jefferson-Adams Letters as a Shrine and National Monument" (*North American Review*, Winter 1937–1938), "National Culture, a Manifesto 1938" (first published in *Impact*), and "An Introduction to the Economic Nature of the United States," written in Italian in 1944, predicate the renaissance of American civilization on the reclamation of an original American culture characterized by a "hierarchy of values" that stood against usury.

Part Six: *Civilization, Money, and History*. The largest section of *Selected Prose* is the heart of the collection, gathering themes introduced in earlier sections around the problem of economics and money. "Provincialism the Enemy" (*New Age*, 12 July 1917) demonstrates how Pound's concern with economics stems from his effort to envision a humanistic society wherein artists could thrive. Several articles from 1920—"Kublai Kahn and His Currency" (*New Age*, 20 May), "Probari Ratio" (*Athenaeum*, 2 April), and "Economic Democracy" (*Little Review*, April)—show Pound already wrestling with Douglas, Keynes, and the question of money. Most of the essays in this section were written in the 1930s when the Great Depression, Pound's meeting with Mussolini, and impending war drove Pound to an intense exploration of the cultural and ethical ramifications of monetary reform. Pound's major economic treatise, *ABC of Economics*, lays out his basic principles, though the simplicity and clarity he hoped for are not evident. Other significant essays of this period include "Murder by Capital" (*Criterion*, July 1933), "The Individual and His Milieu" (*Criterion*, October 1935)—in which Gesellite economics begins to assert an influence on his thinking—and "What Is Money For" (1939). The section contains two works Pound originally wrote in Italian during the war: "A Visiting Card" (1942) and "Gold and Work" (1944). In the former, he attempts a summary of his cultural views along the lines of *Guide to Kulchur*. Pound was never a systematic thinker, preferring repetition to categorization, but in reading these essays, one finds that, as with *The Cantos*, repeated ideas and phrases accrue significance and thereby clarify themselves.

Part Seven: *The Art of Poetry*. This section collects pieces not included in *Literary Essays*. There are two theoretical works, "The Wisdom of Poetry" (*Forum*, April 1912) and "Affirmations—As for Imagism" (*New Age*, 28 January 1915), the latter a clarification of Imagism in light of Vorticism. "The Approach to Paris" (*New Age*, 25 September 1913), "Beddoes and Chronology" (*Future*, September 1917), and "Landor (1775–1864)" (*Future*, November 1917) are critical writings. The section also includes "Prefatio Aut Cimicium Tumulus" (1933), the preface to *Active Anthology*.

Part Eight: *Contemporaries*. The final section includes appreciations of Remy de Gourmont, Marianne Moore, Mina Loy, William Henry Hudson, Wyndham Lewis, and Jean Cocteau and a brief appraisal of Modernism, "D'Artagnan Twenty Years After" (*Criterion*, July 1937). The section also contains four obituaries: "Ford Madox (Hueffer) Ford; Obit" (*Nineteenth Century and After*, August 1939), "For T.S.E." (*Sewanee Review*, Winter 1966), "Obituary: A. R. Orage" (*New English Weekly*, 15 November 1934), and "In the Wounds (Memoriam A. R. Orage)" (*Criterion*, April 1935).

Michael J. Alleman

A Selection of Poems

Published by Faber and Faber in the Sesame Books series in 1940, the volume reprints twenty-eight of Pound's poems from 1909 to 1920, including extracts from *Hugh Selwyn Mauberley* and *Homage to Sextus Propertius*, as well as Cantos 1, 2, and 45. The selection presents Pound as a poet of major and minor *personae*, ranging from Bertran de Born, "The Seafarer," poems from *Cathay*, and *Propertius*. The majority of the shorter poems are from *Riposte* and *Lustra*; the longest single component is "Near Perigord."

Line Henriksen

Sexuality

Pound's thinking regarding sexuality comprises a complex and controversial topos central to his poetics. Rooted in his antagonism toward the Christian dissociation of the mind from the body, Pound's interest in sexuality issues forth in his belief in the capacity of coitus to elicit visions, a belief detectable in his writings from very early on. Pound later brings into focus his understanding of sexuality through idiosyncratic readings of predominantly two sources: Remy de Gourmont's *Physique de l'amour: Essai sur l'instinct sexuel* (Paris, 1903), a profuse text on the erotica of the natural world and physiognomy that Pound translated in 1922 as *The Natural Philosophy of Love*, and to which he added his "Translator's Postscript" and Dr. Louis Berman's *The Glands Regulating Personality*

(1921), a book Pound encountered in 1922. Pound's tangential readings of these texts provide him with parascientific "evidence" to support his highly dimorphic and eccentric sexual theories.

Pound's theory regarding the significance of sex to artistic creativity first arises from his study of the troubadour tradition; by way of his Provençal studies at university, Pound became absorbed in the tradition of courtly love. Indeed, in 1933, Pound wrote to Viola Baxter Jordan that years of his life had been devoted to the investigation of "uplift," of specific kinds of sexuality, and that his interest in Provence reflected this general interest because it was there that the subject had been "properly" understood (Oderman 6). During his early years in London Pound began to develop theories regarding the troubadour tradition that he eventually expressed in his essay on "Psychology and Troubadours" (*SR* 87–100). Here Pound suggests that the troubadours' complex poetry encodes visionary experiences that stem from Hellenistic paganism. Courtly love is thus a remnant religion whose objects of worship are lovers rather than gods. Plainly put, the locus of "Psychology and Troubadours" is that certain kinds of sexual encounters are, for certain individuals, the source of contact with a visionary reality. In *The Spirit of Romance* Pound discreetly circumscribes this subject, often framing his ideas in obscure scientific metaphor. He is also careful to insist that sexuality is but one source of illumination and that not just any sexual experience is capable of invoking visions; instead, it must be characterized by restraint, delay, and tension, and the lover must be composed of "a specific constitution of nerves and intellect." Although Pound discusses sexuality in an oblique fashion, his early thought can be summed up in the following way: Sex has the potential to be a mystical and illuminating experience; when it is, poetry may ensue.

Pound finds support for his developing ideas regarding sexuality in Remy de Gourmont's book *The Natural Philosophy of Love*. Gourmont's observations become fodder for Pound's eccentric speculations. For example, an important distinction made by Gourmont concerns instinct and intelligence, a relationship that he considers dynamically related since he views instinct as "the series of acts which tend to conserve the present condition of the species" and intelligence as "those [acts] which tend to modify that condition" (139). This distinction occasions in Pound sexually dimorphic theories that he formulates as follows:

> [O]ne offers woman as the accumulation of hereditary aptitudes, better than man in the "useful gestures," the perfections; but to man, given what we have of history, the "inventions," the new gestures, the extravagance, the wild shots, the impractical, merely because in him occurs the new up-jut, the new bathing of the cerebral tissues in the residuum, in *la mousse* of the life sap. (204)

Pound again "creatively" explicates Gourmont by appropriating his casual metaphor that seeds cause the "generation of bodies as genius fecundates a generation of minds" ("Postscript" 207). Pound takes Gourmont's poetic analogy to stand for an exact physiological corollary and argues that at the root of invention is the male brain, which Pound hypothesizes is "in origin and development only a sort of great clot of genital fluid held in suspense or reserve" (203). Pound further attempts to establish an actual link between the function of sperm and the brain's imagistic or visionary capacities by insisting that there is an "intimate connection between his sperm and cerebration" (213), the latter hinging on the "relative discharge and retention of the fluid." Excess in discharge, he writes, results in "imbecility," while "retention" or "delay" leads to "genius." Thus, according to his masculinist schema, the postponement of desire during coitus induces vision and creativity. Indeed, as Pound memorably notes, a new idea is "a sensation analogous with the male feeling in copulation" (204).

Thus Pound finds in Gourmont the material out of which he can concretize his masculinist theories of sexuality; it would seem that he believes to have discovered the "scientific" basis he needs to substantiate his hypotheses in Berman's *The Glands Regulating Personality*. Berman's book, a work of popular science, argues that glands are the determining factors in the evolution and performance of the individual. Structurally, Pound's 1922 review of the book is similar to the relation of his "Translator's Postscript" to Gourmont's *Physique de l'Amour*; Pound maintains the same degree of analysis but also departs significantly from the text with personal inferences drawn from his own preoccupations. For example, his review of Berman begins with his summary of Gourmont's physiognomy and continues by using Berman's belief that glands "regulate" personality to attack those who discriminate between the mind and the "evil" body. In his typical manner, Pound focuses on a few of Dr. Berman's phrases that engender in Pound even more eccentric notions. For example, Pound picks up on Berman's reference to "chemical pressure" and surmises that "when the secretions of glands interact in certain ways, they produce definite chemical pressure, and that when this pressure reaches a certain intensity, it forces itself in the consciousness" ("New Therapy" 260). Pound also becomes engrossed by Berman's observation that "the posterior pituitary [is] the gland of hallucination" ("New Therapy" 260); based on this, he tabulates Berman's discussion on glands, focusing on two: the Pineal and the Pituitary, attributing vision to pineal influence and hallucination to pituitary. Reminiscent of his explication of Gourmont's work, Pound is intrigued by visionary experiences but abhors experiences he believes to be hallucinatory. Pound's dissociation of pineal, visionary experience from the pituitary, hallucinatory experience is not to be found in Berman's exposition of glandular effects.

As one might have anticipated, there are divergent readings of Pound's sexuality. Two detectable critical strands are those instigated by Lacanian methodology and those seeking to explore the mystical or occult possibilities of Pound's sexual theories. Alan Durant's *Ezra Pound, Identity in Crisis*, Paul Smith's *Pound Revised*, and Robert Casillo's *Genealogy of Demons* are exemplary Lacanian readings of Pound's sexuality. All three studies are highly critical of Pound and his work as they attempt to explain Pound's more obvious failings such as his fascism, anti-Semitism, and sexual chauvin-

ism in terms of the Lacanian version of the castration complex. While translation into Lacanian terminology does provide a coherent framework in which to consider Pound's "phallocentrism," according to critics like Kevin Oderman, who is interested in the erotic mysticism of Pound's work, the dangers of such readings are that they obscure Pound's own understanding of sexuality and thus are inevitably reductive. Critics such as Oderman, Leon Surette, and Demetres P. Tryphonopoulos, who are predominantly interested in the "mediumistic" and occult potentialities of Pound's work, read his frequent but cryptic references to sexuality in his poetry not as symptomatic of his "phallic consciousness" but as indicative of his stance that coitus is a portal to illumination.

According to Pound's sexual theories, the possibilities for women are obviously ancillary, and indeed, feminist reconsiderations that censure Pound for his inveterate sexism abound. For discussions of Modernism's misogynous discourses, see Gail McDonald's *Learning to Be Modern*, Ann Douglas's *The Feminization of American Culture*, and Sandra Gilbert and Susan Gubar's *No Man's Land: The Place of the Woman Writer in the Twentieth Century*, Vol. 1, *The War of the Words*.

Pound's forays into sexuality, equivocal and eccentric as they are, attest to his continual preoccupation with the notion that the body is not something to be "gotten over" but cultivated. As Oderman writes, though Pound's physiology is at times "naive enough to seem like a fable," his speculations are always fueled by the implicit view that sexuality can be a means into extraordinary experience (49).

Bibliography

Casillo, Robert. *The Genealogy of Demons: Anti-Semitism, Fascism, and the Myths of Ezra Pound.* Evanston: Northwestern UP, 1988.

Douglas, Ann. *The Feminization of American Culture.* New York: Knopf, 1977.

Durant, Alan. *Ezra Pound: Identity in Crisis.* Brighton: Harvester, 1981.

Gilbert, Sandra M., and Susan Gubar. *No Man's Land: The Place of the Woman Writer in the Twentieth Century.* 3 vols. New Haven: Yale UP, 1988–1994.

McDonald, Gail. *Learning to Be Modern: Pound, Eliot, and the American University.* New York: Oxford UP, 1993.

Oderman, Kevin. *Ezra Pound and the Erotic Medium.* Durham: Duke UP, 1986.

Pound, Ezra. "The New Therapy." *New Age* 30.20 (16 March 1922): 259–260.

———. "Postscript to the Natural Philosophy of Love by Remy de Gourmont." *Pavannes and Divagations.* New York: New Directions, 1958.

Smith, Paul. *Pound Revised.* London: Croom Helm, 1983.

Surette, Leon. *The Birth of Modernism: Ezra Pound, T. S. Eliot, W. B. Yeats, and the Occult.* Montreal: McGill–Queen's UP, 1993.

Tryphonopoulos, Demetres P. *The Celestial Tradition: A Study of Pound's The Cantos.* Waterloo: Wilfrid Laurier UP, 1992.

———. "Sacrum, Sacrum, Iluminatio Coitu: Ezra Pound's Sexual Politics." *Nationalism and Sexuality: Crises of Identity.* Ed. Yiorgos Kalogeras and Domna Pastourmatzi. Thessaloniki: Aristotle UP, 1996.

Wilson, Peter. *A Preface to Ezra Pound.* New York: Longman, 1997.

Sheri Benning

Sexuality: Misogyny

Pound's difficult relationships with women remain a contentious issue in critical discourse, and as Demetres P. Tryphonopoulos writes, it seems as easy to censure Pound as to defend him. One approach to Pound's misogynistic behavior describes his phallic preoccupation, impertinent sexism, and offensive language all as symptomatic of a phallocentric consciousness that subordinates the female. Another approach describes Pound's deeply rooted sexism more generally as a reflection of the failures of a patriarchal era. Neither approach is entirely satisfying. The former can be accused of anachronism: "Sexism," though an age-old phenomenon, is a relatively recent concept, and it is somewhat unfair to apply it retrospectively. However, simply studying Pound as a man of his era is also reductive, in that it might too easily explain away his often heinous statements about women. For a fuller understanding, one must consider not only Pound's theoretic and poetic contributions to Modernism's phallocentrism but also his willing support of good writing, regardless of the author's sex.

That early Modernism is a monolithic phenomenon with a unified aesthetic is no longer unchallenged: Recent critics point to the era's plurality and diversity. But one characteristic of Modernism emphasized by feminist analyses is that it is highly gendered as masculine. Indeed, at the very time the *New Freewoman* was promoting women's suffrage and women were defying Victorian gender roles, Male modernists were working with a traditional aesthetic of the feminine ideal. The "men of 1914," writes Helen Dennis, saw the work of their immediate precursors, the Decadents, as degenerate and effeminate. Thus the early Modernists felt compelled to reinscribe patriarchal values into their own productions—as detectable in Pound, who frequently evokes traditional models of the archetypal feminine (264). Just when Pound was working with some of the most radical women of the Modernist era, his writing articulates conservative gender formulations.

Pound's early conception of women derives largely from his study of the Provençal and Renaissance love poets and D. G. Rossetti; his early writing therefore recalls woman's function as a divine emissary who confirms for the male artist the relevance of his enterprise. As Dennis writes, according to the stereotypes of Western culture, women act as intermediaries with the "beyond" that is the poet's life work to translate; at the same time, women must provide the material conditions that make artistic production possible (269). Pound's perception of Margaret Cravens, a young American pianist living in Paris, exemplifies his typecasting of women according to his patriarchal schema. "You have given me so much," he wrote her; "I don't mean the apparent gift—but the restoration of faith . . . the apparent gift comes, as a sort of sign from beyond that my work is accepted. It couldn't have come unless there was some real reason, behind us all, for the work to go on unfettered" (Dennis 269).

Pound's understanding of gender formation became more fully informed by his reading of Remy de Gourmont's *Natural Philosophy of Love.* His "Translator's Postscript" devolves into an exposition of his belief that artistic genius is linked to biological masculinity and that woman's role as "conservator" of culture is linked to her reproductive capacity. Pound draws authority for his argument by combining the rhetoric of scientific objectivity with the persuasive power of myth and by citing his personal experience of heterosexual desire. Pound's theory confers glamor on women insofar as it elevates them to divine status, but it does not allow for political rights to autonomy or equality. Pound's masculinist perceptions are revealed when he speaks of coitus: "[S]ome desire the trivial, some the processional, the stately, the master-work." It would be difficult to argue that this "master-work" merely denotes excellence without implying an exclusively male act that renders the female invisible (Wilson 120).

In Pound's masculinist agenda, women thus fulfill the roles of muse, of spiritual inspirer, of receptacle for the male "master-work." Pound evokes this idea in Canto 29: "Nel ventre tuo, o nella mente mia," "anything properly made," that is, is made in your belly or in my mind (29). Margaret Cravens's suicide in 1912, sometimes attributed to Walter Rummel's sudden marriage, may also have resulted from Pound's courtship of Dorothy Shakespear. Like Hilda Doolittle and Mary Moore of Trenton before her, Cravens was perhaps another discarded victim.

One might assume from this mix of ideology and personal relationships that Pound provided little support for female writers. However, as so often with Pound, his rhetoric is not an accurate indicator of his actions—thus the contradiction between his talk of the feminine ideal and his work as collaborator, promulgator, and colleague to such figures as H. D., Marianne Moore, and Iris Barry. In the case of H. D., Pound helped her launch both the first wave of Imagist poetry and her career as one of the finest Modernist poets. As Peter Wilson notes, however, Pound's support was tailored to promote his own Modernist agenda, and to that extent it was motivated by his sexual politics (121). Women not content to remain in "pleasing attitudes / Of discipleship" (Ruthven 105) suffered Pound's criticism, in which he responded to female strong-mindedness with ridicule. Amy Lowell, who resisted Pound's tight editorial control and instituted her own Imagist anthologies, became a target of Pound's acrimony, sometimes

aimed at her corpulent figure. Indeed "Amygism" was, according to Pound, a flabby alternative to the lean clarity of Imagism (Ruthven 107).

Pound's complex relationship to women is ultimately figured in his relationships with Dorothy Shakespear and Olga Rudge. Hugh Kenner sums it up: "Would Gaudier or would Lewis have come to count for so much in Ezra's mind had not Dorothy lived through her eyes, and had her mother Olivia not purchased Lewises and Gaudiers? His alliance with Miss Rudge was with a musician, as though to redress some balance of the senses, an ear world. For years he loved both women" (493).

An underlying principle in *The Cantos* is a radical revision of religious and symbolic expression through various evocations of Venus/Aphrodite. In Canto 1, Venus is worthy of worship—"Venerandam"—and is addressed throughout the poem as Venus, Cythera, or Kypris. To read these representations of the goddesses merely as part of a patriarchal plot to interpret woman as muse is to deny the importance of Shakespear and Rudge in Pound's life. The thirteenth printing of *The Cantos* ends with "FRAGMENT (1966)": "That her acts / Olga's acts / of beauty / be remembered. // Her name was Courage / & is written Olga // These lines are for the / ultimate CANTO // whatever I may write / in the interim" [24 August 1966]. However flawed Pound's relationships with women were, they were fundamental to the complicated design of his life's work.

Bibliography

Dennis, Helen. "Pound, Women, and Gender." *The Cambridge Companion to Ezra Pound*. Ed. Ira B. Nadel. Cambridge: Cambridge UP, 1999.

Kenner, Hugh. *The Pound Era*. Berkeley: U of California P, 1971.

Ruthven, K. K. *Ezra Pound as Literary Critic*. New York: Routledge, 1990.

Tryphonopoulos, Demetres P. "Sacrum, Sacrum, Illuminatio Coitu: Ezra Pound's Sexual Politics." *Nationalism and Sexuality: Crises of Identity*. Ed. Yiorgos Kalogeras and Domna Pastourmatzi. Thessaloniki: Aristotle UP, 1996.

Wilson, Peter. *A Preface to Ezra Pound*. New York: Longman, 1997.

Sheri Benning

Shakespear, Dorothy (1886–1973)

Dorothy Shakespear was the daughter of a London solicitor, Henry Hope Shakespear, and Olivia Tucker Shakespear, a novelist and art patron who had once been romantically involved with W. B. Yeats. Pound met Olivia at an art lecture, and it was she who introduced him to both Dorothy and Yeats himself. Dorothy was educated in England and spent a year studying in Geneva, where she learned to speak French. She was a painter of talent and considered herself an emancipated woman, but her temperament was probably more attuned to nineteenth-century art than to Modernism. Through Pound's influence, however, she became a Vorticist painter of some note and designed notices and book covers for the Vorticists, including the covers for two of Pound's books (see Gallup A8d and B10) and the initials for many of *The Cantos* (mostly unpublished).

Only after Pound was able to show a regular income from his art, music, and literature reviews did Dorothy's father reluctantly permit them to marry in 1914 and offer them a small allowance. The couple continued to live for the next few years in London and were part of a circle of young avant-garde artists and writers. In 1919 they traveled to Paris and then to southern France, where they were later joined by T. S. Eliot. While Pound and Eliot rambled the troubadour country, Dorothy painted. They returned to England several times but moved to France in 1921. In 1924 they finally settled in Rapallo, Italy.

Dorothy's life with Ezra had been fairly tranquil until he met in Paris and fell in love with the expatriate American violinist Olga Rudge, who followed them to Italy. In July 1925, Olga gave birth to Pound's daughter, Mary. For the next several months, Dorothy traveled around Italy, mostly without Ezra, then spent December to early March in Egypt. She returned from Egypt pregnant and gave birth to a son, Omar, in September 1926, at the American Hospital in Paris. Omar lived for a significant part of his childhood with Olivia Shakespear and was visited at regular intervals by his mother. Pound signed the birth certificate and maintained responsible and affectionate relations with both families.

Following her mother's death in 1938, Dorothy enjoyed a comfortable income; but during World War II things were difficult because it became increasingly difficult to receive money from England. Toward the end of the war the Germans evacuated the Rapallo seafront where the Pounds were living (5 Via Marsala), and they moved into Olga's small house in nearby Sant'Ambrogio, a situation that was difficult for all. After Pound was arrested and sent first to the U.S. Army Disciplinary Training Center (DTC) outside Pisa and then to St. Elizabeths Hospital in Washington, D.C., Dorothy provided unreserved and steadfast support, moving to Washington in early July 1936 to be with Pound and to oversee his care and legal affairs and to visit him every day. When Pound was declared legally incompetent, Dorothy was appointed "Committee" and assumed control of his financial and literary affairs, which also enabled her to restrain his behavior somewhat after his release.

On their return to Italy in 1958, Pound chose to live at Mary's home in the Italian Alps, and Dorothy went with him, but she became increasingly withdrawn. Finally, when Pound was old and ill and Dorothy too frail to care for him, she left for England. Pound remained with Olga, mainly in her small house in Venice, until his death in 1972. Dorothy (and Omar) were not informed of Pound's death until it was too late to get to Italy in time to attend the funeral; she died the following year.

Bibliography

Carpenter, Humphrey. *A Serious Character: The Life of Ezra Pound*. Boston: Houghton Mifflin, 1988.

Pound, Ezra. *Ezra and Dorothy Pound: Letters in Captivity 1945–1946*. Ed. Omar Pound and Robert Spoo. New York: Oxford UP, 1999.

———. *Ezra Pound and Dorothy Shakespear, Their Letters 1909–1914*. Ed. Omar Pound and A. Walton Litz. New York: New Directions, 1984.

Stock, Noel. *The Life of Ezra Pound*. 1970. San Francisco: North Point P, 1982.

Patricia A. Cockram

Shakespear, Olivia (1864–1938)

Born Olivia Tucker in Niton, Isle of Wight, Dorothy Shakespear's mother was the daughter of Major General Henry Tod Tucker, C.B.

(1808–1896), adjutant general of the army in India; through her mother, Harriet Maria Johnson (d. 1900), she was a first cousin of Lionel Johnson (1867–1902), the 1890s poet and member of the Rhymers' Club. In 1885 Olivia married Henry Hope Shakespear, a successful solicitor, who was also an accomplished painter, and their daughter Dorothy was born in 1886. Olivia was a close friend of W. B. Yeats, with whom she had once been romantically involved. She is the "Diana Vernon" of Yeats's autobiographical works, and his "Two Love Poems," published in the *Savoy* (January 1896), are thought to have been written for her. Her stepniece, Dorothy's dear childhood friend Georgie Hyde-Lees, married Yeats in 1917.

Olivia was a widely published novelist, playwright, and literary critic and an avid collector of art. Pound met Olivia, probably through the Australian poet Frederic Manning, in January 1909. She introduced him both to her London literary friends, including Yeats, and to late-nineteenth-century French poetry.

Olivia assumed the responsibility for her grandson Omar, left to her care at the age of eighteen months, and oversaw his education. She died in London in 1938, leaving Dorothy a comfortable income.

Bibliography

Carpenter, Humphrey. *A Serious Character: The Life of Ezra Pound*. Boston: Houghton Mifflin, 1988.

Pound, Ezra. *Erza Pound and Dorothy Shakespear, Their Letters 1909–1914*. Ed. Omar Pound and A. Walton Litz. New York: New Directions, 1984.

Stock, Noel. *The Life of Ezra Pound*. 1970. San Francisco: North Point P, 1982.

Patricia A. Cockram

Sinclair, May (1863–1946)

The English novelist, poet, and critic May Sinclair (Mary Amelia St. Clair Sinclair) published twenty-four novels, including *The Three Sisters* (1914), which Pound admired, and *Mary Olivier* (1919). Herself an innovator, Sinclair actively championed younger avant-garde writers such as H. D., Eliot, and Pound. She sought a new critical vocabulary adequate to Modernist writing: Her 1918 description of Dorothy Richardson's *Pilgrimage* as "stream of consciousness" (William James's term) became a staple of the literary critical lexicon. In 1920, defending Pound against critical attacks, Sinclair published "The Reputation of Ezra Pound," commending his defiance, talent, and generous promotion of other writers.

Bibliography

Sinclair, May. "The Novels of Dorothy Richardson." *Egoist* 5 (April 1918): 57–59.

———. "The Reputation of Ezra Pound." *English Review* 30 (April 1920): 326–335.

Miranda B. Hickman

Social Credit: An Impact

Despite its title, *Social Credit: An Impact* records the impact not so much of Major Douglas's Social Credit ideas, which had already made an indelible mark on Pound, as the impact of Silvio Gesell, author of *The Natural Economic Order* (1916). Though Ezra Pound had been aware of Gesell's work since 1932, after seeing it in action in the Austrian town of Wörgl, he became more interested in Gesell's thinking when he read Hugo Fack's 1935 American edition. Pound's pamphlet, published in 1935, is designed to bring Douglas and Gesell together and, in so doing, to criticize Karl Marx, English leftists, and American New Dealers. Reprinted by Peter Russell in 1951, it is not to be found in Pound's *Selected Prose 1909–1965*.

Pound epitomizes Douglas's economic critique of finance capitalism by stating: "WORK is not a commodity. Money is not a commodity. The state HAS credit, and does not need to rent it from banks" (14). Note the implicit critique of the Marxist axiom that labor is a commodity and therefore the distinction Pound draws between work and labor: Work is what one man does; labor is a mass phenomenon governed by market forces. Pound then turns immediately to quote Gesell: " '*Marx found nothing to criticize in money*,'—S. Gesell" (Pound's emphasis, 15). He continues: "Many vast and heavy books have ended in muddle from failure to see that property and capital are radically different. Property does not imply the enslavement of others. There is a difference between durable and perishable goods, in fact there are all degrees of durability, from that of the fresh-plucked fruit to that of the art works of Chaldea" (15). The heavy books certainly include the three volumes of Marx's *Capital*, and indeed, in that monumental work, Marx has little to say about money. Following the classical economists Adam Smith and David Ricardo, Marx subscribes to the labor theory of value, which is measured by money. Evidently, once the true nature of money is understood, via thin pamphlets like Pound's, economics can be rendered in pithy maxims, not pages of recondite algebra or difficult economic theory.

In this pamphlet, Pound spends little time on Gesell's innovative *Schwundgeld* or "stamp scrip," regarding it as a temporary expedient (14), a "half-way house" (20) on the way to a full Douglasite reform of the money system. Another article written near the same time, "The Individual and His Milieu: A Study of Relations and the Individual" (1935), republished in *Selected Prose*, is a crucial companion piece to this essay.

The pamphlet has four chapters. The first of these is an excellent economic gloss on *The Cantos*. Here one finds the most complete explanation of the difference between "the hell banks" and the Monte Dei Paschi, Pound's ideal bank. Chapter Two contains one of Pound's Populistic pocket economic histories of the United States. Chapter Three is the heart of his explicitly economic argument, as outlined above, while Chapter Four challenges professors ("agglomerates of protoplasm"); New Dealers, Fabians, and Laborites to accept Douglas's teachings.

Bibliography

Marsh, Alec. *Money and Modernity: Pound, Williams, and the Spirit of Jefferson.* Tuscaloosa: U of Alabama P, 1998.

Redman, Tim. *Ezra Pound and Italian Fascism.* New York: Cambridge UP, 1991.

Sieburth, Richard. *Instigations: Ezra Pound and Remy de Gourmont.* Cambridge: Harvard UP, 1978.

Surette, Leon. *A Light from Eleusis: A Study of Ezra Pound's Cantos.* Oxford: Clarendon P, 1979.

———. *Pound in Purgatory: From Economic Radicalism to Anti-Semitism.* Urbana: U of Illinois P, 1999.

Alec Marsh

Sonnets and Ballate of Guido Cavalcanti

In 1912, Ezra Pound published *Sonnets and Ballate of Guido Cavalcanti*, a facing-page translation of thirty-five sonnets, one madrigal, and fourteen *ballate* of Guido Cavalcanti (c. 1250–1300), all of the work generally accepted as his at the time except for the canzone *"Donna mi prega,"* which Pound was to translate twice later in his career. The edition caps a period of intense interest in Cavalcanti, Dante's friend and mentor in the art of lyric poetry, who was discussed in *The Spirit of Romance* (1910) and "I Gather the Limbs of Osiris" (1911), both of which contained versions of some of the poems contained in *Sonnets and Ballate*.

Bilingual editions of early Italian poetry were not the exotica in 1912 that they might seem today, the Temple Classics edition of Dante's *Commedia* that Pound used in college being one example. Pound himself wrote Margaret Cravens in 1910 that the *Sonnets and Ballate* "intends to be the most important contribution to English-Italian Belles lettres since Symonds translation of Mike. Angelos Sonnets" (Pound, *Ezra Pound and Margaret Cravens* 47). A closer model for *Sonnets and Ballate*, in that Pound saw his translations both as guides to the original and as poems in their own right, is Dante Gabriel Rossetti's *Dante and His Circle*. But since Rossetti had already translated twenty-four of Cavalcanti's poems, why do them over again?

One reason for *Sonnets and Ballate* was to present Cavalcanti as more than just Dante's associate. Pound engaged in a lifelong effort to bring Cavalcanti out of the shade of being seen just as part of "Dante and His Circle." All of *Sonnets and Ballate* were included in *The Translations of Ezra Pound* in 1953 and then were republished along with both versions of *"Donna mi prega,"* two essays on Cavalcanti and a one-page foreword by Pound in 1966, the foreword being one of the last things he wrote. It was thus a matter of continuing importance to Pound to present Cavalcanti as an important poetic voice in his own right. Why his voice was important for Pound is best caught in Pound's praise in the introduction to *Sonnets and Ballate*: "Than Guido Cavalcanti no psychologist of the emotions is more keen in his understanding, more precise in his expression; we have in him no rhetoric, but always a true delineation" (2). This focus on "true delineation" or exact representation is, of course, a key theme in Pound's Imagist poetry, which develops immediately after the Cavalcanti translations. Seeing Cavalcanti as a kind of proto-Imagist is another reason why for Pound he needed to be translated again, after Rossetti. Although Pound in his introduction to *Sonnets and Ballate* courteously says that "in the matter of these translations and of my knowledge of Tuscan poetry, Rossetti is my father and my mother," he also goes out of his way to point out mistakes in Rossetti's translation. However, the real limitation to Rossetti's version is that the kind of precise language Pound praised in Cavalcanti is not to be found. Take, for example, Rossetti's rendering of the opening of the famous *ballata "Perch'io non spero"*: "Because I think not ever to return, / Ballad, to Tuscany." This fails in two ways, as Pound would have seen. First, since it does not make it clear that Guido cannot return, sounding instead rather as if he were indecisive about whether he wishes to return, it does not fully convey the sense of the original. Second, Rossetti's desire for a line-by-line translation enables him to reproduce Cavalcanti's second line intact, but at a cost of a word order in line 1 that is not normal English and is markedly less direct than Cavalcanti: *"Perch'io non spero di tornar già mai, / Ballatetta, in Toscana."*

Nonetheless, it has to be said that Pound's 1912 version improves on Rossetti in only one of these respects: "Because no hope is left me, Ballatetta, / Of return to Tuscany." This gives a clearer sense than Rossetti does of the involuntary nature of Cavalcanti's absence. However, it does so only by deviating further than Rossetti does from Cavalcanti's lineation, and the result is no closer to anything anyone would actually say in English. The following line, *"Va tu leggiera e piana,"* rendered by Pound as "Light-foot go thou some fleet way," is rendered much more directly—if also more freely and scarcely more colloquially—in Rossetti's "Go therefore though for me."

If Cavalcanti thus was a force on Pound leading him in the direction of Imagism's poetry of direct statement and closer approximation to the norm of spoken language, it is fair to say that Pound's own translations of Cavalcanti in *Sonnets and Ballate* show rather the distance Pound had to travel to reach this goal. It was left to Eliot in "Ash Wednesday" in 1929, in lines that are the greatest consequence of Pound's early interest in Cavalcanti, to show how these lines can be translated into a colloquial, powerful, and accurate English rendering: "Because I do not hope to turn again." Pound remained the truer Cavalcantian, however, in that the note of exile sounded here as in the *Commedia* was one he sounded in his work virtually wherever he found himself.

Sonnets and Ballate is an important work in Pound's oeuvre, less for the qualities of the translations themselves than for the enduring effect of Cavalcanti on Pound's work. In 1912, the effect was to lead him toward the poetic of Imagism. After Imagism, Pound returns to Cavalcanti's work, and this subsequent equally intense period of immersion in Cavalcanti (roughly 1928 to 1934)—very different from the first—leads to a second book on Cavalcanti, *Guido Cavalcanti Rime*, published in 1932, not to mention an opera based on his life and work.

Bibliography

Gugelberger, Georg M. "The Secularization of Love to a Poetic Metaphor: Cavalcanti, Center of Pound's Medievalism." *Paideuma* 2.2 (1973): 159–174.

Oderman, Kevin. "Cavalcanti: That the Body Is Not Evil." *Paideuma* 11.2 (1982): 257–280.

Paolucci, Anne. "Ezra Pound and Dante Gabriel Rossetti as Translators of Cavalcanti." *Romanic Review* 51 (1960): 256–267.

Pound, Ezra. *Ezra Pound and Margaret Cravens: A Tragic Friendship 1910–1912.* Ed. Omar Pound and Robert Spoo. Durham: Duke UP, 1988.

———. *Pound's Cavalcanti: An Edition of the Translations, Notes, and Essays.* Ed. David Anderson. Princeton: Princeton UP, 1983.

Wilhelm, James J. "Guido Cavalcanti as a Mask for Ezra Pound." *PMLA* 89 (1974): 332–340.

Reed Way Dasenbrock

Spanish Literature

Ezra Pound's involvement in the Spanish-speaking literary world dates back to his early visit to Spain in 1906. His intention was to compile material at the Royal Library of Madrid for his planned doctoral thesis on the function of the *gracioso* in the plays of Lope de Vega, a project that was ultimately left unfinished. Nevertheless, that trip fostered his interest in universal culture and in a reappraisal of Western civilization. To this effect, his fascination with the chanson de geste, and more particularly with the "Cantar del Mío Cid," and the constant allusions in his work to Spanish authors—like Francisco de Quevedo, for representing the proliferation of the active signifier, or Cervantes, who is taken as an essential reference for Joyce's modes of concision—have been rewarded with a torrent of his work translated into Spanish. His poems, literary essays, art criticism, letters, interviews, and writings on economy, politics, and culture have been profusely appearing since 1920, the date when "The Island of Paris: A Letter" was published in the Bilbao magazine *Hermes*, considered his first publication in Spanish. His continual literary presence in books, anthologies, and magazines led to Pound's recognition as a decisive influence on Modern poetry whether in Latin America or Spain. Jorge Guillén, Juan Ramón Jiménez (who visited Pound at St. Elizabeths), Ernesto Cardenal, José Coronel Urtecho, Octavio Paz, and Pere Gimferrer, to mention but a few, openly applauded his literary achievement. As well, avant-garde Spanish poetical tendencies like Ultraism and Creationism also felt the attraction of Pound's poetics.

Possibly Pound's best book in Spanish is his *Cantares completos*, edited and annotated by Javier Coy and with an excellent translation by José Vázquez Amaral, who also writes briefly about his personal relationship with Pound to explain Old Ez's special desire that the Spanish translation of *The Cantos* should be "Cantares," as in the chansons de geste or "Cantar del Mío Cid," because they also deal with the tale of the human tribe. Vázquez Amaral raised many questions and was always challenged by Pound to provide an aesthetic dimension involving complex relations to historical, literary, cultural, and ideological issues. Translations of Pound's work have appeared in nearly all the Spanish-speaking countries, including Argentina, Bolivia, Chile, Colombia, Costa Rica, Mexico, Nicaragua, Peru, Spain, and Venezuela. When appearing in general anthologies of American literature, there is apparently little discernment used so as to include a representative selection of his work. The best approach is achieved in books where he is the only author, anthologized to represent the variety and aesthetic dimensions of his production. His presence in literary magazines has proven almost an obligation for their editors; many separate poems or special issues devoted to his poetry have been published, among them *Reunión* (Autumn 1949, Buenos Aires), *El Zaguán* (1976, Mexico), *Poesía Libre* (October 1983, Managua), and *Otras Palabras* (1985, Medellín). Generally speaking, most translators do not follow Pound's advice to Vázquez Amaral to take the translation as a sort of vision, preferring instead to operate too literally on the basis of the English referent.

Bibliography

Pound, Ezra. *Antología poética*. Ed. and trans. Carlos Viola Soto. Buenos Aires: Fabril, 1963.

———. *Antología poética*. Ed. Manuel Almagro Jiménez. Trans. Antonio Rivero Taravillo. Sevilla: Ediciones Universidad de Sevilla, 1991.

———. *Cantares Completos (I–CXX)*. Trans. José Vázquez Amaral. México: Joaquin Martiz, 1975.

———. *Introducción a Ezra Pound: Antología general de textos*. Trans. Carmen R. de Velasco and Jaime Ferrán. Barcelona: Barral, 1973.

Manuel Brito

The Spirit of Romance

Ezra Pound's first book of prose criticism, *The Spirit of Romance: An Attempt to Define Somewhat the Charm of the Pre-Renaissance Literature of Latin Europe*, was published by Dent in 1910. In a "Post-Postscript" to the New Directions edition dated 1968, Pound describes the book's origin in Hugo Rennert's classes in Spanish, Italian, Old French, and Provençal at the University of Pennsylvania. Plans for the book were formed together with a course of twenty-one public lectures delivered at the London Polytechnic, and Ernest Rhys, founder of Dent's Everyman series, arranged for publication. Pound in 1968 could recall no notice from the press, but there was one perceptive review by Pound's cautious admirer Edward Thomas, who praised the translations but complained that the author was too "restlessly opinionated" (Homberger 68).

The ten original chapters focus on selected major figures—Arnaut Daniel, Dante, the authors of the *Poema del Cid* and the *Chanson de Roland*, Villon, Lope de Vega, Camoens—and on subcanons of medieval literature: the early "transitional" texts, the troubadour *cansos*, the Italian *dolce stil nuovo*, the gestes and romances (where Pound's relative lack of interest is transparent), and the Renaissance Latinists. One additional chapter, "Psychology and Troubadours," appeared as a separate article in 1912 and was added to the book in 1932 and subsequent printings.

The book at one level fits with that class of scholarly popularizations such as J. W. Mackail's 1895 *Latin Literature*, which Pound's introduction "parrots" (see 1929 footnote, page 12), or Ida Farnell's 1896 *Lives of the Troubadours* (62). Pound sometimes seems as fascinated with the legendry of the troubadour lives (compare his 1913 essay "Troubadours: Their Sorts and Conditions") as with the poems themselves, and he notes that the *razos* often give "a great deal of information in very few words" (55). At another level, the book resembles the criticism of Walter Pater, in *The Renaissance* or *Appreciations*: The "charm" of Pound's subtitle perhaps echoes Pater's concept of the particular "virtue" of an author's work, a concept that Pound elaborates in his 1912 "Osiris" essay "On Virtue" to indicate the "donative" quality, the essential transmissible originality of an author.

For *The Spirit of Romance* is a narrative of origins—not Pater's "rebirth" but the birth itself. Chapter 1, "The Phantom Dawn," selects the *Metamorphoses* not of Ovid but of Apuleius, *The Golden Ass*, as his starting point, a "picaresque novel" written in an "incult Latin" that would have disgusted Cicero (12)—and a work whose interpolated tale of Cupid and Psyche reappears in Pater's novel *Marius the Epicurean*

(quoted on page 17). The beginning of the Middle Ages is the anonymous Latin lyric "Pervigilium Veneris," which features metrical tendencies "indigenous to the Italian peninsula" that had been long suppressed (18). Likewise, "Romance literature begins with a Provençal 'Alba,' supposedly of the Tenth Century" (11)—Pound's translation of which stands as the earliest item in Gallup's *Bibliography*. *The Spirit of Romance* oddly dismisses the first known troubadour, William IX of Poitiers (41), whose strong personality dominates Canto 8; but following the lead of Dante in his *De Vulgari Eloquentia*, it dwells on the troubadours collectively as the originators of the vernacular lyric tradition.

Like Dante (and unlike Pater), the twenty-five-year-old Pound locates "charm" largely in technique. The troubadours invented new harmonies depending not on quantity but on rhyme and accent (22). Like Dante (and unlike contemporary scholars), Pound singles out Arnaut Daniel as the master craftsman of the troubadours. Anticipating his Vorticist manifestos, Pound declares that poetry is "a sort of inspired mathematics, which gives us equations, not for abstract figures, triangles, spheres, and the like, but equations for the human emotions" (14). The troubadours teach principles for the construction of stanzas. They show that musical rhymes depend on their "arrangement, not on their multiplicity" (38). Scarce rhymes are preferable to facile. But surprisingly, Pound dwells not on Arnaut's virtuosic versification but on his diction and metaphor, "his refusal to use the 'journalese' of his day" and his "aversion from an obvious familiar vocabulary" (25). He praises Arnaut's "use of the picturesque verb with an exact meaning" (33). Anticipating Imagism, Pound likewise praises Dante's precision, his ability "to reproduce exactly the thing which has been clearly seen" (126). Still, Pound makes clear that technique is not everything. If one test of poetic art is the single line (the quasi-Arnoldian touchstone), a greater test is Coleridge's "continuous undercurrent of feeling . . . everywhere present, but seldom anywhere a separate excitement" (50). If Camoens was master of "that part of the art of poetry which can be taught" (220), Dante's work surpasses all others "not because it is, line for line, better" but because of the "lofty spirit . . . moving behind the verse" (113).

Throughout his book, Pound remains true to his vision of history as living tradition, not the repository of dead fact it seemed to be in the philology of his day. In a frequently quoted passage from his preface, Pound declares: "All ages are contemporaneous. . . . What we need is a literary scholarship, which will weigh Theocritus and Yeats with one balance; it will judge dull dead men as inexorably as dull writers of today" and will likewise "give praise to beauty" wherever it is found (8). The best plays of Lope "are as fresh and playable today as they were in 1600" (197). On the other hand, interest in the prose romances is, with certain exceptions, "archaeological rather than artistic" (85).

Pound's book is in part a redefinition of epic tradition. The line of literary epic that runs from Virgil through Milton, so dominant in the schools, is scarcely mentioned. Likewise the line of allegorical fantasies from Boiardo and Ariosto to Tasso and Spenser. Pound is unexpectedly charitable to the Virgilian Camoens, whose "florid rhetoric . . . is hardly to be surpassed"; but he warns that "epic cannot be written against the grain of its time: the prophet or satirist may hold himself aloof . . . but the writer of epos must voice the general heart" (216). Instead, Pound highlights an alternative tradition in Ovid and above all Dante. Ovid writes with "the clarity of French scientific prose"; his gods are "humanized, their annals . . . written as if copied from a parish register" (15). As for Dante's *Commedia* (in a comment that adumbrates the genre of *The Cantos*), it "must not be considered as an epic; . . . It is in a sense lyric, the tremendous lyric of the subjective Dante" (153). Yet Pound enjoys pitting this nonepical Dante against Milton: "Dante's god is ineffable divinity," he says; "Milton's god is a fussy old man with a hobby. Dante is metaphysical, where Milton is merely sectarian" (156–157).

Pound's Villon chapter ponders the artist outsider: Villon's depravity "is not a pose cultivated for literary effect." In contrast to Whitman, who "having decided that it is disgraceful to be ashamed, rejoices in having attained nudity," Villon "never makes the fatal mistake of glorifying his sin" (169, 171). These outsiders join the group that includes "the bandit" Ruy Diaz, whom Pound prefers to the more conventionally heroic Roland (78), and Dante's heretical friend Guido Cavalcanti. Significantly, Villon and Cavalcanti become the subjects of Pound's two operas.

"Psychology and Troubadours" (subtitled "A Divagation from Questions of Technique"), which first appeared in G.R.S. Mead's Theosophical journal *Quest* (October 1912), adds another dimension to Pound's mix. This essay—described by Surette as the "most theosophical" of all Pound's works (*Birth of Modernism* 198)—is built on an assumption that there is a single tradition of occult wisdom, founded in ancient Greece, coded into myth and the Eleusinian mysteries, and transmitted to the Middle Ages through the troubadours of Provence. There is no clear exposition of these beliefs—such an exposition would violate the secrecy of the secret tradition—and much in the chapter remains circular or opaque. Yet there is a gesture of leaving aside superficials and cutting to the core. "Apart from Arnaut's aesthetic merits," declares Pound, "there is a problem of meaning" (89). "If paganism survived anywhere it would have been, unofficially, in the Langue d'Oc. . . . Did this 'close ring,' this aristocracy of emotion, evolve, out of its half memories of Hellenistic mysteries?" (90). The obscurities of the *trobar clus* seem to invite this kind of speculation; as Peter Makin observes, "Pound's myth always assumed something 'behind' the troubadours" (240). The occult traditions underlying these ideas have been explored by Makin, Miyake, Surette, Tryphonopoulos, and others, and in *The Spirit of Romance* they emerge partly as digression and partly as secret history momentarily revealed. But in the rest of the book, too, Pound's literary history shadows his mystical history: Thus, the famous "inspired mathematics" passage goes on to talk of "spells or incantations" (14), showing Pound's use of scientific rhetoric to mask his occultism. The last part of Apuleius's romance is "a huge parody of the mystic rites," while the "Pervigilium Veneris . . . celebrates a Greek feast which had been transplanted into Italy" (18). And "at the time of *La Regina Avrillouse*, the worshipers of Diana, and the Star of the Sea [i.e., Mary], are moving to the still graver music in cloisters" (40).

For the most part, however, Pound remains an obliging guide to the glories of medieval literature. He never forgets what we still need reminding of: "Art is a joyous thing . . . apropos of which I would in all seriousness plead for a greater levity, a more befitting levity, in our study of the arts" (8).

Bibliography

Homberger, Eric, ed. *Ezra Pound: The Critical Heritage*. London: Routledge, 1972.

Makin, Peter. *Provence and Pound*. Berkeley: U of California P, 1978.

Miyake, Akiko. *Ezra Pound and the Mysteries of Love: A Plan for the Cantos*. Durham: Duke UP, 1991.

Surette, Leon. *The Birth of Modernism: Ezra Pound, T. S. Eliot, W. B. Yeats, and the Occult*. Montreal: McGill–Queen's UP, 1993.

Tryphonopoulos, Demetres P. *The Celestial Tradition: A Study of Ezra Pound's The Cantos*. Waterloo: Wilfrid Laurier UP, 1992.

Stephen J. Adams

Stein, Gertrude (1874–1946)

An expatriate American writer born to German Jewish parents, Gertrude Stein studied under William James at Radcliffe, nearly completed a medical degree at Johns Hopkins, and moved to France in 1902. She acquired an important collection of paintings by Picasso, Braque, and others. Her domestic partnership with Alice B. Toklas made possible Stein's Paris salon. What James Laughlin "came up against" as "automatic dictation" in Stein's writing (129) she regarded as her effort to ensnare "the complete actual present." In her great popular success, *The Autobiography of Alice B. Toklas*, Stein wrote of Pound that she "liked him but did not find him amusing. She said he was a village explainer, excellent if you were a village, but if

you were not, not" (189). She further perceived him as a threat to domestic tranquillity from their meeting in 1921: "All he has to do is to come in and sit down for half an hour. When he leaves, the chair's broken, the lamp's broken. Ez is fine, but I can't afford to have him in the house" (Souhami 149). Pound's negativity toward Stein was more viscerally expressed: "Gertie Stein is supposed to haff a stdyle pecause she writes yittish wit englisch wordts. That is not the way to did it but it shows how effektif it iss yess" (Carpenter 400).

Bibliography

Carpenter, Humphrey. *A Serious Character: The Life of Ezra Pound*. Boston: Houghton Mifflin, 1988.

Cooper, David D., ed. *Thomas Merton and James Laughlin: Selected Letters*. New York: W. W. Norton, 1997.

Souhami, Diane. *Gertrude and Alice*. London: Pandora P, 1991.

Stein, Gertrude. *The Autobiography of Alice B. Toklas. Selected Writings of Gertrude Stein*. Ed. Carl Van Vechten. Modern Library. New York: Random House, 1962.

Evelyn Haller

Stokes, Adrian (1902–1972)

Adrian Stokes was born in Bayswater, London, the son of a self-made stockbroker and a Sephardic Jew of the Montefiori family. Educated at Rugby School and Magdalene College, Oxford, where he studied politics, philosophy, and economics, Stokes had written two immature books of metaphysical speculation before he met Ezra Pound on the tennis courts of Rapallo in November 1926. There he was able to show Pound the frontispiece of his *Sunrise in the West, a Modern Interpretation of Past and Present* (1926), featuring a relief by Agostino di Duccio from the Tempio Malatestiano at Rimini, the Renaissance building that had served Pound as a metaphor of order and aspiration in the "Malatesta Cantos" (1923). Stokes would always jealously protect the independence of his discovery of the Tempio on 5 July 1925 before meeting Pound, but close examination of *Sunrise in the West* reveals possible acquaintance with *The Cantos*.

Pound was impressed by Stokes's evocations of stone and water in an early essay on Agostino of 1928, which responded to the Venetian parts of Canto 17 published in the winter of 1925–1926. Through his influence with T. S. Eliot at the *Criterion* and Faber, Pound secured publication of Adrian Stokes's earliest publications on art, of which the most important were the first two volumes of a trilogy that was never finished: *The Quattro Cento: A Different Conception of the Italian Renaissance* (1932) and *Stones of Rimini* (1934). The first of these not only demonstrates a keen affinity with the outwardness of Pound's Mediterranean aesthetic but also finds in the contrastive dynamic and reserved qualities of Florentine Renaissance funerary monuments a visual equivalent to Pound's literary distinction between Cavalcanti's organic metaphors and Petrarch's extraneous ornaments. Pound reviewed *The Quattro Cento* enthusiastically but was diffident toward *Stones of Rimini*. Not only was the prose style of this second volume more remote from the fragmentary abruptness of Pound's example, but during 1933 Stokes had also evolved a comprehensive theory of the visual arts that categorized them according to the wholesome, objective effects of carving or the willful, subjective effects of modeling, a distinction that drew on Freud's defense of psychoanalysis from hypnotism rather than on anything in Pound and that may have been designed to rival the theory of medieval literature of which Pound had boasted to Stokes in letters and which Stokes had helped him to publish as *Make It New* (1934).

Another factor in their mounting rivalry was a series of essays defending the sculptural art of Ben Nicholson, Barbara Hepworth, and Henry Moore, which Stokes published in the *Spectator* in 1933. These short but brilliant reviews had the effect of making the aggressive masculinity of an older generation of sculptors applauded by Pound in *Gaudier-Brzeska: A Memoir* (1916)

look distinctly old-fashioned, though Pound would soon claim with some justice that Stokes had plagiarized aspects of his *Gaudier* in *Stones of Rimini*. Perhaps the major cause of Pound's tepid response to *Stones* was recognition that Stokes was supporting the visual manifestations of the Italian Renaissance against his own enthusiasm for medieval philosophy and literature. Stokes's support also depended on an overtly bisexual reading of the Tempio reliefs that flew in the face of Pound's use of that building as a focus for the moral, aesthetic, and heterosexual virtues of its patron, Sigismondo Malatesta, foretype of Mussolini in his long, experimental poem.

Despite these challenges to his former mentor, Stokes expressed his bitter disappointment at the review in letters to Pound and subsequently abandoned the third volume of his trilogy. This volume would have returned to "Four essays on the Tempio Malatestiano at Rimini" begun under Pound's guidance from 1927, of which only the third and the first essays, on Agostino and Pisanello, were published in 1929 and 1930, respectively. These early essays were to have served as a historical commentary on *The Cantos* in a format that Stokes's new aesthetic tastes, theories, and artistic allegiances had now outgrown. Not only did his daily sessions in London with the child psychologist Melanie Klein from January 1930 onward curtail his visits to Rapallo; but they are also likely to have undermined Stokes's support for the authoritarian and intolerant qualities that Pound admired in Sigismondo and Mussolini. After-echoes of each other's work are to be found, nevertheless, after 1938, when Stokes saw Pound in Rapallo for the last time.

Bibliography

Read, Richard. *Art and Its Discontents: The Early Life of Adrian Stokes*. Aldershot: Ashgate P; University Park: Pennsylvania State UP, 2002.

Richard Read

T

Tagore, Rabindranath (1861–1941)

Rabindranath Tagore and Ezra Pound met in London in 1912, and Pound immediately championed his work. Tagore translated his original poetry into English prose, and Pound praised its cadence and content, stating, "The Bengali brings to us the pledge of a calm which we need overmuch in an age of steel and mechanics" ("Tagore's Poems," *EPPP* 1.109). Pound secured publication of six Tagore poems in the December 1912 issue of *Poetry*—the first time Tagore's work appeared in the West—and contributed his essay "Tagore's Poems" for the same issue. In 1913, the *Fortnightly Review* included Pound's review of Tagore's *Gitanjali*, and he contributed an essay to the *New Freewoman*, chastising the English public for undervaluing Tagore's work. Pound's enthusiasm for Tagore led to his own translations of poems by the Indian poet Kabir. By the time Tagore received the Nobel Prize in 1913, however, Pound was already losing interest in Tagore's cadenced prose. When Pound reviewed Ernest Fenollosa's *Certain Noble Plays of Japan* in the August 1917 issue of the *Little Review*, he did more than express his excitement for Japanese literature: He publicly denounced Tagore's work and Indian poetry in general.

Ce Rosenow

Terrell, Carroll F. (1917–2003)

Carroll F. Terrell, known to all Ezra Pound scholars as "Terry" Terrell, was born on 17 February 1917 in Richmond, Maine. He graduated from Bowdoin College in 1940 and served as an officer in the U.S. Coast Guard from 1941 to 1946, stationed primarily in the Caribbean. He received an M.A. from the University of Maine in 1950 and a Ph.D. from New York University in 1956, writing a dissertation on Eliot's *Four Quartets*. Terry taught full-time at the University of Maine from 1948 to 1982 and part-time from 1982 to 1988. In the 1960s his research interests shifted increasingly to Ezra Pound. In 1971 he nominated Pound for an honorary Doctor of Literature degree from the University of Maine, and Pound agreed to travel to the United States to accept the degree. However, while the university administration approved the honorary degree, the board of trustees refused to vote the degree on the grounds that Pound was a traitor.

In 1971 Terry founded *Paideuma: A Journal Devoted to Ezra Pound Scholarship*, with Hugh Kenner and Eva Hesse serving as senior editors; the first issue was published in 1972, and the journal remained a primary organ for Pound studies for the next thirty years. While Terry modestly titled himself only the managing editor, he in fact edited *Paideuma* essentially single-handedly from its founding until 1998. In 1974 Terry also initiated a book series under the National Poetry Foundation (NPF) imprint; the first NPF publication was James J. Wilhelm's *Dante and Pound: The Epic of Judgement*, and in the years since, NPF has published more than a dozen additional Pound-related books. NPF also branched out from Pound himself to publish books on poets affiliated with Pound, including in particular the Man and Poet/Woman and Poet Series, which has to date published volumes of biography and critical commentary on such poets as William Carlos Williams, H. D., Marianne Moore, T. S. Eliot, Basil Bunting, Louis Zukofsky, and many others. The *Companion* draws on the work of many Pound scholars, especially the contributors to *Paideuma* during its first ten years of publication, in providing glosses for every reference in the text of *The Cantos*. After 1977 Terry was able to devote most of his time to this project; volume 1 of the *Companion*, covering Cantos 1–71, was published in 1980, followed by volume 2 in 1984.

Terry also made a major contribution to Pound studies by organizing a series of conferences devoted to the poet's work. In 1975, 1980, and 1985, Terry hosted Pound conferences on the campus of the University of Maine, and in 1990 he hosted a Pound/Yeats conference. These conferences brought to the University of Maine such key figures in Pound studies as Hugh Kenner, Marjorie Perloff, M. L. Rosenthal, John J. Espey, Louis Martz, Walter Baumann, Donald Gallup, James Wilhelm, Donald Davie, Hugh Witemeyer, Wendy Flory, David Moody, Leon Surette, Ronald Bush, and many others. Conference participants also included poets such as Donald Hall, Robert Creeley, and Allen Ginsberg; members of Pound's family, including Mary de Rachewiltz and Olga Rudge; and friends of Pound, such as Louis Zukofsky, James Laughlin, David Gordon, Marcella Spann Booth, and Sherri Martinelli. In the 1980s Terry also organized conferences on poets affiliated with Pound, including William Carlos Williams (1984), H. D. (1986), Marianne Moore (1987), and T. S. Eliot (1988).

Terry's own essays on Pound are collected in *Ideas in Reaction: Byways to the Pound Arcana* (Northern Lights P, 1991). Under the NPF imprint, Terry has also published three sections of a long poem modeled on *The Cantos: Smoke and Fire* (1985), *Rod and Lightning* (1985), and *Dark and Light* (1986). In 1993 he published a memoir of his childhood, *Growing Up Kennebec: A Downeast Boyhood* (Northern Lights P, 1993).

Burton Hatlen

Le Testament

Le Testament is an opera in one act, two scenes (circa forty-five minutes), composed from 1920 to 1933 in five different versions, on verse from *Le grande testament* by François Villon, with dialogue by the composer. The first performances of the entire opera were two BBC broadcasts, both in 1931. Its first staged performance with the complete original orchestration from the 1923 version edited by George Antheil took place at the San Francisco Western Opera Theater in Berkeley, California, in 1971.

The scene is Paris circa 1462: a square fronted by a brothel, a bar, and a church. Villon has been condemned to death and a warrant issued for his arrest. Though his capture is imminent, he sits before the tavern writing his last will and irrevocable testament. Too poor to have material goods, he wills his poetry. The world he writes about revolves around him. The old whore Heaulmière sings of her lost charms, a Gallant en route to the brothel sings of love, and Villon's mother sings for the salvation of all. Bozo the brothel-keeper drunkenly sings of his whore Fat Margot as the spent Gallant wobbles out of the brothel only to renounce love and, to the gathering crowd's delight, to collapse atop Bozo. The scene climaxes with the crowd's drinking song, the arrival of the police, and the arrest of Villon. The opera concludes with an eerie preternatural scene: Six corpses strung from the gibbet sing a plea for the salvation of their souls.

While Pound's music basically adheres to the hexatonic vocal range of the late Middle Ages, his dominant instrumental concept is strikingly original. Similar to Webern's *Klangfarbenmelodie* (the melodic line fragmented among a group of instruments), Pound's technique was arrived at independently as a means of reinforcing the accents of Villon's verse. It is possible to speculate that *Le Testament* is minimally harmonized as a result of incompetence. But if Pound felt inadequate at fulfilling the obligations of traditional harmony, it also seems possible that traditional harmony, in turn, had been unable to fulfill its obligation to Pound (and to the most sophisticated composers of his generation). In

Le Testament he obviously sought (in company with Webern, for example) a music that lay beyond or before the harmonic era and was, in essence, melody.

Villon, a baritone, is joined by nine other soloists (soprano, four contralti, two tenors, two baritones) and chorus. A small orchestra of seventeen performers calls for the following instruments: nose-flute, flute, and piccolo (one player), oboe, saxophone, bassoon, trumpet (for two bars only!), horn, two trombones, mandolin, violin, cello, three contrabassi, a variety of drums (including six timpani), tubular chimes, bass bells, gongs, sandpaper, dried bones, and a percussionist whistling.

Less obvious is the complexity of Pound's music structure. Amid a virtual absence of repetition, the form of *Le Testament* is accomplished through both the ingenious juxtaposition of stanzas from the Villon poem and the remarkable sense of development and contrast of non-melodic musical materials. The first third of the opera (Nos. 1–5) is unified by the pointillistic emphasis of the vocal line by instruments, generally at the interval of the unison or octave. As the section progresses, organic growth is achieved by the increasing density with which consonant and dissonant intervals are added. Similarly, there is a growth in rhythmic complexity with, in No. 5, the rapid alternation of meters 7/16, 11/16, 19/32, and 25/32 being characteristic rather than exceptional. The central portion (Nos. 6–14) is characterized by an ongoing enrichment of the harmonic idiom. The introduction of a remarkable fabric of bass bells with three contrabassi tremolandi in the Mother's prayer (No. 9) resolves into the purified echo of simple church bells accompanying the haunting voice of Mère au Saveur (No. 10). Dissonance returns prolonged and in full force in the trombones of No. 12, Bozo's drunken aria, climaxing in the drunken chorus, A Père Noé (No. 14), which makes consistent use of polyrhythms, polytonality, and sharply contrasted timbres of a nasal tone of tough, open-air singing (*GK* 368) against an ostinato of trombone, cello, and bassoon. The final a cappella sextet gradually simplifies harmonically from a rich dissonance at the beginning to end in a poignant unison chant following the last ominous tolling of bass bells. The great aesthetic arc achieved by the conclusion would seem not unworthy of the mind of the major epic poet of our time.

Pound was thirty-five when he began the composition of *Le Testament*. The setting of a poet's words to music became for him the fourth and most intense form of criticism, save for the composition of new work (*LE* 74), and served to actualize his theories about the interrelationship of poetry and music. Pound did not set his own poetry to music. Villon, France's greatest poet of the fifteenth century, literary rogue, and antagonist of officialdom, was a permanent favorite of Pound's. He maintained that Villon's strophes on the whole resisted translation and that music could better convey the cadence and emotion of the poetry. The most salient feature of the opera is Pound's rendering of Villon's speech rhythms in asymmetrical meters.

Pound's ideas about setting two of Villon's poems to music have been documented in the Agnes Bedford correspondence as early as 1919, possibly earlier. He began composing the opera per se in London during the fall of 1920 with the help of Agnes Bedford, to whom he sang the words and plunked out melodies on the piano for her notation. Built upon a string of soliloquies, Pound's opera contains little dialogue or action until the group number, Père Noé, at the end of the main scene. Frères Humains, a sextet, comprises the final short tableaux. Pound wrote Yeats in 1924 that the one-act with its final tableaux of the gibbet recalled the Greek model (Stock 255), a reference to the *ekkuklema*. The influence of the Japanese Noh theater has been suggested in the small extant published commentary on Pound's operas. This latter view takes into account Pound's work as editor of the posthumous publication of Ernest Fenollosa's *"Noh," or Accomplishment* in 1917 and is supported by Pound's auxiliary notes for *Le Testament*. These describe a spare and static stage punctuated by individually stylized body gestures assigned to the masked principal characters. Neither the Noh nor the Greek model is fully supported, however, by Pound's overarching music design, to which visual control and restraint ultimately surrender in a scene of feverish dancing at the opera's climactic Père Noé. Having moved to Paris in early 1921, Pound finished his first version of *Le Testament* in collaboration with Bedford by the fall of that year. Two years later Pound submitted the manuscript to the American composer George Antheil for a more exact transcription, today considered the definitive version of the opera. He beat, dictated, and cantillated the music and words to Antheil in Paris. Notating the results carefully into what Pound called fractional metrics, Antheil transcribed the opera into a full orchestral score, completed on 31 December 1923.

In preparing *Le Testament* for the 1931 broadcast by the adventurous BBC Research Section, Pound worked with E.A.F. Harding, an early experimenter and leader of radio technique. Under Harding's guidance Pound rescripted the opera as a four-scene melodrama with additional characters and locales, providing dialogue in English but keeping the lyrics in Old French. The experience gave Pound his earliest insights into advanced radio techniques almost a decade before he prepared his World War II radio speeches for transmission from Rome Radio to the United States and England.

The opera's reception as a work of music has been mixed, a predictable response in no small part due to the originality of Pound's concept and the difficulty of the music itself. Virgil Thomson wrote of *Le Testament*'s 1926 Paris concert premiere, "The music was not quite a musician's music, though it may well be the finest poet's music since Thomas Campion. . . . Its sound has remained in my memory" (Thomson 83).

Bibliography

Adams, Stephen J. "The Dramatic Background of Pound's Operas." *Literary Modernism and the Occult Tradition*. Ed. Leon Surette and Demetres P. Tryphonopoulos. Orono: NPF, 1996. 147–162.

Fisher, Margaret. *Ezra Pound's Radio Operas: The BBC Experiments 1931–1933*. Cambridge: MIT P, 2002.

Hughes, Robert. "Ezra Pound's Opera." *Paideuma* 2.1 (1973): 11–16.

———. *Le Testament*. San Francisco Western Opera Theater. LP recording, 1972. Fantasy records #12001.

Hughes, Robert, and Margaret Fisher. *Cavalcanti: A Perspective on the Music of Ezra Pound*. Emeryville: Second Evening Art Publishing, 2003. http://www.ezrapoundmusic.com/.

Schafer, R. Murray. "Ezra Pound and Music." *Canadian Music Journal* 5 (Summer 1961): 15–43.

Stock, Noel. *The Life of Ezra Pound*. 1970. San Francisco: North Point P, 1982.

Thomson, Virgil. *Virgil Thomson*. New York: Knopf, 1966.

Robert Hughes and Margaret Fisher

Theater

Pound's relationship to theater was more extensive than is immediately obvious. He was attracted to theater but impatient with its narrative and realistic elements, its performativity, and he sought an alternative to the realistic theater of the day: "The drama is a mixed art," he declared; "it does not rely on the charge that can be put into the word, but calls on gesture and mimicry and 'impersonation' for assistance" (*LE* 29). From the beginning, he sought a poet's theater.

His *paideuma* included the Greek tragedians, and he declared *Agamemnon* the greatest of the plays (*GK* 92), though he noted that, compared with Homer, "even Aeschylus is rhetorical" (*LE* 27). As a student, he contemplated a thesis on Lope de Vega. And he shared the general reverence for Shakespeare, recommending the lyrics for study in "A Retrospect" (*LE* 5). "The plays, especially the series of history plays," he declared, "form the true English EPOS" (*ABCR* 59). On the other hand, Pound's views have some idiosyncracy: The play that fascinated him most was *Pericles* (*GK* 92), and he was not above starting a mischievous argument by comparing Shakespeare unfavorably with Chaucer: "English opinion has been bamboozled for centuries by a love of the stage, the glamour of the theater. . . . Chaucer had a deeper knowledge of life than Shakespeare" (*ABCR* 99). Pound's ambiguities about the stage appear as well in certain omissions: His writings seem virtually silent, for example, on Racine or Molière, Schiller or Victor Hugo.

From youth, Pound kept abreast of modern drama. Hilda Doolittle recalls going with him to see *Peer Gynt* (*End to Torment* 20). But the names appear only rarely. Ibsen is treated with respect (*LE* 62), but Strindberg is a "faddist" and Maeterlinck a "craze" (*LE* 401; *SP* 413). Shaw's presence was nearer at hand. Pound knew him, and they apparently were pleasant to each other; the impudence of Shaw's reviews may have inspired Pound's. But Shaw infuriated Pound by refusing to subscribe to the publication of Joyce's *Ulysses*. A heated exchange of letters ensued, and Pound branded Shaw in print "a ninth rate coward" (*LE* 407).

In 1920, Pound wrote, as "T.J.V.," a series of eighteen drama reviews for the *Athenaeum* before being fired by John Middleton Murry for insulting an actress in print (Carpenter 375). Most of the plays Pound reviewed are forgotten (though the offending remark appeared in a notice of Gogol's *The Government Inspector*). Although this is minor journalism, Pound's adopted pose as man of the theater is amusing, often acerbic, sometimes surprisingly generous. He does make claims for writing over presentation: Sheridan's *The Rivals* is, he says, "an excellent argument for our quixotic belief that the dramatist should contribute something to the general effect of the play" (Carpenter 547).

When Pound settled in Paris, he met Jean Cocteau and formed a high opinion of his work, surveying his writing in 1933, including his adaptations from Greek drama. "Cocteau has the freest mind, and the purest, in Europe"; in his plays, he "has brought not a resuscitated old corpse, but an ephèbe out of the sepulchre." His only competitor was Pirandello: "Thank God for both authors in an otherwise desolate stagescape" (*SP* 434–436). Significantly, Pound took little interest in Eliot's drama or the later plays of Yeats.

On a more personal level, Pound is known to have appeared only once on the stage. William Carlos Williams, in his *Autobiography*, records Pound's student performance in 1903, in the chorus of Euripides's *Iphigenia in Aulis*, in a blonde wig "at which he tore as he waved his arms about and heaved his massive breasts in ecstasies of extreme emotion" (57). Not much of a theater career, perhaps, but the incident points toward Pound's true dramatic love: a stylized, nonrealistic, lyric theater with masks, dance, music.

In his poetry, Pound is highly dramatic. As he wrote to Williams in 1908, his dramatic lyrics are "the poetic part of a drama the rest of which (to me the prose part) is left to the reader's imagination. . . . [T]he rest of the play would bore me" (*L* 3–4). But Pound's felicitous discovery—while working closely with Yeats—of the Japanese Noh through Fenollosa's papers led naturally to an investigation of this art.

The results were Pound's pioneering, if flawed, translations—including his introduction, his most extensive discussion of theater—plus Yeats's "plays for dancers," written on the model of Noh. At the celebrated premiere of Yeats's *At the Hawk's Well* in Lady Cunard's drawing room (April 1916), Pound acted as stage manager (Longenbach 217). One immediate result was Pound's effort to write four plays "Modelled on the Noh" (1916). Pound wisely never sought publication of these works, but his efforts are at least suggestive. All suggest a small, elite audience. One play condenses Wagner's Tristan story into a few pages, in Imagist fashion (a subject he earlier treated in "Threnos"). Two others exploit the supernatural content of the Noh, admired by both Yeats and Pound at this time, one being a translation from de Musset's *A Supper at the House of Mademoiselle Rachel*. Finally, his language in these plays is often a vernacular that resembles the Irish dialect spoken by Synge's characters, an effort to write true vernacular for the stage.

In a "Paris Letter" dated February 1923, Pound describes his difficulties translating the *Agamemnon*, finally giving up: "The Greek play is an *ignis fatuus*," he wrote; "I tried every possible dodge, making the watchman a negro, and giving him a *fihn Géoogiah voyce*; making the chorus talk cockney" (277). Three decades later his efforts came to fruition with Sophocles's *Women of Trachis* (produced by the BBC in 1954); by that time, Pound had decided this play represented "the highest peak of Greek sensibility registered in any of the plays that have come down to us," and he underscored his stage model by dedicating the work to Kitasono Katue, hoping to have it accepted by the Japanese theater. His translation adapts Noh conventions, while attempting a stage speech of sometimes jarring colloquialism. A version of Sophocles's *Elektra* appeared posthumously.

Pound's most important original works for the theater, however, are the two operas, *The Testament of François Villon* (1923) and *Cavalcanti* (1931–1933). Pound's stagecraft in these works also call on Noh conventions—masks, controlled gesture, an implied audience of sophisticates. Both works culminate in a supernatural revelation: At the end of *Villon*, six bodies hanged on a gibbet join in a haunting sextet; at the end of *Cavalcanti*, a statue of the goddess Fortuna sings (a device that recalls both *Don Giovanni* and Shakespeare's *Winter's Tale*). Pound put both works together in the same way: He selected poems (in the original language) that he wanted to set, then constructed a narrative to link them and devised colloquial English dialogue. This method ensured that Pound's operas would foreground the poetic, would fulfill his peculiar understanding of opera as "combining orchestra with songs" (*EP&M* 439). They remain the least known major entries in the Pound canon.

Bibliography

Adams, Stephen J. "Pound in the Theater: The Background of Pound's Operas." *Literary Modernism and the Occult Tradition*. Ed. Leon Surette and Demetres P. Tryphonopoulos. Orono: NPF, 1996. 147–162.

Carpenter, Humphrey. *A Serious Character: The Life of Ezra Pound*. Boston: Houghton Mifflin, 1988.

Doolittle, Hilda. *End to Torment: A Memoir of Ezra Pound*. Ed. Norman Holmes Pearson and Michael King. New York: New Directions, 1979.

Fisher, Margaret. *Ezra Pound's Radio Operas: The BBC Experiments 1931–1933*. Cambridge: MIT Press, 2002.

Longenbach, James. *Stone Cottage: Pound, Yeats, and Modernism*. New York: Oxford UP, 1988.

Pound, Ezra. *Plays Modelled on the Noh (1916)*. Ed. Donald C. Gallup. Toledo: Friends of the U of Toledo Libraries, 1987.

———. "Paris Letter." *Dial* 74 (March 1923): 273–280.

Sophocles. *Women of Trachis*. Trans. Ezra Pound. 1956. New York: New Directions, 1957.

Williams, William Carlos. *The Autobiography of William Carlos Williams*. 1948. New York: New Directions, 1967.

Stephen J. Adams

This Quarter

An itinerant expatriate literary magazine, *This Quarter* was begun by Ernest Walsh in Paris in 1925. A promising poet in his own right, Walsh sought Ezra Pound's help in starting the magazine, and its first number was dedicated to Pound for "his helpful friendship for young and unknown artists." Pound viewed the magazine as a possible outlet for his work and the work of his friends, and he used it to print Cantos 17, 18, and 19. Sadly, Walsh was able to print just two numbers of the magazine before his death in Monte Carlo in October 1926. Ethel Moorhead, Walsh's benefactor and coeditor, believed that Pound had been ungracious, and in the third number she angrily withdrew the earlier dedication to the poet. While *This Quarter* lay dormant until 1929, the threat to expatriate publishing created by Walsh's death moved Pound in the meantime to begin his own magazine *Exile*.

Craig Monk

Tinkham, George Holden (1870–1956)

A Republican congressman from Massachusetts (1915–1943), considered an eccentric by some, Tinkham was an inveterate isolationist and a staunch opponent of Franklin Roosevelt and the New Deal. He and Ezra Pound met in Venice in 1936 and corresponded from 1933 to 1940, sharing their opinions of American political figures and their views on economic conditions and American domestic and foreign policy. "Uncle George," as Pound came to address him, helped keep the poet informed about American political life in the 1930s, sending him government publications, copies of pending legislation, and items from magazines and newspapers. In *Guide to Kulchur*, Pound credits Tinkham, among others, with delaying America's entrance into World War II.

Bibliography

Pound, Ezra. *"Dear Uncle George": The Correspondence Between Ezra Pound and Congressman Tinkham of Massachusetts.* Ed. Philip J. Burns. Orono: NPF, 1996.

E. P. Walkiewicz

Townsman

Launched in January 1938 as the *Townsman*, Ronald Duncan's magazine began by 1942 to use intermittently the title *Scythe*, reflecting its editor's interest in agriculture. By that time, Ezra Pound had ceased publishing there, but in its earlier numbers he too used discussions of rural labor to illustrate economic principles. For a publication of limited scope, the *Townsman* was remarkably receptive of contributions on music, politics, and religion. In its second number, for example, Pound reproduced a version of the "Heaulmière" score from his opera *Villon*. His writings on Christianity in the magazine were particularly critical of its current "semitic inflections," claiming that at its peak the Church had no tolerance whatsoever for the Jewish race.

Craig Monk

transatlantic review

The *transatlantic review* was a monthly magazine founded in Paris in 1923 by Ford Madox Ford. Ezra Pound and James Joyce were enlisted as advisers to Ford, and Pound attempted to convince John Quinn to provide financial backing for the venture. However, Quinn died in July 1924, and for most of its one-year existence, the *transatlantic review* was crippled by a shortage of money. Ford wished to recapture much of the excitement of his earlier venture, editing the *English Review* in 1908–1909; he planned to make this new magazine emphasize the international focus of Modern art, however. While the magazine also brought forth editions in England and the United States, Ford hoped that the French capital would give the *transatlantic review* its energy. However, the subsequent involvement of Ernest Hemingway complicated matters. He disagreed a great deal with Ford over editorial approach, and the numbers on which Hemingway assumed greater responsibility took on a markedly different tone. The divergent personalities of these men helped the magazine forge its identity. In its time, the *transatlantic review* was also noteworthy for printing excerpts of Joyce's "Work in Progress," later published as *Finnegans Wake*, and Gertrude Stein's *The Making of Americans*. But Pound's involvement with the magazine was relatively slight. He published half of the twelfth and all of the thirteenth canto in the first number; his work in the magazine is most important for revealing his great interest in music at the time. He printed "Fiddle Music" in the magazine, as well as musical notes that were later published as *Antheil and the Treatise on Harmony*.

Bibliography

Poli, Bernard J. *Ford Madox Ford and the Transatlantic Review.* Syracuse: Syracuse UP, 1967.

Craig Monk

transition

The expatriate American magazine *transition*, founded in Paris in 1927 by Eugene Jolas, was a competitor for Ezra Pound's own periodical the *Exile*. While Pound never contributed to *transition*, his correspondence suggests that he did acknowledge that publication grudgingly as some threat to his own short-lived project. Intended as a forum for literary experimentation for writers from all countries, *transition* was dismissed by Pound as espousing a vapid internationalism exhausted by Ford Madox Ford in his *transatlantic review*. In fact, Jolas used his magazine over time to develop a detailed challenge to the words used in the work of his literary contemporaries. Two manifestos, "The Revolution of the Word" and "Poetry Is Vertical," proposed the creation of a hermetic language to better express the artist's vision. Pound suggested to John Price, New York agent for the *Exile*, that he should direct unsuccessful contributors to their magazine to send their material instead to Jolas in Paris. For his part, Jolas claimed that he had been snubbed by Pound when he approached the poet to contribute to his *Anthologie de la Nouvelle Poésie Américaine*, a volume of translations meant to introduce young American poets to an audience in France. While Jolas came to believe that Pound would never have begun the *Exile* if he knew *transition* would be so effective in offering expatriates a vehicle for publishing their work in Europe, there is no evidence of this opinion in Pound's letters. *Transition* was noteworthy for serializing much of James Joyce's *Finnegans Wake* as "Work in Progress"; indeed, the frequent appearance in the magazine of this "diarrhoea of consciousness" (*L* 292), as Pound viewed it, remained the lightning rod for the poet's enduring ire until *transition* ceased publication in 1938.

Craig Monk

The Translations of Ezra Pound

Faber and New Directions published *The Translations of Ezra Pound* in 1953. If there was a specific, precise date at which Pound began to translate poetry, we do not know when that might be. His earliest volumes of poetry are filled not only with acknowledged translations (from Latin, Italian, Provençal, French, Spanish, Old English, German, and perhaps from Greek) but with adaptations and imitations, echoes, and allusions drawn from all around the globe. The general reader neither knows nor much cares whether a "Villonaud" is a Villon-ode in translation or a mimetic original, a modern poem deeply inspired by the diction, the rhythms, the forms, and even the language of some ancient and long-dead poet. Pound's insistent search for "delicacy, the absolute sense of beauty" (*SR* 34), often leads both poet-translator and reader onto strange and wonderful paths.

But the manner of that search, the translation tools Pound employs and the translation decisions he makes, can also lead both poet-translator and reader sadly astray. A mere two lines from François Villon (*SR* 173) can nicely illustrate the problems: "Necessitè faict gens mesprendre / E faim saillir le loup des boys." "Necessity makes men run wry, / And hunger drives the wolf from wood." Whatever "run wry" may mean, it is not idiomatic English but a

Poundian construct, more a matter of ear than of lexicon. At this early stage in his career, Pound is all too apt to prefer alliteration or other "matter of sound" to mere meaning. If the reader understands "run wry" to mean "go crooked," it becomes an adequate rendering of "mesprendre," which means "to commit a crime or do something wrong." In any case, Villon's blunt sharpness of diction is deliberately blurred in the interests of poetic music. "Men do wrong when they have to" would be closer to Villon's meaning; it would also better reflect the different syntaxes of French and English. ("Syntax" often seems to mean, for Pound, "word order" rather than "verbal structure.") "Drives" is, again, a rather blurry approximation of "saillir," which not only means "to leap, to spout," but particularly when used of animals means "to copulate." "From wood," though semantically unexceptional, is even less idiomatic than "run wry", worse yet, it has a distinctly primitive flavor, though Villon is both an extremely sophisticated poet as well as a powerfully idiomatic one.

Many of these unfortunate tendencies are exaggerated to a somewhat feverish pitch, in Pound's 1910 versions of Guido Cavalcanti. Guido begins one of his dazzling "sonettos" with this dramatic but tropistic picture of the poet/lover cowering in fear of Love: "O donna mia, non vedestu colui / Che 'n su lo core mi tenea la mano, / Quand'io ti rispondea fiochetto e piano / Per' la temenza de gli colpi sui?" (*T* 30). In plain prose: "Oh my lady, didn't you see him, who put his hand on my heart (?) when I weakly/hoarsely answered you, because I was afraid of his blows/shots/arrows?" Pound's translation is almost incoherent:

> O Lady mine, doth not thy sight allege
> Him who hath set his hand upon my heart,
> When dry words rattle in my throat and start
> And shudder for the terror of his edge? (*T* 31)

Analysis of such desperately contorted lines seems beside the point.

But Pound, who was only twenty-five when the Cavalcanti translations were completed (they were published two years later and revised in 1920), could of course do, and had already done, a good deal better. The versions of Heine, published in *Canzoni* (1911), are magically good:

> I dreamt that I was God Himself
> Whom heavenly joy immerses,
> And all the angels sat about
> And praised my verses. (*CEP* 165)

Not only is this brilliantly evocative of the German original, and masterfully spun, but it turns on a quite incredibly deft rendering of the second line, "Und sitz' im Himmel droben." "Sitting in Heaven up there," says the German: Pound's "heavenly joy immerses" allows for a truly splendiferous rhyme (hammered in place by a sudden downshifting from the expected trimeter to a snappy dimeter). This is the Ezra Pound of whom many, including myself, have said that he is both the father of twentieth-century poetic translation and its greatest practitioner.

Ripostes (1912) gives us Pound's version of the Old English elegy "The Seafarer" (reprinted in *Cathay*, 1915). No other rendering of any Old English poetry has ever come closer, in modern English, to recreating the old tongue's verse music. Of the many who have tried to accomplish such an aural resurrection, Pound alone has succeeded. Yet as this author has elsewhere explained (Raffel, *Ezra Pound* 36–37), the translation is nowhere near so effective as a rendering of the *meaning* of "The Seafarer." There are crabbed phrases, sometimes extremely hard to comprehend. More important, there is an utterly ruthless and misguided suppression of the poem's fervently religious substance, including the literal suppression—that is, elimination—of the twenty-five-line prayer at the end. To quote myself: "Pound translated 'The Seafarer,' as I suspect he translated virtually everything he brought over into English . . . for his own purposes and for his own use." And why should he not, so long as we understand quite clearly what he does and does not set out to do?

Cathay (1915) is yet another miracle of translation, except this time a far more extended one. *Lustra* (1913–1915) incorporates a few Chinese translations; many more of its poems show the clear and deeply clarifying effect of Pound's work on the Fenollosa prose translations. (*Lustra* contains, also, a beautiful rendering from Catullus.) But *Cathay* marches triumphantly through no fewer than seventeen poems, often of considerable length, and does not ever falter: "Constant re-reading cannot detect a weak poem in *Cathay*" (Alexander 84). For a poet and translator of Pound's sometimes staggering inconsistency, this is an even more remarkable feat than it might appear: Fenollosa's English cribs are frequently so bad that Wai-lim Yip has bluntly called them "hopeless" (Yip 88), and Pound "never dealt with the Chinese characters directly, but has always followed a crib" (Yip 82). Yip's praise is cast in extraordinary terms:

> [E]ven when he is given only the barest details, he is able to get into the central consciousness of the original author by what we may perhaps call a kind of clairvoyance. . . . [A]lthough Pound has been sharply limited by his ignorance of Chinese and by much of Fenollosa's crippled text, he possesses a sense of rightness, an intuitive apprehension in poetic organization. . . . [H]e sometimes tends to come closer in sensibility to the original than a literal translation might. (88, 92–93)

Ford Madox Ford declared, "The poems in *Cathay* are things of a supreme beauty"; Amy Lowell wrote, "Ezra's new book *Cathay* is full of the most beautiful things. I have seldom read anything finer" (Raffel, *Possum and Ole Ez* 83).

The single largest body of material included in *Translations* is Pound's 1916 collection of Noh plays. Earl Miner, admiring of Pound as he is, regretfully calls this volume "an impossible task." He adds: "[B]y November, 1927, [Pound] had realized . . . that a goodly number of his translations were fragmentary and that he had not done as well as he might with these plays" (Miner 137, 139). This discussion will not be extended by discussion of these essentially "canceled" translations. Neither will it be possible, here, to deal with Pound's 1920 versions from Rémy de Gourmont's *Dust for Sparrows*, a collection of prose *pensées*.

The *Translations* volume is of course not a complete collection. Pound's translation of two volumes of stories, from the French of Paul Morand—*Fancy Goods* and *Open All Night*—was not published until 1984. And there is undoubtedly a good deal of fugitive and unpublished material: Pound was a writer of great industry and energy.

Among the distinctly miscellaneous items represented on pages 401–448 of *Translations* are work from Egyptian (retranslated from the Italian), Latin, Hindi, French, Provençal, and Italian. The versions from Horace are unremarkable; those from Catullus are very much better (they range in date from 1916 to 1963). Rimbaud's "Cabaret Vert," like the three other Rimbaud poems, was translated in 1957. It is sturdily effective, but none of these versions have quite the sparkle, the vibrancy of Pound at his best. Five translations of the simple lyrics of Saturno Montanari, a young Italian poet, dead at age twenty-three in 1941, are perhaps the best of the lot. They were done in 1951, presumably when Pound was held in St. Elizabeths.

Bibliography

Alexander, Michael. *The Poetic Achievement of Ezra Pound*. London: Faber, 1979.

Minor, Earl Roy. *The Japanese Tradition in British and American Literature*. 1958. Westport: Greenwood, 1976.

Raffel, Burton. *Ezra Pound: The Prime Minister of Poetry*. Hamden: Archon Books, 1984.

———. *Possum and Ole Ez in the Public Eye: Contemporaries and Peers on T. S. Eliot and Ezra Pound 1892–1972*. Hamden: Archon Books, 1985.

Yip, Wai-lim. *Ezra Pound's Cathay*. Princeton: Princeton UP, 1969.

Burton Raffel

Translation Theory

Ezra Pound had theories of translation but not a theory. A brief comparison to a genuine theorist, like Charles Darwin, will be instructive: Both Darwin and Pound are, in their very differing ways, large figures of great importance.

Darwin had a theory, founded on years of passionate, patient exploration and testing. He worked hard at assembling the data he needed and, building on that work, proceeded to think and to theorize both widely and deeply. Pound also worked hard, easily as passionately but not always patiently; he too thought widely, though not always deeply. Darwin was concerned with organizing and making sense of a great range of phenomena; organization and system were only of intermittent and occasional interest to Pound, who was engaged in a lifelong crusade under the twin banners of Poetry and Beauty. Darwin's mind tended to be exact. Pound's was excited, appetant, eager, but always imprecise, fighting to recreate the world *now*. Darwin's words were carefully measured. Pound's were thrown like sparks in all directions. "Pound has never valued his literary criticism except in terms of its immediate impact," wrote his longtime friend T. S. Eliot (*LE* x). "Art is a joyous thing," Pound insisted in his 1910 preface to *The Spirit of Romance*. "I would in all seriousness plead for a greater levity, a more befitting levity, in our study of the arts" (*SR* 8). That preface in fact begins: "This book is not a philological work. I am interested in poetry" (7).

Although the truest record of Pound's approaches to poetic translation is to be found in the bountiful body of his translations, rather than in any coherent assortment of prose statements, it is possible to at least outline three major stages for his mercurial theorizing, drawing on his letters and his critical prose as well as on his translations.

Stage 1. Pound's earliest statements about translation (1910), like the early translations themselves, consistently view the primary purpose of translation as transmissive. But in bringing to the modern English reader as much as possible of the original's music, its rhythms, Pound clearly feels that the "power which implies the man" (*T* 24) stems more from sound than sense. As he does so often, when he finds it necessary, he also pays cheerful respect to a diametrically opposite point of view: "My endeavor was not to display skill in versification. . . . Guido [Cavalcanti] cared more for sense than for music, and I saw fit to emphasize this essential aspect of his work. The music is easily available for anyone who will learn Italian pronunciation. I thought I served my audience best by setting forth the meaning" (1912; Homburger 93). He can and does claim that his rendering of the Old English poem "The Seafarer," in which he repeatedly distorts sense in the interests of sound, gives us that poem "as nearly as I can reproduce it in English" (1911–1912; *SP* 26).

Despite such equivocations, however, music plainly forms the basis of poetry's value for Pound, the bedrock beauty for which he cherishes it in the first place. And no mere theory, he declares, will give the reader the proper "satisfaction" to be derived from "matters of sound (1913; *SP* 369). "It was my first intention to print only [the] poems and an unrhymed gloze," Pound explained of *The Spirit of Romance* in 1910. This was not "practicable," because the reader could not be trusted to "read the Italian for the music after he has read the English for the sense" (*T* 24).

Stage 2. The clear, strong translations from the Chinese, published in 1915 as *Cathay*, represent a brilliantly successful turning away from the archaizing and Victorianizing of his first translations. Employing unmistakably modern language, Pound gives us ancient Chinese material in present-day English dress. Indeed, T. S. Eliot flatly pronounced, in 1928, that "Pound is the inventor of Chinese poetry for our time" (Sullivan 105). But as Ronnie Apter has noted, "[H]aving achieved this revolution, Pound never used the diction of *Cathay* in translation again" (21).

Stage 3. Pound drafted the first versions of the first cantos in 1915; this "epic" production soon came to absorb, for the rest of his life, the bulk of his poetic interest. In 1922, in the course of a long letter to his old teacher Felix Schelling, he said of the first eleven cantos that they were merely "preparation of the palette." He was trying, he explained, to "get down all the colors or elements I want for the poem," adding that he hoped "to bring them into some sort of design and architecture later" (*L* 180).

The Cantos never did acquire any "sort of design and architecture." But the fractured poetics of this huge, unfinished and unfinishable poem

(running to over 800 printed pages) are intimately connected with the third stage of his translational poetics. In 1957, Pound produced an eight-line translation labeled as "from Rimbaud." Titled "Anadyomene" (that is, "she who rises out of the sea," Aphrodite/Venus), this is apparently a translation of a nasty little poem on an unattractive woman seen in a "theater box." But the original is not eight but fourteen lines long, a sonnet describing an unattractive woman washing herself in a bath tub, ending: "Et tout ce corps remue et tend sa large croupe / Belle hideusement d'un ulcére a l'anus" ("This whole body moves and sticks out / protrudes its large rump, hideously beautiful with an ulcer on the anus"). The line with which Pound ends "Anadyomene" has no basis in the French original—but more important, even Rimbaud would not have had a woman, no matter how unattractive, bathing unclothed in a "theater box."

Pound has mistaken one meaning of the word *baignoire* for another. Although it can mean "theater box," in this context *baignoire* takes on another sense, that of "bath tub." But this is a good deal more than a simple error in matters lexical, for it exposes the fragmented Poundian emphasis on microcosmic rather than macrocosmic matters, on color rather than sense, on words and rhythms rather than on syntax and structure. Hugh Kenner nicely says that Pound's attention "tended to fix on the constellated words in ancient texts, not on their syntactic connexions." And then he adds, conjecturing as to the cause of this off-center focus, "It is tenable that he saw diction rather than syntax because not having learned declensions accurately *he could not follow the syntax*" (emphasis added; quoted in Raffel 75). K. K. Ruthven, among others, has noted much the same thing: "Pound's academic respect for the literal sense of a poem is overwhelmed by his poetic interest in what he can make of it by treating it as the starting point for something else" (6). Ruthven admits, as we all must, that he has "tried and failed to systematize [Pound's] methods" of translation.

In short, as this author wrote in 1984, for the most part Pound as a translator, like the Pound of *The Cantos*, is appropriative rather than transmissive. And

> appropriation is not programmatic; it does not dictate exactly what can be obtained in any particular translation, nor does it require that the same things be obtained (or sought) in each and every line of a particular translation. Appropriation is basically as indifferent to consistency as it is, in the final analysis, to the integrity of the text being translated. . . . [A]nything that troubles [the translator] can be omitted, so long as you do not think it central; the mere words of the original arc in no way binding. "The artist seeks out luminous detail and presents it" (*SP* 23). And if the artist is Ezra Pound, much of the time that luminous detail will glow indeed. "Mr. Pound," wrote Ford Madox Ford, "has a genius for words that no one—not excluding Shakespeare in England or Heine in Germany—has ever in modern times much surpassed" (Lindberg-Seyersted, *Pound/Ford* 132). (Raffel 63)

Bibliography

Apter, Ronnie. *Digging for the Treasure: Translation after Pound*. New York: Peter Lang, 1984.

Homburger, Eric, ed. *Ezra Pound: The Critical Heritage*. London: Routledge, 1972.

Raffel, Burton. *Ezra Pound: The Prime Minister of Poetry*. Hamden: Archon Books, 1984.

Ruthven, K. K. *A Guide to Ezra Pound's Personae (1926)*. Berkeley: U of California P, 1969.

Sullivan, J. P., ed. *Ezra Pound: A Critical Anthology*. Harmondsworth: Penguin, 1970.

Burton Raffel

U

Uberti, Ubaldo degli (1881–1945)

Admiral of the Italian Navy and descendant of the Farinata degli Uberti put by Dante in the *Inferno*, he is mentioned several times in *The Cantos* (77, 78, 89, 95, and 97). He became Pound's pen-friend in 1931 after reading a letter in the *Morning Post* in which Pound was making his usual complaint about politically motivated British and American publishers who refused to print his *Jefferson and/or Mussolini*. Degli Uberti translated this letter and had it published in the Italian daily *Il Giornale di Genova*, placing emphasis on and articulating his appreciation for the fascism of a U.S. citizen. Pound responded immediately, writing to confirm his fascist faith but explaining that he was a "left-wing Fascist." This initiated an extensive correspondence (close to 200 letters are deposited at the Beinecke) dealing with political topics. Degli Uberti soon became one of Pound's most dear Italian friends and an appreciated translator to whom Pound often submitted his journalistic prose prior to publication; degli Uberti introduced Pound to many prestigious Italian national periodicals, such as *Quadrante* and *Il Meridiano di Roma*. As well, degli Uberti began translating *The Cantos* into Italian.

In 1944 degli Uberti was appointed admiral of the Republican Navy of the neofascist Repubblica Sociale Italiana, and in 1945, he became the director of the military magazine *Marina Repubblicana*; it was here that Pound first published his two "Italian Cantos," Cantos 72 and 73. Degli Uberti was mistakenly shot by Russian soldiers allied to the Germans, an event recorded by Pound in Canto 95. Degli Uberti's son Dick, also a fascist as well as Pound's friend, is the Italian translator of *Guide to Kulchu*r (*Guida alla Cultura*).

Bibliography

Gallesi, Luca. "Ezra Pound, l'ammiraglio degli Uberti e *Marina Repubblicana*." *Storia contemporanea* 27. 2 (April 1996): 309–326.

Redman, Tim. *Ezra Pound and Italian Fascism*. New York: Cambridge UP, 1991.

Uberti, degli Riccardo Maria (Dick). *Ezra Pound. Da Rapallo a Castel Fontana*. Bolzano: Centro di Studi Atesini, 1985.

Luca Gallesi

Umbra

Published in London by Elkin Mathews in 1920 (1,000 copies were printed), *Umbra* provides Ezra Pound's selection of the poetry written by 1912, the year of the publication of *Ripostes*, which is, except for two components, included in its entirety. Of the verse associated with Imagism, only "The Return" is reprinted; none of the poems first published in *Lustra* or *Cathay* are included. A third of the volume consists of translations from Arnaut Daniel and Guido Cavalcanti and the five poems by T. E. Hulme that had been included in *Ripostes*. The collection provides a step in the process of selection from the early verse, some of which had already been reprinted in the American collection *Provença* (1911), whereas poetry from *Ripostes* was included in the American edition of *Lustra*. *Umbra* establishes Pound's choice from the verse written prior to the *phanopoeia* of Imagism and the satire of *Lustra* and includes archaic and nostalgic tones excluded from *Lustra*.

Umbra is Latin for the ghost of a dead person and thus points to the technique of the *persona* and a poetry concerned with digging up and giving a voice to the past. The past is represented by the troubadours of twelfth-century Provence and *trecento* Tuscany; on their example the poetry is presented as "song" and often concerned with a beloved lady. Components from *Ripostes* such as "Portrait d'une femme" and "N.Y." take us on a brief visit to London, New York, and the contemporary world with touches of the wit and *logopoeia* that characterize *Lustra*. The identity of the poet as artist, isolated from the insensitive crowd, remains central.

The final page of the book provides a "Main outline of E. P.'s work to date," dividing his compositions into "Personae" ("Marvoil," "Cino," "Altaforte"); "Major Personae" ("Seafarer," *Cathay*, and *Homage to Sextus Propertius*); "Sketches" from *Ripostes* and *Lustra*, respectively; and "Etudes," involving Guido Cavalcanti, Arnaut Daniel, and the Langue d'Oc. According to this division, *Umbra* may be characterized as concentrating on *personae*, including the "major *persona*" of the "Seafarer," sketches from *Ripostes*, and etudes.

Bibliography

de Nagy, N. Christoph. *The Poetry of Ezra Pound: The Pre-Imagist Stage*. 1960. Bern: Francke Verlag, 1968.

Grieve, Thomas F. *Ezra Pound's Early Poetry and Poetics*. Columbia: U of Missouri P, 1997.

Jackson, Thomas H. *The Early Poetry of Ezra Pound*. Cambridge: Harvard UP, 1968.

Witemeyer, Hugh. *The Poetry of Ezra Pound: Forms and Renewal, 1908–1920*. Berkeley: U of California P, 1969.

Line Henriksen

Untermeyer, Louis (1885–1977)

A New York poet, anthologist, and critic, Louis Untermeyer was influential as one of the leading American anthologists of Modernist poetry. In reviews in the *New Republic*, *Dial*, and other magazines, Untermeyer praised Ezra Pound's earlier poetry, and the two struck up a correspondence in 1914. Later, Untermeyer became critical of Pound's poetry, and the two

stopped writing to each other. In 1929 Pound again wrote to Untermeyer when he learned that the latter was coming to Rapallo. The two met there and later resumed their correspondence for several years. Nine of Pound's letters, including an autobiographical outline, were edited by J. A. Robbins and published as *EP to LU: Nine Letters Written to Louis Untermeyer by Ezra Pound* (1963). Untermeyer ultimately held a low opinion of Pound's *The Cantos*, describing them in his 1965 memoir *Bygones* as "a jigsaw puzzle of history, scraps of myths, and fragments of literature, of confused significance and violence" (94).

Bibliography

Untermeyer, Louis. *Bygones: The Recollections of Louis Untermeyer*. New York: Harcourt, 1965.

Cameron McWhirter

Upward, Allen (1863–1926)

Allen Upward was an English barrister, amateur sinologist and religions historian, novelist, playwright, poet (one of his poems was included by Ezra Pound in *Des Imagistes*), civil servant, volunteer soldier, and world traveler. Upward moved in the same London Theosophical circles as G.R.S. Mead, A. R. Orage (he was a regular contributor to Orage's *New Age*), W. B. Yeats, and Pound himself. They first met at a gathering of Mead's Quest Society in 1911, and the two became lifelong friends; Pound discovered his work in *Poetry*, and as Upward later recalled, he "rose up and called me an Imagist. (I had no idea what he meant.)" (Tryphonopoulos 74).

Pound read, reviewed, and was influenced by Upward's *The New Word* (1910) and *The Divine Mystery* (1913). A sardonic analysis of contemporary thought, *The New Word* argues that the true source of knowledge is primitive language; the book also endeavors to demonstrate the falsity of the standard definition that assumes that "the universe is made up of matter." Drawing upon contemporary science for many of his examples, Upward puts forth as a model for the real world the image of the "whirl-swirl" or waterspout, which he views as a knot of energy and the point of contact between the human and the divine. Not only do several of Upward's ideas belong to the occult thought of the day, but his concepts of the waterspout and his penchant for scientific analogies also parallel Pound's concept of the vortex and his own frequent use of scientific metaphors in his prose.

In a letter to Dorothy Shakespear, Pound finds *The Divine Mystery* to be a "digested golden bough with a lot more of [Upward's] own intelligence stuck into it"; and in his review of the book in the *New Freewoman*, Pound calls it "the most fascinating book on folk-lore that I have ever opened" (*SP* 403). In his book Upward deals with the origins and development of religions, arguing for their evolution from primitive fertility rites through stellar to solar worship and the parallel evolution of the Divine Man through the phases of the Wizard, Magician, Genius, Sear, Priest, Prophet, and *Chrestos*, or anointed one. According to Upward the universe is composed of vital forces; he proposes that "the secret of genius is sensitiveness" and that the "genius" acts as an antenna ("artists are the antennae of the race" [*LE* 58]) that is sensitive to the universe's vital forces, registers the changes in the cosmic atmosphere, and is "the archetype of all Heroes in all Mysteries." Of course, one easily finds echoes of these notions in Pound's work.

Like Yeats, Upward discovered the material for many of his doctrines and beliefs in occult London circles and in his study of synoptic Hellenistic tradition—the same speculative, metaphysical occultism that Pound became familiar with during his London years.

Upward committed suicide early in 1926.

Bibliography

Tryphonopoulos, Demetres P. *The Celestial Tradition: A Study of Ezra Pound's The Cantos.* Waterloo: Wilfrid Laurier UP, 1992.

Demetres P. Tryphonopoulos

Usury (See Economics: Usury)

Versi Prosaici

Versi Prosaici was published in June 1959 by Salvatore Sciascia, Rome. Some 250 copies were printed. Despite the Italian title and its plural character (and the paratextual claim that this is a *raccolta*, a collection of verse), the book is in English, and its 219 lines seem to form one poem at the length of a canto. Donald Hall talks of its "dense, elliptical prose," yet the style is identical to that of *The Cantos* and can hardly be classifiable as other than verse. Entire lines and passages are repeated from *Rock-Drill* (Cantos 88 and 89 especially). Ezra Pound's source for those cantos is Thomas H. Benton's *Thirty Years' View* to which *Versi Prosaici* adds William Cabell Bruce's *John Randolph of Roanoke 1773–1833*. Themes include money, the just price, and American politics of the 1820s and 1830s: the Bank War and slavery debates.

Five lines listing a series of mainly seventeenth century European jurists were published under the title "Versi Prosaici" in the Yorkshire magazine *Listen* 3.3–4 (Spring 1960). The circumstances of this publication are discussed by Peter Stoicheff in *The Hall of Mirrors* and Donald Hall in *Remembering Poets*.

Bibliography

Hall, Donald. *Remembering Poets*. New York: Harper & Row, 1977.

Stoicheff, Peter. *The Hall of Mirrors: Drafts & Fragments and the End of Ezra Pound's Cantos*. Ann Arbor: U of Michigan P, 1995.

Line Henriksen

Visual Arts: Historical

Ezra Pound searched the art of his predecessors for useful elements of the past to revive in the present, but at the same time he wanted to shirk the limiting aspects of tradition. Not surprisingly, the lens through which he viewed the distant past of the Renaissance and even more distant past of the Greeks was ground by such nineteenth-century aestheticians as Walter Pater (1839–1894) and John Ruskin (1819–1900), and his arguments with Greek and Renaissance aesthetics continued his bickerings with his immediate predecessors.

Pater's aestheticism and Ruskin's art criticism served Pound well as stalking horses for critiques of moribund ways of looking at art. Ruskin became in Pound's art criticism an embodiment of old-fashioned Oxford-donnish appreciation. Pater's flowery language and insistence on the superiority of antique art—what Pound called "Paterine sentimentalesque Hellenism"—had only built a culture of mediocrity, which preferred familiar beauty to the untested waters of Modern art. Nevertheless, Pound read in Pater one of his favorite aesthetic truths: "All arts approach the conditions of music." Pound returned to this notion regularly, and it served as the basis of his third tenet of Imagisme: "As regarding rhythm: to compose in sequence of the musical phrase, not in sequence of the metronome" (*LE* 3).

By the time that Pound did most of his writing about the visual arts, the Pre-Raphaelites seemed like old news. Much like Pater, the work of this group of artists—who tried to create art free of the artificial academic manner that followed the success of Raphael—became for Pound a way of pointing to some contemporary artists' lack of innovation. Whether he referred to this boring contemporary art as "post-pre-Raphaelite" or a tired version of work by Dante Gabriel Rossetti (1828–1882), John Everett Millais (1829–1896), or Sir Edward Burne-Jones (1833–1898), Pound used these tags to mean that a work was pretty but not artistically or intellectually engaging.

Like the Futurists whose influence Pound vehemently denied, Pound questioned the aesthetic valuing of Greek sculpture, preferring the more formally innovative work of Modern artists. The Greeks were appealing, he argued, because their work is "caressable": Under the influence of Paterian aestheticism, the public around him mistook prettiness for beauty. While a pretty statue may serve as an acceptable substitute for a pretty woman dressed in silken finery, ultimately the real, caressable woman is to be preferred. Again following the Futurists, Pound centered his comparison on the *Nike of Samothrace* (c. 190 B.C.E.), noting that for all her rippling draperies and bodily loveliness, she remains "aloft on her pedestal prow." Art, then, should have other goals than to replicate the caressable. While caressable art, he argued, becomes less stimulating as it becomes more familiar, art that interrogates the nature of form ultimately satisfies intellectually. Modern art is an awakening so far as artists have managed to judge the beauty of a work outside the parameters of classical aesthetics. While Pound was quick to note that some classical works were more admirable than others, he cautioned his readership against using such models to judge Modern work.

Similarly, Pound questioned the role that the Renaissance had come to play in his contemporaries' view of the arts. "You can prove anything you like by the Renaissance," he commented in 1915. Nevertheless, Pound found in the Renaissance activities with which he could compare what he considered the most important cultural work of his era, thereby justifying that work

to its opponents. The Modern artists' fascination with machinery, he suggested, resembled Renaissance interest in nature for its own sake. Ernest Fenollosa's discovery in China and Japan of art and poetry widened the Modern artist's scope in the same way that Renaissance rediscoveries of Greek, Arab, and Hebrew writings invigorated that period. He looked to the *quattrocento* for models of patronage. The Modern age, he argued, should learn from the example of Lorenzo de' Medici and Sigismundo Malatesta and value the work of living artists while they are living, rather than placing all value on the work of the dead.

Although Pound rarely had good things to say about America, he found in James Abbott McNeill Whistler (1834–1903) a model of the kind of beautiful art that, after viewing, leads its viewer to find previously unnoticed beauty in familiar things. These kinds of works, Pound thought, admitted viewers to an entirely new world of knowledge and perception. On the occasion of the Tate Gallery's loan exhibition of Whistler's work (September 1912), Pound wrote a critical essay for the *New Age* and his laudatory poem, "To Whistler, American" (*Poetry* 1.1 [1912]: 7): In both works he celebrates not only Whistler's aesthetic sense but also his place at the beginning of a Great American Tradition. An expatriate American like Whistler himself, Pound saw his background as a hindrance to his artistic development. And just as the Pre-Raphaelites and the caressable Greeks had become for Pound metaphors of dead and deadening art, Whistler stood out as a touchstone of the art of engagement.

Although Pound's interest in Chinese and Japanese painting never rivaled his investment in the poetry of the same countries, Pound nevertheless was intrigued by what he learned about Asian art from Laurence Binyon and Ernest Fenollosa. His enthusiasm for the Tang painter-poet Wang Wei (699–759) relied in part on the similarity he perceived to Jules Laforgue. He saw Wang Wei as a true Modern, combining aspects of French and Chinese influences. He was no doubt also interested by the combination of painterly and poetic production. Pound comments on Binyon's writings about Chinese art in *BLAST*, noting that the wisdom of *The Flight of the Dragon* (1911) is occasionally marred by the same mediocrity that Pound had seen in the culture around him. Pound's own mission in returning to the culture of the past—whether Greek or Chinese, ancient or recent—was to reinvigorate that culture, to reveal the links between it and Modernity, and to build an appreciation of things ancient and Modern that was nevertheless bold, innovative, and engaging.

Bibliography

Paul, Catherine E. *Poetry in the Museums of Modernism: Yeats, Pound, Moore, Stein.* Ann Arbor: U of Michigan P, 2002.

Pound, Ezra. *Ezra Pound and the Visual Arts.* Ed. Harriet Zinnes. New York: New Directions, 1980.

Catherine E. Paul

Visual Arts: Twentieth Century

Ezra Pound was an important critic of the visual arts. Although often called upon to comment on the work of academic artists of the 1910s and 1920s, his true appreciation was given to more innovative artists, those who like himself were trying to "make it new." As a result, his art criticism is written to make an uninformed and often lazy public comfortable with Cubism, Futurism, Vorticism, Dadaism, and Surrealism.

Whether readers accept Pound's assertion that he had little interest in Italian Futurism—he denounced it as "an accelerated form of impressionism"—there is much in the English avant-garde movement Vorticism of which he was a part that borrows from the Italian movement. Such Italian Futurist poets and artists as Filippo Marinetti (1876–1944), Gino Severini (1883–1966), and Giacomo Balla (1871–1958) denied traditional modes of representation and valuation, celebrating dynamism—the motion of something rather than the thing itself—and such technological innovations as automobiles, airplanes, bridges, steamers, and locomotives. Such Vorticists as Wyndham Lewis (1882–1957), Edward Wadsworth (1889–1949), and Pound, on the other hand, probed the relationships between such industrial products as steamships and the traditions from which they sprung. The figure of a vortex was useful here, as it represented a circulation with a still center, a mappable point—usually represented as a city or an artist—around which all manners of cultural energies swirled. Whereas Marinetti condemned museums, for example, in his *Futurist Manifesto* (1908), comparing them to cemeteries that merit only obligatory annual visits, Pound praised their ability to educate artists. For Pound, the principal worry came when art was confined to museums, leaving other public spaces without beauty.

In addition to admiring the works of Jacob Epstein and Henri Gaudier-Brzeska, Pound worked for their acceptance by the larger art establishment. He condemned the Tate Gallery for not accepting Epstein's work, claiming that if people do not see his work, they will not learn to appreciate it. He admired the efforts of Capt. Guy Baker, whose collection of contemporary art included works by Wyndham Lewis. He worked tirelessly with John Quinn, New York lawyer and collector of Modern art, to have works by the Vorticists exhibited in the United States. Together with Albert C. Barnes, Ernest Fenollosa, and Charles Lang Freer, Quinn represented for Pound hope for American culture: Art collections, like libraries, decent architecture, and patronage of the arts were necessary if there were to be a "renaissance" in America.

While much of Pound's interest in twentieth-century art centered on the triumvirate of Lewis, Gaudier-Brzeska, and Epstein, he admired many other contemporary artists, relating their innovative work to his own cultural projects. Pound had little use for art enslaved by the imitation of nature or of earlier aesthetic models. He praised the simplified and fluid smoothness of the sculpture of Constantin Brancusi (1876–1957) and how it represented form and form only, free from a sense of the weightiness of real objects. Similarly the "impressions of form" that Pound found in the paintings of Paul Cézanne (1839–1906) contributed to Pound's sense of the role of form in Vorticism—what it means to foreground form and to analyze, whether through sculpture, painting, or poetry, the form of a thing. Marcel Duchamp's (1887–1968) rejection of both traditional forms and those forms devised by his contemporaries meant that he could not bask in the reputation that he had gained but must constantly innovate—a trait that Pound valued for the vitality it gave the arts generally. The way that Alvin Langdon Coburn (1882–1966) experimented with vortography—a process using mirrors to fragment an image to create abstract "photographs"—revolutionized art photography to Pound's mind, not only emphasizing form but also freeing the camera from mindlessly replicating reality. He admired Henri Matisse's (1869–1954) use of vibrant color, his integration of style and content, and the sense that his work could have been produced in any century but would still maintain its essential character. He regularly numbers Pablo Picasso (1881–1973) among important Modern artists and cites him in *BLAST* as an important ancestor of Vorticism. Nevertheless, Pound often dismisses his work from the 1910s as lacking the vitality of Wyndham Lewis's. All these artists carved out new aesthetic territory, and their formal innovations, while not always invested in the tenets of Vorticism, agreed with Pound's aesthetic objectives.

The same cannot be said of the artists he discussed in the "Art Notes" written for the *New Age* under the pseudonym B. H. Dias during the years from November 1917 to April 1920. These critical articles about art exhibitions around London vetted his own critical opinions about art, whether praising the Gaudier-Brzeska exhibition at the Leicester Gallery or condemning the National Portrait Society's artistic contributions "as much nutriment to aesthetic rumination as the contents of the average family photograph album in the most average middle-class family" (*EP&VA* 43). Many of the exhibitions that Pound reviewed contained the kind of art he hated: work that replicated Victorian aesthetic ideals or that was enslaved by the representation of nature or that was merely "caressable," like the sculpture of the Greeks. Employing such touchstones as Epstein, Manet, Picasso, Matisse, or Cézanne, he showed how

these works were derivative and that admiration for them sent England in the wrong direction, culturally speaking. Ceaselessly condemned by Pound was the Royal Academy, the aesthetic value of whose work Pound always doubted. Pound's dismay with this institution sprang as much from their control of Tate Gallery acquisitions through the Chantrey Bequest as from their lack of artistic talent: He saw their self-promotion as yet another element of the culture of mediocrity around him. These columns give readers of Pound's poetry a good sense of the academic and unimaginative art that he would decry as that which "the age demanded" in *Hugh Selwyn Mauberley*. Always driving Pound's writing on the visual arts, whether the work of his contemporaries or ancient monuments, is his project of cultural enrichment. Like the curators of his day, he saw himself as a person of taste with the goal of raising the culture around him to his level.

Bibliography
Paul, Catherine E. *Poetry in the Museums of Modernism: Yeats, Pound, Moore, Stein.* Ann Arbor: U of Michigan P, 2002.
Pound, Ezra. *Ezra Pound and the Visual Arts.* Ed. Harriet Zinnes. New York: New Directions, 1980.
Catherine E. Paul

Vortography
One of the basic concepts of Pound's Vorticism is the contrast between the person who passively receives impressions and the person who actively creates forms. Pound identifies the first with the "retinal" art of Impressionism, which, he declares in *Gaudier-Brzeska*, leads logically to "the cinematograph." As he puts it elsewhere, "[A]ny imbecile can shoot off a Kodak" (*PD* 253).

Pound's remarks caught the attention of photographer Alvin Langdon Coburn, who had created the frontispieces for the New York edition of Henry James and later the Pound portrait that appears in *Lustra*. Coburn thus produced the first nonrepresentational photographs. Two are images of Pound, one a multiple-exposure portrait, the other a double profile in silhouette. Coburn went on to a more conventional though brilliant career. But Pound's ideas about non-representational photography later bore fruit in the landmark avant-garde film by Fernand Léger, Dudley Murphy, and George Antheil, *Ballet Mécanique* (1924).

Bibliography

Gernsheim, Helmut, and Alison Gernsheim. *Alvin Langdon Coburn, Photographer*. New York: Praeger, 1966.

Stephen J. Adams

Vou

Vou was an avant-garde magazine published in Tokyo by the Vou Club and edited by Kitasono Katue (1902–1978). The magazine continued, with occasional suspension, until Kitasono's death in June 1978, the last issue being No. 160. *Vou* (pronounced "vow") had no particular meaning apart from its acoustic value; besides poems, it printed paintings, photographs, and other genres of Modern art. Ezra Pound on receiving some copies of *Vou* with a letter from Kitasono, and later English translations of the poems by Vou Club members, was surprised and wrote an essay, "Vou Club [Introduction]," for *Townsman* (1.1 [1938]: 4). Several of Pound's early poems and a few of his essays were published in *Vou* between 1936 and 1951 in translations by Kitasono.

Bibliography

Solt, John. *Shredding the Tapestry of Meaning: The Poetry and Poetics of Kitasono Katue (1902–1978)*. Cambridge: Harvard UP, 1999.

Sanehide Kodama

Waley, Arthur (1889–1966)

One of twentieth-century Britain's most prolific sinologists, Waley was born in Tunbridge Wells and attended Cambridge University. Between 1912 and 1929, Waley worked in the department of Oriental prints and drawings at the British Museum before embarking upon an impressive academic career at the School of Oriental and African Studies in London. Four years Ezra Pound's junior, Waley came to know him in London. During the World War I years, Pound's lodgings in Kensington, at 5 Holland Place Chambers, near St. Mary Abbots Church, became the pivot for his manifold activities, including a standing invitation to all Pound's friends to assemble there on Thursday evenings at eight o'clock (Goodwin 23); Waley was among the writers that Pound and his wife Dorothy frequently welcomed. Pound's *Cathay* (1915) and Waley's *One Hundred and Seventy Chinese Poems* (1918) together "invented" China for the West. They both translated Confucius's *The Analects* (1938) and *The Book of Songs* (1937) (Pound titled it *The Classic Anthology Defined by Confucius*). Among Waley's other influential works are *The Way and Its Power: A Study of the Tao Te Ching and Its Place in Chinese Thought* (1934), *Poet Li Po, A. D. 701–762* (1919), Wu Ch'eng-en's *Monkey* (1942), and translations from Japanese, notably *The Nō Plays of Japan* (1922) and Murasaki Shikibu's *The Tale of Genji* (1935).

Bibliography

Goodwin, K. L. *The Influence of Ezra Pound*. London: Oxford UP, 1966.

Huang, Guiyou. "Arthur Waley." *Encyclopedia of Literary Translation into English*. Ed. Olive Classe. London: Fitzroy Dearborn, 2000. 2:1483–1484.

Guiyou Huang

What Is Money For?

Published in London in 1939, *What Is Money For?* is the clearest of Pound's money pamphlets. It is available in *Selected Prose*; a shortened version appeared in *Impact* under the title "Integrity of the Word." The task of Pound's pamphlet is to answer the title question: Money is for distributing goods to the people; money is a "measured claim" against those goods. The nature of sovereignty lies in the ability to create money, Pound explains: "It is the business of the STATE to see that there is enough money in the hands of the WHOLE people, and in adequately rapid EXCHANGE, to effect distribution of all wealth produced and produceable" (*SP* 294). Forcefully, Pound addresses the problem of "underconsumption" caused by the Great Depression and suggests a number of ways of augmenting the money supply so that there might be sufficient money to buy what is being produced. Pound argues for a "just price" of goods, an idea he probably got from reading the American economist Irving Fisher. Here he justifies it by going back to canon law.

The credit that would underwrite any just augmentation of the money supply would be the Social Credit of society—"the legacy of mechanical efficiency and scientific advance"—as proposed by Douglas, which Pound sometimes calls "the cultural heritage." However, Pound is by no means a doctrinaire Douglasite. For example, Pound claims that Hitler and Mussolini are already distributing goods and tickets (i.e., money) in ways consistent with Social Credit and also suggests Gesell's stamp scrip as a practical way of increasing the velocity of the money already in existence (*SP* 294–295).

Throughout, Pound suggests that Mussolini and Hitler have got it right and that the so-called liberal democracies are firmly under the thumb of the great usurers, who control the "Jewspapers" and the league of Nations. "USURY is the cancer of the world," Pound concludes, "which only the surgeon's knife of Fascism can cut out of the life of nations" (*SP* 300).

Alec Marsh

Williams, William Carlos (1883–1963)

The American man of letters William Carlos Williams met Pound at the University of Pennsylvania in 1902. Williams was then a freshman student of medicine; later, he pursued a full-time career in obstetrics and pediatrics in his hometown of Rutherford, New Jersey. In addition, he became a prolific writer of poems, plays, short stories, novels, and essays. At college, the two young men shared interests in poetry, theater and acting, French and Spanish literature, fencing, tennis, and pretty girls. An undergraduate comradeship grew into a sixty-year friendship that survived geographical separation, infrequent meetings, and numerous quarrels.

Pound settled in London in 1908. He and Williams exchanged spirited critiques of the poems they both published in 1909. Williams visited Pound in London in March 1910 and saw much of him when Pound spent seven months in Philadelphia and New York later that year. For the next three decades, each was the other's window upon a relinquished world across the Atlantic. Williams gave Pound his most enduring contact with the American literary scene he had left behind. Pound gave Williams a glimpse of the Bohemian adventures he might have enjoyed in London, Paris, and Italy.

In 1913 Pound persuaded his own publisher, Elkin Mathews of London, to bring out Williams's second book of poems, *The Tempers*. Pound also drew his friend into the Imagist

movement of 1912–1914 by including Williams's work in the *Egoist* and in the anthology *Des Imagistes* (1914). During the Great War of 1914–1918, their poems appeared side by side in some of the leading little magazines of the day: the *Egoist*, *Poetry*, the *Little Review*, and *Others*. Williams gathered some of his Imagist work in *Al Que Quiere!* (1917).

The first public dispute between Pound and Williams occurred when Pound prompted the English critic Edgar Jepson to attack *Poetry* in 1918. Jepson criticized the homegrown poets favored by the magazine, and he praised the work of the American expatriate T. S. Eliot. Williams came to the defense of his compatriots in the Prologue to *Kora in Hell: Improvisations* (1919). He criticized the London Yankees—Pound, Eliot, and Hilda Doolittle ("H. D.")—as too deracinated and Europeanized to be representative of American verse. This exchange marked the beginning of an ongoing debate between Williams and Pound about the role of nationality and locale in Modern literature.

When Pound moved to Paris in 1921, he helped to arrange the publication by Three Mountains Press of Williams's *Spring and All* and *The Great American Novel* (both 1923). Williams and his wife visited Pound in Paris in 1924, and Williams later contributed a suite of poems to Pound's journal *Exile*. Pound published an insightful critical essay titled "Dr. Williams' Position" in the *Dial* for November 1928, and he included substantial selections of Williams's work in his anthologies *Profile* (1932) and *Active Anthology* (1933). Williams admired Pound's American History Cantos, and Pound praised Williams's short stories in *Life along the Passaic River* (1938). In a 1934 letter to John Henri Buchi, Pound described Williams as "the best prose writer and poet in America" (Yale Archive), and in 1928 he recommended Williams to Louis Zukofsky as "the best human value on my murkn. visiting list" (*Pound/Zukofsky* 7).

With the onset of the depression, the collaborations of Williams and Pound were severely tested by political disagreements. For a time they found common ground in the advocacy of

Social Credit, for Williams was active in the New York branch of the movement. But their paths diverged sharply in the mid-1930s. Williams thoroughly disapproved of Pound's allegiance to Benito Mussolini and Italian fascism. A left-leaning Democrat who admired the New Deal of President Franklin D. Roosevelt, Williams sympathized with the struggles of peasants and workers in the Soviet Union and actively supported the Republican or antifascist side in the Spanish Civil War. When Pound visited the United States in 1939 to lobby for his beliefs, Williams saw a man with a closed mind, who had come to preach and not to learn. After Pound began to broadcast his pro-Italian views on Rome Radio in 1941, Williams attacked him in an article titled "Ezra Pound: Lord Ga-Ga!"

When Pound was remanded to St. Elizabeths Hospital in late 1945, Williams resumed their correspondence and visited him on occasion, despite his mixed feelings about the man. Williams incorporated four of Pound's postwar letters to him into his long poem *Paterson* (1946–1958), a major work inspired in large part by *The Cantos*. Williams defended the award of the Bollingen Prize to Pound in 1949 and agitated for his release from St. Elizabeths. When Pound was at last discharged in the summer of 1958, he spent his last two nights before sailing for Italy at Williams's home in Rutherford, New Jersey. Several portraits taken by the photographer Richard Avedon on this occasion capture the symbolic quality of their final reunion.

After Pound's return to Italy, the two men corresponded very little. But Pound's last anthology, *Confucius to Cummings* (1964), contains a late poem by Williams, and Williams's last book of verse, *Pictures from Brueghel* (1962), contains a poem titled "To My Friend Ezra Pound." Shortly after Williams's death in March 1963, Pound wrote to his wife: "He bore with me sixty years, and I shall never find another poet friend like him."

Bibliography

Aji, Hélène. *Ezra Pound et William Carlos Williams: Pour une poétique américaine.* Paris: L'Harmattan, 2001.

Hoffman, Daniel, ed. *Ezra Pound and William Carlos Williams: The University of Pennsylvania Conference Papers.* Philadelphia: U of Pennsylvania P, 1983.

Movius, Geoffrey. "Caviar and Bread: Ezra Pound and William Carlos Williams, 1902–1914." *Journal of Modern Literature* 5 (1976): 383–406.

Parkinson, Thomas. "Pound and Williams." *Ezra Pound among the Poets.* Ed. George Bornstein. Chicago: U of Chicago P, 1985. 149–167.

Pound, Ezra. *Pound/Williams: Selected Letters of Ezra Pound and William Carlos Williams.* Ed. Hugh Witemeyer. New York: New Directions, 1996.

———. *Pound/Zukofsky: Selected Letters of Ezra Pound and Louis Zukofsky.* Ed. Barry Ahearn. New York: New Directions, 1987.

Wallace, Emily Mitchell. "Pound and Williams at the University of Pennsylvania." *Pennsylvania Review* 1.2 (1967): 41–53.

Williams, William Carlos. "Ezra Pound: Lord Ga-Ga!" *Decision* 2.3 (1941): 23–24.

Hugh Witemeyer

Women of Trachis

Pound's translation of Sophocles's *Trachiniae* as *Women of Trachis* was first published in full in the Winter 1953–1954 issue of the *Hudson Review* and in book form by New Directions in 1956. There may have been two reasons why Pound chose to render this particular play. First, one may surmise that at St. Elizabeths Pound felt some sort of affinity with the suffering Herakles, as the Greek hero met with an unavoidable fate after a life of fighting and struggling, a fate that seemed to be out of all proportion in relation to the nature of his error. Second, the love triangle in the play between Herakles, Deianeira, and Iole may have reminded the poet of his own relationships with his wife Dorothy Shakespear and his mistress Olga Rudge.

For a long time the *Trachiniae* has been the least admired of Sophocles's tragedies because the play seems to fall into two halves. Deianeira may be seen as the central figure of the first half of the *Trachiniae*, and Herakles of the second, a division that many Classicists found difficult to reconcile with Sophocles's other plays where the unity was provided by one leading character. Pound told Donald Hall in the *Paris Review* interview in 1960 that his interest in the play came from rereading the Fenollosa Noh plays for a new edition and from wanting to use the Noh as the closest Modern equivalent to Greek drama. By linking the Greek play to Noh conventions in which each Noh play embodies "some primary human relation or emotion" that is always fixed "upon idea, not upon personality" (*T* 279), Pound could do away with the notion of one leading figure and look for a unity of theme. Thus he could focus on the play as a description of the events leading up to the death of Herakles and of all those involved.

For Pound, the play's unity resides in the fact that the driving force behind the entire chain of events is the all-powerful eros, or force of violent passion, personified by Aphrodite, who claims both Deianeira and Herakles as victims. Herakles sacked Oechalia out of lust for Iole, which in turn prompted Deianeira, afraid of losing Herakles, to send the robe smeared with the poison given to her by Nessus when Herakles prevented him from satisfying his feelings of lust for Deianeira. At the end of the play, Herakles must suffer the consequences of all these different manifestations of eros. As his note to his translation of line 1174, "SPLENDOUR / IT ALL COHERES" makes clear, Pound seems to have found the play's whole meaning in Herakles's death: "This is the key phrase, for which the play exists." In Pound's view, Herakles realized in that moment of lucidity in agony that now all oracles about his life were being fulfilled and that Nessus and Deianeira were only instruments in the hands of Zeus to die in the manner ordained by him. This also explains why Pound in his list of *dramatis personae* described Herakles as "the solar vitality," the eternal force behind the alternation of human fortune. In his moment of extreme lucidity, Herakles attained the ultimate insight into his human condition, thereby transcending human mortality and its limits, limitations and fragmentary awareness of the forces behind everyday reality. The importance of this unifying image to Pound may be seen in the fact that the poet in a despairing moment used it negatively in Canto 116 as an evaluation of himself and his work.

With regard to the length of the play, one may see that Pound's rendering has 1,242 lines against the 1,278 lines of Sophocles's original. Pound has shortened his version especially at the beginning of the play, namely, in the Prologue, the Parodos, and the First Episode, producing 453 lines against the original's 496. After the First Stasimon, Pound generally stays fairly close to the number of lines of the original, although it must be noted that in the Exodos he compensates his deletion of 22 lines at the beginning of this final part with short extensions of each of the speeches of Herakles.

Pound has made no attempt to transpose the iambic trimeters of the speeches and dialogues of the *Trachiniae* into a regular English equivalent, but he has used the rhythms of everyday speech in lines of variable length. Consequently, the number of stresses in each line depends on its length as well as on its emotional weight, since Pound varies neutral phrasing with emphatic speech, often colloquial and slanglike. The language of his choral lyrics, however, is far more formally poetical and archaic. This is why the overall style of the *Trachis* has generally been deemed inconsistent by most critics.

Bibliography

Hall, Donald. "Ezra Pound." *Writers at Work: The Paris Review Interviews.* Ed. Malcolm Cowley. 2nd Series. New York: Viking, 1963. 35–59.

Ingber, Richard. "Pound's *Women of Trachis*: A Song for the Muses' Garden." *Amerikastudien* 23 (1978): 131–146.

Mason, H. A. "*The Women of Trachis* and Creative Translation." *Anon* 2.1 (1963), 59–81; 2.2 (1963): 105–121. Revised for the *Cambridge Quarterly* 4.3 (1969): 244–272.

Pound, Ezra. "Sophocles. Women of Trachis, a Version by Ezra Pound." *Hudson Review* 6.4 (1953–1954): [487]–523.

Peter Liebregts

Y

Yeats, John Butler (1839–1922)

John Butler Yeats was W. B. Yeats's father. Abandoning law at Trinity College in 1867, he enrolled in Heatherley's art school in London, eventually turning to portrait painting. He met Ezra Pound in New York in 1910. Recalling an outing to Coney Island during this visit, Pound in Canto 80 describes him as "beaming like the prophet Isaiah" while riding on an elephant. Although not relating to Pound as a critic, Yeats admired Pound's poetry for its critique of "surface life." Pound edited *Passages from the Letters of John Butler Yeats* (1917) and reviewed them in *Poetry* (January 1918).

Bibliography

Ellman, Richard. *Yeats: The Man and the Masks*. New York: Macmillan, 1948.

Murphy, William M. *Prodigal Father: The Life of John Butler Yeats*. Ithaca: Cornell UP, 1978.

Pound, Ezra, ed. *Passages from the Letters of John Butler Yeats*. Churchtown, Dundrum: Cuala P, 1917.

———. "The Yeats Letters." *Poetry* 11.4 (1918): 223–225.

Yeats, J. B. *Letters to His Son W. B. Yeats and Others*. Ed. Joseph Hone. London: Secker & Warburg, 1983.

Annie Pulis

Yeats, William Butler (1865–1939)

W. B. Yeats was introduced to Ezra Pound by Olivia Shakespear in London in 1908. By the time the two men had met, Yeats was already a renowned poet, and Pound had studied his work at length. Yeats was impressed by Pound's enthusiasm, and though the two men were a generation apart, they felt immediate kinship. Pound soon became a regular at Yeats's Monday Meetings at Weyburn Buildings.

Pound esteemed "Uncle William" as an experienced and eminent poet; but nearly from the beginning of their acquaintance, Pound unabashedly critiqued the older poet's work and relentlessly encouraged Yeats to eschew his "nineties" Symbolist background and cultivate a more modern poetics. In 1912, Yeats gave Pound some poems to be published in *Poetry*, but Pound took the liberty of editing them for "abstractions" before their submission. Liberties such as these not surprisingly irritated Yeats, if only temporarily. During the winter months of 1913 through 1916, Yeats and Pound set up a sort of poets' retreat at Stone Cottage in Ashdown Forest, Sussex. With his eyesight rapidly failing, the aging Yeats needed a secretary, so Pound took on the duties of managing Yeats's correspondence and reading aloud for him. Watching the war from their cottage's doorstep, the two poets read and studied together, arguing extensively about the nature of poetry and the value of vers libre. Pound published his highly favorable review of Yeats's *Responsibilities* in *Poetry* in April 1914, a volume of poems coming out of their discussion and which Pound considered to be an important departure from Yeats's earlier work. One of the poems from *Responsibilities*, "The Peacock," is referred to in Canto 83, with Yeats incanting "a great Peeeeacock / in the proide ov his oiye" in a way sounding like the wind in the chimney as he composed downstairs in the cottage. Ultimately, the "Stone Cottage" years proved to play a key role in the development of high Modernist aesthetics.

Pound's interest in "world" literatures also had an effect on the older poet. Yeats had been involved in theater for many years and had started the Abbey Theater with Lady Augusta Gregory in Dublin (1898) to encourage an Irish theater culture. When Pound introduced him to Fenollosa's *Epochs of Chinese and Japanese Art*, Yeats became fascinated with Japanese Noh plays, which revolve around secrets, spirits, and revelation. Together with Pound, Arthur Waley, and Edmund Dulac, Yeats formed an enclave of Noh enthusiasts and wrote a preface to Pound's volume of translated Noh plays published by the Cuala Press. Eventually Yeats's interest in Noh drama moved him to develop his Cuchulain plays in a new direction. In general, the Cuchulain plays depicted dramatic stories of Irish heroism on the level of mystical Symbolism. In *At the Hawk's Well* (1916), the first play in the Cuchulain cycle influenced by Noh drama, Yeats had his characters wear masks and gave them archetypal identities. This new, more abstract dramatic strategy allowed Yeats to reconcile more completely his ongoing interests in spiritual ideas and Irish nationalism.

In October 1917, Yeats married Georgie Hyde-Lees, a young woman with a gift for automatic writing, who came to play a role in the construction of Yeats's large, mysticopoetical work *A Vision*. In *A Packet for Ezra Pound*, an introductory segment of *A Vision* added to the second, revised edition of 1931, Yeats largely attributes the mathematical symbology of *A Vision*'s "Great Wheel" to discussions with Pound concerning images, spheres, vortices, and the cycles of history. The core of *A Vision*'s system, "The Great Wheel," comprised a sort of aesthetic link in *A Vision* between Yeats's spiritualistic tendencies and Poundian ideas of Modern, Imagistic poetics. In this same work, Yeats develops the idea of the Unity of Being, wherein a human soul achieves its greatest perfection through the balance of subjective and objective tendencies. This notion resonated against Pound's views on history as well as the representational unity of the poetic image and epigram that Pound valued. Absorbed in marriage and children for the next several years, Yeats did not meet Pound again until 1925 in Rapallo, Italy. In 1927–1928, the Yeatses came to stay with Pound and his wife Dorothy in Rapallo so that Yeats could recover from a persistent, nervous illness. Yeats's association with the Pound circle at Rapallo continued for almost five years, in which time his poetics were further influenced by the younger, dynamic generation. After a slow decline in health, Yeats died in France on 28 January 1939.

Bibliography
Aldritt, Keith. *W. B. Yeats: The Man and the Milieu.* New York: Clarkson Potter, 1997.
Ellmann, Richard. *Eminent Domain: Yeats among Wilde, Joyce, Pound, Eliot and Auden.* London: Oxford UP, 1967.
Longenbach, James. *Stone Cottage: Pound, Yeats, and Modernism.* New York: Oxford UP, 1988.
Materer, Timothy. "Daemonic Images: From W. B. Yeats to Ezra Pound." *Modernist Alchemy: Poetry and the Occult.* Ithaca: Cornell UP, 1995. 25–47.

Annie Pulis

Z

Zukofsky, Louis (1904–1978)

Louis Zukofsky brought himself to Pound's attention by sending him "Poem Beginning 'The' " in 1927. Pound promptly accepted it for inclusion in the third issue of *Exile*. Shortly thereafter, Pound began urging Zukofsky to form a literary group in the New York area. Although such a group never came to be, it was thanks to Pound's advice that Zukofsky became acquainted with William Carlos Williams, who became a lifelong friend. A few years later, Zukofsky, with the assistance of George Oppen, created To Publishers. To reprinted *The Spirit of Romance* in 1932. This was intended to be the first in a series of volumes reprinting Pound's collected prose, but To went out of business before any further volumes appeared. One other volume, edited by Zukofsky and published by To, *An "Objectivists" Anthology* (1932), was dedicated to Pound and contained his "Yittischer Charleston" poem. The following year Pound included Zukofsky in the *Active Anthology*, giving his poems a considerable amount of space. Pound also dedicated *Guide to Kulchur* (1938) to Zukofsky and Basil Bunting.

The years between 1927 and 1941 saw the most intensive period of exchange between Pound and Zukofsky. Pound even helped finance Zukofsky's trip to Europe in 1933, during which Zukofsky stayed for several weeks at Rapallo. They met again during Pound's visit to New York in 1939, but after World War II they corresponded infrequently. Their final meeting took place in 1954, when Zukofsky brought his wife and son to visit Pound at St. Elizabeths, an event recalled in chapter 33 of Zukofsky's novel *Little* (1970).

Zukofsky's two most important considerations of Pound are his essay "Ezra Pound" (1929) and his statement *"Work/Sundown"* (1948). In the first of these Zukofsky praises Pound's translations, precision of language, and the method of *The Cantos*. In the second he addresses the issue of Pound's World War II radio broadcasts—and subsequent indictment and arrest—by once again pointing to Pound's poetic skill. Here Zukofsky also notes that he never felt "the least trace of anti-Semitism in his presence." Pound's comments on Zukofsky were brief. The most extensive—no more than a few sentences—are in the preface to *Active Anthology*.

Pound's public reticence about his younger friend obscured the depth of the relationship. The complexity of their friendship was not widely recognized until the publication of *Pound/Zukofsky: Selected Letters* (1987). Among other things, it became clear that Pound had frequently apprised Zukofsky of periodicals where he might place his work. He also wrote letters of recommendation on Zukofsky's behalf to the Guggenheim Foundation. It was Pound's enthusiasm for Zukofsky's work that prompted Harriet Monroe to name Zukofsky as the editor of the "Objectivists" issue of *Poetry* (February 1931). In their correspondence, Pound assumed the role of mentor, or literary father, while Zukofsky obligingly played the literary son. As the 1930s wore on, however, Pound's political and economic views so clashed with Zukofsky's that the tone of their exchanges sometimes became rancorous. Nevertheless, they kept writing to each other and still found common ground for agreement in poetry. Pound even approved of

Zukofsky's "A"-8 (1937), which in terms of content can be interpreted as a Stalinist poem. For his part, Zukofsky's approach to Pound's poetry emphasized its skill and innovation while slighting its "message." As he wrote to Pound in 1937 in regard to *The Fifth Decad of Cantos*, he was not as interested in the *Fifth Decad*'s comments on interest rates and the issuance of money as in "the fact that you have used word and sounds, cadence & beat . . . like strokes of the Chinese characters, that it is a development of technique 20 years after Cathay, the outgrowth but not at all like *Cathay* (whatever its beauties)" (193). Although Pound was not as expansive when discussing Zukofsky's work, a 1954 letter responding to a gift of Zukofsky's book of poems *Anew* (1946) acknowledged that Zukofsky had found his own style. "I note that you have got OUT of influence of E. P. and Possum [Eliot]" (208). Zukofsky had the final word in the relationship. Hearing that Pound had denigrated his own work, Zukofsky wrote to him in 1963, "And anyway when I can't read myself, happens too, I can still read ol' Ez . . . & for the rest the *song* carries along, yours, always right" (218).

Bibliography

Comens, Bruce. *Apocalypse and After: Modern Strategy and Postmodern Tactics in Pound, Williams, and Zukofsky.* Tuscaloosa: U of Alabama P, 1995.

Perelman, Bob. *The Trouble with Genius: Reading Pound, Joyce, Stein, and Zukofsky.* Berkeley: U of California P, 1994.

Pound, Ezra. *Pound/Zukofsky: Selected Letters of Ezra Pound and Louis Zukofsky.* Ed. Barry Ahearn. New York: New Directions, 1987.

Sharp, Frederick Thomas. "'Objectivists' 1927–1934: A Critical History of the Work and Association of Louis Zukofsky, William Carlos Williams, Charles Reznikoff, Carl Rakosi, Ezra Pound, George Oppen." Diss. Stanford U, 1982.

Barry Ahearn

Selected Bibliography

PRIMARY SOURCES

Original Writings

ABC of Economics. London: Faber, 1933. Reprinted in *SP*.

ABC of Reading [*ABCR*]. 1934. New York: New Directions, 1960.

Antheil and the Treatise on Harmony. Paris: Three Mountains Press, 1924. Reprinted in *EP&M*.

Canti postumi. Ed. Massimo Bacigalupo. Milan: Mondadori, 2002.

The Cantos of Ezra Pound. New York: New Directions, 1972. Contains: *A Draft of XXX Cantos* (1930); *Eleven New Cantos* (1934); *The Fifth Decad of Cantos* (1937); *Cantos LII–LXXI* (1940); *Cantos LXXII–LXXIII* (1944); *The Pisan Cantos* (1948); *Section: Rock-Drill de los Cantares* (1955); *Thrones de los Cantares* (1959); and *Drafts and Fragments of Cantos CX–CXVII* (1969). (*Note*: The first printing of Cantos 1–117 in one volume dates to 1970. Subsequent printings vary, particularly in the inclusion of Cantos 72–73 and the contents and arrangement of *Drafts and Fragments*.)

Cavalcanti: A Perspective on the Music of Ezra Pound. Ed. Robert Hughes and Margaret Fisher. Emeryville: Second Evening Art, 2003. Includes score of *Cavalcanti*.

Certain Radio Speeches of Ezra Pound. Ed. William Levy. Rotterdam: Cold Turkey P, 1975.

Collected Early Poems of Ezra Pound [*CEP*]. Ed. Michael King. New York: New Directions, 1976. Contains: *A Lume Spento* (1908); *A Quinzaine for This Yule* (1908); *Personae* (1909); *Exultations* (1909); *Canzoni* (1911); and *Ripostes* (1912).

Ezra Pound and Music: The Complete Criticism [*EP&M*]. Ed. R. Murray Schafer. New York: New Directions, 1977.

Ezra Pound and the Visual Arts [*EP&VA*]. Ed. Harriet Zinnes. New York: New Directions, 1980.

Ezra Pound e la scienza: Scritti inediti o rari [*EP&S*]. Ed. Maria Luisa Ardizzone. Milano: Libri Scheiwiller, 1987.

"Ezra Pound Speaking": Radio Speeches of World War II [*RSWWII*]. Ed. Leonard W. Doob. Westport: Greenwood, 1978.

Ezra Pound's Poetry and Prose: Contributions to Periodicals [*EPPP*]. Ed. Lea Baechler, A. Walton Litz, and James Longenbach. 11 vols. New York: Garland, 1991.

Gaudier-Brzeska: A Memoir [*GB*]. 1916. New York: New Directions, 1970.

Guide to Kulchur [*GK*]. 1938. New York: New Directions, 1970.

Hilda's Book. In Hilda Doolittle, *End to Torment: A Memoir of Ezra Pound*. Ed. Norman Holmes Pearson and Michael King. New York: New Directions, 1979.

I Cantos. Ed. Mary de Rachewiltz. Milan: Mondadori, 1985.

"IF THIS BE TREASON . . ." Siena: Tip. Nuova, [1948]; Venice: Tip Litografia Armena, 1983.

Imaginary Letters. Paris: Black Sun P, 1930.

Impact: Essays on Ignorance and the Decline of American Civilization. Ed. Noel Stock. Chicago: Henry Regnery, 1960.

Instigations of Ezra Pound, Together with an Essay on the Chinese Written Character by Ernest Fenollosa. New York: Boni and Liveright, 1920.

Jefferson and/or Mussolini [*J/M*]. 1935. New York: Liveright, 1970.

Literary Essays of Ezra Pound [*LE*]. Ed. T. S. Eliot. 1954. New York: New Directions, 1972.

Love Poems of Ancient Egypt. Trans. Ezra Pound and Noel Stock. Norfolk: New Directions, n.d.

Machine Art and Other Writings: The Lost Thought of the Italian Years. Ed. Maria Luisa Ardizzone. Durham: Duke UP, 1996.

Make It New [*MIN*]. 1934. New Haven: Yale UP, 1935.

Patria Mia [*PM*]. Chicago: Ralph Fletcher Seymour, 1950. Reprinted in *SP* (American ed.).

Pavannes and Divagations [*PD*]. New York: New Directions, 1958.

Personae: The Shorter Poems of Ezra Pound [*P*]. Ed. Lea Baechler and A. Walton Litz. 1926. New York: New Directions, 1990.

Plays Modelled on the Noh (1916). Ed. Donald C. Gallup. Toledo: Friends of the U of Toledo Libraries, 1987.

Poems and Translations. Ed. Richard Sieburth. New York: Library of America, 2003.

Polite Essays. 1937. Norfolk: New Directions, 1940.

Selected Cantos of Ezra Pound. London: Faber, 1967; New York: New Directions, 1970.

Selected Poems. Ed. T. S. Eliot. London: Faber and Gwyer, 1928.

Selected Poems. New York: New Directions, 1949.

Selected Prose 1909–1965 [*SP*]. Ed. William Cookson. New York: New Directions, 1973. Contains: *Patria Mia* (1950, American ed. only); *An Introduction to the Economic Nature of the United States* (1944/1950); *ABC of Economics* (1933); *What Is Money For?* (1939); *A Visiting Card* (1942/1952); and *Gold and Work* (1944/1951).

The Spirit of Romance [*SR*]. 1910. New York: New Directions, 1968.

A Variorum Edition of "Three Cantos" by Ezra Pound: A Prototype. Ed. Richard Taylor. Bayreuth: Boomerang P, 1991.

A Walking Tour in Southern France: Ezra Pound among the Troubadours. Ed. Richard Sieburth. New York: New Directions, 1992.

Translations and Edited Works

Cathay. London: Elkin Matthews, 1915.

Cavalcanti, Guido. *Pound's Cavalcanti*. Ed. David Anderson. Princeton: Princeton UP, 1983.

The Classic Anthology Defined by Confucius. Cambridge: Harvard UP, 1954.

Confucius. New York: New Directions, 1969. Contains: *Ta Hio* (1928); *The Unwobbling Pivot* (1947); and *The Analects* (1950).

de Gourmont, Remy. *The Natural Philosophy of Love*. Postscript by Ezra Pound. New York: Boni & Liveright, 1922.

Fenollosa, Ernest. *The Chinese Written Character as a Medium for Poetry*. Foreword and Notes by Ezra Pound. 1920. London: S. Nott, 1936.

Forked Branches: Translations of Medieval Poems. Ed. Charlotte Ward. Iowa City: U of Iowa P, 1985.

Love Poems of Ancient Egypt. With Noel Stock. Norfolk: New Directions, [1962].

Morand, Paul. *Fancy Goods; Open All Night*. Ed. Breon Mitchell. New York: New Directions, 1984.

Pea, Enrico. *Moscardino*. Milano: All'Insegna del pesce d'oro, 1955.

Por, Odon. *Italy's Policy of Social Economics, 1939–1940*. Trans. Ezra Pound. Bergamo: Istituto italiano d'arti grafiche, 1941.

Pound, Ezra, ed. *Active Anthology*. London: Faber, 1933.

———. *Profile*. Milano: Giovanni Scheiwiller, 1932.

———. *The Translations of Ezra Pound* [*T*]. Ed. Hugh Kenner. 1953. New York: New Directions, 1963.

Pound, Ezra, and Ernest Fenollosa. *The Classic Noh Theater of Japan*. New York: New Directions, 1959.

Pound, Ezra, and Marcella Spann, eds. *Confucius to Cummings: An Anthology of Poetry*. New York: New Directions, 1964.

Pound's Cavalcanti: An Edition of the Translations, Notes, and Essays. Ed. David Anderson. Princeton: Princeton UP, 1983.

Pound's Translations of Arnaut Daniel: A Variorum Edition with Commentary from Unpublished Letters. Ed. Charlotte Ward. New York: Garland, 1991.

Sophocles. *Elektra: A Play*. With Rudd Fleming. Ed. Richard Reid. New York: New Directions, 1990.

———. *Women of Trachis*. 1956. New York: New Directions, 1957.

Correspondence

Note: After the first two items, collections are listed alphabetically by the name of Pound's correspondent.

Ezra Pound/Japan: Letters and Essays. Ed. Sanehide Kodama. Redding Ridge: Black Swan, 1987.

The Selected Letters of Ezra Pound, 1907–1941 [*L*]. Ed. D. D. Paige. 1950. New York: New Directions, 1971.

"I Cease Not to Yowl": Ezra Pound's Letters to Olivia Rossetti Agresti. Ed. Demetres P. Tryphonopoulos and Leon Surette. Urbana: U of Illinois P, 1998.

Pound/The Little Review: The Letters of Ezra Pound to Margaret Anderson [*L/MA*]. Ed. T. L. Scott and M. J. Friedman, with J. Bryher. New York: New Directions, 1988.

The Correspondence of Ezra Pound and Senator William Borah. Ed. Sarah Holmes. Urbana: U of Illinois P, 2001.

Ezra Pound and Margaret Cravens: A Tragic Friendship 1910–1912. Ed. Omar Pound and Robert Spoo. Durham: Duke UP, 1988.

Pound/Cummings: The Correspondence of Ezra Pound and E. E. Cummings. Ed. Barry Ahearn. Ann Arbor: U of Michigan P, 1996.

Ezra Pound and Senator Bronson Cutting: A Political Correspondence 1930–1935. Ed. E. P. Walkiewicz and Hugh Witemeyer. Albuquerque: U of New Mexico P, 1995.

Dk/Some Letters of Ezra Pound. Ed. Louis Dudek. Montreal: DC Books, 1974.

Pound/Ford: The Story of a Literary Friendship. Ed. Brita Lindberg-Seyersted. New York: New Directions, 1982.

The Letters of Ezra Pound to Alice Corbin Henderson [L/ACH]. Ed. Ira B. Nadel. Austin: U of Texas P, 1993.

Ezra Pound: Letters to Ibbotson, 1935–1952. Ed. Vittoria I. Mondolfo and Margaret Hurley. Orono: NPF, 1979.

Pound/Joyce: The Letters of Ezra Pound to James Joyce, with Pound's Critical Essays and Articles about Joyce [L/JJ]. Ed. Forrest Read. New York: New Directions, 1967.

Ezra Pound and James Laughlin: Selected Letters. Ed. David M. Gordon. New York: Norton, 1994.

Pound/Lewis: The Letters of Ezra Pound and Wyndham Lewis [L/WL]. Ed. Timothy Materer. New York: New Directions, 1985.

Charles Olson & Ezra Pound: An Encounter at St. Elizabeths. Ed. Catherine Seelye. New York: Paragon House, 1975.

Ezra and Dorothy Pound: Letters in Captivity 1945–1946. Ed. Omar Pound and Robert Spoo. New York: Oxford UP, 1999.

Selected Letters of Ezra Pound to John Quinn, 1915–1924. Ed. Timothy Materer. Durham: Duke UP, 1991.

Ezra Pound and Dorothy Shakespear, Their Letters 1909–1914 [L/DS]. Ed. Omar Pound and A. Walton Litz. New York: New Directions, 1984.

Pound, Thayer, Watson, and the Dial: A Story in Letters. Ed. Walter Sutton. Gainesville: Florida UP, 1994.

Ezra Pound/John Theobald Letters. Ed. Donald Pearce and Herbert Schneidau. Redding Ridge: Black Swan, 1984.

"Dear Uncle George": The Correspondence Between Ezra Pound and Congressman Tinkham of Massachusetts. Ed. Philip J. Burns. Orono: NPF, 1996.

EP to LU: Nine Letters Written to Louis Untermeyer by Ezra Pound. Ed. J. A. Robbins. Bloomington: Indiana UP, 1963.

Ezra Pound's Letters to William Watt. Ed. William Watt. Marquette: Northern Michigan UP, 2001.

Pound/Williams: Selected Letters of Ezra Pound and William Carlos Williams. Ed. Hugh Witemeyer. New York: New Directions, 1996.

Pound/Zukofsky: Selected Letters of Ezra Pound and Louis Zukofsky. Ed. Barry Ahearn. New York: New Directions, 1987.

SECONDARY SOURCES

Reference

Bischoff, Volker. *Ezra Pound Criticism 1905–1985: A Chronological List of Publications in English.* Marburg: Universitätsbibliotek Marburg, 1991.

Dilligan, Robert J., J. W. Paris, and Todd K. Bender. *A Concordance of Ezra Pound's Cantos.* New York: Garland, 1981.

Edwards, John Hamilton, and William W. Vasse. *Annotated Index to the Cantos of Ezra Pound: Cantos I–LXXXIV.* Berkeley: U of California P, 1957.

Gallup, Donald. *A Bibliography of Ezra Pound.* 1963. Charlottesville: UP of Virginia, 1983.

Lane, Gary. *A Concordance to Personae: The Shorter Poems of Ezra Pound.* New York: Haskell House, 1972.

Ricks, Beatrice. *Ezra Pound: A Bibliography of Secondary Works.* Metuchen: Scarecrow P, 1986.

Ruthven, K. K. *A Guide to Ezra Pound's Personae (1926).* Berkeley: U of California P, 1969.

Terrell, Carroll F. *A Companion to the Cantos of Ezra Pound.* 2 vols. Berkeley: U of California P, 1980, 1984.

Biographical and Critical Works

Accame, Giano. *Ezra Pound economista.* Rome: Europa Libreria, 1995.

Ackroyd, Peter. *Ezra Pound and His World.* London: Thames & Hudson, 1980.

Aji, Hélène. *Ezra Pound et William Carlos Williams: Pour une poétique américaine.* Paris: L'Harmattan, 2001.

Albright, Daniel. *Quantum Poetics: Yeats, Pound, Eliot and the Science of Modernism.* New York: Cambridge UP, 1997.

Alexander, Michael. *The Poetic Achievement of Ezra Pound*. London: Faber, 1979.

Alexander, Michael, and James MacGonigal, eds. *Sons of Ezra: British Poets and Ezra Pound*. Amsterdam: Rodopi, 1995.

Alldritt, Keith. *Modernism in the Second World War: The Later Poetry of Ezra Pound, T. S. Eliot, Basil Bunting and Hugh MacDiarmid*. New York: P. Lang, 1989.

Andrews, Norwood, Jr. *The Case against Camões: A Seldom Considered Chapter from Ezra Pound's Campaign to Discredit Rhetorical Poetry*. New York: P. Lang, 1988.

Anonymous. *Pound's Artists: Ezra Pound and the Visual Arts in London, Paris, and Italy*. London: Tate Gallery Publications, 1985.

Apter, Ronnie. *Digging for the Treasure: Translation after Pound*. 1984. New York: Paragon, 1987.

Ardizzone, Maria Luisa. *Ezra Pound e la scienza. Scritti inediti o rari*. Milano: Scheiwiller, 1987.

Bacigalupo, Massimo. *The Forméd Trace: The Later Poetry of Ezra Pound*. New York: Columbia UP, 1980.

Baumann, Walter. *The Rose in the Steel Dust: An Examination of the Cantos of Ezra Pound*. 1967. Coral Gables: U of Miami P, 1970.

———. *Roses from the Steel Dust: Collected Essays on Ezra Pound*. Orono: NPF, 2000.

Beach, Christopher. *ABC of Influence: Ezra Pound and the Remaking of American Poetic Tradition*. Berkeley: U of California P, 1992.

Bell, Ian F. A. *Critic as Scientist: The Modernist Poetics of Ezra Pound*. London: Methuen, 1981.

———, ed. *Ezra Pound: Tactics for Reading*. Totowa: Barnes & Noble, 1982.

Bell, Michael. *Literature, Modernism and Myth: Belief and Responsibility in the Twentieth Century*. Cambridge: Cambridge UP, 1997.

Bernstein, Michael André. *The Tale of the Tribe: Ezra Pound and the Modern Verse Epic*. Princeton: Princeton UP, 1980.

Berryman, Jo Brantley. *Circe's Craft: Ezra Pound's "Hugh Selwyn Mauberley."* Ann Arbor: UMI, 1983.

Bloom, Harold, ed. *Ezra Pound*. New York: Chelsea House, 1987.

Bornstein, George, ed. *Ezra Pound among the Poets*. Chicago: U of Chicago P, 1985.

———. *Poetic Remaking: The Art of Browning, Yeats, and Pound*. University Park: Pennsylvania State UP, 1988.

———. *The Post-Romantic Consciousness of Ezra Pound*. Victoria: U of Victoria, 1977.

Brooker, Peter. *A Student's Guide to the Selected Poems of Ezra Pound*. London: Faber, 1979.

Brooke-Rose, Christine. *A Structural Analysis of Pound's Usura Canto*. The Hague: Mouton, 1976.

———. *A ZBC of Ezra Pound*. Berkeley: U of California P, 1971.

Brown, Dennis. *Intertextual Dynamics within the Literary Group—Joyce, Lewis, Pound and Eliot: The Men of 1914*. New York: St. Martin's P, 1990.

Bucknell, Brad. *Literary Modernism and Musical Aesthetics: Pater, Pound, Joyce, and Stein*. New York: Cambridge UP, 2001.

Bush, Ronald. *The Genesis of Ezra Pound's Cantos*. Princeton: Princeton UP, 1976.

Carne-Ross, D. S. *Instaurations: Essays in and out of Literature, Pindar to Pound*. Berkeley: U of California P, 1979.

Carpenter, Humphrey. *A Serious Character: The Life of Ezra Pound*. Boston: Houghton Mifflin, 1988.

Carson, Luke. *Consumption and Depression in Gertrude Stein, Louis Zukofsky, and Ezra Pound*. New York: St. Martin's P, 1999.

Casillo, Robert. *The Genealogy of Demons: Anti-Semitism, Fascism, and the Myths of Ezra Pound*. Evanston: Northwestern UP, 1988.

Chace, William. *The Political Identities of T. S. Eliot and Ezra Pound*. Stanford: Stanford UP, 1973.

Cheadle, Mary Paterson. *Ezra Pound's Confucian Translations*. Ann Arbor: U of Michigan P, 1997.

Childs, John Steven. *Modernist Form: Pound's Style in the Early Cantos*. Selinsgrove: Susquehanna UP, 1986.

Clearfield, Andrew M. *These Fragments I Have Shored: Collage and Montage in Early Modernist Poetry*. Ann Arbor: UMI, 1984.

Comens, Bruce. *Apocalypse and After: Modern Strategy and Postmodern Tactics in Pound, Williams, and Zukofsky*. Tuscaloosa: U of Alabama P, 1995.

Conover, Anne. *Olga Rudge and Ezra Pound: "What Thou Lovest Well . . ."* New Haven: Yale UP, 2001.

Cookson, William. *A Guide to The Cantos of Ezra Pound*. London: Croom Helm, 1985.

Cornell, Julian. *The Trial of Ezra Pound*. New York: J. Day, 1966.

Coyle, Michael, ed. *Ezra Pound and African American Modernism*. Orono: NPF, 2001.

———. *Ezra Pound, Popular Genres, and the Discourse of Culture*. University Park: Pennsylvania State UP, 1995.

Craig, Cairns. *Yeats, Eliot, Pound, and the Politics of Poetry: Richest to the Richest*. London: Croom Helm, 1982.

Dasenbrock, Reed Way. *Imitating the Italians: Wyatt, Spenser, Synge, Pound, Joyce.* Baltimore: Johns Hopkins UP, 1991.

———. *The Literary Vorticism of Ezra Pound and Wyndham Lewis: Towards the Condition of Painting.* Baltimore: Johns Hopkins UP, 1985.

Davenport, Guy. *Cities on Hills: A Study of I–XXX of Ezra Pound's Cantos.* Ann Arbor: UMI, 1983.

Davidson, Peter. *Ezra Pound and Roman Poetry: A Preliminary Survey.* Amsterdam: Rodopi, 1995.

Davie, Donald. *Ezra Pound.* Chicago: U of Chicago P, 1975.

———. *Ezra Pound: Poet as Sculptor.* New York: Oxford UP, 1964.

———. *Studies in Ezra Pound.* Manchester: Carcanet, 1991.

———. *Trying to Explain.* Ann Arbor: U of Michigan P, 1979.

Davis, Earle K. *Vision Fugitive: Ezra Pound and Economics.* Lawrence: UP of Kansas, 1968.

Davis, Kay. *Fugue and Fresco: Structures in Pound's Cantos.* Orono: NPF, 1984.

Dekker, George. *Sailing after Knowledge: The Cantos of Ezra Pound.* London: RKP, 1963.

Dembo, L. S. *Conceptions of Reality in American Poetry.* Berkeley: U of California P, 1966.

———. *The Confucian Odes of Ezra Pound: A Critical Appraisal.* Berkeley: U of California P, 1963.

de Nagy, N. Christoph. *Ezra Pound's Poetics and Literary Tradition: The Critical Decade.* Bern: Francke Verlag, 1966.

———. *The Poetry of Ezra Pound: The Pre-Imagist Stage.* 1960. Bern: Francke Verlag, 1968.

D'Epiro, Peter. *A Touch of Rhetoric: Ezra Pound's Malatesta Cantos.* Ann Arbor: UMI, 1983.

Dickie, Margaret. *On the Modernist Long Poem.* Iowa City: U of Iowa P, 1986.

Diepeveen, Leonard. *Changing Voices: The Modern Quoting Poem.* Ann Arbor: U of Michigan P, 1993.

Doolittle, Hilda. *Collected Poems, 1912—1944.* Ed. Louis L. Martz. New York: New Directions, 1983.

———. *End to Torment: A Memoir of Ezra Pound.* Ed. Norman Holmes Pearson and Michael King. New York: New Directions, 1979.

Driscoll, John. *The China Cantos of Ezra Pound.* Uppsala: Ubsaliensis S. Academiae, 1983.

Durant, Alan. *Ezra Pound: Identity in Crisis.* Brighton: Harvester, 1981.

Eastham, Scott. *Paradise and Ezra Pound: The Poet as Shaman.* Lanham: UP of America, 1983.

Eastman, Barbara. *Ezra Pound's Cantos: The Story of the Text 1948–1975.* Orono: NPF, 1979.

Eder, Doris. *Three Writers in Exile: Pound, Eliot and Joyce.* Troy: Whitston, 1984.

Eliot, T. S. "Ezra Pound: His Metric and Poetry." *To Criticize the Critic: Eight Essays on Literature and Education.* New York and London: Faber, 1965. 162–182.

Ellmann, Maud. *The Poetics of Impersonality: T. S. Eliot and Ezra Pound.* Brighton: Harvester P, 1987.

Emery, Clark. *Ideas into Action: A Study of Pound's Cantos.* 1958. Coral Gables: U of Miami P, 1969.

Emig, Rainer. *Modernism in Poetry: Motivation, Structure, and Limits.* New York: Longman, 1995.

Espey, John. *Ezra Pound's Mauberley: A Study in Composition.* Berkeley: U of California P, 1955.

Fang, Achilles. *Confucius: The Great Digest & Unwobbling Pivot.* New York: New Directions, 1951.

Fisher, Margaret. *Ezra Pound's Radio Operas: The BBC Experiments 1931–1933.* Cambridge: MIT P, 2002.

Flory, Wendy Stallard. *The American Ezra Pound.* New Haven: Yale UP, 1989.

———. *Ezra Pound and The Cantos: A Record of Struggle.* New Haven: Yale UP, 1980.

Fogelman, Bruce. *Shapes of Power: The Development of Ezra Pound's Poetic Sequences.* Ann Arbor: UMI, 1988.

Froula, Christine. *A Guide to Ezra Pound's Selected Poems.* New York: New Directions, 1982.

———. *To Write Paradise: Style and Error in Pound's Cantos.* New Haven: Yale UP, 1984.

Furia, Philip. *Pound's Cantos Declassified.* University Park: Pennsylvania State UP, 1984.

Gage, John T. *In the Arresting Eye: The Rhetoric of Imagism.* Baton Rouge: Louisiana State UP, 1981.

Gallesi, Luca, ed. *Ezra Pound educatore.* Milano: Terziaria, 1997.

———, ed. *Ezra Pound e il turismo colto a Milano.* Milano: Ares, 2001.

———, ed. *Ezra Pound e l'economia.* Milano: Ares, 2001.

Gallup, Donald. *T. S. Eliot & Ezra Pound: Collaborators in Letters.* New Haven: H. W. Wenning/C. A. Stonehill, 1970.

Géfin, Laszlo. *Ideogram: History of a Poetic Method.* Austin: U of Texas P, 1982.

Gelpi, Albert. *A Coherent Splendor: The American Poetic Renaissance 1910–1950.* Cambridge: Cambridge UP, 1987.

Gibson, Andrew, ed. *Pound in Multiple Perspective.* London: Macmillan, 1993.

Gibson, Mary Ellis. *Epic Reinvented: Ezra Pound and the Victorians.* Ithaca: Cornell UP, 1995.

Giovannini, Giovanni. *Ezra Pound and Dante*. New York: Haskell House, 1974.

Goodwin, K. L. *The Influence of Ezra Pound*. London: Oxford UP, 1966.

Grieve, Thomas F. *Ezra Pound's Early Poetry and Poetics*. Columbia: U of Missouri P, 1997.

Gross, Harvey. *The Contrived Corridor: History and Fatality in Modern Literature*. Ann Arbor: U of Michigan P, 1971.

Grover, Philip, ed. *Ezra Pound: The London Years 1908–1920*. New York: AMS P, 1978.

———, ed. *Ezra Pound and the Troubadours: Selected Papers from the Ezra Pound Conference, Brantôme, 1995*. Gardonne: Fédérop, 2000.

Gugelberger, Georg M. *Ezra Pound's Medievalism*. Frankfurt: P. Lang, 1978.

Hall, Donald. "Ezra Pound." *Writers at Work: The Paris Review Interviews*. 2nd Series. Ed. Malcolm Cowley. New York: Viking, 1963. 35–59.

Hamilton, Scott. *Ezra Pound and the Symbolist Inheritance*. Princeton: Princeton UP, 1992.

Harmon, William. *Time in Ezra Pound's Work*. Chapel Hill: U of North Carolina P, 1977.

Hayot, Eric. *Chinese Dreams: Pound, Brecht, Tel Quel*. Ann Arbor: U of Michigan P, 2004.

Hesse, Eva, ed. *New Approaches to Ezra Pound*. Berkeley: U of California P, 1969.

Heymann, C. David. *Ezra Pound: The Last Rower*. New York: Viking, 1976.

Hoffman, Daniel, ed. *Ezra Pound and William Carlos Williams: The University of Pennsylvania Conference Papers*. Philadelphia: U of Pennsylvania P, 1983.

Homberger, Eric, ed. *Ezra Pound: The Critical Heritage*. London: Routledge, 1972.

Hooley, Daniel M. *The Classics in Paraphrase: Ezra Pound and Modern Translators of Latin Poetry*. Selingsgrove: Susquehanna UP, 1988.

Hsieh, Ming. *Ezra Pound and the Appropriation of Chinese Poetry: Cathay, Translation, and Imagism*. New York: Garland, 1999.

Huang, Guiyou. *Whitmanism, Imagism, and Modernism in China and America*. Selingsgrove: Susquehanna UP, 1997.

Hutchins, Patricia. *Ezra Pound's Kensington: An Exploration 1885–1913*. Chicago: Regnery, 1965.

Jackson, Thomas H. *The Early Poetry of Ezra Pound*. Cambridge: Harvard UP, 1968.

Jones, Peter, ed. *Imagist Poetry*. Harmondsworth: Penguin, 1972.

Joseph, Terri Brint. *Ezra Pound's Epic Variations: The Cantos and Major Long Poems*. Orono: NPF, 1995.

Juhasz, Suzanne. *Metaphor and the Poetry of Williams, Pound, and Stevens*. Lewisburg: Bucknell UP, 1974.

Kaye, Jacqueline, ed. *Ezra Pound and America*. New York: St. Martin's P, 1992.

Kayman, Martin A. *The Modernism of Ezra Pound: The Science of Poetry*. Houndsmills: Macmillan, 1986.

Kearns, George. *Ezra Pound: The Cantos*. Cambridge: Cambridge UP, 1989.

———. *Guide to Ezra Pound's Selected Cantos*. New Brunswick: Rutgers UP, 1980.

Kenner, Hugh. *Gnomon: Essays in Contemporary Literature*. New York: McDowell Obolensky, 1958.

———. *The Poetry of Ezra Pound*. 1951. Lincoln: U of Nebraska P, 1985.

———. *The Pound Era*. Berkeley: U of California P, 1971.

Knapp, James F. *Ezra Pound*. Boston: Twayne, 1979.

Korg, Jacob. *Ritual and Experiment in Modern Poetry*. New York: St. Martin's P, 1995.

———. *Winter Love: Ezra Pound and H. D.* Madison: U of Wisconsin P, 2003.

Korn, Marianne. *Ezra Pound: Purpose, Form, Meaning*. London: Middlesex Polytechnic P, 1983.

———, ed. *Ezra Pound and History*. Orono: NPF, 1985.

Kuberski, Philip. *A Calculus of Ezra Pound: Vocations of the American Sign*. Gainesville: UP of Florida, 1992.

Kyburz, Mark. *Voi Altri Pochi: Ezra Pound and His Audience 1908–1925*. Basel: Birkhäuser Verlag, 1996.

Laughlin, James. *Pound as Wuz: Essays and Lectures on Ezra Pound*. Saint Paul: Greywolf P, 1987.

Leary, Lewis, ed. *Motive and Method in the Cantos of Ezra Pound*. New York: Columbia UP, 1954.

Levenson, Michael. *The Genealogy of Modernism: A Study of English Literary Doctrine, 1908–1922*. Cambridge: Cambridge UP, 1984.

Levin, Harry. *Ezra Pound, T. S. Eliot, and the European Horizon*. Oxford: Clarendon P, 1975.

Levy, Alan. *Ezra Pound: The Voice of Silence*. Sag Harbor: Permanent P, 1983.

Liebregts, P.Th.M.G. *Ezra Pound and Neoplatonism*. Madison: Farleigh Dickinson UP, 2004.

Lindberg, Kathryne V. *Reading Pound Reading: Modernism after Nietzsche*. New York: Oxford UP, 1987.

Longenbach, James. *Modernist Poetics of History: Pound, Eliot, and the Sense of the Past*. Princeton: Princeton UP, 1987.

———. *Stone Cottage: Pound, Yeats, and Modernism*. New York: Oxford UP, 1988.

Makin, Peter. *Pound's Cantos*. London: Allen & Unwin, 1985.

———. *Provence and Pound*. Berkeley: U of California P, 1978.

Marsh, Alec. *Money and Modernity: Pound, Williams, and the Spirit of Jefferson*. Tuscaloosa: U of Alabama P, 1998.

Materer, Timothy. *Modernist Alchemy: Poetry and the Occult*. Ithaca: Cornell UP, 1995.

———. *Vortex: Pound, Eliot, and Lewis*. Ithaca: Cornell UP, 1979.

McDonald, Gail. *Learning to Be Modern: Pound, Eliot, and the American University*. New York: Oxford UP, 1993.

McDougal, Stuart Y. *Ezra Pound and the Troubadour Tradition*. Princeton: Princeton UP, 1972.

Merritt, Robert. *Early Music and the Aesthetics of Ezra Pound: Hush of Older Song*. Lewiston: Edwin Mellen P, 1993.

Miller, James E., Jr. *The American Quest for a Supreme Fiction: Whitman's Legacy in the Personal Epic*. Chicago: U of Chicago P, 1979.

Miyake, Akiko. *Ezra Pound and the Mysteries of Love: A Plan for the Cantos*. Durham: Duke UP, 1991.

Miyake, Akiko, Sanehide Kodama, and Nicholas Teele, eds. *A Guide to Ezra Pound and Ernest Fenollosa's Classic Noh Theatre of Japan*. Orono: NPF/EP Foundation Japan, 1994.

Morrison, Paul. *The Poetics of Facism: Ezra Pound, T. S. Eliot, Paul de Man*. New York: Oxford UP, 1996.

Nadel, Ira B., ed. *The Cambridge Companion to Ezra Pound*. Cambridge: Cambridge UP, 1999.

———. *Ezra Pound: A Literary Life*. New York: Palgrave Macmillan, 2004.

Nänny, Max. *Ezra Pound: Poetics for an Electric Age*. Bern: Francke Verlag, 1973.

Nassar, Eugene Paul. *The Cantos of Ezra Pound: The Lyric Mode*. Baltimore: Johns Hopkins UP, 1975.

Nicholls, Peter. *Ezra Pound: Politics, Economics, and Writing: A Study of The Cantos*. Atlantic Highlands: Humanities P, 1984.

Nolde, John J. *Blossoms from the East: The China Cantos of Ezra Pound*. Orono: NPF, 1983.

Norman, Charles. *The Case of Ezra Pound*. New York: Funk and Wagnalls, 1968.

———. *Ezra Pound*. New York: Macmillan, 1960.

North, Michael. *The Political Aesthetic of Yeats, Eliot, and Pound*. Cambridge: Cambridge UP, 1991.

Oderman, Kevin. *Ezra Pound and the Erotic Medium*. Durham: Duke UP, 1986.

Paul, Catherine E. *Poetry in the Museums of Modernism: Yeats, Pound, Moore, Stein*. Ann Arbor: U of Michigan P, 2002.

Pearlman, Daniel D. *The Barb of Time: On the Unity of Ezra Pound's Cantos*. New York: Oxford UP, 1969.

Pearson, Norman H. Foreword. In Hilda Doolittle, *Tribute to Freud*. New York: New Directions, 1984.

Perelman, Bob. *The Trouble with Genius: Reading Pound, Joyce, Stein, and Zukofsky*. Berkeley: U of California P, 1994.

Perloff, Marjorie. *The Dance of the Intellect: Studies in the Poetry of the Pound Tradition*. Evanston: Northwestern UP, 1985.

———. *The Futurist Moment: Avant-garde, Avant Guerre, and the Language of Rupture*. Chicago: U of Chicago P, 1986.

———. *The Poetics of Indeterminacy: Rimbaud to Cage*. Princeton: Princeton UP, 1981.

Pratt, William. *Ezra Pound, Nature and Myth*. New York: AMS P, 2002.

———. *The Imagist Poem: Modern Poetry in Miniature*. 1963. Ashland: Story Line P, 2001.

Pratt, William, and Robert Richardson, eds. *Homage to Imagism*. New York: AMS P, 1992.

Qian, Zhaoming. *Ezra Pound and China*. Ann Arbor: U of Michigan P, 2003.

———. *The Modernist Response to Chinese Art: Pound, Moore, Stevens*. Charlottesville: U of Virginia P, 2003.

———. *Orientalism and Modernism: The Legacy of China in Pound and Williams*. Durham: Duke UP, 1995.

Rabaté, Jean-Michel. *Language, Sexuality and Ideology in Ezra Pound's Cantos*. Albany: State U of New York P, 1986.

Rachewiltz, Mary de. *Discretions: Ezra Pound, Father and Teacher*. Boston: Little, Brown, 1971.

Rae, Patricia. *The Practical Muse: Pragmatist Poetics in Hulme, Pound, and Stevens*. Lewisburg: Bucknell UP, 1997.

Raffel, Burton. *Ezra Pound: The Prime Minister of Poetry*. Hamden: Archon Books, 1984.

———. *Possum and Ole Ez in the Public Eye: Contemporaries and Peers on T. S. Eliot and Ezra Pound 1892–1972*. Hamden: Archon Books, 1985.

Rainey, Lawrence S. *Ezra Pound and the Monument of Culture: Text, History and the Malatesta Cantos*. Chicago: U of Chicago P, 1991.

———. *Institutions of Modernism: Literary Elites and Public Culture*. New Haven: Yale UP, 1998.

———, ed. *A Poem Containing History: Textual Studies in The Cantos*. Ann Arbor: U of Michigan P, 1997.

Read, Forrest. *'76: One World and the Cantos of Ezra Pound*. Chapel Hill: U of North Carolina P, 1981.

Read, Richard. *Art and Its Discontents: The Early Life of Adrian Stokes*. University Park: Pennsylvania State UP, 2002.

Reck, Michael. *Ezra Pound: A Close-up*. New York: McGraw-Hill, 1973.

Redman, Tim. *Ezra Pound and Italian Fascism*. New York: Cambridge UP, 1991.

Ricciardi, Caterina. *Eikones: Ezra Pound e il Rinascimento*. Napoli: Liguori, 1991.

Rosenthal, M. L. *A Primer of Ezra Pound*. New York: Macmillan, 1960.

———. *Sailing into the Unknown: Yeats, Pound and Eliot*. New York: Oxford UP, 1978.

Rosenthal, M. L., and Sally M. Gall. *The Modern Poetic Sequence: The Genius of Modern Poetry*. New York: Oxford UP, 1983.

Ruthven, K. K. *Ezra Pound as Literary Critic*. New York: Routledge, 1990.

———. *A Guide to Ezra Pound's Personae (1926)*. Berkeley: U of California P, 1969.

Sanders, Frederick K. *John Adams Speaking*. Orono: U of Maine P, 1975.

Schneidau, Herbert N. *Ezra Pound: The Image and the Real*. Baton Rouge: Louisiana State UP, 1969.

Schwartz, Sanford. *The Matrix of Modernism: Pound, Eliot, and Early Twentieth-Century Thought*. Princeton: Princeton UP, 1985.

Sherry, Vincent. *Ezra Pound, Wyndham Lewis, and Radical Modernism*. New York: Oxford UP, 1993.

Shioji, Ursula. *Ezra Pound's Pisan Cantos and the Noh*. Frankfurt: P. Lang, 1998.

Sicari, Stephen. *Pound's Epic Ambition: Dante and the Modern World*. Albany: State U of New York P, 1991.

Sieburth, Richard. *Instigations: Ezra Pound and Remy de Gourmont*. Cambridge: Harvard UP, 1978.

Simpson, Louis. *Three on the Tower: The Lives and Works of Ezra Pound, T. S. Eliot, and William Carlos Williams*. New York: Morrow, 1975.

Singh, G. *Ezra Pound as Critic*. New York: St. Martin's P, 1994.

Smith, Marcel, and William A. Ulmer, eds. *Ezra Pound: The Legacy of Kulchur*. Tuscaloosa: U of Alabama P, 1988.

Smith, Paul. *Pound Revised*. London: Croom Helm, 1983.

Smith, Stan. *The Origins of Modernism: Eliot, Pound, Yeats, and the Rhetorics of Renewal*. New York: Harvester Wheatsheaf, 1994.

Stead, C. K. *Pound, Yeats, Eliot, and the Modernist Movement*. New Brunswick: Rutgers UP, 1986.

Stock, Noel, ed. *Ezra Pound Perspectives: Essays in Honor of His Eightieth Birthday*. 1965. Westport: Greenwood, 1977.

———. *Ezra Pound's Pennsylvania*. Toledo: Friends of U of Toledo Libraries, 1976.

———. *The Life of Ezra Pound*. 1970. San Francisco: North Point P, 1982.

———. *Poet in Exile: Ezra Pound*. Manchester: Manchester UP, 1964.

———. *Reading the Cantos: A Study of Meaning in Ezra Pound*. London: Routledge, 1966.

Stoicheff, Peter. *The Hall of Mirrors: Drafts & Fragments and the End of Ezra Pound's Cantos*. Ann Arbor: U of Michigan P, 1995.

Sullivan, J. P., ed. *Ezra Pound: A Critical Anthology*. Harmondsworth: Penguin, 1970.

Sullivan, J. P. *Ezra Pound and Sextus Propertius: A Study in Creative Translation*. Austin: U of Texas P, 1964.

Surette, Leon. *The Birth of Modernism: Ezra Pound, T. S. Eliot, W. B. Yeats, and the Occult*. Montreal: McGill–Queen's UP, 1993.

———. *A Light from Eleusis: A Study of Ezra Pound's Cantos*. Oxford: Clarendon P, 1979.

———. *Pound in Purgatory: From Economic Radicalism to Anti-Semitism*. Urbana: U of Illinois P, 1999.

Surette, Leon, and Demetres P. Tryphonopoulos, eds. *Literary Modernism and the Occult Tradition*. Orono: NPF, 1996.

Sutton, Walter, ed. *Ezra Pound: A Collection of Critical Essays*. Twentieth-Century Views STC-9. Englewood Cliffs: Prentice-Hall, 1963.

Symons, Julian. *Makers of the New: The Revolution in Literature 1912–1939*. New York: Random House, 1987.

Taupin, René. *The Influence of French Symbolism on Modern American Poetry*. 1929. Trans. William and Anne Rich Pratt. 1965. New York: AMS P, 1985.

Taylor, Richard, and Claus Melchior, eds. *Ezra Pound and Europe*. Amsterdam: Rodopi, 1993.

Terrell, Carroll F. *Ideas in Reaction: Byways to the Pound Arcana*. Orono: Northern Lights P, 1991.

Thomas, Ron. *The Latin Masks of Ezra Pound*. Ann Arbor: UMI, 1983.

Tiffany, Daniel. *Radio Corpse: Imagism and the Cryptaesthetic of Ezra Pound*. Cambridge: Harvard UP, 1995.

Torrey, E. Fuller. *The Roots of Treason: Ezra Pound and the Secret of St. Elizabeths*. New York: McGraw-Hill, 1984.

Tryphonopoulos, Demetres P. *The Celestial Tradition: A Study of Ezra Pound's The Cantos*. Waterloo: Wilfrid Laurier UP, 1992.

Tsukui, Nobuko. *Ezra Pound and Japanese Noh Plays*. Washington: UP of America, 1983.

Tytell, John. *Ezra Pound: The Solitary Volcano*. New York: Anchor P, 1987.

Ueda, Makoto. *Zeami, Basho, Yeats, and Pound: A Study in Japanese and English Poetics*. The Hague: Mouton, 1965.

Walker, Jeffrey. *Bardic Ethos and the American Epic Poem: Whitman, Pound, Crane, Williams, Olson*. Baton Rouge: Louisiana State UP, 1989.

Wilhelm, James J. *The American Roots of Ezra Pound*. New York: Garland, 1985.

————. *Dante and Pound: The Epic of Judgment*. Orono: U of Maine P, 1974.

————. *Ezra Pound: The Tragic Years 1925–1972*. University Park: Pennsylvania State UP, 1994.

————. *Ezra Pound in London and Paris 1908–1925*. University Park: Pennsylvania State UP, 1990.

————. *The Later Cantos of Ezra Pound*. New York: Walker, 1977.

————. *Il Miglior Fabbro: The Cult of the Difficult in Daniel, Dante, and Pound*. Orono: NPF, 1982.

Wilson, Peter. *A Preface to Ezra Pound*. New York: Longman, 1997.

Witemeyer, Hugh. *The Poetry of Ezra Pound: Forms and Renewal, 1908–1920*. Berkeley: U of California P, 1969.

Wolfe, Cary. *The Limits of American Literary Ideology in Pound and Emerson*. Cambridge: Cambridge UP, 1993.

Woodward, Anthony. *Ezra Pound and the Pisan Cantos*. London: Routledge, 1980.

Woodward, Kathleen M. *At Last, the Real Distinguished Thing: The Late Poems of Eliot, Pound, Stevens, and Williams*. Columbus: Ohio State UP, 1980.

Yao, Steven G. *Translation and the Languages of Modernism: Gender, Politics, Language*. New York: Palgrave, 2002.

Yip, Wai-lim. *Ezra Pound's Cathay*. Princeton: Princeton UP, 1969.

Index

This general index includes as entries the topics of this encyclopedia's entries (in **bold**), of persons, and of titles of Ezra Pound works. The titles of Pound's works are not listed in an Ezra Pound index entry; instead, they are listed alphabetically. This index does not include as entries place names, ideas, or titles of works by writers other than Pound. Moreover, it does not include the names of writers of scholarly work on Pound—these are available in the Selected Bibliography and in the bibliographical notes which accompany most topic entries.

About the Contributors

STEPHEN J. ADAMS is Professor of English at the University of Western Ontario, London, Canada. He has published on Pound's music and prosody and is the author of *R. Murray Schafer* (1984) and *Poetic Designs: An Introduction to English Meters, Verse Forms, and Figures of Speech* (1997).

BARRY AHEARN is Professor of English at Tulane. His publications include *William Carlos Williams and Alterity: The Early Poetry* (1994) and two collections of Pound letters, *Pound/Zukofsky* (1987) and *Pound/Cummings* (1996), as well as correspondence of Zukofsky and Williams.

HÉLÈNE AJI is Associate Professor of American Poetry at the Université de Paris–Sorbonne. She has written widely on Modernist and contemporary poetry. Her publications include *Ezra Pound et William Carlos Williams: Pour une poétique américaine* (2001) and *William Carlos Williams: un plan d'action* (2004). She is the editor of *Ezra Pound and Referentiality* (2003).

MICHAEL J. ALLEMAN is Associate Professor of Humanities at Collin County Community College, Plano, Texas.

JONATHAN AUSUBEL is Associate Professor of English at Chaffey College, Rancho Cucamonga, California. He has published encyclopedia entries, book reviews, and articles on poetry in *Connotations, Twentieth Century Literature,* and *Paideuma*.

MASSIMO BACIGALUPO is Professor of American Literature at the University of Genoa. He lives in Rapallo. His many books include *The Formèd Trace: The Later Poetry of Ezra Pound* (1980) and *Ezra Pound: Canti postumi* (2002). He was the recipient of the Italian National Translation Prize for 2001 and President of the Italian Association for American Studies (2001–2004).

GREG BARNHISEL is Director of First-Year Writing at Duquesne University in Pittsburgh. He is the author of *Media and Messages: Strategies and Readings in Public Rhetoric* (2004) and *James Laughlin, New Directions, and the Remaking of Ezra Pound* (2005).

MADELINE BASSNETT has an M.A. in English from the University of New Brunswick, Fredericton, Canada, and is now pursuing her doctorate at Dalhousie University in Halifax, Nova Scotia.

WALTER BAUMANN taught German Studies at the Universities of Toronto and Ulster, Northern Ireland. He has been a regular speaker at the International Ezra Pound Conferences, for which he has provided photographic records since 1990. A regular contributor to *Paideuma,* he is author of *The Rose in the Steel Dust* (1967) and *Roses from the Steel Dust* (2000).

SHERI BENNING has completed her M.A. in English and Creative Writing at the University of New Brunswick, Fredericton, Canada. Her first book of poetry, *Earth after Rain,* came out in 2001.

JOEL BETTRIDGE has a Ph.D. in Modern Language and Literature from the State University of New York at Buffalo. He is a widely published poet.

JONATHAN BLACKWOOD is a Lecturer in Cultural & Media Studies at the School of Humanities and Social Sciences, University of Glamorgan, Pontypridd, United Kingdom. His Ph.D. is from the Courtauld Institute of Art, University of London. His main publications concern visual cultures and national identities in the twentieth century.

RICHARD L. BLEVINS is Professor of English and Chair of the Humanities Division, University of Pittsburgh at Greensburg. *Fogbow Bridge*, a book of selected poems, appeared in 2000. He is editor of the Charles Olson–Robert Creeley correspondence.

GEORGE BORNSTEIN has written five critical books on nineteenth- and twentieth-century literature, most recently *Material Modernism: The Politics of the Page* (2001). He has also produced editions of Modernist works and edited several collections of essays. He is currently C. A. Patrides Professor of Literature at the University of Michigan at Ann Arbor.

MANUEL BRITO teaches American Literature at the Universidad de La Laguna. He is the founder of Zasterle, a publisher of poetry books since 1989 out of La Laguna, Canary Islands.

RONALD BUSH is Drue Heinz Professor of American Literature at Oxford University. His many books include *The Genesis of Ezra Pound's Cantos* (1976) and *T. S. Eliot: A Study in Character and Style* (1984). He is nearly finished with a study of the composition of *The Pisan Cantos*.

MARK S. BYRON completed his Ph.D. dissertation in 2001 at the University of Cambridge, titled "Exilic Modernism and Textual Ontogeny: Ezra Pound's *Pisan Cantos* and Samuel Beckett's *Watt*." He is currently teaching at the University of Sydney, Australia.

FRANCESCA CADEL (Ph.D. in Italian Studies, Sorbonne, 1999; Ph.D. in Comparative Literature, City University of New York, 2002) teaches in the Department of Italian at Yale University. She is the author of *La lingua dei desideri. Il dialetto secondo Pier Paolo Pasolini* (2002) and is currently writing a book on the Italian cultural landscape in Ezra Pound's poetry.

STEPHEN CAIN teaches Poetry and Canadian Literature at Wilfrid Laurier University, Waterloo, Canada. His primary area of research is publishing and cultural production, and he is the author of the poetry collections *dyslexicon* (1998) and *Torontology* (2001).

LANCE CALLAHAN teaches at the University of New Brunswick and Saint Thomas University in Fredericton, Canada. He is author of *"In the Shadows of Divine Perfection": Derek Walcott's Omeros* (2003).

STEFANO MARIA CASELLA is Assistant Professor of English and American Literature at the Istituto Universitario di Lingue Moderne (now Libera Università di Lingue e Comunicazione) in Milan and Feltre and at the University of Padua. He has published on Pound, Eliot, and comparative literature as well as translations of poetry.

MARY PATERSON CHEADLE earned her Ph.D. at the University of California at Berkeley. An independent scholar living in Seattle, she is the author of *Ezra Pound's Confucian Translations* (1997).

PATRICIA A. COCKRAM teaches in the English Department at Lehman College, New York, where she specializes in twentieth-century British, Irish, and American literatures, feminist studies, and hypertext and cyber theories. She is the author of *Tard, très tard: Dominique de Roux et la tardive découverte d'Ezra Pound en France* (forthcoming) and is at work on a book about Ezra Pound and France.

CHRISTOPHER K. COFFMAN, a Ph.D. candidate at The Catholic University of America, is writing a dissertation on James Merrill and Modernism. He lectures at the Catholic and American Universities in Washington, D.C.

WILLIAM COLE is the Instructional Technology Director at Morehead State University, Morehead, Kentucky.

MICHAEL COYLE is Professor of English at Colgate University, Hamilton, New York. He is author of *Ezra Pound, Popular Genres, and the Discourse of Culture* (1995) and has edited *Ezra Pound and African American Modernism* (2001) and *Raymond Williams & Modernism* (2002). He has a forthcoming book, *Professional Attention: Ezra Pound and the Career of Modern Criticism*.

REED WAY DASENBROCK is Dean of the College of Arts and Sciences and Professor of English at the University of New Mexico, Albuquerque. His numerous books include *The Literary Vorticism of Ezra Pound and Wyndham Lewis* (1985) and *Imitating the Italians: Wyatt, Spenser, Synge, Pound, Joyce* (1991).

PATRICK DEANE is Vice President (Academic) and Provost and Professor of English at the University of Winnipeg. He is the author of *At Home in Time: Forms of Neo-Augustanism in Modern English Poetry* (1994) and editor of *History in Our Hands: A Critical Anthology of Writings on Literature, Culture and Politics from the 1930s* (1998).

JULIE DENNISON is a Canadian poet who teaches at the University of Prince Edward Island in Canada.

DANNAH EDWARDS is an Assistant Professor of French at the University of Dallas. Her Ph.D. dissertation deals with Pound's response to French poets.

MARGARET FISHER, who is an independent scholar, choreographer, and video director, is author of *Ezra Pound's Radio Operas: The BBC Experiments 1931–1933* (2002) and the companion booklet to the audio CD *"Ego scriptor cantilenae": Music of Ezra Pound* (2004). She coauthored, with Robert Hughes, *Cavalcanti: A Perspective on the Music of Ezra Pound* (2003).

PEGGY L. FOX is the Vice President and Managing Director of New Directions Publishing Corporation. A coexecutor of James Laughlin's literary estate, she is coediting, with Thomas Keith, *Correspondence of James Laughlin and Tennessee Williams*.

ANDRE FURLANI is Associate Professor of English at Concordia University in Montreal. His publications are primarily in the fields of nineteenth- and twentieth-century British and American literature, rhetoric, Milton, Canadian literature, and Postmodernism. Forthcoming is a book on Guy Davenport.

LUCA GALLESI teaches and works in Milan, has organized several International Ezra Pound Conferences in Italy, and has edited, among other volumes, *Ezra Pound educatore* (1997) and *Ezra Pound e l'economia* (2001).

ANITA GEORGE, who wrote her Ph.D. dissertation on the Hellenistic poetics of Pound and Eliot at the University of Toronto, teaches in Ottawa, Canada. Her area of special interest is literary translation and the theory of translation.

JOHN GERY is Research Professor of English at the University of New Orleans and Founding Director of the Ezra Pound Center for Literature, Brunnenburg Castle, Dorf Tirol, Italy. He is author of four collections of poetry as well as a book-length poem, *Davenport's Version* (2003), and the critical study *Nuclear Annihilation and Contemporary American Poetry: Ways of Nothingness* (1996).

MARY ELLIS GIBSON is Professor of English at the University of North Carolina at Greensboro. She is the author of *History and the Prism of Art: Browning's Poetic Experiments* (1987) and *Epic Reinvented: Ezra Pound and the Victorians* (1995) and the editor of *Critical Essays on Robert Browning* (1992).

JONATHAN P. GILL, who teaches at Columbia University, has published on Jewish studies, modern American poetry, African American literature, and vernacular American musics. *The Wishing Tree: A History of Harlem* is forthcoming.

WILLARD GOODWIN worked as a librarian at the Harry Ransom Humanities Research Center, University of Texas at Austin. He compiled *Kenner on Joyce: A Bibliography* (1991) and *Hugh Kenner: A Bibliography* (2001).

THOMAS F. GRIEVE is Associate Professor of English at Simon Fraser University in British Columbia. He is the author of *Ezra Pound's Early Poetry and Poetics* (1997).

MICHAEL GRODEN is Professor of English at the University of Western Ontario, London, Canada. Author of *"Ulysses" in Progress* (1977) and *James Joyce's Manuscripts: An Index* (1980), he is the general editor of the sixty-three-volume *James Joyce Archive* (1977–1979), and he has coedited, with Martin Kreiswirth, *The Johns Hopkins Guide to Literary Theory and Criticism* (1994).

EVELYN HALLER is Professor of English and Chair at Doane College in Crete, Nebraska, near Lincoln. She has published on Pound as well as Virginia Woolf, Willa Cather, and William Butler Yeats. She was a contributing editor to *The Feminist Companion to Literature in English: Women Writers from the Middle Ages to the Present* (1990).

BURTON HATLEN is Professor of English, University of Maine, Orono, and the Director of the National Poetry Foundation. He has edited *George Open, Man and Poet* (1981) and, with Demetres P. Tryphonopoulos, *William Carlos Williams and the Language of Poetry* (2002).

ARCHIE HENDERSON, who wrote a Ph.D. dissertation titled "Pound and Music: The Paris and Early Rapallo Years" (1983), is a lawyer and independent scholar in Dallas, Texas.

LINE HENRIKSEN (M.A., University of York, United Kingdom; Ph.D., University of Copenhagen), is an independent scholar who lives in Copenhagen and Brussels.

MIRANDA B. HICKMAN is Associate Professor of English at McGill University. Her forthcoming book *The Geometry of Modernism* will appear in 2005. She has published on Pound, H. D., and Raymond Chandler. She is currently working on an annotated critical edition of the correspondence between Ezra Pound and publisher Stanley Nott.

MATTHEW R. HOFER is trained principally as an Anglo-American Modernist. He has written on Mina Loy and Langston Hughes and published on Ezra Pound, W. S. Merwin, and Paul Celan. He teaches at the University of New Mexico.

GUIYOU HUANG is Professor of English and Director of the Honors College at Grand Valley State University, Michigan. His numerous books include *Whitmanism, Imagism, and Modernism in China and America* (1997) as well as several articles on Pound.

ROBERT HUGHES conducted the world premiere of *Cavalcanti* and the 1923 Pound/Antheil *Le Testament*, recorded *The Testament of François Villon* and *"Ego scriptor cantilenae": Music of Ezra Pound*, and edited *Complete Violin Works of Ezra Pound* (2004). He is coauthor, with Margaret Fisher, of *Cavalcanti: A Perspective on the Music of Ezra Pound* (2003).

LIONEL KELLY is a retired Professor of English at the School of English and American Literature, University of Reading, United Kingdom. He is the editor of *Tobias Smollett: The Critical Heritage* (1987).

ROBERT E. KIBLER, Associate Professor of English at the Minot State University in North Dakota, has particular expertise in Pound's relationship with Chinese language and culture.

DENNIS KLINCK, Professor in the Faculty of Law, McGill University, has a Ph.D. in English

Literature from the University of London. He is the author of *The Word of the Law: Approaches to Legal Discourse* (1992).

SANEHIDE KODAMA is President Emeritus, Doshisha Women's College in Kyoto, Japan. He is the author of *American Poetry and Japanese Culture* (1984) and has edited *A Guide to Ezra Pound and Ernest Fenollosa's Classic Noh Theatre of Japan* (with Akiko Miyake and Nicholas Teele, 1994) and *Ezra Pound & Japan: Letters & Essays* (1987).

LAURIAT LANE JR. is Professor Emeritus, University of New Brunswick, Fredericton, Canada. He edited *Approaches to Walden* (1961) and coedited *The Dickens Critics* (1961) with George Ford. He served as editor of *English Studies in Canada* for its first ten years (1975–1984).

ANTHONY LEYLAND has a Ph.D. from the University of York (United Kingdom); his thesis was titled "Ezra Pound and the Italian Renaissance 1915–1930."

PETER LIEBREGTS graduated in Classics, University of Utrecht, and obtained his doctorate at the University of Leiden, where he now works as an Associate Professor, Department of English. Besides numerous articles, he has published *Centaurs in the Twilight: W. B. Yeats's Use of the Classical Tradition* (1993) and *Ezra Pound and Neoplatonism* (2004).

BRITA LINDBERG-SEYERSTED, Professor of American Literature at the University of Oslo, died in 2002. She was editor of *Pound/Ford: The Story of a Literary Friendship* (1982) and author of *The Voice of the Poet: Aspects of Style in the Poetry of Emily Dickinson* (1968).

ALEC MARSH is Associate Professor of English at Muhlenberg College, Allentown, Pennsylvania. His *Money & Modernity: Pound, Williams, and the Spirit of Jefferson* (1998) won the first Ezra Pound Society book prize.

TIMOTHY MATERER is Professor of English at the University of Missouri. He is the author of *Wyndham Lewis, the Novelist* (1976), *Vortex: Pound, Eliot, Lewis* (1979), *Modernist Alchemy: Poetry and the Occult* (1995), and *James Merrill's Apocalypse* (2000), and he has also edited two volumes of Ezra Pound's letters.

GAIL McDONALD is Associate Professor in the Department of English at the University of North Carolina at Greensboro. She is the author of *Learning to Be Modern: Pound, Eliot, and the American University* (1993).

STUART Y. McDOUGAL is DeWitt Wallace Professor of English and Chair of the English Department at Macalester College, St. Paul, Minnesota. Among his books are *Ezra Pound and the Troubadour Tradition* (1972) and *Dante among the Moderns* (1985).

PATRICK McGINNESS is Sir Win and Lady Bischoff Fellow and Tutor of French at St. Anne's College, Oxford University. He specializes in nineteenth- and twentieth-century French literature and Modern British poetry.

CAMERON McWHIRTER is a journalist for the *Atlanta Journal-Constitution*. He is a graduate of Hamilton College, Pound's alma mater, and the Columbia Graduate School of Journalism. His scholarly work on Pound correspondence has appeared in *Paideuma*.

ROBERT MERRITT is Professor of English and Chair, Division of Language, Literature and Communications, at Bluefield College, Bluefield, Virginia. He is the author of *Early Music and the Aesthetics of Ezra Pound: Hush of Older Song* (1993).

CRAIG MONK is Associate Professor in the Department of English at the University of Lethbridge in Alberta, Canada. His interests extend to nineteenth- and twentieth-century American literature, twentieth-century Anglo-Irish literature, interdisciplinary Modernism, bibliography, and publishing history.

A. DAVID MOODY is Emeritus Professor at the University of York, United Kingdom. His many books include *Thomas Stearns Eliot: Poet* (1979, 1994) and *Tracing T. S. Eliot's Spirit* (1996). Currently he is at work on a critical biography of Pound. He is the editor of *The Cambridge Companion to T. S. Eliot* (1994) and has published many articles on Pound.

PAUL MORRISON is Professor of English at Brandeis University. He is author of *The Poetics of Fascism* (1996) and *The Explanation of Everything: Essays on Sexual Subjectivity* (2001).

IRA B. NADEL, Professor of English at the University of British Columbia, is the General Editor of *The Cambridge Companion to Ezra Pound* (1999) and editor of *The Letters of Ezra Pound to Alice Corbin Henderson* (1993). His biography *Ezra Pound: A Literary Life* appeared in 2004. His previous biographies include Leonard Cohen and Tom Stoppard.

PETER A. NICHOLLS is Professor of English and American Literature at the University of Sussex, United Kingdom. His many publications include *Ezra Pound: Politics, Economics and Writing: A Study of The Cantos* (1984) and *Modernisms: A Literary Guide* (1995). He is currently working on *George Open and the Fate of Modernism*, a project funded by a Leverhulme Research Fellowship.

MICHAEL J. O'DRISCOLL is an Associate Professor of English at the University of Alberta, where he teaches in the areas of twentieth-century American literature, critical theory, and poetics. He has edited, with Tilottama Rajan, *After Poststructuralism: Writing the Intellectual History of Theory* (2002).

CATHERINE E. PAUL is Associate Professor of English, Clemson University. She is the author of *Poetry in the Museums of Modernism: Yeats, Pound, Moore, Stein* (2002).

MARJORIE PERLOFF is Sadie D. Patek Professor Emerita of Humanities at Stanford University. Her most recent books are *21st-Century Modernism* (2002), *The Vienna Paradox* (2004), and *Differentials: Poetry, Poetics, Pedagogy* (2004), which contains a long essay on Pound's nominalism. She is President-Elect of the Modern Language Association.

OMAR POUND has published numerous translations from Persian and Arabic, as well as Latin and French. He is coeditor of *Ezra Pound and Dorothy Shakespear, Their Letters 1909–1914* (with A. Walton Litz, 1984), *Ezra Pound and Margaret Cravens: A Tragic Friendship 1910–1912* (with Robert Spoo, 1988), and *Ezra and Dorothy Pound: Letters in Captivity 1945–1946* (with Robert Spoo, 1999).

WILLIAM PRATT is retired Professor of English, University of Miami, Oxford, Ohio. He has edited *The Imagist Poem; Modern Poetry in Miniature* (1963), *Homage to Imagism* (with Robert Richardson, 1992), and *Ezra Pound, Nature and Myth* (2002). With Anne Rich Pratt he translated René Taupin's *Influence of French Symbolism on Modern American Poetry* (1965).

ROXANA PREDA is Assistant Professor at the Kennedy Institute, Freie Universität, Berlin. Her most recent book is *Ezra Pound's (Post)Modern Poetics and Politics: Logocentrism, Language, and Truth* (2001).

ANNIE PULIS completed her Ph.D. at the University of Missouri at Columbia in 2000. Her dissertation was titled "The Vanishing Inquiry: Modernists in Pursuit of Spirit (Dorothy Richardson, Anais Nin, William Butler Yeats, Ireland)." She lives and works in the Seattle area.

ZHAOMING QIAN is Research Professor of English at the University of New Orleans. Among his books are *Orientalism and Modernism: The Legacy of China in Pound and Williams* (1995) and *The Modernist Response to Chinese Art: Pound, Moore, Stevens* (2003). He has edited *Ezra Pound and China* (2003).

BURTON RAFFEL until 2003 held an Endowed Chair in Arts and Humanities, University of Louisiana at Lafayette. He has published many volumes of poetry, fiction, translation, and literary and cultural commentary. Among these works are *Ezra Pound, the Prime Minister of Poetry* (1984) and *Possum and Ole Ez in the Public Eye: Contemporaries and Peers on T. S. Eliot and Ezra Pound, 1892–1972* (1985).

RICHARD READ is Associate Professor, School of Architecture, Landscape and Visual Arts at the University of Western Australia. He is the author of *Art and Its Discontents: The Early Life of Adrian Stokes* (2002).

TIM REDMAN, Professor of English at the University of Texas at Dallas, is the author of *Ezra Pound and Italian Fascism* (1991). He is working on a Pound biography.

BRIAN M. REED is Assistant Professor of English, University of Washington, Seattle. He is the author of *Hart Crane: After His Lights* (forthcoming) and has coedited with Nancy Perloff *Situating El Lissitzky: Vitebsk, Berlin, Moscow* (2003).

DIANE REID is an M.A. candidate at the University of New Brunswick, Fredericton, Canada. Her thesis deals with Pound, H. D., and mythology.

MATTHEW ROBINSON is a Ph.D. candidate at the University of New Brunswick, Fredericton, Canada. His dissertation deals with H. D. and occultism.

TIM ROMANO is an independent scholar. He has a B.A. from Swarthmore College and an M.A. from the University of Pennsylvania.

CE ROSENOW is a Visiting Professor of Literature in the Clark Honors College at the University of Oregon. Her research focuses on American Modernisms with an emphasis on the intersections of American and Japanese literatures. She is currently working on *Pictures of the Floating World: American Modernist Poetry and Cultural Translations of Japan*.

HERBERT N. SCHNEIDAU, a retired Professor of English, taught at the University of Arizona. He is the author of *Ezra Pound: The Image and the Real* (1969), *Sacred Discontent: The Bible and Western Tradition* (1977), and *Waking Giants: The Presence of the Past in Modernism* (1991). In 1984 he coedited with Donald Pearce Pound's letters to John Theobald.

F. RICHARD SEDDON is an independent scholar in New Mexico.

STEPHEN SICARI is Professor and Chair of English at St. John's University in New York City. He has written extensively on Pound, including *Pound's Epic Ambition* (1991). His most recent book is *Joyce's Modernist Allegory: Ulysses and the History of the Novel* (2001).

ROBERT SPOO, formerly Professor of English at the University of Tulsa, now practices law but still maintains his literary interests. Among his numerous publications are the two volumes of Pound correspondence he has coedited with Omar Pound: *Ezra Pound and Margaret Cravens: A Tragic Friendship 1910–1912* (1988) and *Ezra and Dorothy Pound: Letters in Captivity 1945–1946* (1999).

ELLEN KECK STAUDER is Professor of English and Humanities at Reed College, Portland, Oregon. She has published on Pound, Loy, Pater, Keats, and Doty and is currently at work on a book on Pound's prosody, *Form Cut into Time: The Poetics of Rhythm in the Poetry of Ezra Pound*.

PETER STOICHEFF is Professor of English at the University of Saskatchewan. He is author of *The Hall of Mirrors: Drafts & Fragments and the End of Ezra Pound's Cantos* (1995).

HELEN SWORD, a former Associate Professor of English at Indiana University, is now a Lecturer in the Centre for Professional Development at the University of Auckland in New Zealand. She is the author of *Engendering Inspiration: Visionary Strategies in Rilke, Lawrence, and H. D.* (1995) and *Ghostwriting Modernism* (2002).

RICHARD TAYLOR is Professor Emeritus of English and Comparative Literature at Universität Bayreuth. Among his works is the *Variorum Edition of "Three Cantos": A Prototype* (1991). He is at work on *The Variorum of Ezra Pound's Cantos.*

CHARLES TIMBRELL is Professor of Music at Howard University in Washington, D.C. He has presented major piano recitals in New York, Washington, London, Paris, Rome, European festivals, and radio. He is the author of *French Pianism* (1992), *Prince of Virtuosos: A Life of Walter Rummel, American Pianist* (2005), and numerous articles.

TONY TREMBLAY is an Associate Professor of Canadian and Cultural Studies at St. Thomas University in Fredericton, Canada. His work includes numerous articles and chapters on Pound's Canadians, notably Marshall McLuhan and Louis Dudek.

DEMETRES P. TRYPHONOPOULOS is Professor of English at the University of New Brunswick in Fredericton, Canada. He is author of *The Celestial Tradition: A Study of Ezra Pound's Cantos* (1992) and has edited, with Leon Surette, *Literary Modernism and the Occult Tradition* (1996) and *"I Cease Not to Yowl": Ezra Pound's Letters to Olivia Rossetti Agresti* (1998).

E. P. WALKIEWICZ is Professor of English at Oklahoma State University, Stillwater. He is the author of *John Barth* (1986) and *Ulysses, Order, Myth: Classification and Modern Literature* (1995); and he has edited, with Hugh Witemeyer, *Ezra Pound and Senator Bronson Cutting: A Political Correspondence, 1930–1935* (1995).

HUGH WITEMEYER taught Victorian and Modern Literature at the University of New Mexico from 1973 to 2004. His first book, *The Poetry of Ezra Pound: Forms and Renewal 1908–1920* (1969), is still standard. More recent work includes *Ezra Pound and Senator Bronson Cutting: A Political Correspondence 1930–1935* (1995), coedited with E. P. Walkiewicz, and *Pound/Williams: Selected Letters of Ezra Pound and William Carlos Williams* (1996).

STEVEN G. YAO, Assistant Professor of English at Hamilton College, Clinton, New York, holds a Ph.D. in English from the University of California at Berkeley. He is the author of *Translation and the Languages of Modernism* (2002).